W9-BNC-886

ITU	International Telecommunications Union	PSTN	Public-switched telephone network
		PTT	Post telephone and telecommunications (authority)
JTM	Job transfer and manipulation		
		QPSX	Queued-packet, distributed-switch
LAN	Local area network		
LAPB	Link access procedure balanced	RF	Radio frequency
LED	Light-emitting diode	ROSE	Remote operations service element
LLC	Logical link control		
LSAP	Link service access point	SAP	Service access point
		SASE	Specific application service element
MAN	Metropolitan area network	SDLC	Synchronous data link control
MHS	Message handling service	SE	Session entity
MIB	Management information base	SEL	Selector
MMS	Manufacturing messaging service	SI	Subnet identifier
MUX	Multiplexer	SMTP	Simple mail transfer protocol
		SNA	Systems network architecture (IBM)
NAK	Negative acknowledgement	SNMP	Simple network management protocol
NBS	National Bureau of Standards	SPF	Shortest path first
NMS	Network management system	SSAP	Session service access point
NRM	(Unbalanced) normal response mode		
NRZ	Non-return to zero	TCP	Transmission control protocol
NRZI	Non-return to zero inverted	TDM	Time-division multiplexing
NS	Network service	TE	Transport entity
NSAP	Network service access point	TP_4	(OSI) Transport protocol class 4
NSDU	Network service data unit	TSE	Terminal switching exchange
		TTL	Transistor transistor logic
OSI	Open systems interconnection	TSAP	Transport service access point
PA	Point-of-attachment	UART	Universal asynchronous receiver transmitter
PAD	Packet assembler–disassembler	UE	User element
PBX	Private branch exchange	UDP	User datagram protocol
PDN	Public data network	USRT	Universal synchronous receiver transmitter
PDU	Protocol data unit		
PE	Presentation entity		
PPSDN	Public packet-switched data network	VPN	Virtual private network
PSAP	Presentation service access point	VT	Virtual terminal
PSDN	Packet-switched data network		
PSK	Phase-shift keying	WAN	Wide area network

DATA COMMUNICATIONS, COMPUTER NETWORKS AND OPEN SYSTEMS

ELECTRONIC SYSTEMS ENGINEERING SERIES

Consulting editors   **E.L. Dagless**
University of Bristol
J. O'Reilly
University College of Wales

OTHER TITLES IN THE SERIES

THIRD EDITION

DATA COMMUNICATIONS, COMPUTER NETWORKS AND OPEN SYSTEMS

FRED HALSALL

Newbridge Professor of Communications Engineering,
University of Wales, Swansea

ADDISON-WESLEY PUBLISHING COMPANY

Wokingham, England · Reading, Massachusetts · Menlo Park, California · New York
Don Mills, Ontario · Amsterdam · Bonn · Sydney · Singapore
Tokyo · Madrid · San Juan · Milan · Paris · Mexico City · Seoul · Taipei

© 1992 Addison-Wesley Publishers Limited
© 1992 Addison-Wesley Publishing Company, Inc.

All rights reserved. No part of this publication may be reproduced, stored in a retrieval system, or transmitted in any form or by any means, electronic, mechanical, photocopying, recording, or otherwise, without prior written permission of the publisher.

The programs presented in this book have been included for their instructional value. They have been tested with care but are not guaranteed for any particular purpose. The publisher does not offer any warranties or representations, nor does it accept any liabilities with respect to the programs.

Many of the designations used by manufacturers and sellers to distinguish their products are claimed as trademarks. Addison-Wesley has made every attempt to supply trademark information about manufacturers and their products mentioned in this book.

Cover design by Chris Eley.
Illustrations by Chartwell Illustrators.
Typeset by CRB Typesetting Services, Ely, Cambs.
Printed in the United States of America.

First printed 1992.

British Library Cataloguing in Publication Data
A catalogue record for this book is available from the British Library.

Library of Congress Cataloging in Publication Data
Halsall, Fred
    Data communications, computer networks, and open systems / Fred Halsall.—3rd ed.
        p.   cm.
    Rev. ed. of Data communications, computer networks, and OSI. c1988.
    Includes bibliographical references and index.
    ISBN 0-201-56506-4
    1. Data transmission systems.   2. Computer networks.   3. Local area networks (Computer networks)   4. Computer network protocols.
I. Halsall, Fred. Data communications, computer networks, and OSI.
II. Title.
TK5105.H35   1992
004.6--dc20   91-40180
                                                                    CIP

Preface

Objectives

Computers are now found in every walk of life: in the home, in the office, in banks, in schools and colleges, in industry, and so on. Although in some instances the computers carry out their intended function in a standalone mode, in others it is necessary to exchange information with other computers. This means that an essential consideration in the design of most forms of computing equipment installed today is the type of data communication facility that is to be used to allow it to communicate with other computers. In many instances, this necessitates a knowledge not only of the alternative types of data transmission circuits that may be used but also an understanding of the interface requirements to the many different types of computer communication networks available for this purpose. Data communications and the allied subject of computer networks have thus become essential topics in all modern courses on computer systems design.

In many applications of computer networks, providing a means for two systems to exchange information solves only part of the problem. In an application that involves a distributed community of heterogeneous (or dissimilar) computers exchanging files of information over a computer network, for example, such issues as the use of different operating (and hence file) systems and possibly different character sets and word sizes must also be addressed if the systems are to communicate in an unconstrained (open) way. It is thus essential when considering the applications of computer networks also to gain an understanding of the various application-oriented communication protocols that have now been defined to create communication environments in which computers from different manufacturers can exchange information in an open way. The three parts of this book – data communications, computer networks and open systems – consider each of these issues.

Intended readership

This book has been written primarily as a course text book for students studying the subjects of data communications, computer networks and open systems. Typically, the students will be on electronic engineering, computer engineering, computer systems or computer science courses. In addition, it is felt suitable for practicing engineers and computer professionals who wish or need to gain a working knowledge of these subjects.

Within most colleges and universities the subjects addressed are introduced at different points in a course. In some instances, one or more of the subjects are found in first-degree level courses whilst in others they are first introduced at a graduate level. For this reason, care has been taken not to assume too much background knowledge when introducing each subject except that which is found in all foundation courses taken by such students. Thus the only prerequisites are an understanding of basic logic circuits and computer architectures and a working knowledge of a high-level structured programming language.

The book does not attempt to cover the theory of digital communications since this is primarily the domain of the electronics engineer. Rather, it starts by simply identifying the characteristics of the different types of transmission media that can be used to transmit data and then proceeds to identify the hardware and software that are needed to enable two or more geographically distributed computers to communicate to achieve a specific distributed application function.

In practice, beyond the basic data transmission level, the majority of communication protocols that are needed in each computer are implemented in software. When discussing the various protocols that are used, in addition to describing their operation in a qualitative way, it is felt essential also to present a methodology that can be adopted for their implementation.

Furthermore, it is equally important for the reader to gain an understanding of how a collection of such protocols cooperate and communicate one with another in order to achieve the overall communication function. This book addresses both these issues in some detail and this is seen as one of its major strengths.

Organization

The organization of the book closely follows the structure of the ISO reference model for open systems interconnection. Thus the first part – data communications – concentrates on the fundamental issues that need to be addressed to achieve the reliable transfer of data across a serial data link.

Part Two – computer networks – builds on this and describes the operation of the different types of computer networks that are used to provide a switched communication facility over which a distributed set of computers can communicate one with another.

The third part – open systems – introduces and describes the operation of the additional protocols that are required in order to enable a distributed set of application processes that are running in these computers to exchange data in an open way in order to carry out a range of distributed application functions; that is, irrespective of any differences that may exist between the character sets, word sizes or the way local services are provided in each computer.

New in this edition

Since the last edition of this book was published, a number of important developments have taken place in each of the three subjects considered. The primary aim of this edition, therefore, has been to incorporate these developments and, in general, to bring the material covered more up to date. Also, the author has now given lecture courses on each of these subjects, at graduate and postgraduate level, and has given many in-house courses to practicing engineers and computer scientists. The experience gained from this has also been incorporated into the new edition.

In the field of data communications, intelligent modems have been introduced which incorporate data compression. Also, digital leased circuits are now widely available from most public carriers. Hence both of these subjects have been introduced into the chapter on data transmission – Chapter 3. In addition, since it is felt essential for a newcomer to the area to have a sound understanding of the fundamentals of communication protocols together with their formal specification and implementation methodology, a new chapter devoted to this subject has been introduced – Chapter 4.

In the field of computer networks, the continuing demand for higher transmission bandwidth has resulted in high-speed local area networks (LANs) being introduced. These include FDDI and DQDB, both of which are now discussed. Also, as the size of LANs has increased, so most installations now incorporate intelligent bridges into their design. A new chapter covering both of these topics has thus been introduced into this section – Chapter 7.

Probably the most significant development in computer networks has been the widespread introduction of interconnection environments that comprise multiple linked networks of different types. Such environments are known as internetworks. A new chapter specifically devoted to the protocols associated with internetworks has also been introduced in this section – Chapter 9.

In the section on open systems, the most notable addition is the introduction of detailed descriptions of the various protocols that make up the TCP/IP protocol suite. In the previous edition, this section was devoted entirely to the OSI protocols but the new edition now gives equal coverage to both protocol suites. This has been done to reflect the widespread support for both protocol suites in creating open systems interconnection environments.

Coverage of the OSI protocols has also been expanded and now includes a description of all the application protocols that have been introduced. These include the X.400 message handling protocols, the X.500 directory service protocols and the SNMP and CMISE protocols associated with the increasingly important subject of network management.

Intended usage

To the lecturer

The book is based on three separate lecture courses given by the author to electronic engineering, computer systems and computer science students at both undergraduate and graduate levels, as well as to teams of practicing professionals involved in the implementation of data and computer communication systems. Care has been taken, therefore, to assume only a fundamental knowledge of each subject. This includes an understanding of basic logic circuits and computer architectures, and a working knowledge of a structured high-level programming language.

Users of the previous edition of the book have cited three main advantages compared with similar texts. Firstly, the protocols are presented in a form that enables students readily to see how they can be implemented in program code. Secondly, it explains how the various protocols that make up a complete protocol suite interact and communicate with one another to achieve a particular distributed information processing task. Thirdly, the extensive range of figures help to explain the many detailed issues considered and significantly reduce lecture preparation time. These three features, therefore, have been retained in the new edition.

There is now sufficient material in the book to cover three complementary courses: one on data communications, one on computer networks and one on open systems. Courses on data communications should be based on Part One of the book and the topic of forward error correction from Appendix A. Also, if the students have the necessary background, transmission control circuits from Appendix B.

The material in Part Two forms a comprehensive course on computer networks. However, if this is the only course being taught, then selected topics on transport protocols from Chapter 10 can also be included. The material in Part Three then forms the basis of a good course on the application-oriented protocols of open systems that includes both the TCP/IP and OSI protocol suites. Again, if this is the only course being taught, selected topics on internetworking from Chapter 9 could also be included. Alternatively, the material from Parts One and Two can be combined to give a single longer course on data communications and computer networks or, the material from Parts Two and Three can be combined to give a single longer course on computer communications and open systems.

To the student

The book is suitable for self study: worked examples are included in most chapters and the large number of figures help considerably to explain many of the topics covered. Also, to test understanding, a list of exercises is included at the end of each chapter.

To give some structure to the range of topics covered in each chapter, their order and interrelationships are summarized at the end of each chapter in a diagrammatic, flowchart-like style. These include not only the interrelationships of the topics covered within the chapter, but also how they relate to the material covered in other chapters.

Acknowledgements

I would like to take this opportunity to acknowledge the detailed responses to a questionnaire relating to the previous edition which helped me to formulate the structure and content of the new edition.

P.T. Tan Department of Information Engineering, Nanyang Technological University, Nanyang, Singapore
D. Hutchison Computing Department, Lancaster University, Lancaster, UK
S.J. Knapskög Division of Computer Systems and Telematics, The Norwegian Institute of Technology, The University of Trondheim, Trondheim, Norway
M.H. Barton Department of Electrical and Electronic Engineering, University of Bristol, Bristol, UK
M. Sloman Department of Computing Science, Imperial College of Science and Technology, London, UK
J.A.M. Frishert Department of Electrical Engineering, Hogeschool Eindhoven, Eindhoven, the Netherlands
B. Christianson Division of Computer Science, Hatfield Polytechnic, Hertfordshire, UK
A.R. Warman Department of Information Systems, The London School of Economics and Political Science, London, UK
L. Christoff Department of Computer Systems, Uppsala University, Uppsala, Sweden
R.D. Boyce School of Computer Studies, University of Leeds, Leeds, UK
C. Smythe Centre for Satellite Engineering Research, University of Surrey, Surrey, UK
P. Mars School of Engineering and Computer Science, University of Durham, Durham, UK
S.R. Wilbur Department of Computer Science, University College London, London, UK
B. Plattner Swiss Federal Institute of Technology (ETH), Zurich, Switzerland
A. Simmonds School of Engineering Information Technology, Sheffield Polytechnic, Sheffield, UK
W.K. Wong Department of Electronic Engineering, City Polytechnic of Hong Kong, Kowloon, Hong Kong
T. Walasek Department of Computer Systems, Uppsala University, Uppsala, Sweden
Marvin Solomon Computer Science Department, University of Wisconsin – Madison, Wisconsin, USA
Mostafa Ammar College of Computing, Georgia Institute of Technology, Georgia, USA
Jack Decker Computer Information Science, Washburn University, Kansas, USA
Imrich Chiamtac University of Massachusetts a- Amherst, Massachusetts, USA
Michael Faiman Department of Computer Science, University of Illinois at Urbana-Champaign, Illinois, USA
Graham Campbell Illinois Institute of Technology, Chicago, USA
Jerrold Siegel Math and Computer Science Department, University of MO at St Louis, Missouri, USA
Ron Greve Computer Science Department, South Dakota State University, South Dakota, USA
David Cheriton Computer Science Department, Stanford University, California, USA

Finally, I would like to take this opportunity to express my sincere thanks, firstly to Agnes George for her help with typing the manuscript and making numerous corrections, alterations and additions without a word of criticism; secondly, to Riaz Ahmad, one of my research assistants, for his help with the simulation results presented in Chapters 6 and 7 and to the British IEE for permission to publish them; and finally, to my wife Rhiannon for her unwavering support, patience and understanding while I was writing the book. It is to her that I dedicate the book

Fred Halsall
January 1992

Contents

To my wife Rhiannon

PART ONE

DATA COMMUNICATIONS

The need for data communications has evolved almost from the earliest days of computing. However, although the reader of this book is likely to be aware of the basic terminology and devices associated with computers themselves – bits and bytes, gates and highways, BASIC and Pascal, etc – equally, there is a fundamental set of techniques and terminology associated with data communications and these are often less well understood. Before describing the different types of computer network, therefore, the first part of this book is devoted to a review of the fundamentals and terminology associated with data communications on which all forms of distributed system are based. In particular, it is concerned with the different techniques that are utilized to achieve the reliable transfer of data between two devices. The physical separation of two devices may vary from a few tens of metres – for example, between two locally connected computers – to several hundreds of kilometres, if the two devices are connected by a transmission path through a national telephone network, for example.

Chapter 1 describes the historical development of distributed computing systems that has taken place as a result of advancing technology and identifies the different types of data communication networks that have evolved for use in such systems. Also, it identifies the intended application domain of each network type and the standards that have been defined for use with them. It thus lays the foundation for the remainder of the book.

Chapter 2 is concerned with the electrical characteristics of the different types of physical transmission medium used. It also outlines the various international standards that have been defined both for encoding data and for interfacing a device to the different media types.

As will be seen, data is normally transmitted between two devices bit serially in blocks comprising varying numbers of binary digits (bits). Chapter 3 describes the various techniques that enable the receiving device to determine, firstly, the start and end of each block being transmitted and, secondly, if any errors (bit corruptions) have occurred during transmission. It also discusses the subject of data compression and the different types of multiplexer equipment.

Chapter 4 presents the different techniques that are used, firstly, to overcome the effect of transmission errors and, secondly, to control the rate of flow of data across a data link. Both these functions form part of the protocol associated with the data link. The chapter also describes how protocols are specified and a methodology for their implementation in program code.

Chapter 5 builds on the general principles introduced in Chapter 4 to describe the standard data link protocols that are in widespread use for controlling the exchange of data between a distributed community of computers.

1

Data communication networks and open system standards

CHAPTER OBJECTIVES

When you have completed studying the material in this chapter you should be able to:

- identify the different applications of computer communication networks;
- appreciate the different types of data communication networks that are used in these applications;
- understand the concept of layering and structure of the ISO Reference Model for open systems interconnection;
- describe the functionality of each layer in the ISO Reference Model;
- know the protocols associated with the TCP/IP protocol suite and how they relate to the ISO Reference Model;
- know some of the standard protocol suites that are based on the ISO protocols.

1.1 BACKGROUND

Computers are now used in every walk of life. In the home, for example, for games playing and word processing, in the office for word processing, spreadsheet and database management, in banks and other financial institutions for the maintenance of customer accounts, in travel agencies for airline and other reservations, in schools and colleges for computer-aided instruction, in universities and other research establishments for the analysis of scientific and other experimental data, in the process industry for the control of chemical and other plants, in manufacturing industries for the control of machine tools and robots, in department stores for point-of-sale accounting, and so on.

Although in many instances computers are used to perform their intended role in a stand-alone mode, in others there is a need to interwork and exchange data with other computers. In the home, for example, to transfer a file of data from one personal computer to another or to access information from a public database using the switched telephone network, in the office for the exchange of electronic mail either within the same establishment or between establishments, in financial institutions to carry out funds transfers from one institution computer to another, in travel companies to access the reservation systems belonging to various airlines, in schools and colleges to share the use of an expensive peripheral such as a laser printer, in universities and other research establishments to access the results produced by a remote supercomputer, in the process industry to coordinate the control of the instrumentation equipment associated with a plant, in manufacturing industry to control the transfer of parts and related data from one automated unit to another, in department stores for stock-control and the automatic ordering of goods, and so on.

This book is concerned specifically with the issues that must be considered when communicating data between two computers in such applications. It provides not only an understanding of the different data and computer networks that are now available, but also details of the hardware and software that is required within each computer to interface with these facilities. In addition, it describes how application programs running in different computers with different word sizes and character sets cooperate to achieve a specific distributed application function. Figure 1.1 shows the three basic issues that must be considered.

The fundamental requirement in all applications that involve two or more computers is the provision of a suitable data communications facility. In practice, however, a wide range of different types of communications facility may be utilized, each intended for a specific application domain. For example, if the requirement is simply to transfer a file of data from one computer to another similar computer in the same room or office, then the communications facility will be much simpler than if data is to be transferred between different computers at different sites.

Irrespective of the type of data communications facility being used, in most applications data is transmitted between computers in a **bit-serial mode**.

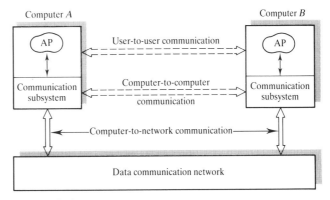

Computer A   Computer B

User-to-user communication

AP   AP

Communication   Computer-to-computer   Communication
subsystem   communication   subsystem

Computer-to-network communication

Data communication network

FIGURE 1.1

Computer
communication
schematic.

AP = Application process

Consequently, since data is transferred between subsystems within a computer in a **word-parallel mode**, it is necessary to perform a **parallel-to-serial conversion** operation at the computer interface prior to outputting data, and the reverse **serial-to-parallel** function on input. Also, the type of transmission mode and circuits that are required vary and depend on the physical separation of the computers and the data transmission rate.

In addition, once data is transmitted outside of a computer, there is a much increased probability that bit errors (corruptions) will occur. In most applications, therefore, it is necessary to incorporate not only a means to detect when bit (transmission) errors occur but also a way to obtain another (hopefully-correct) copy of the affected data. This is known as **error control** and is just one issue that must be considered when transmitting data between two computers. Other issues include regulating the rate at which data is transferred – known as **flow control** – and, if an intermediate data network is involved, establishing a communications path across the network.

In some instances, the application software can use this basic computer-to-computer communications facility directly whilst in others additional functionality must be added. For example, in some applications the communicating computers may be of different types which means that their internal representation of characters and numerical values may be different. Hence a means of ensuring the transferred data is interpreted in the same way in each computer must be incorporated. Also, the computers may use different operating systems; for example, one may be a small single-user computer whilst another may be a large multi-user system. This means that the interface between user (application) programs – normally referred to as **application processes** or **APs** – and the underlying computer-to-computer communications services will also be different. All these issues must be considered when communicating data between computers.

1.2 DATA COMMUNICATION NETWORKS

As may be concluded from the foregoing, the type of data communications facility used is a function of the nature of the application, the number of computers involved, and their physical separation. Typical data communication facilities are shown in Figures 1.2 through 1.6.

If only two computers are involved and both are in the same room or office, then the transmission facility can comprise just a simple point-to-point wire link. However, if they are located in different parts of a town or country, **public-carrier** facilities must be used. Normally this will involve the **public switched telephone network (PSTN)** which requires a device known as a **modem** to be used for transmitting data. The general arrangement is as shown in Figure 1.2.

When more than two computers are involved in the application, a switched communication facility (network) is normally provided to enable all the computers to communicate with one another at different times. If all the computers are distributed around a single office or building, it is possible to install one's own network. Such networks are known as **local area (data) networks** or

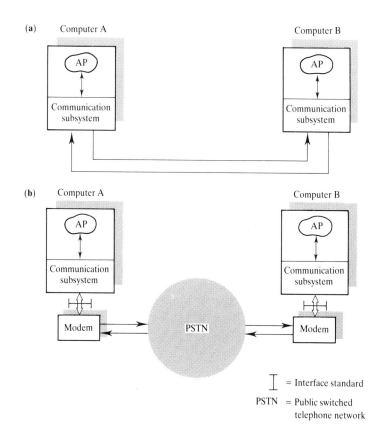

FIGURE 1.2

Simple computer-to-computer alternatives: (a) point-to-point wire link; (b) PSTN + modem link.

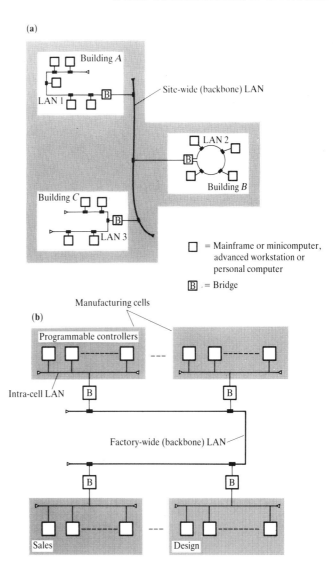

FIGURE 1.3

LAN-based distributed
systems: (a) technical
and office automation;
(b) manufacturing
automation.

LANs. A wide range of such networks and allied equipment is available. Two
LAN-based systems are shown in Figure 1.3.

When the computers are located in different establishments (sites),
public-carrier facilities must again be used. The resulting network is known as a
wide area network or **WAN**. The type of WAN used will depend on the nature of
the application. For example, if all the computers belong to the same enterprise
and there is a requirement to transfer substantial amounts of data between sites,
one approach is simply to lease transmission lines (circuits) from the public
carriers and install a private switching system at each site to create what is known
as an **enterprise-wide private network**. Many large enterprises choose to do this;

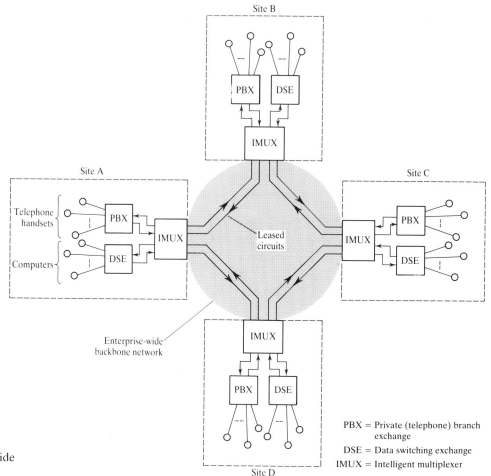

FIGURE 1.4

Typical enterprise-wide
private network.

such networks normally incorporate both voice and data communications. The
general scheme is shown in Figure 1.4.

Such solutions are only viable for large enterprises since only then is there
sufficient inter-site traffic to justify the cost of leasing lines and installing and
running a private network. In most other instances, therefore, public-carrier
networks must be used. In addition to providing a public switched telephone
service, most public carriers now provide a public switched data service. Indeed,
such networks, like the PSTN, are now interconnected internationally and have
been designed specifically for the transmission of data rather than voice. Consequently, for applications that involve computers distributed around a country or
perhaps internationally, a **public switched data network (PSDN)** is normally
used. Alternatively, many public carriers are now converting their existing
public switched telephone networks to enable data to be transmitted without

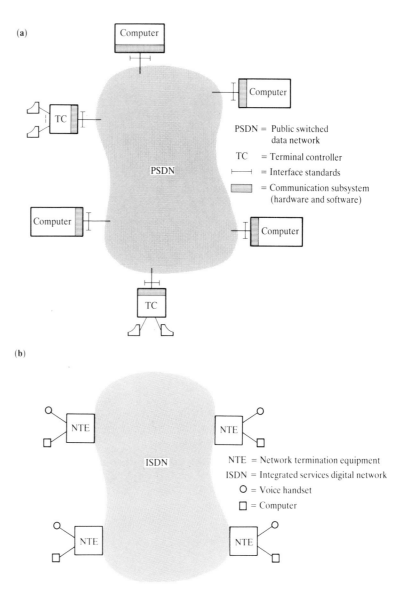

(a)

PSDN = Public switched
        data network

TC   = Terminal controller

├──┤ = Interface standards

▨▨▨ = Communication subsystem
        (hardware and software)

(b)

NTE = Network termination equipment

ISDN = Integrated services digital network

O   = Voice handset

□   = Computer

FIGURE 1.5

Public-carrier data
networks: (a) public
switched data network;
(b) integrated services
digital network.

modems. The resulting networks, which operate in an all-digital mode, are
known as **integrated services digital networks** or **ISDN**. When ISDNs are in
widespread use, this type of facility may also be considered. The general
schemes are shown in parts (a) and (b) of Figure 1.5.

   In all these applications it has been assumed that all the computers are
attached to the same LAN or WAN. In some applications, however, the data
communications facility embraces multiple networks such as LAN–WAN–LAN.
For example, a workstation (computer) attached to a LAN in one establishment

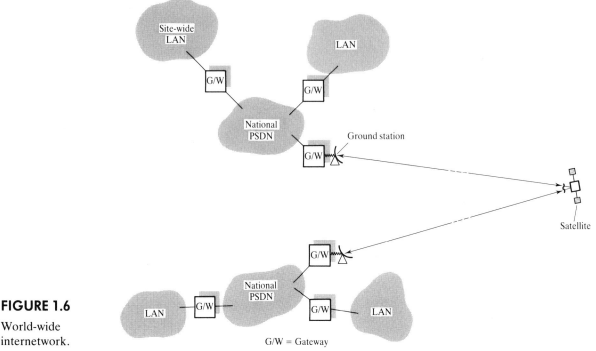

FIGURE 1.6

World-wide
internetwork.

may require to communicate with a computer that is attached to a LAN in a
different establishment with the two LANs being interconnected by, say, a
public switched data network. This type of communications facility, which is
known as an **internetwork** or **internet**, requires additional issues to be addressed
both in relation to the network itself and when interfacing computers to such
networks. An example of such a network is shown in Figure 1.6.

1.3 STANDARDS

Until recently, the standards established for use in the computer industry by the
various international bodies were concerned primarily with either the internal
operation of a computer or the connection of a local peripheral device. The result
was that early hardware and software communications subsystems offered by
manufacturers only enabled their own computers, and so-called **plug-compatible
systems**, to exchange information. Such systems are known as **closed systems**,
since computers from other manufacturers cannot exchange information unless
they adhere to the (proprietary) standards of a particular manufacturer.

In contrast, the various international bodies concerned with public-carrier
networks have for many years formulated internationally agreed standards for
connecting devices to these networks. The **V-series recommendations**, for example, are concerned with the connection of equipment – normally referred to as a

data terminal equipment (DTE) – to a modem connected to the PSTN; the X-series recommendations for connecting a DTE to a public data network; and the I-series recommendations for connecting a DTE to the emerging ISDNs. The recommendations have resulted in compatibility between the equipment from different vendors, enabling a purchaser to select suitable equipment from a range of manufacturers.

Initially, the services provided by most public carriers were concerned primarily with data transmission, and hence the associated standards only related to the method of interfacing a device to these networks. More recently, however, the public carriers have started to provide more extensive distributed information services, such as the exchange of electronic messages (**Teletex**) and access to public databases (**Videotex**). To cater for such services, the standards bodies associated with the telecommunications industry have formulated standards not only for interfacing to such networks but also so-called higher level standards concerned with the format (syntax) and control of the exchange of information (data) between systems. Consequently, the equipment from one manufacturer that adheres to these standards, can be used interchangeably with equipment from any other manufacturer that complies with the standards. The resulting system is then known as an **open system** or, more completely, as an **open system interconnection environment (OSIE)**. A summary of the evolution of standards, together with the major standards organizations, is shown in diagrammatic form in Figure 1.7.

In the mid 1970s, as different types of distributed systems (based on both public and private data networks) started to proliferate, the potential advantages of open systems were acknowledged by the computer industry. As a result, a range of standards started to be introduced. The first was concerned with the

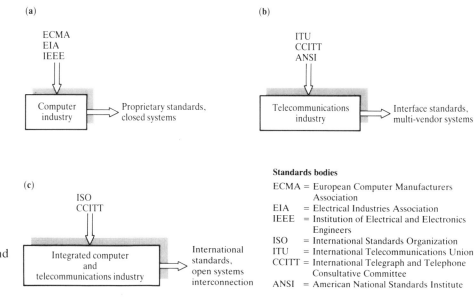

FIGURE 1.7

Standards evolution and major standardization organizations.

overall structure of the complete communication subsystem within each computer. This was produced by the **International Standards Organization (ISO)** and is known as the **ISO Reference Model** for **Open Systems Interconnection (OSI)**.

The aim of the ISO Reference Model is to provide a framework for the coordination of standards development and to allow existing and evolving standards activities to be set within a common framework. The aim is to allow an application process in any computer that supports a particular set of standards to communicate freely with an application process in any other computer that supports the same standards, irrespective of its origin of manufacture.

Some examples of application processes that may wish to communicate in an open way are:

- a process (program) executing in a computer and accessing a remote file system;
- a process acting as a central file service (server) to a distributed community of (client) processes;
- a process in an office workstation (computer) accessing an electronic mail service;
- a process acting as an electronic mail server to a distributed community of (client) processes;
- a process in a supervisory computer controlling a distributed community of computer-based instruments or robot controllers associated with a process or automated manufacturing plant;
- a process in an instrument or robot controller receiving commands and returning results to a supervisory system;
- a process in a bank computer that initiates debit and credit operations on a remote system.

Open systems interconnection is concerned with the exchange of information between such processes. The aim is to enable application processes to cooperate in carrying out a particular (distributed) information processing task irrespective of the computers on which they are running.

1.4 ISO REFERENCE MODEL

A communication subsystem is a complex piece of hardware and software. Early attempts at implementing the software for such subsystems were often based on a single, complex, unstructured program (normally written in assembly language) with many interacting components. The resulting software was difficult to test and often very difficult to modify.

To overcome this problem, the ISO has adopted a layered approach for the reference model. The complete communication subsystem is broken down into a number of layers each of which performs a well defined function. Conceptually, these layers can be considered as performing one of two generic functions: network-dependent functions and application-oriented functions. This in turn gives rise to three distinct operational environments:

(1)   The **network environment**, which is concerned with the protocols and standards relating to the different types of underlying data communication networks.

(2)   The **OSI environment**, which embraces the network environment and adds additional application-oriented protocols and standards to allow end systems (computers) to communicate with one another in an open way.

(3)   The **real systems environment**, which builds on the OSI environment and is concerned with a manufacturer's own proprietary software and services, which have been developed to perform a particular distributed information processing task.

This is shown in diagrammatic form in Figure 1.8.

Both the network-dependent and application-oriented (network-independent) components of the OSI model are implemented as a number of layers. The boundaries between each layer, and the functions performed by each layer, have been selected on the basis of experience gained during earlier standardization activity.

Each layer performs a well defined function in the context of the overall communication subsystem. It operates according to a defined **protocol** by exchanging messages, both user data and additional control information, with a corresponding **peer** layer in a remote system. Each layer has a well defined interface between itself and the layer immediately above and below. Consequently, the implementation of a particular protocol layer is independent of all other layers.

FIGURE 1.8

Operational environments.

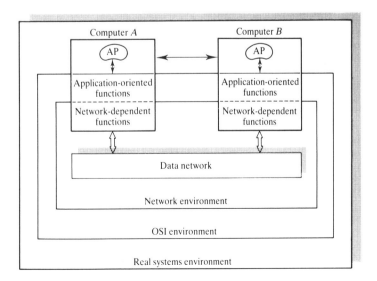

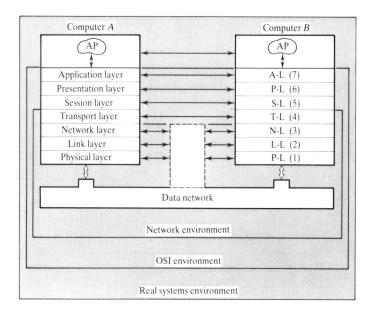

FIGURE 1.9

Overall structure of the
ISO Reference Model.

The logical structure of the ISO Reference Model is made up of seven protocol layers, as shown in Figure 1.9. The three lowest layers (1–3) are network dependent and are concerned with the protocols associated with the data communication network being used to link the two communicating computers. In contrast, the three upper layers (5–7) are application oriented and are concerned with the protocols that allow two end user application processes to interact with each other, normally through a range of services offered by the local operating system. The intermediate transport layer (4) masks the upper application-oriented layers from the detailed operation of the lower network-dependent layers. Essentially, it builds on the services provided by the latter to provide the application-oriented layers with a network-independent message interchange service.

The function of each layer is specified formally as a protocol that defines the set of rules and conventions used by the layer to communicate with a similar peer layer in another (remote) system. Each layer provides a defined set of services to the layer immediately above. It also uses the services provided by the layer immediately below it to transport the message units associated with the protocol to the remote peer layer. For example, the transport layer provides a network-independent message transport service to the session layer above it and uses the service provided by the network layer below it to transfer the set of message units associated with the transport protocol to a peer transport layer in another system. Conceptually, therefore, each layer communicates with a similar peer layer in a remote system according to a defined protocol. However, in practice the resulting protocol message units of the layer are passed by means of the services provided by the next lower layer. The basic functions of each layer are summarized in Figure 1.10.

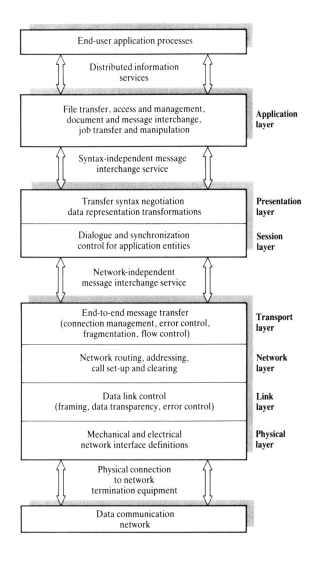

FIGURE 1.10

Protocol layer summary.

1.4.1 The application-oriented layers

The application layer

The **application layer** provides the user interface – normally an application program/process – to a range of network-wide distributed information services. These include file transfer access and management, as well as general document and message interchange services such as electronic mail. A number of standard protocols are either available or are being developed for these and other types of service.

Access to application services is normally achieved through a defined set of primitives, each with associated parameters, which are supported by the local operating system. The access primitives are the same as other operating system calls (as used for access to, say, a local file system) and result in an appropriate operating system procedure (process) being activated. These operating system procedures use the communication subsystem (software and hardware) as if it is a local device – similar to a disk controller, for example. The detailed operation and implementation of the communication subsystem is thus transparent to the (user) application process. When the application process making the call is rescheduled (run), one (or more) status parameters are returned indicating the success (or otherwise) of the network transaction that has been attempted.

In addition to information transfer, the application layer provides such services as:

- identification of the intended communication partner(s) by name or by address;
- determination of the current availability of an intended communication partner;
- establishment of authority to communicate;
- agreement on privacy (encryption) mechanisms;
- authentication of an intended communication partner;
- selection of the dialogue discipline, including the initiation and release procedures;
- agreement on responsibility for error recovery;
- identification of constraints on data syntax (character sets, data structures, etc).

The presentation layer

The **presentation layer** is concerned with the representation (syntax) of data during transfer between two communicating application processes. To achieve true open systems interconnection, a number of common **abstract data syntax** forms have been defined for use by application processes together with associated **transfer** (or **concrete**) **syntaxes**. The presentation layer negotiates and selects the appropriate transfer syntax(es) to be used during a transaction so that the syntax (structure) of the messages being exchanged between two application entities is maintained. Then, if this form of representation is different from the internal abstract form, the presentation entity performs the necessary conversion.

To illustrate the services provided by the presentation layer, consider a telephone conversation between a French speaking person and a Spanish speaking person. Assume each uses an interpreter and that the only language understood by both interpreters is English. Each interpreter must translate from their local language to English, and vice versa. The two correspondents are thus analogous to two application processes with the two interpreters representing presentation layer entities. French and Spanish are the local syntaxes and English the transfer or concrete syntax. Note that there must be a universally understood language which must be defined to allow the agreed transfer language (syntax) to be negotiated. Also note that the interpreters do not necessarily understand the meaning (semantics) of the conversation.

Another function of the presentation layer is concerned with data security. In some applications, data sent by an application is first encrypted (enciphered) using a **key**, which is (hopefully) known only by the intended recipient presentation layer. The latter decrypts (deciphers) any received data using the corresponding key before passing it on to the intended recipient. Although this is not currently part of the standard, the subject of encryption is discussed in Chapter 11 in the context of the presentation layer.

The session layer

The **session layer** provides the means that enable two application layer protocol entities to organize and synchronize their dialogue and manage their data exchange. It is thus responsible for setting up (and clearing) a communication (dialogue) channel between two communicating application layer protocol entities (presentation layer protocol entities in practice) for the duration of the complete network transaction. A number of optional services are provided, including:

- Interaction management: The data exchange associated with a dialogue may be duplex or half-duplex. In the latter case it provides facilities for controlling the exchange of data (dialogue units) in a synchronized way.

- Synchronization: For lengthy network transactions, the user (through the services provided by the session layer) may choose periodically to establish synchronization points associated with the transfer. Then, should a fault develop during a transaction, the dialogue may be restarted at an agreed (earlier) synchronization point.

- Exception reporting: Non-recoverable exceptions arising during a transaction can be signalled to the application layer by the session layer.

The transport layer

The **transport layer** acts as the interface between the higher application-oriented layers and the underlying network-dependent protocol layers. It provides the session layer with a message transfer facility that is independent of the underlying network type. By providing the session layer with a defined set of message transfer facilities the transport layer hides the detailed operation of the underlying network from the session layer.

The transport layer offers a number of **classes of service** which cater for the varying **quality of service (QOS)** provided by different types of network. There are five classes of service ranging from:

- class 0, which provides only the basic functions needed for connection establishment and data transfer, to

- class 4, which provides full error control and flow control procedures.

As an example, class 0 may be selected for use with a PSDN while class 4 may be used with a PSTN. This will be expanded upon in Chapter 10 when the transport layer is discussed in detail.

1.4.2 The network-dependent layers

As the lowest three layers of the ISO Reference Model are network dependent, their detailed operation varies from one network type to another. In general, however, the **network layer** is responsible for establishing and clearing a network-wide connection between two transport layer protocol entities. It includes such facilities as network routing (addressing) and, in some instances, flow control across the computer-to-network interface. In the case of internetworking it provides various harmonizing functions between the interconnected networks.

The **link layer** builds on the physical connection provided by the particular network to provide the network layer with a reliable information transfer facility. It is thus responsible for such functions as error detection and, in the event of transmission errors, the retransmission of messages. Normally, two types of service are provided:

(1) **Connectionless**, which treats each information frame as a self-contained entity that is transferred using a best-try approach; that is, if errors are detected in a frame then the frame is simply discarded.

(2) **Connection oriented**, which endeavours to provide an error-free information transfer facility.

Finally, the **physical layer** is concerned with the physical and electrical interfaces between the user equipment and the network terminating equipment. It provides the link layer with a means of transmitting a serial bit stream between the two equipments.

1.5 OPEN SYSTEM STANDARDS

The ISO Reference Model has been formulated simply as a template for the structure of a communication subsystem on which standards activities associated with each layer may be based. It is not intended that there should be a single standard protocol associated with each layer. Rather, a set of standards is associated with each layer, each offering different levels of functionality. Then, for a specific open systems interconnection environment, such as that linking numerous computer-based systems in a fully-automated manufacturing plant, a selected set of standards is defined for use by all systems in that environment.

The three major international bodies actively producing standards for computer communications are the ISO, the American Institution of Electrical and Electronic Engineers (IEEE) and the International Telegraph and Telephone Consultative Committee (CCITT). Essentially, ISO and IEEE produce standards for use by computer manufacturers while CCITT defines standards for connecting equipment to the different types of national and international public network. As the degree of overlap between the computer and telecommunications industries increases, however, there is an increasing level of cooperation and commonality between the standards produced by these organizations.

In addition, prior to and concurrently with ISO standards activity, the United States Department of Defense has for many years funded research into computer communications and networking through its **Defense Advanced Research Projects Agency (DARPA)**. As part of this research, the computer networks associated with a large number of universities and other research establishments were linked to those of DARPA. The resulting internetwork, known as **ARPANET**, has recently been extended to incorporate internets developed by other government agencies. The combined internet is now known simply as the **Internet**.

The protocol suite used with the Internet is known as **Transmission Control Protocol/Internet Protocol (TCP/IP)**. It includes both network-oriented protocols and application support protocols. Because TCP/IP is in widespread use with an existing internet, many of the TCP/IP protocols have been used as the basis for ISO standards. Moreover, since all the protocol specifications associated with TCP/IP are in the public domain – and hence no licence fees are payable – they have been used extensively by commercial and public authorities for creating open system networking environments. In practice, therefore, there are two major open system (vendor-independent) standards: the TCP/IP protocol suite and those based on the evolving ISO standards.

Figure 1.11 shows some of the standards associated with the TCP/IP protocol suite. As can be seen, since TCP/IP has developed concurrently with the ISO initiative, it does not contain specific protocols relating to all the ISO layers.

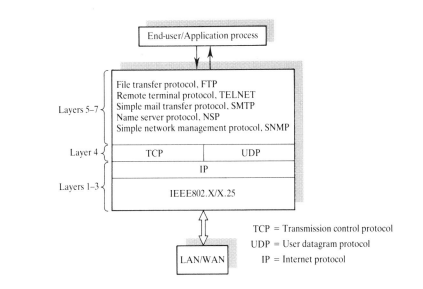

FIGURE 1.11

TCP/IP protocol suite.

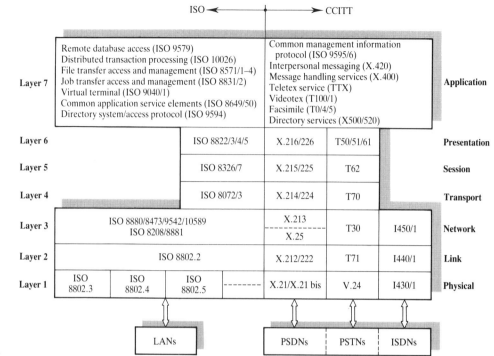

FIGURE 1.12

Standards summary.

Moreover, the specification methodology used for the TCP/IP protocols differs from that used for the ISO standards. Nevertheless, most of the functionality associated with the ISO layers is embedded in the TCP/IP suite.

In the case of ISO/CCITT standards, as can be seen in Figure 1.12, a range of standards is associated with each layer. Collectively they enable the administrative authority that is establishing the open system environment to select the most suitable set of standards for the application. The resulting protocol suite is known as the **open system interconnection profile**. A number of such profiles have now been defined, including: **TOP**, a protocol set for use in technical and office environments; **MAP**, for use in manufacturing automation; US and UK **GOSIP** for use in US and UK government projects, respectively; and a similar suite used in Europe known as the **CEN functional standards**. The latter has been defined by the Standards Promotion and Application Group (**SPAG**), a group of twelve European companies.

As Figure 1.12 shows, the lower three layers vary for different network types. CCITT has defined V, X and I series standards for use with public-carrier networks. The V series is for use with the existing switched telephone network (PSTN), the X series for use with existing switched data networks (PSDN) and the I series for use with the emerging integrated services digital networks (ISDN). X and I series are discussed in Chapter 8. Those produced by ISO/IEEE for use with local area networks are discussed in Chapters 6, 7 and 9.

Although different numbering systems are used by ISO and CCITT, the function and specification of the transport, session and presentation layers are almost identical. There is then a range of application layer standards, some defined by ISO for private networks and others by CCITT for public-carrier services. The function and operation of the application-oriented (network-independent) protocol layers are described in Chapters 10, 11 and 12.

1.6 SUMMARY

This chapter has reviewed several applications of computer communication networks. The different types of data communication networks used in these applications have also been discussed. The standards pertaining to computer communications have been reviewed and the structure and standards associated with the ISO Reference Model identified. The most widely used open system standard is the TCP/IP protocol suite developed by the US Defense Advanced Research Projects Agency (DARPA). The structure and protocols associated with TCP/IP have also been reviewed. Finally, some of the protocol suites that have been defined based on the ISO protocols have been identified. The structure and contents of the remaining chapters in the book are outlined in Figure 1.13.

The chapters are grouped into three sections. The first section, which is concerned with the issues involved in creating a basic data communications facility, describes alternative data transmission methods and error control. It also introduces the subject of protocols and describes some widely-used data link protocols.

The second section is concerned with the mode of operation and protocols relating to both local area and wide area computer networks as well as with issues relating to internetworks. The standard protocols used for interfacing a computer to these networks are also discussed.

The third section covers the issues and protocols relating to the higher-layer protocols that must be considered when interworking between hetero-geneous computer systems. Standard protocols that have been defined for use in different applications are identified and their functionality explained. Finally, there is a discussion on how the various protocols associated with an open system stack cooperate and interact to provide selected application services.

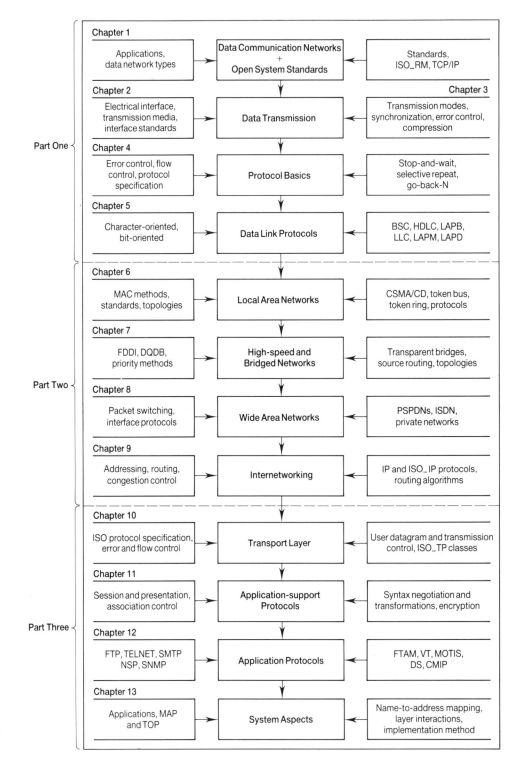

FIGURE 1.13

Chapter summary and contents.

2

The electrical interface

CHAPTER CONTENTS

CHAPTER OBJECTIVES

When you have completed studying the material in this chapter you should be able to:

- describe the different types of physical transmission media that are used to transmit data;
- appreciate the characteristics and limitations of each type of medium.
- explain the different forms of electrical signal that are used with some of the alternative transmission media;
- appreciate that standards have been defined for connecting a computer to data circuit terminating equipment, which include the type of transmission medium, the form of the electrical signals to be used and the use of additional control lines to regulate the flow of data across the interface;
- understand the function of a number of additional control lines that are used with some of the more common standards;
- appreciate that a modem must be used when data is transmitted over the PSTN;
- describe some of the alternative designs for the modulator and demodulator sections of a modem;
- understand the derivation and structure of digital leased circuits.

2.1 INTRODUCTION

To transmit binary data over a transmission line, the binary digits making up each element to be transmitted must be converted into electrical signals. For example, a binary 1 may be transmitted by applying a voltage signal (or level) of amplitude +V volts to the sending end of a transmission line and a binary 0 by applying −V volts. On receiving these signals, the receiving device interprets +V volts as a binary 1 and −V volts as a binary 0. In practice, however, transmitted electrical signals are **attenuated** (smaller) and **distorted** (misshapen) by the transmission medium, so that at some stage the receiver is unable to discriminate between the binary 1 and 0 signals, as shown in Figure 2.1. The extent of attenuation and distortion is strongly influenced by:

- the type of transmission medium;
- the bit rate of the data being transmitted; and
- the distance between the two communicating devices.

The various sources of impairment will be expanded upon later in the chapter.

As attenuation and distortion can be quantified for different types of transmission media and physical separations, international standards have been defined for the electrical interface between two items of data communications equipment. These standards not only define the electrical signal levels to be used but also the use and meaning of any additional control signals and conventions that are used at the physical interface. The two bodies that formulate standards for interconnecting data communications equipment are the **International Telegraph**

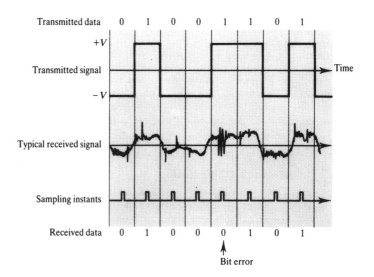

FIGURE 2.1

Effect of imperfect transmission medium.

and Telephone Consultative Committee (CCITT) in Europe and the **Electrical Industries Association (EIA)** in the United States. Although the standards defined by both bodies use slightly different terminology, the basic signals and their meanings are the same.

This chapter is divided into four sections: the first describes the most widely used transmission media; the second, the different forms of electrical signals; the third, the characteristics of public carrier circuits; and the fourth, some additional aspects of the more common physical layer interface standards. Although in most instances we will consider the interface of a computer to the different data communication interfaces, it is normal to use the more general term data terminal equipment or DTE rather than computer since this implies any type of equipment.

2.2 TRANSMISSION MEDIA

The transmission of an electrical signal requires the use of a transmission medium which normally takes the form of a **transmission line**. In some cases, this consists of a pair of conductors or wires. Common alternatives are a beam of light guided by a glass fibre and electromagnetic waves propagating through free space. The type of transmission medium is important, since it determines the maximum number of bits (**binary digits**) that can be transmitted per second or **bps**. The more common types of transmission media are discussed in the following sections.

2.2.1 Two-wire open lines

A **two-wire open line** is the simplest transmission medium. Each wire is insulated from the other and both are open to free space. This type of line is adequate for connecting equipment that is up to 50 m apart using moderate bit rates (less than, say, 19.2 kbps). The signal, which is typically a voltage or current level relative to some ground reference, is applied to one wire while the ground reference is applied to the other.

Although a 2-wire open line can be used to connect two computers (DTEs) directly, it is used mainly for connecting a DTE to local data circuit terminating equipment (DCE) – a modem, for example. As will be seen, such connections usually utilize multiple lines, the most common arrangement being a separate insulated wire for each signal and a signal wire for the common ground reference. The complete set of wires is then either enclosed in a single protected **multicore cable** or moulded into a **flat ribbon cable** as shown in Figure 2.2(a).

With this type of line, care is needed to avoid cross coupling of electrical signals between adjacent wires in the same cable. This is known as **crosstalk** and is caused by **capacitive coupling** between the two wires. In addition, the open structure makes it susceptible to the pick-up of spurious **noise signals** from other electrical signal sources caused by **electromagnetic radiation**. The main problem with interference signals is that they may be picked up in just one wire – the signal wire, for example – creating an additional difference signal between the two wires. Since the receiver normally operates using the difference signal between the two wires, this can give rise to an erroneous interpretation of the combined (signal plus noise) received signal. These factors all contribute to the limited lengths of line and bit rates that can be used reliably.

2.2.2 Twisted pair lines

Much better immunity to spurious noise signals can be achieved by employing a **twisted pair line** in which a pair of wires are twisted together. The proximity of the signal and ground reference wires means that any interference signal is picked up by both wires reducing its effect on the difference signal. Furthermore, if multiple twisted pairs are enclosed within the same cable, the twisting of each pair within the cable further reduces crosstalk. A schematic of a twisted pair line is shown in Figure 2.2(b).

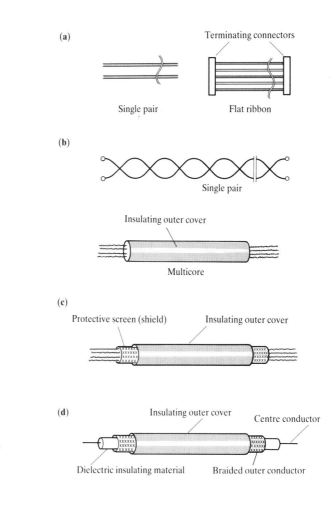

FIGURE 2.2

Copper wire transmission media: (a) two-wire open lines; (b) unshielded twisted pair; (c) shielded twisted pair; (d) coaxial cable.

Twisted pair lines are suitable, with appropriate line driver and receiver circuits that exploit the potential advantages gained by using such a geometry, for bit rates in the order of 1 Mbps over short distances (less than 100 m) and lower bit rates over longer distances. More sophisticated driver and receiver circuits enable similar or even higher rates to be achieved over much longer distances. Such lines, known as **unshielded twisted pairs**, or **UTP**, are used extensively in telephone networks and (with special integrated circuits) in many data communication applications. With some twisted pair cables, a protective screen or shield is used to reduce further the effects of interference signals. This is referred to as a **shielded twisted pair** or **STP** (see Figure 2.2(c)).

2.2.3 Coaxial cable

The main limiting factor of a twisted pair line is caused by a phenomenon known as the **skin effect**. As the bit rate (and hence frequency) of the transmitted signal increases, the current flowing in the wires tends to flow only on the outer surface of the wire, thus using less of the available cross-section. This increases the electrical resistance of the wires for higher frequency signals leading to higher attenuation. In addition, at higher frequencies, more signal power is lost as a result of radiation effects. Hence, for applications that demand a bit rate higher than 1 Mbps, either more sophisticated driver and receiver electronics or another type of transmission medium must be used.

Coaxial cable minimizes both these effects. Figure 2.2(d) shows that the signal and ground reference wires take the form of a solid centre conductor running concentrically (coaxially) inside a solid (or braided) outer circular conductor. Ideally the space between the two conductors should be filled with air, but in practice it is normally filled with a dielectric insulating material with a solid or honeycomb structure.

The centre conductor is effectively shielded from external interference signals. Also only minimal losses occur as a result of electromagnetic radiation and the skin effect. Coaxial cable can be used with a number of different signal types, but typically 10 Mbps over several hundred metres – or higher with modulation – is perfectly feasible. Also, as will be expanded upon later, coaxial cable is applicable to both point-to-point and multipoint topologies.

2.2.4 Optical fibre

While the geometry of coaxial cable significantly reduces the various limiting effects, the maximum signal frequency, and hence the information rate that can be transmitted using a solid (normally copper) conductor, although very high, is limited. This is also the case for twisted pair lines. **Optical fibre cable** differs from both these transmission media in that it carries the transmitted information in the form of a fluctuating beam of light in a glass fibre, rather than as an electrical signal on a wire. Light waves have a much wider bandwidth than electrical waves enabling optical fibre cable to achieve transmission rates of hundreds of megabits per second. Furthermore, light waves are immune to electromagnetic interference and crosstalk. Consequently, optical fibre cable is also extremely useful for the transmission of lower bit rate signals in electrically noisy environments – steel plants, for example, which employ much high-voltage and current-switching equipments. It is also being used increasingly where security is important, since it is difficult to physically tap an optical fibre cable.

An optical fibre cable consists of a single glass fibre for each signal to be transmitted, contained within a protective coating which also shields the fibre from any external light sources. A diagram of such a cable is shown in Figure 2.3(a). The light signal is generated by an optical transmitter, which performs the conversion from normal electrical signals as used in a DTE. Similarly, an optical receiver is used to perform the reverse function at the receiving end. Typically, the transmitter uses a **light-emitting diode (LED)** or **injection laser**

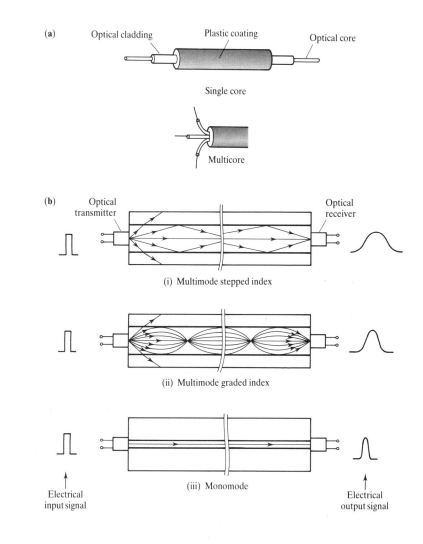

FIGURE 2.3

Optical fibre principles:
(a) cable structure;
(b) transmission modes.

diode (ILD) to perform the conversion operation while the receiver uses a light-sensitive **photodiode** or **photo transistor**.

The fibre itself consists of two parts: the glass core and a glass cladding with a lower refractive index. Light propagates along the optical fibre core in one of three ways depending on the type and width of core material used. These are shown in Figure 2.3(b).

In a **multimode stepped index fibre** the cladding and core material each has a different but uniform refractive index. All the light emitted by the diode at an angle less than the critical angle is reflected at the cladding interface and propagates along the core by means of multiple (internal) reflections. Depending on the angle at which the light is emitted by the diode, light will take a variable amount of time to propagate along the cable. The received signal thus has a wider pulse width than the input signal with a corresponding decrease in the maximum permissible bit rate. This type of cable is thus used primarily for modest bit rates with relatively inexpensive LEDs.

Dispersion can be reduced by using a core material that has a variable (rather than constant) refractive index. As shown in Figure 2.3 part (ii), in such a **muiltimode graded index fibre** light is refracted by an increasing amount as it moves away from the core. This has the effect of narrowing the pulse width of the received signal compared with stepped index fibre, allowing a corresponding increase in maximum bit rate.

Further improvements can be obtained by reducing the core diameter to that of a single wavelength (3–10 μm) so that all the emitted light propagates along a single path. Consequently the received signal is of a comparable width to the input signal. This **singlemode fibre**, which is normally used with ILDs, can operate at hundreds of megabits per second.

2.2.5 Satellites

All the transmission media mentioned so far have used a physical line to carry the transmitted information. However, data can also be transmitted using electromagnetic (radio) waves through free space as in **satellite** systems. A collimated **microwave beam**, onto which the data is modulated, is transmitted to the satellite from the ground. This beam is received and retransmitted (relayed) to the predetermined destination(s) using a directional antenna and an on-board circuit known as a **transponder**. A single satellite has many such transponders each covering a particular band of frequencies. A typical satellite channel has an extremely high bandwidth (500 MHz) and can provide many hundreds of high bit rate data links using a technique known as **multiplexing**. This will be described in more detail later but, essentially, the total available capacity of the channel is divided into a number of subchannels, each of which can support a high bit rate link.

Satellites used for communication purposes are normally **geostationary**, which means that the satellite orbits the earth once every 24 hours in synchronism with the earth's rotation and hence appears stationary from the ground. The orbit of the satellite is chosen so that it provides a line-of-sight communication path to the transmitting station(s) and receiving station(s). The degree of the collimation of the microwave beam retransmitted by the satellite can be either coarse, so that the signal can be picked up over a wide geographical area, or finely focused, so that it can only be picked up over a limited area. In the second case the signal power is higher allowing smaller diameter receivers known as **antennas** or **dishes** (known as **very small aperture terminals** or **VSATs**) to be used. Satellites are widely used for data transmission applications ranging from interconnecting different national computer communication networks to providing high bit rate paths to link communication networks in different parts of the same country.

A typical satellite system is shown in Figure 2.4(a). Only a unidirectional transmission path is shown but a duplex path is used in most practical applications. The up and down channels associated with each ground station then operate at different frequencies. Other common configurations involve a central hub ground station that communicates with a number of VSAT ground stations distributed around the country. Typically, a computer is connected to each VSAT and can communicate with a central computer connected to the hub, as shown in Figure 2.4(b). Normally, the central site broadcasts to all VSATs on a single frequency, whilst in the reverse direction each VSAT transmits at a different frequency.

To communicate with a particular VSAT, the central site broadcasts the message with the identity of the intended VSAT at the head of the message. For applications that require VSAT-to-VSAT communication, all messages are first sent to the central site – via the satellite – which then broadcasts them to the intended recipients. With the next generation of higher-powered satellites, however, it will be possible for the routing to be carried out on-board the satellite without passing through a central site. Thus direct VSAT-to-VSAT communication is possible.

2.2.6 Terrestrial microwave

Terrestrial microwave links are widely used to provide communication links when it is impractical or too expensive to install physical transmission media; for example, across a river or perhaps a swamp or desert. As the collimated microwave beam travels through the earth's atmosphere, it can be disturbed by

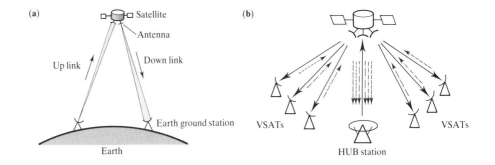

FIGURE 2.4

Satellite transmission:
(a) point-to-point;
(b) multipoint.

such factors as man-made structures and adverse weather conditions. With a satellite link, on the other hand, the beam travels mainly through free space and is therefore less prone to such effects. Nevertheless, line-of-sight microwave communication through the earth's atmosphere can be used reliably over distances in excess of 50 km.

2.2.7 Radio

Lower frequency **radio transmission** is also used in place of fixed wire links over more modest distances using ground-based transmitters and receivers. For example, to connect a large number of data gathering computers distributed throughout a rural area to a remote data logging/monitoring computer, or for connecting computers (or computer-based terminals) within a town or city to a local or remote computer.

Clearly, it would be expensive to install fixed-wire cables for such applications. Hence radio is often used to provide a **cordless (wireless) link** between a fixed-wire termination point and the distributed computers. A radio transmitter (known as the base station) is placed at the fixed-wire termination point, as shown in Figure 2.5(a), providing a cordless link between each computer and the central site.

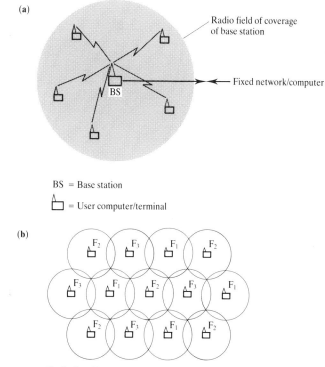

FIGURE 2.5

Ground-based radio transmission: (a) single cell; (b) multiple cells.

Multiple base stations must be used for applications that require a wider coverage area or a higher density of users. The coverage area of each base station is restricted – by limiting its power output – so that it provides only sufficient channels to support the total load in that area. Wider coverage is achieved by arranging multiple base stations in a cell structure, as shown in Figure 2.5(b). In practice, the size of each cell varies and is determined by such factors as the terminal density and local terrain.

Each base station operates using a different band of frequencies from its neighbours. However, since the field of coverage of each base station is limited, it is possible to re-use its frequency band in other parts of the network. Base stations are connected to the fixed network as before. Normally, the usable data rate available to each of the computers within a cell is tens of kilobits per second.

A similar arrangement can be utilized within a building to provide cordless links to computer-based equipment within each office. In such cases one or more base stations are located on each floor of the building and connected to the fixed network. Each base station then provides cordless links to the fixed network for all the computers in its field of coverage. Clearly, this avoids re-wiring whenever a new computer is installed or moved, but at the cost of providing a radio unit to convert the data into and from a radio signal. Also, the usable data rate is often much lower than with fixed wiring.

2.3 ATTENUATION AND DISTORTION SOURCES

The various attenuation and distortion effects that can degrade a signal during transmission are shown in Figure 2.6. Any signal carried on a transmission medium will be affected by attenuation, limited bandwidth, delay distortion and noise. Although all are present and produce a combined effect, each impairment will be considered separately.

Attenuation

As a signal propagates along a transmission medium (line) its amplitude decreases. This is known as **signal attenuation**. Normally, to allow for attenuation, a limit is set on the length of the cable that can be used to ensure that the receiver circuitry can reliably detect and interpret the received attenuated signal. If the cable is longer, one or more **amplifiers** – also known as **repeaters** – must be inserted at intervals along the cable to restore the received signal to its original level.

Signal attenuation increases as a function of frequency. Hence, since a signal comprises a range of frequencies, the signal is also distorted. To overcome this problem, the amplifiers are designed to amplify different frequency signals by varying amounts. Alternatively devices known as **equalizers** are used to equalize the attenuation across a defined band of frequencies.

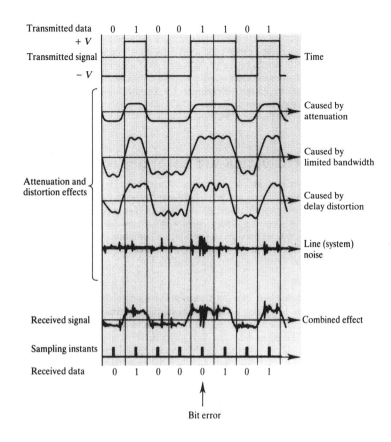

FIGURE 2.6

Sources of attenuation
and distortion.

Limited bandwidth

Since a typical digital signal consists of a large number of frequency components, only those components that are within the bandwidth of the transmission medium are received. It may be recalled that the amplitude of each frequency component making up a digital signal diminishes with increasing frequency. It can be concluded, therefore, that the larger the bandwidth of the medium, the more higher frequency components are passed and hence a more faithful reproduction of the original (transmitted) signal is received.

A formula derived by **Nyquist** can be used to determine the maximum information (data) rate of a transmission medium as a function of its bandwidth. If a system or transmission line has a bandwidth of B hertz, Nyquist showed that the maximum data rate, assuming just two levels per signalling element, is $2B$. More generally, the Nyquist formula for determining the maximum data transfer rate of a line or system, C, assuming M levels per signalling element, is given by:

$$C = 2B \log_2 M \text{ bps}$$

EXAMPLE

A modem to be used with a PSTN uses an AM-PSK modulation scheme with eight levels per signalling element. If the bandwidth of the PSTN is 3100 Hz, deduce the Nyquist maximum data transfer rate.

$$
\begin{aligned}
C &= 2B \log_2 M \\
&= 2 \times 3100 \times \log_2 8 \\
&= 2 \times 3100 \times 3 \\
&= 18\,600\,\text{bps}
\end{aligned}
$$

In practice the data transfer rate will be less than this because of other effects such as noise.

Delay distortion

The rate of propagation of a sinusoidal signal along a transmission line varies with the frequency of the signal. Consequently, when transmitting a digital signal the various frequency components making up the signal arrive at the receiver with varying delays, resulting in **delay distortion** of the received signal. The amount of distortion increases as the bit rate of the transmitted data increases for the following reason: as the bit rate increases, so some of the frequence components associated with each bit transition are delayed and start to interfere with the frequency components associated with a later bit. Delay distortion is also known therefore as **intersymbol interference**; its effect is to vary the bit transition instants of the received signal. Since the received signal is normally sampled at the nominal centre of each bit cell, this can lead to incorrect interpretation of the received signal as the bit rate increases.

Noise

In the absence of a signal, a transmission line or channel will ideally have zero electrical signal present. In practice, however, there will be random perturbations on the line even when no signal is being transmitted. This is known as the **line noise level**. In the limit, as a transmitted signal becomes attentuated, its level is reduced to that of the line (background) noise. An important parameter associated with a transmission medium, therefore, is the ratio of the power in a received signal, S, to the power in the noise level, N. The ratio S/N is known as the **signal-to-noise ratio** and normally is expressed in **decibels** or **dB** as:

$$
\frac{S}{N} = 10 \log_{10}\left(\frac{S}{N}\right) \text{dB}
$$

Clearly, a high S/N ratio means a high power signal relative to the prevailing noise level, resulting in a good quality signal. Conversely, a low S/N ratio means a low quality signal. The theoretical maximum information (data) rate of a transmisson medium is related to the S/N ratio and can be determined using a formula attributed to Shannon and Hartley. Known as the **Shannon–Hartley Law**, this formula states:

$$C = B \log_2\left(1 + \frac{S}{N}\right) \text{ bps}$$

where C is the information rate in bps, B is the bandwidth of the line (or system) in Hz, S is the signal power in watts and N is the random noise power in watts.

EXAMPLE

Assuming that a PSTN has a bandwidth of 3000 Hz and a typical signal-to-noise ratio of 20 dB, determine the maximum theoretical information (data) rate that can be achieved.

$$\frac{S}{N} = 10 \log_{10}\left(\frac{S}{N}\right)$$

Therefore:

$$20 = 10 \log_{10}\left(\frac{S}{N}\right)$$

Hence:

$$\frac{S}{N} = 100$$

Now:

$$C = B \log_2\left(1 + \frac{S}{N}\right)$$

Therefore:

$$C = 3000 \times \log_2(1 + 100)$$
$$= 19963 \text{ bps}$$

One source of noise, crosstalk, was identified earlier when discussing open-wire and twisted pair transmission lines. It is caused by unwanted electrical coupling between adjacent lines. This results in a signal being transmitted in one line being picked up by adjacent lines as a small but finite (noise) signal. An example of crosstalk is when one hears another call in the background when using the telephone; even though one is not talking oneself, a signal is still present on the line.

In practice, there are several types of crosstalk but in most cases the most limiting impairment is **near-end crosstalk** or **NEXT**. This is also known as **self-crosstalk** since it is caused by the strong signal output by a transmitter circuit being coupled (and hence interfering) with the much weaker signal at the input to the local receiver circuit. As explained in the text associated with Figure 2.6, the received signal is normally significantly attenuated and distorted and hence the amplitude of the coupled signal from the transmit section can be comparable with the received signal.

Special integrated circuits known as **adaptive NEXT cancellers** are now used to overcome this type of impairment. A typical arrangement is shown in Figure 2.7. The canceller circuit adaptively forms an inverted replica of the crosstalk signal that is coupled into the receive line from the local transmitter and adds this to the signal at the input to the receiver. Such circuits are now used in many applications involving unshielded twisted pair cable, for example, to transmit data at high bit rates.

Another related form of noise pick-up is **impulse noise**. This, as its name implies, is caused by impulses of electrical energy associated with external activity or equipment being picked up by a signal line. An example is a lightning discharge or, in the case of a telephone network, electrical impulses associated with the switching circuits used in old telephone exchanges. Normally, this takes the form of loud clicks on the line and, although unimportant during a telephone conversation, such sources can be particularly troublesome when transmitting

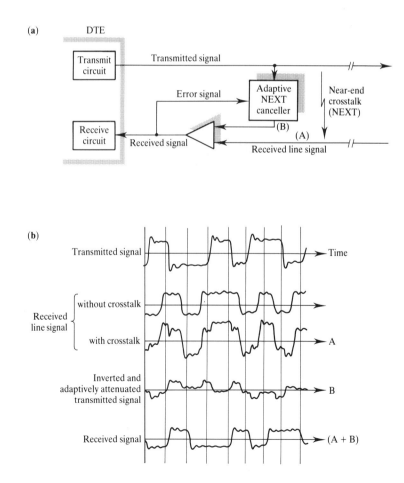

FIGURE 2.7

Adaptive NEXT cancellers: (a) circuit schematic; (b) example waveforms.

data. An impulse (click) of, say, one-half a second might corrupt 1200 bits of data at a transmission rate of 2400 bps. Fortunately, such sources of noise are relatively infrequent.

Both crosstalk and impulse noise are caused by electrical activity that is external to the transmission line. In contrast, a third type of noise, known as **thermal noise**, is present in all electronic devices and transmission media irrespective of any external effects. It is caused by the thermal agitation of electrons associated with each atom in the device or transmission line material. At all temperatures above absolute zero, all transmission media experience thermal noise. It is made up of random frequency components (across the complete frequency spectrum) of continuously varying amplitude. It is also known, therefore, as **white noise**.

It should be stressed that the Shannon–Hartley Law gives the theoretical maximum information rate. When considering the effect of noise in practice, it is important to determine the minimum signal level that must be used, relative to the noise level, to achieve a specific minimum **bit error rate**; that is, over a defined period, an acceptably low probability that a single bit will be misinterpreted by the receiver. For example, a bit error rate of 10^{-4} means that, on average, 1 bit in every 10^4 received will be misinterpreted. The energy measured in joules (= watts × seconds) per bit in a signal is given by the formula:

$$E = ST$$

where S is the signal power in watts and T is the time period for 1 bit in seconds. Now the data transmission rate R equals $1/T$ and hence:

$$E = \frac{S}{R} \text{ watts bit}$$

The level of (thermal) noise in a bandwidth of 1 Hz in any transmission line is given by the formula:

$$N_0 = kT$$

where N_0 is the noise power density in watts Hz^{-1}, k is Boltzmann's constant (1.3803×10^{-23} joule K^{-1}) and T is the temperature in degrees Kelvin (K).

To quantify the effect of noise, the energy per bit E is expressed as a ratio of the noise energy per hertz N_0:

$$\frac{E}{N_0} = \frac{S/R}{N_0} = \frac{S/R}{kT}$$

In practice, the value of E/N_0 used to achieve a particular bit error rate varies for the different modulation schemes. It can readily be deduced from the foregoing, however, that the signal power level S required to achieve an acceptable E/N_0 ratio – and hence the minimum bit error rate – increases with the temperature T and bit rate R.

2.4 SIGNAL TYPES

When two items of equipment (DTEs) are close to one another and only modest bit rates are used, data can be transmitted using two-wire open lines and simple interface circuits, which change the signal levels used within the equipment to a suitable level for use on the interconnecting cable. However, as the physical separation between the DTEs and the bit rate increase, more sophisticated circuits and techniques must be employed. Moreover, if the DTEs are in different parts of the country (or world) and no public data communication facilities are available, the only cost-effective approach is to use lines provided by the PTT authorities for telephony. When using this type of communication medium, it is normally necessary to convert the electrical signals output by the source DTE into a form analogous to the signals used to convey spoken messages. Similarly, on reception these signals must be converted back into a form suitable for use by the destination DTE. The equipment used to perform these functions is known as a **modem**. Some of the different signal types used by modems and other forms of transmission lines are discussed in the following sections.

2.4.1 RS-232C/V.24

The RS-232C interface (defined by EIA) and the V.24 interface (defined by CCITT) were originally defined as the standard interface for connecting a DTE to a PTT-supplied (or approved) modem, thereby allowing manufacturers of different equipment to use the transmission facilities available in the switched telephone network. The physical separation between the DTE and modem is therefore relatively short and the maximum possible bit rate relatively low (9600 bps). Since their introduction, these interfaces have been adopted as the standard for connecting any character-oriented peripheral device (for example, a VDU or a printer) to a computer, thus allowing peripherals from different manufacturers to be connected to the same computer.

Because of the short distances (less than a few centimetres) between neighbouring subunits within a DTE, the signal levels used to represent binary data are often quite small. For example, a common logic family used in digital equipment is **transistor transistor logic**, or **TTL**. This uses a voltage signal of between 2.0 V and 5.0 V to represent a binary 1 and a voltage of between 0.2 V and 0.8 V to represent a binary 0. Voltages between these two levels can yield an indeterminate state: in the worst case, if the voltage level is near one of the limits, even modest signal attenuation or electrical interference can lead to misinterpretation. Consequently, the voltage levels used when connecting two items of equipment are normally greater than those used to connect subunits within the equipment.

The signal levels defined for use with the RS.232C (V.24) interface are shown in Figure 2.8 together with the appropriate interface circuits. The voltage signals used on the lines are symmetric with respect to the ground reference signal and are at least 3 V: +3 V for a binary 0 and −3 V for a binary 1. In

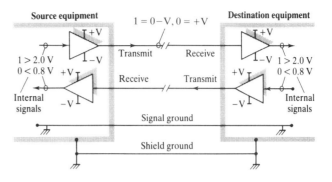

FIGURE 2.8

RS-232C/V.24 signal
levels – single ended/
unbalanced.

practice, the actual voltage levels used are determined by the supply voltages applied to the interface circuits, $\pm12\,V$ or even $\pm15\,V$ not being uncommon. The transmit circuits convert the low-level signal voltages used within the equipment to the higher voltage levels used on the transmission lines. Similarly, the receive circuits perform the reverse function. Interface circuits, known as **line drivers** and **line receivers**, respectively, perform the necessary voltage inversion functions.

The relatively large voltage levels used with this interface mean that the effects of signal attenuation and noise are much less significant than at, say, TTL logic levels. The RS-232C (V.24) interface normally uses a flat ribbon or multi-core cable with a single ground reference wire for connecting the equipment. Noise picked up in a signal wire can therefore be troublesome. To reduce crosstalk, it is not uncommon to connect a **capacitor** across the output of the transmitter circuit. This rounds off the transition edges of the transmitted signals, which in turn removes some of the troublesome higher frequency components in the signal. As the line length or signal bit rate increases, the attenuation of the line reduces the received signal levels to the point at which even low amplitude external noise signals produce erroneous operation. The RS-232C and V.24 standards specify maximum physical separations of less than 15 m and bit rates lower than 9.6 kbps, although larger values are often used when connecting a peripheral to a computer.

2.4.2 20 mA current loop

An alternative to the RS-232C standard is the 20 mA current loop. This, as the name implies, utilizes a current signal, rather than a voltage. Although it does not extend the available bit rate, it substantially increases the potential physical separation between two communicating devices. The basic approach is shown in Figure 2.9.

Essentially, the state of a switch (relay or other similar device) is controlled by the bit stream to be transmitted: the switch is closed for a binary 1, thus passing a current (pulse) of 10 mA, and opened for a binary 0, thus stopping the current flow. At the receiver, the flow of the current is detected by a matching current-sensitive circuit and the transmitted binary signal reproduced.

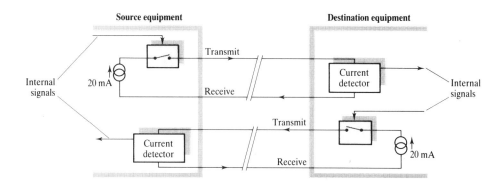

FIGURE 2.9

20 mA current loop.

The noise immunity of a current loop interface is much better than a basic voltage-driven interface since, as can be seen from Figure 2.9, it uses a pair of wires for each signal. This means that any external noise signals are normally picked up in both wires – often referred to as **common-mode noise** or **pick-up** – which has a minimal effect on the basic current-sensitive receiver circuit. Consequently, 20 mA current loop interfaces are particularly suitable for driving long lines (up to 1 km), but at modest bit rates because of the limited operational rate of the switches and current-sensitive circuits. It is for this reason that some manufacturers often provide two separate RS-232C output interfaces with a piece of equipment, one producing voltage output signals and the other 20 mA current signals. The user can then decide which interface to use depending on the physical separation between the equipment.

2.4.3 RS-422/V.11

If the physical separation and the bit rate are both to be increased, then the alternative RS-422/V.11 signal definition should be used. This is based on the use of a twisted pair cable and a pair of **differential** (also referred to as **balanced** or **double-ended**) **transmitter and receiver circuits**. A typical circuit arrangement is shown in Figure 2.10.

A differential transmitter produces twin signals of equal and opposite polarity for every binary 1 or 0 signal to be transmitted. As the differential receiver is sensitive only to the difference between the two signals on its two inputs, noise picked up by both wires will not affect receiver operation. Differential receivers, therefore, are said to have good **common-mode rejection** properties. A derivative of the RS-422, the RS-423, can be used to accept single-ended (**unbalanced**) voltages output by an RS-232C interface with a differential receiver. The RS-422 is suitable for use with twisted pair cable for physical separations of, say, 100 m at 1 Mbps, or greater distances at lower bit rates.

An important parameter of any transmission line is its **characteristic impedance** (Z_0) because a receiver only absorbs all of the received signal if the line is terminated by a resistor equal to Z_0. If this is not the case, **signal**

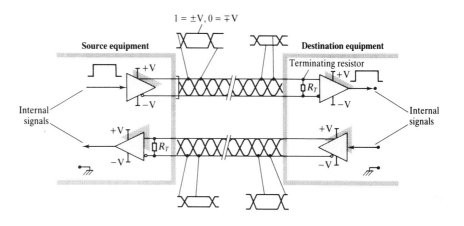

FIGURE 2.10

RS-422/V.11 signal levels – differential/ balanced.

reflections occur, which further distort the received signal. Lines are therefore normally terminated by a resistor equal to Z_0, with values from 50 to $200\,\Omega$ being common.

2.4.4 Coaxial cable signals

In contrast to the low bandwidth available with a connection through an analogue-switched telephone network, the usable bandwidth with a coaxial cable can be as much as $350\,\mathrm{MHz}$ (or higher). This potentially high bandwidth can be utilized in one of two ways:

(1) **Baseband mode**, in which all the available bandwidth is used to derive a single high bit rate ($10\,\mathrm{Mbps}$ or higher) transmission path (channel).

(2) **Broadband mode**, in which the available bandwidth is divided to derive a number of lower bandwidth subchannels (and hence transmission paths) on one cable.

Baseband

In baseband mode, normally the cable is driven from a single-ended voltage source. Because of the geometry of coaxial cable, however, the effect of external interference is very low. A number of matching transmit and receive interface circuits are available for use with coaxial cable. A typical connection is shown in Figure 2.11(b), which also shows the effect of terminating a line with the correct terminating resistance, Z_0. Such arrangements are suitable for transmitting data at up to $10\,\mathrm{Mbps}$ over a distance of several hundred metres.

In some applications, the cable is used exclusively for the transmission of data between two systems – that is, **point-to-point** – while in others the normally high bit rate transmission channel is time-shared by a number of systems – referred to as **multipoint** or **multidrop** configuration. Both arrangements are shown in Figure 2.11(b).

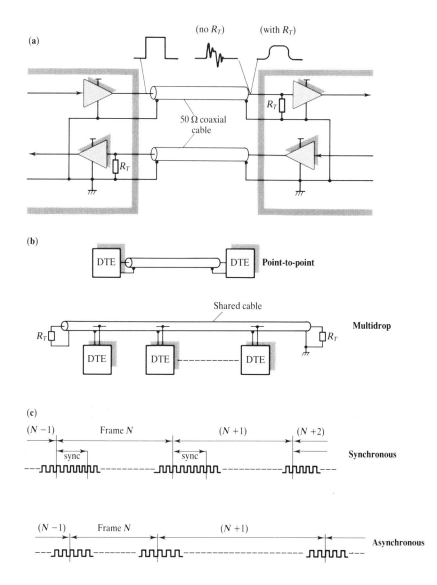

FIGURE 2.11

Baseband principles:
(a) coaxial cable signals;
(b) connection
methods; (c) TDM
methods.

Time division multiplexing or **TDM** is used to share the available capacity of a baseband transmission channel. Two types of TDM are used:

(1) Synchronous (or fixed cycle): Each user has access to the channel at precisely defined (synchronized) time intervals.

(2) Asynchronous (or on demand): Users have random access to the channel and, once a user has acquired access, is the sole user of the channel for the duration of the transmission.

These two forms of TDM are shown diagrammatically in Figure 2.11(c).

As will be described in Chapter 3, data is normally transmitted between two systems (DTEs) in the form of **frames** and, with synchronous TDM, each frame is of a fixed length. To ensure that all systems connected to the (shared) cable transmit data at their allotted time, a special bit pattern, known as the **synchronizing** (or simply **sync**) **pattern** is transmitted at the beginning of each frame. From this, each system can determine both the start of each frame and the position of the frame (frame number) in a complete cycle of frames. With asynchronous TDM, a mechanism must be employed to ensure that each system can gain access to the channel in a fair way, since each system has random access to the channel. As will be described in Chapter 6, asynchronous TDM is used in certain types of **local area data network**.

Broadband

Using the broadband mode, multiple (independent and concurrent) transmission channels are derived from a single distribution (coaxial) cable using a technique known as **frequency-division multiplexing** or **FDM**. FDM requires a device known as a **radio frequency** or **rf modem** – cf. (audio frequency) modems with the PSTN – between each connected device and the cable. The term radio frequency is utilized because the frequencies used for each channel are in the radio frequency spectrum, but otherwise the principles are the same as those described for baseband in the previous section. Thus, the selected (carrier) frequency for the transmit (forward) direction is modulated with the data to be transmitted and the selected frequency for the receive (reverse) direction is demodulated to derive the received data.

The bandwidth required for each channel is determined by the desired data (bit) rate and the modulation method. It is typically between 0.25 and 1.0 bits per Hz. Thus, a 9600 bps channel may require a bandwidth of about 20 kHz and a 10 Mbps channel around 18 MHz.

The principles of broadband working and the subunits within an rf modem are summarized in Figure 2.12. Normally, modulation (and demodulation) within a modem is carried out in two phases. First, a selected frequency signal is modulated using phase- or frequency-shift keying, by the data to be transmitted. Then, the modulated signal is mixed (multiplied) with a second frequency so that the frequency-translated signal is in the assigned frequency band. The filters shown in the figure allow only the signals associated with the assigned frequency band to be transmitted (on output) or processed (on input).

2.4.5 Optical fibre

There are a variety of forms of optical signal encoding. One, based on a bipolar encoding scheme, is shown in Figure 2.13. This type of encoding produces a three-level optical output which makes it suitable for operating the cable from dc (zero frequency equivalent to a continuous string of binary 0s or 1s) up to

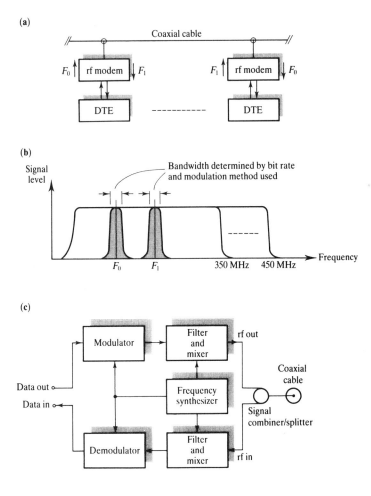

FIGURE 2.12

Broadband principles:
(a) cable schematic;
(b) bandwidth; (c) rf
modem schematic.

50 Mbps. The three optical power output levels are zero, half-maximum power and maximum power. The transmit module performs the conversion from the internal binary voltage levels to the three-level optical signal that is applied to the fibre using special connectors and a high-speed LED.

At the receiver, the fibre is terminated with a special connector to a high-speed photodiode housed within a special receiver module. This contains the control electronics needed to convert the electrical signal output by the photodiode, which is proportional to the light level, into the internal voltage levels corresponding to binary 1s and 0s.

Currently, optical fibre is used mainly in a point-to-point mode but, as with baseband coaxial cable, the transmission capacity available may be utilized either for a single high bit rate channel or, with (normally synchronous) TDM, to derive multiple lower bit rate channels on a single link.

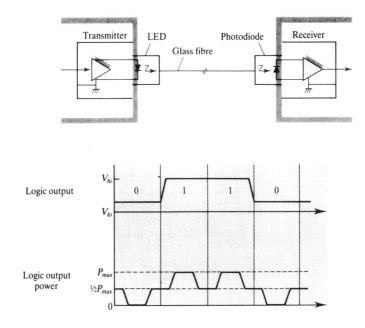

FIGURE 2.13

Optical fibre signals.

2.4.6 Satellite and radio

As indicated earlier, transmission channels in satellite and other radio-based systems are obtained by frequency division multiplexing. In addition, the available (baseband) capacity of each channel is normally further subdivided using synchronous time division multiplexing techniques.

A number of different **access control methods** are used to control access to the available capacity including:

- random access: all stations compete for a transmission channel in a random (uncontrolled) way;
- fixed assignment: both the channel frequency and the channel time slot are preassigned to each ground or cordless station;
- demand assignment: when a station wishes to transmit data, it first requests channel capacity from a central site which assigns the required capacity (time slots) to the requesting station.

Random access is the oldest type of access control method and was first used to control access to a single (shared) satellite channel. It will only work in those applications in which firstly, the total offered load is only a small fraction of the available channel capacity and secondly, all transmissions are randomly distributed. The technique is known as **Aloha** since it was first used by the University of Hawaii to link a community of computers distributed around several islands to a central computer located on the island of Oahu. The two versions of the scheme are shown in Figure 2.14(a).

With pure Aloha, when a station has a message (data) to transmit, it simply transmits (broadcasts) it. Clearly, if a second station starts to transmit while the first station is transmitting its message, both transmissions will be corrupted and a **collision** is said to have occurred. Thus the scheme will only work satisfactorily if the probability of two transmissions overlapping is small. Assuming randomly generated messages, the mean achievable throughput with this scheme is less than 20% of the available capacity. This can be improved, however, by establishing a synchronous time slot structure and constraining all transmissions to be carried out in these time slots. This scheme is known as **slotted Aloha** and, because a transmission can only corrupt another transmission in the same time slot, utilizations in excess of 30% are possible.

With **fixed assignment**, both the channel frequency and/or channel time slot are preassigned to each station in advance. In general, the preassignment of frequency channels is easier than time slot assignment. Hence in satellite applications based on a central hub, for example, a fixed frequency channel is normally preassigned to each VSAT and the central site then broadcasts on

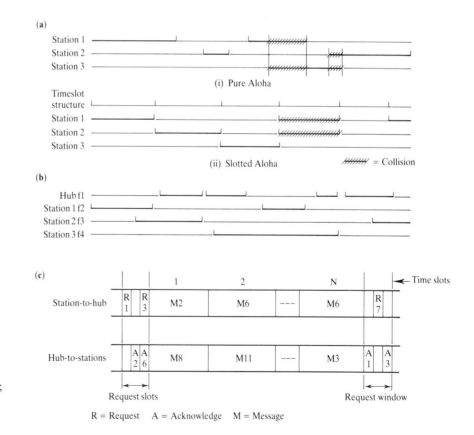

FIGURE 2.14

Satellite and radio access control methods:
(a) Aloha;
(b) Preassigned FDMA;
(c) Demand assigned TDMA.

another preassigned frequency channel. Generally, since there is only a single hub-to-VSAT channel, the frequency band (and hence bit rate) of this is wider than those used for VSAT-to-hub transmissions. Typical bit rates are 64 kbps for each VSAT-to-hub channel and up to 2 Mbps for the hub-to-VSAT broadcast channel. This type of access control scheme, known as **preassigned frequency division multiple access** or **preassigned FDMA**, is shown in Figure 2.14(b).

Much better channel utilization can be achieved by using a **demand assignment** access control method. This scheme provides a number of time slots – known as **request time slots** – in which a VSAT or cordless station can make a request to the hub or base station site for the use of one or more message time slots. If free capacity is available, the central site assigns specific message time slots for that transmission and informs the requesting station in a corresponding **acknowledge time slot**. Figure 2.14(c) illustrates this scheme which is known as **demand-assigned TDMA**.

As can be seen, a request slot is much shorter than normal message slots. A request message includes the identity of the requesting station and, assuming multiple time slots per message, the number of message time slots required. The corresponding request acknowledge message then indicates which message time slots should be used. All transmissions from the central site are made directly with the identity of the intended recipient station at the head of the message. To decrease the probability of a collision occurring in request slots, a station randomly selects a slot to use. However, if a collision does occur (indicated by no response) then the station tries again in the next **request window**.

Finally, it should be stressed before leaving the subject of radio that the bit error rate of a radio link (channel) is, in general, much higher than for a fixed-wire link. Consequently, as will be expanded upon in the next chapter, small message blocks are normally used and more sophisticated error detection and correction methods employed.

2.5 SIGNAL PROPAGATION DELAY

There is always a short but finite time delay for a signal (electrical, optical or radio) to propagate (travel) from one end of a transmission medium to the other. This is known as the **transmission propagation delay** of the medium. At best, signals propagate (radiate) through free space at the speed of light $(3 \times 10^8 \, \text{ms}^{-1})$. In contrast the speed of propagation for twisted pair wire or coaxial cable is a fraction of this figure. Typically, it is in the region of $2 \times 10^8 \, \text{ms}^{-1}$; that is, a signal will take $0.5 \times 10^{-8}\text{s}$ to travel 1 m through the medium. Although this may seem insignificant, in some situations the resulting delay is important.

As will be seen in subsequent chapters, data is normally transmitted in blocks (also known as frames) of bits. On receipt of a block, an acknowledgement of correct (or otherwise) receipt is returned to the sender. An important parameter associated with a data link, therefore, is the **round-trip delay** associated with the link; that is, the time delay between the first bit of a block being transmitted by the sender and the last bit of its associated acknowledge-ment being received. Clearly, this will be a function not only of the time taken to transmit the frame at the link bit rate but also on the propagation delay of the link. The relative weighting of the two times will vary for different types of data link and hence the two times are often expressed as a ratio a such that:

$$a = \frac{T_p}{T_x}$$

where

T_p = propagation delay

$$= \frac{\text{physical separation } S \text{ in metres}}{\text{velocity of propagation } V \text{ in metres per second}}$$

and:

T_x = transmission delay

$$= \frac{\text{number of bits to be transmitted } N}{\text{link bit rate } R \text{ in bits per second}}$$

EXAMPLE

A 1000-bit block of data is to be transmitted between two DTEs. Determine the ratio of the propagation delay to the transmission delay a for the following types of data link.

(a)   100m of twisted pair wire and a transmission rate of 10 kbps.
(b)   10 km of coaxial cable and a transmission rate of 1 Mbps.
(c)   50 000 km of free space (satellite link) and a transmission rate of 10 Mbps.

Assume that the velocity of propagation of an electrical signal within each type of medium is $2 \times 10^8 \text{ms}^{-1}$.

(a) $T_p = \dfrac{S}{V} = \dfrac{100}{2 \times 10^8} = 5 \times 10^{-7} \text{ s}$

$T_x = \dfrac{N}{R} = \dfrac{1000}{10 \times 10^3} = 0.1 \text{ s}$

$a = \dfrac{T_p}{T_x} = \dfrac{5 \times 10^{-7}}{0.1} = 5 \times 10^{-6}$

(b) $T_p = \dfrac{S}{V} = \dfrac{10 \times 10^3}{2 \times 10^8} = 5 \times 10^{-5} \text{ s}$

$T_x = \dfrac{N}{R} = \dfrac{1000}{1 \times 10^6} = 1 \times 10^{-3} \text{ s}$

$a = \dfrac{T_p}{T_x} = \dfrac{5 \times 10^{-5}}{1 \times 10^{-3}} = 5 \times 10^{-2}$

(c) $\quad T_p = \dfrac{S}{V} = \dfrac{5 \times 10^7}{2 \times 10^8} = 2.5 \times 10^{-1}$ s

$\quad T_x = \dfrac{N}{R} = \dfrac{1000}{10 \times 10^6} = 1 \times 10^{-4}$ s

$\quad a = \dfrac{T_p}{T_x} = \dfrac{2.5 \times 10^{-1}}{1 \times 10^{-4}} = 2.5 \times 10^{-3}$

It may be concluded from the foregoing results that:

- if a is less than 1, then the round-trip delay is determined primarily by the transmission delay;
- if a is equal to 1, then both delays have equal effect;
- if a is greater than 1, then the propagation delay dominates.

Furthermore, in case (c) it is interesting to note that, providing blocks are transmitted contiguously, there will be:

$$10 \times 10^6 \times 2.5 \times 10^{-1} = 2.5 \times 10^6 \text{ bits}$$

in transit between the two DTEs at any one time; that is, the sending DTE will have transmitted 2.5×10^6 bits before the first bit arrives at the receiving DTE. The implications of this will be discussed further in later chapters.

2.6 PUBLIC CARRIER CIRCUITS

When data is to be transmitted between two DTEs in the same building or establishment, this is (relatively) simply achieved by installing a cable. Typically, this may be unshielded or shielded twisted pair, coaxial cable or optical fibre. In some instances, radio may be used. When data is to be transmitted between two DTEs in different establishments, however, this can only be achieved by using microwave or satellite links, or lines from one of the public-carrier telephone companies. The last solution is widely used; both switched circuits and leased (dedicated) circuits are possible.

Switched circuits can be set up using the analogue public switched telephone network (PSTN) or an integrated services digital network (ISDN), depending on availability. Although the analogue PSTN was designed specifically for voice communications, it is also possible to transmit data using a modem. In the case of an ISDN, calls can be set up and data transmitted directly. Also much higher bit rates are possible.

In the case of leased circuits, although in some circumstances it is still necessary to use leased PSTN lines – and hence modems – in most cases leased circuits are now all-digital for reasons that will be given later in the section. Since public carrier circuits are used extensively in many data communication applications, this section describes the characteristics of such circuits in terms of their usage.

2.6.1 Analogue PSTN circuits

When data is to be transmitted using existing PSTN transmission lines, it is necessary to convert the electrical signals output by the source DTE into a form that is acceptable to the PSTN. The latter was designed for speech communications which are assumed to be made up of a mix of (audio) frequencies in the range 400 to 3400 Hz, as shown in Figure 2.15.

The range of signal frequencies that a circuit passes is known as its **bandwidth**. Thus, the PSTN is said to have a bandwidth of from 400 to 3400 Hz or simply 3000 Hz. This means that a telephone line will not pass low frequency signals that could occur if, for example, the data stream to be transmitted is made up of a continuous string of binary 1s or 0s. For this reason, it is not possible simply to apply two voltage levels to the telephone line, since zero output would be obtained for both levels if the binary data stream was all 1s or all 0s. Instead, it is necessary to convert the binary data into a form compatible with a speech signal at the sending end of the line and to reconvert this signal back into its binary form at the receiver. The circuit that performs the first operation is known as a **modulator**, and the circuit performing the reverse function a **demodulator**. Since each end of a data link normally both sends and receives data, the combined device is known as a modem.

Using modems, data can be transmitted through the PSTN either by dialling and thereby setting up a switched path through the network, as with a normal telephone call, or by leasing a **dedicated** (or **leased**) **line** from the PTT. Since leased lines bypass the normal switching equipment (exchange) in the network and are set up on a permanent or long-term basis, they are only economically justifiable for applications having a high utilization factor. An added advantage of a leased line is that its operating characteristics can be more accurately quantified than for a short-term switched circuit, making it feasible to use higher signalling (bit) rates. For clarity, the modulation and demodulation functions will be considered separately.

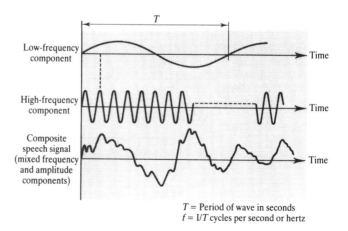

FIGURE 2.15

Speech waveform frequency components.

T = Period of wave in seconds
f = 1/T cycles per second or hertz

Modulation

Three basic types of modulation are employed for the conversion of a binary signal into a form suitable for transmission on a PSTN: amplitude modulation, frequency modulation and phase modulation. The general principle of each is illustrated in Figure 2.16.

With **amplitude modulation (AM)** the level or amplitude of a single frequency audio tone is switched or **keyed** between two levels at a rate determined by the transmitted binary data signal. The single frequency audio tone, known simply as the **carrier**, is selected to be within the acceptable range of frequencies for use in the PSTN. This type of modulation, although the simplest, is affected by varying signal attenuation caused, for example, by varying propagation conditions on different routes through the PSTN. In its basic form, therefore, this type of modulation is not often used, although it is utilized in conjunction with phase modulation in more sophisticated modem designs primarily used on leased lines.

In **frequency modulation (FM)** the frequency of a fixed amplitude carrier signal is changed according to the binary stream to be transmitted. Since only two frequencies (audio tones) are required for binary data, this type of modulation is also known as **digital FM** or **frequency-shift keying (FSK)**. It is the method most frequently used with lower bit rate modems (300 to 1200 baud) designed to operate with switched connections across the PSTN since the demodulation circuitry is relatively simple and the bandwidth requirements are low.

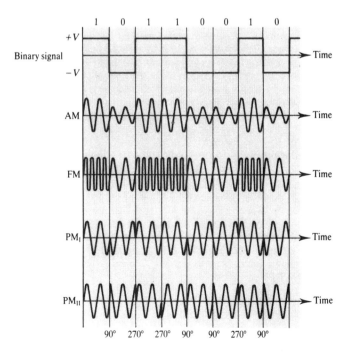

FIGURE 2.16

Modulation methods.

In the case of **phase modulation (PM)**, the frequency and amplitude of the carrier signal are kept constant while the carrier is shifted in **phase** as each bit in the data stream is transmitted. One form of PM uses two fixed carrier signals, for binary 1 and binary 0, with a 180 degree phase difference (equivalent to a signal reversal) between them. This is known as **phase-shift keying (PSK)**. As this type of PM must maintain a reference carrier signal at the receiver against which the phase of the received signal is compared, it is also known as **phase-coherent PSK**. In practice, such an arrangement can involve complex demodulation circuitry. Also this type of modulation is very susceptible to random phase changes in the transmitted waveform. Consequently an alternative form of PM is often used which employs shifts in phase at each bit transition determined by the state of the next bit to be transmitted relative to the current bit. A phase shift of 90 degrees relative to the current signal indicates a binary 0 is being transmitted whereas a phase shift of 270 degrees indicates a binary 1. Thus the demodulation circuitry need only determine the magnitude of each phase shift rather than the absolute value. This type of PM is therefore known as **differential PSK**.

Demodulation

To understand how the various modulated signals shown in Figure 2.16 are demodulated at the receiver to reproduce the transmitted data stream, it is necessary to understand some basic properties of these types of signal. As it is outside the scope of this book to derive the complex mathematical expressions for the waveforms produced by the different modulation methods, the aim here is to outline in a qualitative way the various effects that must be considered during the demodulation process. Some of these effects are shown in Figure 2.17. The following points should be noted when interpreting the figure:

(1) When a carrier signal of fixed frequency f_c is modulated by a second fixed frequency signal f_m, a number of additional frequency components known as **sidebands** are produced (Figure 2.17(a)). With AM, just two sidebands are produced, at $f_c + f_m$ and $f_c - f_m$, each containing a fraction of the power contained within the carrier. Note, however, that it is the sidebands that contain the required information f_m. With both FM and PM, many sidebands are produced at multiples of f_m from the carrier $(f_c + f_m, f_c + 2f_m,$ etc), the amplitudes of which are derived using **Bessel functions.**

(2) Using a mathematical technique known as **Fourier analysis**, it can be shown that a **square wave** – equivalent to a repetitive binary data string of 0, 1, 0, 1, 0, 1, and so on – is made up of an infinite number of sinusoidal frequency components. These comprise a **fundamental frequency**, f_n, equal to one-half the bit rate in **cycles per second** or **hertz**, and multiples of this frequency $(3f_n, 5f_n, 7f_n,$ etc), known as **harmonics**, the amplitudes of which decrease with increasing frequency.

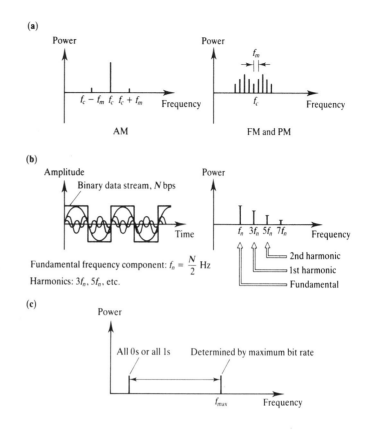

FIGURE 2.17

Modulation: (a) power–
frequency spectrum;
(b) square wave
frequency components;
(c) fundamental
frequency of binary
data stream.

(3)   When a binary data stream is transmitted, the bit pattern changes continuously. Hence, the fundamental frequency (and the associated harmonics) will also change continuously. At one extreme, the data stream
may be a square wave (equivalent to a string of 0, 1 transitions) while at
the other it may be a zero frequency (dc) signal (equivalent to a continuous string of 0s or 1s).

It can be concluded, therefore, that the signal produced after modulating
a sinusoidal carrier signal with a binary data stream is made up of the carrier plus
a possibly infinite number of additional frequency components which contain the
required information. Because most power is contained in the fundamental
frequency of the modulating bit stream and the primary sidebands of the resulting modulated signal, it is possible in practice to determine the transmitted
information by detecting just a limited band of frequencies either side of the
carrier and ensuring that this band embraces the primary sidebands produced by
the maximum modulation frequency. This, in turn, is determined by the bit rate
being used, since the sidebands produced by any lower bit rate signals in the
transmitted data stream will automatically be nearer to the carrier and hence
within this band.

For example, an FSK modulated signal can be considered as being made up of two separate carrier frequencies – one for binary 0 and one for binary 1 – each of which is keyed on and off at the maximum bit rate frequency as shown in Figure 2.18(a). The **frequency spectrum** of this type of signal is shown in Figure 2.18(b). Now, if the maximum bit rate is, say, 300 bps, this has a maximum fundamental frequency component of 150 Hz. The frequency spectrum, therefore, will contain primary sidebands spaced at 150 Hz on each side of the carriers. Hence, if a frequency separation between the two carriers of, say, 200 Hz is selected, this will embrace the primary sidebands of each carrier. Similarly, if the maximum bit rate is 1200 bps, this has a maximum fundamental frequency component of 600 Hz, so a frequency separation in the order of 1000 Hz is normally selected. It should be noted, however, that a bit rate of 9600 bps has a maximum fundamental frequency component of 4800 Hz, which exceeds the bandwidth of a PSTN line. Thus this rate of operation cannot be achieved with the basic modulation techniques outlined.

Figure 2.19(a) illustrates how a pair of channels is obtained from a single pair of wires derived from a connection through a PSTN. The two channels

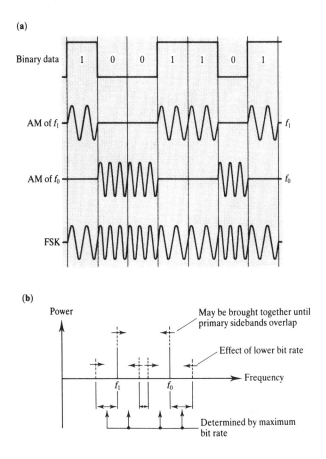

FIGURE 2.18

FSK frequency components: (a) FSK modulation components; (b) power–frequency spectrum.

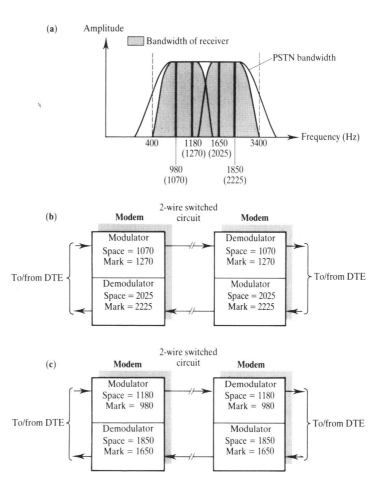

FIGURE 2.19

300 bps full-duplex modem: (a) frequency spectrum; (b) US frequency assignments; (c) CCITT frequency assignments.

would be used, typically, to provide a full-duplex 300 bps link between two DTEs. This type of modem uses FSK with the lower pair of frequencies carrying data in one direction and the higher pair data in the reverse direction. The actual frequencies used for this type of modem differ from one country (and hence public carrier) to another. Figures 2.19(b) and (c) show two alternative frequency assignments.

Hybrid modulation techniques

To derive higher bit rate channels from a normal telephone line, it is necessary to use more sophisticated modulation techniques. In the examples discussed so far, the bit rate was the same as the **signalling rate**, that is, the number of times per second the amplitude, frequency or phase of the transmitted signal changes per second. The signalling rate is measured in **bauds**; in the examples the bit rate has been equal to the baud rate. It is possible, however, when transmitting a signal across a PSTN line to utilize more than two different values, four or eight not being uncommon. This means that each signal element may contain two (four values) or three (eight values) bits of encoded information. The bit rate is then two or three times the baud rate.

An example is provided by PM where four different phase changes (0, 90, 180, and 270) can be employed instead of just two, enabling the phase change of each signal to convey two bits. This is shown in two different forms in Figures 2.20(a) and (b). Also, the different modulation techniques may be combined to produce, for example, **amplitude modulated-phase shift keying (AM-PSK)**, as shown in schematic form in Figure 2.20(c). It should be noted, however, that although it is possible to increase the information content of the signal by increasing the number of signal changes per transmitted element, the bandwidth of the line always imposes a maximum limit on the information (bit) rate. This was discussed earlier in Section 2.3.

2.6.2 Digital leased circuits

Digital leased circuits are used not only to provide a direct connection between two DTEs but also as the basis of most private data (and voice) networks. Such networks will be described later in Chapter 8 when wide area networks are discussed. Normally, they are used when a single organization or enterprise has a very high level of inter-site traffic.

All the information relating to calls – voice and data – associated with most public carrier networks is now transmitted between the switching exchanges within the network in digital form. Moreover, the digital mode of working is steadily being extended to many customer premises. The resulting network is then known as an **integrated services digital network** or **ISDN** since

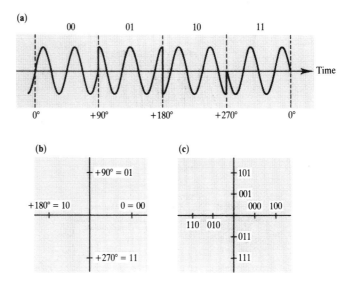

FIGURE 2.20

Alternative modulation techniques: (a) phase–time; (b) phase diagram; (c) AM–PSK.

the user can readily transmit data with voice without the use of modems. The transmission of data using an ISDN will be discussed later in Chapter 8. One result of these developments is that it is now possible to lease from many public carrier operators all digital circuits operating at from tens of kilobits per second to tens of megabits per second.

Such circuits are derived from – and hence must coexist with – those being used for normal inter-exchange traffic. When using such circuits, therefore, it is necessary to know how they are organized in terms of usable capacity. This section provides this knowledge.

Digitization

It may be concluded from the foregoing that digital circuits have evolved from the requirement to transmit voice in digital form. As described in the previous section, voice transmissions are limited to a maximum bandwidth of less than 4 kHz. To convert such signals into digital form, the **Nyquist sampling theorem** states that their amplitude must be sampled at a minimum rate of twice the highest frequency component. Hence to convert a 4 kHz voice signal into digital form, it must be sampled at 8000 times per second. The general arrangement is shown in Figure 2.21(a); parts (b) and (c) illustrate more detailed aspects.

In part (b) a single (analogue) frequency signal is shown, although a typical voice signal will comprise a mix of frequencies. As can be seen, the sampled signal is first converted into a pulse stream, the amplitude of each pulse being equal to the amplitude of the original analogue signal at the sampling instant. The resulting signal is thus known as a **pulse amplitude modulated** or **PAM signal**.

The PAM signal is still analogue since its amplitude can vary over the full amplitude range. It is converted into an all-digital form by **quantizing** each pulse into its equivalent binary form. Eight binary digits (bits) are used to quantize each PAM signal which includes one bit to indicate the sign of the signal – positive or negative. This means 256 distinct levels are used – from eight 0 bits to eight 1 bits. The resulting digital signal has a bit rate of 64 kbps – 8000 samples per second each of 8 bits – and is the minimum unit of transmission capacity available with a digital leased circuit.

As can be deduced from the single frequency (sinusoidal) signal in part (a), the rate of change of the amplitude of the signal various at different parts of the cycle. In particular, the signal changes faster at low amplitudes than high amplitude. Hence if the signal is linearly quantized over its complete amplitude range, a phenomenon known as **quantization distortion** occurs. To overcome this, the amplitude of the PAM signals are first categorized into eight segment levels prior to quantization. As this technique compresses larger signals and expands smaller signals it is known as **companding**. It is illustrated in part (c) of the figure.

The effect of companding is that the digitized (quantized) value of each PAM signal is made up of three parts: a single polarity bit (0 = positive and 1 = negative), three segment code bits (giving eight segments), and four quantization

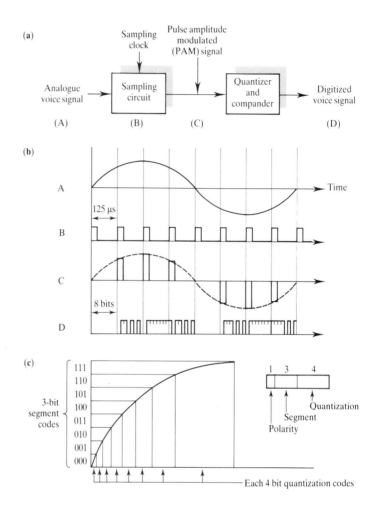

FIGURE 2.21

Digitization principles:
(a) coder schematic;
(b) coder signals;
(c) companding.

bits (giving sixteen quantization levels within each segment). The companding laws used in North America and Japan – known as μ **laws** – are slightly different from the A law used in Europe and many other parts of the world. Thus conversion is needed when using leased circuits that span both continents. Fortunately, this is only necessary for voice communications and not data.

Multiplexing

Circuits that link exchanges carry multiple calls concurrently. This is achieved in a digital form by time division multiplexing (TDM). It may be recalled that with TDM, digital signals from multiple sources are each assigned a specific **time slot** in a higher bit rate aggregate link. Since each analogue signal is sampled 8000 times per second, this produces an 8-bit sample once every 125 microseconds. The aggregate link bit rate, therefore, is a function of the number of voice channels it carries. In North America and Japan, 24 voice channels are grouped together whereas 30 channels are used in countries that comply with CCITT recommendations. This yields aggregate bit rates of 1.544 Mbps and 2.048 Mbps, respectively. The general scheme is shown in Figure 2.22(a).

It is also necessary to include additional bits (or channels) for other purposes (Figure 2.22(b)). These include bits to indicate the start of each frame – frame synchronization – and bits for call setup (signalling). Frame synchronization in the North American system uses a single bit at the start of each frame

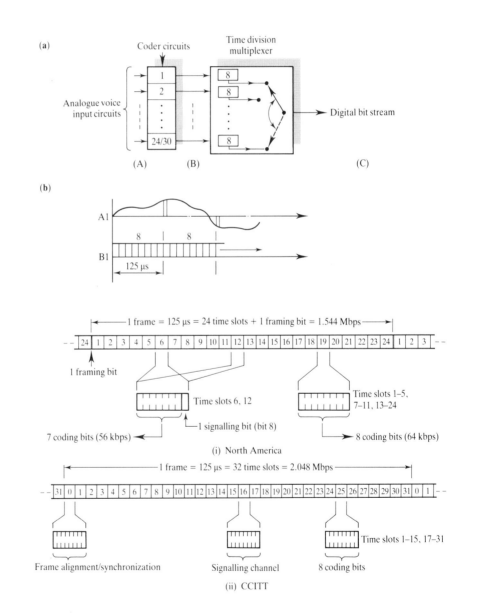

FIGURE 2.22

Multiplexing hierarchy:
(a) TDM schematic;
(b) framing structures.

which toggles (alternates) between 1 and 0 for consecutive frames. Signalling information is carried in the first bit of time slots 6 and 12 leaving just seven user bits in these slots. Thus the aggregate bit rate is $(24 \times 64 + 8)$ kbps = 1.544 Mbps. Such circuits are known as **DS1** or **T1 links**.

In the CCITT recommended system, time slot 0 (zero) is used for frame synchronization – also known as **frame alignment** since it allows the receiver to interpret the time slots in each frame on aligned boundaries. Signalling information is then carried in time slot 16 yielding an aggregate bit rate of $32 \times 8 =$ 2.048 Mbps. Such circuits are referred to as **E1 links**. In the two systems, the lower bit rates are known as **fractional T1/E1**.

Higher aggregate link bit rates are achieved by multiplexing together several such groups. The range of bit rates for the two systems, together with their names, are as follows:

	Circuit	Bit rate (Mbps)	Voice/Data channels
North America:	DS1	1.544	24
	DS1C	3.152	48
	DS2	6.312	96
	DS3	44.736	672
	DS4	274.176	4032
CCITT:	E1	2.048	30
	E2	8.448	120
	E3	34.368	480
	E4	139.264	1920
	E5	565.148	7680

These higher bit rate links require additional bits for framing and control. For example, $4 \times 2.048 = 8.192$ and hence 0.256 Mbps is used for control functions. The various bit rates are often abbreviated to 1.5, 3, 6, 44, 274 and 2, 8, 34, 140, 565 respectively.

2.7 PHYSICAL LAYER INTERFACE STANDARDS

The preceding sections have been concerned with some of the alternative transmission media and the associated electrical signals that may be used to transmit a binary data stream between two DTEs. However, it is important to note that the various standards introduced not only define the form of the electrical signals to be used, but also a complete range of additional signals that control the order and timing of data transfer across the appropriate interfaces. Collectively, these are said to form the **physical layer interface standard**. Although it is not practicable in a book of this type to describe the complete range of signal definitions presented in the various standards documents, some of the additional control signals used with the various interface standards introduced previously will now be described.

2.7.1 RS-232C/V.24

As was mentioned earlier, the RS-232C/V.24 standards were originally defined as a standard interface for connecting a DTE to a PTT-supplied (or approved) modem, which is more generally referred to as a **data circuit-terminating equipment** or **DCE**. A schematic indicating the position of the interface standard with respect to the two communicating DTEs is shown in Figure 2.23(a). Some additional control signals that have been defined for use with the RS-232C/V.24 standard are shown in Figure 2.23(b).

The transmit data (TxD) and receive data (RxD) lines are the lines that transmit and receive the data, respectively. The other lines collectively perform the timing and control functions associated with the setting up and clearing a switched connection through a PSTN. All the lines use the same electrical signal levels described earlier. The function and sequence of operation of the various signals is outlined in Figure 2.24. To illustrate the function of each line, this shows how a connection (call) is first established and a half-duplex data interchange carried out. It assumes that the calling DTE is a user at a terminal and that the called DTE is a remote computer with automatic answering facilities. The latter is normally switch selectable on the modem.

The connection is established by the user dialling the number associated with the remote computer in the usual way and waiting for the call to be

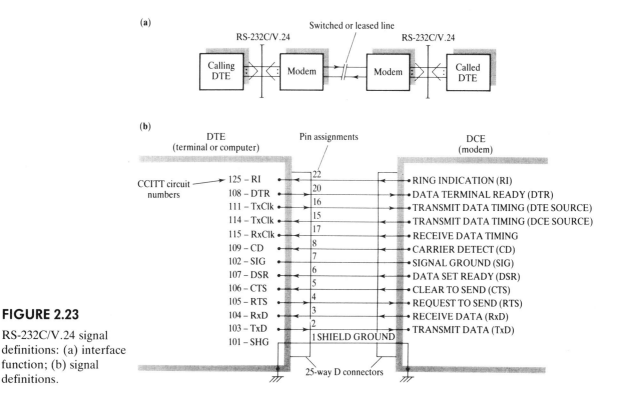

FIGURE 2.23

RS-232C/V.24 signal definitions: (a) interface function; (b) signal definitions.

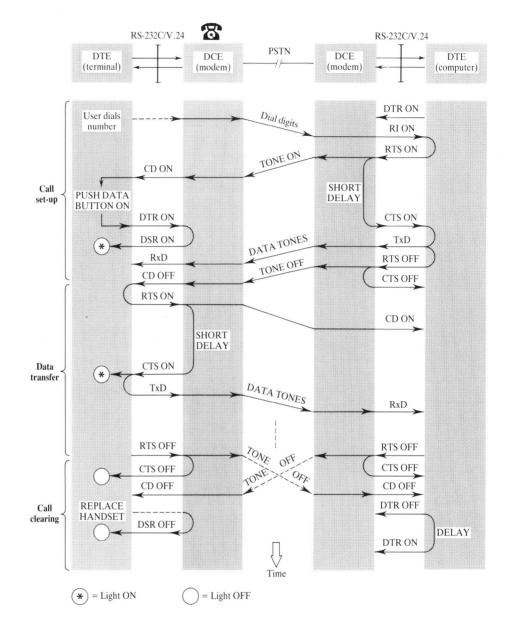

FIGURE 2.24

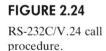

RS-232C/V.24 call
procedure.

answered. Note that autodial facilities are normally used if the calling DTE is a
computer. If the remote computer line is free and the computer is ready to
communicate, the ringing tone stops and the user hears a single audio tone. The
user then proceeds by pressing the **data button** on the handset. This initiates the
connection of the terminal to the set-up line and the local modem responds by
setting the data set ready (DSR) line to on. An indicator lamp normally

associated with this line then comes on, indicating that a link has been established with the remote computer.

When the number is dialled, the modem at the remote computer sets the ring indicator (RI) line to on. If the computer is ready to receive a call – the data terminal ready (DTR) line is set to on – it responds by setting the request-to-send (RTS) line to on. This has two effects:

(1)   it results in the modem sending a carrier signal (a single audio tone) to the calling modem to indicate that the call has been accepted by the remote computer, and

(2)   after a short delay, to allow the remote modem to prepare to receive data, the modem responds by setting the clear-to-send (CTS) line to on to indicate to the called computer that it may start sending data.

Typically, the called computer responds by sending a short invitation-to-type message or character to the calling terminal via the set-up link. Having done this, the computer prepares to receive the user's response by switching the RTS line to off, which in turn results in the carrier signal being switched off. When the calling modem detects that the carrier has been switched off, it sets the carrier detect (CD) line to off. The terminal then sets the RTS line to on and, on receipt of the CTS signal from the modem, the user types the response message. (An indicator lamp normally associated with the CTS signal comes on at this point.) Finally, after the complete transaction has taken place, both carriers are switched off and the set-up link (call) is released (cleared).

The use of a half-duplex switched connection has been described here to illustrate the meaning and use of some of the control lines available with the RS-232C/V.24 standard. However, it should be noted that in practice the time taken to change from the receive to transmit mode with a half-duplex circuit, known as the **turnaround** time, is not insignificant. Hence, it is preferable to operate with a full-duplex circuit whenever possible even if only half-duplex working is required. When a full-duplex circuit is used the transmit and receive functions can take place simultaneously. In such cases, the RTS line from both devices is normally left permanently set and, under normal operation, both modems maintain the CTS line on and a carrier signal to the remote modem.

When synchronous transmission is used, as will be described in Chapter 3, it is necessary to have a clock signal for bit synchronization. Furthermore, if a synchronous modem is used, the modulation and demodulation functions both require a clock signal to perform signal encoding and decoding. Thus, it is necessary for the modem to supply the transmit and receive clocks to the interface control circuits in the DTEs (terminal and computer). The clock signal is passed from the modem to the DTE using the transmit signal element timing (DCE source) control line and the receive signal element timing line. These are assigned pins 15 and 17, respectively, in the connector. If a single bit per signalling element is used by the modem, then the clock signal supplied to the DTE to control the transmission and reception rates is the same as the baud rate of the channel. However, if two bits per signalling element are used, the clock supplied to the DTE is twice the baud rate, and so on.

With an asynchronous modem, on the other hand, the baud and bit rates are the same and no clock is used within the modem. Thus, if synchronous transmission is used, it is necessary for the clock to be extracted from the incoming data stream by the interface circuits within the DTE. The **digital phase-lock loop circuit**, which will be described in Chapter 3, is an example of a circuit suitable for use with an asynchronous modem. To minimize the additional circuitry required to interface a terminal (or computer) to a modem, the interface control circuits (UARTs and USRTs: see Chapter 3) normally have a modem control section that automatically handles the RTS/CTS and DSR/DTR control lines.

The null modem

With the signal assignments shown in Figure 2.23 the terminal and computer both receive and transmit data on the same lines, since the modem provides the same function for both devices. Since its original definitions, however, the RS-232C/V.24 standard has been adopted as a standard interface for connecting character-oriented peripherals (VDUs, printers, etc) to a computer. For this type of use, therefore, it is necessary to decide which of the two devices – peripheral or computer – is going to emulate the modem, since clearly both devices cannot transmit and receive data on the same lines. The same applies when linking the serial ports associated with two computers.

There are three possible alternatives in this situation:

(1) the terminal emulates the modem and the appropriate line definitions are used accordingly,

(2) the computer emulates the modem, or

(3) both the terminal and computer remain unchanged and the interconnecting wiring is modified.

The disadvantage of the first two is that the terminal or computer cannot be used directly with a modem. Nevertheless, a common approach is for the computer RS-232C port to be wired to emulate a modem, enabling an unmodified terminal to be connected directly to it. The third alternative is also widely used, but requires a **null modem** (or **switch box**) to be inserted between the terminal and computer to modify the interconnecting lines, as shown in Figure 2.25.

As can be seen, in addition to reversing the transmit and receive data lines, some of the control lines are also reversed. For example, since a computer and terminal normally operate in full-duplex mode, the RTS and CTS lines are connected together at each end and this signal is then connected to the CD input line of the other device. Similarly, the DSR and RI lines are connected together at each end and these signals are cross-connected to the DTR inputs. The signal and shield ground lines are connected directly.

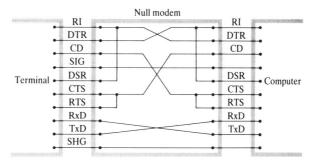

FIGURE 2.25

Null modem
connections.

When the two devices communicate via a synchronous data link, the transmit clock from each device is normally cross-connected and is used as the receive clock by the other device. In some instances, neither device contains a clock source and the clock to be used by both devices is generated within the null modem which is then known as a **modem eliminator**.

2.7.2 RS-449

The RS-449 interface is used with RS-422/423 electrical signals when longer DTE/DCE separations are needed. It uses a 37-pin connector. Some of the control signals used with this standard are shown in Figure 2.26(a). The differential signals used with RS-422 mean that each line requires a pair of wires. As can be seen, some of the control signals are the same as those used with the RS-232C standard. Also, the data mode and receiver ready lines correspond to the DSR and DTR lines in the RS-232C standard. Test mode is a new mandatory signal specific to the RS-449 standard which is included for testing the communication equipment. Essentially, it provides a facility for looping the output of the DTE (terminal or computer) back again through the DCE (modem): that is, the TxD output line is automatically looped back to the RxD input line. In this way, a series of tests can be carried out by the DTE to determine which (if any) piece of communication equipment (DCE) is faulty.

In practice, there are two separate specifications depending on whether RS-422 (balanced) or RS-423 (unbalanced) receivers are used. Both specifications operate with either an asynchronous or a synchronous transmission mode. The maximum separations and bit rates are summarized in Figure 2.25(a).

2.7.3 V.35

The V.35 interface is used to interface a DTE to a wideband (analogue) high bit rate modem. As this is a synchronous modem, additional control lines are incorporated into the interface for the transmit and receive clock lines. The interface uses a 34-pin connector. Bit rates are in the range 48–168 kbps.

As V.35 signals are a mixture of unbalanced (V.24/RS-232C) and balanced (RS-422), the maximum separation between the DTE and modem is the

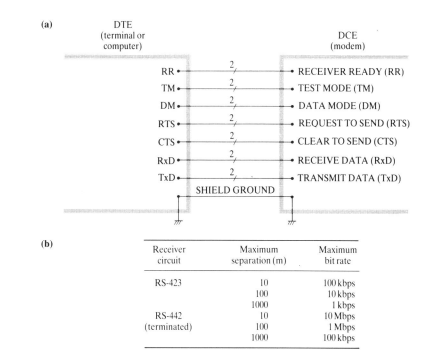

FIGURE 2.26

RS-449 interface:
(a) some signal
definitions;
(b) maximum
separations/bit rate.

Receiver circuit	Maximum separation (m)	Maximum bit rate
RS-423	10	100 kbps
	100	10 kbps
	1000	1 kbps
RS-442	10	10 Mbps
(terminated)	100	1 Mbps
	1000	100 kbps

same as for V.24. In some applications, however, only the transmit and receive data lines (with clocks) are used. Because the latter all use balanced (differential) lines, in such cases longer separations can be used.

2.7.4 X.21

The synchronous X.21 interface has been defined for interfacing a DTE to the DCE of a public data network. Examples of public data networks (see Chapter 8) include X.25 packet-switching networks and circuit-switched networks. X.21 is also used with high bit rate digital circuits.

In addition to the normal transmit and receive data line definitions, the standard also defines a procedure for setting up connections using these lines. This aspect of the interface will be described in Chapter 8.

A variation of X.21, known as X.21 bis, is also sometimes used to interface a DTE that is designed for use with a synchronous modem to a public data network. The normal call-control lines associated with V-series interfaces are then used.

2.7.5 Standards summary

The various standards discussed here are only part of the full range of standards that have been defined by CCITT for use with public telephone networks. Collectively, they are known as the V-series standards. Some of them are summarized in Figure 2.27(a).

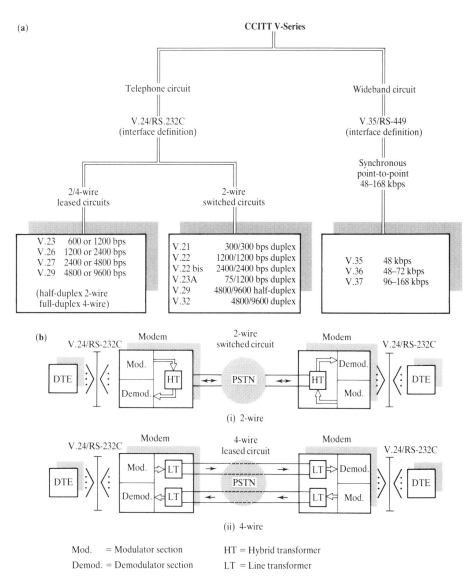

FIGURE 2.27

Modem summary:
(a) CCITT V-series
standards; (b) modem
alternatives.

As the figure shows, the two physical interface standards are V.24
(RS-232C) and V.35 (RS-449). The former is intended for use with normal (and
hence low bit rate) telephone circuits and the latter with wider bandwidth (**wideband**) circuits. These wider bandwidth circuits are normally leased from the PTT
authority. Because they bypass the normal switching circuits, they provide a
direct point-to-point circuit (link) between two sites. Typically, such circuits can
operate at data rates of from 48 to 168 kbps. As will be described in Chapter 3, a
synchronous mode of transmission must be used on these circuits because of
their relatively high data rates.

The various standards listed in Figure 2.27(a) are rigidly defined and include a precise definition of both the type of modulation scheme that must be used and the number and use of the additional interface control lines. In this way, a user buying a modem that adheres to, say, the V.21 standard, can readily use it with a V.21 compatible modem from a different manufacturer.

Some modems are designed to be used with 2-wire switched connections whilst others can be used with both 2-wire switched circuits (connections) and 4-wire leased circuits. The two different circuit arrangements are shown in part (b) of the figure.

With 4-wire leased (permanent) circuits, a pair of circuits is set up through the PSTN and leased to the user. One pair is used for transmission and the other for reception thus providing a full-duplex capability. Such circuits are used for permanent connections between two DTEs. Because of their high running cost, they are used for applications involving high user traffic densities.

For applications that require a switched connection or do not have sufficient traffic to justify a permanent circuit, a normal switched connection must be used. Such connections use only a single pair of lines (2-wire); duplex (two-way) operation is achieved by a device known as a 4-wire to 2-wire **hybrid transformer**. With such a device, the modulated (analogue) signal output from the modulator section of the modem is only coupled to the 2-wire line. Similarly, the signal received from the 2-wire line is coupled only to the input of the demodulator section.

Because of imperfections in hybrid transformers, a fraction of the signal output from the modulator section – known as the **echo signal** – is received at the input to the local demodulator section. Therefore, only half-duplex (two-way alternate) working is normally used with this type of circuit. Using more sophisticated modulation techniques and additional circuits known as **echo cancellers**, it is now possible to have duplex (two-way simultaneously) operation over 2-wire switched circuits at high bit rates (9600 bps). This approach is used in V.32 modems, which also include error correction facilities built into the modem. This feature will be expanded upon in Chapter 5 under the heading link access procedure for modems, LAPM.

EXERCISES

2.1   Give a brief description of the application and limitations of the following types of transmission media:

    (a)   two-wire open lines,
    (b)   twisted pair lines,
    (c)   coaxial cable,
    (d)   optical fibre,
    (e)   microwaves.

2.2   With the aid of sketches, explain the differences between the following transmission modes used with optical fibre:

    (a)   multimode stepped index,
    (b)   multimode graded index,
    (c)   monomode.

2.3   The maximum distance between two terrestrial microwave dishes, d, is given by the expression:

$$d = 7.14\sqrt{Kh}$$

where h is the height of the dishes above ground and K is a factor that allows for the curvature of the earth. Assuming $K = 4$, determine d for selected values of h.

2.4   With reference to Figure 2.5(b), determine the frequency assignments for a cellular system assuming a 7-cell repeat pattern. Explain the advantages of this over the 3-cell repeat pattern shown in the figure.

2.5   With the aid of sketches, explain the effect on a transmitted binary signal of the following:

(a)   attenuation,
(b)   limited bandwidth,
(c)   delay distortion,
(d)   line and system noise.

2.6   Explain the meaning of the term NEXT canceller and how such circuits can improve the data transmission rate of a line.

2.7   Describe the principle of operation of the following satellite/radio access control methods:

(a)   Aloha,
(b)   preassigned FDMA,
(c)   demand assigned TDMA.

2.8   Explain the meaning of the terms signal propagation delay and transmission delay. Assuming the velocity of propagation of an electrical signal is equal to the speed of light, determine the ratio of the signal propagation delay to the transmission delay, a, for the following types of data link:

(a)   100 m of UTP wire and a transmission rate of 1 Mbps.
(b)   2.5 km of coaxial cable and a transmission rate of 10 Mbps.
(c)   a satellite link and a transmission rate of 512 kbps.

2.9   Make a sketch showing the interface circuits and the associated signal levels used to transmit binary data between two DTEs using the following signal types and transmission media:

(a)   RS-232C/V.24 and open lines,
(b)   20 mA current loop and open lines,
(c)   RS-422 and twisted pair,
(d)   coaxial cable,
(e)   optical fibre.

Outline the properties of each signal type.

2.10   (a)   Why must a modem be used to transmit binary data through a PSTN? Use sketches and additional text to describe the following modulation methods:

        (i)   amplitude modulation,
        (ii)   frequency modulation,
        (iii)   phase-coherent PSK,
        (iv)   differential PSK.

(b)   Discuss the factors that influence the choice of carrier frequency and the bandwidth used by the demodulator section of a modem.

2.11   Deduce the maximum theoretical information rates associated with the following transmission channels:

(a)   telex (international message switching) network with a bandwidth of 500 Hz and a signal to noise ratio of 5 dB,

(b)   switched telephone network with a bandwidth of 3100 Hz and a signal to noise ratio of 20 dB.

2.12   Data is to be transmitted using a modem at 9600 bps. Determine the minimum bandwidth of the system with the following modulation methods:

(a)   FSK,

(b)   AM-PSK.

2.13   Data is to be transmitted though a PSTN at 4800 bps with a minimum bit error rate of 10^{-6} using a PSK modem. If the E/N_0 ratio needed to achieve this error rate is 10 dB with PSK modulation, deduce the minimum received signal level that is required assuming a temperature of 20°C.

2.14   List the main signals used with the RS-232C/V.24 standard interface and state their functions. Derive a time sequence diagram to show the use of each line. Use as an example a user at a terminal establishing a half-duplex connection through a PSTN to carry out a transaction involving the exchange of data between the terminal and a remote computer.

2.15   (a)   What is the function of a null modem? Show the internal connections used within a null modem and explain the significance of each connection.

(b)   List the main signals used with the RS-449/V.35 standard interface and state their functions.

2.16   With aid of sketches, explain the meaning of the following terms relating to the digitization of an analogue voice single:

(a)   sampling and PAM signals,

(a)   quantization,

(a)   companding.

2.17   Explain the digital hierarchy used in North America and the CCITT recommendation relating to leased digital circuits.

Use sketches of the frame structure used in each of these schemes to show how the basic multiplexing groups are derived and hence derive the usable data rate with each circuit.

CHAPTER SUMMARY

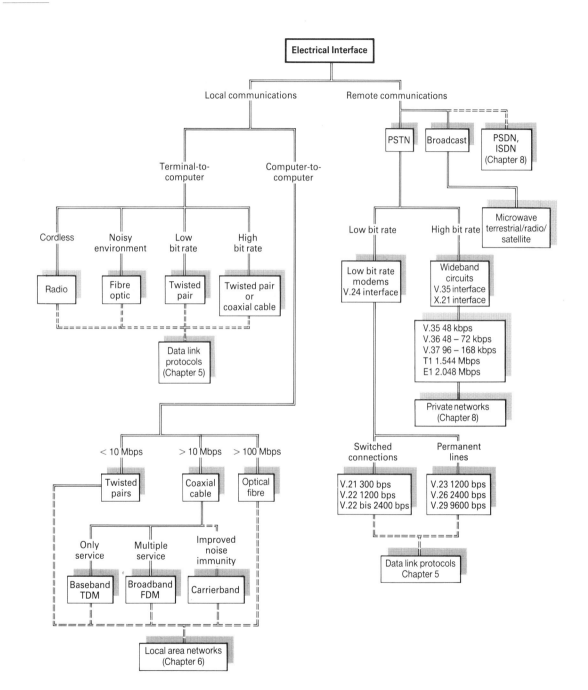

3

Data transmission

CHAPTER CONTENTS

CHAPTER OBJECTIVES

When you have completed studying the material in this chapter you should be able to:

- know the structure of the two most common information interchange codes;
- understand the difference between an asynchronous and a synchronous transmission control scheme;
- explain the bit (clock) and character (byte) synchronization methods associated with asynchronous transmission and the different encoding methods used;
- explain some of the alternative techniques that are employed to obtain bit (clock) synchronization with synchronous transmission;
- describe how frame synchronization is achieved with asynchronous and character-oriented synchronous transmission;
- understand the terms data transparency, and character and bit stuffing;
- explain the operation and application areas of some of the alternative methods that can be employed to detect transmission (bit) errors;
- describe some of the most widely used methods for the compression of data;

- • **explain the principle of operation of the different types of multiplexer equipment.**

3.1 INTRODUCTION

Data communication is concerned with the exchange of digitally encoded information between two DTEs. The physical separation of the two pieces of equipment may vary from a few tens of metres – for example, between two personal computers – to several hundreds of kilometres, if the two devices are connected using a public-carrier network, for example.

Within the data communication community, the term 'data' is normally reserved for describing a set or block of one or more digitally encoded alphabetic and numeric characters being exchanged between two devices. Typically, these represent a string of numbers or the contents of a computer file containing a stored document. When using a data communication facility to transfer this type of data, it is necessary for the two communicating parties (DTEs) to exchange additional control messages; for example, to overcome the effect of transmission errors within the communication facility. To discriminate between the two types of message, therefore, the more general term **information** is used to describe the actual user data being exchanged across the data communication facility.

In any digital system, the loss or corruption of a single **bit (binary digit)** of information can be critical. It is thus essential when designing a data communication facility to ensure that adequate precautions are taken to detect and, if necessary, correct for any possible loss or corruption of information during transmission. Data communication is concerned, therefore, not only with the way data is transmitted over the physical transmission medium but also with the techniques that may be adopted to detect and, if necessary, correct transmission errors. It is also concerned with the control of the data transfer rate, the format of the data being transferred and related issues.

Both this chapter and the next are concerned with the fundamental concepts associated with data communication and, in particular, with the techniques that are used to achieve the reliable (error free and no losses or duplicates) transfer of information across a **bit-serial transmission medium** connecting two DTEs. As was seen in the last chapter, the transmission medium may be a physical circuit – twisted pair, coaxial cable or optical fibre – or a radio-based channel. In many instances, therefore, the more general term **data link** is used to describe the link connecting two DTEs. This chapter deals with the basic techniques and circuits used for the transmission of data between two DTEs, while Chapter 4 describes the basic techniques employed for the control of data transfer between the two communicating parties. It should be stressed that, irrespective of the type of error-detection (and correction) scheme adopted, it is impossible to detect all possible combinations of transmission errors with 100% certainty. In practice, therefore, the aim of the various error-detection and correction techniques is to make the probability that undetected errors are present in a received message acceptably low.

3.2 DATA TRANSMISSION BASICS

When entering data into a computer via a keyboard, each selected keyed element – an alphabetic or numeric character, for example – is **encoded** by the electronics within the keyboard into an equivalent binary-coded pattern using one of the standard coding schemes that are used for the interchange of information. In order to represent all the characters on a keyboard with a unique pattern, seven or eight binary digits (bits) are utilized. The use of seven bits means that 128 different elements can be represented, while eight bits can represent 256 elements. A similar procedure is followed on output except in this case the printer will **decode** each received binary-coded pattern to print the corresponding character. The coded bit patterns for each character are often referred to as **codewords**.

The two most widely used codes that have been adopted for this function are the **Extended Binary Coded Decimal Interchange Code (EBCDIC)** and the **American Standards Committee for Information Interchange (ASCII)**. The EBCDIC code is an 8-bit code that is used with most equipment manufactured by IBM. As such it is a **proprietary code** but, owing to the widespread use of IBM equipment in the computer industry, it is frequently used. The codeword definitions used with EBCDIC are shown in Figure 3.1(a).

The ASCII code is the same as that defined by the CCITT – known as **International Alphabet Number 5** or **IA5** – and also that used by the International Standards Organization known as ISO 645. Each is a 7-bit code; the codeword definitions used are shown in Figure 3.1(b).

Both coding schemes cater for all the normal alphabetic, numeric and punctuation characters – collectively referred to as **printable characters** – plus a range of additional **control characters** – also known as **non-printable characters**. Examples of the latter include format control characters – BS (backspace), LF (line feed), CR (carriage return), SP (space), DEL (delete), ES (escape) and FF (form feed) – information separators – FS (file separator) and RS (record separator) – and transmission control (TC) characters – SOH (start-of-heading), STX (start-of-text), ETX (end-of-text), ACK (acknowledge), NAK (negative acknowledgement) and SYN (synchronous idle). The use of some of these will be described later in this chapter.

Although such codes are used for input and output, once numerical data has been input into the computer, it is normally converted and stored in an equivalent, fixed-length binary form. Typically the latter are either 8, 16 or 32 bits. An 8-bit binary pattern is referred to as a **byte** while longer patterns are known as **words**. Because of the range of bits used to represent each word, it is usual when communicating data between two DTEs to use multiple, fixed-length elements each of eight bits. Thus in some instances the eight bits being transmitted across a data link may represent a binary-encoded printable character (seven bits plus an additional bit for error detection purposes) while in others it may represent an 8-bit component of a larger value. In the latter case, the element is referred to either as a byte or, for communication purposes, as an **octet**.

(a)

Bit positions — top header (columns labelled by bits 4 3 2 1), rows labelled by bits 8 7 6 5:

8765 \ 4321	0000	0001	0010	0011	0100	0101	0110	0111	1000	1001	1010	1011	1100	1101	1110	1111
0000	NUL	SOH	STX	ETX	PF	HT	LC	DEL			SMM	VT	FF	CR	SO	SI
0001	DLE	DC$_1$	DC$_2$	DC$_3$	RES	NL	BS	IL	CAN	EM	CC		IFS	IGS	IRS	IUS
0010	DS	SOS	FS		BYP	LF	EOB	PRE			SM			ENQ	ACK	BEL
0011			SYN		PN	RS	UC	EOT					DC$_4$	NAK		SUB
0100	SP										¢	.	<	(	+	|
0101	&										!	$	*	)	;	¬
0110	−	/										'	%	_	>	?
0111											:	#	@	,	=	''
1000		a	b	c	d	e	f	g	h	i						
1001		j	k	l	m	n	o	p	q	r						
1010			s	t	u	v	w	x	y	z						
1011																
1100		A	B	C	D	E	F	G	H	I						
1101		J	K	L	M	N	O	P	Q	R						
1110			S	T	U	V	W	X	Y	Z						
1111	0	1	2	3	4	5	6	7	8	9						□

(b)

Bit positions — top header (columns labelled by bits 7 6 5), rows labelled by bits 4 3 2 1:

4321 \ 765	000	001	010	011	100	101	110	111
0000	NUL	DLE	SP	0	@	P	\	p
0001	SOH	DC1	!	1	A	Q	a	q
0010	STX	DC2	''	2	B	R	b	r
0011	ETX	DC3	#	3	C	S	c	s
0100	EOT	DC4	$	4	D	T	d	t
0101	ENQ	NAK	%	5	E	U	e	u
0110	ACK	SYN	&	6	F	V	f	v
0111	BEL	ETB	'	7	G	W	g	w
1000	BS	CAN	(	8	H	X	h	x
1001	HT	EM	)	9	I	Y	i	y
1010	LF	SUB	*	:	J	Z	j	z
1011	VT	ESC	+	;	K	[	k	{
1100	FF	FS	,	<	L	\	l	|
1101	CR	GS	−	=	M	]	m	}
1110	SO	RS	.	>	N	^	n	~
1111	SI	US	/	?	O	_	o	DEL

FIGURE 3.1

Standard interchange codes: (a) EBCDIC; (b) ASCII/IA5.

3.2.1 Bit-serial transmission

Within a piece of equipment, the distances and hence lengths of wire used to connect each subunit are short. Thus it is normal practice to transfer data between subunits using a separate wire to carry each bit of the data. This means that there are multiple wires connecting each subunit and data is said to be exchanged using a **parallel transfer mode**. This mode of operation results in minimal delays in transferring each word.

When transferring information between two physically separate pieces of equipment, especially if the separation is more than a few metres, for reasons of cost and varying transmission delays in the individual wires, it is more usual to use a single pair of lines. Each octet making up the data is transmitted a single bit at a time using a fixed time interval for each bit. This mode of operation is known as **bit-serial transmission**.

The two alternative modes of operation are shown in Figure 3.2. A binary digit is normally represented within a piece of digital electronic equipment as a

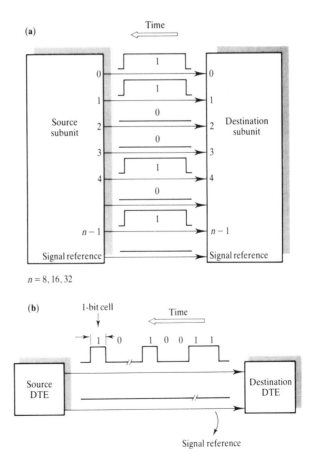

FIGURE 3.2

Transmission modes:
(a) parallel; (b) serial.

specific voltage level relative to a reference level. In the figure, a high signal relative to the reference indicates the transmission of a binary 1 while a low signal level, equal to the reference, represents a binary 0. In contrast, as was described in the last chapter, with serial transmission the high and low level signals are normally positive and negative voltages relative to the reference.

3.2.2 Communication modes

When a person is giving a lecture or speech, information is primarily conveyed in one direction. During a conversation between two people, however, it is usual for spoken messages (information) to be exchanged in both directions. These messages are normally exchanged alternately but can, of course, be exchanged simultaneously! Similarly, when data is transmitted between two pieces of equipment, three analogous modes of operation can be used:

(1)   **Simplex**: This is used when data is to be transmitted in one direction only; for example, in a data logging system in which a monitoring device returns a reading at regular intervals to the data gathering facility.

(2)   **Half-duplex**: This is used when the two interconnected devices wish to exchange information (data) alternately; for example, if one of the devices only returns some data in response to a request from the other. Clearly, it is necessary for the two devices to be able to switch between send and receive modes after each transmission.

(3)   **Duplex**: This is also referred to as full-duplex and is used when data is to be exchanged between the two connected devices in both directions simultaneously; for example, if for throughput reasons data can flow in each direction independently.

The alternative communication modes are important since in many distributed systems the circuits (lines) used to provide the communication facilities are often leased from the PTT authorities, and it is less expensive to lease a single circuit, rather than two circuits, if only simplex operation is required, for example.

3.2.3 Transmission modes

As has been mentioned, data is normally transmitted between two DTEs in multiples of a fixed length unit, typically of eight bits. In some instances, for example, if a computer is transferring a data file comprising, say, a source program, the data will be made up of a string (block) of 8-bit binary-encoded characters. In others, for example, if the file comprises the object (compiled) code of the program, then the data will be made up of a block of 8-bit bytes.

Since each character or byte is transmitted bit serially, the receiving DTE receives one of two signal levels which vary according to the bit pattern (and hence character string) making up the message. For the receiving device to decode and interpret this bit pattern correctly, it must be able to determine:

(1)   the start of each bit cell (in order to sample the incoming signal in the middle of the bit cell);

(2)   the start and end of each element (character or byte);

(3)   the start and end of each complete message block (the latter is also known as a **frame**).

These three tasks are known as **bit** or **clock synchronization**, **character** or **byte synchronization**, and **block** or **frame synchronization**, respectively.

In general, synchronization is accomplished in one of two ways, the method being determined by whether the transmitter and receiver clocks are independent (asynchronous) or synchronized (synchronous). With **asynchronous transmission**, each character (byte) is treated independently for clock (bit) and character (byte) synchronization purposes and the receiver resynchronizes at the start of each character received. With **synchronous transmission**, the complete frame (block) of characters is transmitted as a contiguous string of bits and the receiver endeavours to keep in synchronism with the incoming bit stream for the duration of the complete frame (block).

Asynchronous transmission

This method of transmission is used primarily when the data to be transmitted is generated at random intervals – for example, by a user at a keyboard communicating with a computer. Clearly, with this type of communication, the user keys in each character at an indeterminate rate, with possibly long random time intervals between each successive typed character. This means that the signal on the transmission line will be in the idle (known as **marking**) state for long time intervals between characters. With this type of communication, therefore, it is necessary for the receiver to be able to resynchronize at the start of each new character received. To accomplish this, each transmitted character or byte is encapsulated between an additional **start bit** and one or more **stop bits**, as shown in Figure 3.3.

Although primarily used for the transmission of characters between a keyboard (or more generally a terminal) and a computer, asynchronous transmission can also be used for the transmission of blocks of characters (or bytes) between two computers. In this case, the start bit of each subsequent character immediately follows the stop bit(s) of the previous character since the characters in a block are transmitted one after the other with no delay between them.

As can be seen from Figure 3.3, the polarity of the start and stop bits is different. This ensures that there is always a minimum of one transition $(1 \rightarrow 0 \rightarrow 1)$ between each successive character, irrespective of the bit sequences in the characters being transmitted. The first $1 \rightarrow 0$ transition after an idle period is then used by the receiving device to determine the start of each new character. In addition, by utilizing a clock whose frequency is N times higher than the

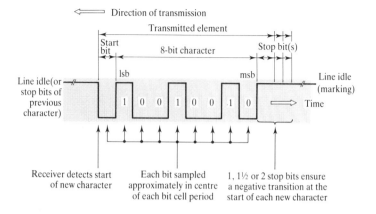

FIGURE 3.3

Asynchronous
transmission basics.

transmitted bit rate frequency ($N = 16$ is typical), the receiving device can determine (to a good approximation) the state of each transmitted bit in the character by sampling the received signal approximately at the centre of each bit cell period. This is shown in the figure and will be discussed further in the next section.

It can be deduced from the foregoing that to transmit each item of user data, 10 (one start bit and one stop bit) or possibly 11 (one start bit and two stop bits) bits are utilized. Assuming a single start bit and two stop bits per 8-bit element and a data transmission rate of, say, 1200 bps, the data rate is 1200/11 or about 110 bytes per second. The useful data rate is, in fact, less than this for reasons that will be described later.

When defining the transmission rate of a line, the term 'baud' is often used by communication engineers. When correctly used, however, the term baud indicates the number of line signal transitions per second. Thus, if each transmitted signal can be in one of two states, the term baud and bits per second (bps) are equivalent. However, as was described in Chapter 2, in some instances the line signal can take on more than two states, and hence each transmitted cell can be used to convey more than a single binary digit of information. To avoid confusion, therefore, the term **signalling rate** is used to define the number of line signal transitions per second (in baud) while the data or information transfer rate represents the number of data bits per second (bps). For example, a signalling rate of 300 baud with four bits per signalling element would yield a data rate of 1200 bps. The most common data rates in use on asynchronous lines are 110, 300, 1200, 4800, 9600 and 19 200 bps although higher rates are also used over short distances.

Finally, when blocks of characters (or bytes) are being transmitted, each block is encapsulated between a pair of reserved (transmission control) characters to achieve block (frame) synchronization. This ensures that the receiver, on receipt of the opening character (byte) after an idle period, can determine that a new frame is being transmitted. Similarly, on receipt of the closing character (byte), that the end of the frame has been reached.

Synchronous transmission

As indicated, asynchronous transmission is normally used either when the rate at which characters are generated is indeterminate, or for the transmission of blocks of characters at relatively low data rates. In such applications, the use of additional bits per character for character synchronization and the relatively coarse bit synchronization method used, are both acceptable. For the transmission of large blocks of data at higher bit rates, however, the synchronous transmission alternative is used.

With synchronous transmission, the complete block or frame of data is transmitted as a contiguous bit stream with no delay between each 8-bit element. To enable the receiving device to achieve the various levels of synchronization:

(1)   the transmitted bit stream is suitably encoded so that the receiver can be kept in bit synchronism;

(2)   all frames are preceded by one or more reserved bytes or characters to ensure the receiver reliably interprets the received bit stream on the correct character or byte boundaries (character or byte synchronization);

(3)   the contents of each frame are encapsulated between a pair of reserved characters or bytes for frame synchronization.

In the case of synchronous transmission, during the period between the transmission of successive frames, either idle (sync) characters (or bytes) are continuously transmitted to allow the receiver to retain bit and byte synchronism, or each frame is preceded by two or more special synchronizing bytes or characters to allow the receiver to regain synchronism. This is shown in Figure 3.4.

The alternative bit-encoding methods that are used to achieve bit synchronization will be described in Section 3.4. Also, as with asynchronous transmission, it is necessary to ensure that the start and end-of-frame characters (bytes) are unique; that is, they are not present in the contents of the frame being transmitted. Clearly, if the frame contains, say, the contents of a binary

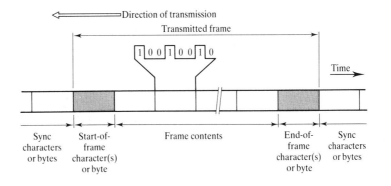

FIGURE 3.4

Synchronous
transmission basics.

code file, this cannot be guaranteed and hence additional steps have to be taken to allow for this possibility. These aspects will be discussed in more detail in later sections.

EXAMPLE

Deduce the number of additional bits required to transmit a message comprising one hundred 8-bit characters over a data link using each of the following transmission control schemes:

(a)   asynchronous with one start bit and two stop bits per character and a single start and end-of-frame character per message;

(b)   synchronous with two synchronization characters and a single start and end-of-frame character per message.

(a)   Number of bits per character = 1 + 2 = 3. Therefore, 3 × 102 = 306 additional bits are required.

(b)   With synchronous transmission, the number of additional bits is simply the two synchronization characters and one start and one end-of-frame character; that is, 4 × 8 = 32 bits.

3.2.4 Error control

During the transmission of a serial bit stream between two DTEs, it is very common – especially when the physical separation is large and, say, the switched telephone network is being used – for the transmitted information to become corrupted; that is, the signal level corresponding to a binary 0 is modified and, in the limit, is interpreted by the receiver as the level for a binary 1, and vice versa. It is normal when data is being transmitted between two devices, therefore, to provide a means for detecting possible transmission errors and, should they arise, a means for correcting for such errors.

A number of alternative schemes can be used, but the one selected is normally determined by the transmission method. When asynchronous transmission is used, for example, since each character is treated as a separate entity, it is normal to embed an additional binary digit (bit) within each transmitted character. This additional digit is known as a **parity bit**; its function will be described in Section 3.5.1.

In contrast, when synchronous transmission is used, it is more usual to determine possible transmission errors on the complete frame, as the basic unit of transmission is a frame. Moreover, since the contents of a frame may be large, the probability of more than one bit being corrupted increases. Consequently, a more sophisticated error check sequence must be used. Again, this may take a number of different forms but, in general, the transmitting device computes a sequence of error check digits, based on the contents of the frame being transmitted, and appends these to the tail of the frame either after the character or before the byte signalling the end of the frame.

During transmission of the frame, the receiver can recompute a new set of error check digits based on the received contents and, on receipt of the end-of-frame characters or byte, can compare this with the transmitted check digits. If these are not equal, a transmission error is assumed.

Both schemes only allow the receiver to detect the occurrence of transmission errors. Consequently, a scheme is necessary to enable the receiver to obtain another copy of the transmitted information when errors are detected. Again, a number of schemes are possible. For example, consider the case of a terminal and a computer transmitting data using asynchronous transmission. As the user keys in each character, the encoded character is normally transmitted to the computer as already outlined. The character corresponding to the received bit stream is then 'echoed' back by the computer and displayed on the screen of the user terminal. If the displayed character is different from the selected keyed character, the user may send a special (delete) character to inform the computer to ignore the last (erroneous) character received. This is referred to as **error control**. A way of performing the same function when blocks of characters are being transmitted must be employed. Some of the more common error control methods are discussed in Chapter 4.

3.2.5 Flow control

If the amount of data to be transmitted between two devices is small, it is possible for the sending device to transmit all the data immediately because the receiving device will have sufficient resources (storage space) to hold the data. In many data communication situations, however, this is not the case. Thus it is often necessary to adopt a method to control the flow of data transfer to ensure that the receiver does not lose any of the transmitted data because if has insufficient storage. This is particularly important when the two devices are communicating through an intermediate data communication network as very often the network will only buffer a limited amount of data. If the two devices operate at different data rates, it is often necessary to control the mean output rate of the faster device to prevent the communication network from becoming congested. The control of the flow of information between two DTEs is known as **flow control**. Some of the alternative methods used will be introduced in Chapter 4.

3.2.6 Data link protocols

Error and flow control are two essential components of the more general topic of data link control protocols. Essentially, a protocol is a set of conventions or rules that must be adhered to by both communicating parties to ensure that information being exchanged across a serial data link is received and interpreted correctly. In addition to error and flow control, a data link protocol also defines such things as:

- the format of the data being exchanged – that is, the number of bits per element and the type of encoding scheme being used; and

- the type and order of messages that are to be exchanged in order to achieve reliable (error free and no duplicates) information transfer between the two communicating parties.

For example, it is normal before transferring any data from one DTE to another to set up a connection between them to ensure that the receiving DTE is free and ready to receive the data. This is often accomplished by the sending device transmitting a specific control message – a call or connect request, for example – and the receiver returning a defined response message – a call connected or reject, for example. A number of different data link control protocols will be discussed in subsequent chapters of the book.

3.3 ASYNCHRONOUS TRANSMISSION

As has been outlined, data is normally transmitted between two DTEs bit serially in multiple 8-bit elements (characters or bytes) using either asynchronous or synchronous transmission. Within the DTEs, however, each element is normally stored, processed and transferred in a parallel form. Consequently, the transmission control circuits within each DTE, which form the interface between the device and the serial data link, must perform the following functions:

- parallel-to-serial conversion of each character or byte in preparation for its transmission on the data link;

- serial-to-parallel conversion of each received character or byte in preparation for its storage and processing in the device;

- a means for the receiver to achieve bit, character and frame synchronization;

- the generation of suitable error check digits for error-detection and the detection of such errors at the receiver should they occur.

Parallel-to-serial conversion is performed by a **parallel-in, serial-out (PISO) shift register**. This, as its name implies, allows a complete character or byte to be loaded in parallel and then shifted out bit serially. Similarly, serial-to-parallel conversion is performed by a **serial-in, parallel-out (SIPO) shift register** which performs the reverse function.

To achieve bit and character synchronization, the receiving transmission control circuit (which is normally programmable) must be set to operate with the same characteristics as the transmitter in terms of the number of bits per character and the bit rate being used.

3.3.1 Bit synchronization

In asynchronous transmission, the receiver clock (which is used to shift the incoming signal into the SIPO) runs asynchronously – out of synchronism – with respect to the incoming signal. In order for the reception process to work reliably, therefore, it is necessary to devise a scheme whereby the local (asynchronous) receiver clock samples (and hence shifts into the SIPO) the incoming signal as near to the centre of the bit cell as possible.

To achieve this, a local receiver clock of N times the transmitted bit rate ($N = 16$ is common) is used and each new bit is shifted into the SIPO after N cycles of this clock. The first $1 \rightarrow 0$ transition associated with the start bit of each character is used to start the counting process. Each bit (including the start bit) is sampled at (approximately) the centre of each bit cell. Hence, after the first transition is detected, the signal (the start bit) is sampled after $N/2$ clock cycles and then subsequently after N clock cycles for each bit in the character. The general scheme is shown in Figure 3.5(a) and three examples of different clock rate ratios in Figure 3.5(b).

Remembering that the receiver clock (RxC) is running asynchronously with respect to the incoming signal (RxD), the relative positions of the two

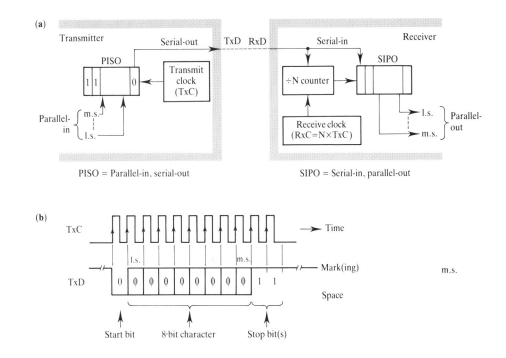

FIGURE 3.5

Asynchronous transmission:
(a) principle of operation;
(b) transmit timing.

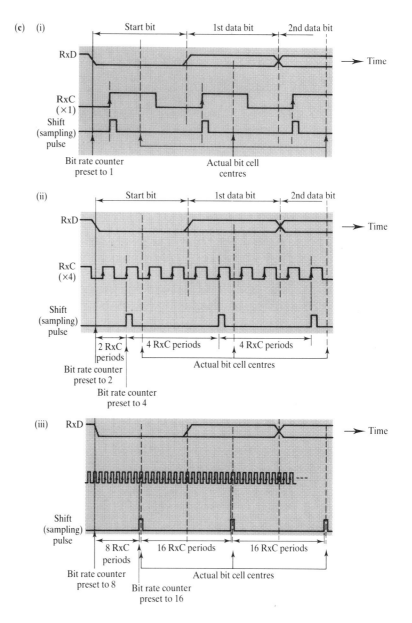

FIGURE 3.5 (cont.)

(c) Receiver timing examples.

signals can be anywhere within a single cycle of the receiver clock. Those shown are just arbitrary positions. Nevertheless, it can be deduced from these examples that the higher the clock rate ratio, the nearer the sampling instant will be to the nominal bit cell centre. Because of this mode of operation, the maximum bit rate normally used with asynchronous transmission is 19.2 kbps.

EXAMPLE

A block of data is to be transmitted across a serial data link. If a clock of 19.2 kHz is available at the receiver, deduce the suitable clock rate ratios and estimate the worst-case deviations from the nominal bit cell centres, expressed as a percentage of a bit period, for each of the following data transmission rates:

(a)   1200 bps;
(b)   2400 bps;
(c)   9600 bps.

It can readily be deduced from Figure 3.5 that the worst-case deviation from the nominal bit cell centres is approximately one cycle of the receiver clock. Hence:

(a)   At 1200 bps, the maximum RxC ratio can be $\times 16$. The maximum deviation is thus 6.25%.

(b)   At 2400 bps, the maximum RxC ratio can be $\times 8$. The maximum deviation is thus 12.5%.

(c)   At 9600 bps, the maximum RxC ratio can be $\times 2$. The maximum deviation is thus 50%.

Clearly, the last case is unacceptable. With a low quality line, especially one with excessive delay distortion, even the second may be unreliable. It is for this reason that a $\times 16$ clock rate ratio is used whenever possible.

3.3.2 Character synchronization

As has been indicated, the receiving transmission control circuit is programmed to operate with the same number of bits per character and the same number of stop bits as the transmitter. After the start bit has been detected and received, the receiver achieves character synchronization simply by counting the programmed number of bits. It then transfers the received character (byte) into a local **buffer register** and signals to the controlling device (a microprocessor, for example) that a new character (byte) has been received. It then awaits the next line signal transition that indicates a new start bit (and hence character) is being received.

3.3.3 Frame synchronization

When messages comprising blocks of characters – normally referred to as **information frames** – are being transmitted, in addition to bit and character synchronization, it is necessary for the receiver to be able to determine the start and end of each frame. This is known as **frame synchronization**.

When transmitting blocks of printable characters, the simplest method is to encapsulate the complete block between two special (non-printable) characters: STX (start-of-text) which indicates the start of a new frame after an idle period, and ETX (end-of-text) which indicates the end of the frame. Because of their function, they are known as **transmission control characters**. As the frame contents consist only of printable characters, the receiver can interpret the receipt of an STX character as signalling the start of a new frame and an ETX character as signalling the end of the frame. This is shown in Figure 3.6(a).

Although the scheme shown is satisfactory for the transmission of blocks of printable characters, when transmitting blocks of data that comprise pure binary data (for example, the contents of a file containing a compiled program), the use of a single ETX character to indicate the end of a frame is not sufficient. In the case of binary data it is possible for one of the bytes to be the same as an ETX character, which would cause the receiver to terminate the reception process abnormally.

To overcome this problem, when transmitting binary data the two transmission control characters STX and ETX are each preceded by a third transmission control character known as **data link escape** or **DLE**. The modified format of a frame is then as shown in Figure 3.6(b).

It must be remembered that the transmitter knows the number of bytes in each frame being transmitted. After transmitting the start-of-frame sequence

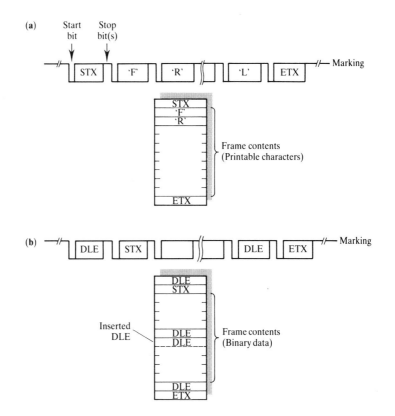

FIGURE 3.6

Frame synchronization:
(a) printable characters;
(b) binary data.

(DLE–STX), it inspects each byte in the frame prior to transmission to determine if it is the same as the DLE character pattern. If it is, irrespective of the next byte, it transmits a second DLE character (byte) before the next byte. This procedure is repeated until the appropriate number of bytes in the frame have been transmitted. It then signals the end of the frame by transmitting the unique DLE–ETX sequence.

This procedure is known as **character** or **byte stuffing**. On receipt of each byte after the DLE–STX start-of-frame sequence, the receiver determines whether it is a DLE character (byte). If it is, it then processes the next byte to determine whether that is another DLE or an ETX. If it is a DLE, the receiver discards it and awaits the next byte. If it is an ETX, however, this can reliably be taken as being the end of the frame.

3.4 SYNCHRONOUS TRANSMISSION

The use of an additional start bit and one or more stop bits per character or byte means that asynchronous transmission is relatively inefficient in its use of transmission capacity, especially when transmitting messages that comprise large blocks of characters. Also, the bit (clock) synchronization method used with asynchronous transmission becomes less reliable as the bit rate increases. Synchronous transmission is normally used to overcome these problems. As with asynchronous transmission, however, a suitable method must be adopted to enable the receiver to achieve bit (clock), character (byte) and frame (block) synchronization. In practice, there are two synchronous transmission control schemes: character-oriented and bit-oriented. Both will be discussed separately but, since they both use the same bit synchronization methods, these will be discussed first.

3.4.1 Bit synchronization

Although the use of a start bit and stop bit(s) with each character is often used to discriminate between asynchronous and synchronous transmission, the fundamental difference between the two methods is that with asynchronous transmission the receiver clock runs asynchronously (unsynchronized) with respect to the incoming (received) signal, whereas with synchronous transmission the receiver clock operates in synchronism with the received signal.

As was indicated earlier, start and stop bits are not used with synchronous transmission. Instead each frame is transmitted as a contiguous stream of binary digits. The receiver then obtains (and maintains) bit synchronization in one of two ways. Either the clock (timing) information is embedded into the transmitted signal and subsequently extracted by the receiver, or the receiver has a local clock (as with asynchronous transmission) but this time it is kept in synchronism with the received signal by a device known as a **digital phase-lock-loop**. As will be seen, the latter exploits the $1 \rightarrow 0$ or $0 \rightarrow 1$ bit transitions in the received signal

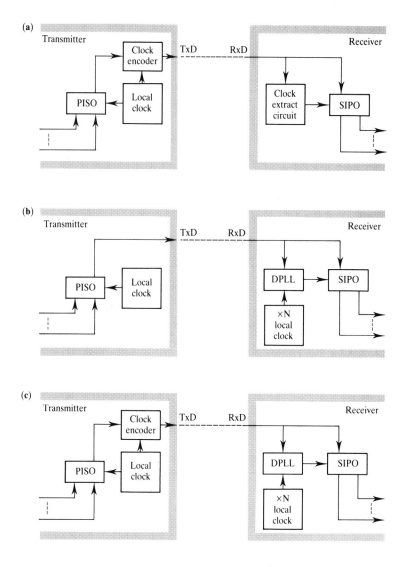

FIGURE 3.7

Synchronous
transmission clock
synchronization
alternatives: (a) clock
encoding; (b) DPLL;
(c) hybrid.

to maintain bit (clock) synchronism over an acceptably long period. Hybrid
schemes that exploit both methods are also used. The principles of operation of
these schemes are shown in Figure 3.7.

Clock encoding and extraction

Three alternative methods of embedding timing (clock) information into a
transmitted bit stream are shown in Figure 3.8. In part (a), the bit stream to be
transmitted is encoded so that a binary 1 is represented by a positive pulse and
binary 0 by a negative pulse. This is known as **bipolar encoding**. Each bit cell in

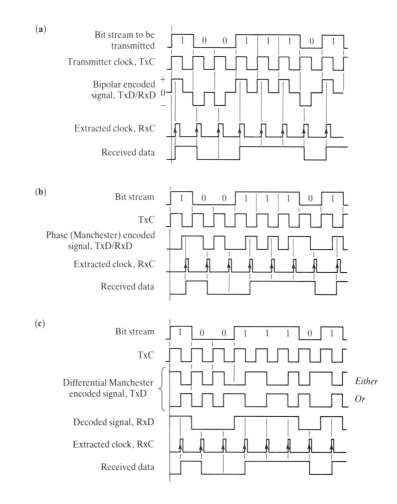

FIGURE 3.8

Clock encoding methods: (a) bipolar; (b) Manchester; (c) differential Manchester.

the bipolar encoded signal contains clocking information. A simple electronic circuit enables the clock signal to be extracted from the received bipolar signal. Since the encoded signal returns to the zero level after each encoded bit (positive or negative), this type of signal is also referred to as a **return-to-zero** or **RZ signal.**

Three distinct amplitude levels $(+, 0, -)$ are utilized with bipolar encoding. In contrast, the scheme shown in part (b) requires only two levels. The resulting signal is thus known as a **non-return-to-zero** or **NRZ signal** and the encoding scheme **phase** or **Manchester encoding**. With this scheme a binary 1 is encoded as a low–high signal and a binary 0 as a high–low signal. However, there is always a transition $(1 \rightarrow 0$ or $0 \rightarrow 1)$ at the centre of each bit cell. This is used by the clock extraction circuit to produce a clock pulse in the centre of the second half of the bit cell. At this point, the received (encoded) signal is either high (for binary 1) or low (for binary 0) and hence the correct signal will be shifted into the SIPO shift register.

The scheme shown in part (c) is known as **differential Manchester encoding**. This differs from Manchester encoding in that although there is still a transition at the centre of each bit cell, a transition at the start of the bit cell only occurs if the next bit to be encoded is a 0. This has the effect that the encoded output signal may take on one of two forms depending on the assumed start level (high or low). As can be seen, however, one is simply an inverted version of the other. This can be a useful feature with, say, point-to-point twisted pair links since, if differential drivers and receivers are being used, it does not matter which way round the two terminating wires at the receiver are connected. With a non-differential encoding scheme, the output will be inverted giving incorrect operation. The extracted clock is generated at the centre of each bit cell and the transitions in the decoded signal are triggered by signal changes at the start of the bit cell.

All of the schemes are **balanced codes** which means there is no mean (d.c.) value associated with them. This is so since a string of binary 1s (or 0s) will always have transitions associated with them rather than a constant (d.c.) level. This is also an important feature since it means that the received signal can then be **a.c. coupled** to the receiver electronics using, for example, a **transformer**. The receiver electronics can then operate using its own power supply since this is effectively isolated from the power supply of the transmitter.

Digital phase-lock-loop

An alternative approach to encoding the clock in the transmitted bit stream is to utilize a stable clock source at the receiver which is kept in time synchronism with the incoming bit stream. However, as there are no start and stop bits with a synchronous transmission scheme, it is necessary to encode the information in such a way that there are always sufficient bit transitions ($1 \rightarrow 0$ or $0 \rightarrow 1$) in the transmitted waveform to enable the receiver clock to be resynchronized at frequent intervals. One approach is to pass the data to be transmitted through a **scrambler** which randomizes the transmitted bit stream, removing continuous strings of 1s or 0s. Alternatively, the data may be encoded in such a way that suitable transitions will always be present.

The bit pattern to be transmitted is first differentially encoded as shown in Figure 3.9(a), the resulting encoded signal being referred to as a **non-return-to-zero-inverted (NRZI)** waveform. With NRZI encoding the signal level (1 or 0) does not change for the transmission of a binary 1, whereas a binary 0 causes a change. This means that there will always be bit transitions in the incoming signal of an NRZI waveform, providing there are no contiguous streams of binary 1s. On the surface, this may seem no different from the normal NRZ waveform but, as will be described later, if a bit-oriented scheme with zero bit insertion is used, an active line will always have a binary 0 in the transmitted bit stream at least every five bit cells. Consequently, the resulting waveform will contain a guaranteed number of transitions, since long strings of 0s cause a

(a)

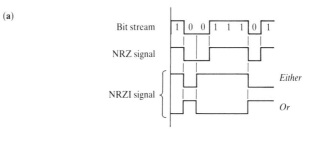

(b)

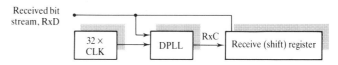

(c)

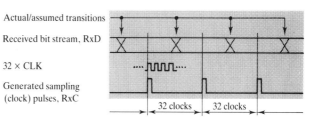

(d)

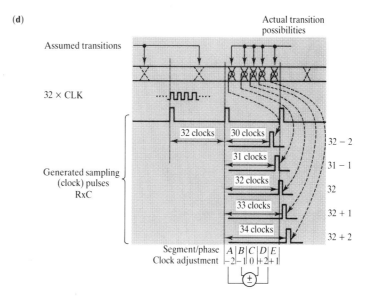

FIGURE 3.9

DPLL operation: (a) bit encoding; (b) circuit schematic; (c) in phase; (d) clock adjustment rules.

transition every bit cell. This enables the receiver to adjust its clock so that it is in synchronism with the incoming bit stream.

The circuit used to maintain bit synchronism is known as a **digital phase-lock-loop (DPLL)**. A **crystal-controlled oscillator** (clock source), which can hold its frequency sufficiently constant to require only very small adjustments at irregular intervals, is connected to the DPLL. Typically, the frequency of the clock is 32 times the bit rate used on the data link and is used by the DPLL to derive the timing interval between successive samples of the received bit stream.

Hence, assuming the incoming bit stream and the local clock are in synchronism, the state (1 or 0) of the incoming signal on the line will be sampled (and hence clocked into the SIPO) at the centre of each bit cell with exactly 32 clock periods between each sample. This is shown in part (c) of the figure.

Now assume that the incoming bit stream and local clock drift out of synchronism because of small variations in the latter. The sampling instant is adjusted in discrete increments as shown in part (d). If there are no transitions on the line, the DPLL simply generates a sampling pulse every 32 clock periods after the previous one. Whenever a transition ($1 \rightarrow 0$ or $0 \rightarrow 1$) is detected, however, the time interval between the previously generated sampling pulse and the next is determined according to the position of the transition relative to where the DPLL thought it should occur. To achieve this, each bit period is divided into five segments, shown as A, B, C, D and E in Figure 3.9(d). If, for example, a transition occurs during segment A, this indicates that the last sampling pulse was too close to the next transition and hence late. The time period the next pulse is therefore shortened to 30 clock periods. Similarly, if a transition occurs in segment E, this indicates that the previous sampling pulse was too early relative to the transition. The time period to the next pulse is therefore lengthened to 34 clock periods. Transitions in segments B and D are clearly nearer to the assumed transition and hence the relative adjustments are less (-1 and $+1$, respectively). Finally, a transition in segment C is deemed to be close enough to the assumed transition to warrant no adjustment.

In this way, successive adjustments keep the generated sampling pulses close to the centre of each bit cell. In practice, the widths of each segment (in terms of clock periods) are not equal. The outer segments (A and E), being further away from the nominal centre, are made longer than the three inner segments. For the circuit shown, a typical division might be A = E = 10 and B = C = D = 4. It can then be readily deduced that in the worst case the DPLL will require ten bit transitions to converge to the nominal bit centre of a waveform: five bit periods of coarse adjustments (± 2) and five bit periods of fine adjustments (± 1). Hence when using a DPLL, it is usual before transmitting the first frame on a line, or following an idle period between frames, to transmit a number of characters to provide a minimum of ten bit transitions. Two characters each composed of all 0s, for example, will provide 16 transitions with NRZI encoding. This ensures that the DPLL will generate sampling pulses at the nominal centre of each bit cell by the time the opening character or byte of a frame is received. It should be stressed, however, that once in synchronism (lock) only minor adjustments will normally take place during the reception of a frame.

It can be deduced from the figure, that with NRZI encoding the maximum rate at which the encoded signal changes polarity is one half that of bipolar and Manchester encoding. If the bit period is T, with NRZI encoding the maximum rate is $1/T$ whereas with bipolar or Manchester encoding it is $2/T$. The latter are known as the **modulation rate**. As described in the last chapter, the highest fundamental frequency component of each scheme is $1/T$ and $2/T$, respectively. This means that for the same data rate, bipolar and Manchester encoding require twice the transmission bandwidth of an NRZI encoded signal, that is, the higher the modulation rate the wider the required bandwidth.

The effect of this is that Manchester and differential Manchester encoding are both used extensively in applications such as local area networks (LANs) while schemes like NRZI are used primarily in wide area networks (WANs). LANs operate in a single office or building and hence use relatively short cable runs. This means that even though they operate at high bit rates – for example 10 Mbps and higher – the attenuation and bandwidth of the transmission medium are not generally a problem.

In contrast, in WANs twisted pair cable is often used with relatively high bit rates and over distances of several kilometres. Hence encoding schemes such as NRZI are often used with each bit occupying a full-width pulse. Examples of the encoding schemes used in WANs are shown in Figure 3.10. All are differentially encoded signals and use multiple levels per cell period. The use of differential encoding means that the signals shown may all be inverted if a different polarity start point is chosen. Also, the use of multiple levels with alternative

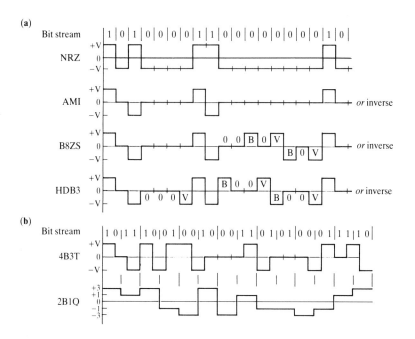

FIGURE 3.10

Some alternative coding schemes used with WANs.

transitions means that any errors that result in a violation of this rule can be identified.

The three codes in part (a) use a three-level code (+V, 0, −V) to represent the bit stream. With **AMI (alternate mark inversion)**, signal transitions are triggered by a binary 1 (mark) in the input bit stream. The disadvantage of this basic scheme is that a long string of binary 0s will have no associated signal transitions. Consequently, the DPLL associated with the circuit may lose bit synchronization whenever a string of 0s is present.

To overcome this problem, a derivative of the basic AMI encoding scheme known as **B8ZS (bipolar with 8 zeros substitution)** is often used. It is basically the same as AMI except that if a string of eight zeros is detected then these are encoded as 0 0 B 0 V B 0 V prior to transmission where B represents a normal (opposite polarity) transition and V a violation (same polarity). Thus the maximum number of zero bits that can be obtained is seven. This scheme is widely used in the North American integrated services digital network (ISDN).

An alternative scheme that is used outside North America is known as **HDB3 (high density bipolar 3)**. This operates by replacing any string of four zeros by three zeros followed by a violation that is of the same polarity as the previous transition. Thus in the example the first string of four zeros is replaced by 000V. With this basic rule, however, the presence of a long string of zeros will lead to a mean d.c. level being introduced into the signal as each set of four zeros is encoded in the same way. To avoid this with a long string of zeros the encoding of each successive four zeros is changed to B00V, producing a signal of alternating polarity. It can be deduced that with HDB3 the maximum number of zeros without a transition is three. This and the previous two schemes are often referred to as the **modulation format**.

The two coding schemes shown in Figure 3.10(b) are used on the access circuits to an ISDN network. As will be expanded upon in Chapter 8, these operate at bit rates of 160 kbps over twisted pair wire and span distances up to several kilometres. Both codes are examples of **baud rate reduction codes** which means that more than one bit is represented in a single pulse (time cell). The major advantage is that crosstalk is reduced owing to the smaller signal amplitude variations between adjacent pulses.

Both codes are classified as **mBnL codes** which means that a sequence of m input bits is represented by n pulses each of L levels where $n < m$ and $L > 2$. Thus with the **4B3T code** – also known as **modified monitoring state 43** or **MMS 43** – the T indicates three (ternary) levels, represented by the symbols +, −, 0. Hence four input bits are represented by three pulses each of three levels. The **baud rate** is thus 3/4 giving a **baud rate reduction** of 1/4.

The three symbol codes transmitted for each 4-bit input sequence are selected from one of the four columns in Table 3.1. Associated with each code in a column is a number (1–4) that indicates the next column from which the following code should be chosen. Thus in the example, the first 4-bit sequence 1011 is chosen from column 1 (+ 0 −) and the next column is 2. The next sequence 1001 is thus chosen from column 2 (+ − +) and the next column is 3, and so on. It can be deduced from the table that there are 27 different

Table 3.1   4B3T encoding patterns.

Binary sequence	1		2		3		4	
	Code	Next col.	Code	Next col.	Code	Next col.	Code	Next col.
0001	0 − +	1	0 − +	2	0 − +	3	0 − +	4
0111	− 0 +	1	− 0 +	2	− 0 +	3	− 0 +	4
0100	− + 0	1	− + 0	2	− + 0	3	− + 0	4
0010	+ − 0	1	+ − 0	2	+ − 0	3	+ − 0	4
1011	+ 0 −	1	+ 0 −	2	+ 0 −	3	+ 0 −	4
1110	0 + −	1	0 + −	2	0 + −	3	0 + −	4
1001	+ − +	2	+ − +	3	+ − +	4	− − −	1
0011	0 0 +	2	0 0 +	3	0 0 +	4	− − 0	2
1101	0 + 0	2	0 + 0	3	0 + 0	4	− 0 −	2
1000	+ 0 0	2	+ 0 0	3	+ 0 0	4	0 − −	2
0110	− + +	2	− + +	3	− − +	2	− − +	3
1010	+ + −	2	+ + −	3	+ − −	2	+ − −	3
1111	+ + 0	3	0 0 −	1	0 0 −	2	0 0 −	3
0000	+ 0 +	3	0 − 0	1	0 − 0	2	0 − 0	3
0101	0 + +	4	− 0 0	1	− 0 0	2	− 0 0	3
1100	+ + +	4	− + −	1	− + −	2	− + −	3

(*Note:* the symbol 000 is decoded into the binary sequence 0000)

codewords. Since there are only 16 possible input sequences (four bits), the code contains redundancy which can be exploited for error control. Also, the contents of the table are chosen such that with a random input sequence the mean bandwidth required is lower than when coding is not used.

The second code is known as **2B1Q**, the Q indicating four (quaternary) level pulses – known as **quats**. Hence each 2-bit input sequence is transmitted in one 4-level pulse. As can be seen in the example, the four levels are represented by the symbols $+3, +1, -1, -3$ to indicate symmetry about zero and equal spacing between states. The first bit in each pair of binary digits determines the sign ($1 = +, 0 = -$) and the second bit the magnitude ($1 = 1, 0 = 3$). There is no redundancy with this code but the baud rate is 1/2 compared with 3/4 with 4B3T. This is now the most widely adopted code.

Hybrid schemes

As the bit rate increases, so it becomes increasingly difficult to obtain and maintain clock (bit) synchronization. Hence, although Manchester and DPLL schemes are both widely used, additional hybrid schemes are also used. A typical scheme is shown in Figure 3.11(a). It uses a combination of Manchester encoding and a DPLL.

The DPLL is used to keep the local clock in synchronism with the incoming received signal. The use of Manchester encoding, however, means that

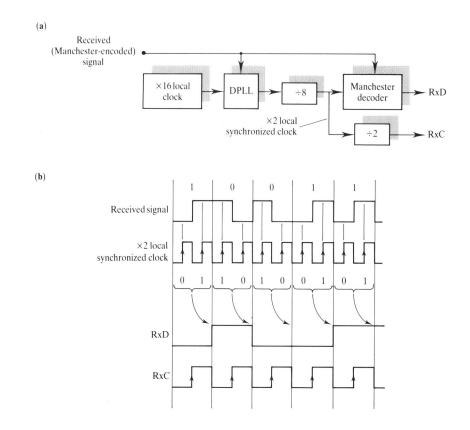

FIGURE 3.11

Bit synchronization using Manchester-encoding and a DPLL.

there is at least one signal transition every bit cell rather than, say, one per five bits with an NRZI signal. The local clock thus keeps in synchronism more reliably and, as can be deduced from the waveform set shown in part (b) of the figure, the availability of a local ($\times 2$) clock in synchronism with the incoming signal provides a reliable means of decoding the received (Manchester-encoded) signal. The price to pay is the increased bandwidth required for Manchester encoding compared with NRZI.

3.4.2 Character-oriented

As indicated earlier, there are two types of synchronous transmission control scheme: character-oriented and bit-oriented. Both use the same bit synchronization methods. The major difference between the two schemes is the method used to achieve character and frame synchronization.

Character-oriented transmission is used primarily for the transmission of blocks of characters, such as files of ASCII characters. Since there are no start or stop bits with synchronous transmission, however, an alternative way of achieving character synchronization must be utilized. This is achieved by the transmitter adding two or more transmission control characters, known as **synchronous idle** or **SYN** characters, before each block of characters. These have two functions. First they allow the receiver to obtain (or maintain) bit synchronization. Second, once this has been done, they allow the receiver to start to interpret the received bit stream on the correct character boundaries – **character synchronization**. The general scheme is shown in Figure 3.12.

Part (a) of the figure shows that frame synchronization (with character-oriented synchronous transmission) is achieved in just the same way as for asynchronous transmission by encapsulating the block of characters – the frame contents – between an STX–ETX pair of transmission control characters. Thus the SYN control characters used to enable the receiver to achieve character synchronization precede the STX start-of-frame character. Hence once the receiver has obtained bit synchronization it enters what is known as the **hunt mode**. This is shown in part (b) of the figure.

When the receiver enters the hunt mode, it starts to interpret the received bit stream in a window of 8-bits as each new bit is received. In this way, as each bit is received, it checks whether the last eight bits were equal to the known SYN character. If they are not, it receives the next bit and repeats the check. If they are, then this indicates it has found the correct character boundary and hence the following characters are then read after each subsequent eight bits have been received.

FIGURE 3.12

Character-oriented transmission: (a) frame format; (b) character synchronization; (c) data transparency (character stuffing).

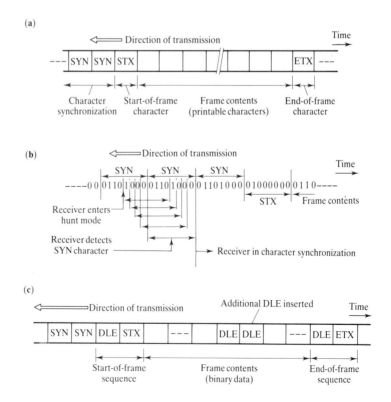

Once in character synchronization (and hence reading each character on the correct bit boundary), the receiver starts to process each subsequently received character in search of the STX character indicating the start of the frame. On receipt of the latter, it proceeds to receive the frame contents and terminates this process when it detects the ETX character. On a point-to-point link, the transmitter normally then reverts to sending SYN characters to allow the receiver to maintain synchronism. Alternatively, the above procedure must be repeated each time a new frame is transmitted.

Finally, as indicated in part (c) of the figure, when binary data is being transmitted, data transparency is achieved in the same way as described previously by preceding the STX and ETX characters by a DLE (data link escape) character and inserting (stuffing) an additional DLE character whenever it detects one in the frame contents. In this case, therefore, the SYN characters precede the first DLE character.

3.4.3 Bit-oriented

The need for a pair of characters at the start and end of each frame for frame synchronization, coupled with the additional DLE characters to achieve data transparency, means that a character-oriented transmission control scheme is relatively inefficient for the transmission of binary data. Moreover, the format of the transmission control characters varies for different character sets, so the scheme can only be used with a single type of character set, even though the frame contents may be pure binary data. To overcome these problems, a more universal scheme known as **bit-oriented transmission** is now the preferred control scheme as it can be used for the transmission of frames comprising either printable characters or binary data. The three main bit-oriented schemes are shown in Figure 3.13. They differ mainly in the way the start and end of each frame is signalled.

The scheme shown in part (a) is used primarily on point-to-point links. The start and end of a frame are both signalled by the same unique 8-bit pattern 01111110, known as the **flag byte** or **flag pattern**. The term **bit-oriented** is used because the received bit stream is searched by the receiver on a bit-by-bit basis for both the start-of-frame flag and, during reception of the frame contents, for the end-of-frame flag. Thus in principle the frame contents need not necessarily comprise multiples of eight bits.

To enable the receiver to obtain bit synchronism, the transmitter sends a string of **idle bytes** (each comprising 11111111) preceding the start-of-frame flag. On receipt of the opening flag, the received frame contents are read and interpreted on 8-bit (byte) boundaries until the closing flag is detected. The reception process is then terminated.

To achieve data transparency with this scheme, it is necessary to ensure that the flag pattern is not present in the frame contents. This is accomplished by using a technique known as **zero bit insertion** or **bit stuffing**. The circuit that performs this function is located at the output of the PISO register, as shown in part (ii). It is only enabled by the transmitter during transmission of the frame

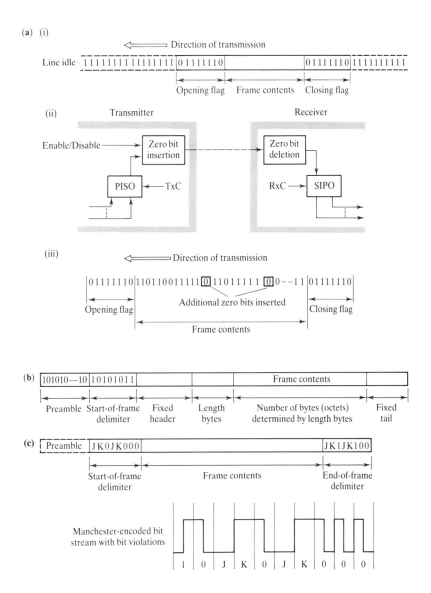

FIGURE 3.13

Bit-oriented
transmission frame
synchronization
methods: (a) flags;
(b) start-of-frame
delimiter and length
indication; (c) bit-
encoding violations.

contents. When enabled, the circuit detects whenever it has transmitted a sequence of five contiguous binary 1 digits, then automatically inserts an additional binary 0 digit. In this way, the flag pattern 01111110 can never be present in the frame contents between the opening and closing flags.

A similar circuit at the receiver located prior to the input of the SIPO performs the reverse function. Whenever a zero is detected after five contiguous 1 digits, it automatically removes (deletes) it from the frame contents. Normally the frame will also contain additional error detection digits preceding the closing flag which will be subjected to the same bit stuffing operation as the frame contents. An example stuffed bit pattern is shown in part (iii).

The scheme shown in part (b) is used with some **local area networks (LANs)**. In such networks, as will be explained in a later chapter, the transmission medium is a broadcast medium and is shared by all the attached DTEs (stations). Thus when a station wants to send a frame, it simply transmits it on the medium with the address (identity) of the intended recipient station at the head of the frame.

To enable all the other stations to obtain bit (clock) synchronization, the sending station precedes the fame contents with a bit pattern, known as the **preamble**, which comprises a string of 10 (binary) bit-pairs. Once in bit synchronism, the receiver searches the received bit stream on a bit-by-bit basis until it detects the known start of frame byte – 10101011 – known as the **start-of-frame delimiter**. A fixed header then follows, which includes the address of the intended recipient. It is followed by two **length bytes** which indicate the number of bytes in the contents field. Thus with this scheme the receiver simply counts the appropriate number of bytes (octets) to determine the end of each frame.

The scheme shown in part (c) is also used with LANs. The start and end of a frame are both signalled by the use of non-standard bit encoding patterns known as **bit violations**. For example, if Manchester encoding is being used instead of a signal transition occurring in the centre of the bit cell, the signal level either remains at the same level as the previous bit for the complete bit period (J) or at the opposite level (K).

Again, to detect the start and end of each frame, the receiver searches the received bit stream on a bit-by-bit basis, first for the start delimiter – JK0JK000 – and then for the end delimiter – JK1JK111. Since the J and K symbols are non-standard bit encodings, then the frame contents will not contain such symbols and data transparency is achieved.

Each of the schemes will be discussed in more detail when the different network types and protocols are introduced in later chapters.

3.5 ERROR DETECTION METHODS

As was indicated in the last chapter, when data is being transmitted between two DTEs it is very common, especially if the transmission lines are in an electrically noisy environment such as the switched telephone network, for the electrical signals representing the transmitted bit stream to be changed by electromagnetic interference induced in the lines by neighbouring electrical devices. This means that signals representing a binary 1 will be interpreted by the receiver as a binary 0 signal and vice versa. To ensure that information received by a destination DTE has a high probability of being the same as that transmitted by the sending DTE, there must be some way for the receiver to deduce, to a high probability, when received information contains errors. Furthermore, should errors be detected, a mechanism is needed to obtain a copy of the (hopefully) correct information.

There are two approaches for achieving this:

(1) **Forward error control**, in which each transmitted character or frame contains additional (redundant) information so that the receiver can not only detect when errors are present but also determine where in the received bit stream the errors are. The correct data is then obtained by inverting these bits.

(2) **Feedback (backward) error control**, in which each character or frame includes only sufficient additional information to enable the receiver to detect when errors are present but not their location. A retransmission control scheme is then used to request that another, hopefully correct, copy of the erroneous information be sent.

In practice, the number of additional bits required to achieve reliable forward error control increases rapidly as the number of information bits increases. Hence, feedback error control is the predominant method used in the types of data communication and networking systems discussed in this book. Nevertheless, a brief introduction to the subject of forward error control is given in Appendix A.

Feedback error control can be divided into two parts: firstly, the techniques that are used to achieve reliable error detection, and secondly, the control algorithms that are available to perform the associated retransmission control schemes. This section is concerned with the most common error-detection techniques currently in use. Some of the alternative retransmission control algorithms are then discussed in Chapter 4.

The two factors that determine the type of error detection scheme used are the **bit error rate (BER)** of the line or circuit and the type of errors, that is, whether the errors occur as random single-bit errors or as groups of contiguous strings of bit errors. The latter are referred to as **burst errors.** The BER is the probability P of a single bit being corrupted in a defined time interval. Thus a BER of 10^{-3} means that, on average, 1 bit in 10^3 will be corrupted during a defined time period.

If we are transmitting single characters using asynchronous transmission (say eight bits per character plus 1 start and 1 stop bit), the probability of a character being corrupted is $1 - (1 - P)^{10}$ which is approximately 10^{-2}. Alternatively, if we are transmitting blocks of characters using synchronous transmission (say 125 characters per block, each of eight bits), then the probability of a block (frame) containing an error is approximately 1. This means that on average every block will contain an error and must be retransmitted. Clearly, this length of frame is too long for this type of line and must be reduced to obtain an acceptable throughput.

The type of errors present is important since, as we will see, the different types of error detection scheme detect different types of error. Also, the number of bits used in some schemes determines the burst lengths that are detected. The three most widely used schemes are parity, block sum check and cyclic redundancy check. Each will be considered separately.

3.5.1 Parity

The most common method used for detecting bit errors with asynchronous and character-oriented synchronous transmission is the **parity bit method**. With this scheme the transmitter adds an additional bit – the parity bit – to each transmitted character prior to transmission. The parity bit used is a function of the bits that make up the character being transmitted. Hence, on receipt of each character, the receiver can perform a similar function on the received character and

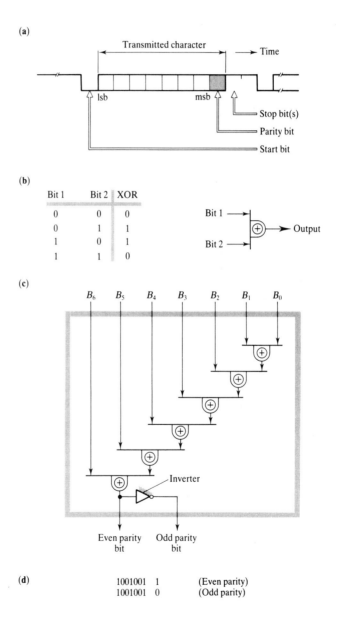

FIGURE 3.14

Parity bit method:
(a) position in character; (b) XOR gate truth table and symbol; (c) parity bit generation circuit; (d) two examples.

compare the result with the received parity bit. If they are equal, no error is assumed, but if they are different, then a transmission error is assumed to have occurred.

To compute the parity bit for a character, the number of 1 bits in the code for the character are added together (modulo 2) and the parity bit is then chosen so that the total number of 1 bits (including the parity bit itself) is either even – **even parity** – or odd – **odd parity**. The principles of the scheme are shown in the Figure 3.14.

The two examples shown in part (d) of the figure show that the parity bit method will only detect single (or an odd number of) bit errors and that two (or an even number of) bit errors will go undetected.

The circuitry used to compute the parity bit for each character comprises a set of **exclusive–OR (XOR) gates** connected as shown in part (c) of the Figure. The XOR gate is also known as a **modulo-2 adder** since, as shown by the **truth table** in Figure 3.14(b), the output of the exclusive–OR operation between two binary digits is the same as the addition of the two digits without a carry bit. The least significant pair of bits are first XORed together and the output of this gate is then XORed with the next (more significant) bit, and so on. The output of the final gate is the required parity bit which is loaded into the transmit PISO register prior to transmission of the character. Similarly, on receipt, the recomputed parity bit is compared with the received parity bit. If it is different, this indicates that a transmission error has been detected.

3.5.2 Block sum check

When blocks of characters are being transmitted, there is an increased probability that a character (and hence the block) will contain a bit error – the block error rate. Hence when blocks of characters (frames) are being transmitted, an extension to the error detecting capabilities obtained by the use of a single parity bit per character (byte) can be achieved by using an additional set of parity bits computed from the complete block of characters (bytes) in the frame. With this method, each character (byte) in the frame is assigned a parity bit as before (**transverse** or **row parity**). In addition, an extra bit is computed for each bit position (**longitudinal** or **column parity**) in the complete frame. The resulting set of parity bits for each column is referred to as the **block (sum) check character**. An example shown in Figure 3.15 uses odd parity for the row parity bits and even parity for the column parity bits. It assumes that the frame contains printable characters.

It can be deduced from this example that although two bit errors in a character will escape the row parity check, they will be detected by the corresponding column parity check. This is true, of course, only if no two bit errors occur in the same column at the same time. Clearly, the probability of this occurring will be much less than the probability of two bit errors in a single character occurring. Hence the use of a block sum check significantly improves the error detection properties of the scheme.

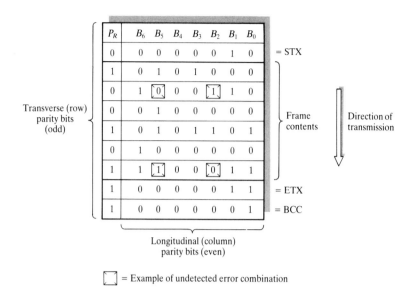

FIGURE 3.15

Block sum check example.

3.5.3 Cyclic redundancy check

The previous two schemes are best suited to applications in which random single-bit errors are present. When bursts of errors are present, however, a more rigorous method must be used. An **error burst** begins and ends with an erroneous bit, although the bits in between may or may not be corrupted. Thus, an error burst is defined as the number of bits between two successive erroneous bits including the incorrect two bits. Furthermore, when determining the length of an error burst, the last erroneous bit in a burst and the first erroneous bit in the following burst must be separated by B or more correct bits, where B is the length of the error burst. An example showing two different error burst lengths is shown in Figure 3.16. Notice that the first and third bit errors could not be used to define a single 11-bit error burst since an error occurs within the next 11 bits.

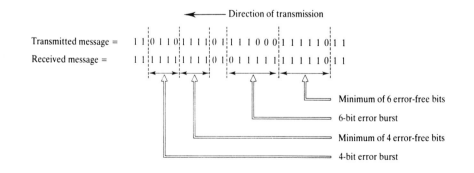

FIGURE 3.16

Error burst examples.

Parity, or its derivative block sum check, does not provide a reliable detection scheme against error bursts. In such cases, the most common alternative is based on the use of **polynomial codes**. Polynomial codes are used with frame (or block) transmission schemes. A single set of check digits is generated (computed) for each frame transmitted, based on the contents of the frame, and is appended by the transmitter to the tail of the frame. The receiver then performs a similar computation on the complete frame and check digits. If no errors have been induced, a known result should always be obtained; if a different answer is found, this indicates an error.

The number of check digits per frame is selected to suit the type of transmission errors anticipated, although 16 and 32 bits are the most common. The computed check digits are referred to as the **frame check sequence (FCS)** or the **cyclic redundancy check (CRC)** digits.

The underlying mathematical theory of polynomial codes is beyond the scope of this book but, essentially, the method exploits the following property of binary numbers if modulo-2 arithmetic is used. Let:

M = a k-bit number (the message to be transmitted)
R = an n-bit number such that k is greater than n (the remainder)
G = an $(n + 1)$-bit number (the divisor or generator)

Then if:

$$\frac{M \times 2^n}{G} = Q + \frac{R}{G}, \text{ where } Q \text{ is the quotient,}$$

$$\frac{M \times 2^n + R}{G} = Q, \text{ assuming modulo-2 arithmetic.}$$

This result can be readily confirmed by substituting the expression for $M \times 2^n / G$ into the last equation, giving:

$$\frac{M \times 2^n + R}{G} = Q + \frac{R}{G} + \frac{R}{G}$$

which is equal to Q since any number added to itself modulo-2 will result in zero; that is, the remainder is zero.

To exploit this, the complete frame contents M together with an appended set of zeros equal in number to the number of FCS digits to be generated (which is equivalent to multiplying the message by 2^n, where n is the number of FCS digits) are divided module-2 by a second binary number G, the **generator polynomial** containing one more digits than the FCS. The division operation is equivalent to performing the exclusive–OR operation bit-by-bit in parallel as each bit in the frame is processed. The remainder R is then the FCS which is transmitted at the tail of the information digits. Similarly, on receipt, the received bit stream including the FCS digits is again divided by the same generator polynomial – that is, $(M \times 2^n + R)/G$ – and, if no errors are present, the remainder is all zeros. If an error is present, however, the remainder is non-zero.

EXAMPLE

A series of 8-bit message blocks (frames) is to be transmitted across a data link using a CRC for error detection. A generator polynomial of 11001 is to be used. Use an example to illustrate the following:

(a)   the FCS generation process,

(b)   the FCS checking process.

Generation of the FCS for the message 11100110 is shown in Figure 3.17. First, four zeros are appended to the message, which is equivalent to

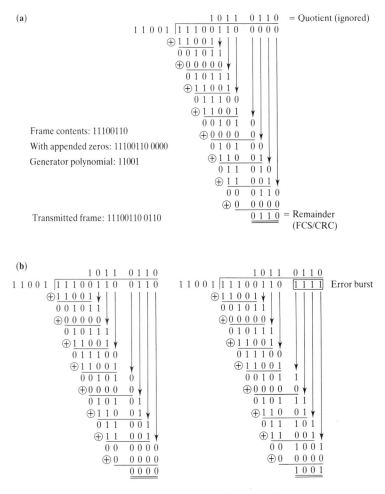

Frame contents: 11100110

With appended zeros: 11100110 0000

Generator polynomial: 11001

Transmitted frame: 11100110 0110

FIGURE 3.17

CRC example.

multiplying the message by 2^4, since the FCS will be four bits. This is then divided (modulo-2) by the generator polynomial (binary number). The modulo-2 division operation is equivalent to performing the exclusive–OR operation bit-by-bit in parallel as each bit in the dividend is processed. Also, with modulo-2 arithmetic, a division can be performed into each partial remainder, providing the two numbers are of the same length, that is, the most significant bits are both 1s. The relative magnitude of both numbers is not considered. The resulting 4-bit remainder (0110) is the FCS, which is then appended at the tail of the original message when it is transmitted. The quotient is not used.

At the receiver, the complete received bit sequence is divided by the same generator polynomial as used at the transmitter. Two examples are shown in Figure 3.17(b). In the first, no errors are assumed to be present, so that the remainder is zero – the quotient is again not used. In the second, however, an error burst of four bits at the tail of the transmitted bit sequence is assumed. Consequently, the resulting remainder is non-zero, indicating that a transmission error has occurred.

The choice of generator polynomial is important since it determines the types of error that are detected. For example, an error pattern that is identical, or has a factor identical, to the generator polynomial will generate the same check bits as the correct transmission and be undetectable. A polynomial which is prime, in the modulo-2 sense, is therefore normally chosen.

EXAMPLE

Assuming the same requirements as were used in the previous example, deduce an example of a received frame that will not be detected.

Any number multiplied by another number will give zero remainder when subsequently divided by the same number:

$$
\begin{array}{r}
11100110 = \text{Arbitrary message (multiplicand)} \\
11001 = \text{Generator polynomial (multiplier)} \\
\hline
\left.\begin{array}{r}
111001100000 \\
11100110000 \\
11100110
\end{array}\right\} \text{Partial products} \\
\hline
100110110110 = \text{Final product (modulo-2 sum of partial products)}
\end{array}
$$

Thus, if a received frame (information plus FCS bits) is 100110110110, it will yield zero remainder when divided by 11001, irrespective of the contents of the transmitted frame.

A generator polynomial of R bits will detect:

- all single-bit errors,
- most double-bit errors,
- most odd number of bit errors,
- all error bursts $< R$,
- most error bursts $\geq R$.

The standard way of representing a generator polynomial is to show those positions that are binary 1 as powers of X. Some examples of CRCs used in practice are thus:

$$CRC\text{--}16 \quad = X^{16} + X^{15} + X^2 + 1$$
$$CRC\text{--}CCITT = X^{16} + X^{12} + X^5 + 1$$
$$CRC\text{--}32 \quad = X^{32} + X^{26} + X^{23} + X^{16} + X^{12} + X^{11} + X^{10} + X^8 + X^7 + X^5 + X^4 + X^2 + X + 1$$

Hence CRC–16 is equivalent in binary form to:

1 1000 0000 0000 0101

With such a generator polynomial, 16 zeros would be appended to the frame contents before generation of the FCS. The latter would then be the 16-bit remainder. This will detect all error bursts of less than 16 bits and most error bursts greater than or equal to 16 bits. CRC–16 and CRC–CCITT are both used extensively with wide area networks, while CRC–32 is used in most local area networks.

Although the requirement to perform multiple (modulo-2) divisions may appear to be relatively complicated, in practice it can be done quite readily in either hardware or software. To illustrate this, a hardware implementation of the scheme used in the earlier example is given in Figure 3.18(a).

In this example, since four FCS digits are to be generated, only a 4-bit shift register is needed to represent bits x^3, x^2, x^1 and x^0 in the generator polynomial. These are often referred to as the **active bits** of the generator. With this generator polynomial, digits x^3 and x^0 are binary 1 while digits x^2 and x^1 are binary 0. Hence the new states of shift register elements x^1 and x^2 simply take on the states of x^0 and x^1 directly; the new states of elements x^0 and x^3 are determined by the state of the feedback path XOR-ed with the preceding digit.

The circuit operates as follows. The FCS shift register is cleared and the first 8-bit byte in the frame parallel loaded into the PISO transmit shift register. This is then shifted-out to the transmission line, most significant bit first, at a rate determined by the transmitter clock TxC. In time synchronism with this, the same bit stream is XOR-ed with x^3 and passed via the feedback path to the selected inputs of the FCS shift register. As each subsequent 8-bit byte is loaded into the transmit shift register and transmitted to line, the procedure repeats. Finally, after the last byte in the frame has been output, the transmit shift register is loaded with zeros and the feedback control signal changes from 1 to 0

(a)

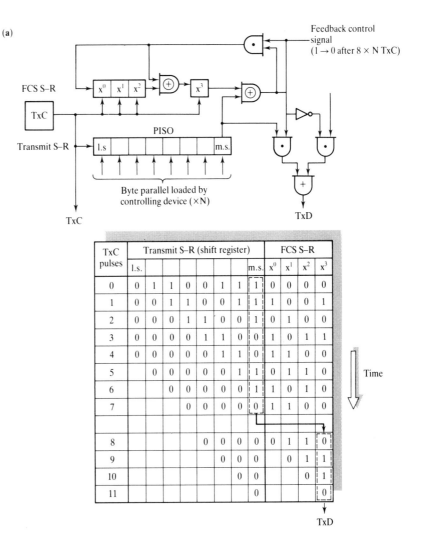

TxC pulses	Transmit S-R (shift register)								FCS S-R			
	l.s.							m.s.	x^0	x^1	x^2	x^3
0	0	1	1	0	0	1	1	1	0	0	0	0
1	0	0	1	1	0	0	1	1	1	0	0	1
2	0	0	0	1	1	0	0	1	0	1	0	0
3	0	0	0	0	1	1	0	0	1	0	1	1
4	0	0	0	0	0	1	1	0	1	1	0	0
5		0	0	0	0	0	1	1	0	1	1	0
6			0	0	0	0	0	1	1	0	1	0
7				0	0	0	0	0	1	1	0	0
8					0	0	0	0	0	1	1	0
9						0	0	0		0	1	1
10							0	0			0	1
11								0				0

Time

TxD

FIGURE 3.18

CRC hardware
schematic:
(a) generation.

so that the current contents of the FCS shift register – the computed remainder –
follow the frame contents onto the transmission line.

The contents of the transmit and FCS shift registers shown in the example
assume just a single-byte frame ($N = 1$), and hence correspond to that shown in
the earlier example in Figure 3.17. The figure shows the contents of both the
transmit and FCS shift registers after each shift (transmit clock) pulse. Thus the
transmitted bit stream is as shown in the hashed boxes.

The corresponding receiver hardware is similar to that used at the transmitter, as shown in Figure 3.18(b). The received data (RxD) is sampled (shifted)
into the SIPO receive shift register in the centre (or later with Manchester
encoding) of the bit cell. Also, as before, in time synchronization with this the

(b)

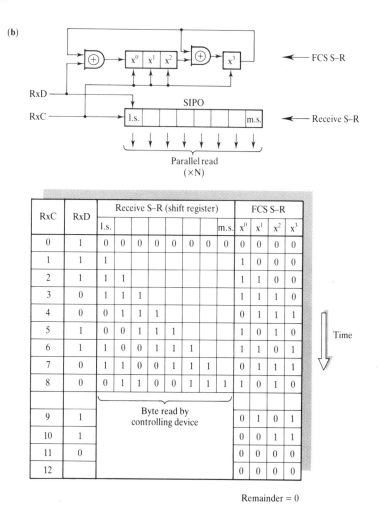

RxC	RxD	Receive S-R (shift register)								FCS S-R			
		l.s.							m.s.	x^0	x^1	x^2	x^3
0	1	0	0	0	0	0	0	0	0	0	0	0	0
1	1	1								1	0	0	0
2	1	1	1							1	1	0	0
3	0	1	1	1						1	1	1	0
4	0	0	1	1	1					0	1	1	1
5	1	0	0	1	1	1				1	0	1	0
6	1	1	0	0	1	1	1			1	1	0	1
7	0	1	1	0	0	1	1	1		0	1	1	1
8	0	0	1	1	0	0	1	1	1	1	0	1	0
9	1	Byte read by controlling device								0	1	0	1
10	1									0	0	1	1
11	0									0	0	0	0
12										0	0	0	0

Time

Remainder = 0

FIGURE 3.18 (cont.)

(b) Checking.

bit stream is XOR-ed with x^3 and fed into the FCS shift register. As each 8-bit byte is received, it is read by the controlling device. Again, the example frame contents shown are for a frame comprising just a single byte of data.

The hardware shown in Figure 3.18 is normally incorporated into the transmission control circuits associated with bit-oriented transmission. In some instances, however, a CRC is used in preference to a BSC with character-oriented transmission. In such cases, the CRC must normally be generated in software by the controlling device rather than in hardware. Again this is relatively straightforward as can be seen from the pseudo-code shown in Figure 3.19.

The code assumes an 8-bit generator polynomial (divisor) and that the preformatted frame – STX, ETX, etc – is stored in an array. The same code can be used for CRC generation and checking; for generation the array will contain a NUL byte/character (all zeros) at its tail, and for checking the received CRC.

{ Assume a preformatted frame to be transmitted (including a zero byte at its tail) or a received frame is stored in a byte array buff[1 .. count]. Also that the 8 active bits of a 9-bit divisor are stored in the most-significant 8 bits of a 16-bit integer CRCDIV. The following function will compute and return the 8-bit CRC }

```
function CRC : byte;
var      i, j : integer;
         data : integer

begin    data := buff[1] shl 8;
         for j := 2 to count do
             begin
                 data := data + buff[j];
                 for i := 1 to 8 do
                     if ((data and $8000) = $8000) then
                         begin data := data shl1;
                               data := data xor CRCDIV; end
                     else    data := data shl 1;
             end;

         CRC := data shr 8;
end;
```

FIGURE 3.19

Pseudo-code for 8-bit computation/checking.

3.6 DATA COMPRESSION

It has been assumed until now that the contents of transmitted frames (blocks) are comprised of the original (source) data in the form of strings of fixed-length characters or bytes. Although this is the case in many data communication applications, there are applications in which the source data is **compressed** prior to transmission. This is mainly done in applications involving public transmission facilities, such as the PSTN, in which charges are based on time (duration) and distance. Hence, for a particular call, if the time to transmit each block of data can be reduced, it will automatically reduce the call cost.

For example, assume we are transmitting data at, say, 4800 bps over the PSTN and the time needed to transmit the data associated with the call is 20 minutes. Clearly, if by using data compression we can halve the amount of data to be transmitted, a 50% saving in transmission costs will be obtained. This is the same as saying we can achieve the same performance with, say, a 4800 bps modem with compression as with a 9600 bps modem without compression.

In practice, a range of compression algorithms can be employed, each suited to a particular type of data. Some modems – often referred to as **intelligent modems** – now offer an **adaptive compression** feature which selects a particular compression algorithm depending on the type of data being transmitted. Some of the more common types of data compression algorithm are described in this section.

3.6.1 Packed decimal

When frames comprising just numeric characters are being transmitted, significant savings can be obtained by reducing the number of bits per character from seven to four by using simple binary-coded-decimal encoding instead of ASCII. It can be deduced from the table of ASCII codes shown in Figure 3.1, that the ten numeric digits (0–9) all have 011 in their three high-order bit positions. Normally, these are needed to discriminate between numeric and alphabetic (and other) characters in the codeset. If the data comprises only numeric digits, however, these three bits are redundant and need not be transmitted, as shown in Figure 3.20(a).

As can be seen, if character-oriented transmission is being used, it is not possible simply to insert the compressed binary-coded digits between the STX and ETX control characters since the digit pair 0, 3 would be interpreted as an ETX. Hence at the start of the data a (known) control character code is used to indicate that packed decimal follows, then a second character (byte) indicating the number of digits in the run. Two characters in the same column – for example, ':' and ';' – are often used as a decimal point and space, respectively.

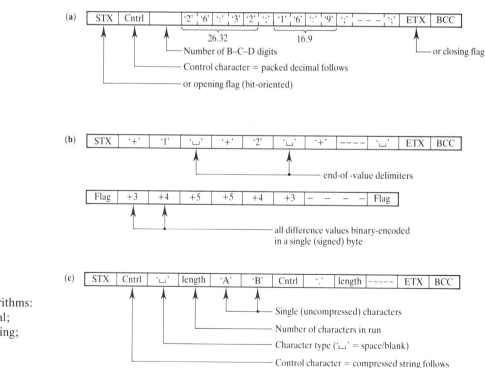

FIGURE 3.20

Some example compression algorithms:
(a) packed decimal;
(b) relative encoding;
(c) character suppression.

3.6.2 Relative encoding

An alternative to packed decimal when transmitting numeric data that has only small differences between successive values is to send only the difference in magnitude between each value together with a known reference value. This is known as **relative encoding** and can be particularly effective in data logging applications.

For example, if the water level of a river is being remotely monitored, it is normal to read the level at set time intervals and to store (log) these prior to transmission. Then, when a preset number of readings has been obtained, they are transmitted to the central monitoring site using, for example, the PSTN and an **autodial modem**. To minimize the time needed to transmit the readings, instead of sending the absolute water level values, just the difference values are sent. An example frame content with this scheme is shown in Figure 3.20(c) which shows that the savings will be a function of the format of the difference values, binary values with a bit-oriented protocol being best.

3.6.3 Character suppression

A variation of the above scheme that can be used in a more general way to compress other character types is shown in part (b) of Figure 3.20. Normally, when frames comprising printable characters are being transmitted, there are often sequences in the frame when the same character repeats, for example the space character. The control device at the transmitter scans the frame contents prior to transmission and, if a continuous string of three or more characters is located, replaces these with the three-character sequence shown in the figure.

The sequence comprises a (known) control character indicating that a compressed string follows, the character type and a count of the number of characters in the string. Normally, the count is in binary form, but since it is preceded by a known control character the receiver can discriminate between a count value of 3 and the ETX control character. Any character can be compressed in this scheme. The receiver, on detecting the compression control character, simply reads the following character type and count values and inserts the appropriate number of these characters into the received frame at this point. This scheme is an example of a more general run-length encoding technique.

3.6.4 Huffman coding

Huffman coding exploits the property that not all symbols in a transmitted frame occur with the same frequency. For example, in a frame comprising strings of characters, certain characters will occur more often than others. Hence, instead of using a fixed number of bits per character, a different encoding scheme is used in which the most common characters are encoded using fewer bits than less frequent characters. It is thus a form of **statistical encoding**. Because of the variable number of bits per character, bit-oriented transmission must be used.

First the character string to be transmitted is analysed and the character types and their relative frequency determined. The coding operation then involves creating an **unbalanced tree** with some branches (and hence codewords, in practice) shorter than others. The degree of imbalance is a function of the relative frequency of occurrence of the characters; the larger the spread, the more unbalanced the tree. The resulting tree is known as the **Huffman code tree**.

A Huffman (code) tree is a **binary tree** with branches assigned the value 0 or 1. The base of the tree, normally the geometric top, in practice, is known as the **root node**, and the point at which a branch divides as a **branch node**. The termination point of a branch is known as a **leaf node** to which the symbols being encoded are assigned. An example of a Huffman tree is shown in part (a) of Figure 3.21. This corresponds to the string of characters AAABBCD.

As each branch divides, a binary value of 0 or 1 is assigned to each new branch: a binary 0 for the left branch and a binary 1 for the right branch. The codewords used for each character (shown in the leaf nodes) are determined by tracing the path *from* the root node out to each leaf and forming a string of the binary values associated with each branch traced. It can be deduced from the codes that it would take

$$4 \times 1 + 3 \times 2 + 2 \times 2 + 1 \times 1 = 19 \text{ bits}$$

to transmit the complete string AAAABBCD compared with $8 \times 8 = 64$ bits using ASCII codewords.

In practice, this is not a fair comparison since, with Huffman coding, it is necessary for the receiver to know the reduced character set being transmitted and the corresponding codewords, that is, their frequency of occurrence or Huffman tree. A better comparison is to consider the number of bits required with normal binary coding: four characters (A–D) would require two bits for each character, so a total of 20 bits would be required to transmit the ten characters. Clearly, the savings are nominal. In general, Huffman coding is most efficient when the frequency distribution of the characters being transmitted is wide and long character strings are involved. Conversely, it is not suitable for the transmission of binary-coded computer data since the 8-bit bytes generally occur with about the same frequency.

To illustrate how the Huffman tree shown in part (a) of Figure 3.21 is determined, information concerning the frequency of occurrence of each character as listed in part (b) of the figure must be added. The characters are listed in a column in decreasing (weight) order. The tree is derived as follows.

The first two leaf nodes at the base of the list – C1 and D1 – are assigned to the (1) and (0) branches respectively of a branch node. These are then replaced by a branch node whose weight is the sum of these two weights – 2. A new column is formed containing the new node, combined with the remaining nodes from the first column, again arranged in their correct weight order. This procedure is repeated until only two nodes remain.

To derive the resulting codewords for each character, one starts with the character in the first column and then proceeds to list the branch numbers – 0 or 1 – as they are encountered. Thus for character A the first (and only) branch

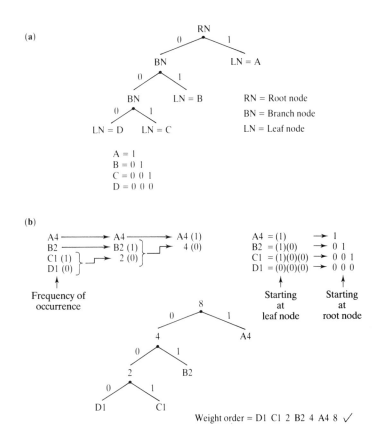

FIGURE 3.21

Huffman code tree construction: (a) final tree with codes; (b) tree derivation.

number is (1) in the last column while for C the first is (1) then (0) at branch node 2 and finally (0) at branch node 4. However, the codewords start at the root and not the leaf node hence the actual codewords are the reverse of these numbers. The Huffman tree can then be readily constructed from these.

A check is then made to ensure that this is the optimum tree – and hence set of codewords – by listing the resulting weights of all the leaf and branch nodes in the tree starting with the smallest weight and proceeding from left-to-right and from bottom-to-top. The codewords are optimum if the resulting list increments up in weight order.

EXAMPLE

A character file is to be transmitted that is made up of the characters A through H only. Determine a Huffman code tree, and hence the corresponding codewords for each character, to transmit the following files:

(a)   9 As, 9 Bs, 5 Cs, 5 Ds, 2 Es, 2 Fs, 2 Gs, 2 Hs,

(b)   18 As, 10 Bs, 2 Cs, 2 Ds, 1 E, 1 F, 1 G, 1 H.

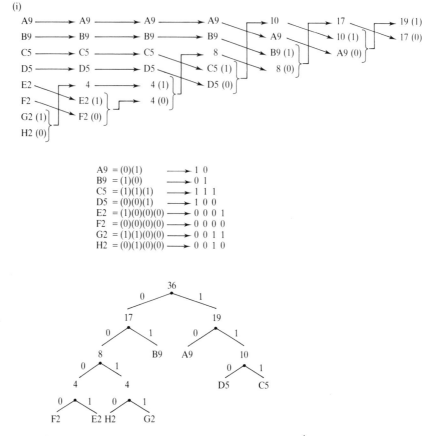

FIGURE 3.22

Huffman code tree derivation for two alternative frequency distributions of the character set ABCDEFGH.

Deduce the savings in transmission capacity in each case relative to normal binary encoding.

The derivation of the codewords is shown in parts (i) and (ii) of Figure 3.22.

For each case, the characters are first listed in weight order and the two characters at the bottom of the list are assigned to the (1) and (0) branches. This time, however, when the two nodes are combined, the weight of the resulting branch node, 4, is greater than the weight of the two characters E2 and F2. Hence the ordered list in the second column shows a combined branch and node higher than these two characters. This procedure is repeated until there are only two nodes remaining. The number of bits required is:

$$9 \times 2 + 9 \times 2 + 5 \times 3 + 5 \times 3 + 2 \times 4 + 2 \times 4 + 2 \times 4 + 2 \times 4 = 98 \text{ bits}$$

With normal binary encoding, three bits are required to represent the eight characters and hence the number of bits = $36 \times 3 = 108$ bits.

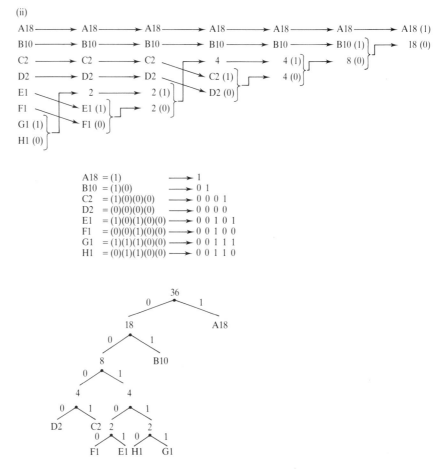

FIGURE 3.22 (cont.)   Weight order = F1 E1 H1 G1 D2 C2 2 2 4 4 8 B10 18 A18 ✓

This procedure is followed in part (ii). The number of bits required is:

$18 \times 1 + 10 \times 2 + 2 \times 4 + 2 \times 4 + 4 \times 5 = 74$ bits

The resulting codewords and Huffman tree for parts (i) and (ii) are as shown in the figure. It can be concluded from this, therefore, that the larger the imbalance, the more efficient the codings become.

Since each character in its encoded form has a variable number of bits, then the received bit stream must be interpreted (decoded) in a bit-oriented way rather than on fixed 8-bit boundaries. Because of the order in which bits are assigned during the encoding procedure, however, Huffman codewords have the unique property that a shorter codeword will never form the start of a longer

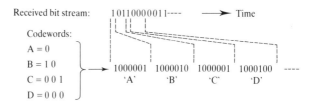

FIGURE 3.23

Decoding of a received
bit string assuming
codewords derived in
Figure 3.21.

codeword. If, say, 011 is a valid codeword, then there cannot be any longer codewords starting with this pattern. This can be confirmed by considering the codes derived in the earlier examples.

This property, known as the **prefix property**, means that the received bit stream can be decoded simply by carrying out a recursive search bit-by-bit until each valid codeword is found. The ASCII codes corresponding to the received string of codewords are then written into the receive buffer. An example is given in Figure 3.23.

As the Huffman code tree (and hence codewords) varies for different sets of characters being transmitted, for the receiver to perform the decoding operation, it must know the codewords relating to the data being transmitted. This can be done in two ways. Either the codewords relating to the next set of data are sent before the data is transmitted, or the receiver knows in advance what codewords are being used.

The first approach leads to a form of **adaptive compression** since the codewords can be changed to suit the type of data being transmitted. The disadvantage is the overhead of having to send the new set of codewords (and corresponding characters) whenever a new type of data is to be sent. An alternative is for the receiver to have one or more different sets of codewords and for the sender to indicate to the receiver (through an agreed message) which codeword set to use for the next set of data.

For example, since a common requirement is to send text files generated by a word processor (and hence containing normal textual information), detailed statistical analyses have been carried out into the frequency of occurrence of the characters in the English alphabet in normal written text. This information has been used to construct the Huffman code tree for the alphabet. If this type of data is being sent, the transmitter and receiver would automatically use this set of codewords. Other common data sets have been analysed in a similar way; the interested reader should consult the bibliography at the end of the book for further examples.

3.6.5 Dynamic Huffman coding

The basic Huffman coding method requires both the transmitter and receiver to know the table of codewords relating to the data being transmitted. An alternative method allows the transmitter (encoder) and receiver (decoder) to build the

Huffman tree – and hence codeword table – dynamically as the characters are transmitted/received. This is known as **dynamic Huffman coding**.

With this method, if the character to be transmitted is currently present in the tree its codeword is determined and sent in the normal way. If it is not present – that is, it is the first occurrence of this character – it is transmitted in its uncompressed form. The encoder proceeds to update its Huffman tree either by incrementing the frequency of occurrence of the transmitted character or introducing the new character into the tree.

Each transmitted codeword is encoded in such a way that the receiver, in addition to being able to determine the character that is received, can also carry out the same modifications to its own copy of the tree so that it can interpret the next codeword received according to the new updated tree structure.

To describe the details of the method, assume that the data (file) to be transmitted starts with the character string:

This is simple ...

The steps taken by the transmitter are shown in parts (a)–(g) of Figure 3.24.

Both transmitter and receiver start with a tree that comprises the root node and a single **empty leaf node** – a leaf node with a zero frequency of occurrence – assigned to its 0-branch. There is always just one such node in the tree and its position – and codeword – varies as the tree is being constructed. It is represented in the figure as e0.

The encoder then starts by reading the first character – T – and assigning this to the 1-branch of the root. Since this is the first occurrence of this character, it is shown as T1 and it is transmitted in its uncompressed – say, ASCII – form. Since the decoder's tree is also empty, it interprets the received bit string as an uncompressed character and proceeds to assign the character to its tree in the same way – part (a).

For each subsequent character, the encoder first checks whether the character is already present in the tree. If it is, then it sends the codeword for the character in the normal way, the codeword being determined by the position of the character in the tree. If it is not, then it sends the current codeword for the empty leaf – again determined by its position in the tree – followed by the uncompressed codeword for the character. Since the decoder has the same tree as the encoder, it can readily deduce from the received bit string whether it is the codeword of a (compressed) character or that of the empty leaf followed by the character in its uncompressed form.

The encoder and decoder proceed to update their copy of the tree based on the last character that has been transmitted/received. If it is a new character, the existing empty leaf node in the tree is replaced with a new branch node, the empty leaf being assigned to the 0-branch and the character to the 1-branch – part (b).

If the character is already present in the tree, then the frequency of occurrence of the leaf node is incremented by unity. On doing this, the position of the leaf node may not now be in the optimum position in the tree. Hence, each time the tree is updated – either by adding a new character or incrementing

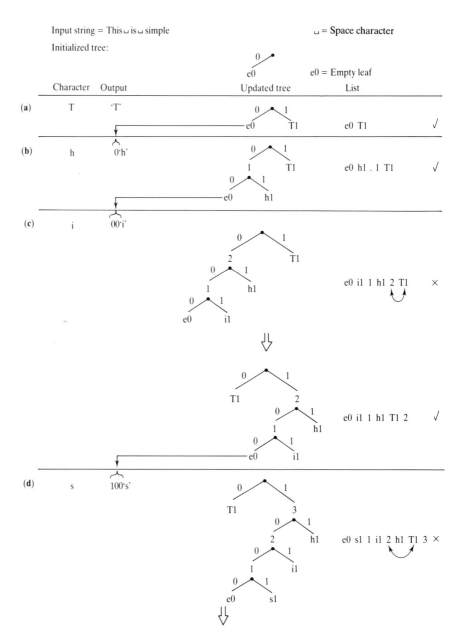

FIGURE 3.24

Dynamic Huffman coding example.

the frequency of occurrence of an existing character – both the encoder and decoder proceed to check, and if necessary modify, the current position of all the characters in the tree.

To ensure that both the encoder and decoder do this in a consistent way, they first list the weights of the leaf and branch nodes in the updated tree from

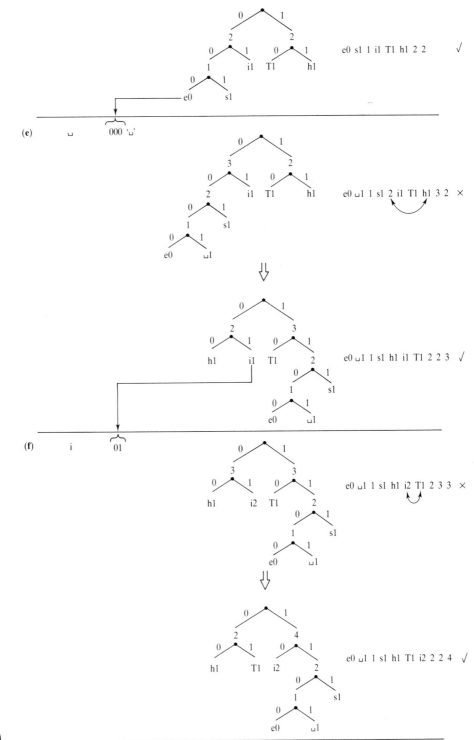

FIGURE 3.24 (cont.)

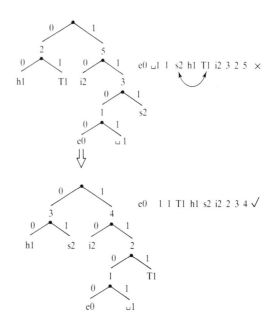

FIGURE 3.24 (cont.)

left-to-right and bottom-to-top starting at the empty leaf. If they are all in weight order, all is well and the tree is left unchanged. If there is a node out of order, the structure of the tree is modified by exchanging the position of this node with the other node in the tree – together with its branch and leaf nodes – to produce an incremented weight order. The first occurrence is in part (c) and other examples are in parts (d)–(g).

The steps followed when a character to be transmitted has previously been sent are shown in part (f). At this point, the character to be transmitted is 'i' and when the encoder searches the tree, it determines it is already present and transmits its existing codeword – 01. It then proceeds to increment its weight – frequency of occurrence – by unity to i2 and updates the position of the modified node as before. Another example is shown in part (g) when the character 's' is to be transmitted.

It can be deduced from this example that the savings in transmission bandwidth only start to be obtained when characters begin to repeat themselves. In practice, however, the savings with text files can be significant and dynamic Huffman coding is now used in many data communication applications. An example is the data compression algorithm that is used in V.32 modems.

3.6.6 Facsimile compression

Although compression ratios of up to 2:1 can be obtained with character files using Huffman coding, the most pronounced savings are realized for the transmission of the digitized images produced by the scanners associated with

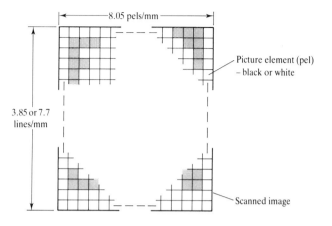

FIGURE 3.25

Facsimile scanned
image schematic.

facsimile (fax) machines. As can be seen in Figure 3.25, these scan a page with a
vertical resolution of 3.85 or 7.7 lines per millimetre – approximately 100 to 200
lines per inch. Each scan line is digitized at the rate of 8.05 **picture element** or
pels per millimetre – a 0 for white and a 1 for black. Thus a typical scanned page
produces about two million binary digits. To transmit this in its uncompressed
form at, say, 4800 bps, would require in excess of 6 minutes.

In practice, in most documents, many scanned lines comprise only long
strings of white pels whilst others comprise a mix of long strings of white and
long strings of black pels. Since facsimile machines are normally used with public
carrier networks, CCITT has produced standards relating to them. These are T2
(Group 1), T3 (Group 2), T4 (Group 3) and T5 (Group 4). The first two are
earlier standards and are now rarely used. The last two, however, both operate
digitally, Group 3 with modulation for use with an analogue PSTN and Group 4
all-digital for use with digital networks such as the ISDN. Both use data compression, and compression ratios in excess of 10:1 are common with most
document pages. Consequently the time taken to transmit a page is reduced to
less than a minute with Group 3 machines and, because of the added benefit of a
higher transmission rate (64 kbps), less than a few seconds with a Group 4
machine.

As part of the standardization process, extensive analyses of typical
scanned document pages were made. Tables of codewords were produced based
on the relative frequency of occurrence of the number of contiguous white and
black pels found in a scanned line. The resulting codewords are fixed and
grouped into two separate tables: the **termination–codes table** and the **make-up
codes table**. The codewords in each table are shown in Figure 3.26.

Codewords in the termination-codes table are for white or black run
lengths of from 0 to 63 pels in steps of 1 pel; the make-up codes table contains
codewords for white or black run lengths that are multiples of 64 pels. A
technique known as overscanning is used which means that all lines start with a
minimum of one white pel. In this way, the receiver knows the first codeword

White run length	Code word	Base 64 rep	Black run length	Code word
0	00110101	0	0	0000110111
1	000111	1	1	010
2	0111	2	2	11
3	1000	3	3	10
4	1011	4	4	011
5	1100	5	5	0011
6	1110	6	6	0010
7	1111	7	7	00011
8	10011	8	8	000101
9	10100	9	9	000100
10	00111	a	10	0000100
11	01000	b	11	0000101
12	001000	c	12	0000111
13	000011	d	13	00000100
14	110100	e	14	00000111
15	110101	f	15	000011000
16	101010	g	16	0000010111
17	101011	h	17	0000011000
18	0100111	i	18	0000001000
19	0001100	j	19	00001100111
20	0001000	k	20	00001101000
21	0010111	l	21	00001101100
22	0000011	m	22	00000110111
23	0000100	n	23	00000101000
24	0101000	o	24	00000010111
25	0101011	p	25	00000011000
26	0010011	q	26	000011001010
27	0100100	r	27	000011001011
28	0011000	s	28	000011001100
29	00000010	t	29	000011001101
30	00000011	u	30	000001101000
31	00011010	v	31	000001101001
32	00011011	w	32	000001101010
33	0010010	x	33	000001101011
34	00010011	y	34	000011010010
35	00010100	z	35	000011010011
36	00010101	A	36	000011010100
37	00010110	B	37	000011010101
38	00010111	C	38	000011010110
39	00101000	D	39	000011010111
40	00101001	E	40	000001101100
41	00101011	F	41	000001101101
42	00101010	G	42	000011011010
43	00101100	H	43	000011011011
44	00101101	I	44	000001010100
45	00000100	J	45	000001010101
46	00000101	K	46	000001010110
47	00001010	L	47	000001010111
48	00001011	M	48	000001100100
49	01010010	N	49	000001100101
50	01010011	O	50	000001010010
51	01010100	P	51	000001010011
52	01010101	Q	52	000000100100
53	00100100	R	53	000000110111

(a)

White run length	Code word	Base 64 rep	Black run length	Code word
54	00100101	S	54	000000111000
55	01011000	T	55	000000100111
56	01011001	U	56	000000101000
57	01011010	V	57	000001011000
58	01011011	W	58	000001011001
59	01001010	X	59	000000101011
60	01001011	Y	60	000000101100
61	00110010	Z	61	000001011010
62	00110011	*	62	000001100110
63	00110100	=	63	000001100111

(a) *cont.*

White run length	Code word	Base 64 rep	Black run length	Code word
64	11011	1	64	0000001111
128	10010	2	128	000011001000
192	010111	3	192	000011001001
256	0110111	4	256	000001011011
320	00110110	5	320	000000110011
384	00110111	6	384	000000110100
448	01100100	7	448	000000110101
512	01100101	8	512	0000001101100
576	01101000	9	576	0000001101101
640	01100111	a	640	0000001001010
704	011001100	b	704	0000001001011
768	011001101	c	768	0000001001100
832	011010010	d	832	0000001001101
896	011010011	e	896	0000001110010
960	011010100	f	960	0000001110011
1024	011010101	g	1024	0000001110100
1088	011010110	h	1088	0000001110101
1152	011010111	i	1152	0000001110110
1216	011011000	j	1216	0000001110111
1280	011011001	k	1280	0000001010010
1344	011011010	l	1344	0000001010011
1408	011011011	m	1408	0000001010100
1472	010011000	n	1472	0000001010101
1536	010011001	o	1536	0000001011010
1600	010011010	p	1600	0000001011011
1664	011000	q	1664	0000001100100
1728	010011011	r	1728	0000001100101
EOL	00000000001		EOL	00000000001

(b)

FIGURE 3.26

CCITT Group 3 and 4 facsimile conversion codes:
(a) termination-codes;
(b) make-up codes.

always relates to white pels and then alternatives between black and white. Since the scheme uses two sets of codewords (termination and make-up) they are known as **modified Huffman codes**. As an example, a run length of 12 white pels would be coded directly as 001000. Similarly, a run length of 128 black pels would be coded directly as 000011001000. A run length of 140 block pels, however, would be encoded as 000011001000 + 0000111; that is, 128 + 12 pels.

There is no error correction protocol with Group 3. From the list of codewords, it can be deduced that should one or more bits be corrupted by transmission errors, the receiver will start to interpret subsequent codewords on the wrong bit boundaries. It thus becomes unsynchronized and cannot decode the received bit string. To enable the receiver to regain synchronism, each scanned line is terminated with a known **end-of-line (EOL) code**. In this way, if the receiver fails to decode a valid codeword after the maximum number of bits in a codeword have been scanned (parsed), it starts to search for the EOL pattern. Also, if it fails to decode an EOL after a preset number of lines, it aborts the reception process and informs the sending machine.

In contrast, Group 4 fax machines incorporate an error correction protocol of the type described in the next chapter. Because of the need to retain a copy of more than one scanned line of data, a more sophisticated compression scheme known as **modified–modified read (MMR) coding** is used. It is also known as **two-dimensional** or **2-D coding** since it identifies black and white run lengths by comparing adjacent scan lines. 'Read' stands for **relative element address designate**, and modified since it is a modified version of an earlier (modified) coding scheme.

MMR coding exploits the fact that most scanned lines differ from the previous line by only a few pels. For example, if a line contains a black run then the next line will normally contain the same run plus or minus three pels. With MMR coding the run lengths associated with a line are identified by comparing the line contents relative to the immediately preceding line, known as the **reference line**. The first reference line is always assumed to be an (imaginary) all-white line and the first line proper is encoded relative to this. Next the encoded line becomes the reference line for the following line and so on. To ensure that the complete page is scanned, the scanner head always starts to the left of the page, so each line always starts with at least one white pel.

The run lengths associated with a line are identified as being one of three possibilities or **modes** relative to the reference line. Examples of the three modes are shown in Figure 3.27. The three modes are identified by the position of the next black run length in the reference line $(b_1 b_2)$ relative to the start and end of the next pair of white and black run lengths in the coding line $(a_0 a_1$ and $a_1 a_2)$. The three possibilities are:

(1)   **Pass mode:** this is the case when the black run length in the reference line $(b_1 b_2)$ is to the left of the next black run length in the coding line $(a_1 a_2)$; that is, b_2 is to the left of a_1. An example is given in part (a) of the figure; for this mode, the run length $b_1 b_2$ is coded.

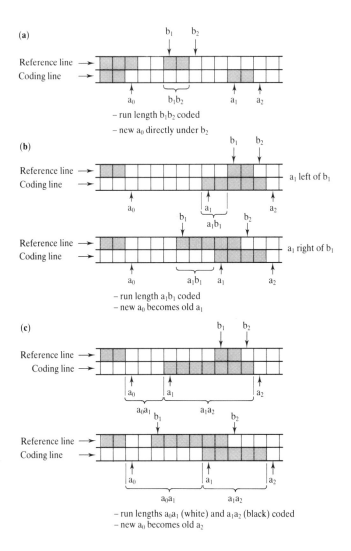

FIGURE 3.27

Some example run
length possibilities:
(a) pass mode;
(b) vertical mode;
(c) horizontal mode.

(2)   **Vertical mode:** this is the case when the black run length in the reference line $(b_1 b_2)$ overlaps the next black run length in the coding line $(a_1 a_2)$ by a maximum of plus or minus 3 pels. Two examples are given in part (b) of the figure; for this mode, just the difference run length $a_1 b_1$ is coded. Most codewords will be in this category.

(3)   **Horizontal mode:** this is the case when the black run length in the reference line $(b_1 b_2)$ overlaps the next black run length $(a_1 a_2)$ by more than plus or minus 3 pels. Two examples are given in part (c) of the figure; for this mode, the two run lengths $a_0 a_1$ (white) and $a_1 a_2$ (black) are coded.

Table 3.2 Two-dimensional code table contents.

Mode	Run length to be encoded	Abbreviation	Codeword
Pass	$b_1 b_2$	P	$0001 + b_1 b_2$
Horizontal	$a_0 a_1, a_1 a_2$	H	$001 + a_0 a_1 + a_1 a_2$
Vertical	$a_1 b_1 = 0$	V(0)	1
	$a_1 b_1 = -1$	$V_R(1)$	011
	$a_1 b_1 = -2$	$V_R(2)$	000011
	$a_1 b_1 = -3$	$V_R(3)$	0000011
	$a_1 b_1 = +1$	$V_L(1)$	010
	$a_1 b_1 = +2$	$V_L(2)$	000010
	$a_1 b_1 = +3$	$V_L(3)$	0000010
Extension			0000001000

After the run length(s) associated with the identified mode have been coded, the start of the next run in the coding line a_0 is updated to the appropriate position. The new $a_1 a_2$ and $b_1 b_2$ are located and the position of b_2 relative to a_1 is again compared. If it is to the left, this indicates pass mode. If it isn't, then the magnitude of $a_1 b_1$ is used to determine if the mode is vertical or horizontal. This procedure repeats until the end of the line is detected. The current coding line then becomes the new reference line and the next scanned line the new coding line.

Since the coded run lengths relate to one of the three modes, additional codewords are used either to indicate to which mode the following codeword(s) relate – pass or horizontal – or to specify the length of the codeword directly – vertical. The additional codewords are given in a third table known as the **two-dimensional code table**. Its contents are shown in Table 3.2. The final entry in the table, known as the **extension mode**, is a unique codeword that aborts the encoding operation prematurely before the end of the page. This has been provided to allow a portion of a page to be sent in its uncompressed form or possibly with a different coding scheme should this be required.

3.7 TRANSMISSION CONTROL CIRCUITS

Most major semiconductor manufacturers offer a range of integrated circuits (ICs) to perform all the functions discussed in this chapter. In the case of asynchronous transmission, there are ICs that perform the clock (bit) and character synchronization functions and generate and check the parity bit per character. Similarly, in the case of synchronous transmission, there are ICs to perform the character-synchronization and parity generation and checking functions in relation to character-oriented transmission. Others are available for the zero bit insertion and deletion and CRC generation and checking functions with bit-oriented transmission. Normally, the clock encoding and decoding functions are carried out by separate integrated circuits, especially at high bit rates. Again, a range of ICs are available.

Most transmission control circuits are **programmable** which means that the user can define the precise mode of operation of the device – asynchronous/ synchronous, character-oriented/bit-oriented, parity/CRC etc – by writing defined bit patterns into selected internal registers. They are also referred to, therefore, as **universal communication interface circuits**. Normally, a single circuit will provide one, two or even four separate (full-duplex) transmission line interface circuits.

The device controlling the operation of the circuit – a microprocessor, for example – first programs the desired operating mode by writing a defined byte (bit pattern) into the **mode register**. It is then made ready to transmit and/or receive characters/bytes by writing a second byte into a **command register**. The transmit and receive channels are always **double-buffered** which means that the controlling device has a full character (or byte) time to process each character (byte) prior to transmission or after reception, rather than a single bit time.

The names and functions of the most common devices are as follows:

Universal asynchronous receiver transmitter – UART:
- – start and stop bit insertion and deletion,
- – bit (clock) synchronization,
- – character synchronization,
- – parity bit generation and checking per character (BSC computed by controlling device).

Universal synchronous receiver transmitter – USRT:
- – low bit rate DPLL clock synchronization,
- – character synchronization,
- – synchronous idle character generation,
- – parity generation and checking per character (BSC computed by controlling device).

Universal synchronous/asynchronous receiver transmitter — USART
- – can be programmed to operate as either a UART or a USRT,
- – has all the programmable features of both devices.

Bit-oriented protocol circuits – BOPs:
- – opening and closing flag insertion and deletion,
- – zero bit insertion and deletion,
- – CRC generation and checking,
- – idle pattern generation.

Universal communications control circuits
- – can be programmed to operate either as a UART, a USRT or a BOP,
- – has all the programmable features of each circuit.

3.8 COMMUNICATIONS CONTROL DEVICES

In many data communication applications, a common requirement is to have a distributed community of terminals – personal computers, for example – that all require to access a central computing facility. This facility could operate a central electronic mail service for an enterprise, or house a central database to which the distributed community of terminals requires access.

If all the terminals are situated in different locations, the only solution is to provide a separate communications line for each terminal, as shown in Figure 3.28. In part (a) it is assumed that the terminals are distributed around a single establishment, whereas in part (b) it is assumed that they are each located in different establishments. In the latter case, it is likely that modems will be required operating over switched connections or leased lines, depending on the amount of data to be transferred and the frequency of calls. In the case of switched connections, the terminals will normally have autodial facilities associated with the communications interface.

For applications in which a number of terminals are located together, a device known as a **multiplexer** can be used to minimize the number of transmission lines required. Such devices are used with a single transmission line that

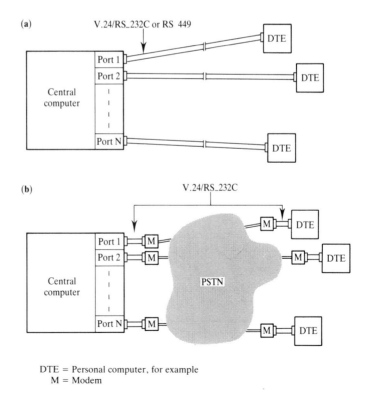

FIGURE 3.28

Simple terminal networks:
(a) locally distributed;
(b) remotely distributed.

DTE = Personal computer, for example
M = Modem

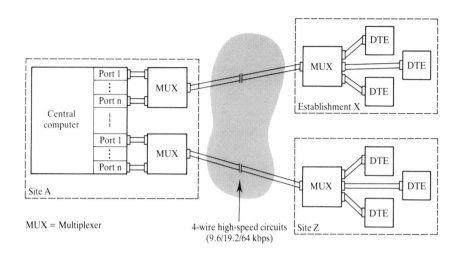

FIGURE 3.29

Multiplexer-based
network schematic.

MUX = Multiplexer

4-wire high-speed circuits
(9.6/19.2/64 kbps)

operates at a higher bit rate than the individual user terminal rates. As shown in
Figure 3.29, a similar multiplexer is normally used at each end of the link. In this
way the presence of the multiplexers is transparent to both the terminals and the
central computer.

In practice, there are two types of multiplexer: time division multiplexers
and statistical multiplexers. A time division multiplexer assigns each terminal a
dedicated portion of the transmission capacity of the shared line. In contrast, a
statistical multiplexer allocates transmission capacity on an on-demand or statistical basis.

3.8.1 Time division multiplexer

A typical **time division multiplexer** application is shown in Figure 3.30(a). The
terminals located in each establishment associated with an enterprise all require
access to the central computer. It is assumed that each site has a large number of
terminals that generate sufficient inter-site traffic to justify high bit rate leased
circuits being used to link the various sites to the central site. Typically, these
will be 64 kbps or higher, depending on the number of terminals.

Figure 3.30(b) shows the internal architecture of each MUX. Typically,
each terminal operates in an asynchronous transmission mode and is therefore
connected to a UART. The controlling microprocessor within the MUX then
controls the transfer of characters between the UARTs and the high-speed link
interface circuit. As the latter normally operates in a character-oriented synchronous transmission mode it will comprise a USRT.

To ensure that the presence of the MUXs is transparent to the terminals/
computer, the transmission capacity associated with the high bit rate circuit is
divided in such a way that the UARTs in the terminal and computer ports can
operate at their programmed rate. This is achieved by a technique known as **rate**

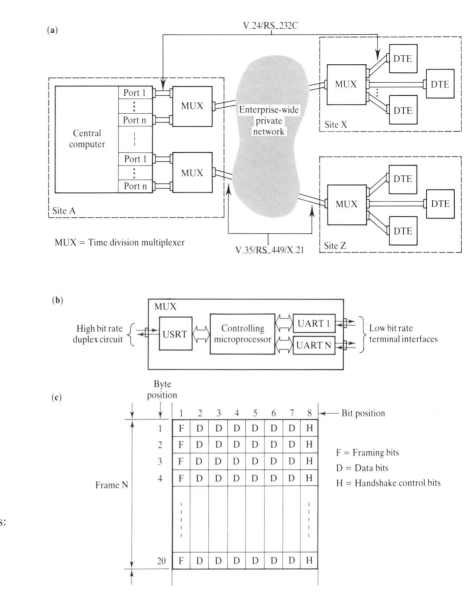

FIGURE 3.30

Time division
multiplexer principles:
(a) application;
(b) multiplexer
schematic; (c) rate
adaption.

adaption which involves the available link capacity being broken down into a
number of frames as shown in part (c) of the figure.

Each frame comprises N bytes such that the bit rate associated with a
single byte position in each frame forms a suitable basic multiplexing rate. The
bit rates associated with each terminal are then derived by using multiple bytes
per frame. However, not all the bits in each byte are used for user data. The first
bit in each byte is used for framing; a fixed repetitive bit pattern is sent in this bit
position of all bytes in a frame so that the receiver can determine the start and

end of each frame. Also, the eighth bit is used to transmit the state of the handshake control bits – DSR/DTR and RTS/CTS, for example – associated with the V.24/RS-232C interface control lines of each UART.

As an example, assume the bit rate of the high-speed circuit is 64 kbps and that a frame length of 20 bytes is being used. The user data rate associated with the six D bits in each byte will then be 2400 bps. Thus the high-speed circuit could be used to support one of:

20	2400 bps	terminals,
10	4800 bps	terminals,
5	9600 bps	terminals,
1	48 kbps	terminal.

Alternatively, a suitable mix of these such as:

8	2400 bps	terminals,
4	4800 bps	terminals,
1	9600 bps	terminal.

To perform the multiplexing operation, the microprocessor uses two 2-byte buffers for each UART – one pair for transmission and the other for reception. For transmission, each byte received from a UART – a 7-bit character plus a parity bit, for example – is simply stored in a repetitive way in the 2-byte (circular) buffer. Concurrently with this happening, the microprocessor reads the current contents of each 2-byte buffer in 6-bit segments in synchronism with the high-speed link bit rate. The reverse procedure is used for reception from the high-speed link using the other 2-byte buffer. The handshake control bits are then set in an agreed way to reflect the state of the corresponding lines associated with the respective interface.

3.8.2 Statistical multiplexer

Each terminal in a time division multiplexer is allocated a fixed character slot in each frame. If the terminal or computer has no character ready to transmit when the controlling microprocessor polls the associated UART, the microprocessor must insert a NUL character in this slot, thus leading to inefficiencies in the use of the available transmission bandwidth. If the data link is a private line, this is not necessarily important, but if PTT lines are used, it can be costly. A more efficient method is to use a **statistical multiplexer** or **stat mux**.

Statistical multiplexers operate on the principle that the mean data rate of characters entered at a terminal keyboard is often much lower than the available transmission capacity of the line – certainly the case with a human user. Hence if the mean user data rate is used rather than the transmission line rate, the bit rate of the common data link can be much lower, with the effect that transmission line costs are substantially reduced. For example, suppose a remote location has eight terminals that need to be connected to a single remote central computer over a PTT line, which has a maximum bit rate of, say, 4800 bps. Using a basic multiplexer and a single line, the nominal operating rate of each terminal would have to be less than 600 bps – say 300 bps. The effect of this limit is that the response time of the computer to each character keyed in at the terminal would be relatively slow or, if a block of characters was being transmitted to the terminal, the delay would be noticeable. Alternatively, if the mean data rate of the terminal is, say, 300 bps, then with a statistical multiplexer the data could be transmitted by a terminal at the maximum available bit rate of 4800 bps. Thus, the average response time to each keyed character is much improved.

To implement this scheme, the controlling microprocessor within the statistical multiplexer must not only perform the normal polling function associated with the terminal UARTs, but also provide and manage a limited amount of buffer storage facilities to allow for possible transient overload conditions on the common data link when a number of terminals are active simultaneously. Because characters are being transmitted on the common data link on a statistical rather than a preallocated basis, each character or group of characters transmitted must also carry identification information.

Another function of the microprocessor in a statistical multiplexer is related to error control. With a normal multiplexer, simple echo checking is often a perfectly acceptable mode of working, since each terminal and computer port is allocated a fixed character slot in each frame on the duplex link. However, because of the statistical mode of working of a statistical multiplexer, it is more common to perform error control on a block of characters on the shared data link. A typical arrangement is shown in Figure 3.31(a).

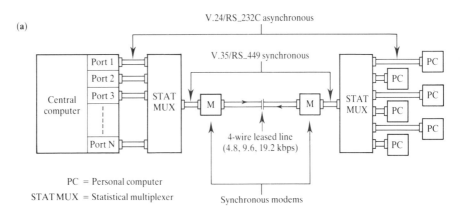

FIGURE 3.31

Statistical multiplexer principles: (a) network schematic; (b) framing alternatives.

To reduce the overheads associated with each transmitted character, it is usual to group a number of characters together for transmission on the shared data link. This can be done in a number of ways, two examples of which are shown in part (b) of the figure. In one, the controlling microprocessor waits until it has a number of characters from a single terminal – a string of characters making up a single line, for example – and then transmits them as a complete block with a single terminal (channel) identifier at the head. In the other, each block contains a mix of characters from all currently active terminals each with a separate terminal identifier. As can be seen from the figure, the assembled characters collectively occupy the I-field of each block or frame transmitted on the shared data link. The communication protocol used on the link is normally a character-oriented or a bit-oriented synchronous protocol, details of which are given in the next chapter.

3.8.3 Block-mode devices

More sophisticated terminals, bank data entry terminals and department store point-of-sale terminals, normally operate in a block mode rather than a character mode. In this mode, as each character is keyed in it is echoed to the display screen directly by the terminal's local processor. The data is then passed to the central computing complex where it is processed when a complete block of data (a message) has been assembled. Consequently, such terminals normally support a more sophisticated block-oriented communication protocol to control the transfer of messages. Also, because the acceptable response time to each transmitted message can be much slower than that expected with an interactive character-mode network, equipment aimed at reducing the communication line costs at the expense of the response time is often used in block-mode terminal networks.

Multidrop lines

A common method of reducing transmission line costs in block-mode terminal networks is to employ **multidrop** (also known as **multipoint**) lines. A schematic of a network that uses multidrop lines is shown in Figure 3.32(a). Instead of each terminal being connected directly to the central computer by a separate line, a number of terminals share the line. In this way, the number of lines (and hence modems or line drivers, depending on the geographical scope of the network) is greatly reduced. Clearly, however, with only one line for each community of terminals, only one message block can be sent at a time, either by a terminal or the central computer. All transmissions on each line are therefore controlled by the central computer using an arbitration procedure known as **poll-select**.

Poll-select

To ensure that only one message is transmitted at any instant on each shared communication line, the central computer, or its agent, either **polls** or **selects** each terminal connected to the line in a particular sequence. As each terminal

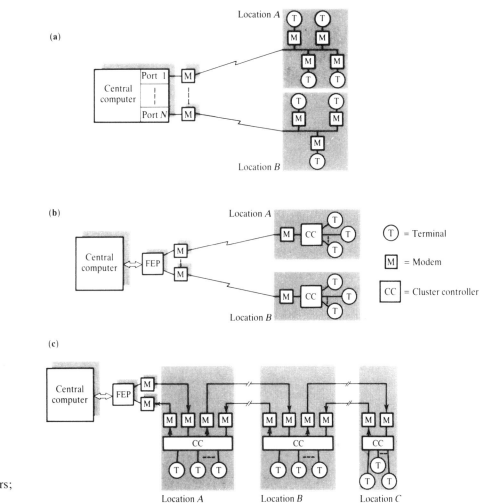

FIGURE 3.32

Polling network
alternatives:
(a) multidrop;
(b) cluster controllers;
(c) hub polling.

connected to the shared line is allocated a unique identifier, the central computer communicates with a terminal by sending it messages with the identity of the terminal at the head. Messages can be of two types: control or data.

Periodically the central computer sends each terminal, in turn, a poll control message, which effectively invites the polled terminal to send a message should it have one waiting. If it has, it is returned in a data message, otherwise it responds with a nothing-to-send control message. Similarly, whenever the central computer wishes to send a message to a terminal, it sends a select control message addressed to the particular terminal. Assuming the selected terminal is able to receive a message, it responds by returning a ready-to-receive control message. The central computer then sends the data message. Finally, the terminal acknowledges correct receipt of the data message and the central computer continues by either polling or selecting another terminal. This type of polling, known as **roll call polling**, results in quite long response times for larger networks since each terminal in the network must be polled or selected before it can send or receive a message. The communication overheads imposed on the central computer can be very high.

To overcome these problems, a more common type of multidrop network uses a **cluster controller** to reduce the response time of the network and a **front-end processor (FEP)** to reduce the communication overheads on the central computer. An example of such a network is as shown in Figure 3.32(b). Effectively, each cluster controller acts as an agent for the central computer by polling and selecting the terminals connected to it, thereby managing all message transfers to and from the terminals. Then the central computer, or the FEP, in practice, only needs to poll or select each controller.

An FEP is typically a small computer that is closely coupled to the central computer. It is programmed to handle all the polling and selection procedures, allowing the central computer to devote its time to the main task of application processing. The advantage of an FEP is that the central computer need only be involved when a data message has been received or is to be sent. Furthermore, since all the communication overheads associated with each message transfer are handled by the FEP, the central computer need only initiate the transfer of each message to and from the FEP.

If terminal clusters are widely separated, an alternative mechanism known as **hub polling** is sometimes cost justified. This is shown in Figure 3.32(c). In this configuration each cluster controller is connected to its nearest neighbour rather than to the central computer. As before, the central computer manages all transfers to and from the cluster controllers. The central computer selects and sends a data message to any of the controllers at any time by means of the top line of the figure.

To receive messages from the controllers, the central computer sends a poll control message to the furthest controller which responds by sending either a data message or a nothing-to-send control message on the bottom (return) line to its nearest-neighbour controller. On receipt of this message, the next controller interprets this as a poll message and, if it has a message waiting, responds by adding its own data message to the tail of the received message from its upstream neighbour. The composite message is then forwarded to its downstream neighbour, again on the return line. This procedure continues down the chain, each controller adding its own response message as it relays the message towards the central computer. Finally, on receipt of the composite response message, the FEP disassembles the message and passes on any valid data messages contained within it to the central computer for further processing.

EXERCISES

3.1 (a) Explain the difference between asynchronous and synchronous transmission.

(b) Assuming asynchronous transmission, one start bit, two stop bits, one parity bit and two bits per signalling element, derive the useful information transfer rate in bps for each of the following signalling (baud) rates:

(i) 300,
(ii) 600,
(iii) 1200,
(iv) 4800.

3.2 With the aid of a diagram, explain the clock (bit) and character synchronization methods used with an asynchronous transmission control scheme. Use a receiver clock rate ratio of $\times 1$ and $\times 4$ of the transmitter clock.

3.3 With the aid of diagrams, explain how clock synchronization can be achieved using:

(a) bipolar encoding,
(b) phase (Manchester) encoding,
(c) differential Manchester encoding.

3.4 Use example waveform sets to illustrate the main features associated with the following encoding schemes:

(a) AMI,
(b) B8ZS,
(c) HDB3,
(d) 2B1Q.

Comment on the relative advantages of each scheme.

3.5 (a) Explain under what circumstances data encoding and a DPLL circuit may be used to achieve clock synchronization. Also, with the aid of a diagram, explain the operation of the DPLL circuit.

(b) Assuming the receiver is initially out of synchronism, derive the minimum number of bit transitions required for a DPLL circuit to converge to the nominal bit centre of a transmitted waveform. How may this be achieved in practice?

3.6 Assuming a synchronous transmission control scheme, explain how character and frame synchronization are achieved:

(a) with character-oriented transmission,
(b) with bit-oriented transmission.

3.7 Explain what is meant by the term data transparency and how it may be achieved using:

(a) character stuffing,
(b) zero bit insertion.

3.8 Explain the operation of the parity bit method of error detection and how it can be extended to cover blocks of characters.

Draw a circuit to compute the parity bit for a character and explain the difference between the terms odd and even parity.

3.9   With the aid of examples, define the terms:

(a)   single-bit error,

(b)   double-bit error,

(c)   error burst.

Produce a sketch showing the contents of a frame to illustrate the type of transmission errors that are not detected by a block sum check.

3.10   (a)   Explain the principle of operation of a CRC error detection method.
By means of an example, show how:

(i)   the error detection bits are generated,

(ii)   the received frame is checked for transmission errors.

Use the generator polynomial

$$x^4 + x^3 + 1$$

(b)   Use an example to show how an error pattern equal to the generator polynomial used in (a) will not be detected. List other error patterns that would not be detected with this polynomial.

3.11   (a)   Produce sketches of circuits to generate and check the CRC of a transmitted frame using a generator polynomial of

$$x^4 + x^3 + 1$$

Show the contents of the transmit and FCS shift registers as the data is being transmitted and received to and from the line.

(b)   Develop an algorithm in pseudo-code form to show how the generation and check functions can be carried out in software.

3.12   Use examples to explain the operation of the following data compression algorithms:

(a)   packed decimal,

(b)   relative encoding,

(c)   character suppression.

3.13   With the aid of an example, illustrate the rules that are used to construct the Huffman code tree for a transmitted character set.

3.14   The following character string is to be transmitted using Huffman coding:

A B A C A D A B A C A D A B A C A B A B

(a)   derive the Huffman code tree,

(b)   determine the savings in transmission bandwidth over normal ASCII and binary coding.

3.15   With reference to the example shown in Figure 3.25 relating to dynamic Huffman coding:

(a)   Write down the actual transmitted bit pattern corresponding to the character string:

'This is '

assuming ASCII coding is being used.

(b)   Deduce the extensions to the existing Huffman tree if the next word transmitted is 'the'.

3.16   Given a scanned line from a Group 3 fax machine stored in a binary array, deduce an algorithm to:

(a)   determine the transmitted codewords,

(b)   decode the received string of codewords.

Use the Huffman tables in Figure 3.26 as a guide.

3.17   With the aid of example pel patterns, explain the meaning of the terms:

(a)   pass mode,

(b)   vertical mode,

(c)   horizontal mode,

as used with Group 4 fax machines.

Use your examples to deduce an algorithm to perform the encoding operation.

3.18   Explain the difference between a time division multiplexer and a statistical multiplexer.

Produce a sketch showing the internal architecture of a time division multiplexer and explain its operation. Describe the organization of the shared data link and how the controlling device determines the destination of each received character.

3.19   Make a sketch of a terminal network that uses a statistical multiplexer. Describe the organization of the shared data link with such a device and how the controlling device determines the destination of each character.

3.20   Make a sketch of a typical block-mode terminal network that uses multidrop lines and a poll-select control protocol. Explain the operation of the network and describe how the computer sends and receives messages to and from each terminal.

3.21   (a)   Explain the function of

       (i)   a cluster controller, and

       (ii)   a front-end processor.

       (b)   Distinguish between roll call polling and hub polling. Make a sketch of each polling method and explain its operation.

CHAPTER SUMMARY

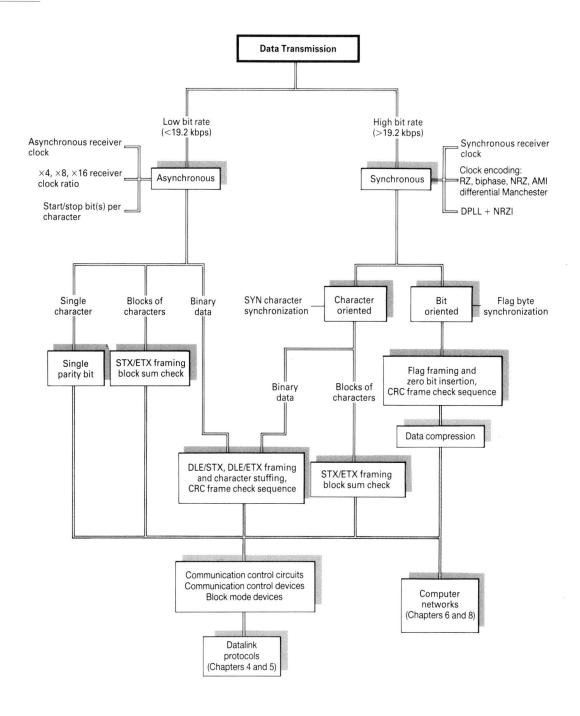

4

Protocol basics

CHAPTER CONTENTS

CHAPTER OBJECTIVES

When you have completed studying the material in this chapter you should be able to:

- appreciate that a data link protocol is made up of a number of functional components that include error control, flow control and connection management;
- know the different methods that are used to specify the operation of a protocol;
- understand the principles behind a layered architecture;
- explain the operation of the idle RQ and continuous RQ error control schemes and produce frame sequence diagrams to illustrate their operation;
- know the difference between a selective repeat and go-back-N error control scheme;
- explain the operation of the sliding window flow control method and its effect on the sequence numbers used for error control purposes;
- determine the utilization of link capacity with an idle RQ, selective repeat, and a go-back-N error control scheme;
- specify the operation of each error control method in the form of a state transition diagram, an event–state table, and structured program code;
- understand and explain the role of connection management with respect to a protocol.

4.1 INTRODUCTION

Chapter 3 described the circuits and techniques that can be employed to transmit a frame of information between two DTEs across a point-to-point data link. In addition, the various error-detection schemes were described which allow the receiving DTE to determine, to a known probability, the presence of any errors in the transmitted bit stream. Alternatively, if forward error correction is used, the receiver can deduce from the received bit stream, again to a known probability, the information being transmitted even when errors are present.

In general, however, the techniques described provide only the basic mechanism for transmitting information and for the receiver to detect the presence of any transmission errors. Clearly, when a transmission error is detected, even if it is only a single (unknown) bit, then the complete data block must be discarded. This type of scheme is thus known as **best-try transmission** or, for reasons discussed later in the chapter, **connectionless mode** transmission.

In addition to this mode of operation, therefore, an alternative operating mode known as **reliable transmission** or **connection-oriented** is also used in many applications. With this mode, in addition to detecting when errors are present, it is necessary to define a set of rules or control procedures that must be adopted by both communicating parties to ensure the reliable (that is, to a high probability, free of errors and duplicates and in the correct sequence) transfer of messages. Normally this is accomplished by the controlling device at the destination informing the source that an error has been detected and that another copy of the affected frame should be sent. The combined error detection/correction cycle is thus known as **error control**. In addition, there are often other control mechanisms that must be observed by the two communicating parties. Collectively these constitute the **data link control protocol** for the link. Some of the basic components of a data link protocol will be considered in this chapter and the descriptions of practical realizations of the basic protocols introduced will be given in the next chapter.

4.2 ERROR CONTROL

When data is entered into a computer by means of a keyboard, as each key is pressed the resulting codeword is normally transmitted to the computer bit-serially using a UART and asynchronous transmission. The program in the computer controlling the input process then reads and stores the received character and initiates its output to the display screen. Hence if the displayed character is different from what was entered or intended, then the user simply enters a suitable control character – a *delete* or *back space*, for example. When this is received, the control program discards the previously entered character and removes it from the screen. In this way the user is performing a form of **manual error control**.

A similar procedure is used when a terminal is connected to a remote computer via, say, the analogue PSTN and a modem. Instead of each entered character being displayed directly on the terminal display, it is first transmitted to the remote computer. The latter reads and stores the character and retransmits it back to the terminal which displays it. If this is different from what was keyed in or intended, the user can again initiate the transmission of a suitable delete character. This mode of error control is known as **echo checking**.

In contrast, when a computer is transferring blocks of characters (frames) across a serial data link to another computer, the program in the receiving computer controlling the reception process must perform the error control procedure automatically without any intervention from the user. Typically this involves the receiving computer checking the received frame for possible transmission errors and then returning a short control message (frame) to either acknowledge its correct receipt or to request that another copy of the frame is sent. This type of error control is therefore known as **automatic repeat request** or **ARQ**.

In practice, there are two basic types of ARQ: **idle RQ**, which is used with character-oriented (or byte-oriented) data transmission schemes, and **continuous RQ**, which employs either a **selective repeat** or a **go-back-N retransmission strategy**. Continuous RQ is used primarily with bit-oriented transmission schemes. Hence, although idle RQ is being replaced in many applications by the more efficient continuous RQ scheme, there are still many data link protocols in use based on idle RQ. More importantly, however, since it is the simplest type of error control scheme, it forms an ideal vehicle for explaining many of the more general issues relating to data link control protocols. Hence both the idle RQ and continuous RQ schemes will be discussed.

4.3 IDLE RQ

The idle RQ error control scheme has been defined to enable blocks (frames) of printable and formatting control characters to be reliably transferred – that is, to a high probability, without error or replication and in the same sequence as they were submitted – over a serial data link between a source DTE and a destination DTE. To discriminate between the sender (source) and receiver (destination) of data frames – more generally referred to as **information** or **I-frames** – the terms **primary (P)** and **secondary (S)** are normally used, respectively. Thus the idle RQ error control scheme is concerned with the reliable transfer of I-frames between a primary and a secondary across a serial data link.

The idle RQ protocol operates in a half-duplex mode since the primary, after sending an I-frame, must wait until it receives an indication from the secondary as to whether the frame was correctly received or not. The primary then either sends the next frame, if the previous frame was correctly received, or retransmits a copy of the previous frame if it was not.

There are two ways of implementing this scheme. In **implicit retransmission** S only acknowledges correctly received frames and P interprets the absence of an acknowledgement as an indication that the previous frame was corrupted. Alternatively, when S detects that a frame has been corrupted, it returns a **negative acknowledgement** to request that another copy of the frame is transmitted – **explicit request**.

Some example frame sequences with the implicit retransmission control scheme are shown in Figure 4.1(a). The following points should be noted when interpreting the frame sequences:

- P can have only one I-frame outstanding (awaiting an **acknowledgement** or **ACK-frame**) at a time;
- on receipt of an error-free I-frame, S returns an ACK-frame to P;
- on receipt of an error-free ACK frame, P can transmit another I-frame – part (i);
- when P initiates the transmission of an I-frame it starts a timer;

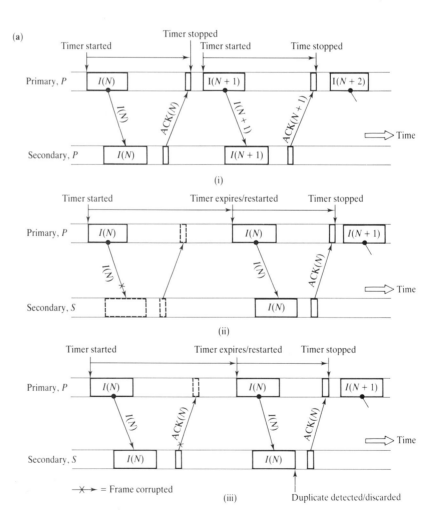

FIGURE 4.1

Idle RQ operation: (a) implicit retransmission.

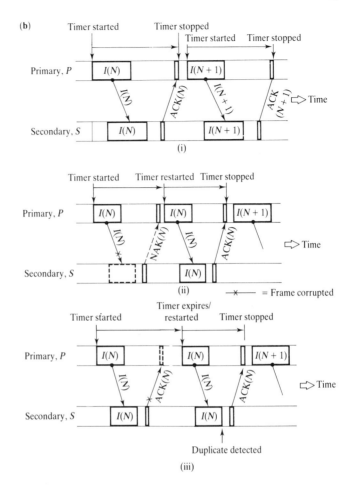

FIGURE 4.1 (cont.)

(b) Explicit request.

- if S receives an I-frame or P receives an ACK-frame containing transmission errors, the frame is discarded;

- if P does not receive an ACK-frame within a predefined time interval (the **timeout interval**), then P retransmits the waiting I-frame – part (ii),

- if an ACK-frame is corrupted, then S receives another copy of the frame and hence this is rejected by S – part (iii).

As can be seen in part (i), after initiating the transmission of a frame, P must wait a minimum time before transmitting the next frame. The wait time is equal to the time the I-frame takes to be received and processed by S plus the time for the acknowledgement frame to be transmitted and processed. In the worst case, P must wait a time equal to the timeout interval, which must exceed the minimum time by a suitable margin, to avoid an ACK-frame being received after another copy of the previous frame has been retransmitted.

The relative magnitude of each component making up the minimum time varies for different types of data link. It is determined by such factors as the physical separation of the two communicating systems (P and S) and the data transmission rate of the link. In general, however, a significant improvement in the utilization of the available link capacity can be obtained by S informing P immediately whenever it receives a corrupted I-frame. This is done by S returning a **negative acknowledgement** or **NAK-frame**. Some example frame sequence diagrams with this scheme are shown in Figure 4.1(b).

The following points should be noted when interpreting the frame sequences:

- as with the implicit acknowledgement scheme, on receipt of an error-free I-frame, S returns an ACK-frame to P;

- on receipt of an error-free ACK-frame, P stops the timer and can then initiate the transmission of another I-frame – part (i);

- if S receives an I-frame containing transmission errors, the frame is discarded and it returns a NAK-frame – part (ii);

- if P does not receive an ACK-frame (or NAK-frame) within the timeout interval, P retransmits the waiting I-frame – part (iii).

Since with the idle RQ scheme the primary must wait for an acknowledgement after sending a frame, it is also known as **send-and-wait** or **stop-and-wait**. As can be seen from the two sets of examples, it ensures that S receives at least one copy of each frame transmitted by P. With both schemes, however, it is possible for S to receive two (or more) copies of a particular I-frame. These are known as **duplicates**. In order for S to discriminate between the next valid I-frame (as it expects) and a duplicate, each frame transmitted contains a unique identifier known as the **sequence number** (N, $N + 1$ etc) as shown in the figure. S must therefore retain a record of the sequence number contained within the last I-frame it correctly received. If it receives another copy of this frame, then the copy is discarded. To enable P to resynchronize, S returns an ACK-frame for each correctly received frame with the related I-frame identifier within it.

The improvement in link utilization by using an explicit request scheme can be deduced by considering the frame sequences in part (ii) of each scheme. With implicit retransmission, the time before the next I-frame can be transmitted is the timeout interval, whereas it is much shorter with a NAK-frame. The relative improvement in link utilization will be determined ultimately by the bit error rate (BER) of the link and hence the number of frames that are corrupted and need to be retransmitted. However, most data communication applications for which the idle RQ protocol is suitable use the explicit request scheme with NAK-frames.

The sequence number carried in each I-frame is known as the **send sequence number** or **N(S)**, and the sequence number in each ACK and NAK frame as the **receive sequence number** or **N(R)**. As described in the last chapter, the ASCII (and EBCDIC) character sets contain a number of control characters (for example, STX, ETX), some of which are used for transmission control.

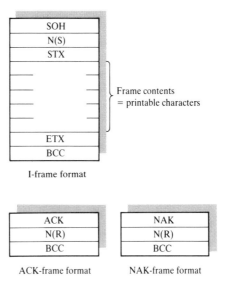

FIGURE 4.2

Idle RQ frame (PDU) formats.

Three other transmission control characters are needed to implement the basic idle RQ error control procedure: SOH, NAK and ACK. Their use is shown in Figure 4.2

Each I-frame must contain a sequence number at the head of the frame and, as can be seen, this precedes the STX character. The SOH (start-of-header) character is then inserted at the head of the complete block.

The ACK and NAK control characters used for acknowledgement purposes are followed by the receive sequence number. Again, to enhance the error detection probability, the complete NAK or ACK frame contains a block sum check character. Collectively, the three frames – I-frame, ACK-frame, and NAK-frame – are known as the **protocol data units** or **PDUs** of the idle RQ protocol, and P and S as the primary and secondary **protocol entities**.

4.3.1 Layered architecture

The frame sequence diagrams shown in Figure 4.1 illustrate the essential features of the operation of the idle RQ protocol. Before proceeding with more details relating to the protocol, however, it is necessary to introduce the concept of **layering**. This involves decoupling the combined application and communication tasks to create two well-defined subtasks or **layers** with a formal interface between them.

To illustrate this, consider an **application process** (program) running in one computer transferring a file of data to another similar application process (AP) running in a second computer across a serial data link using an idle RQ error control protocol. As has been described, the idle RQ protocol will endeavour to send a series of blocks of information – printable characters or bytes –

across the data link in a reliable way. Also, depending on the **bit error rate (BER)** of the link, a maximum block size will be specified that ensures, to a high probability, that a good percentage of I-frames transmitted will be free of errors.

The idle RQ **protocol layer** in the source computer thus offers a defined **service** to the user AP layer above it to transfer a series of blocks of information each of a defined maximum length, to a similar (peer) AP in the destination computer. The two peer idle RQ protocol entities are thus concerned with the various issues discussed earlier relating to error detection: the generation and return of acknowledgement frames, timeouts, and the delivery of blocks of information in the same sequence as they were submitted.

In contrast, the two peer APs are concerned only with the transfer of the file of data using the service provided by the communications (idle RQ) layer. They are thus concerned with issues such as the name of the file, its length, the segmentation of the file contents into smaller blocks prior to submitting them to the communications layer and the reassembly of the blocks into a complete file on receipt. Thus for each application, there is a need to define the sequence of message blocks expected, their syntax and structure. This implies an AP-to-AP protocol with its own set of (AP-to-AP) protocol data units. The two AP protocol entities then use the services of the lower communications layer to transfer their own PDUs. To the communications layer, however, these are all simply blocks of information which are transferred in the same way.

Normally, the service provided by a communications layer is expressed in the form of a **service primitive** with the data to be transferred – normally referred to as **user data** – as a **parameter**. Since the service is associated with the link layer (L) and for the transfer of data (blocks of information), the user service primitive at the sending interface is expressed in the form L_DATA.request and that at the interface with the recipient AP as L_DATA.indication. This is shown in Figure 4.3(a).

In many instances, since the users of a layer are concerned only with the service provided rather than how the service is implemented, when defining the services associated with a (protocol) layer it is normal to represent them in the form shown in part (b) of the figure. This is known as a (service) **time sequence diagram**. Also, to decouple the two layers in a clean way, a **queue** is introduced between them, as shown in part (c) of the figure. This is simply a data structure that implements a **first-in, first-out (FIFO)** queueing discipline. There is thus a **head** and a **tail** associated with it; elements are added to the tail of the queue and are removed from the head.

Normally, the user service primitive(s) associated with a layer is (are) passed between layers using a data structure known as an **event control block** or **ECB**. Generally this is a record or structure with the primitive type in the first field and a character or byte array containing the user data in a second field. Hence whenever the source AP – or higher protocol layer – wishes to send a message block, it first obtains a free ECB, writes the segment of user data in a character or byte array, sets the primitive type field to L_DATA.request and inserts the ECB at the tail of the link layer (LS-user) input queue ready for reading by the idle RQ primary.

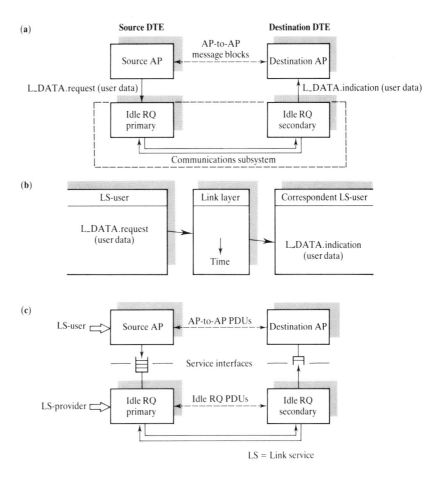

FIGURE 4.3

Layered architecture:
(a) service primitives;
(b) time sequence
diagram; (c) service
interfaces.

When the idle RQ protocol entity software is next run, it detects the presence of an entry (ECB) in the link service (LS-user) input queue, reads the entry from the head of the queue, and proceeds to create an I-frame with the message block – the contents of the character/byte array – as the frame contents and the appropriate header and trailer characters. It then initiates the transmission of the frame to the secondary protocol entity. Assuming the received frame is error free, the secondary protocol entity strips off the header and trailer characters, and passes the frame contents – the message block – up to the destination AP in an ECB using the link service (LS-provider) output queue with the primitive type set to L_DATA.indication. It then creates and returns an ACK-frame to P.

When the destination AP is next run, it detects and reads the ECB from the LS-provider queue and proceeds to process the contents of the message block according to the defined AP-to-AP protocol. Typically, if this is the first message block containing, say, the file name, it will involve creating a file with this name and opening it ready for subsequent write/append file operations.

At the sending side, assuming the ACK-frame is received free of errors, the primary frees the memory buffer holding the acknowledged I-frame and checks the LS-user input queue for another waiting ECB. If there is one, the procedure is repeated until all the file segments have been transferred. Normally this will involve the source AP sending an end-of-transfer message block to inform the destination AP that the complete file contents have been transferred.

It can be concluded that the adoption of a layered architecture means that each layer performs its own well-defined function in the context of the overall communications task (file-transfer, for example). Also, that the lower (data link control) layer offers a defined service to the layer above it and operates according to a defined protocol. As will be expanded upon in later chapters, the adoption of a layered architecture means that more sophisticated communication subsystems can be implemented simply by adding layers between the application layer and the lower link layer, each concerned with a complementary function.

4.3.2 Protocol specification

Although the three frame sequence diagrams shown in Figure 4.1, coupled with the descriptive text, are probably sufficient to illustrate the operation of an idle RQ protocol, with more sophisticated protocols it is often not practicable to describe fully the operation of the protocol using just this method. Indeed, as will be seen in this and later chapters, it is very complex to define the operation of a protocol allowing for all the possible events and error conditions that can arise. In general, therefore, protocols are specified using one of a number of more precise methods and formalisms. Frame sequence diagrams of the type shown in Figure 4.1 are normally used simply to illustrate selected aspects of a protocol, rather than as a means of specifying the protocol.

The three most common methods used for specifying a communication protocol are: **state transition diagrams**, **event–state tables** and high-level **structured programs**. In many instances, however, a protocol is defined as a combination of these and is coupled with time sequence diagrams to illustrate the user service primitives associated with the protocol.

Irrespective of the specification method used, a protocol is modelled as a **finite state machine** or **automaton**. This means that the protocol – or, more accurately, the protocol entity – can be in just one of a finite number of defined **states** at any instant. For example, it might be idle waiting for a message to send, or waiting to receive an acknowledgement. Transitions between states take place as a result of an **incoming event**; for example, a message becomes ready to send, or an ACK-frame is received. As a result of an incoming event, an associated **outgoing event** is normally generated; for example, on receipt of a message, send the created I-frame on the link, or on receipt of a NAK-frame, retransmit the waiting I-frame.

As is apparent from this example, some incoming events may lead to a number of possible outgoing events. The particular outgoing event selected is then determined by the computed state of one or more **predicates** (boolean variables). As an example, predicate P1 may be true if the N(R) in a received

ACK-frame is the same as the N(S) in the I-frame waiting to be acknowledged. Hence, if P1 is true, then free the memory buffer in which the I-frame is being held; if it is false, initiate retransmission of the frame.

Finally, an incoming event, in addition to generating an outgoing event (and possibly a change of state), may also have one or more associated **local** or **specific actions**. Examples include *start a timer* and *increment the send sequence variable*. Each of the foregoing issues associated with the specification of a protocol will now be expanded upon by considering the specification of the error control procedure associated with the idle RQ protocol.

4.3.3 Idle RQ specification

All finite state machines – and hence protocol entities – operate in an **atomic way**. This means that once an incoming event has started to be processed, all processing functions associated with the event, including the generation of any outgoing event(s), local (specific) actions and a possible change in state, are all carried out in their entirety (that is, in an indivisible way) before another incoming event is accepted.

To ensure this happens, the various incoming (and outgoing) event interfaces are decoupled from the protocol entity itself by means of queues as shown in Figure 4.4. There is thus an additional pair of queues between the protocol entity and the transmit–receive procedure that controls the particular transmission

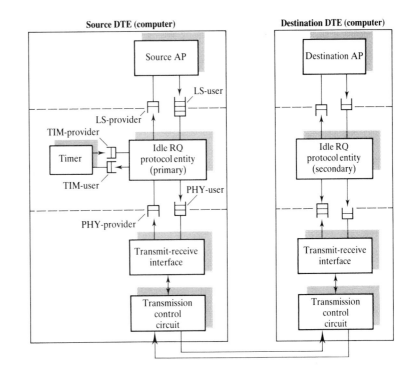

FIGURE 4.4

Communications subsystem architecture and protocol entity interfaces.

control circuit being used. Similarly, there is a pair of queues between the protocol entity and the timer procedure. Normally, the latter is run at regular (tick) intervals by means of an **interrupt** and, if a timer is currently running, its current value is decremented by the tick value. If the value goes to zero, a **timer expired** message is returned to the protocol entity via the appropriate queue.

The role of the transmit–receive procedure is simply to transmit a preformatted frame passed to it or to receive a frame from the link and queue the frame for processing by the protocol entity. This procedure may also be run as a result of an interrupt, but this time from the transmission control circuit. Finally, although in principle only a single input and output queue is necessary to interface the primary and secondary to their respective APs, in practice a pair of queues is necessary at each interface.

To simplify the specification procedure, the various incoming events, outgoing events, predicates, specific actions and states associated with each protocol entity are each given an abbreviated name. Prior to specifying the

(a) **Incoming events**

Name	Interface	Meaning
LDATAreq	LS_user	L_DATA.request service primitive received
ACKRCVD	PHY_provider	ACK-frame received from S
TEXP	TIM_provider	Wait ACK timer expires
NAKRCVD	PHY_provider	NAK-frame received from S

States

Name	Meaning
IDLE	Idle, no message transfer in progress
WTACK	Waiting an acknowledgement

Outgoing events

Name	Interface	Meaning
TxFRAME	PHY_user	Format and transmit an I-frame
RetxFRAME	PHY_user	Retransmit I-frame waiting acknowledgement
ERRORind	LS_user	Error message: frame discarded for reason specified

Predicates

Name	Meaning
P0	N(S) in waiting I-frame = N(R) in ACK-frame
P1	Block sum check (BSC) in ACK/NAK-frame okay

Specific actions

[1] = Start_timer using TIM-user queue
[2] = Increment V(S)
[3] = Stop_timer using TIM-user queue
[4] = Increment RetxCount
[5] = Increment ErrorCount
[6] = Reset RetxCount to zero

State variables

VS = Send sequence variable
PresentState = Present state of protocol entity
ErrorCount = Number of erroneous frames received
RetxCount = Number of retransmissions for this frame

FIGURE 4.5

Abbreviated names used in idle RQ specifications: (a) primary.

protocol, the various abbreviated names are normally listed; all subsequent references are then made using these names. For the error control component of the idle RQ protocol, the list of abbreviated names for the primary and secondary are as shown in Figure 4.5(a) and (b), respectively.

Since each protocol entity is essentially a sequential system, it is necessary to retain information that may vary as different incoming events are received. This information is held in a number of **state variables**. Examples are, for the primary, the send sequence variable V(S) which holds the sequence number to be allocated to the next I-frame to be transmitted, the PresentState variable which holds the present state of the protocol entity, RetxCount which is used to limit the number of retransmissions of a frame, and ErrorCount which is a count of the number of erroneous frames received. Typically, if either RetxCount or ErrorCount reaches its maximum limit then the frame is discarded, an error message is sent to the AP layer above and the protocol (entity) re-initializes.

Just two state variables are needed for the secondary: the receive sequence variable V(R) is used to hold the sequence number of the last correctly received I-frame and ErrorCount is used to keep a record of the number of erroneous frames received. Again, if this reaches its defined maximum limit an error message is sent to the AP-layer above.

(b)   **Incoming events**

Name	Interface	Meaning
IRCVD	PHY_provider	I-frame received from P

States

Name	Meaning
WTIFM	Waiting a new I-frame from P

Outgoing events

Name	Interface	Meaning
LDATAind(X)	LS_provider	Pass contents of received I-frame with N(S) = X to user AP with an L_DATA.indication primitive
TxACK(X)	PHY_user	Format and transmit an ACK-frame with N(R) = X
TxNAK(X)	PHY_user	Format and transmit a NAK-frame with N(R) = X
LERRORind	LS_provider	Issue error message for reason specified

Predicates

Name	Meaning
P0	N(S) in I-frame = Vr
P1	Block sum check (BSC) in I-frame correct
P2	N(S) in I-frame = Vr − 1

FIGURE 4.5 (cont.)

(b) Secondary.

Specific actions	**State variables**
[1] = Increment Vr	Vr = Reserve sequence variable
[2] = Increment ErrorCount	ErrorCount = Number of erroneous frames received

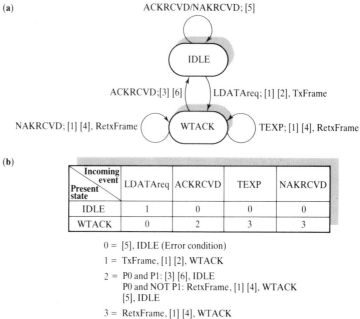

FIGURE 4.6

Idle RQ specification –
primary: (a) state
transition diagram;
(b) event–state table.

0 = [5], IDLE (Error condition)

1 = TxFrame, [1] [2], WTACK

2 = P0 and P1: [3] [6], IDLE
    P0 and NOT P1: RetxFrame, [1] [4], WTACK
    [5], IDLE

3 = RetxFrame, [1] [4], WTACK

The formal specification of both the primary and secondary (protocol entities) are shown in Figure 4.6 and Figure 4.7, respectively. The figures illustrate the specification of the primary and secondary in state transition diagram form and event–state table form.

Using the state transition diagram method, the possible states of the protocol entity are shown in circles with the particular states written within them. **Directional arrows** (also known as **arcs**) indicate the possible transitions between the states, with the incoming event causing the transition and any

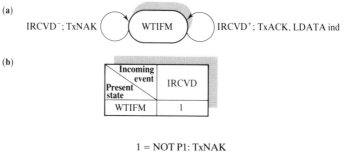

FIGURE 4.7

Idle RQ specification –
secondary: (a) state
transition diagram;
(b) event–state table.

1 = NOT P1: TxNAK
    P1 and P2: TxACK,
    P0 and P1: LDATAind, TxACK, [1] [2]

resulting outgoing event and specific actions, written alongside. If, for example, an L_DATA.request (LDATAreq) is received from the LS-user interface, then the frame is formatted and output to the PHY-user interface (TxFrame), a timer is started for the frame [1], the send sequence variable incremented [2], and the WTACK state entered. Similarly, if an ACK-frame is received with an N(R) equal to the N(S) in the waiting frame and the block sum check is correct, then the timer is stopped and the retransmission count reset to zero [3], and the IDLE state entered. The other transitions can be interpreted in a similar way.

Although state transition diagrams are useful for showing the correct operation of a protocol, because of space limitations it is not always practicable to show all possible incoming event possibilities including error conditions. Hence most state transition diagrams are incomplete specifications. Moreover, with all but the simplest of protocols, it is necessary to have many such diagrams to define even the correct operation of a protocol. It is for these reasons that the event–state table and the structured program code methods are used.

Using the **event–state table method**, as can be seen in the figure, all the possible incoming events and protocol (present) states are shown in the form of a table. Then, for each state, the table entry defines the outgoing event, any specific action(s), and the new state for all possible incoming events. Also, if predicates are involved, the alternative set of action(s). Clearly, it is a far more rigorous method since all possible incoming-event, present-state combinations are allowed for.

When interpreting the actions to be followed if predicates are involved, it should be noted that these are shown in the order in which they should be interpreted. Hence the action to be followed if the primary is in the WTACK state and an ACK-frame is received (ACKRCVD), is first to determine if P0 and P1 are both true. If they are, then carry out specific action [3] and enter the IDLE state. Else, determine if P0 and NOTP1 are both true and so on. As shown, if neither condition is true then an error is suspected and the actions are as shown.

A feature of the event–state table is that it lends itself more readily to implementation in program code than a state transition diagram. This is best seen by considering an example: implementation of the idle RQ primary and secondary. Their outline structures are shown in parts (a) and (b) of Figure 4.8, respectively. They are written in a high-level pseudo-code for readability and each is shown as a separate program. In practice, they may be procedures but this will not affect their basic operation.

When each program is first run, the Initialize procedure is invoked. This performs such functions as initializing all state variables to their initial values and the contents of the EventStateTable array to those in the event–state table. The program then enters an infinite loop waiting for an incoming event to arrive at one of its input queues.

The incoming event causing the program to run is first assigned to Event-Type. The current contents of PresentState and EventType are then used as indices to the EventStateTable array to determine the integer – 0, 1, 2 or 3 – that defines the processing actions associated with that event. For example, if the

```
(a)    program  IdleRQ_Primary;
       const    MaxErrCount;
                MaxRetxCount;
       type     Events = (LDATAreq, ACKRCVD, TEXP, NAKRCVD);
                States  = (IDLE, WTACK);
       var      EventStateTable = array [Events, States] of 0 .. 3;
                PresentState : States;
                Vs, ErrorCount, RetxCount : integer;
                EventType : Events;
       procedure Initialize;        } Initializes state variables and contents of EventStateTable
       procedure TxFrame;           ⎫
       procedure RetxFrame;         ⎬ Outgoing event procedures
       procedure LERRORind;         ⎭
       procedure Start_timer;       ⎫ Specific action procedures
       procedure Stop_timer;        ⎭
       function  P0 : boolean;      ⎫ Predicate functions
       function  P1 : boolean;      ⎭

       begin    Initialize;
                repeat Wait receipt of an incoming event
                       EventType := type of event
                       case EventStateTable [EventType, PresentState] of
                           0 : begin ErrorCount := ErrorCount + 1; PresentState = IDLE;
                                    if(ErrorCount = MaxErrCount) then ERRORind end;
                           1 : begin TxFrame; Start_timer; Vs := Vs + 1; PresentState := WTACK end;
                           2 : begin if(P0 and P1) then begin Stop_timer; RetxCount := 0; PresentState := IDLE end;
                                    else if(P0 and NOTP1) then begin RetxFrame; Start_timer;
                                                        RetxCount := RetxCount = 1;
                                                        PresentState := WTACK end;
                                    else begin PresentState := IDLE; ErrorCount := ErrorCount + 1;
                                            if(ErrorCount = MaxErrorCount) then begin LERRORind; Initialize; end;
                                    end;
                           3 : begin RetxFrame; Start_timer; RetxCount := RetxCount + 1; PresentState := WTACK;
                                    if(RetxCount = MaxRetxCount) then begin LERRORind; Initialize; end;
                                    end;
                until Forever;
       end.
```

FIGURE 4.8

Idle RQ specification:
(a) psuedo-code for
primary.

accessed integer is 2, this will result in the predicate functions P0 and P1 being invoked and, depending on their computed state (true or false), the invocation of the appropriate outgoing event procedure, coupled with any specific action procedure(s) as defined in the specification; for example, starting or resetting the timer, and updating PresentState.

The pseudo-code has been simplified to highlight the structure of each program and hence the implementation methodology. Hence no code is shown for the various outgoing event procedures nor for the predicate functions. In practice, these must be implemented in an unambiguous way using the necessary steps listed in the specification.

Although many protocols are specified in the form of an event–state table, some protocols are specified in a **structured program code form**. In practice, this type of specification is similar to the pseudo-code implementations

(b)

```
program  IdleRQ_Secondary;
const.    MaxErrorCount;
type      Events = IRCVD;
          States  = WTIFM;
var       EventStateTable = array[Events, States] of 1;
          EventType : Events;
          PresentState : States;
          Vr, X, ErrorCount : integer;
procedure Initialize;        } Initializes state variables and contents of EventStateTable
procedure LDATAind(X); ⎤
procedure TxACK(X);     ⎪
procedure TxNAK(X);     ⎬ Outgoing event procedures
procedure LERRORind;   ⎦
function  P0 : boolean; ⎤
function  P1 : boolean; ⎬ Predicate functions
function  P2 : boolean; ⎦

begin     Initialize;
          repeat Wait receipt of incoming event; EventType := type of event;
                  case EventStateTable[EventType, PresentState] of
                     1 : X := N(S) from I-frame;
                        if(NOTP1) then TxNAK(X);
                        else if(P1 and P2) then TxACK(X);
                        else if(P0 and P1) then begin LDATAind(X); TxACK(X); Vr := Vr + 1; end;
                        else begin ErrorCount := ErrorCount + 1; if(ErrorCount = MaxErrorCount) then
                                begin LERRORind; Initialize; end
                           end;
                  until Forever;
          end.
```

FIGURE 4.8 (cont.)

(b) Pseudo-code for secondary.

shown in parts (a) and (b) of Figure 4.8. However, they are more formal since all the variables required and the various outgoing event and specific action procedures and functions are all shown in detail. Hence their implementation is much simplified and less prone to errors.

An outline structure of the error control procedure of the idle RQ primary using the structured code method is shown for comparison purposes in Figure 4.8(c). The approach is known as the **extended state transitional model**. As can be seen, in general this is similar in structure to the specifications in parts (a) and (b) except that the actual protocol entity is defined in the form of a **module** and all the possible transitions are defined separately in a more formal way. In practice only a small number of specifications are in this form; the majority are in event–state table form. By applying the outlined implementation methodology, similar structured program code can be produced.

4.3.4 Link utilization

Before considering the error control procedures associated with the two types of continuous RQ protocol, it is perhaps helpful first to quantify the efficiency of utilization of the available link capacity with the idle RQ protocol. The

(c)   – Type and constant definitions
       – Interface definitions { interface queue names and ECB record structure definitions }
       – Formal finite state machine definition.

     module
      – states
      – incoming events
      – outgoing event procedures
      – specific action procedures
      – predicate functions
     trans (* begin state transition definitions *)
      from IDLE *to* IDLE
      when PHY_provider.ACKRCVD
       begin
       end;
      from IDLE *to* IDLE
      when TIM_provider.TEXP
       begin
       end;

       .
       .
       .

      from WTACK *to* IDLE
      provided P0 *and* P1
      when PHY_provider.ACKRCVD
       begin
       end;

       .
       .
       .

     end.

FIGURE 4.8 (cont.)

(c) Outline of the
structure of the primary
in Estelle.

efficiency of utilization U is a ratio of two times, each measured from the point in time the transmitter starts to send a frame. It is defined as:

$$U = \frac{T_{ix}}{T_t}$$

where T_{ix} = time for transmitter to transmit a frame and $T_t = T_{ix}$ plus any time the transmitter spends waiting for an acknowledgement.

To quantify the link utilization with idle RQ, a frame sequence diagram with the various component times identified is given in Figure 4.9. In practice, in most cases for which the idle RQ protocol is adequate, the time to process an I-frame T_{ip} and its associated ACK-frame T_{ap} are both short compared with their transmission times T_{ix} and T_{ax}. Also, since an ACK-frame is much shorter than an I-frame, T_{ax} is negligible compared with T_{ix}. Hence the minimum total time before the next frame can be transmitted is often approximated to $T_{ix} + 2T_p$. An approximate expression for U is thus:

$$U = \frac{T_{ix}}{T_{ix} + 2T_p}$$

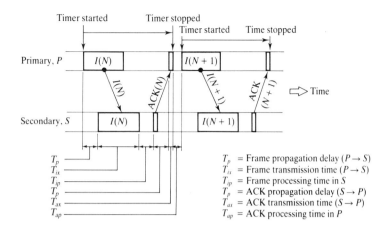

FIGURE 4.9

Idle RQ link utilization schematic.

or

$$U = \frac{1}{1 + 2T_p/T_{ix}}$$

As was described in Chapter 2, the ratio T_p/T_{ix} is often given the symbol a and hence

$$U = \frac{1}{1 + 2a}$$

As was shown, a can range from a small fraction for low bit rate links of modest length, to a large integer value for long links and high bit rates. For these two extremes, U varies between near unity (100%) and a small fraction.

EXAMPLE

A series of 1000-bit frames is to be transmitted using an idle RQ protocol. Determine the link utilization for the following types of data link assuming a data transmission rate of (i) 1 kbps and (ii) 1 Mbps. The velocity of propagation of the link is $2 \times 10^8 \, \text{ms}^{-1}$ and the bit error rate is negligible.

(a)   a twisted pair cable 1 km in length,

(b)   a leased line 200 km in length,

(c)   a satellite link of 50 000 km.

The time taken to transmit a frame T_{ix} is given by:

$$T_{ix} = \frac{\text{number of bits in frame } N}{\text{bit rate } R \text{ in bps}}$$

At 1 kbps:

$$T_{ix} = \frac{1000}{10^3} = 1 \, \text{s}$$

At 1 Mbps:

$$T_{ix} = \frac{1000}{10^6} = 10^{-3}\,s$$

$$T_p = \frac{S}{V} \text{ and } U = \frac{1}{1 + \frac{2T_p}{T_{ix}}} = \frac{1}{1 + 2a}$$

(a) $T_p = \dfrac{10^3}{2 \times 10^8} = 5 \times 10^{-6}\,s$

  (i) $a = \dfrac{5 \times 10^{-6}}{1} = 5 \times 10^{-6}$ and hence $(1 + 2a) \simeq 1$ and $U = 1$

  (ii) $a = \dfrac{5 \times 10^{-6}}{10^{-3}} = 5 \times 10^{-3}$ and hence $(1 + 2a) \simeq 1$ and $U = 1$

(b) $T_p = \dfrac{200 \times 10^3}{2 \times 10^8} = 1 \times 10^{-3}\,s$

  (i) $a = \dfrac{1 \times 10^{-3}}{1} = 1 \times 10^{-3}$ and hence $(1 + 2a) \simeq 1$ and $U = 1$

  (ii) $a = \dfrac{5 \times 10^{-3}}{1} = 5 \times 10^{-3}$ and hence $(1 + 2a) > 1$ and $U = \dfrac{1}{1 + 2}$

$$= 0.33$$

(c) $T_p = \dfrac{50 \times 10^6}{2 \times 10^8} = 0.25\,s$

  (i) $a = \dfrac{0.25}{1} = 0.25$ and hence $(1 + 2a) > 1$ and $U = \dfrac{1}{1 + 0.5} = 0.67$

  (ii) $a = \dfrac{0.25}{10^{-3}} = 250$ and hence $(1 + 2a) > 1$ and $U = \dfrac{1}{1 + 500}$

$$= 0.002$$

The results are summarized in Figure 4.10 from which some interesting observations can be made. Firstly, for relatively short links for which a is less than 1, the link utilization is (to a good approximation) 100% and is independent of the data rate. This means that an idle RQ protocol is perfectly adequate for short links and modest data rates. Examples are networks based on modems and the analogue PSTN. Secondly, for longer terrestrial links, the link utilization is high for low data rates (and hence values of a) but falls off significantly as the data rate (and hence a) increases. Thirdly, the link utilization is poor for satellite links, even at low data rates. It can be concluded that an idle RQ protocol is unsuitable for such applications and also for those that involve high bit rate

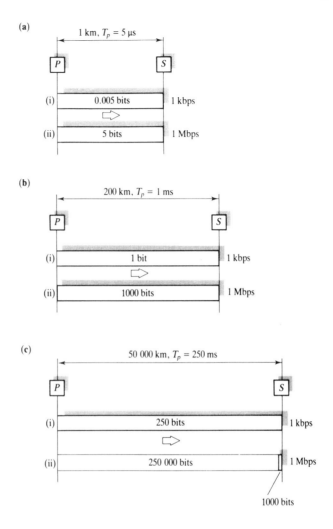

FIGURE 4.10

Effect of propagation delay as a function of data transmission rate; corresponding to parts (a), (b) and (c) of the example.

terrestrial links, such as local area networks (Chapter 6) and most public carrier wide area networks (Chapter 8).

The link utilizations calculated in the example assumed no transmission errors, although in practice, the links will have a non-zero bit error rate. Hence, to successfully transmit a frame, an average N_r transmission attempts will be required. The expression for link utilization can be modified, therefore, to give:

$$U = \frac{T_{ix}}{N_r T_{ix} + 2N_r T_p} = \frac{1}{N_r\left(1 + \dfrac{2T_p}{T_{ix}}\right)}$$

The value of N_r can be derived from a knowledge of the bit error rate P of the link. If P is the probability that a bit will be corrupted then, assuming random errors, the probability P_f that a frame will be corrupted is given by:

$$P_f = 1 - (1 - P)^{N_i}$$
$$\simeq N_i P \text{ if } N_i P \ll 1$$

For example, a bit error rate of 10^{-4} means that, on average, 1 bit in 10^4 will be corrupted. Hence for, say, 1000-bit frames:

$$P_f = 1 - (1 - 10^{-4})^{1000} = 0.095$$

or

$$P_f = 10^3 \times 10^{-4} = 0.1$$

Now, if P_f is the probability that a frame is corrupted, then $(1 - P_f)$ is the probability that an uncorrupted frame will be received. Hence:

$$N_r = \frac{1}{1 - P_f}$$

For example, if $P_f = 0.5$, $N_r = 2$; that is, if on average 50% of the frames are corrupted, then each frame will have to be transmitted twice. This is so since 50% of the retransmitted frames will also be corrupted, assuming ACK frames are not corrupted. Because of their short length relative to I-frames, this is a reasonable assumption. In practice, therefore, all the link efficiency values must be divided by N_r. That is,

$$U = \frac{1 - P_f}{1 + 2a}$$

The major advantage of the idle RQ scheme is that it requires a minimum of buffer storage for its implementation, since both P and S need only contain sufficient storage for one frame. In addition, S must retain only a record of the identifier of the last correctly received frame to enable it to detect duplicates. In general, the various retransmission schemes trade buffer storage requirements for transmission efficiency. Because of its low storage requirements, however, idle RQ is used extensively in applications that involve a relatively simple device (such as a terminal or personal computer) at one end of the link.

4.4 CONTINUOUS RQ

With a continuous RQ error control scheme, link utilization is much improved at the expense of increased buffer storage requirements. An example illustrating the transmission of a sequence of I-frames and their returned ACK-frames is shown in Figure 4.11.

The following points should be noted when interpreting the operation of the scheme:

● P sends I-frames continuously without waiting for an ACK-frame to be returned;

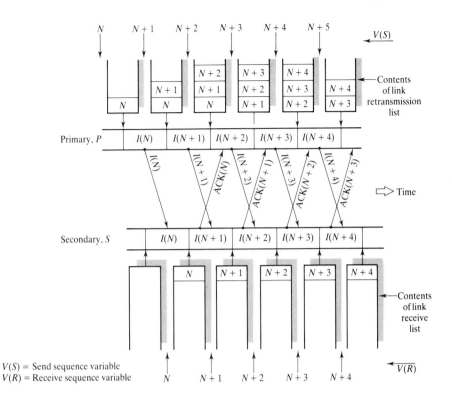

FIGURE 4.11

Continuous RQ frame
sequence.

$V(S)$ = Send sequence variable
$V(R)$ = Receive sequence variable

- since more than one I-frame is waiting acknowledgement, P retains a copy of each I-frame transmitted in a **retransmission list** that operates on a first-in, first-out (FIFO) queue discipline;

- S returns an ACK-frame for each correctly received I-frame;

- each I-frame contains a unique identifier which is returned in the corresponding ACK-frame;

- S retains an ordered list, the **receive list**, which contains the identifiers from the last n (see later) correctly received I-frames;

- on receipt of an ACK-frame, the corresponding I-frame is removed from the retransmission list by P.

As described earlier in the chapter, the interface between the higher layer software and the communication protocol software normally takes the form of two FIFO queues. It should be stressed, however, that there is no relationship between these and the link retransmission list (at P) and the link receive list (at S). The latter are for internal use by the communications layer to ensure the reliable transfer of message blocks between the two higher-layer entities.

To implement the scheme, it is necessary for P to retain a **send sequence variable V(S)**, which indicates the send sequence number N(S) to be allocated to the next I-frame to be transmitted. Also, S must maintain a **receive sequence variable V(R)**, which indicates the next in-sequence I-frame it expects to receive.

It can be concluded from Figure 4.11 that, in the absence of transmission errors, the link utilization of a continuous RQ scheme (to a reasonable approximation) will always be 100% providing the sending of I-frames by P is unrestricted. As will be seen later, however, this is not necessarily the case, as normally there is a limit set on the number of I-frames that P can send before the corresponding ACK-frame is received. Further discussion of the link utilization with a continuous RQ scheme will, therefore, be delayed until later in the chapter.

The example assumed that no transmission errors occur. When an error does occur, one of two retransmission strategies may be followed:

- S detects and requests the retransmission of just those frames in the sequence that are corrupted – **selective repeat**;
- S detects the receipt of an out-of-sequence I-frame and requests P to retransmit all outstanding unacknowledged I-frames from the last correctly received, and hence acknowledged, I-frame – **go-back-N**.

It should be noted that with all continuous RQ schemes, corrupted frames are discarded and retransmission requests are only triggered after the next error-free frame is received.

4.4.1 Selective repeat

As with the idle RQ error control scheme, selective repeat can be implemented in one of two ways; either by S acknowledging correctly received frames and P determining from the sequence of ACK-frames received that a frame has been lost – **implicit retransmission** – or by S returning a specific negative acknowledgement for a frame that is missing from the sequence – **explicit request**.

Two frame sequence diagrams illustrating aspects of the first scheme are shown in Figure 4.12(a) and (b). In part (a), all ACK-frames are assumed to be received correctly, while in part (b) the effect of a corrupted ACK-frame is illustrated. To follow the sequence in part (a) the following should be noted:

- assume I-frame $N + 1$ is corrupted;
- S returns an ACK-frame for each correctly received I-frame as before;
- S returns an ACK-frame for I-frames $N, N + 2, N + 3, \ldots$;
- on receipt of the ACK for I-frame $N + 2$, P detects that frame $N + 1$ has not been acknowledged;
- P removes I-frame $N + 2$ from the retransmission list and retransmits I-frame $N + 1$ before transmitting frame $N + 5$.

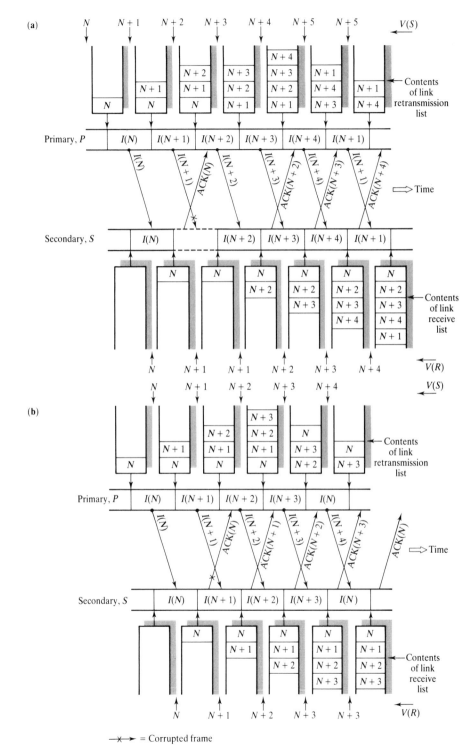

FIGURE 4.12

Selective repeat –
implicit retransmission:
(a) corrupted I-frame;
(b) corrupted
ACK-frame.

$\xrightarrow{\quad\times\quad}$ = Corrupted frame

The frame sequence shown in part (b) of the figure relates to the situation in which all the I-frames are received correctly but ACK-frame N is corrupted. It should be noted:

- on receipt of ACK-frame $N + 1$, P detects that I-frame N is still awaiting acknowledgement and hence retransmits it;

- on receipt of the retransmitted I-frame N, S determines from its receive list that this has already been received correctly and is therefore a duplicate;

- S discards the frame but returns an ACK-frame for it to ensure P removes it from the retransmission list.

Operation of the above scheme relies on the receipt of ACK-frames relating to following frames to initiate the retransmission of an earlier corrupted frame. The alternative approach is to use an explicit negative acknowledgement frame to request for a specific frame to be retransmitted. The negative acknowledgement is known as **selective reject**. Figure 4.13 shows two example frame sequence diagrams showing the operation of the scheme. Again the sequence

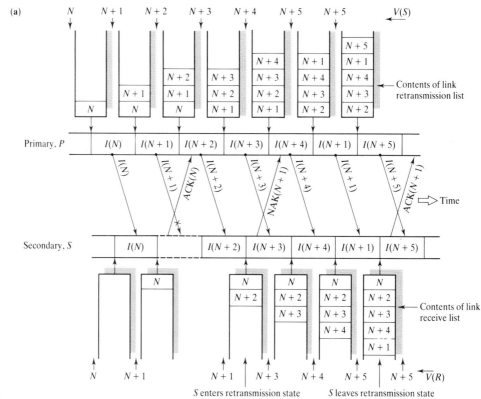

FIGURE 4.13

Selective repeat – explicit request: (a) correct operation.

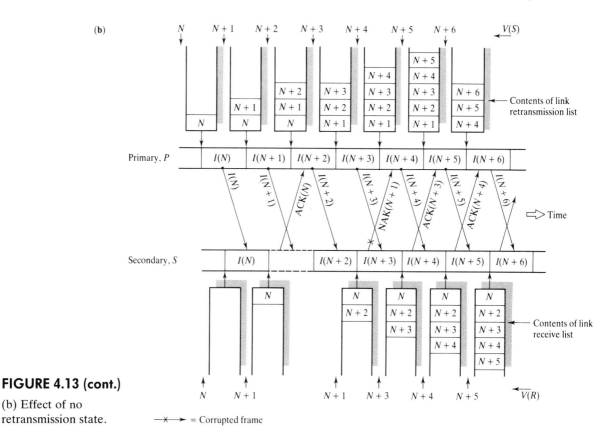

FIGURE 4.13 (cont.)

(b) Effect of no
retransmission state.

$\longrightarrow\!\!\!\times\!\!\!\longrightarrow$ = Corrupted frame

shown in part (a) assumes no acknowledgements are corrupted, while the sequence in part (b) shows the effect of a lost acknowledgement.

The following should be noted:

- an ACK-frame acknowledges all frames in the retransmission list up to and including the I-frame with the sequence number the ACK contains;

- assume I-frame $N + 1$ is corrupted;

- S returns an ACK-frame for I-frame N;

- when S receives I-frame $N + 2$ it detects I-frame $N + 1$ is missing and hence returns a NAK frame containing the identifier of the next correctly received I-frame $N + 2$;

- on receipt of NAK $(N + 1)$, P interprets this as acknowledging I-frame $N + 2$ but detects frame $N + 1$ is still awaiting an acknowledgement and hence retransmits it;

- when S returns a NAK frame it enters the **retransmission state**;

- when in the retransmission state, the return of ACK-frames is suspended;

- on receipt of I-frame $N + 1$, S leaves the retransmission state and resumes returning ACK-frames;
- NAK $N + 1$ acknowledges all frames up to and including frame $I + 1$;
- a timer is used with each NAK-frame to ensure that if it is corrupted (and hence frame $N + 1$ is not received), it is retransmitted.

To understand why only one NAK-frame can be outstanding at a time, consider the frame sequence diagram shown in part (b) of the figure. The following should be noted:

- assume I-frame $N + 1$ is again corrupted;
- S returns NAK $N + 1$ as before but this time it is corrupted;
- on receipt of ACK-frame $N + 3$, this would acknowledge all frames including I-frame $N + 1$ and hence this will not be retransmitted;
- I-frame $N + 1$ would be lost.

It is readily deduced from the frame sequences shown that although S receives a correct copy of each frame sent by P, the order of reception is not maintained. For example, in the examples S receives I-frames $N + 2$, $N + 3$ and $N + 4$ before frame $N + 1$. Selective repeat is used primarily, therefore, when either the frames being transmitted are self-contained entities (that is, the order of reception is not important), or all the frames relate to the same message (or larger frame) and messages (frames) are being reassembled by the secondary. An example of the latter is when a high BER link is being used (such as a radio link) and hence the maximum frame size associated with the link is small. The normal approach is to use selective repeat for the small frame fragments relating to each larger frame and to reassemble the smaller fragments (frames) back into a single larger frame before the frame is delivered. A single NAK is then used to request retransmission of any lost fragments.

In many applications, however, frames must be delivered in the same sequence as they were submitted. Hence frames received out of sequence must be buffered (held) by S until the missing frame(s) is (are) received. Since the frames can often be large, and the number of frame buffers required can also become large, making the buffer storage capacity required in the communications subsystem unacceptably high. For this reason most applications of the type outlined as well as most terrestrial networks, use the go-back-N retransmission control scheme.

4.4.2 Go-back-N

With go-back-N, as the name implies, when the secondary detects an out-of-sequence frame, it informs the primary to start to retransmit frames from a specified frame number. It does this by returning a special negative acknowledgement frame known as a **reject**. Two frame sequences illustrating the operation of go-back-N are shown in Figure 4.14(a) and (b). The following should be noted when interpreting the sequence in part (a):

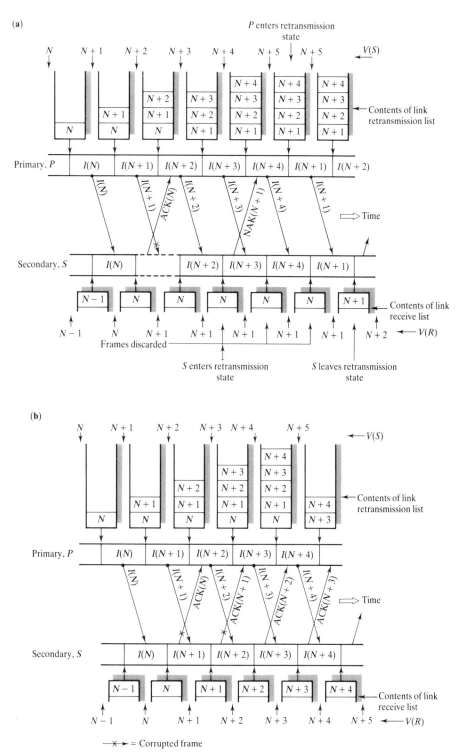

FIGURE 4.14

Go-back-N
retransmission strategy:
(a) corrupted I-frame;
(b) corrupted
ACK-frame.

- assume I-frame $N + 1$ is corrupted;

- S receives I-frame $N + 2$ out of sequence;

- on receipt of I-frame $N + 2$, S returns NAK $N + 1$ informing P to go back and start to retransmit from I-frame $N + 1$;

- S then enters the retransmission state and waits for I-frame $N + 1$;

- on receipt of I-frame $N + 1$, S leaves the retransmission state and continues as before;

- to allow for NAK frame $N + 1$ being corrupted, S starts a timer for receipt of I-frame $N + 1$ and retransmits NAK $N + 1$ if it does not receive it before the expired timeout interval.

Again, it has been assumed in this example that an I-frame was corrupted and that the acknowledgement frames were received correctly. The effect of a corrupted acknowledgement on the frame transmission sequence is shown in Figure 4.14(b). The following points should be noted regarding its operation:

- S receives each transmitted I-frame correctly;

- assume ACK-frames N and $N + 1$ are both corrupted;

- on receipt of ACK-frame $N + 2$, P detects that there are two outstanding I-frames in the retransmission list (N and $N + 1$);

- since it is an ACK-frame rather than a NAK-frame, P assumes that the two ACK-frames for I-frames N and $N + 1$ have both been corrupted and hence accepts ACK $N + 2$ as an acknowledgement for the two outstanding frames.

This example shows that with a go-back-N strategy, the correct frame sequence is maintained, thus minimizing the buffer storage required for its implementation. However, since some correctly received frames must be retransmitted, it is less efficient in its use of the available transmission capacity than a selective retransmission scheme. There is thus the trade-off between buffer storage requirements and link utilization.

Finally, it was assumed in all the earlier frame sequence diagrams relating to continuous RQ that the loss of an I-frame was detected only after the next I-frame had been correctly received. Clearly this requires a continuous stream of I-frames being ready to send, otherwise unacceptably long delays would be experienced while S waits for the next I-frame to be transmitted.

To allow for this possibility, P normally employs an additional timeout mechanism similar to the one outlined for the idle RQ control scheme. A number of alternative timeout schemes are possible, but the one selected in the earlier protocol definitions assumes a separate timer is started each time an I-frame is transmitted by P, and is stopped (reset) when an acknowledgement indicating its correct receipt is received. Then, if an acknowledgement for a

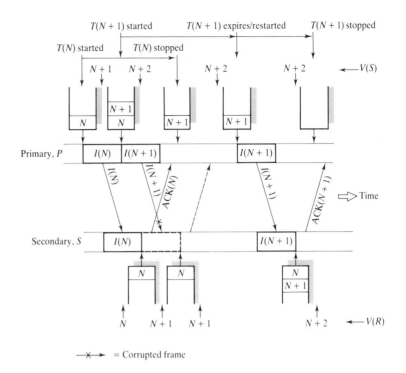

FIGURE 4.15

Timeout mechanism.

$\longrightarrow\!\!\times\!\!\longrightarrow$ = Corrupted frame

frame is not received before its timeout interval expires, the frame is retransmitted. This is shown in Figure 4.15.

Clearly, the timeout interval selected must be greater than the worst-case propagation delay between transmitting a frame and receiving the associated acknowledgement. Also, with a timeout mechanism it is possible for S to receive duplicate copies of a frame even if it is correctly received by S since the resulting acknowledgement frame may be corrupted on its return to P. In the absence of an acknowledgement, P assumes that the initial frame has been corrupted and erroneously retransmits another copy.

With a go-back-N control scheme, this does not create a problem since the N(S) in the duplicate frame(s) will not be equal to the current V(R) held by S and will be discarded automatically. With a selective retransmission scheme, however, the possibility of one or more duplicate frames being sent by P is allowed for by S retaining an ordered list (the receive list) of the sequence numbers of the last *N* correctly received I-frames. In this way, it can check if a received frame is a duplicate of an already correctly received (and therefore acknowledged) frame or a new frame. The number of frames to be retained *N* is influenced by the flow control algorithm.

For clarity, all of the foregoing examples have assumed that information frames flow in one direction and that the return path is used simply for acknowledgement. Normally, however, most communication links that use continuous RQ are duplex links and carry information frames in both directions. To accommodate this, each side of such links contains both a primary and a secondary: the first controlling the sequence of I-frames transmitted and the second controlling the sequence of I-frames received. Thus, each side of the link contains both a V(S), which is controlled by the primary, and a V(R), which is controlled by the secondary. Also, although separate ACK and NAK frames are utilized, since there is the possibility of an I-frame awaiting transmission in the reverse direction when an ACK or NAK is to be retuned, to improve link utilization some protocols utilize the I-frames flowing in the return direction to carry acknowledgement information relating to the transmission of I-frames in the forward direction. Each I-frame transmitted then contains both an N(S), indicating the send sequence number, and an N(R), containing acknowledgement information for the reverse direction. This scheme is referred to as **piggyback acknowledgement**. A protocol that uses this technique is the high-level data link control (HDLC) protocol described in the next chapter.

Finally, although all the ACK and NAK frames in the foregoing examples carried an N(R) that is the same as the N(S) to which they relate, in practice the V(R) at the secondary is incremented immediately the I-frame is received and hence before the acknowledgement is generated. This means that with most practical protocol implementations ACK N acknowledges frame $N - 1$. Again HDLC is an example.

4.4.3 Flow control

Error control is only one component of a data link protocol. Another important and related component is **flow control**. As the name implies, it is concerned with controlling the rate of transmission of characters or frames on a link so that the receiver always has sufficient buffer storage resources to accept them prior to processing. With a character-oriented terminal-to-computer link, for example, if the remote computer is servicing many terminals, it may become temporarily overloaded and be unable to process all the characters sent to it at the available transmission rates. Similarly, with a frame-oriented selective retransmission scheme, the receiver may run out of buffer storage capacity if it is endeavouring to buffer an indeterminate number of frames. The two most common flow control schemes will now be considered.

X-ON/X-OFF

It may be deduced from the discussion in Section 4.2 that echo checking, in addition to performing (manual) error control, implicitly performs flow control since, if the remote computer runs out of buffer storage, it will cease echoing characters back to the terminal screen. Hence the user will automatically stop keying-in further characters. Normally, however, the lack of echoed characters from the computer is caused by the computer becoming temporarily overloaded. In this case, if the user does not cease transmitting new characters, the computer will incur further and unnecessary processing overheads by simply reading each character and then discarding it.

Consequently an additional automatic flow control facility is often invoked to ensure that a terminal does not send any further characters until an overload condition has been cleared. This mechanism is achieved by the computer returning a special control character **X-OFF** to the controlling device within the terminal instructing it to cease transmission. On receipt of the X-OFF character, the terminal either ignores any further characters entered at the keyboard or buffers them in a local buffer until the overload has been cleared. In this way, the computer does not incur any unnecessary processing overheads. Then, when the overload condition decays and the computer becomes able to accept further characters, it returns a companion control character **X-ON** to inform the terminal control device that it may restart sending characters. This mechanism is also used when a computer is sending characters to a printer or other terminal that cannot sustain the same rate of output as the computer. In such cases, however, it is the controlling device within the printer (or terminal) that controls the flow of characters.

As was explained in Chapter 2, the RTS/CTS handshake control lines associated with the RS-232C/V.24 interface can be used to perform a similar function. To discriminate between the two methods, therefore, the latter is referred to as **out-of-band flow control** whilst X-ON/X-OFF is an example of **in-band flow control**.

Sliding window

To control the flow of frames across a data link, an alternative mechanism known as a **sliding window** is used. Recall that an idle RQ error control scheme, although inefficient in its use of transmission bandwidth, requires a minimum of buffer storage capacity since, after a frame is transmitted by P, it must wait until an acknowledgement is returned by S before transmitting the next frame. The flow of I-frames across the link is therefore automatically tightly controlled.

With a continuous RQ error control scheme, however, P may send I-frames continuously before receiving any acknowledgements. Hence, with this type of scheme it is possible for the destination to run out of available buffer storage if, for example, it is unable to pass on the frames at the rate they are received. To allow for this possibility, it is usual to introduce an additional regulating action into such schemes. The approach has many similarities to the one inherent in the idle RQ control scheme in that it essentially sets a limit on the number of I-frames that P may send before receiving an acknowledgement. This is accomplished by P monitoring the number of outstanding (unacknowledged) I-frames currently held in the retransmission list. Then, if the destination side of the link becomes unable to pass on the frames sent to it, S will stop returning acknowledgement frames, the retransmission list at P will build up and this in turn can be interpreted as a signal for P to stop transmitting further frames until acknowledgements start to flow again.

To implement this scheme, a maximum limit is set on the number of I-frames that can be awaiting acknowledgement and hence are outstanding in the retransmission list. This limit is referred to as the **send window** for the link.

Clearly, if this is set to 1, the transmission control scheme reverts to idle RQ with a consequent drop in transmission efficiency. The limit is normally selected so that, providing the destination is able to pass on or absorb all frames it receives, the send window does not impair the flow of I-frames across the link. Factors such as the maximum frame size, available buffer storage, link propagation delay and transmission bit rate must all be considered when selecting the send window.

Operation of the scheme is shown in Figure 4.16. As each I-frame is transmitted, the **upper window edge (UWE)** is incremented by unity. Similarly, as each I-frame is acknowledged, the **lower window edge (LWE)** is incremented by unity. The acceptance of any new frames (message blocks), and hence the flow of I-frames, is stopped if the difference between UWE and LWE becomes equal to the send window K. Assuming error-free transmission, K is a fixed window that moves (slides) over the complete set of frames being transmitted. The technique is thus known as **sliding window**.

The use of a timeout mechanism to overcome the problem of lost (corrupted) acknowledgements can also result in duplicate frames being received by S. To allow for this possibility, S must retain a list of the identifiers of the last n frames correctly received so that, on receipt of each frame, it can deduce whether a correct copy of the frame has previously been received. The number of identifiers is referred to as the **receive window** for the link.

With a go-back-N control scheme, n need only be 1 since, if any out-of-sequence frames are received, S will simply discard them and wait until it receives the next in-sequence frame. With a selective retransmission scheme, however, n must be large enough to ensure that S can determine whether a frame has already been received. It may be deduced that adopting a maximum

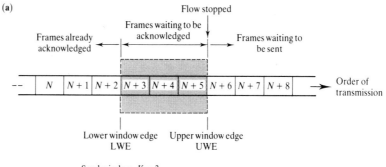

FIGURE 4.16

Flow control principle: (a) sliding window example; (b) send and receive window limits.

(a)

	Protocol	Send window	Receive window
(b)	Idle RQ	1	1
	Selective repeat	K	K
	Go-back-N	K	1

limit on the number of I-frames that P may send before receiving any acknowl-edgement (the send window), means that the number of identifiers to be retained by S need only be the same. Thus, with selective retransmission it is normal to operate the link with equal send and receive windows so that, in the worst case, S can always determine if a received frame is a valid retransmitted frame or a duplicate.

4.4.4 Sequence numbers

Until now, it has been assumed that the sequence number inserted into each frame by P is simply the previous sequence number plus one and that the range of numbers available is infinite. Defining a maximum limit on the number of I-frames that may be in the process of being transferred across a link not only limits the size of the link retransmission and receive lists, but also makes it possible to limit the range of sequence numbers that are required to identify each transmitted frame uniquely. The number of identifiers required is a func-tion of both the retransmission control scheme and the size of the send and receive windows.

For example, with an idle RQ control scheme, the send and receive windows are both 1 and hence only two identifiers are required to allow S to determine whether a particular I-frame received is a new frame or a duplicate. Typically, the two identifiers would be 0 and 1; the send sequence variable would then be incremented modulo-2 by P.

With a go-back-N control scheme and a send window of, say, K, the number of identifiers must be at least $K + 1$. This can best be seen by consider-ing the example shown in Figure 4.17(a).

The following should be noted when interpreting the example:

- the send window used in the example is 3;
- P sends its full window of three I-frames;
- the three I-frames are correctly received by S;
- the three ACK-frames returned by S are all corrupted;
- P times-out each I-frame and retransmits them;
- S discards each duplicate I-frame and acknowledges all of them with a single ACK-frame, ACK 2.

Now, if only three identifiers were used – that is, the same number as the send window – S would not be able to determine whether I-frame I(0) was a new frame or a duplicate, since 0 would then be the next in-sequence identifier. Hence, with four identifiers (the send window + 1), S knows that the next in-sequence I-frame would have an identifier of 3, whereas the retransmitted (duplicate) frame would have an identifier of 0. It therefore correctly discards the latter.

With a selective repeat scheme and a send and receive window of K, the number of identifiers must not be less than $2K + 1$. Again, this can be deduced

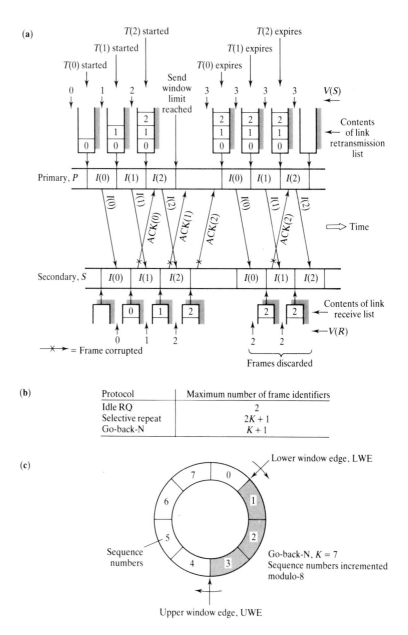

FIGURE 4.17

Sequence numbers:
(a) maximum range
example; (b) maximum
number for each
protocol; (c) example
assuming eight
sequence numbers.

by considering the case when P sends a full window of K frames and all
subsequent acknowledgements are corrupted. S must be able to determine if any
of the next K frames are new frames. The only way of ensuring that S can deduce
this is to assign a completely new set of K identifiers to the next window of
I-frames transmitted, which requires at least $2K + 1$ identifiers. The limits for
each scheme are shown in part (b) of the figure.

In practice, since the identifier of a frame is in binary form, a set number of binary digits must be reserved for its use. For example, with a send window of, say, 7 and a go-back-N control scheme, three binary digits would be required for the send and receive sequence numbers yielding eight possible identifiers: 0 through 7. The send and receive variables would then be incremented modulo-8 by P and S, respectively. This is shown in part (c) of the figure.

4.4.5 Protocol specification

The frame sequence diagrams and accompanying text in the preceding sections provide a qualitative description of the error control and flow control components of the continuous RQ protocol. It is now possible to derive a more formal specification based on the methodology described earlier in section 4.3.2.

First the various interfaces associated with each protocol entity are identified. These are shown in Figure 4.18. A go-back-N error control strategy, together with a window flow control mechanism, have then been used as the basis of the two specifications shown in Figures 4.19 and 4.20. The primary is specified in Figure 4.19 and the secondary in Figure 4.20.

In both specifications, first the abbreviated names to be used are defined; they are given in part (a) of the figures. The specifications of each protocol – primary and secondary – using the three methods are then presented in parts (b), (c) and (d). As can be deduced from each specification, although the state

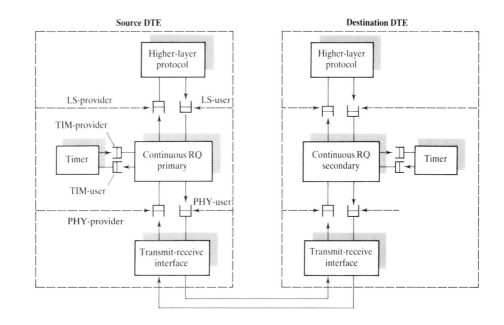

FIGURE 4.18

Continuous RQ protocol layer interfaces.

(a)   **Incoming events**

Name	Interface	Meaning
LDATAreq	LS_user	L_DATA.request service primitive received
ACKRCVD	PHY_provider	ACK-frame received from S
TEXP	TIM_provider	Wait ACK timer for frame expires
NAKRCVD	PHY_provider	NAK-frame received from S

States

Name	Meaning
DATA_TRANSFER	Data transfer

Outgoing events

Name	Interface	Meaning
TxFrame(X)	PHY_user	Format a frame with N(S) = X and transfer to tail of PHY_user queue
RetxFrame(X)	PHY_user	Transfer frame to tail of PHY_user queue

Predicates

Name	Meaning
P0	Send window open

Specific actions

[1] = Start_timer (X) using TIM_user queue
[2] = Stop_timer (X) using TIM_user queue
[3] = Increment Va
[4] = Decrement Va
[5] = Increment Vs
[6] = Get frame from head of retransmission list
[7] = Put frame at tail of retransmission list

State variables

Vs = Send sequence variable
PresentState = Preset state of protocol entity
Va = Number of unacknowledged frames in retransmission list

(b)

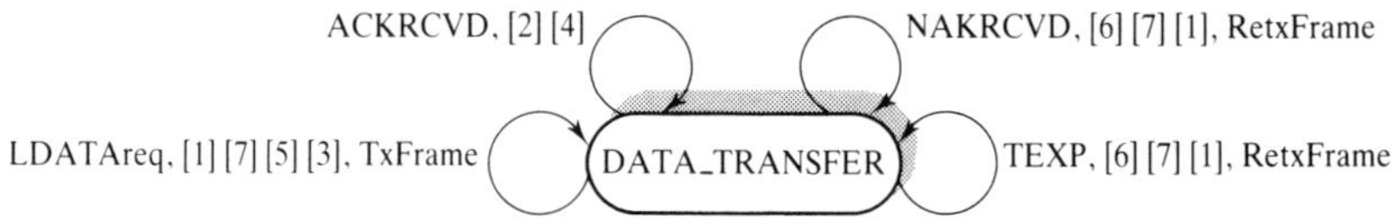

(c)

Incoming event / Present state	LDATAreq	ACKRCVD	TEXP	NAKRCVD
DATA_TRANSFER	1	2	3	4

1 = P0: TxFrame, [1] [7] [5] [3]
2 = [2] [4]
3 = RetxFrame, [6] [7] [1]
4 = RetxFrame, [6] [7] [1]

FIGURE 4.19

Continuous RQ (go-back-N) specification: (a) abbreviated names; (b) state transition diagram; (c) event–state table.

(d)   *program*   Continuous RQ_Primary;
           const   K; { Send Window Limit }
           type   Events = (LDATAreq, ACKRCVD, TEXP, NAKRCVD);
                        States = DATA_TRANSFER;
           var   EventStateTable = *array* [Events, States] *of* 1 .. 3;
                        EventType : Events;
                        PresentState : States;
                        Vs = 0 .. K;
                        Va = 0 .. K − 1;
                        RetxList; { FIFO queue holding I-frame buffer pointers awaiting acknowledgement }
           procedure Initialize; { Initializes contents of EventStateTable and state variables }
           procedure TxFrame (X : integer); ⎫
           procedure RetxFrame (X : integer); ⎬ Outgoing event procedures
           procedure Start_timer (X : integer); ⎫
           procedure Stop_timer (X : integer); ⎬ Specific action procedures
           procedure Get_frame; ⎪
           procedure Put_frame; ⎭
           function   P0 : *boolean*;   ⎬ Predicate function

           begin
                     repeat Wait for an incoming event;
                              EventType := type of incoming event;
                              case EventStateTable[EventType, PresentState] *of*
                                  1 : *begin if* P0 *then* TxFrame(Vs); Start_timer(Vs); Put_frame;
                                               Vs := Vs + 1; Va := Va + 1;
                                          if SW = K *then* P0 := false *end*;
                                  2 : *repeat* Get_frame; X := N(R) from frame; Stop_timer(X)
                                               Va := Va − 1; P0 := true;
                                      until   X = N(R) in ACK-frame;
                                  3 : *begin*   Get_frame; X := N(S) from frame; RetxFrame(X);
                                               Start_timer(X); Put_frame; *end*;
                                  4 : *repeat* Get_frame; X := N(S) from frame; RetxFrame(X);
                                               Start_timer(X); Put_frame;
                                      until   X = N(R) in NAK-frame;
                     until Forever;
           end.

FIGURE 4.19 (cont.)

(d) Structured pseudo-code.

transition diagrams give a good overview of the basic operation of each protocol, it is not possible to illustrate all possible aspects of their operation using this method.

The event–state tables allow more detail to be included since they allow predicates to be embedded into the specification. Also, the specification of each protocol in structured (pseudo) code can then be carried out in a systematic way. The resulting pseudo-code specifications are given in part (d) of the figures. The approach in subsequent chapters will be to derive the event–state tables for the various protocols discussed, or the essential features of them. The reader is then left to apply the same methodology to derive the corresponding structured code.

(a) **Incoming events**

Name	Interface	Meaning
IRCVD	PHY_provider	I-frame received from P

States

Name	Meaning
DATA	Waiting for next I-frame with N(S) = Vr
NAK_SENT	Waiting for missing I-frame with N(S) = Vr

Outgoing events

Name	Interface	Meaning
LDATAind(X)	LS_provider	Pass contents of I-frame with N(S) = X to layer above
TxACK(X)	PHY_user	Format and transmit an ACK-frame with N(R) = X
TxNAK(X)	PHY_user	Format and transmit a NAK-frame with N(R) = X
LERRORind	LS_provider	Issue an error message

Predicates

Name	Meaning
P0	N(S) in I-frame received = Vr

Specific actions

[1] = Start_timer
[2] = Stop_timer
[3] = Increment Vr
[4] = Increment RetxCount
[5] = Increment ErrorCount
[6] = Discard frame

State variables

Vr = Receive sequence variable
RetxCount = Number of NAK-frames retransmitted
ErrorCount = Number of error conditions
PresentState = Present state of protocol entity

(b)

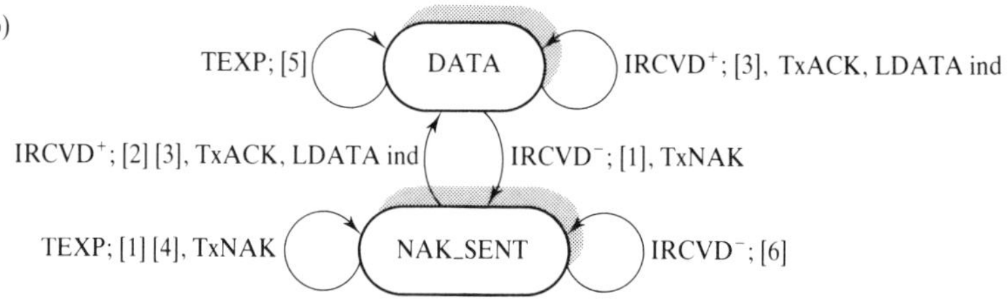

(c)

Present State \ Incoming Event	IRCVD	TEXP
DATA	1	0
NAK_SENT	2	3

0 = [5]

1 = P0: TxACK, LDATAind, [3]
    NOT P0: TxNAK, [1], NAK_SENT

2 = P0: TxACK, LDATAind, [2] [3], DATA
    NOT P0: [6]

3 = TxNAK, [1] [4]

FIGURE 4.20

Continuous RQ (go-back-N) specification – secondary: (a) abbreviated names; (b) state transition diagram; (c) event–state table.

```
(d)   program   Continuous RQ_Secondary;
      const      MaxRetxCount;
                 MaxErrorCount;
      type       Events = (IRCVD, TEXP);
                 States  = (DATA, NAKSENT);
      var        EventStateTable = array[Events, States] of 0 .. 3;
                 EventType : Events;
                 PresentState : States;
                 Vr, RetxCount, ErrorCount : integer;
      procedure Initialize; { Initializes contents of EventStateTable and state variables }
      procedure LDATAind(X);  ⎫
      procedure TxACK(X);     ⎪
      procedure TxNAK(X);     ⎬  Outgoing event procedures
      procedure LERRORind;    ⎭
      procedure Start_timer;  ⎫
      procedure Stop_timer;   ⎬  Specific action procedures
      procedure DiscardFrame; ⎭
      function  P0 : boolean;  } Boolean function

      begin     Initialize;
                repeat Wait for an incoming event; EventType = type of event;
                      case EventStateTable[EventType, PresentState] of
                          0 : begin ErrorCount := ErrorCount − 1; if(ErrorCount = MaxErrorCount) then
                                      begin LERRORind; Initialize; end;
                              end;
                          1 : X := N(S) from I-frame received;
                              begin if P0 then begin TxACK(X); LDATAind(X); Vr := Vr + 1; end;
                                      else begin TxNAK(X); Start_timer; PresentState := NAK_SENT; end;
                              end;
                          2 : X := N(S) from I-frame received;
                              begin if P0 then begin TxACK(X); LDATAind(X); Vr := Vr + 1; Stop_timer; end;
                                      else DiscardFrame;
                              end;
                          3 : begin TxNAK(Vr); Start_timer; RetxCount := RetxCount + 1;
                                      if(RetxCount = MaxRetxCount) then begin LERRORind; Initialize; end;
                              end;
                until Forever;
      end.
```

**FIGURE 4.20
(cont.)**

(d) Structured
pseudo-code.

4.4.6 Link utilization

During the discussion of the idle RQ protocol, it was shown that to a good approximation the link utilization U is a function of the time T_{ix} to transit an I-frame and the propagation delay of the link T_p. However, for links with a T_p greater than T_{ix}, the link utilization is also influenced by the send window K.

Recall that the example in the section on idle RQ (Figure 4.10) showed that with a typical satellite link, T_p is often much greater than T_{ix}. In this example, T_{ix} was derived to be 1 ms and T_p about 250 ms for a 1 Mbps channel and 1000-bit frames. Theoretically, therefore, it is possible for 250 such frames to be in transit between P and S at any one time. Hence, to achieve a link efficiency of 100%, a send window in excess of 500 is required, since an

ACK-frame for the first frame in the sequence will not be received until 500 ms $(2T)$ later.

In general, the link utilization U for a send window of K is given by:

$$U = 1$$

if K is greater than or equal to $1 + 2a$ and:

$$U = \frac{KT_{ix}}{T_{ix} + 2T_p} = \frac{K}{1 + \frac{2T_p}{T_{ix}}} = \frac{K}{1 + 2a}$$

if K is less than $1 + 2a$.

This can best be seen by considering the case when $T_p = T_{ix}$. In this case, the last bit of a frame sent by P will not be received until $2T_p$ (and hence $2T_{ix}$) later. The associated ACK-frame will then take a further T_p (and hence T_{ix}) to be received by P. If $K = 1$ (idle RQ), then $U = 1/3$. To raise this to 100% (K greater than $1 + 2a$), K must be in excess of 3; that is, three or more frames must be sent by P before an ACK is received.

EXAMPLE

A series of 1000-bit frames is to be transmitted using a continuous RQ protocol. Determine the link efficiency for the following types of data link if the velocity of propagation is $2 \times 10^8 \, \text{ms}^{-1}$ and the bit error rates of the links are all negligibly low:

(a)   a 1 km link of 1 Mbps and a send window $K = 2$,
(b)   a 10 km link of 200 Mbps and a send window $K = 7$,
(c)   a 50000 km satellite link of 2 Mbps and a send window $K = 127$.

$$T_p = \frac{S}{V} \quad T_{ix} = \frac{N_i}{R} \quad a = \frac{T_p}{T_{ix}}$$

(a) $T_p = \dfrac{10^3}{2 \times 10^8} = 5 \times 10^{-6} \text{s}$

$T_{ix} = \dfrac{1000}{1 \times 10^6} = 10^{-3} \text{s}$

Hence:

$$a = \frac{5 \times 10^{-6}}{1 \times 10^{-3}} = 5 \times 10^{-3}$$

Now $K = 2$ is greater than $1 + 2a$ and hence $U = 1$.

(b) $T_p = \dfrac{10 \times 10^3}{2 \times 10^8} = 5 \times 10^{-5} \text{s}$

$T_{ix} = \dfrac{1000}{200 \times 10^6} = 5 \times 10^{-6} \text{s}$

Hence:

$$a = \frac{5 \times 10^{-5}}{1 \times 10^{-6}} = 10$$

Now $K = 7$ is less than $1 + 2a$ and hence:

$$U = \frac{K}{1 + 2a} = \frac{7}{1 + 20} = 0.33$$

(c)
$$T_p = \frac{50 \times 10^6}{2 \times 10^8} = 0.25\,s$$

$$T_{ix} = \frac{1000}{2 \times 10^6} = 5 \times 10^{-4}\,s$$

Hence:

$$a = \frac{0.25}{5 \times 10^{-4}} = 500$$

Now $K = 127$ is less than $1 + 2a$ and hence:

$$U = \frac{K}{1 + 2a} = \frac{127}{1 + 1000} = 0.127.$$

It can be deduced from these results that the choice of K has a strong impact on the link utilization in certain cases. As can be seen, even with a K of 127, the link utilization of a satellite link is still very low. It is for this reason that a large K (and hence sequence number range) is utilized. This also applies to terrestrial links operating at high bit rates in later chapters.

The results calculated in the example assumed no transmission errors. Any errors will further reduce the link utilization since some frames must be retransmitted. However, the effect differs slightly for the two retransmission schemes. For example, with a selective repeat scheme, U is reduced simply by the number of attempts to transmit each frame N_r since only the corrupted frame is retransmitted. If P_f is the frame error rate of the link then, assuming random errors:

$$N_r = \frac{1}{1 - P_f}$$

The modified value of U is thus:

$$U = \frac{K}{N_r(1 + 2a)} = \frac{K(1 - P_f)}{1 + 2a}$$

for K less than $1 + 2a$. For values of K greater than or equal to $1 + 2a$, U is found simply by substituting $K = 1 + 2a$ in this expression, since $1 + 2a$ is the maximum number of frames that can be transmitted before receiving an acknowledgement in time $T_{ix} + 2T_p$. Hence:

$$U = \frac{(1 + 2a)(1 - P_f)}{1 + 2a} = 1 - P_f$$

for K greater than or equal to $1 + 2a$.

With a go-back-N scheme, the link utilization is reduced further since, if a frame is corrupted, more than one frame must be retransmitted. Again, the number of additional frames to be transmitted will be determined by the magnitude of K relative to $1 + 2a$.

For K less than $1 + 2a$, the number of times $(K - 1)$ frames must be retransmitted is simply $P_f(K - 1)$. Now, for each occurrence, a further $1 + 2a$ delay will occur. The modified expression is thus:

$$U = \frac{K(1 - P_f)}{(1 + 2a) + (1 + 2a)P_f(K - 1)} = \frac{K(1 - P_f)}{(1 + 2a)(1 + P_f(K - 1))}$$

for K less than $1 + 2a$, and

$$U = \frac{(1 + 2a)(1 - P_f)}{(1 + 2a)(1 + P_f(K - 1))} = \frac{1 - P_f}{1 + P_f(K - 1)}$$

for K greater than or equal to $1 + 2a$.

It should be stressed that these formulae are only approximations and will only give meaningful results if the earlier approximations hold. Nevertheless, they give a good guide both to the level of performance that can be expected and the relative performance of each method.

EXAMPLE

A series of 1000-bit frames is to be transmitted across a data link 100 km in length at 20 Mbps. If the link has a velocity of propagation of $2 \times 10^8 \, ms^{-1}$ and a bit error rate of 4×10^{-5}, determine the link utilization using the following link protocols:

(a)   idle RQ,

(b)   selective repeat and a send window of 10,

(c)   go-back-N and a send window of 10.

$$T_p = \frac{S}{V} = \frac{100 \times 10^3}{2 \times 10^8} = 5 \times 10^{-4} s$$

$$T_{ix} = \frac{N_i}{R} = \frac{1000}{20 \times 10^6} = 5 \times 10^{-5} s$$

$$a = \frac{T_p}{T_{ix}} = \frac{5 \times 10^{-4}}{5 \times 10^{-5}} = 10$$

Hence:

$$1 + 2a = 21$$

Now:

$$\therefore P_f \simeq N_i P = 1000 \times 4 \times 10^{-5} = 4 \times 10^{-2}$$

Hence:

$$1 - P_f = 96 \times 10^{-2}$$

(a) $\quad U = \dfrac{(1 - P_f)}{1 + 2a} = \dfrac{96 \times 10^{-2}}{21} = 0.046$

(b) $\quad$ For K less than $1 + 2a$

$$U = \frac{K(1 - P_f)}{1 + 2a} = \frac{10 \times 96 \times 10^{-2}}{21} = 0.46$$

(c) $\quad$ For K less than $1 + 2a$

$$U = \frac{K(1 - P_f)}{(1 + 2a)(1 + P_f(K - 1))} = 0.336$$

4.5 LINK MANAGEMENT

Error and flow control are both concerned with the correct transfer (in sequence and without error or duplication) of frames across an imperfect communication line. For the schemes outlined to function correctly, it has been assumed that both communicating parties have been initialized so that they are ready to exchange information. For example, it is necessary to ensure that both sides of the link start with the same send and receive sequence variables before any information frames are transmitted. In general, this is known as the initialization or **link set-up** phase. Normally after all data has been exchanged across a link, there is a **link disconnection phase**. Since the link set-up and disconnection phases are not concerned with the actual transfer of user data, they are collectively referred to as **link management**.

For a link between a terminal and a computer with a relatively short separation (up to, say, 20m), management functions can be achieved by exchanging signals on additional handshake (control) lines associated with the physical interface. This is known as a **handshake procedure**. A user wishing to open a dialogue with the computer first switches the terminal on. This results in one of the control lines becoming set (active), indicating to the computer that the terminal is ready to send characters – data terminal ready. The terminal must then wait until the computer responds by setting a corresponding response control line to indicate that it is ready to receive characters. The exchange of characters can then commence.

When both communicating devices are computers and they are transferring frames across a data link, the link is established (set up) by the link-level protocol within each computer exchanging an agreed set of **control** or **supervisory frames**. In the previous example, the link was established by the user switching on the terminal. However, in the case of a computer-to-computer link, the setting up of a link is normally initiated by higher layer software (an application program, for example) in one of the computers signalling to the communication software that it wishes to open a dialogue with a remote computer. Typically, this might take the form of a send or transfer request statement (primitive) being executed in the application program which, in turn, causes the communication software to be invoked. In practice, as will be seen in later chapters, the communication software is normally made up of a number of separate protocol layers, each responsible for a specific function in the overall communication task. Before any data is sent, each layer is first initialized. As an example, the initialization primitives associated with the data link layer are as shown in Figure 4.21(a).

As can be seen, prior to sending any data – using the L_DATA.request service – the LS-user (layer) first sends an **L_CONNECT.request** service primitive to the link layer. Unlike the L_DATA service, this is known as a **confirmed service** since, when the source link protocol entity has established a link (logical connection) with the destination (link) protocol entity, it returns an **L_CONNECT.confirm** primitive to the source LS-user. Note, however, that this only confirms that a logical link has been set up with the destination link protocol entity and not with the destination LS-user. As will be seen in later chapters, the latter is normally the case for all higher protocol layers.

On receipt of an L_CONNECT.request primitive, using an event control block as described previously, the link protocol entity at the source initializes all state variables and then creates a **link SETUP** frame (PDU). This is sent to the correspondent (peer) link protocol entity in the destination DTE using the selected transmission mode. On receipt of the SETUP frame, the destination DTE initializes its own state variables and proceeds by sending an **L_CONNECT.indication** primitive to the correspondent LS-user and an acknowledgement frame back to the source.

Since this acknowledgement does not relate to an I-frame, it does not contain a sequence number. It is known, therefore, as an **unnumbered acknowledgement** or **UA-frame**. On receipt of this UA-frame, the source protocol entity issues the L_CONNECT.confirm primitive to the LS-user and the link is now ready for the transfer of data using the L_DATA service. Finally, after all data has been transferred, the setup link is released using the L_DISCONNECT service, which is also a confirmed service. The corresponding frame, known as a **disconnect** or **DISC frame**, is acknowledged using a UA-frame. This mode of operation is also known as a **connection-oriented mode**.

Clearly, adding the link management function will affect the idle RQ and continuous RQ protocol specifications given earlier. To illustrate this, the modifications to the state transition diagram for the primary are as shown in Figure 4.21(b).

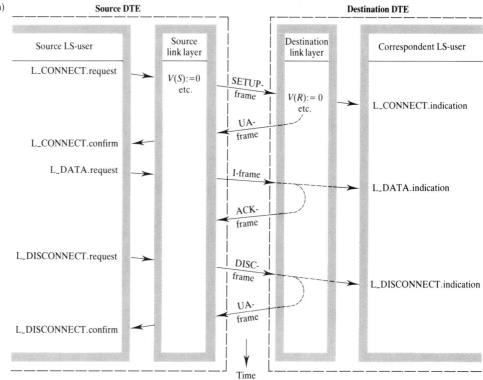

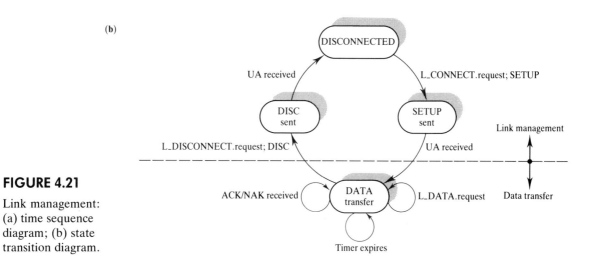

FIGURE 4.21

Link management: (a) time sequence diagram; (b) state transition diagram.

As can be seen, three new states are needed; the incoming events that cause the transitions between these and the DATA transfer state are as shown in the figure. A similar extension to the state transition diagram for the secondary can readily be developed. Moreover, the structure of both the event–state table and the corresponding pseudo-code is such that the same additions can readily be incorporated into these without any major changes to their structure.

EXERCISES

4.1   Assume a terminal is connected to a computer. Explain the two techniques that are used to achieve error control and flow control. Clearly outline the effect of each mechanism on the user of the terminal.

4.2   Explain the meaning of the following terms relating to a data link control protocol:

(a)   connectionless,
(b)   connection-oriented.

4.3   With the aid of frame sequence diagrams and assuming an idle RQ error control procedure, describe the difference between an implicit and an explicit retransmission control scheme.

4.4   With the aid of frame sequence diagrams and assuming an idle RQ error control procedure with explicit retransmission, describe the following:

(a)   the factors influencing the minimum time delay between the transmission of two consecutive information frames,
(b)   how the loss of a corrupted information frame is overcome,
(c)   how the loss of a corrupted acknowledgement frame is overcome.

4.5   Explain the meaning of the following terms relating to a protocol:

(a)   protocol layer,
(b)   user services,
(c)   time sequence diagram,
(d)   interlayer queue.

4.6   Explain the meaning of the following terms relating to a protocol specification:

(a)   finite state machine or automaton,
(b)   protocol state,
(c)   incoming event,
(d)   outgoing event,
(e)   predicate,
(f)   local or specific action.

4.7   Use the frame sequence diagrams derived for question 4.4 to define the operation of the primary and secondary sides of a link that is operating with an idle RQ error control scheme using:

(a)   a state transmission diagram,
(b)   an event–state table,
(c)   structured program code written in a pseudo high-level language.

4.8 A series of information frames with a mean length of 100 bits is to be transmitted across the following data links using an idle RQ protocol. If the velocity of propagation of the links is $2 \times 10^8 \text{ms}^{-1}$, determine the link efficiency (utilization) for each type of link.

(a) A 10 km link with a bit error rate of 10^{-4} and a data transmission rate of 9600 bps.

(b) A 500 m link with a bit error rate of 10^{-6} and a data transmission rate of 10 Mbps.

4.9 With the aid of frame sequence diagrams, describe the difference between an idle RQ and a continuous RQ error control procedure. For clarity, assume that no frames are corrupted during transmission.

4.10 With the aid of frame sequence diagrams and assuming a selective repeat error control scheme, describe how the following are overcome using both implicit and explicit retransmission:

(a) a corrupted information frame,

(b) a corrupted ACK/NAK frame.

4.11 Use the frame sequence diagrams derived for question 4.10 to define the operation of the primary and secondary sides of a link that is operating with a continuous RQ and selective repeat error control scheme using:

(a) a state transition diagram,

(b) an event–state table,

(c) structured program code written in pseudo high-level code.

Deduce the factors that influence the maximum size of the link receive list with a selective repeat retransmission strategy.

4.12 With the aid of frame sequence diagrams and assuming a go-back-N error control scheme, describe how the following are overcome:

(a) a corrupted information tree,

(b) a corrupted acknowledgement frame,

(c) a corrupted NAK-frame.

Include in these diagrams the contents of the link retransmission and link receive lists in addition to the state of the send and receive sequence variables as each frame is transmitted and received.

4.13 Using a continuous RQ error control scheme as an example, describe how the operation of the primary and secondary side of a link may be defined in the form of a finite-state machine and:

(a) a state transition diagram,

(b) a state transition table,

(c) a high-level language program segment written in pseudo-code.

4.14 What is the function of a timeout mechanism? Use frame sequence diagrams to illustrate how a timeout interval may be used to overcome the effect of a corrupted information frame assuming:

(a) idle RQ,

(b) selective repeat,

(c) go-back-N.

Deduce the factors that determine the duration of the timeout interval to be used with each scheme and how duplicates are detected.

4.15   Discriminate between the send window and receive window for a link and how they are related with:

(a)   a selective repeat retransmission scheme,
(b)   a go-back-N control scheme.

4.16   With the aid of frame sequence diagrams, illustrate the effect of a send window flow control limit being reached. Assume a send window of 2 and a go-back-N error control procedure.

4.17   Assuming a send window of K, deduce the minimum range of sequence numbers (frame identifiers) required with each of the following error control schemes:

(a)   idle RQ,
(b)   selective repeat,
(c)   go-back-N.

Clearly identify the condition when the maximum number of identifiers is in use.

4.18   A series of information frames with a mean length of 1000 bits is to be transmitted across a data link 4000 km long at a data rate of 2 Mbps. If the link has a velocity of propagation of $2 \times 10^8 \mathrm{ms}^{-1}$ and a bit error rate of 10^{-4}, determine the link efficiency using the following link protocols:

(a)   idle RQ,
(b)   selective retransmission and a send window of 7,
(c)   go-back-N and a send window of 127.

Indicate the effect of bit errors on each of the results obtained.

4.19   Explain what is meant by the term link management. Use an example set of user primitives and a time sequence diagram to show how a logical communication path is established (setup) between two systems and subsequently cleared (disconnected).

4.20   Assuming the user primitives used in question 4.19 and an idle RQ error and flow control scheme, derive:

(a)   a state transition diagram,
(b)   an event–state table,

for the protocol. Outline how the protocol can be defined in a pseudo high-level code form.

CHAPTER SUMMARY

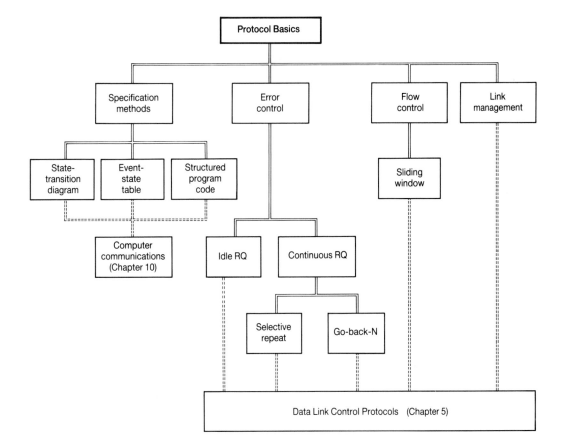

Data link control protocols

CHAPTER CONTENTS

CHAPTER OBJECTIVES

When you have completed studying the material in this chapter you should be able to:

- know the different types of character-oriented and bit-oriented data link control protocols that are in use and the application domains of each protocol type;
- understand the application and operation of the simplex, character-oriented protocol Kermit;
- describe the character-oriented binary synchronous control protocol as used in poll-select, multipoint networks;
- explain the operation of a duplex character-oriented protocol;
- understand the frame formats and frame types used in the high-level data link control (HDLC) protocol and explain selected aspects of its operation;
- know the differences between a single link and a multi-link control procedure;
- explain the operation and application domains of the various derivatives of HDLC including LAPB, LAPM, LAPD and LLC.

5.1 INTRODUCTION

The data link control layer – often abbreviated simply to data link layer – is concerned with the transfer of data over a serial data link. The link can be either a point-to-point physical circuit (twisted-pair wire, coaxial cable or optical fibre), a radio-based channel such as a satellite link, or a physical or logical link through a switched network. The transmission mode may be either asynchronous or synchronous and based on either a character-oriented or bit-oriented transmission control protocol. The data link layer is thus fundamental to the operation of all data communication applications.

In simple point-to-point applications, the data link layer normally serves the application layer directly. In more sophisticated applications, such as those

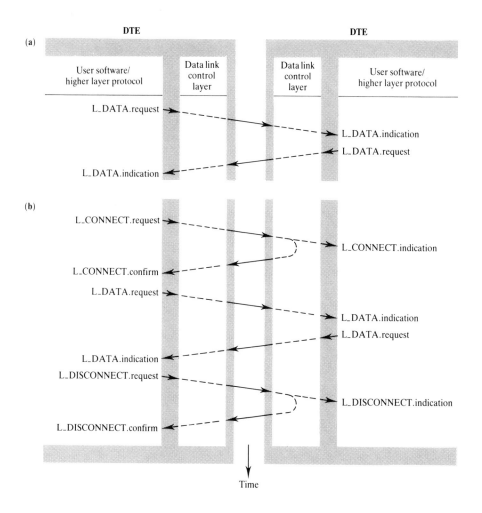

FIGURE 5.1

Data link control layer – user service primitives: (a) connectionless (best-try); (b) connection-oriented (reliable).

utilizing switched networks, it provides a defined service to a set of (higher) protocol layers. Depending on the application, the user service provided by the data-link layer may be either a simple **best-try (connectionless) service** or a **reliable (connection-oriented) service**. The two types of service are shown in the time sequence diagram of Figure 5.1.

The connectionless (best-try) service means that although error check bits are used to detect errors, any frames that are found to contain transmission errors are simply discarded by the link layer protocol entity. It is also referred to, therefore, as an **unacknowledged service** and retransmission becomes a function of a higher protocol layer. This is done in applications based on switched networks, for example, in which the bit error rate of the transmission lines is very low and hence the probability of retransmissions is relatively small. Examples are local area computer networks and integrated services digital networks.

The user service primitives associated with the connection-oriented mode are the same as those discussed in the last chapter. As may be recalled, with this type of service the data link protocol employs error and flow control procedures to provide a reliable service. This means that there is a high probability that the data will be error free without duplicates and that messages (data blocks) will be delivered in the same sequence as they were submitted. To achieve this, prior to sending any data (information frames), a logical connection between the two data link protocol entities is established using the L_CONNECT service. All data is then transferred using a suitable retransmission and flow control protocol. Then, when all data (information) has been exchanged, the logical connection is cleared using the L_DISCONNECT service.

Because of the range of applications of the data link layer, some of the different application environments to which they relate are first identified in the next section. The detailed operation of the different protocols is then presented in subsequent sections.

5.2 APPLICATION ENVIRONMENTS

Some application environments are shown in Figure 5.2. As can be seen, in some instances the data link protocols are located in the two communicating DTEs – computers, for example – and the protocol is then said to operate on an **end-to-end basis**. In others, it operates over the local link connecting, for example, the DTE to a network. The protocol is then said to have only **local significance**.

In part (a), the data link is a point-to-point circuit which can be either a direct physical connection (twisted-pair wire, coaxial cable or fibre), a circuit set-up through the analogue switched telephone network using modems, a circuit through a private multiplexer network or a radio-based link such as a satellite or terrestrial microwave link. The data link thus operates on an end-to-end basis and, in many such applications, serves the application directly. A reliable connection-oriented service is therefore normally used.

The type of data link protocol used is a function of the physical separation of the two communicating DTEs and the bit rate of the link. For lower bit rate

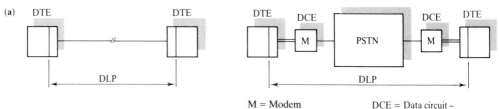

(a)

M = Modem

DCE = Data circuit –
terminating equipment

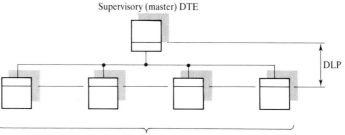

(b)

Supervisory (master) DTE

DLP

Slave DTEs

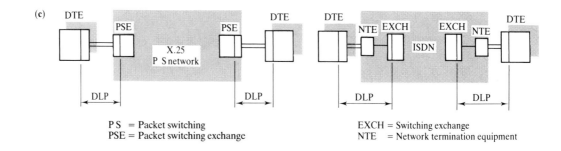

(c)

P S = Packet switching
PSE = Packet switching exchange

EXCH = Switching exchange
NTE = Network termination equipment

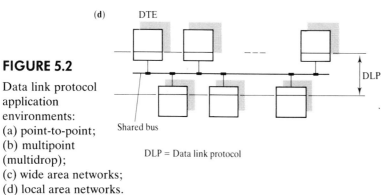

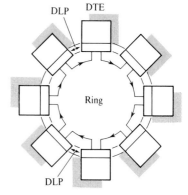

(d)

Shared bus

DLP = Data link protocol

Ring

DLP

FIGURE 5.2

Data link protocol
application
environments:
(a) point-to-point;
(b) multipoint
(multidrop);
(c) wide area networks;
(d) local area networks.

links such as those used with modems, a character-oriented idle RQ (stop and wait) protocol is often used. Examples of such protocols are **Kermit** and **X-modem**. Both are simple file transfer protocols that are used extensively for PC-to-PC communications. They are thus very similar to the basic idle RQ protocol described in the last chapter.

For higher bit rate links, and especially those involving long physical separations such as radio-based satellite links or circuits through private multiplexer networks, the alternative (and more efficient) continuous RQ protocol known as **high-level data link control** or **HDLC** is used. This is a bit-oriented protocol and can be used in many different operational modes.

The application architecture shown in part (b) of the figure is known as a **multipoint** or **multidrop topology**. As can be seen, a single transmission line – known as a **bus** or **data highway** – is used to connect all the computers together. Hence a means must be employed to ensure that all transmissions are carried out in a controlled way and no two transmissions occur simultaneously. Such architectures are normally used in applications that involve a single **master (supervisory) computer** communicating with a distributed community of **slave computers**. Examples are a **back-of-store computer** controlling a distributed set of point-of-sale terminals (computers) in a department store or a supervisory computer in a process plant controlling a distributed community of intelligent (computer-based) instruments. All transmissions are between the master and a selected slave computer, so the master controls the order of all transmissions.

In order to control access to the shared transmission medium in an equitable way, a connection-oriented data link protocol is used. Earlier protocols for use with such architectures are based on a development of the character-oriented idle RQ protocol known as **binary synchronous control (BSC)** or **bisync**. More recent implementations are based on one of the alternative operating modes of the bit-oriented HDLC protocol known as **normal response mode** or **NRM**. Both bisync and NRM operate in a **poll-select mode** in which when the master wishes to receive data from a slave it sends the slave a **poll message**, and if it wants to send data to, it sends a **select message.**

The two architectures shown in part (c) of the figure both relate to applications involving switched wide-area data networks. In the first example, the link protocol has only local significance and operates between the DTE and the local data circuit-terminating equipment (DCE), as in an **X.25 packet-switching network**. The X.25 protocol set used with such networks applies only to the local link between the DTE and DCE. The data link protocol with X.25 is also based on HDLC and is known as **link access procedure, balanced** or **LAPB**.

The second arrangement is used with circuit-switched data networks such as an ISDN. Once a circuit (connection) has been set-up through the network it provides the equivalent of a point-to-point link – known as a virtual circuit – for the data transfer phase. The protocol can be either connection-oriented (reliable) or connectionless (best-try) – known as **frame switching** and **frame relay**, respectively. In addition, the call set-up procedure associated with ISDN is carried out using a separate link known as the **signalling** or **D channel**. This uses a link protocol which is a variation of HDLC known as **link access procedure, D channel** or **LAPD**.

Finally, the two configurations shown in part (d) of the figure relate to applications involving **local area networks** or **LANs**. A feature of such networks is the use of relatively short, low bit error rate links that operate at high bit rates (~ 10 Mbps). The overall result is that errors are relatively infrequent and the end-to-end frame transfer time is very fast. Such networks, therefore, normally operate in a connectionless, best-try mode. In this mode, all retransmission and flow control functions are left to a higher protocol layer in the two end systems (DTEs). The link protocol used with LANs is a subclass of HDLC known as **logical link control** or **LLC**.

In summary, a range of data link protocols are available, each of which is intended for use in a particular application environment.

5.3 CHARACTER-ORIENTED PROTOCOLS

Character-oriented protocols are in use in both point-to-point and multipoint applications. They are characterized by the use of selected transmission control characters to perform the various transmission control functions associated with link management, start-of-frame and end-of-frame delimiting, error control and data transparency.

In the discussions relating to character-oriented protocols in the last chapter, a point-to-point data link and a simplex (undirectional) flow of information frames was considered to introduce the various issues relating to link protocols. In most practical applications, however, it is necessary to extend the concepts introduced to allow for data (information) to be transferred in both directions. Also, if more than two communicating parties are involved in a multipoint configuration, a method is needed for controlling access to the shared transmission medium. All of these issues will be addressed as the different protocols are discussed.

5.3.1 Simplex protocols

This class of protocol is the simplest since it allows just a simplex – one direction only – transfer of data from one computer (DTE) to another over a point-to-point data link. It is thus used with the topologies shown in Figure 5.2(a). A typical application is the transfer of data files from one computer to another. One of the most widely used protocols for this function is **Kermit** and hence this will be considered as an example.

Kermit is used extensively for the transfer of the contents of a specified file or group of files from one computer – for example, a personal computer – to another over a point-to-point data link. The link can be either a circuit set-up through the switched telephone network using modems or a pair of twisted-pair lines with appropriate line drivers and receivers. Normally synchronous transmission is used. It is a practical example of the idle RQ (stop-and-wait) protocol described in the last chapter.

There are a number of versions of Kermit that allow it to be used to transfer files either between two personal (single-user) computers or between a personal computer and a file server or mainframe computer. The basic file transfer mechanism associated with each version is the same, however. The main differences are associated with how the user of the source computer gains access – through the Kermit program – to the Kermit program in the destination machine at start-up. The version used for the transfer of files between two single-user computers will be considered for descriptive purposes.

A simple set of commands is available to the two users after the Kermit programs have been run in both systems. These are shown in the time sequence diagram of Figure 5.3.

If modems are being used then one modem must be set into the **originate mode** and the other the **answer mode**. Both modems must of course be set to operate at the same baud rate. Each user runs the Kermit program and then enters the CONNECT command, resulting in a physical link being setup between the two systems. The user in the system that wants to receive a file (or files) then enters the RECEIVE command and the user in the sending system the SEND command followed by the file name. Kermit in the sending system then transfers the file(s) in its (their) entirety. As each file segment is transferred, a message is output on both user screens. After all file segments have been transferred, both users exit Kermit and return to the local operating system

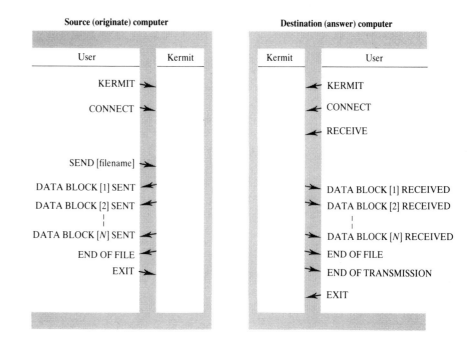

FIGURE 5.3

Kermit user commands.

(a)

SOH = Marks start of a frame
LEN = The number of characters/bytes in the frame following
this character up to and including BCC. The number is
encoded in excess-32 notation using a single character in
the range from ASCII # (decimal 35) to ASCII ~
(decimal 126) where # indicates a length of 3 (no data)
and ~ indicates the maximum length of 91
SEQ = The send sequence number of the frame. The sequence
number is incremented modulo-64 and is again encoded
as a single character in the range ASCII SP (decimal 32)
for zero to ASCII _ (decimal 95) for 63
TYPE = The type of frame encoded using a single character:
S = Send initiation (parameters)
F = Filename
D = File data
Z = End of file
B = End of transaction
Y = Acknowledgement (ACK)
N = Negative acknowledgement (NAK)
E = Fatal error
Data = Frame contents
BCC = Block check character
CR = End of block marker (ASCII carriage return)

FIGURE 5.4

Kermit operation:
(a) frame format and
types.

by giving an EXIT command. To transfer files in the opposite direction, the
order of the commands is reversed.

It can be seen that Kermit is not simply a data link protocol since it
performs a number of additional functions such as file reading/writing and file
segmentation and reassembly. It also has frame types associated with each of
these functions as can be seen from the standard frame format shown in
Figure 5.4(a).

There are two main differences between the frame format used with
Kermit and those discussed in the last chapter. Firstly, a length character is used
to specify the length of each frame instead of an ETX transmission control
character, and secondly, information (data) and ACK and NAK frames all have
the same basic format. Also, an additional (redundant) control character –
carriage return (CR) – is used at the end of each frame. The use of a length
character has the added benefit that the frame (and hence file) contents can be
either text characters or binary bytes since the receiver simply receives and
appends the appropriate number of characters or bytes (as specified in the frame
header) as the file is being reassembled. Normally the user in the receiving
computer either knows the file type or can deduce it from the name.

The contents of a text file are sent as a sequence of 80 character blocks
each terminated by a pair of carriage-return/line-feed characters. Binary files,
however, are sent simply as a string of 8-bit bytes. Any format control characters

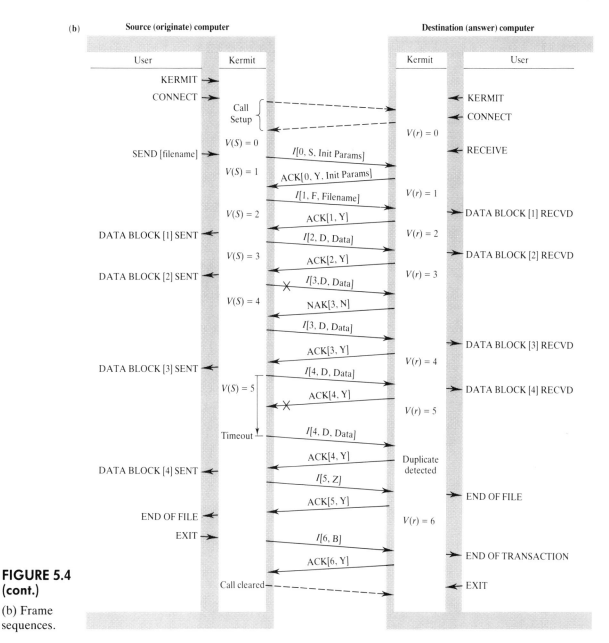

FIGURE 5.4 (cont.)

(b) Frame sequences.

in the file contents – text or binary – are encoded prior to transmission to ensure that they do not affect the state of the communication equipment during transfer. This is a feature of the flow control operation of some modems. Each control character detected is converted into a two-character printable character sequence consisting of a control prefix character – ASCII # – followed by the

ASCII printable character that is in the same row of the ASCII table and either column 4 or 5 corresponding to columns 0 or 1, respectively. Thus Ctrl-A becomes #A, CR becomes #M and FS becomes #\. Any # characters are preceded by an additional #.

The sequence of frames exchanged by the Kermit protocol entities to transfer a file are shown in Figure 5.4(b). The first information frame sent prior to initiating the transfer of a file is a send-invitation (S) frame. It includes a list of parameters associated with the protocol, such as the maximum frame length and the timeout interval to be used for retransmission. The receiver returns an acknowledgement (Y) frame with the agreed transmission control parameters.

The sender then proceeds to transfer the file contents. First a file header (F) frame containing the file name is sent, followed by a sequence of data (D) frames containing the frame contents. After the last data frame in the file has been sent, the receiver is informed by sending an end-of-file (Z) frame. Other files can then be sent in the same way. Finally, when all file transfers have been carried out, the source sends an end-of-transaction (B) frame.

As indicated, Kermit is an idle RQ protocol. Hence, after sending each information (I) frame, the source waits until it receives either a positive acknowledgement (Y) frame — BCC correct – or a negative acknowledgement (N) frame – BCC incorrect. Also, to allow for the possibility of either of the these two frames being corrupted, a timer is started each time a new frame is sent. The send sequence number in each I-frame increments modulo-64 and the receive sequence number in each ACK (Y) and NAK (N) frame carries the same sequence number as the I-frame being positively, or negatively, acknowledged.

The features described are the minimum features associated with Kermit. The reader should refer to the bibliography relating to this chapter for books containing a more detailed coverage.

5.3.2 Half-duplex protocols

Most character-oriented protocols operate in the half-duplex, stop-and-wait mode. Large computer manufacturers frequently have their own versions which differ slightly. Probably the best known is that developed by IBM and known as **binary synchronous control**, often shortened to **Bisync** or **BSC**. As it is the basis of the ISO character-oriented protocol known as **Basic Mode**, BSC will be used as an example.

As the name implies, it is normally used with a synchronous transmission control scheme. It is a connection-oriented protocol and is used primarily in multipoint (multidrop) applications in which there is a single master station (computer) which controls all message transfers to and from a community of slave stations. The slave stations are connected to the master by either a **multipoint network** if all the stations are located in different establishments and modems are being used, or a **multidrop bus network** if all the stations are at the same site and line drivers/receivers are being used. The two configurations are shown in Figure 5.5(a) and (b).

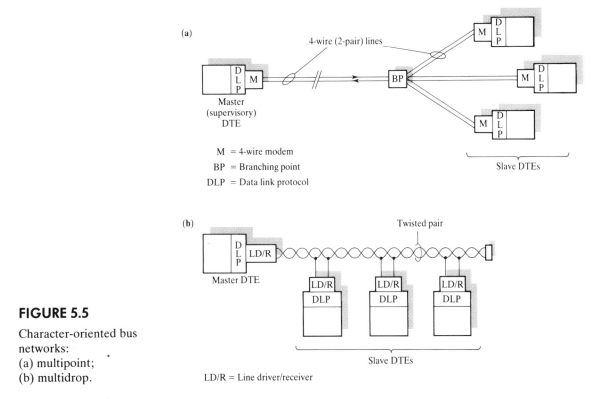

FIGURE 5.5

Character-oriented bus
networks:
(a) multipoint;
(b) multidrop.

Frame formats

It may be recalled that to perform the various functions associated with link management, control frames are needed in addition to normal information (data carrying) frames (blocks). Also, that with character-oriented synchronous transmission the receiver must be able to achieve both character (byte) and frame synchronization.

With BSC, these functions are carried out using selected EBCDIC (or ASCII/IAS with Basic Mode) transmission control characters. The role of some of these characters was described in the last chapter. A more complete list together with their functions, is given in Table 5.1.

The different types of information frame – known as data blocks in BSC – are shown in Figure 5.6(a). As indicated, BSC uses character-oriented synchronous transmission and hence all data (and control) blocks transmitted are preceded by at least two SYN characters to allow the receiver to achieve character synchronization. Short user messages (less than the defined maximum length) are transmitted in a single data block while longer messages are transmitted in multiple blocks. The header field, when present, is for general use and normally defines how the data field is to be interpreted. In addition, with Basic Mode a single **block check character (BCC)** is used after the end-of-block

Table 5.1 Transmission control characters used with BSC.

Character	Function
SOH (TC1)	Start of header: used to indicate the start of the header (if one is present) of an information frame (block)
STX (TC2)	Start of text: used both to terminate a header (if one is present) and to signal the start of a text string
ETX (TC3)	End of text: used to signal the end of a text string
EOT (TX4)	End of transmission: used to indicate the end of the transmission of one or more text (information) blocks and to terminate (clear) the connection
ENQ (TC5)	Enquiry: used as a request for a response from a remote station – the response may include the identity and/or status of the station
ACK (TC6)	Acknowledge: positive acknowledgement transmitted by a receiver in response to a message from the sender
DLE (TC7)	Data link escape: used to change the meaning of other selected transmission control characters
NAK (TC8)	Negative acknowledge: negative response transmitted by a receiver to a message from the sender
SYN (TC9)	Synchronous idle: used to provide the means for a receiver to achieve or retain (idle condition) character synchronization with a synchronous transmission control scheme
ETB (TC10)	End of transmission block: used to indicate the end of a block of data when a message is divided into a number of such blocks (frames)

delimiter (ETX or ETB) which is a longitudinal (column) parity check (see Chapter 3). It starts the check with the STX character and ends with the particular end-of-block delimiter character being used. As parity has only limited error detection capabilities, BSC often uses a two-character (byte) CRC computed using CRC–16 instead of a single BCC. Both schemes set a limit on the number of characters allowed in each transmitted data block. This is determined by the bit error rate of the link being used, the maximum block size being chosen to ensure that most blocks are received error free. Longer messages are then transmitted as a sequence of shorter fixed-sized data blocks, each terminated with an ETB control character. The last data block of such a sequence terminates with an ETX control character.

The different control frames associated with the BSC protocol are shown in part (b) of Figure 5.6. The ACK and NAK control characters have two functions:

- as an acknowledgement: one or other is returned in response to a previously transmitted data block and hence contains an identifier (sequence number);

- as a response to a select control message: an ACK indicates that the selected station is able to receive a data block whereas a NAK indicates that it is not.

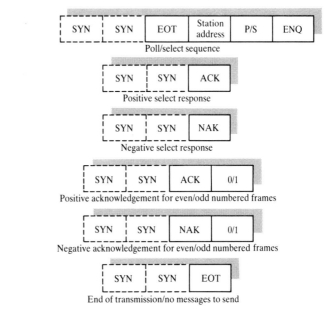

FIGURE 5.6

BSC block/frame formats: (a) data; (b) supervisory.

The ENQ control character is used in both poll and select control frames. The address of the polled or selected slave station is followed by either a P (for poll) or an S (for select) character, which is in turn followed by the ENQ character.

Finally, the EOT control character has two functions:

- to signal the end of a complete message exchange sequence and clear the logical link between the two communicating parties;

- to provide a means of resetting the link to the idle state.

Data transparency

The use of the DLE character to achieve data transparency when transmitting pure binary data rather than character strings was described in Chapter 3. Essentially, the various framing character sequences shown in Figure 5.6 are modified to be DLE/STX, DLE/ETX, etc. Also, whenever the transmitter detects a binary pattern corresponding to a DLE character in the text, it adds (inserts) an extra DLE. The receiver performs a similar check. Whenever the receiver detects two consecutive DLEs, it removes the inserted DLE before passing the data on for further processing.

A further difference when operating in the transparent mode is concerned with error control. Under normal operation, the eighth bit of each transmitted character is used as a parity bit and hence features in the error-detection procedure. Consequently, if a block contains a transparent sequence of 8-bit binary values, this cannot be used. Hence, when transmitting binary data in the transparent mode, an alternative error-detection procedure is normally used. Instead of a simple 8-bit longitudinal parity check per block, a more sophisticated polynomial code is used. Each block is thus terminated by a 16-bit CRC rather than an 8-bit BCC.

Protocol operation

As was described earlier, the master computer (station) is responsible for scheduling all transmissions on each shared data link. The poll control message is used to request a specific slave computer to send any waiting data message it may have; the select control message is used to ask the selected slave whether it is ready to receive a data message.

Figure 5.7(a) shows a typical poll and select sequence. A typical sequence of frames exchanged on a multidrop line is shown in parts (b) and (c). Part (b) shows both a successful and an unsuccessful sequence associated with a select operation while part (c) shows two sequences associated with a poll operation.

To select a particular slave station, the master station sends an ENQ select control message with the address of the slave station preceding the ENQ character. Assuming the selected station is ready to receive a message, it responds with an ACK control message. The master station then sends the message either as a single data block (as shown in the figure) or as a sequence of data blocks with the last block terminating with an ETX character. As each data block is received and stored, the slave station recomputes the parity check sequence and, assuming there are no transmission errors, responds with an ACK control message for each block. Finally, after the complete message has been sent, the master station sends an EOT control message, which terminates the message transfer and clears the logical connection.

In some situations, when selecting a station it is not always necessary to wait for an acknowledgement to the ENQ control message before sending a message. For example, if a station has been selected previously and the logical connection has not been closed. In such cases the master station sends the

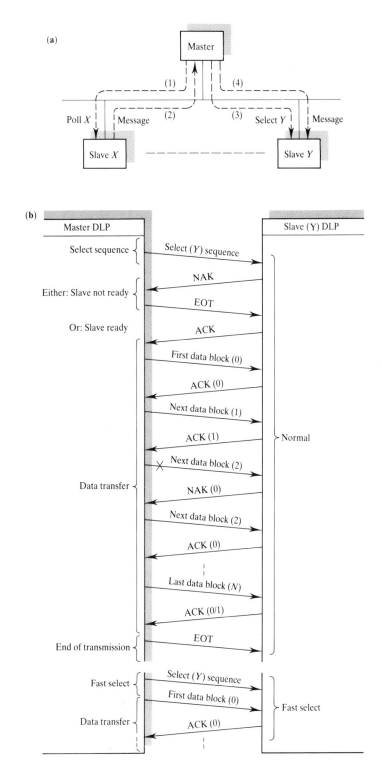

FIGURE 5.7

BSC frame sequences:
(a) poll-select
schematic; (b) select.

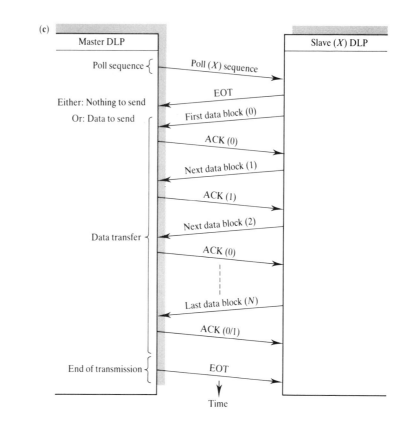

FIGURE 5.7 (cont.)

(c) Poll.

message immediately after the select control message, without waiting for an ACK (or NAK) response. This is known as a **fast select sequence**.

During the polling phase, the master station first sends an ENQ poll control message with the address of the polled slave station preceding the ENQ character. Then, assuming the polled station has a message awaiting transmission, it responds by sending the message. On receipt of the data block, the master station recomputes the parity check sequence and, assuming no transmission errors, acknowledges its correct receipt. Finally, after the complete message has been transferred and acknowledged, the logical connection is cleared with an EOT control message.

Figure 5.7 illustrates the fact that BSC is an idle RQ protocol because, after sending each data block, the transmitter waits for either an ACK or a NAK control message before sending the next block and, in the latter case, retransmits the corrupted block. The use of an additional NAK control message ensures that a corrupted data block will be retransmitted on receipt of the NAK message rather than after the timeout interval. As was described in Chapter 4, if the transmitted block is completely corrupted, an additional timeout mechanism is required to ensure that the affected block is retransmitted. The identifier (send sequence number) is then used to enable the receiver to detect duplicates.

Note that in BSC the send sequence number simply increments up (modulo an agreed number), whereas the receive sequence number in ACK and NAK frames simply increments modulo-2 (0 or 1). As a result, a receive sequence number of 0 refers to even numbered frames while 1 refers to odd numbered frames. Since only a single duplicate frame is possible, this is sufficient to enable the receiver to detect them.

User interface

It is important to discriminate between the services provided by the link layer and the detailed operation of the link-layer protocol entity. To illustrate this, the relationship between the user services and the various message blocks (control and data) associated with the BSC protocol are shown in Figure 5.8(a) and (b). As can be seen, the initial select control message is acknowledged and hence this is used as a confirmation that the remote station is ready to accept a message. With the poll sequence, however, an ACK is not returned in response to the initial poll message and so the confirm primitive has to be generated by the local protocol entity after the poll message has been transmitted. A similar procedure is also followed with the link disconnection procedure.

In common with the Kermit protocol, BSC performs a segmentation and reassembly function. Hence, on receipt of a L_DATA.request primitive (with the message as a parameter), the sending protocol entity segments the message into a sequence of data blocks for transmission. Similarly, the receiving entity reassembles the blocks into a complete message before passing it to the user using an L_DATA.indication primitive.

Because BSC is effectively a half-duplex protocol, BSC cannot exploit full-duplex transmission even if it is supported by the physical link. Nevertheless, as it needs minimal buffer storage facilities, it is still widely used for networks of the type considered. However, in recent years there has been a shift towards the more flexible and potentially more efficient bit-oriented protocols. This is certainly the case for computer networks which require transparent working.

Protocol performance

The basic link efficiency (utilization) achieved with the idle RQ protocol was discussed in the last chapter. However, the major use of BSC is in applications where there is a single master (primary) station which sends and receives messages to and from multiple slave (secondary) stations. An important additional performance parameter with such configurations is the average time taken to poll or select all the slave stations on a link.

In practice, because of the low-link utilization of idle RQ relative to continuous RQ, idle RQ protocols are used primarily with multidrop links operating at data rates of up to, say, 64 kbps. In such links, the time taken to transmit a message is the dominant time in a poll or select sequence. For example, if an average message is 1000 bits and the data rate is 10 kbps, the time

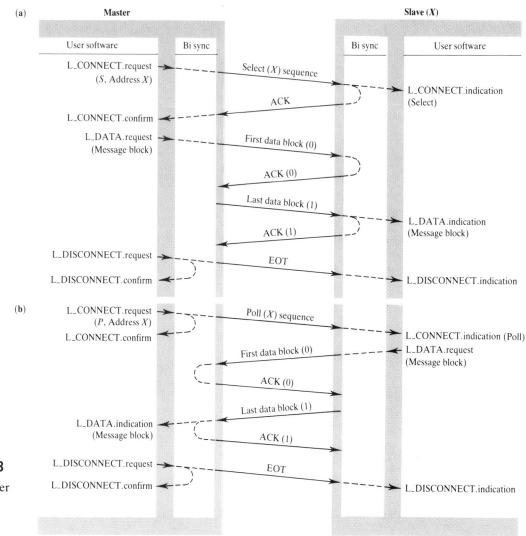

FIGURE 5.8

User/link layer
interactions:
(a) select;
(b) poll.

required to transmit a message is 0.1s. In contrast, the control messages
associated with a poll (or select) sequence are short (say 30 bits), so the time to
transmit these messages is also short (0.003s at 10kbps). Even allowing a small
additional time of, say, 0.001s to process these messages, the total time for each
poll (or select) sequence (0.004s) is still small compared with the message
transmission time.

In the absence of any messages to send, the minimum time required to
poll all secondaries is N times the time taken to poll a single secondary, where N
is the number of secondaries on the link. As messages become ready to transmit,
the average time to poll all secondaries increases and depends on the average
rate at which messages are generated. Clearly, the maximum poll time occurs

when the average rate at which messages are generated approaches the link bit rate since, beyond this rate, the link becomes overloaded and delays progressively increase.

In general, the average time to poll each secondary can be expressed as:

$$T_{avr} = \frac{T_{min}}{1 - M_r T_{ix}}$$

where T_{min} is the minimum time to poll all secondaries, M_r is the average rate at which messages are generated and T_{ix} is the time to transmit an average-sized message. If M_r is low compared with T_{ix}, then T_{avr} is approximately T_{min}; as M_r increases, however, so does T_{avr}.

EXAMPLE

A BSC protocol is to be used to control the flow of messages between a computer (master station) and ten block-mode terminals (secondaries) over a multipoint data link. The link data rate is 10 kbps and the average length of a message is 1000 bits. If a poll message and its associated ACK is 30 bits and the total time to process these messages is 1 ms, determine the average time each terminal will be polled if the average rate at which messages are generated is:

(a)   one message per minute

(b)   six messages per second.

The bit error rate and signal propagation delay times of the link can be assumed to be negligible.

The time to transmit an average message is:

$$\frac{N_i}{R} = \frac{1000}{10^4} = 100\,\text{ms}$$

The time to transmit a poll and its ACK is:

$$\frac{30}{10^4} = 3\,\text{ms}$$

The time to poll a single secondary is:

$$3 + 1 = 4\,\text{ms}$$

The minimum time to poll all secondaries is:

$$T_{min} = 10 \times 4 = 40\,\text{ms}$$

Now:

$$T_{avr} = \frac{T_{min}}{1 - M_r T_{ix}}$$

(a) M_r = one message per minute = $\dfrac{10^{-3}}{60}$ messages/ms. Hence:

$$T_{avr} = \frac{40}{1 - \dfrac{10^{-3}}{60} \times 100} = 40\,\text{ms}$$

(b) M_r = six messages per second = 6×10^{-3} messages/ms. Hence:

$$T_{avr} = \frac{40}{1 - 6 \times 10^{-3} \times 100} = \frac{40}{0.4} = 100\,\text{ms}$$

5.3.3 Duplex protocols

A few character-oriented protocols operate in a (full) duplex mode. As an example, the data link protocol used in the early **ARPANET** network to control the flow of information frames across the links connecting the internal network switching nodes – known as **interface message processors (IMPs)** – will be considered. The protocol thus operates over the point-to-point duplex links that connect two switching nodes.

The protocol supports the transmission of information frames in both directions simultaneously – duplex – and utilizes a continuous RQ transmission control scheme for both directions. It operates with an effective send window of either eight for terrestrial links or sixteen for satellite links. To ensure a continuous flow of frames, eight (or sixteen for satellite) separate stop-and-wait information flows can be in progress at any instant.

To achieve this, the single physical link is operated as eight (or sixteen) separate **logical links**, the flow of frames over each link being controlled by its own stop-and-wait protocol machine. The send sequence number in the header of each frame transmitted on the physical link is thus a concatenation of two fields: a single-bit sequence number – 0 or 1 – which is the normal send sequence number associated with the idle RQ (send-and-wait) protocol, and a **logical channel number (LCN)** which indicates the logical channel to which the frame relates.

In common with most duplex schemes, character-oriented and bit-oriented, acknowledgement information relating to the flow of information frames flowing in one direction is **piggybacked** in the header of information frames flowing in the reverse direction. Thus a single type of frame is used and the various fields in its header relate to a specific function. The general frame format and the fields in the header that are associated with the data link protocol are shown in Figure 5.9, together with the general operation of the protocol.

To support a duplex flow of frames, the forward and reverse physical links both support eight (or sixteen) logical links. Thus, for each logical channel, the data link protocol at each side of the link maintains a separate send and receive sequence variable. The send sequence variable – 0 or 1 – is the send sequence number that will be assigned to the next new frame to be transmitted on the

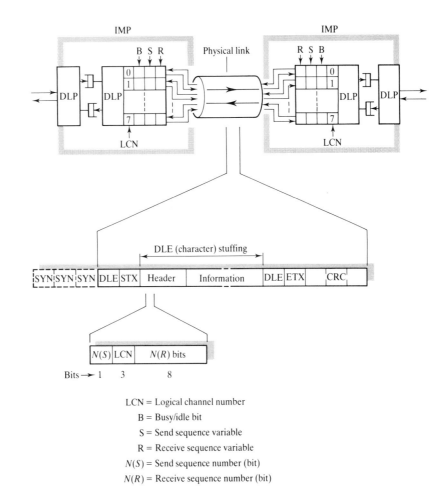

FIGURE 5.9

ARPANET IMP-to-
IMP data link protocol
detail.

LCN = Logical channel number

B = Busy/idle bit

S = Send sequence variable

R = Receive sequence variable

$N(S)$ = Send sequence number (bit)

$N(R)$ = Receive sequence number (bit)

forward channel, while the receive sequence variable is the sequence number of
the next information frame expected to be received on the reverse channel. In
addition, to ensure each forward channel operates in a stop-and-wait mode, each
side also has a busy/idle bit associated with each channel that indicates whether
the channel is busy, that is, an acknowledgement is still outstanding on this
channel.

Within the ARPANET network, each frame is treated as a separate
entity, that is, the frames relating to the same (user) message are treated
independently. Hence, on receipt of a frame to be forwarded, the sending data
link protocol simply scans the busy/idle bit associated with each logical channel
to determine whether a channel is free and, if so, inserts the appropriate send
sequence number – 0 or 1 – and logical channel number in the frame header,
starts a timer for the frame and initiates its transmission. If a channel is not free,
the frame is left in the input queue to wait for a free channel.

The protocol uses a 24-bit (3 byte) CRC for error detection. Error correction uses an acknowledgement byte in the header of each frame. The eight bits are a concatenation of the eight receive sequence numbers relating to the flow of frames in the eight logical channels of the reverse path. On receipt of a frame, the data link protocol reads the acknowledgement byte and, for all active channels, interprets the corresponding bit according to the idle RQ protocol described in the last chapter. In this way, acknowledgement information relating to all channels is received every time a new frame is received. This has the same effect as utilizing a send window of eight (or sixteen) for the link. Also, it means that an implicit acknowledgement scheme – ACK only – can be used.

In conclusion, although many character-oriented protocols are still widely used, the availability of inexpensive integrated circuits that support the more efficient bit-oriented protocols means that all new (and many current) protocols are of the bit-oriented type.

5.4 BIT-ORIENTED PROTOCOLS

All new data link protocols are bit-oriented protocols. As may be recalled, such protocols use defined bit patterns rather than transmission control characters to signal the start and end of a frame. The receiver searches the received bit stream on a bit-by-bit basis for the known start and end of frame bit pattern. Three methods of signalling the start and end of a frame – known as **frame delimiting** – were shown in Figure 3.12. These were:

- unique start and end of frame bit patterns, known as flags (01111110), together with zero bit insertion;

- a unique start of frame bit pattern, known as the start delimiter (10101011), and a length (byte) count in the header at the start of the frame;

- unique start and end of frame delimiters that include bit **encoding viola-tions.**

In general, the first is used with the **high-level data link control** or **HDLC** protocol while the other two are used with the **logical link control** or **LLC** protocol. In practice, all the bit-oriented protocols are derivates of the HDLC protocol and hence this will be described first.

5.4.1 High-level data link control

The HDLC protocol is an international standard that has been defined by ISO for use on both point-to-point and multipoint (multidrop) data links. It supports full-duplex, transparent-mode operation and is now extensively used in both multipoint and computer networks. Although the acronym HDLC is now widely accepted, a number of large manufacturers and other standards bodies still use

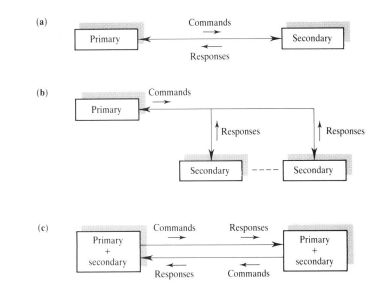

FIGURE 5.10

Alternative HDLC network configuration: (a) point-to-point with single primary and secondary; (b) multipoint with single primary and multiple secondary; (c) point-to-point with two primaries and two secondaries.

their own acronym. These include IBM's **SDLC (synchronous data link control)**, which was the forerunner of HDLC, and **ADCCP** (advanced data communications control procedure), which is used by the American National Standards Institute (ANSI).

Because HDLC has been defined as a general purpose data link control protocol, it can be used in a number of different network configurations. These are shown in Figure 5.10. In HDLC, the frames sent by the primary station to the secondary station are known as **commands** and those from the secondary to the primary as **responses**. The two configurations shown in parts (a) and (b) have a single primary station and are known as **unbalanced configurations** while that in part (c) has two primary stations and is known as a **balanced configuration**. In the third configuration, since each station has both a primary and a secondary, they are also known as **combined stations**.

HDLC has three operational modes:

(1) **Normal Response Mode (NRM)**: this is used in unbalanced configurations. In this mode, slave stations (or secondaries) can only transmit when specifically instructed by the master (primary) station. The link may be point-to-point or multipoint. In the latter case only one primary station is allowed.

(2) **Asynchronous Response Mode (ARM)**: this is also used in unbalanced configurations. It allows a secondary to initiate a transmission without receiving permission from the primary. This is normally used with point-to-point configurations and duplex links and allows the secondary to send frames asynchronously with respect to the primary.

(3)   **Asynchronous balanced mode (ABM)**: this is used mainly on duplex point-to-point links for computer-to-computer communication and for connections between, say, a computer and a packet switched data network. In this mode, each station has an equal status and performs both primary and secondary functions. It is the mode used in the protocol set known as X.25 which will be described in a later chapter.

Frame Formats

Unlike BSC, using HDLC both data and control messages are carried in a standard format frame. This format is shown in Figure 5.11 together with the different frame types that are defined in the control field of the frame header. Three classes of frame are used in HDLC:

(1)   **Unnumbered frames**: these are used for such functions as link set-up and disconnection. The name derives from the fact that they do not contain any acknowledgement information, which is contained in sequence numbers.

(2)   **Information frames**: these carry the actual information or data and are normally referred to simply as I-frames. I-frames can be used to piggyback acknowledgement information relating to the flow of I-frames in the reverse direction when the link is being operated in ABM or ARM.

(3)   **Supervisory frames**: these are used for error and flow control and hence contain send and receive sequence numbers.

The use of the flag field as a start-of-frame and end-of-frame delimiter, together with zero bit insertion and deletion to achieve data transparency, was described in Chapter 3 and is not repeated here.

The frame check sequence (FCS) is a 16-bit cyclic redundancy check for the complete frame contents enclosed between the two flag delimiters. The generator polynomial used with HDLC is normally CRC–CCITT:

$$x^{16} + x^{12} + x^5 + 1$$

The FCS is generated by the procedure described in Chapter 3 enhanced by procedures to make the check more robust. An example is adding sixteen 1s to the tail of the dividend prior to division (instead of zeros) and inverting the remainder. This has the effect that the remainder computed by the receiver is not all zeros but a special bit pattern – 0001 1101 0000 1111.

The contents of the address field depend on the mode of operation. In NRM, as used on a multidrop line, for example, every secondary station is assigned a unique address. Whenever the primary station communicates with a secondary, the address field contains the address of the secondary. Certain addresses known as **group addresses** can be assigned to more than one secondary station. All frames transmitted with a group address are received by all stations in that group. Also, a **broadcast address** can be used to transmit a frame to all secondary stations on the link.

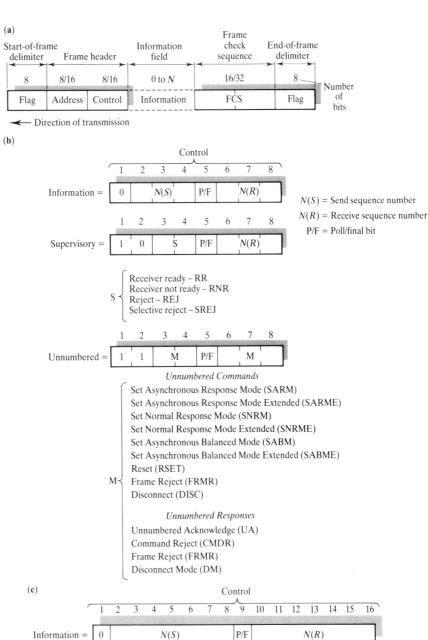

FIGURE 5.11

HDLC frame format and types: (a) standard/ extended format; (b) standard control field bit definitions; (c) extended control field bit definitions.

When a secondary station returns a response message (frame) to the primary, the address field always contains the unique address of that secondary. In the case of large networks containing a large number of secondaries, the address field may be extended beyond eight bits. The least significant bit (lsb) of each 8-bit field is then used to indicate whether there is another octet to follow (lsb = 0) or whether it is the last or only octet (lsb = 1). Note that the address field is not used in this way in ABM because only direct point-to-point links are involved. Instead, it is used to indicate the direction of commands and their associated responses.

The various control field bit definitions are defined in Figure 5.11(b). The S-field in supervisory frames and the M-field in unnumbered frames are used to define the specific frame type. The send and receive sequence numbers – N(S) and N(R) – are used in conjunction with the error and flow control procedures.

The **P/F bit** is known as the **poll/final bit**. A frame of any type is called a **command frame** if it is sent by the primary station and a **response frame** if it is sent by a secondary station. The P/F bit is called the poll bit when used in a command frame and, if set, indicates that the receiver must acknowledge this frame. The receiver acknowledges this frame by returning an appropriate response frame with the P/F bit set; it is then known as the final bit.

The use of three bits for N(S) and N(R) means that sequence numbers can range from 0 through 7. This, in turn, means that a maximum send window of seven can be selected. Although this is large enough for many applications, those involving very long links (satellite links, for example) or very high bit rates, require a larger send window if a high link utilization is to be achieved. The **extended format** uses seven bits (0 through 127), thereby increasing the maximum send window to 127.

The address field identifies the secondary station that sent the frame, and is therefore not needed with point-to-point links. With multipoint links, however, the address field can be either eight bits – normal mode – or multiples of eight bits – extended mode. In the latter case, bit 1 of the least significant address octet(s) is (are) set to 0 and bit 1 is set to 1 in the last octet. The remaining bits then form the address. In both modes, an address of all 1s is used as an all-stations broadcast address.

Frame types

Before describing the operation of the HDLC protocol, it is perhaps helpful to list some of the frame types and to outline their function. Three classes of frame are used. Some of the different types of frame in each class are listed in Figure 5.11(b).

Unnumbered frames are used for link management. SNRM and SABM frames, for example, are used both to set up a logical link between the primary and a secondary station and to inform the secondary station of the mode of operation to be used. A logical link is subsequently cleared by the primary station sending a DISC frame. The UA frame is used as an acknowledgement to the other frames in this class.

Although there are four types of supervisory frame, only RR and RNR are used in both NRM and ABM. These frames are used both to indicate the willingness or otherwise of a secondary station to receive an I-frame(s) from the primary station, and for acknowledgement purposes. REJ and SREJ frames are used only in ABM which permits simultaneous two-way communication across a point-to-point link. The two frames are used to indicate to the other station that a sequence error has occurred, that is, an I-frame containing an out-of-sequence N(S) has been received. The SREJ frame is used with a selective repeat transmission procedure, whereas the REJ frame is used with a go-back-N procedure.

Protocol operation

This section highlights some of the more important features of the HDLC protocol, rather than giving a full description of its operation. The two basic functions are link management and data transfer (including error and flow control).

Link management.   Before any information (data) may be transmitted, either between the primary and a secondary station on a multidrop link or between two stations connected by a point-to-point link, a logical connection between the two communicating parties must be established. This is accomplished by the exchange of two unnumbered frames, as shown in Figure 5.12.

In a multidrop link (Figure 5.12(b)), an SNRM frame is first sent by the primary station with the poll bit set to 1 and the address of the appropriate secondary in the address field. The secondary responds with a UA frame with the final bit set and its own address in the address field. As can be seen, the set-up procedure has the effect of initializing the sequence variables held by each station. These variables are used in the error and flow control procedures. Finally, after all data has been transferred, the link is cleared by the primary sending a DISC frame and the secondary responding with a UA.

The procedure followed to set up a point-to-point link is the same as that used for a multidrop link. In the example shown in Figure 5.12(b), however, ABM has been selected and hence an SABM frame is sent first. In this mode, both sides of the link may initiate the transfer of I-frames independently so each station is often referred to as a **combined station**, since it must act as both a primary and a secondary. Either station may initiate the setting up or clearing of the link in this mode. In the example, station A initiates link set-up while station B initiates the clearing of the (logical) connection. A single exchange of frames sets up the link in both directions. Also, as can be seen, the address field is used to indicate the direction of the command frame (SABM/DISC) and its associated response.

If the receiver wishes to refuse a set-up command in either mode, a disconnected mode (DM) frame is returned in response to the initial mode setting frame (SNRM or SABM). The DM frame indicates the responding station is logically disconnected.

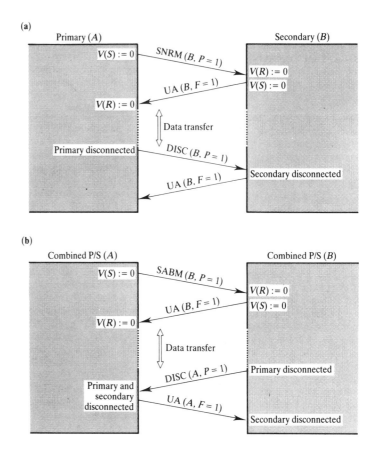

FIGURE 5.12

Link management procedure: (a) normal response mode – multipoint link; (b) asynchronous balanced mode – point-to-point link.

Data transfer. In NRM, all data (I-frames) is transferred under the control of the primary station. The unnumbered poll (UP) frame with the P bit set to 1 is normally used by the primary to poll a secondary. If the secondary has no data to transmit, it returns an RNR frame with the F bit set. If data is waiting, it transmits the data, typically as a sequence of I-frames, with the F bit set to 1 in the last frame of the sequence.

The two most important aspects associated with the data transfer phase are error control and flow control. Essentially, error control uses a continuous RQ procedure with either a selective repeat or a go-back-N retransmission strategy, while flow control is based on a window mechanism. The basic operation of both these procedures was described in Chapter 4 and hence only typical frame sequences will be given here to illustrate the use of the different frame types.

Figure 5.13(a) gives an example illustrating the basic acknowledgement and retransmission procedure; it only uses RR frames and assumes a go-back-N strategy. Only a undirectional flow of information frames is shown in the figure, so all acknowledgement information must be returned using specific acknowledgement supervisory frames. As can be seen, each side of the link maintains

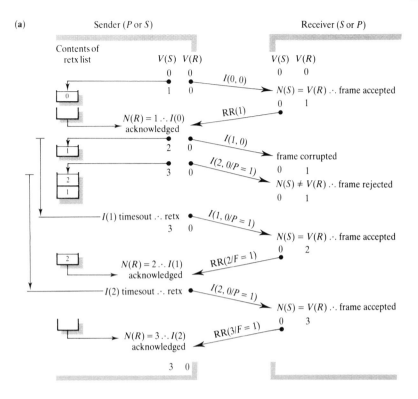

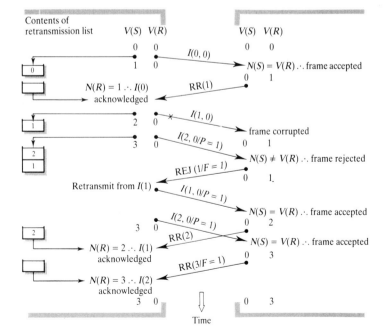

FIGURE 5.13

Use of acknowledgement frames: (a) positive acknowledgement (RR) only; (b) use of negative acknowledgement (REJ).

both a send and a receive sequence variable, respectively. The V(S) indicates the next send sequence number N(S) which is allocated to an I-frame transmitted by that station, and V(R) the send sequence number of the next in-sequence I-frame expected by that station.

Each RR (positive acknowledgement) supervisory frame contains a receive sequence number N(R) which acknowledges correct receipt of all previously transmitted I-frames up to and including that with an N(S) equal to [N(R) − 1]. Similarly, part (b) of the figure shows that each REJ (negative acknowledgement) supervisory frame contains an N(R) which indicates that an out-of-sequence I-frame has been received and the sender must start to retransmit from the I-frame with N(S) equal to N(R).

As can be seen from part (a), any I-frames received out of sequence are simply discarded. Hence on receipt of frame I(2, 0/P = 1) – the P bit set because the previous frame has not been acknowledged – it is discarded and no action is taken by the receiver. In the absence of acknowledgements, the timer associated with frames I(1) and I(2) will expire and hence both are retransmitted. The example assumes each is received correctly and hence is acknowledged using a RR frame.

In part (b), negative acknowledgement (REJ) frames are used. When the receiver detects that frame I(2, 0) – that is, the last frame in the sequence with P = 1 – is out of sequence, it returns an REJ frame with the F bit set. The sender then retransmits frames I(1, 0) and I(2, 0) with the P bit again set to 1 in frame I(2, 0). The receiver acknowledges correct receipt of each frame with the F bit set to 1 in the last RR frame. If selective retransmission were being used, then frame I(2, 0) would be accepted and an SREJ frame returned to request that frame I(1, 0) be retransmitted.

The frame sequence shown in Figure 5.13 is typical of information transfer over a multidrop link operating in NRM. However, for a point-to-point link in ABM, a bidirectional flow of I-frames is possible. Consequently, acknowledgement information relating to the flow of I-frames in one direction can be piggybacked in I-frames flowing in the reverse direction. An example illustrating this is given in Figure 5.14. For clarity, no transmission errors are shown.

As each I-frame is received, its N(S) and N(R) are both read. N(S) is first compared with the receiver's V(R). If they are equal, the frame is in the correct sequence and is accepted; if they were not equal, the frame would be discarded and an REJ or SREJ frame returned. N(R) is then examined and used to acknowledge any outstanding frames in the retransmission list. Finally, as no further I-frames are awaiting transmission, an RR frame is used to acknowledge the outstanding unacknowledged frames in each retransmission list.

Flow control is particularly important when two-way simultaneous working is used and the link is being operated in ABM. Clearly, with NRM, if the primary experiences transient overload conditions, it can simply suspend polling, thereby allowing the overload to subside. However, when both sides of the link are operating independently, an alternative mechanism must be used. The flow control procedure used in HDLC is based on a sliding window mechanism similar to that already discussed in Chapter 4.

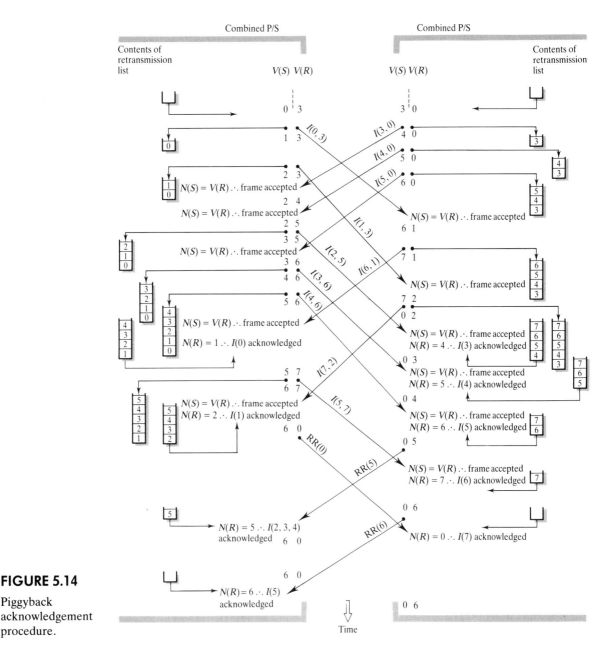

FIGURE 5.14

Piggyback acknowledgement procedure.

As has been seen in the examples, the send and receive sequence numbers are incremented modulo-8 so the maximum send window K that can be used is 7. Thus a maximum of 7 I-frames can be awaiting acknowledgement in the retransmission list at any time. Each side of the link maintains a separate variable known as the retransmission count (RetxCount) which is initialized to zero when the logical link is set up. It is incremented each time an I-frame is transmitted, and hence each time a frame is placed in the retransmission list, and is decremented whenever a positive acknowledgement is received, and hence each time a frame is removed from the retransmission list. The primary stops sending I-frames when the retransmission count reaches K and does not resume until a positive acknowledgement is received either as a separate RR supervisory frame or piggybacked in an I-frame flowing in the reverse direction. It can be concluded, therefore, that transmission of I-frames is stopped when:

$$V(S) = \text{last } N(R) \text{ received} + K$$

It should be noted that the window mechanism controls the flow of I-frames in only one direction and that supervisory and unnumbered frames are not affected by the mechanism. Hence, these frames can still be transmitted when the window is operating. An example illustrating this is shown in Figure 5.15; for clarity, only the flow of I-frames in one direction is affected.

The use of a window mechanism means that the sequence numbers in all incoming frames must lie within certain boundaries. On receipt of each frame, therefore, the secondary must check to establish that this is the case and, if not, take corrective action. It can be readily deduced that each received $N(S)$ and $N(R)$ must satisfy the following conditions:

(1) $N(R) - 1$ is less than or equal to $N(S)$ which is less then $V(R) + K$.

(2) $V(S)$ is greater than $N(R)$ which is greater than or equal to $V(S) - $ RetxCount.

Clearly, if $N(S)$ equals $V(R)$, then all is well and the frame is accepted. If $N(S)$ is not equal to $V(R)$ but is still within the range, then a frame has simply been corrupted and a REJ (go-back-N) or a SREJ (selective repeat) frame is returned, indicating to the primary that a sequence error has occurred and from which frame to start retransmission. This was illustrated in Figure 5.13.

If $N(S)$ or $N(R)$ is outside the range, however, then the sequence numbers at both ends of the link have become unsynchronized and the link must be reinitialized (set up). This is accomplished by the secondary, on detecting an out-of-range sequence number, discarding the received frame and returning a **frame reject (FRMR)** – ABM – or a **command reject (CMDR)** – NRM – frame to the primary. The latter discards all waiting frames and proceeds to set up the link again by sending an SABM/SNRM and waiting for a UA response. On receipt of this response, both sides of the link reset their sequence and window variables enabling the flow of I-frames to be resumed. In fact, this is only one reason why a link may be reset; another is the receipt of an unnumbered frame, such as a UA, during the data transfer phase which indicates that the primary and secondary have become unsynchronized.

The flow control procedure just outlined is controlled by the primary side of the link controlling the flow of I-frames according to the send window. In addition, it may be necessary for the secondary to stop the flow of I-frames as a

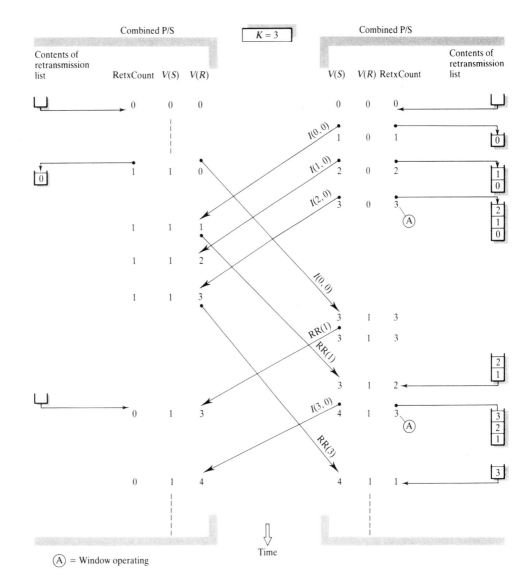

FIGURE 5.15

Window flow control procedure.

(A) = Window operating

result of some event occurring at its side of the link. For example, with a go-back-N retransmission strategy the receive window is 1 and it is reasonably straightforward to ensure that there are sufficient memory buffers available at the receiver. If selective retransmission is used, however, it is possible for the secondary to run out of free buffers to store any new frames. Hence, when the secondary approaches a point at which all its buffers are likely to become full, it returns an RNR supervisory frame to the primary to instruct the latter to stop sending I-frames. Acknowledgement frames are not affected, of course. When the number of full buffers drops below another preset limit, the secondary returns an RR frame to the primary with an N(R) indicating from which frame to restart transmission.

User interface

The relationship between the link layer user services shown earlier in Figure 5.1 and the various protocol message units associated with HDLC can now be established. These are shown in Figure 5.16.

On receipt of the initial L.CONNECT.request from the user, the link layer protocol entity in the calling system first sends an SNRM/SABM supervisory frame to the link layer protocol entity in the called system. On receipt of this frame, the latter creates and passes an L.CONNECT.indication primitive to the called user. In addition, it creates a UA frame and returns this to the calling side. When the calling side receives the UA frame it creates an L.CONNECT.confirm primitive and passes it to the user so that the transfer of user data can commence using the L.DATA service. Finally, after all data (information) has been exchanged, the link is disconnected using the DISC and UA supervisory frames.

A summary of the various service primitives and frame types (protocol data units) associated with HDLC is given in Figure 5.17(a). In practice, there

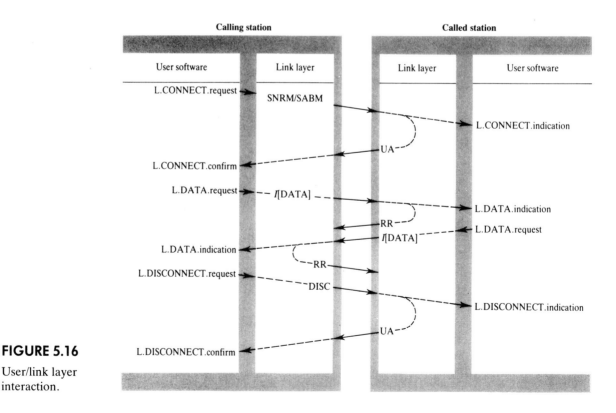

FIGURE 5.16

User/link layer interaction.

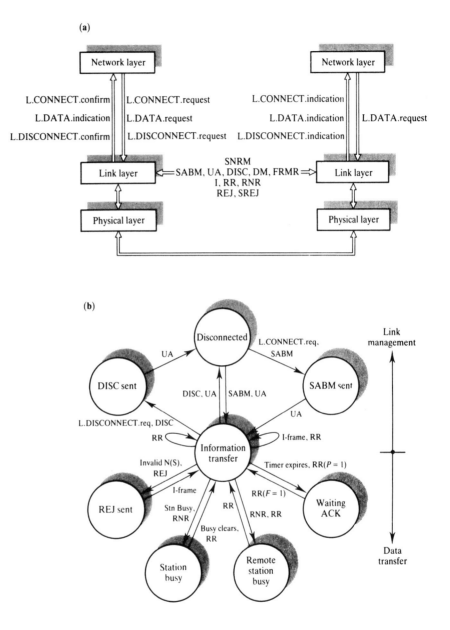

FIGURE 5.17

LAPB summary:
(a) service primitives;
(b) state transition
diagram (ABM).

are more unnumbered frames associated with HDLC than shown in the figure
but, as mentioned earlier, the aim is simply to highlight selected aspects of
HDLC operation. To further reinforce understanding, however, a (simplified)
state transition diagram for HDLC is given in Figure 5.17(b). The first entry
alongside each arc is the incoming event causing the transition (if any); the
second entry is the resulting action. Note that a state transition diagram shows
only the correct operation of the protocol entity and so normally would be

accompanied by a more complete definition in the form of an event–state table and/or pseudo-code.

5.4.2 Link access procedure balanced

Link access procedure balanced or **LAPB** is a subset of HDLC that is used to control the transfer of information frames across a point-to-point duplex data link that connects a computer to a public (or private) packet-switching network. Such networks are normally referred to as X.25 networks and will be discussed in more detail in the later chapter on wide area networks. LAPB is in fact an extended version of an earlier subset known simply as **link access procedure** or **LAP**.

The applicability of LAPB was shown earlier in Figure 5.2(c). The computer is the DTE and the packet switching exchange is known as the data circuit-terminating equipment or DCE. LAPB is used to control the transfer of information frames across the local DTE–DCE interface and is said, therefore, to have local significance.

LAPB uses asynchronous balanced mode with the DTE and DCE as combined stations and all information frames treated as command frames. The earlier LAP protocol used an asynchronous response mode and did not use REJ or RNR frames as command frames. A summary of the frames used with LAP and LAPB are given in Table 5.2. The RR and REJ frames are used for error control and RNR for flow control. It does not support selective repeat (SREJ). The example frame sequences shown in the earlier figures relating to the operation of HDLC thus apply directly to LAPB. As indicated, the sending of an information (command) frame with the P bit set results in the receiving station returning a supervisory frame with the F bit set. Either station can set up the link. To discriminate between the two stations, the DTE and DCE addresses used are as shown in Table 5.3. If a DTE that is not logically operational receives a set-up request frame (SABM/SABME), it must reply with a DM (disconnected mode) frame.

Table 5.2

Type	LAP		LAPB	
	Commands	Responses	Commands	Responses
Supervisory	RR	RR	RR	RR
		RNR	RNR	RNR
		REJ	REJ	REJ
Unnumbered	SARM	UA	SABM	UA
	DISC	CMDR	DISC	DM
				FRMR
Information	I		I	

Table 5.3

| | Addresses | |
Direction	Commands	Responses
DTE → DCE	01 Hex (B)	03 Hex (A)
DCE → DTE	03 Hex (A)	01 Hex (B)

A summary of the use of the P/F bit with LAPB is as follows:

Command frame sent with P = 1	Response frame returned with F = 1
SABM/SABME	UA/DM
I-frame	RR, REJ, RNR, FRMR
RR, REJ, RNR	RR, REJ, RNR, FRMR
DISC	UA/DM

It may be recalled that in the normal SABM mode a single octet is used for the control field. The send and receive sequence numbers are each three bits – eight sequence numbers – allowing a maximum send window of 7. If the extended mode (SABME) is selected, however, two octets are used for the control field. The send and receive sequence numbers are thus extended to seven bits – 128 sequence numbers – which in turn allows for a much larger window. This is used, for example, with very long links and/or high bit rate links.

Integrated circuits are now available that implement LAPB in firmware-preprogrammed memory. These are often referred to as X.25 circuits although they only implement the LAPB protocol rather than the full X.25 protocol set. The availability of these circuits, however, has significantly increased the use of LAPB for many additional computer-to-computer communication applications.

5.4.3 Multilink procedure

The foregoing described the use of HDLC for controlling the transfer of information frames across a single duplex link. It is thus known as a **single link procedure** or **SLP**. In some instances, however, the throughput (or reliability) available with just a single link is not sufficient to meet the requirements of the application, so multiple (physical) links must be used. To allow for this possibility, therefore, an extension to LAPB, known as **multilink procedure** or **MLP**, has been defined.

As can be seen in Figure 5.18(a), the transfer of frames across each physical link is controlled by a separate single link procedure in the way just described. The single MLP operates above these and simply treats them as a pool of links available to transfer user information. This means that the user

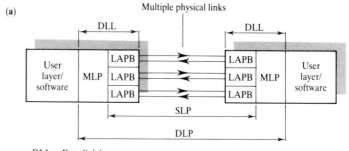

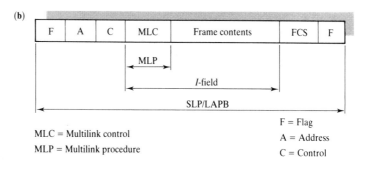

FIGURE 5.18

Multilink procedure:
(a) position in relation
to data link layer;
(b) frame format.

software is unaware of multiple physical links being used and is presented with a
single (logical) link interface as before.

As indicated, the MLP simply treats the set of single link procedures as a
pool of links over which to transfer user frames. It thus operates with its own set
of sequence numbers and error and flow control procedures which are independent of those being used by each SLP. Hence if an SLP becomes unoperational,
then the MLP will initiate the retransmission of frames in the normal way but
using the reduced set of links (SLPs) available.

To implement this scheme, the MLP adds an additional control field to
the head of each frame it receives for transmission prior to passing the frame to
an SLR. This is known as the **multilink control** field or **MLC** and is effectively
transparent to an SLP. The SLP treats the combined MLC and frame contents as
the information field and proceeds to add its own address (A) and control (C)
field as shown in part (b) of the figure. The error and flow control mechanisms
associated with MLP are essentially the same as those used with LAPB.

The multilink control field comprises two octets and contains a 12-bit
sequence number. This provides 4096 (0 through 4095) sequence numbers and
hence a maximum window size of 4095, allowing a significant number of links to
be used, each possibly operating at a high data rate. An example is when two

X.25 packet-switching networks are being connected together. This will be expanded upon in the later chapter on wide area networks.

5.4.4 Link access procedure for modems

Link access procedure for modems or **LAPM** is the protocol used in error correction modems, such as the **V.32 modem**. The latter accept asynchronous (start-stop) data from the DTE but transmit the data in frames using bit-oriented synchronous transmission and an HDLC-based error correcting protocol. The applicability of LAPM is shown in Figure 5.19(a).

Each modem comprises two functional units: a user (DTE) interface part – **UIP** – and an error correcting part – **ECP**. The LAPM protocol is associated with the latter while the UIP is concerned with the transfer of single characters/ bytes across the local V.24 interface and with the interpretation of any flow control signals across this interface.

The UIP communicates with the ECP using a defined set of service primitives, as shown in the time sequence diagram in part (b) of the figure. The different HDLC frame types used by the LAPM protocol machine to implement the various services are also shown.

Before establishing a (logical) link, the originating and responding ECPs must agree on the operational parameters to be used with the protocol. These parameters include the maximum number of octets in I-frames, the acknowledgement timer setting, the maximum number of retransmission attempts and the window size. Default values are associated with each of these, but if they are not used, the originating UIP must issue an L_SETPARM.request primitive with the desired operational parameter values. The values are negotiated by the two ECPs exchanging two special unnumbered frames, known as **exchange identification** or **XID**, one as a command and the other as a response.

Once the operational parameters have been agreed, a link can then be set-up by the UIP issuing an L_ESTABLISH.request primitive. This, in turn, results in an SABM (normal) or SABME (extended) supervisory frame being sent by the ECP. The receiving ECP then issues an L_ESTABLISH.indication primitive to its local UIP and, on receipt of the response primitive, returns a UA frame. On receipt of this frame, the originating ECP issues a confirm primitive and the (logical) link is now set-up. Data transfer can then be initiated using the L_DATA service.

Typically, the UIP first assembles a block of data, comprising characters or bytes received over the V.24 interface, then passes the complete block to the ECP using a L_DATA.request primitive. The ECP packs the data into the information field of an I-frame as a string of octets and transfers this using the normal error correcting procedure of the HDLC protocol. The receiving ECP then passes the (possibly error corrected) block of data to its local UIP which transfers it a character (byte) at a time across the local V.24 interface.

If a flow control (break) condition is detected during the data transfer phase – for example, an X-OFF character being received or the DTR line becoming inactive – then the UIP stops outputting data to the local DTE and

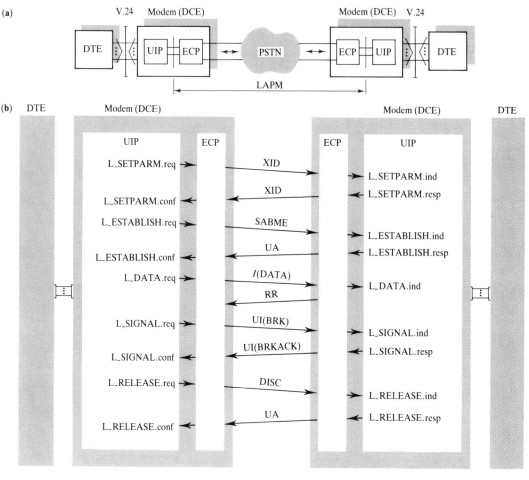

(a)

UIP = User interface part   ECP = Error control part

FIGURE 5.19

LAPM: (a) operational
scope; (b) user service
primitives and
corresponding frame
types.

immediately issues a L_SIGNAL.request primitive to its local ECP. The latter
then informs the distant ECP to (temporarily) stop sending any more data by
sending a BRK (break) message in a special information frame known as an
unnumbered information or **UI frame**. This, as the name implies, does not
contain sequence numbers since it bypasses any error/flow control mechanisms.
The receiving ECP then issues an L_SIGNAL.indication primitive to its local
UIP and acknowledges receipt of the break message by returning a BRKACK
message in another UI frame. The UIP then initiates the same flow control
signal across its own V.24 interface.

Finally, after all data has been transferred, the link is cleared by the
originating UIP issuing a L_RELEASE.request primitive. Again this is a confirmed service and the associated LAPM frames are DISC and UA.

5.4.5 Link access procedure D-channel

Link access procedure D-channel or **LAPD** is the HDLC subset for use with the **integrated services digital network, ISDN**. It has been defined to control the flow of information frames associated with the signalling (call set-up) channel. The latter is known as the **D-channel**, hence the term LAPD. It is also used in a slightly extended form to control the flow of information frames over a user channel associated with a service known as **frame relay**. More details relating to ISDN will be deferred until Chapter 8 when wide area networks are discussed. This section will simply discuss the basic operation of LAPD and how it relates to HDLC.

Two types of service have been defined for use with LAPD. A time sequence diagram showing the two sets of service primitives is shown in Figure 5.20. As can be seen, both an unacknowledged (best-try) and an acknowledged

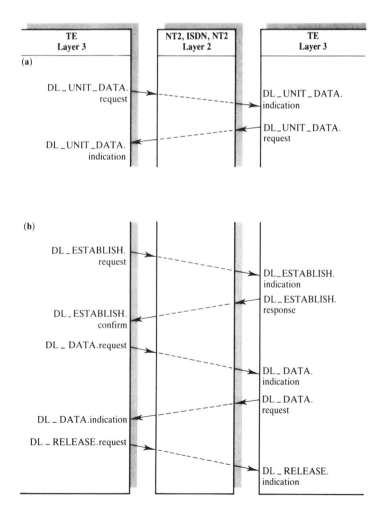

FIGURE 5.20

LAPD user services primitives:
(a) connectionless;
(b) connection-oriented.

(connection-oriented) service are supported. The ISDN, like the analogue PSTN it is replacing, is basically a circuit-switched network which means that a circuit – a **virtual path**, in practice – must be established before any user information is transferred. This is done using a separate signalling channel – the D-channel – which has its own protocol set of which LAPD is a constituent part.

The connection-oriented service is used to transfer call set-up messages between an item of user equipment – a telephone or a DTE – and the local exchange. The associated protocol thus incorporates error control. The connectionless service is used for the transfer of management-related messages and the associated protocol uses a best-try, unacknowledged approach.

As will be expanded upon in Chapter 8, up to eight different items of terminal equipment – telephones, DTEs or combinations of the two – can share a basic access circuit (and hence D-channel) between a customer's premises and

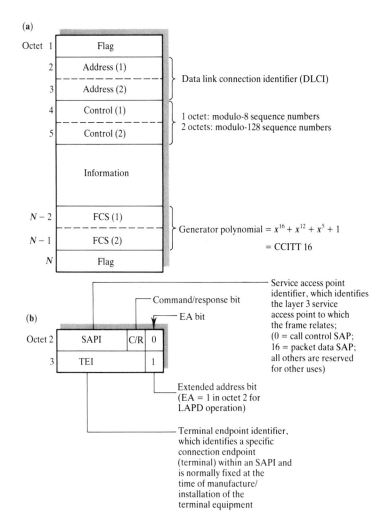

FIGURE 5.21

LAPD: (a) frame format; (b) address field usage.

the local ISDN exchange. All (higher layer) call set-up messages, however, are sent to a specific terminal equipment using the LAPD address field. This is similar in principle to the addressing mechanism used in the NRM mode except that with LAPD there is no master and the physical bus structure to which the terminal equipments are attached allows each terminal to access the bus in a fair way. The general structure of each LAPD frame is shown in Figure 5.21.

Two octets are used for the address field. These consist of two sub-addresses: a **service access point identifier (SAPI)** and a **terminal endpoint identifier (TEI)**. Essentially, the SAPI identifies the class of service to which the terminal relates – voice, data, voice and data – and the TEI then uniquely identifies the terminal within that class. There is also a broadcast address – all binary 1s – that allows a message to be sent to all terminals in a class. This can be used, for example, to allow all telephones to receive an incoming call set-up request message.

The various control field formats – octets 4 and 5 – associated with LAPD are summarized in Figure 5.22, which also shows which frames can be sent as command frames and which as response frames.

In LAPD, as with LAPM, the additional unnumbered frame known as **unnumbered information** or **UI** is used. LAPD uses this with the connectionless

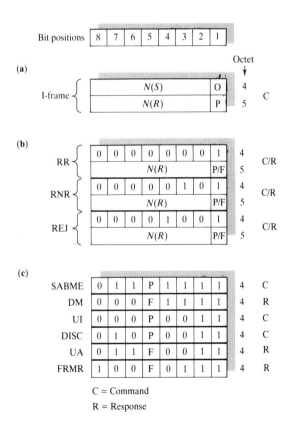

FIGURE 5.22

LAPD control field bit definitions:
(a) information;
(b) supervisory;
(c) unnumbered.

service. Since there is no error control associated with this service (best-try), all information is sent with a single control field with no N(S) or N(R). Such frames do have an FCS field; should this fail, then the frame is simply discarded. Normally with this service the higher (user) layer must then detect this – for example, by the lack of a suitable response (also in a UI frame) – and make another attempt. As will be described in the next section, this is also used in local area networks.

The LAPD service definition and protocol specification are specified in CCITT recommendations I.440 and I.441 respectively. In practice, these are the same as recommendations Q.920 and Q.921.

5.4.6 Logical link control

Logical link control or **LLC** is the HDLC derivative used with local area networks or LANs. These will be discussed in detail in the next chapter but the general arrangement of the two basic types of LAN topology – bus and ring – together with the scope of the DLP – LLC – was shown earlier in Figure 5.2.

Both topologies utilize a shared transmission medium – the bus or ring – which is used to carry all frame transmissions. As with a multipoint network, therefore, a way of controlling the order in which frames are transmitted is needed. Unlike multipoint networks, there is not a single master computer, so a distributed algorithm is used which ensures that the medium is used in a fair way by all the connected DTEs – workstations, servers etc. With LANs, the data link layer is comprised of two **sublayers**, the **medium access control** or **MAC sublayer**, which implements the distributed access control algorithm, and the LLC sublayer. The detailed operation of the different MAC sublayers will be described in the next chapter when LANs are discussed; this section concentrates on the operation of the LLC sublayer. It should be noted that with a LAN, since there are no switching exchanges within the network itself, the LLC (DLP) layer operates on a peer basis, that is, between the LLC sublayer in the two communicating DTEs.

User services

Two types of user service are provided by the LLC layer: an unacknowledged connectionless service and a set of connection-oriented service. The **unacknowledged connectionless service** provides the user with the means of initiating the transfer of service data units with a minimum of protocol overheads. Typically, this service is used when functions such as error recovery and sequencing are being provided in a higher protocol layer and need not be replicated in the LLC layer. Alternatively, the connection-oriented services provide the user with the means needed to establish a link-level logical connection before initiating the transfer of any service data units and, should it be required, to implement error recovery and sequencing of the flow of these units across an established connection.

In certain real-time LAN applications, such as in the process control industry for interconnecting computer-based instrumentation equipment distributed around a chemical plant, the time overhead of setting up a logical connection prior to sending data is often unacceptable. Nevertheless, some acknowledgement of correct receipt of a transmitted item of data is often needed, so the basic unacknowledged connectionless service is not acceptable. An additional service, known as the **acknowledged connectionless service**, is provided to cater for this type of requirement. Similarly, a service is provided to allow an item of data to be requested from a remote user without a connection first being established. This is known as the **obtain reply service.**

The various primitives associated with the two sets of services are shown in the time sequence diagram of Figure 5.23. Each of the primitives illustrated has parameters associated with it. These include a specification of the source (local) and destination (remote) addresses. The source and destination addresses, which are present in all primitives, specify at a minimum, the physical addresses to be used on the network medium. Normally, however, both addresses are a concatenation of the addresses used on the physical medium and the local service access point identifier (LLC-SAP). The meaning of the latter will be expanded upon in the next chapter.

With the unacknowledged connectionless service, when the LLC protocol entity receives a data transfer request primitive (L.DATA.request), it makes a best attempt to send the accompanying data using the MAC sublayer. There is no confirmation that the transfer has been successful or unsuccessful. With the acknowledged connectionless service, however, the user is notified of the success or failure of the passing of the L.DATA_ACKNOWLEDGE.indication to the remote user by means of the L.DATA_ACKNOWLEDGE_STATUS.indication primitive.

The various primitives associated with the obtain reply service allow a user:

- to request the contents of a message buffer maintained by a remote LLC entity – L.REPLY.request/indication;

- to update the contents of a message buffer that is maintained by its local LLC entity – L.REPLY_UPDATE.request and L.REPLY_UPDATE_STATUS.indication.

With the connection-oriented service, a logical connection must be established using the L.CONNECT primitives prior to any data transfer. Similarly, after all data transfers have taken place over this connection, the connection must be cleared using the L.DISCONNECT primitive. During the data transfer phase, the receipt of each error-free data unit is acknowledged by the remote LLC entity which is converted by the local entity into an L.DATA_CONNECT.confirm primitive and passed to the user.

The RESET and FLOWCONTROL service primitives are provided to allow the user to control the flow of service data units across an established

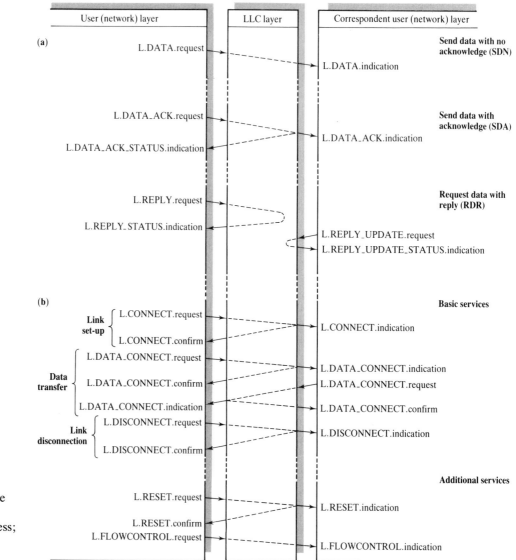

FIGURE 5.23

LLC user service
primitives:
(a) connectionless;
(b) connection-
oriented.

connection. The RESET service has an abortive action as it results in any
unacknowledged data being discarded. It is only used, therefore, if the network
layer protocol entity loses track of the sequence of data units being transferred.

The two flow control primitives have only local significance: the
L.FLOWCONTROL.request primitive specifies the amount of data the user is
prepared to accept from its local LLC protocol entity and the L.FLOW-
CONTROL.indication primitive the amount of data the LLC protocol entity is
prepared to accept from the user, both related to a specific connection. If the

specified amount is zero, then the flow of data is stopped; if the amount is infinite, no flow control is to be applied on the connection. The amount of data allowed is dynamically updated by each request.

Protocol operation

The format of each LLC frame is shown in Figure 5.24(a). The source and destination address fields both refer to the LLC service access point only; they do not contain the addresses to be used on the network medium. Also, there is no FCS field. Essentially, the complete LLC frame is passed to the MAC sublayer in the form of a primitive which includes the frame and the address to be used on the network medium as parameters. It is thus the MAC sublayer that handles the network addressing and error-detection functions. It is for this reason that, in the context of the ISO Reference Model, the link layer is equivalent to a combination of the LLC and a portion of the MAC sublayers.

The control field in each frame is a single octet. It defines the type of the frame and, where appropriate, the send and receive sequence numbers for error and sequence control. The use of the various bits in this field are shown in more detail in Figure 5.24(b).

The LLC protocol entity supports two types of operation: type 1 to support the unacknowledged connectionless service and type 2 to support the

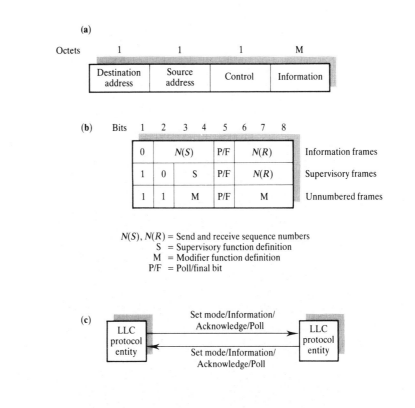

FIGURE 5.24

Aspects of LLC protocol: (a) frame format; (b) control field bit definitions; (c) data link control function (type 2).

connection-oriented service. Type 2 is in practice very similar to the HDLC protocol except that the framing and error-detection functions are provided by the MAC sublayer.

The data link control functions for type 2 operation are shown in Figure 5.24(c). The major difference between the LLC protocol and HDLC is the provision of the unacknowledged connectionless (type 1) service. The set of commands and responses supported in type 1 are:

Commands	Responses
UI	—
XID	XID
TEST	TEST

The UI command frame is used to send a block of data (information) to one or more LLCs. Since there is no acknowledgement or sequence control associated with type 1 operation, the UI frame does not contain an N(S) or N(R) field. Also, there is no response to a UI.

The exchange identification (XID) and TEST command frames are optional. However, if they are sent, the receiving LLC(s) is (are) obliged to respond. The uses of these commands include:

- The XID command with a group address is used to determine the current membership of the group. Each member of the group responds to the command by returning an XID response frame addressed specifically to the originating LLC entity.

- An LLC entity may use an XID command with a broadcast (global) destination address to announce its presence on the network medium.

- The TEST command is used to provide a loopback test facility on each LLC to LLC transmission path.

MAC services

Irrespective of the mode of operation of the underlying MAC sublayer, a standard set of user services are defined for use by the LLC layer to transfer LLC frames to a correspondent LLC layer. The user service primitives supported are:

- MA.DATA.request,
- MA.DATA.indication,
- MA.DATA.confirmation.

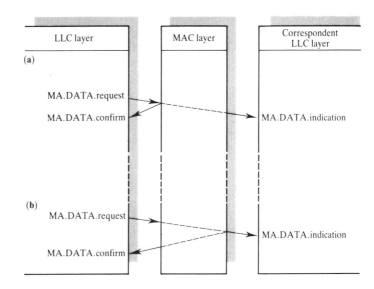

FIGURE 5.25

MAC sublayer user
service primitives:
(a) local confirm;
(b) remote confirm.

A time sequence diagram illustrating their use is shown in Figure 5.25. For some LANs, the confirm primitive indicates that the request has been successfully (or not) transmitted – part (a) – while for others it indicates that the request has been successfully delivered (or not) — part (b).

Each service primitive has associated parameters. The MA.DATA. request primitive includes: the required destination address (this may be an individual, group or broadcast address), a service data unit (containing the LLC frame) and the required class of service associated with the frame. The last one is used with some types of LAN when a prioritized medium access control protocol is being used.

The MA.DATA.confirm primitive includes a parameter that specifies the success or failure of the associated MA.DATA.request primitive. As can be seen from the figure, however, the confirmation primitive is not generated as a result of a response from the remote LLC layer but rather by the local MAC entity. If the parameter is successful, this simply indicates that the MAC protocol entity (layer) was successful in transmitting the service data unit on to the network medium; if unsuccessful, the parameter indicates why the transmission attempt failed. This and other MAC-related issues will be expanded upon in the next chapter.

Figure 5.26 summarizes the various services associated with the LLC and MAC layers and lists the various LLC frame types that are exchanged between two LLC protocol entities. As can be seen, apart from the UI, XID and TEST these are the same as those used with HDLC.

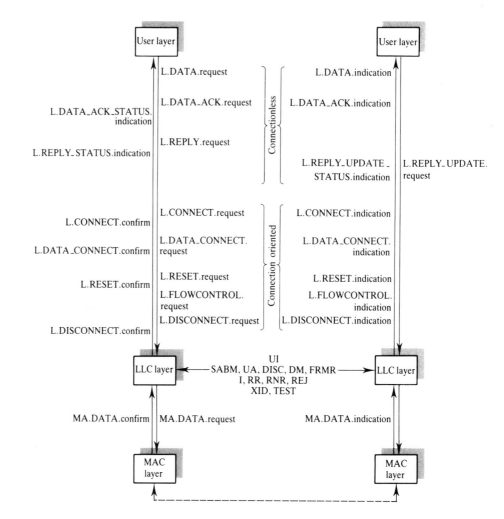

FIGURE 5.26

LLC sublayer
summary.

EXERCISES

5.1   Explain the meaning of the following terms relating to data link protocols:

    (a)   character-oriented,

    (b)   bit-oriented,

    (c)   framing and data transparency,

    (d)   poll-select,

    (e)   primary and secondary.

5.2   Produce a sketch of a time sequence diagram showing the user service primitives
associated with the data link control layer assuming a

    (a)   connectionless (best-try),

    (b)   connection-oriented (reliable),

    operational mode.

5.3 With the aid of sketches, identify the scope of operation of the data link protocol in the following application environments:

(a) point-to-point,
(b) multipoint (multidrop),
(c) wide area networks,
(d) local area networks.

5.4 Explain the operation of the Kermit protocol used for the transfer of files of data from one computer to another. Include in your description:

(a) the user commands,
(b) the frame format and frame types used,
(c) example frame sequences, including retransmissions.

5.5 List the ten transmission control characters from the ASCII character set and explain their function in character-oriented protocols.

5.6 Produce sketches of the various data and supervisory frames (blocks) used with the binary synchronous control (BSC) protocol showing clearly the position of the various transmission control characters.

5.7 Discriminate between the terms poll, select and fast-select in relation to the BSC protocol.
Produce sketches of typical data and supervisory frame (block) sequences to illustrate these three operational modes of BSC.

5.8 Produce a sketch of the frame format used and explain how a continuous duplex flow of I-frames is maintained with the ARPANET data link protocol.
Identify the state variables that are required at each side of the data link to implement the combined error control scheme.

5.9 With the aid of sketches, identify the direction of commands and responses associated with the high-level data link control (HDLC) protocol for the following network configurations;

(a) point-to-point with a single primary and secondary,
(b) point-to-point with combined stations,
(c) multipoint with a single primary.

5.10 Produce a sketch of the basic and extended frame formats associated with the HDLC protocol. Show clearly the structure of the control field in each case and explain the meaning and use of each sub-field.

5.11 Assuming an HDLC protocol, distinguish between the NRM and ABM modes of working. Sketch typical frame sequences to show how a link is first set up (established) and then cleared (disconnected) for each mode. Clearly show the different frame types used and the use of the address and poll/final bit in each frame.

5.12 Define the supervisory frames used for acknowledgement purposes in the HDLC protocol. Assuming a unidirectional flow of I-frames, sketch a typical frame sequence to illustrate the acknowledgement procedure used in the HDLC protocol. Include in the diagram the contents of the link retransmission list and the state of the send and receive sequence variables as each frame is transmitted and received. Also show the send and receive sequence numbers contained within each frame and the state of the poll/final bit, where appropriate.

5.13 Explain the meaning of the term piggyback acknowledgement. Sketch a typical frame sequence to illustrate how piggyback acknowledgements are used in the HDLC protocol. Clearly show the send and receive sequence numbers contained within each frame transmitted and the contents of the retransmission lists and send and receive variables at each side of the link.

5.14 Outline the operation of a window flow control mechanism. Assuming a send window of K and a send window variable $V(W)$, deduce the range within which the send and receive sequence numbers contained within each received frame should be, assuming both sides of the link are in synchronism.

Assuming a send window of 3 and a unidirectional flow of I-frames, sketch a frame sequence to illustrate the operation of the window flow control mechanism used with the HDLC protocol.

5.15 Explain the meaning of the term multi-link procedure in relation to data link protocols.

Use a diagram to illustrate its relationship to a single link procedure and show how the frame format is extended to include additional sequence numbers.

5.16 Produce a time sequence diagram to show the user service primitives associated with the LAPD protocol with

(a)   unacknowledged (best-try),
(b)   acknowledged

information transfer.

Sketch the frame format associated with LAPD and clearly explain the structure and use of the address field octets.

5.17 With the aid of a time sequence diagram, list the user service primitives associated with the LLC protocol with

(a)   connectionless,
(b)   connection-oriented

operation.

In relation to the above, discriminate between the terms:

(a)   send data with no acknowledge,
(b)   send data with acknowledge,
(c)   request data with reply.

5.18 Use a time sequence diagram to show the user service primitives associated with the medium access control (MAC) sublayer used in the data link layer of LANs.

Hence show how the supervisory and information frames associated with the above LLC sublayer user services are transferred using the various MAC user primitives.

CHAPTER SUMMARY

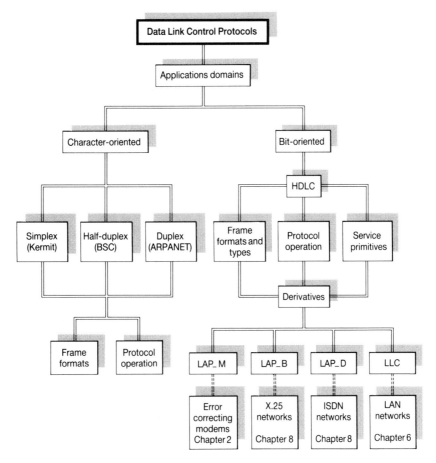

PART TWO

COMPUTER NETWORKS

Part Two of the book is concerned with the mode of operation of the different types of data network that are used to interconnect a distributed community of computers and the various interface standards and protocols associated with them. When the computers are distributed over a localized area, such as a building or campus, the network used is known as a local area network. Alternatively, when the computers are distributed over a wider geographical area, such as a country, the network is known as a wide area network.

Chapter 6 describes the operation and interface protocols associated with the different types of local area network that are now international standards.

In Chapter 7, the operation of two new types of high-speed local area networks are described. The operation and protocols associated with the devices known as bridges, which are used to extend the capacity and field of coverage of local area networks, are also discussed in this chapter.

Chapter 8 describes the operation and interface protocols associated with the two types of wide area networks: public data networks and private networks. The former are installed and managed by the public carriers while private networks are installed, managed and run by large national and multinational companies.

Chapter 9 discusses the issues that must be addressed and the additional protocols that are needed when the network comprises an interconnected set of networks such as a mix of local and wide area networks. Such networks are known as internetworks and the issues include addressing and routing.

6

Local area networks

CHAPTER CONTENTS

CHAPTER OBJECTIVES

When you have completed studying the material in this chapter you should be able to:

- describe the different topologies and transmission media commonly used in local area networks;
- know the difference between baseband and broadband working;
- describe the alternative medium access control methods used in local area networks;
- describe the major components and mode of operation of a CSMA/CD bus network;
- describe the major components and mode of operation of a token ring network;
- describe selected aspects of the operation of a token bus network;
- appreciate the function of the various network-dependent protocols used with local area networks and be able to describe the services and operation of the logical link control and network protocol layers.

6.1 INTRODUCTION

Local area data networks, normally referred to simply as **local area networks** or **LANs** are used to interconnect distributed communities of computer-based DTEs located within a single building or localized group of buildings. For example, a LAN may be used to interconnect workstations distributed around offices within a single building or a group of buildings such as a university campus. Alternatively, it may be used to interconnect computer-based equipment distributed around a factory or hospital complex. Since all the equipment is located within a single establishment, however, LANs are normally installed and maintained by the organization. Hence they are also referred to as **private data networks**.

The main difference between a communication path established using a LAN and a connection made through a public data network is that a LAN normally offers much higher data transmission rates because of the relatively short physical separations involved. In the context of the ISO Reference Model for OSI, however, this difference manifests itself only at the lower network-dependent layers. In many instances the higher protocol layers in the reference model are the same for both types of network. This chapter, therefore, is primarily concerned with a description of the different types of LAN and the function and operation of the associated network-dependent protocol layers.

6.2 SELECTION ISSUES

Before describing the structure and operation of the different types of LAN, it is perhaps helpful to first identify some of the selection issues that must be considered. A summary of some of these issues is given in Figure 6.1. It should be stressed that this is only a summary; there are also many possible links between the tips of the branches associated with the figure. Each of the issues identified will now be considered in some detail.

6.2.1 Topology

Most wide area networks, such as the PSTN, use a **mesh** (sometimes referred to as a **network**) topology. With LANs, however, the limited physical separation of the subscriber DTEs allows simpler topologies to be used. The four topologies in common use are star, bus, ring and hub, as shown in Figure 6.2.

Perhaps the best example of a LAN based on a **star topology** is the digital **private automatic branch exchange (PABX)**. A connection established through a traditional analogue PABX is in many ways similar to a connection made through an analogue PSTN in that all paths through the network are designed to carry limited-bandwidth analogue speech. To use them to carry data, therefore, requires modems as discussed in Chapter 2. However, most modern PABXs use digital-switching techniques within the exchange and are therefore also referred

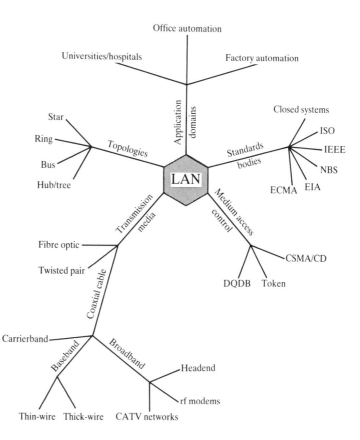

FIGURE 6.1

LAN selection issues.

to as **private digital exchanges (PDX)**. Moreover, the availability of inexpensive integrated circuits to perform the necessary **analogue-to-digital** and **digital-to-analogue** conversion functions means that it is rapidly becoming common practice to extend the digital mode of working right back to the subscriber outlets. This means that a switched 64 kbps path, which is the digitizing rate normally used for digital voice, is available at each subscriber outlet, which can therefore be used for both voice and data.

The main use of a PDX, however, is likely to be to provide a switched communication path between a local community of integrated voice and data terminals (workstations) for the exchange of electronic mail, electronic documents, etc, in addition to normal voice communications. Furthermore, the use of digital techniques within the PDX enables it to be used to provide such services as **voice store-and-forward** (that is, a subscriber may leave (store) a voice message for another subscriber for later retrieval (forwarding)) and teleconferencing (multiple subscribers taking part in a single call).

The preferred topologies for LANs designed to function as data communication subnetworks for the interconnection of local computer-based equipment are bus (linear) and ring. In practice, bus networks are normally extended

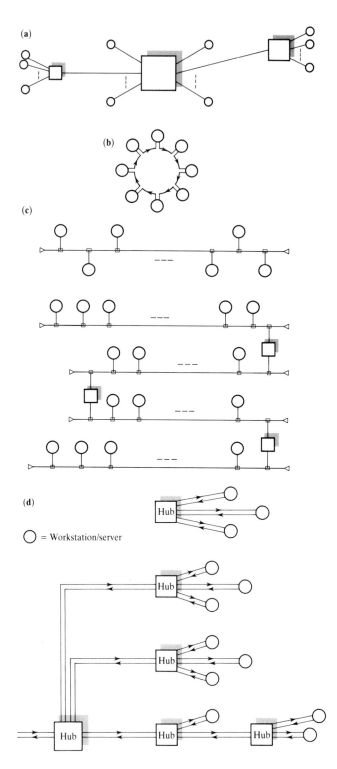

FIGURE 6.2

LAN topologies:
(a) star; (b) ring;
(c) bus; (d) hub/tree.

into an interconnected set of buses and thus more closely resemble an **unrooted tree**. Typically, with a **bus topology** the single network cable is routed through those locations (offices, for example) that have a DTE to be connected to the network and a physical connection (tap) is made to the cable to allow the user DTE to access the network services supported. Appropriate medium access control circuitry and algorithms are then used to share the use of the available transmission bandwidth between the attached community of DTEs.

With a **ring topology**, the network cable passes from one DTE to another until the DTEs are interconnected in the form of a loop or ring. A feature of a ring topology is that there is a direct point-to-point link between each neighbouring DTE which is unidirectional in operation. Appropriate medium access control algorithms then ensure the use of the ring is shared between the community of users.

The data transmission rates used with both ring and bus topologies (typically from 1 to 10 Mbps) mean that they are best suited for interconnecting local communities of computer-based equipment, such as workstations in an office environment or intelligent controllers around a process plant.

A variation of the bus and ring, known as a **hub topology**, is also used. This is shown in part (d) of Figure 6.2. Although such networks have the appearance of a star topology, in practice the hub is simply the bus or ring wiring collapsed into a central unit. The wires used to connect each DTE to the bus or ring are then extended out from the hub. Unlike a PDX, therefore, the hub does not perform any switching function but simply consists of a set of repeaters that retransmit all the signals received from DTEs to all other DTEs in the same way as the bus or ring network. As can be seen, hubs can also be connected in a hierarchical way to form a **tree topology**. The combined topology again functions as a single ring or bus network or an interconnected set of such networks. Practical examples will be discussed later.

6.2.2 Transmission media

Twisted pair, coaxial cable and optical fibre are the three main types of transmission medium used for LANs.

Twisted pair – both **unshielded** and **shielded** – is used primarily in star and hub networks. Because it is less rigid than coaxial cable or fibre, twisted pair can be most readily installed. Also, since wiring ducts suitable for twisted-pair cable are already in place to most office desks for telephony, it is less costly to install additional twisted pairs for data purposes than it is to install new cable ducts for coax or fibre. The general scheme is shown in Figure 6.3(a).

As was indicated in Chapter 2, there is a maximum limit on the length of twisted pair depending on the bit rate being used. Typically the limit is 100 m at 1 Mbps or, with the aid of additional circuits to remove crosstalk, 100 m at 10 Mbps. A typical arrangement, therefore, is to use twisted pair between each DTE and the nearest wiring closet on a floor and then coaxial cable to link the floor wiring closets to the main building hub. For an installation involving multiple buildings, fibre is normally used to link each building hub to a main

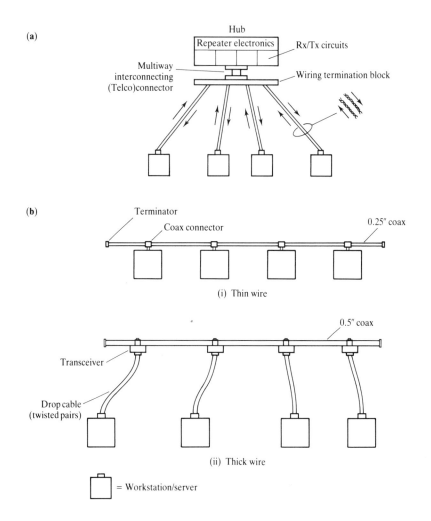

FIGURE 6.3

Transmission media:
(a) twisted-pair;
(b) baseband coaxial
cable.

central hub. The latter normally works at a higher bit rate and is logically configured as a ring network. This type of arrangement is often referred to as **structured wiring**.

Coaxial cable is also widely used for LANs, primarily with bus networks, operating with either **baseband** or **broadband** transmission. The basic operation of these were described in Chapter 2. Two types of cable are used with baseband: one known as **thin wire** and the other as **thick wire**. The terms refer to the cable diameter: thin wire 0.25 inch diameter and thick wire 0.5 inch diameter. Normally, both operate at the same bit rate – 10 Mbps – but thin wire cable results in greater signal attenuation, the maximum length of thin wire cable between repeaters is 200 m compared with 500 m with thick wire. It may be recalled that a repeater is used to regenerate a received signal to its original form. The two alternative operating modes are known as **10 Base 2** – 10 Mbps, baseband, 200 m maximum length – and **10 Base 5**, respectively.

Thin wire coax is often used to interconnect workstations in the same office or laboratory, for example. The physical connector to the coaxial cable then attaches directly to the interface card in the workstation. The cable bus thus takes the form of a daisy chain as it passes from one DTE to the next.

In contrast, thick coax, because of its more rigid structure, is normally installed away from the workstations along a corridor, for example. Additional wiring – known as a **drop cable** – and transmit and receive electronics – known as a **transceiver** – must therefore be used between the main coaxial cable tapping (connection) point – known as the **attachment unit interface** or **AUI** – and the point of attachment to each workstation. This arrangement is more expensive and is, therefore, used primarily when the workstations are each located in different offices or for interconnecting thin-wire segments. Both are illustrated in Figure 6.3(b).

As was described in Chapter 2, with broadband transmission, instead of transmitting information on to the cable in the form of, say, two voltage levels corresponding to the bit stream being transmitted (baseband), the total available bandwidth (frequency range) of the cable is divided into a number of smaller subfrequency bands or channels. Each subfrequency band is then used, with the aid of a pair of special modems, to provide a separate data communication channel. This style of working is known as **frequency-division multiplexing** and, since the frequencies used are in the radio frequency band, the modems are **rf modems**. This principle, known as broadband working, is also widely used in the **community antenna television (CATV)** industry to multiplex a number of TV channels on to a single coaxial cable.

A typical CATV system is shown in Figure 6.4(a). Each TV channel is allocated a particular frequency band, typically of 6 MHz bandwidth. Each received video signal (from the various antenna or aerials) is then used to **modulate** a **carrier frequency** in the selected frequency band. The modulated carrier signals are then transmitted over the cable network and are thus available at each subscriber outlet. The subscriber selects a particular TV channel by tuning to the appropriate frequency band.

In a similar way, it is possible to derive a range of data transmission channels from a single cable by allocating each channel a portion of the total bandwidth, the bandwidth for each channel being determined by the required data rate. For data communication, however, a two-way (duplex) capability is normally required. This may be achieved in two ways:

(1) **Single-cable system:** The transmit and receive paths are assigned two different frequency bands on the same cable.

(2) **Dual-cable system:** Two separate cables are used, one for the transmit path and the other for the receive path.

A schematic of each type of system is shown in Figure 6.4(b). The main difference between them is that a dual-cable system requires twice the amount of cable and cable taps to install. Nevertheless, with this system the total cable

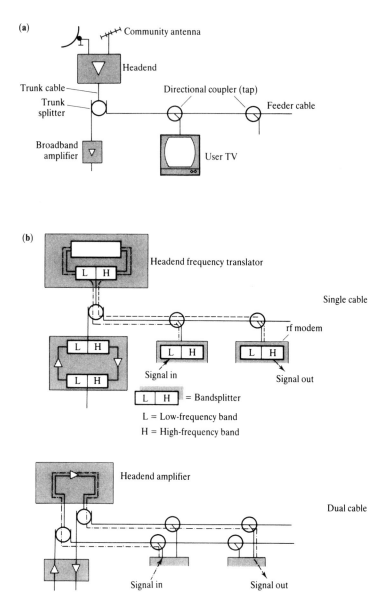

FIGURE 6.4

Broadband coaxial
cable systems: (a) basic
CATV system
components; (b) data
network alternatives.

bandwidth (typically 5 to 450 MHz) is available in each direction. Moreover, the
headend equipment is simply an amplifier, whereas with a single-cable system a
frequency translator is required to translate the incoming frequency signals
associated with the various receive paths to the corresponding outgoing frequencies used for the transmit paths.

A sinusoidal signal in the selected frequency band in the reverse direction
(that is, to the headend) is first modulated by the data to be transmitted using an

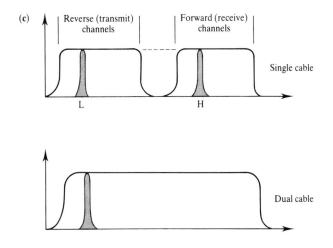

FIGURE 6.4 (cont.)

(c) Frequency usage.

rf modem. This signal is fed on to the cable using a special **directional coupler** or **tap** which is designed so that most of the transmitted signal flows in the reverse direction to the cable **headend (HE)**. Another device, known as a **frequency translator**, is then used to convert (translate) the signals received on the different receive frequency bands to a corresponding set of forward frequency bands. The received modulated signal is thus frequency-translated by the headend and the rf modem associated with the receiving DTE tuned to receive the matching frequency-translated signal frequency band. The transmitted data is then demodulated from the received signal by the receiving modem and passed on to the attached DTE.

It may be deduced from this that a single pair of frequencies provides just a simplex (unidirectional) data path between the two DTEs. Consequently, two separate pairs of frequencies must be used to support duplex communication. Nevertheless, a 9.6 kbps simplex data channel only requires in the order of 20 kHz of the total available bandwidth, so a pair of 6 MHz subfrequency bands can be used to provide 300 such channels or 150 full-duplex channels. Higher data rate channels then require progressively more of the available bandwidth; for example, two 6 MHz bands for a 5 Mbps full-duplex channel or three 6 MHz bands for a 10 Mbps full-duplex channel.

The price to pay for deriving this multiplicity of different data channels from a single cable is the relatively high cost of each pair of rf modems. However, a broadband coaxial cable can be used over longer distances than a baseband cable. The primary use of broadband coaxial cable, therefore, tends to be as a flexible transmission medium for use in manufacturing industry or in establishments comprising multiple buildings, especially when the buildings are quite widely separated (up to tens of kilometres, for example). When used in this way, other services, such as closed-circuit television and voice, can readily be integrated on to the cable being used for data. Hence broadband is a viable alternative to baseband for networks providing a range of services.

Optical fibre, as was described in Chapter 2, is made of glass or plastic and can operate at data rates well in excess of those possible with twisted-pair or coaxial cable. Since data is transmitted via a beam of light, the signal is not affected by electromagnetic interference. It is thus best suited to applications that demand either a very high data rate or high levels of immunity to electromagnetic interference, such as industrial plants containing large electrical equipment. Also, since the fibres do not emit electromagnetic radiation, they are suited to applications that demand high levels of security.

Because data is transmitted using a beam of light, special electrical-to-optical and optical-to-electrical transmitter and receiver electronics must be used. Also, the physical connectors used with optical fibre are more expensive than those used with twisted-pair or coaxial cable, and it is also more difficult to make physical taps to a fibre cable. For these reasons, optical fibre is used either in hub configurations or high-speed ring and other networks that employ point-to-point transmission paths. Two examples of the latter are the fibre distributed data interface (FDDI) and the distributed-queue, dual-bus (DQDB) networks to be described in the next chapter.

6.2.3 Medium access control methods

When a communication path is established between two DTEs through a star network, the central controlling element (a PDX, for example) ensures that the transmission path between the two DTEs is reserved for the duration of the call. With both the ring and bus topologies, however, there is only a single logical transmission path linking all the DTEs together. Consequently, a discipline must be imposed on all the DTEs connected to the network to ensure that the transmission medium is accessed and used in a fair way. The two techniques that have been adopted for use in the various standards documents are **carrier-sense-multiple-access with collision detection (CSMA/CD)**, for use with bus network topologies, and **control token**, for use with either bus or ring networks. An access method based on a **slotted ring** is also widely used with ring networks.

CSMA/CD

The CSMA/CD access method is used solely with bus networks. With this network topology, all DTEs are connected directly to the same cable, which is therefore used for transmitting all data between any pair of DTEs. The cable is thus said to operate in a **multiple access (MA) mode**. All data is transmitted by the sending DTE first encapsulating the data in a frame with the required destination DTE address at the head of the frame. The frame is then transmitted (or **broadcast**) on the cable. All DTEs connected to the cable detect whenever a frame is being transmitted and, when the required destination DTE detects that the frame currently being transmitted has its own address at the head of the frame, it continues reading the data contained within the frame and responds according to the defined link protocol. The source DTE address is included as part of the frame header so that the receiving DTE can direct its response to the originating DTE.

With this style of operation, it is possible for two DTEs to attempt to transmit a frame over the cable at the same time, causing the data from both sources to be corrupted. To reduce the possibility of this, before transmitting a frame, the source DTE first **listens** – electronically – to the cable to detect whether a frame is currently being transmitted. If a **carrier** signal is **sensed (CS)**, the DTE defers its transmission until the passing frame has been transmitted, and only then does it attempt to send the frame. Even so, two DTEs wishing to transmit a frame may simultaneously determine that there is no activity (transmission) on the bus, and hence both start to transmit their frames simultaneously. A **collision** is then said to occur since the contents of both frames will collide and hence be corrupted. This is shown in diagrammatic form in Figure 6.5.

To allow for this possibility, a DTE simultaneously monitors the data signal on the cable when transmitting the contents of a frame on to the cable. If the transmitted and monitored signals are different, a collision is assumed to

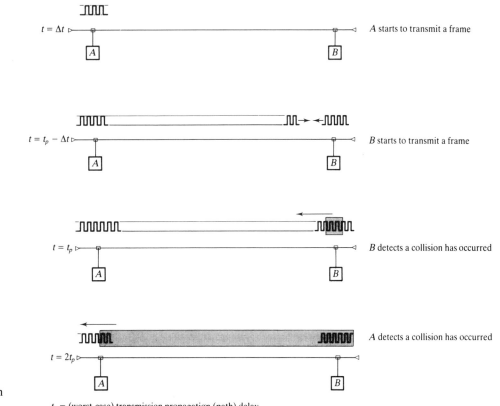

FIGURE 6.5

CSMA/CD collision schematic.

t_p = (worst-case) transmission propagation (path) delay

have occurred – **collision detected (CD)**. To ensure that the other DTE(s) involved in the collision is (are) aware that a collision has occurred, it first enforces the collision by continuing to send a random bit pattern for a short period. This is known as the **jam sequence**. The two (or more) DTEs involved then wait for a further short random time interval before trying to retransmit the affected frames. It can be concluded that access to a CSMA/CD bus is probabilistic and depends on the network (cable) loading. It should be stressed, however, that since the bit rate used on the cable is very high (up to 10 Mbps), the network loading tends to be low. Also, since the transmission of a frame is initiated only if the cable is inactive, the probability of a collision occurring is in practice also low.

Control token

Another way of controlling access to a shared transmission medium is by the use of a **control (permission) token**. This token is passed from one DTE to another according to a defined set of rules understood and adhered to by all DTEs connected to the medium. A DTE may only transmit a frame when it is in possession of the token and, after it has transmitted the frame, it passes the token on to allow another DTE to access the transmission medium. The sequence of operation is as follows:

- A logical ring is first established which links all the DTEs connected to the physical medium, and a single control token is created.

- The token is passed from DTE to DTE around the logical ring until it is received by a DTE waiting to send a frame(s).

- The waiting DTE then sends the waiting frame(s) using the physical medium, after which it passes the control token to the next DTE in the logical ring.

Monitoring functions within the active DTEs connected to the physical medium provide a basis for initialization and recovery of both the connection of the logical ring and from loss of the token. Although the monitoring functions are normally replicated amongst all the DTEs on the medium, only one DTE at a time carries the responsibility for recovery and re-initialization.

The physical medium need not be a ring topology; a token can also be used to control access to a bus network. The establishment of a logical ring on the two types of network is shown in Figure 6.6.

With a physical ring (Figure 6.6(a)), the logical structure of the token-passing ring is the same as the structure of the physical ring, with the order of token passing being the same as the physical ordering of the connected DTEs. With a bus network (Figure 6.6(b)), however, the ordering of the logical ring need not be the same as the physical ordering of the DTEs on the cable. Moreover, with a token access method on a bus network, all DTEs need not be (logically) connected into the logical ring. For example, DTE H is not part of the

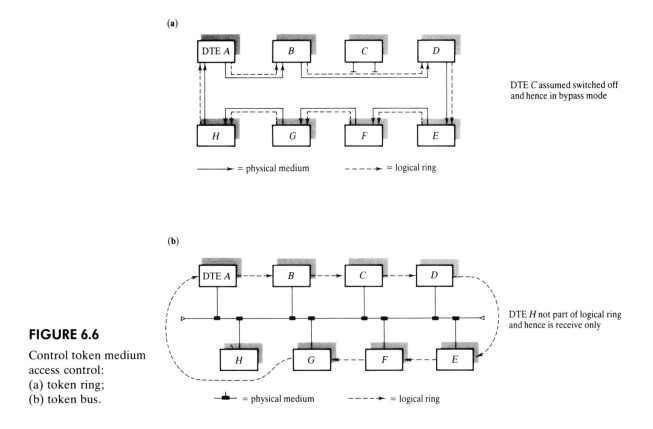

FIGURE 6.6

Control token medium
access control:
(a) token ring;
(b) token bus.

logical ring shown in Figure 6.6(b). This means that DTE H can only operate in
a receive mode, since it will never own the control token. Another feature of the
token access method is that it is possible to associate a priority with the token,
thereby allowing higher priority frames to be transmitted first. This and other
aspects will be expanded upon in later sections.

Slotted ring

Slotted rings are used solely for controlling access to a ring network. The ring is
first initialized to contain a fixed number of binary digits by a special node in the
ring known as a **monitor**. This stream of bits continuously circulates around the
ring from one DTE to another. Then, as each bit is received by a DTE, the DTE
interface examines (reads) the bit and passes (repeats) it on to the next DTE in
the ring, and so on. The monitor ensures that there is always a constant number
of bits circulating in the ring, irrespective of the number of DTEs making up the
ring. The complete ring is arranged to contain a fixed number of **slots**, each
made up of a set number of bits and capable of carrying a single, fixed-size frame
of information. The format of a frame slot is shown in Figure 6.7(a).

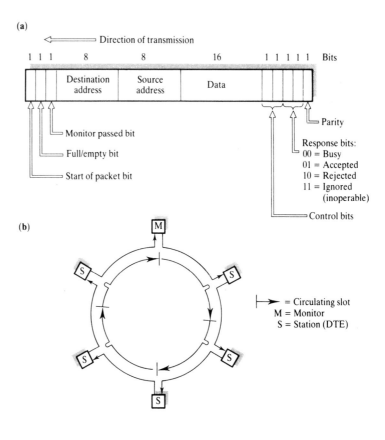

FIGURE 6.7

Slotted ring principles:
(a) bit definitions of
each slot; (b) outline
topology.

Initially, all the slots are marked empty by the monitor setting the full/empty bit at the head of each slot to the empty state. When a DTE wishes to transmit a frame, it waits until an empty slot is detected. It then marks the slot as full and proceeds to insert the frame contents into the slot with both the required destination DTE address and the source DTE address at the head of the frame and the response bits at the tail of the frame, both set to 1. The slot containing this frame then circulates around the physical ring from one DTE to another. Each DTE in the ring examines the destination address at the head of any slot marked full and, if it detects its own address, and assuming it is willing to accept the frame, reads the frame contents from the slot while at the same time repeating the unmodified frame contents around the ring. After reading the frame contents, it modifies the pair of response bits at the tail of the slot to indicate that it has read the frame contents or, alternatively, if the addressed DTE is either busy or inoperable, the response bits are marked accordingly or left unchanged (inoperable).

The source DTE, after initiating the transmission of a frame, waits until the frame has circulated the ring by counting the (fixed number) of slots that are repeated at the ring interface. Then, on receipt of the first bit of the slot used to transmit the frame, it marks the slot as empty once again and waits to read the response bits from the tail of the slot to determine what action to take next.

The monitor-passed bit is used by the monitor to detect whether a DTE fails to release a slot after it has transmitted a frame. This bit is reset by the source DTE as it transmits a frame on to the ring. The monitor subsequently sets the bit in each full slot as it is repeated at its ring interface. Hence, if the monitor detects that the monitor-passed bit is set when it repeats a full slot, it assumes that the source DTE has failed to mark the slot as empty and hence resets the full/empty bit at the head of the slot. The two control bits at the tail of each slot are for use by the higher protocol software layers within each DTE and have no meaning at the medium access level.

It should be noted that with a slotted ring medium access method each DE can only have a single frame in transit on the ring at a time. Also, it must release the slot used for transmitting a frame before trying to send another frame. In this way, access to the ring is fair and shared between the various interconnected DTEs. The main disadvantages of a slotted ring are that:

(1)   a special (and hence vulnerable) monitor node is required to maintain the basic ring structure;

(2)   the transmission of each complete link-level frame normally requires multiple slots, since each slot can carry only 16 bits of useful information.

With a token ring, of course, once a DTE receives the control token it may transmit a complete frame containing multiple bytes of information as a single unit.

6.2.4 Standards

As LANs evolved in the late 1970s and early 1980s, a wide range of different network types were proposed and implemented. However, because of small differences between them, such networks could only be used to interconnect computers or workstations provided by the supplier of the LAN. Such networks are known, therefore, as **closed systems**.

To alleviate this situation, some major initiatives were launched by various national standards bodies with the aim of formulating an agreed set of standards for LANs. The major contributor to this activity was the IEEE which formulated the IEEE 802 series of standards, which have now been adopted by ISO as international standards. As can be concluded from the previous sections, there is not just a single type of LAN. Rather, there is a range of different types, each with its own topology, medium access control method and intended application domain. Some of the different types of LAN in the standards documents will now be described; the protocols associated with them are presented later in the chapter.

6.3 LOCAL AREA NETWORK TYPES

The two dominant types of LAN that have been developed for interconnecting local communities of computer-based equipment are bus and ring. Currently, there are numerous varieties of both types, although many do not adhere to the international standards for LANs. The three types in the standards documents are CSMA/CD bus, token ring and token bus, hence the descriptions that follow will be restricted to these three types.

6.3.1 CSMA/CD bus

CSMA/CD bus networks are used extensively in technical and office environments. For historical reasons, a CSMA/CD bus network is also known as **Ethernet**. Normally, it is implemented as a 10 Mbps baseband coaxial cable network, although other cable media are supported in the standards documents. These include:

10 Base 2 – thin wire (0.25 inch diameter) coaxial cable with a maximum segment length of 200 m;

10 Base 5 – thick wire (0.5 inch diameter) coaxial cable with a maximum segment length of 500 m;

10 Base T – hub (star) topology with twisted pair drop cables;

10 Base F – hub (star) topology with optical fibre drop cables.

Although different media are used, they all operate using the same MAC method. With thin and thick wire coax, the major difference is the location of the transceiver electronics. In the case of thick wire this is located with the cable tap, which is thus known as an **integrated tap and transceiver unit**. With thin wire the cable connects directly to the interface board in the DTE and hence the transceiver is located on the latter. Thin wire coax networks, therefore, are also known as **cheapernets** since they are less costly to install than thick wire networks.

The various components associated with a thick wire configuration are shown in Figure 6.8. A **tap** is used to make a non-intrusive – that is, the cable does not need to be cut – physical connection to the cable. This comprises a screw mechanism that pierces the outer protective shield of the cable and makes contact with the centre conductor. The outer part of the screw also makes contact with the outer screen of the cable thus completing the electrical connection.

The transceiver contains the necessary electronics to:

- send and receive data to and from the cable;
- detect collisions on the cable medium;
- provide electrical isolation between the coaxial cable and cable interface electronics;

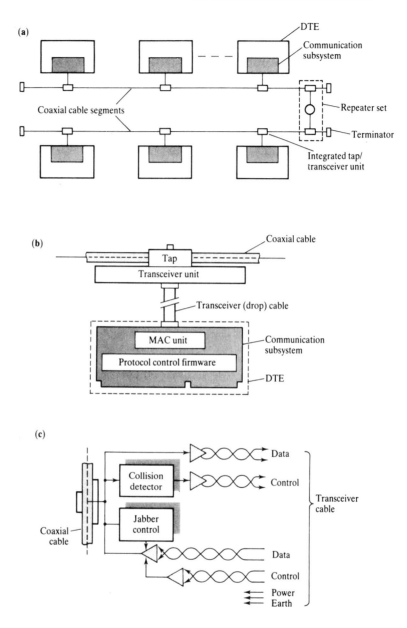

FIGURE 6.8

Thick wire CSMA/CD bus network components: (a) cable layout; (b) DTE interface; (c) transceiver schematic.

- protect the cable from any malfunctions in either the transceiver or attached DTE.

The last function is often referred to as **jabber control** since without the appropriate protection electronics, if a fault develops, it is possible for a faulty transceiver (or DTE) continuously to transmit random data on to the cable medium (jabber) and hence inhibit or corrupt all other transmissions. The jabber control isolates the transmit data path from the cable if certain defined time limits are violated. For example, all frames transmitted on the cable have a defined maximum length; if this is exceeded, the jabber control inhibits further output data from reaching the cable.

The transceiver unit is connected to its host DTE by a shielded cable containing five sets of twisted pair wires: one for carrying power to the transceiver from the DTE, two for data (one send and one receive) and two for control purposes (one to allow the transceiver to signal a collision to the DTE and the other for the DTE to initiate the isolation of the transmit data path from the cable). The four signal pairs are differentially driven, which means that the host DTE may be up to 50m from the transceiver and hence from the cable tapping point.

With a hub configuration, as with thin wire coax, the collision detection function is located on the interface board within the DTE. The function of the hub, therefore, is purely to receive and retransmit (repeat) electrical signals reliably. A hub configuration and the repeater electronics function are shown in Figure 6.9.

As can be seen, there are two twisted-pair (or optical fibre) wires connecting each DTE to the hub – a transmit pair and a receive pair. To enable the

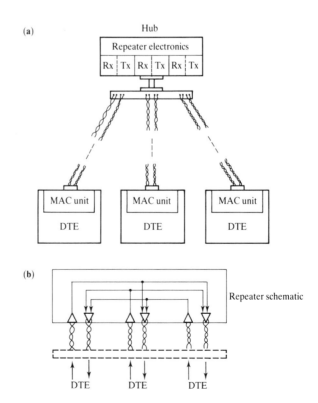

FIGURE 6.9

Hub configuration principles: (a) topology; (b) repeater schematic.

collision detection electronics to function at the DTE, the repeater electronics within the hub retransmit the signal received on an input pair on all the other output pairs. The major task of the repeater electronics, therefore, is to ensure that the (strong) retransmitted signal being output on the outgoing pairs does not interfere with the received signal on the input pair which is relatively weak as a result of attenuation. This effect is known as **far end crosstalk** or **FEXT**. Special integrated circuits known as **adaptive crosstalk echo cancellation circuits** are needed to ensure reliable operation at 10 Mbps with 100 m wire lengths.

Irrespective of the transmission media being used, the communications controller card within each DTE comprises:

- A **medium access control (MAC) unit**, which is responsible for such functions as the encapsulation and de-encapsulation of frames for transmission and reception on the cable, error detection and implementation of the medium access control algorithm.

- A separate microprocessor, which implements both the network-dependent protocols (to be described in a later section) and selected higher level protocols to be described in Chapters 10 through 12.

In this way the complete communication subsystem is normally self-contained on a single printed circuit card that slots into the host system bus and provides a defined set of network (application) services to the host software. Normally, most commercial cards provide multiple connectors to support the different types of transmission medium.

Frame format and operational parameters

The format of a frame and the operational parameters of a typical CSMA/CD bus network are shown in Figure 6.10. The meaning and use of the various parameters will be described as the operation of the MAC unit is presented.

Each frame transmitted on the cable has eight fields. All the fields are of fixed length except the data and associated padding fields.

The **preamble field** is sent at the head of all frames. Its function is to allow the receiving electronics in each MAC unit reliably to achieve bit synchronization before the actual frame contents are received. The preamble pattern is a sequence of seven octets, each equal to the binary pattern 10101010. All frames are transmitted on the cable using Manchester encoding. As was described in Chapter 3, the preamble results in a periodic waveform being received by the receiver electronics in each DTE. The **start-of-frame delimiter (SFD)** is the single octet 10101011 which immediately follows the preamble and signals the start of a valid frame to the receiver.

The **destination** and **source network addresses** specify the identity of both the intended destination DTE(s) and the originating DTE, respectively. Each address field can be either 16 or 48 bits, but for any particular LAN installation the size must be the same for all DTEs. The first bit in the destination address

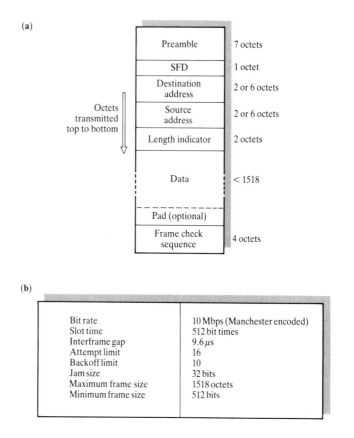

FIGURE 6.10

CSMA/CD bus network
characteristics:
(a) frame format;
(b) operational
parameters.

field specifies whether the address is an **individual address** or a **group address**. If
an individual address is specified, the transmitted frame is intended for a single
destination DTE. If a group address is specified, the frame is intended either for
a logically related group of DTEs (group address) or for all other DTEs connected to the network (**broadcast** or **global address**). In the latter case, the
address field is set to all binary 1s.

The **length indicator** is a two-octet field which indicates the number of
octets in the data field. If this value is less than the minimum number required
for a valid frame (minimum frame size), a sequence of octets is added, known as
padding. Finally, the **FCS field** contains a four-octet (32-bit) cyclic redundancy
check value that is used for error-detection.

Frame transmission

When a frame is to be transmitted, the frame contents are first encapsulated by
the MAC unit into the format shown. To avoid contention with other transmissions on the medium, the medium access control section of the MAC unit first
monitors the carrier sense signal and, if necessary, defers to any passing frame.

Then, after a short additional delay (known as the **interframe gap**) to allow the passing frame to be received and processed by the addressed DTE(s), transmission of the frame is initiated.

As the bit stream is transmitted, the transceiver simultaneously monitors the received signal to detect whether a collision has occurred. Assuming a collision has not been detected, the complete frame is transmitted and, after the FCS field has been sent, the MAC unit awaits the arrival of a new frame, either from the cable or from the controlling microprocessor. If a collision is detected, the transceiver immediately turns on the collision detect signal. This, in turn, is detected by the MAC unit which enforces the collision by transmitting the jam sequence to ensure that the collision is detected by all other DTEs involved in the collision. After the jam sequence has been sent, the MAC unit terminates the transmission of the frame and schedules a retransmission attempt after a short randomly selected time interval.

In the event of a collision, retransmission of the frame is attempted up to a defined maximum number of tries known as the **attempt limit**. Since repeated collisions indicate a busy medium, the MAC unit tries to adjust to the medium load by progressively increasing the time delay between repeated retransmission attempts. The scheduling of retransmissions is controlled by a process called **truncated binary exponential backoff** which works as follows. When transmission of the jam sequence is complete, and assuming the attempt limit has not been reached, the MAC unit delays (backs off) a random integral number of **slot times** before attempting to retransmit the affected frame. A given DTE can experience a collision during the initial part of its transmission, the **collision window**, which is effectively twice the time interval for the first bit of the preamble to propagate to all parts of the cable medium (network). The slot time is thus the worst-case time delay a DTE must wait before it can reliably know a collision has occurred. It is defined as:

$$\text{Slot time} = 2 \times (\text{transmission path delay}) + \text{safety margin}$$

where **transmission path delay** is the worst-case signal propagation delay going from any transmitter to any receiver on the cable network. This includes any delays experienced in repeaters. The slot time is double this delay (to allow for the corrupted signal to propagate back to the transmitting DTE) plus a safety margin. The slot time used is made equal to this figure rounded up to be a multiple number of octets at the bit rate used. As an example, for a 10 Mbps baseband coaxial cable network with a maximum of 2.5 km between any transmitter and any receiver, it is equal to 512 bit times or 64 octets. The number of slots times before the Nth retransmission attempt is then chosen as a uniformly distributed random integer R in the range $0 \leqslant R \leqslant 2^K$, where $K = \min(N, \text{backoff limit})$. A flow chart summarizing the frame transmission sequence is shown in Figure 6.11(a).

Frame reception

Figure 6.11(b) summarizes the frame reception process. At each active DTE connected to the cable, the MAC unit first detects the presence of an incoming

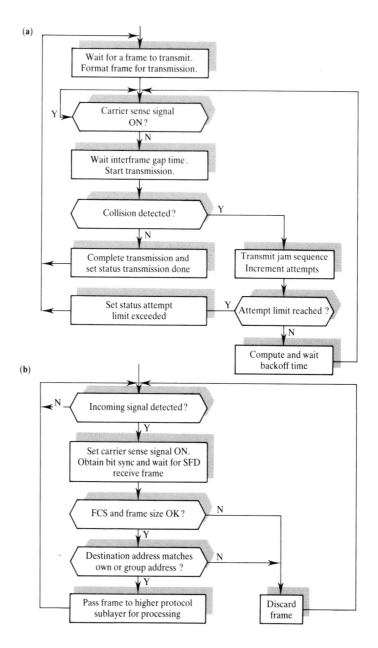

FIGURE 6.11

CSMA/CD MAC
sublayer operation:
(a) transmit;
(b) receive.

signal from the transceiver and switches on the carrier sense signal to inhibit any new transmissions from this DTE. The incoming preamble is then used to achieve bit synchronization and, after synchronization has been achieved, the Manchester-encoded data stream is translated back into normal binary form. The incoming bit stream is then processed.

First, the remaining preamble bits are discarded together with the start-of-frame delimiter, when this is detected. The destination address field is then processed to determine whether the frame should be received by this DTE. If so, the frame contents comprising the destination and source addresses and the data field are loaded into a frame buffer to await further processing. The received FCS field is then compared with that computed by the MAC unit during reception of the frame and, if they are equal, the start address of the buffer containing the received frame is passed to the next higher protocol layer, in the form of a service primitive, for further processing. Other validation checks are also made on the frame before initiating further processing. These include checks to ensure that the frame contains an integral number of octets and that it is neither too short nor too long. If any of these checks fail, the frame is discarded and an error status is sent to the higher sublayer. The latter will be expanded upon later.

Initially, the transmitted bit stream resulting from a collision is received by each active DTE in the same way as a valid frame. After the colliding DTEs have detected the collision and transmitted the jam sequence, they cease transmission. Fragments of frames received in this way therefore violate the minimum frame size limit and hence are discarded by the receiving DTEs. Also, the adoption of a **maximum frame size** means that the length of the frame buffers used for transmission and reception can be quantified. The FCS field is a 32-bit sequence generated using CRC–32 which, as may be recalled from Chapter 3, has a generator polynomial of degree 32.

6.3.2 Token ring

Token ring networks are also used primarily in technical and office environments. Their principle of operation is illustrated in Figure 6.12. Whenever a DTE (station) wishes to send a frame, it first waits for the token. On receipt of the token, it initiates transmission of the frame, which includes the address of the intended recipient at its head. The frame is repeated (that is, each bit is received and then retransmitted) by all DTEs in the ring until it circulates back to the initiating DTE, where it is removed. In addition to repeating the frame, however, the intended recipient retains a copy of the frame and indicates that it has done this by setting the **response bits** at the tail of the frame.

A DTE releases the token in one of two ways depending on the bit rate (speed) of the ring. With slower rings (4 Mbps), the token in released only after the response bits have been received. With higher speed rings (16 Mbps), it is released after transmitting the last bit of a frame. This is known as **early (token) release**.

A typical token ring network is shown in Figure 6.13(a) and the various components needed to connect a DTE to the cable medium are illustrated in Figures 6.13(b) and (c). The (trunk) cable medium is typically a screened twisted-pair which, since each segment around the ring forms a point-to-point link, is differentially driven at a bit rate of between 4 and 16 Mbps.

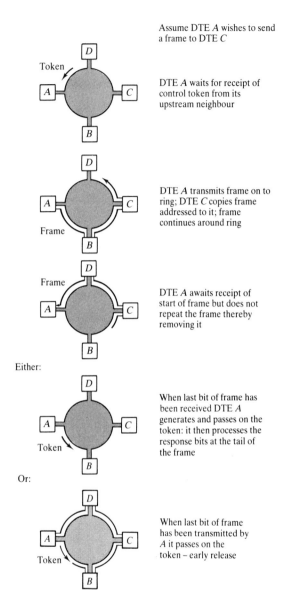

Assume DTE *A* wishes to send a frame to DTE *C*

DTE *A* waits for receipt of control token from its upstream neighbour

DTE *A* transmits frame on to ring; DTE *C* copies frame addressed to it; frame continues around ring

DTE *A* awaits receipt of start of frame but does not repeat the frame thereby removing it

When last bit of frame has been received DTE *A* generates and passes on the token: it then processes the response bits at the tail of the frame

When last bit of frame has been transmitted by *A* it passes on the token – early release

FIGURE 6.12

Token ring network: principle of operation.

As shown in Figure 6.13(b), a DTE can be connected directly to the ring or through a **concentrator**. This device connects directly to the main trunk cable and, in turn, provides direct drop connections to a number of DTEs. A concentrator is often used to simplify the wiring within a building. Typically, it is located at the point where the trunk cable enters (and leaves) an office. Direct drop connections are then used to connect each DTE in the office to the concentrator. It is also known, therefore, as a **wiring concentrator**; a typical installation may use many such devices.

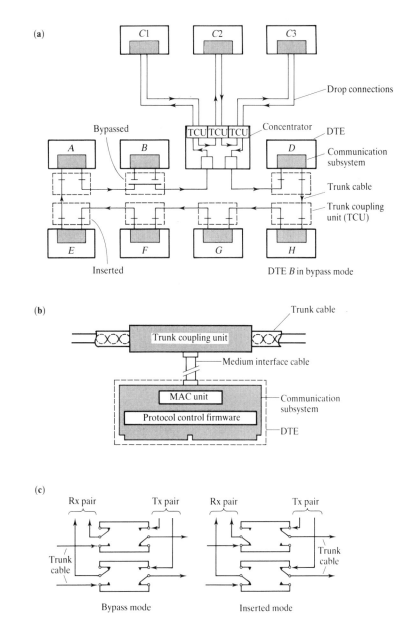

FIGURE 6.13

Token ring network
components:
(a) ring configuration;
(b) DTE interface;
(c) TCU schematic.

Ring interface

The **trunk coupling unit (TCU)** forms the physical interface with the cable
medium. It contains a set of relays and additional electronics to drive and receive
signals to and from the cable. The relays are so arranged that whenever the DTE

is switched off, the TCU is in the **bypass state** and a continuous transmission path through the TCU is maintained. The insertion of a DTE into the ring is controlled by the MAC unit on the communication controller card within the DTE. The MAC unit initiates the insertion of the DTE by activating both pairs of relays in the TCU. As can be seen in Figure 6.13(c), when inserted, this causes all received signals to be routed through the MAC unit. The receive/transmit electronics in the MAC unit then either simply read and relay (repeat) the received signal to the transmit side, if this DTE is not the originator of the frame, or remove the received signal from the ring, if it initiated the transmission.

The use of two pairs of relays connected in this way means that the MAC unit can detect certain open-circuit and short-circuit faults in either the transmit or receive pair of signal wires. Also, in the bypass state the MAC unit can conduct self-test functions, since any data output on the transmit pair are looped back on the receive pair. The DTE is connected to the TCU by a shielded cable containing two twisted-pair wires: one for transmission and the other for reception.

The MAC unit is responsible for such functions as frame encapsulation and de-encapsulation, FCS generation and error detection, and the implementation of the medium access control algorithm. Also, it supplies the ring master clock which is used for data encoding and decoding when the DTE is the active ring monitor (see later). Each circulating bit stream is differentially Manchester encoded by the active ring monitor and all other DTEs on the ring then frequency and phase lock to this bit stream using a **digital phase-locked loop (DPLL) circuit**. In addition, when the DTE is the active ring monitor, it ensures the ring has a **minimum latency time**. This is the time, measured in bit times at the ring data transmission rate, taken for a signal to propagate once around the ring. The ring latency time thus includes the signal propagation delay through the ring transmission medium together with the sum of the propagation delays through each MAC unit. Hence, for the control token to circulate continuously around the ring when none of the DTEs requires to use the ring (that is, all DTEs are simply in the repeat mode), the ring must have a minimum latency time of at least the number of bits in the token sequence to ensure that the token is not corrupted.

The token is 24 bits in length, so when a DTE is the active ring monitor, its MAC unit provides a fixed 24-bit buffer, which effectively becomes part of the ring to ensure its correct operation under all conditions. Although the mean data signalling rate around the ring is controlled by a single master clock in the active monitor, the use of a separate PLL circuit in each MAC unit means that the actual signalling rate may vary slightly around the ring. The worst-case variation is when the maximum number of DTEs (250) are all active, which is equivalent to plus or minus three bits. Unless the latency of the ring remains constant, however, bits will be corrupted as the latency of the ring decreases, or additional bits added as the latency increases. To maintain a constant ring latency, therefore, an additional **elastic (variable) buffer** with a length of six bits is added to the fixed 24-bit buffer. The resulting 30-bit buffer is initialized to 27 bits, then, if the received signal at the master MAC unit is faster than the master oscillator, the buffer is expanded by a single bit. Alternatively, if the received signal is slower, the buffer is reduced by a single bit. In this way the ring always comprises sufficient bits to allow the token to circulate continuously around the ring in the quiescent (idle) state.

Frame formats

Two basic formats are used in token rings: one for the control token and the other for normal frames. The control token is the means by which the right to transmit (as opposed to the normal process of repeating) is passed from one DTE to another, whereas a normal frame is used by a DTE to send either data or medium access control information around the ring. The format of the two types of frame is given in Figure 6.14 together with the bit sequence used for each field.

The start delimiter (SD) and end delimiter (ED) fields are special bit sequences used to achieve data transparency. They exploit the symbol encoding method used on the cable medium: all information bits transmitted on the medium are Manchester encoded, except for selected bits in the SD and ED fields. In contrast, the J and K symbols depart from the normal encoding rules,

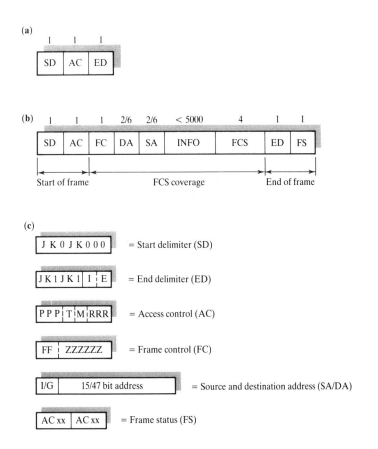

FIGURE 6.14

Token ring network frame formats and field descriptions: (a) token format; (b) frame format; (c) field descriptions.

being used instead to represent constant levels for the complete bit cell period. The J symbol has the same polarity as the preceding symbol whereas a K symbol has the opposite polarity to the preceding symbol. In this way the receiver can reliably detect the start and end of each transmitted token or frame irrespective of its contents or length. It should be noted, however, that only the first six symbols (JK1JK1 in the figure) are used to indicate a valid end of frame. The other two bits, I and E, have other functions:

- In a token, both the I and E bits are 0.

- In a normal frame, the I bit is used to indicate whether the frame is the first (or an intermediate) frame in a sequence (I = 1) or the last (or only) frame (I = 0).

- The E bit is used for error-detection. It is set to 0 by the originating DTE but, if any DTE detects an error while receiving or repeating the frame (FCS error, for example), it sets the E bit to 1 to signal to the originating DTE that an error has been detected.

The access control (AC) field comprises the priority bits, the token and monitor bits, and the reservation bits. As the name implies, it is used to control access to the ring. When it is part of the token, the priority bits (P) indicate the priority of the token and hence which frames a DTE may transmit on receipt of the token. The token bit (T) is used to discriminate between a token and an ordinary frame (a 0 indicates a token and a 1 a frame). The monitor bit (M) is used by the active monitor to prevent a frame from circulating around the ring continuously. Finally, the reservation bits (R) allow DTEs holding high-priority frames to request (in either repeated frames or tokens) that the next token to be issued should be of the requisite priority.

The frame control (FC) field defines the type of the frame (medium access control or information) and certain control functions. If the frame type bits (F) indicate a MAC frame, all DTEs on the ring interpret and, if necessary, act on the control bits (Z). If it is an I-frame, the control bits are only interpreted by the DTEs identified in the destination address field.

The source address (SA) and destination address (DA) fields can be either 16 bits or 48 bits in length, but for any specific LAN they are the same for all DTEs. The DA field identifies the DTE(s) for which the frame is intended. The first bit of the field indicates whether the address is an individual address (0) or a group address (1); individual addresses identify a specific DTE on the ring while group addresses are used to send a frame to multiple destination DTEs. The SA is always an individual address and identifies the DTE originating the frame. In addition, a DA consisting of all 1s is known as a broadcast address and denotes that the frame is intended for all DTEs on the ring.

The information (INFO) field is used to carry either user data or additional control information when included in a MAC frame. Although no maximum length is specified for the information field, it is limited in practice by the maximum time for which a DTE is allowed to transmit a frame when holding the control token. A typical maximum length is 5000 octets.

The frame check sequence (FCS) field is a 32-bit CRC. Finally, the frame status (FS) field is made up of two fields: the address-recognized bits (A) and the frame-copied bits (C). Both the A and C bits are set to 0 by the DTE originating the frame. If the frame is recognized by one or more DTEs on the ring, the DTE(s) sets the A bits to 1. Also, if it copies the frame, it sets the C bits to 1. In this way, the originating DTE can determine whether the addressed DTE(s) is non-existent or switched off, is active but did not copy the frame or is active and copied the frame.

Frame transmission

On receipt of a service request to transmit a data message (which includes the priority of the data as a parameter), the data are first encapsulated by the MAC unit into the standard format shown in Figure 6.14. The MAC unit then awaits the reception of a token with a priority less than or equal to the priority of the assembled frame. Clearly, in a system that employs multiple priorities, a procedure must be followed to ensure that all DTEs have an opportunity to transmit frames in the correct order of priority. This works as follows.

After formatting a frame and prior to receiving an appropriate token (that is, one with a priority less than or equal to the priority of the waiting frame), each time a frame or a token with a higher priority is repeated at the ring interface, the MAC unit reads the value of the reservation bits contained within the AC field. If these are equal to or higher than the priority of the waiting frame, the reservation bits are simply repeated unchanged. If it is lower, however, the MAC unit replaces the current value with the priority of the waiting frame. Then, assuming there are no other higher priority frames awaiting transmission on the ring, the token is passed on by the current owner (user) with this priority. On receipt of the token, the waiting MAC unit detects that the priority of the token is equal to the priority of the frame it has waiting to be transmitted. It therefore accepts the token by changing the token bit in the AC field to 1, prior to repeating this bit, which effectively converts the token to a start-of-frame sequence for a normal frame. The MAC unit then stops repeating the incoming signal and follows the converted start-of-frame sequence with the preformatted frame contents. While the frame contents are being transmitted, the FCS is computed and subsequently appended after the frame contents, before transmitting the end-of-frame sequence.

Once transmission of the waiting frame(s) has been started, the MAC unit stops repeating, thus removing the transmitted frame(s) after it has circulated the ring. In addition, it notes the state of the A and C bits in the FS field at the tail of the frame(s) to determine whether the frame(s) has (have) been copied or ignored. It then generates a new token and forwards this on the ring to allow another waiting DTE to gain access to the ring. It is possible to send more than one frame providing, firstly, that the priority of the other waiting frame(s) is (are) greater than or equal to the priority of the token and, secondly, that the total time taken to transmit the other frame(s) is within a defined limit known as the **token holding time**. The default setting for the latter is 10 ms. Flow charts describing the frame transmission and reception operation are given in Figure 6.15.

Frame reception

In addition to repeating the incoming signal (bit) stream, the MAC unit within each active DTE on the ring detects the start of each frame by recognizing the special start-of-frame bit sequence. It then determines whether the frame should simply be repeated or copied. If the F bits indicate that it is a MAC frame (see later section on ring management), the frame is copied and the C bits are interpreted and, if necessary, acted upon. However, if the frame is a normal data-carrying frame and the DA matches either the DTE's individual address or relevant group address, the frame contents are copied into a frame buffer and passed on for further processing. In either case, the A and C bits in the frame status field at the tail of the frame are set accordingly prior to being repeated. A flow chart describing the reception operation operation is given in Figure 6.15(b).

Priority operation

The priority assigned to a token by a MAC unit after it has completed transmitting any waiting frame(s) is determined by a mechanism that endeavours to ensure that:

(1)   frames with a higher priority than the current ring service priority are always transmitted on the ring first, and

(2)   all DTEs holding frames with the same priority have equal access rights to the ring.

This is accomplished by using both the P and R bits in the AC field of each frame coupled with a mechanism that ensures that a DTE that raises the service priority level of the ring returns the ring to its original level after the higher priority frames have been transmitted.

To implement this scheme, each MAC unit maintains two sets of values. The first set comprises three variables Pm, Pr and Rr. Pm specifies the highest priority value contained within any of the frames currently awaiting transmission at the DTE. Pr and Rr are known as **priority registers** and contain, respectively, the priority and reservation values held within the AC field of the most recently repeated token or frame. The second set of values comprises two stacks known as the Sr and Sx stacks which are used as follows.

All frames transmitted by a DTE on receiving a usable token are assigned a priority value in the AC field equal to the present ring service priority Pr, and a reservation value of zero. After all waiting frames at or greater than the current ring priority have been transmitted, or until the transmission of another frame

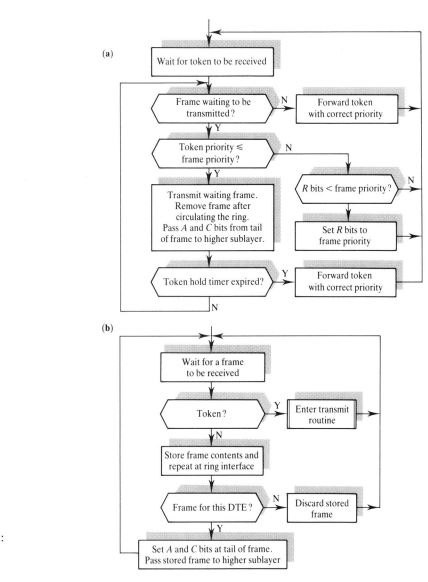

FIGURE 6.15

Token ring MAC
sublayer operation:
(a) transmit;
(b) receive.

would not be completed before the token holding time expires, the MAC unit generates a new token with:

(1) $P = Pr$ and R = the greater of Rr and Pm

if the DTE does not have any more waiting frames with a priority (as contained in register Pm) equal to or greater than the current ring service priority (as contained in register Pr), or does not have a reservation request (as contained in register Rr) greater than the current priority.

(2)   P = the greater of Rr and Pm   and R = 0

if the DTE has another waiting frame(s) with a priority (as contained in Pm) greater than the current priority Pr, or if the current contents of Rr are greater than the current priority.

Since in the latter case the DTE effectively raises the service priority level of the ring, it becomes what is known as a **stacking station** (DTE) and, as such, stores the value of the old ring service priority (Pr) on stack Sr and the new ring service priority (P) on stack Sx. These values are saved as it is the responsibility of the DTE that becomes the stacking station to lower the ring service priority level when there are no frames ready to transmit, at any point on the ring, with a priority equal to or greater than the P stacked on Sx. Also, a stack is used rather than a single register because a stacking station may need to raise the service priority of the ring more than once before the service priority is returned to a lower priority level. The different values assigned to the P and R bits of the token and the actions performed on the two stacks are summarized in Figure 6.16(a).

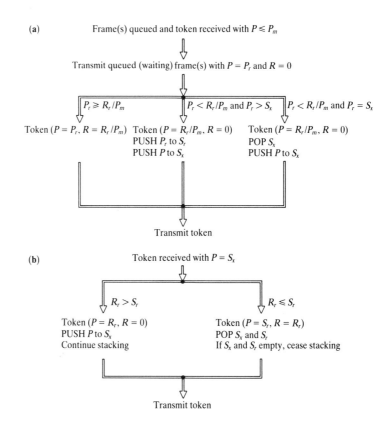

FIGURE 6.16

Token generation and stack modifications: (a) token generation [*Note:* Sx = 0 if stack empty]; (b) stack modification.

Having become a stacking station, the MAC unit claims every token that it receives with a priority equal to that stacked on Sx to examine the value in the R bits of the AC field to determine if the service priority of the ring should be raised, maintained or lowered. The new token is then transmitted with:

(1) $P = Rr$ and $R = 0$

if the value contained in the R bits (the current contents of register Rr) is greater than Sr. The new ring service priority (P) is stacked (PUSHed) on to Sx and the DTE continues its role as a stacking station.

(2) $P = Sr$ and $R = Rr$ (unchanged)

if the value contained in the R bits is less than or equal to Sr. Both values currently on the top of stacks Sx and Sr are POPped from the stack and, if both stacks are then empty, the DTE discontinues its role as a stacking station. These two operations are summarized in Figure 6.16(b).

Ring management

The preceding sections were primarily concerned with the transmission of frames and tokens during normal operation of the ring. Before this can take place, however, the ring must be set up. Also, if a DTE wishes to join an already operational ring, that DTE must first go through an initialization procedure to ensure that it does not interfere with the correct functioning of the established ring. In addition, during normal operation it is necessary for each active DTE on the ring to monitor continuously its correct operation and, if a fault develops, to take corrective action to try to re-establish a correctly functioning ring. Collectively, these functions are known as **ring management**. A list of the various MAC frame types associated with these functions is given in Figure 6.17.

Frame type	Function
Duplicate address test (DAT)	This is used during the initialization procedure to enable a station to determine that no other stations in the ring are using its own address
Standby monitor present (SMP)	Again, this is used in the initialization procedure to enable a station to determine the address of its upstream neighbour (successor) in the ring
Active monitor present (AMP)	These types of frames are transmitted at regular intervals by the currently active monitor and each station monitors their passage
Claim token (CT)	This is used in the procedure to determine a new active monitor if the current one fails
Purge (PRG)	This is used by a new active monitor to initialize all stations into the idle state
Beacon (BCN)	This is used in the beaconing procedure

FIGURE 6.17

Token ring management of MAC frame types.

Initialization When a DTE wishes to become part of the ring after being switched on or being reset, an initialization sequence is entered to ensure that no other DTEs in the ring are using the same address and to inform its immediate downstream neighbour that it has (re)entered the ring.

The initialization procedure starts with the transmission of a duplicate address test (DAT) MAC frame by the DTE with the A bits in the FS field set to 0. On receipt of a DAT frame, each active DTE in the ring inspects the DA field and, if it determines that it is the same as its own address, sets the A bits to 1. Hence, if the DAT frame returns to its originator with the A bits set to 1, the originator informs the network management sublayer and returns to the bypass state. The latter (as will be described in Chapter 10) then determines whether it should try again to become part of the ring. Alternatively, if the A bits are still set to 0 when the DAT frame returns to its originator, the DTE continues the initialization sequence by transmitting a standby monitor present (SMP) MAC frame.

A DTE that receives an SMP frame with the A and C bits set to 0 regards the frame as having originated from its immediate upstream neighbour and hence records the SA as the upstream neighbour's address (UNA). This is required for fault detection and monitoring functions as will be described later. The initialization phase is then complete.

Standby monitor Upon completion of the initialization sequence, the DTE can start to transmit and receive normal frames and tokens. In addition, the DTE enters the standby monitor state to monitor continuously the correct operation of the ring. It does this by monitoring the passage of tokens and special active monitor present (AMP) MAC frames, which are periodically transmitted by the currently active monitor, as they are repeated at the ring interface. If tokens or AMP frames are not detected periodically, the standby monitor times out (it maintains two timers for this function) and enters the claim token state.

In the claim token state, the DTE continuously transmits claim token (CT) MAC frames and inspects the SA in any CT frames it receives. Each CT frame transmitted contains, in addition to the SA of the originating DTE, the latter's stored UNA. Consequently, if a CT frame is received with an SA that matches its own address and a UNA that matches its own stored UNA, this means that the CT frame has successfully circulated around the ring. Consequently the DTE becomes the new active ring monitor. Alternatively, if a CT frame is received with an SA greater than its own address, this means that another DTE has made an earlier bid to become the new monitor. In this case the DTE effectively relinquishes its bid by returning to the standby monitor state.

Active monitor If the DTE is successful in its bid to become the new active monitor, it first inserts its latency buffer into the ring and enables its own clock. (Note that there is only one active monitor in the ring at any point in time.) It then initiates the transmission of a purge (PRG) MAC frame to ensure that there are no other tokens or frames on the ring before it initiates the transmission of a new token. When the DTE receives a PRG frame containing an SA equal to its own address, this indicates that the ring has been successfully purged. The DTE then initiates the neighbour notification process by broadcasting an AMP MAC frame. After a short delay, this is followed by the transmission of a new control token.

The DTE immediately downstream of the active monitor detects that the A bits in the AMP frame are 0 and hence reads the UNA from within the frame and updates its existing UNA variable. It then sets the A and C bits to 1 and repeats the frame. Subsequent DTEs around the ring detect that the A bits are non-zero and hence just record the passage of the AMP frame by resetting the AMP timer.

In addition, the DTE immediately downstream from the active monitor, after repeating the AMP frame, continues the neighbour notification process by broadcasting a similar SMP frame. In turn the next DTE downstream detects that the A bits are set to 0 in this frame, updates its UNA variable, sets the A and C bits to 1 and repeats the frame. It continues the process by broadcasting a new SMP frame with the A bits again set to 0. This procedure is carried out by each DTE around the ring and is subsequently re-initiated by the active monitor transmitting a new AMP frame at regular intervals. In this way, each active DTE in the ring can detect such failures as a DTE jabbering (continuously sending tokens, for example): the absence of AMP frames flowing around the ring means that the AMP timer in all the other DTEs will expire, thus initiating the transmission of CT frames followed, if the fault is still present, by entering a failure diagnostic procedure known as beaconing.

Beaconing   If a serious failure, such as a broken cable, arises in the ring, a procedure known as **beaconing** informs each DTE on the ring that the token-passing protocol has been suspended (until the affected failure domain has been located and repaired). The failure domain consists of:

- the DTE reporting the failure, which is referred to as the **beaconing station;**
- the DTE upstream of the beaconing station;
- the ring medium between them.

As an example, Figure 6.18(a) illustrates a failure domain assuming a break has occurred in the ring medium between DTEs *F* and *G*. In this example, *G* is the beaconing station and *F* its upstream neighbour. Normally, the beaconing state is entered if the timers associated with the AMP or token-passing procedures expire. When in this state, beacon (BCN) supervisory frames are continuously transmitted until either a beacon frame is received or a timer expires. If the latter occurs, the network management sublayer is notified and transmissions cease. Alternatively, if a beacon frame is received by a DTE with an SA equal to its own address, the failure is assumed to have cleared and the DTE enters the claim token state or, if a beacon frame is received with an SA different from the DTE address, the DTE enters the standby monitor state.

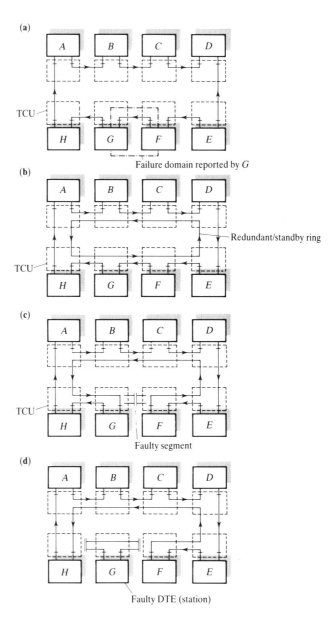

FIGURE 6.18

Ring fault detection and isolation: (a) failure detection; (b) redundant ring configuration; (c) segment isolation; (d) DTE (station) isolation.

Clearly, if the network comprises just a single ring, in the event of a failure it is necessary to repair the faulty segment before network transmissions can be resumed. An optional feature with the token ring, therefore, is to utilize a second, redundant ring transmitting in the opposite direction to the first ring. This network configuration is shown in Figure 6.18(b).

In such networks the TCU not only supports the functions outlined earlier, but can also be used to bypass a faulty ring segment or DTE. As an example, Figure 6.18(c) shows how the faulty ring segment (failure domain) illustrated in Figure 6.18(a) is bypassed. Essentially, once the failure domain has been located and reported, the relays in the TCU of *F* and *G* are activated to (hopefully) re-establish a continuous ring. If isolating the suspected faulty segment does not remove the fault, however, the next step is to initiate the isolation of DTE *G* completely, as shown in Figure 6.18(d). It should be noted from these figures that the redundant ring does not have a direct path to the MAC unit and is used simply to provide a means of bypassing a section of the ring. In this way, the order of the DTEs on a re-established ring is the same as that in the original ring.

It can be concluded from the foregoing that the medium access control procedures used with a token ring network are quite complicated, certainly compared with a CSMA/CD bus, for example. It should be remembered, however, that most of the procedures are implemented in special controller integrated circuits within the MAC unit, so their operation is transparent to the user. Moreover, many of these ring management procedures are only invoked when faults develop and so the overheads associated with them are, on the whole, modest.

6.3.3 Token bus

The third type of LAN supported in the standards documents is the **token bus** network. Because of the deterministic nature of a token medium access control method and the ability to prioritize the transmission of frames, token bus networks are used in the manufacturing industry (for factory automation) and other related domains, such as the process control industry. Under normal (error-free) conditions, the operation of this type of network is similar to that of the token ring network. However, because of differences in the two medium access methods (broadcast for bus, sequential for ring), the procedures used for handling management of the logical ring, such as initialization and lost token, are inevitably different. To avoid repetition, this section will concentrate mainly on the management procedures associated with token bus networks.

Various aspects of the operation and components associated with token bus networks are shown in Figure 6.19. Token bus networks normally utilize coaxial cable as the transmission medium and operate in either a broadband mode or a modified baseband mode known as **carrierband**. The modulation and interface control circuitry, as illustrated in Figure 6.19(a), performs such functions as:

- transmit data encoding (modulation),
- receive data decoding (demodulation),
- clock generation.

There is a standard interface between the physical interface module (PIM) and the attached DTE. In some cases, the PIM is integrated on to the communication board in the DTE.

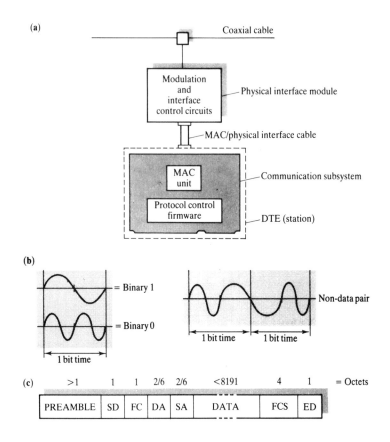

FIGURE 6.19

Token bus network principles: (a) DTE interface schematic; (b) carrierband encoding; (c) frame format.

The principle of operation of the carrierband mode is shown in Figure 6.19(b). Although the carrierband mode is the same as baseband in that each transmission occupies the complete cable bandwidth, in carrierband mode all data is first modulated before transmission using phase-coherent, frequency-shift keying. As can be seen, a binary 1 is transmitted as a single cycle of a sinusoidal signal of frequency equal to the bit rate, normally between 1 and 5 Mbps, while a binary 0 is transmitted as two cycles of a signal of twice the bit rate frequency. Notice also that there is no change of phase at the bit cell boundaries, hence, the term phase coherent.

It may be recalled from Chapter 2 that any extraneous noise signals picked up in the cable consist of an infinite number of frequency components. Furthermore, a basic baseband signal (waveform) is also made up of a possibly infinite number of frequency components. In contrast, a carrierband waveform has only two frequency components. This means that it is possible to use a filter at the receiver which only passes these two frequencies, thereby effectively blocking most of the noise signal, thereby significantly improving the noise immunity of the system. Clearly, this cannot be done with baseband since the filter would also affect the data signal.

The frame format used with token bus networks is shown in Figure 6.19(c). As can be seen, it is almost identical to that used with a token ring network. However, the J and K non-data bits, which are used in the SD and ED fields of a token ring to achieve data transparency, are replaced in carrierband mode by pairs of special non-data symbols.

Basic operation

Figure 6.20 illustrates the basic operation of a token bus network. There is a single control token and only the possessor of the token can transmit a frame. All DTEs that can initiate the transmission of a frame are linked in the form of a **logical ring**. The token is passed physically using the bus around the logical ring. Thus, on receipt of the token from its *predecessor* (upstream neighbour) on the ring, a DTE may transmit any waiting frames up to a defined maximum. It then passes the token on to its known *successor* (downstream neighbour) on the ring.

Before describing the various ring management procedures, it is perhaps helpful to restate two basic properties of bus networks. Firstly, with a bus network all DTEs are connected directly to the transmission medium. Hence, when a DTE transmits (broadcasts) a frame on the medium, it is received (or heard) by all active DTEs in the network. Secondly, there is a maximum time a DTE need wait for a response to a transmitted frame before it can assume that either the transmitted frame is corrupted or the specified destination DTE is inoperable. This time is known as the slot time (not the same as that used with a CSMA/CD bus) and can be defined as:

Slot time = 2 × (transmission path delay + processing delay)

where transmission path delay is the worst-case transmission propagation delay going from any transmitter to any receiver in the network, and processing delay is the maximum time for the MAC unit within a DTE to process a received frame and generate an appropriate response. A safety margin is then added and the slot time value is expressed in bit times rounded up to a multiple number of octets.

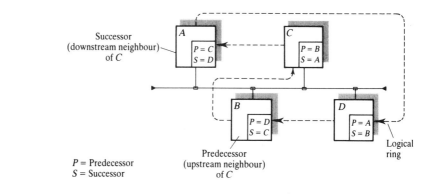

FIGURE 6.20

Token bus network principle of operation.

P = Predecessor
S = Successor

Frame type	Function
Claim token	This is used during the initialization sequence of the (logical) ring
Solicit successor	This is used during both the recovery procedure when a station leaves the ring and the procedure that allows a station to (re)enter the ring
Who follows me	This is used during the procedure that enables a station to determine the address of the station that is its successor in the ring
Resolve contention	This is used during the procedure that allows a new station to enter the ring
Set successor	This is used to allow a new station entering the ring to inform its new predecessor that it has joined the ring
Token	This is the control token frame

FIGURE 6.21

Token bus ring management of MAC frame types.

Under normal operation, the token is passed from one DTE in the logical ring to another using a short token frame. Each DTE need only know, therefore, the address of the next (downstream neighbour or successor) DTE in the logical ring. If a DTE fails to accept the token, however, the sending DTE uses a series of recovery procedures to find a new successor; these procedures get progressively more drastic if the DTE fails to evoke a response from a neighbouring DTE. Other procedures are concerned with the initialization of the ring and maintaining the correct operation of the ring as DTEs enter and leave the ring. Although it is possible to prioritize the token, as with a token ring, only a single priority ring will be considered initially. The MAC frame types used with the various ring management procedures to be described, together with a brief explanation of their use, are shown in Figure 6.21. More detailed explanations will be given as the various procedures are discussed.

Token passing

On receipt of a valid token frame, a DTE may transmit any frames it has waiting. It then passes the token to its known successor. After sending the token, the DTE listens to any subsequent activity on the bus to make sure that its successor is active and has received the token. If it hears a valid frame being transmitted, it assumes that all is well and that its successor received the token correctly. However, if it does not hear a valid frame being transmitted after the slot time interval, it must take corrective action.

If, after sending the token, the DTE hears a noise burst or frame with an incorrect FCS, it continues to listen for up to four more slot times. Then, if nothing more is heard, the DTE assumes that the token itself has become corrupted during transmission and repeats the token transmission. Alternatively, if a valid frame is heard during the delay of four slot times, it again assumes that its successor has the token. If a second noise burst is heard during this interval, the DTE treats this as a valid frame being transmitted by its successor and assumes that the token has been passed.

If, after repeating the token-passing operation and the monitoring procedures, the successor does not respond to the second token frame, the DTE assumes that its successor has failed and hence proceeds to establish a new successor. The sender first broadcasts a who-follows-me frame with its current successor's address in the data field of the frame. On receipt of this type of frame, all DTEs compare the address in the data field of the frame with its own predecessor address, that is, the address of the DTE that normally sends it the token. Then, the DTE whose predecessor is the same as the successor contained within the frame, responds by sending its own address in a set-successor frame. The DTE holding the token has thus established a new successor and in so doing has bridged around the failed DTE.

If the sending DTE does not receive a response to a who-follows-me frame, it repeats the frame a second time. If there is still no response, it takes more drastic action by sending a solicit-successor frame with its own address in the DA field. This effectively asks any DTE in the network to respond to it. If any operational DTEs hear the frame, they respond and the logical ring is re-established using a procedure known as **response window**. Alternatively, if no response is received, the DTE assumes that a catastrophe has occurred, for example, all other DTEs have failed, the medium has broken, or the DTE's own receiver section has failed (and hence cannot hear the response(s) from other DTEs to its own requests). Under these conditions, the DTE becomes silent but continues to listen for another DTE's transmissions.

Response window

This procedure is followed at random time intervals to allow new DTEs to enter an operational logical ring. The response window is the interval for which a DTE needs to wait for a response after transmitting a frame, and is thus the same as the network slot time. Each **solicit-successor** frame transmitted by a DTE specifies an SA and a DA; the frame is responded to by a DTE that wishes to enter the ring and has an address between the two addresses specified. Each DTE sends a solicit-successor frame at random intervals whenever it is the owner of the token.

When a DTE sends a solicit-successor frame, it is said to have opened a response window since, after sending this type of frame, the sending DTE waits for a response within the response window period. Then, if a DTE with an address within the range specified in the solicit-successor frame is waiting to enter the ring, it responds by sending a request to the sender of the frame to become its new successor in the logical ring. If the sender hears the response, called a set-successor frame, it allows the new DTE to enter the ring by making it its new successor and, in turn, passes it the token. Clearly, the specified address range may contain multiple DTEs all waiting to enter the ring in which case the response frames returned by each DTE will be corrupted. Should this happen, the soliciting DTE must try to identify a single responder by entering an arbitration procedure which works as follows.

Having ascertained that more than one DTE in the specified address range is waiting to enter the ring, the soliciting DTE starts to sequence through them by sending a **resolve-contention** frame. This procedure continues until it receives a positive reply. Any DTEs that responded to the earlier solicit-successor frame but which did not subsequently receive the token, each choose a value in the range 0 to 3 and listen for any further activity on the bus for this number of slot times. Then, if a DTE hears a tranmsission during its selected time, it delays its request and waits for another opportunity to become part of the ring; that is, when the next response window is opened. Alternatively, if it does not hear a transmission during its selected time, it continues to wait for the possible receipt of a resolve-contention frame. In this way, the worst-case delay the soliciting DTE need spend resolving the contention is limited.

Initialization

The initialization procedure is built on top of the response window procedure. Each DTE in the network monitors all transmissions on the bus and, whenever a transmission is heard, resets a timer, known as the **inactivity timer**, to a preset value. If a DTE loses the token during normal operation, this inactivity timer expires and the DTE enters the initialization phase, at which point it sends a **claim-token** frame. Clearly, as before, a number of DTEs may try to send a claim-token frame simultaneously, so the following procedure is followed to ensure that only a single token is generated.

Each potential initializer sends a claim-token frame with an information field length that is in integer number of slot times. The integer is either 0, 2, 4 or 6, the choice being based on the first two bits in the DTE's network address. After sending its claim-token frame, the DTE waits a further slot time before listening to the transmission medium. If it hears a transmission, it knows that another DTE(s) has sent a longer claim-token frame and so that DTE simply eliminates itself from trying to become the first owner of the token. If a transmission is not heard, however, the DTE repeats the above process using the next two bits from its address field. Again, if no transmission is detected, it uses the next pair of bits and so on until all address bits have been used. Then, if the medium is still quiet, the DTE has successfully become the first owner of the token. The unique owner of the token then continues the initialization process by using the response window procedure to allow the other waiting DTEs to enter the logical ring.

Although a DTE may remove itself from the logical ring at any time simply by not responding when the token is passed to it, a cleaner method is for the DTE to wait until it receives the token and then send a **set-successor** frame to its predecessor with the address of its own succesor in the information field. The DTE then sends the token to its own successor, as usual, in the knowledge that it is no longer part of the (logical) ring.

Priority operation

As with a token ring network, it is also possible to implement a priority mechanism with a token bus network. However, the access method used with a token bus only distinguishes four priority levels, called **access classes**. These are named 0, 2, 4 and 6, with 6 being the highest priority. As was mentioned earlier, token bus networks are used primarily in application domains such as manufacturing automation and process control. Hence typical usages of the four access classes are:

- Class 6: Urgent messages such as those relating to critical alarm conditions and associated control functions.

- Class 4: Messages relating to normal control actions and ring management functions.

- Class 2: Messages relating to routine data gathering for data logging.

- Class 0: Messages relating to program downloading and general file transfers, that is, long low-priority messages.

Each DTE has two timers which control the transmission of frames: the **token hold timer (THT)** and the **high-priority token hold timer (HP-THT)**. The latter controls the transmission of high priority frames to ensure that the available ring capacity (bandwidth) is shared between all DTEs. Thus when a DTE receives the token, it first sends any high-priority frames it has waiting up to a maximum determined by the HP-THT. Then, assuming the DTE is using the priority mechanism and providing the THT has not expired, the DTE begins to transmit any waiting lower priority frames using the following control algorithm.

Each DTE in the logical ring keeps a timer which indicates the time that has expired since it last received the token. This is held in a variable known as the **token rotation timer (TRT)**. When the DTE next receives the token, it first transfers the current value in the TRT into the THT and resets the contents of the TRT to zero. It then transmits any waiting high-priority frames, increasing the TRT at the same time, and computes the difference between a fixed time known as the **target token rotation time (TTRT)** and its current THT. If the difference is positive, the DTE can send any waiting lower priority frames until the TTRT is reached; if the difference is zero or negative, the DTE cannot send any lower priority frames on this pass of the token. Each DTE using the priority mechanism can transmit any waiting frames working from higher to lower access class until the TTRT is reached.

To illustrate the operation of this mechanism, consider the example shown in Figure 6.22. For clarity, the example assumes only two access classes. Also, all frames transmitted are assumed to be of a fixed length so the various times are directly proportional to the number of frames. The example assumes DTEs 9 and 1 only send high-priority frames each time they receive the token whereas DTEs 7 and 5 send lower priority frames whenever possible. Note that the logical ring is built so that the physcial DTE addresses are in descending numerical order. Also, the TTRT for the lower priority frames is fixed at a value equivalent to eight frames. The values in the left-hand column under each DTE labelled TRT are the token rotation times measured by that DTE for the previous rotation of the token. The values in the right-hand column labelled

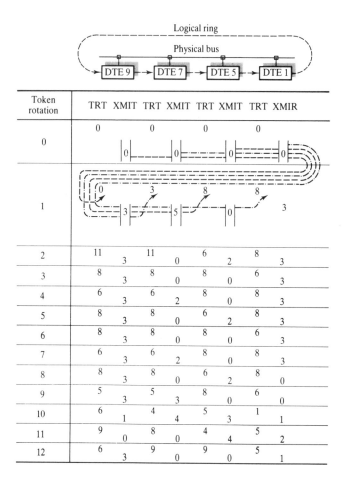

FIGURE 6.22

Prioritized ring example.

XMIT are the number of frames transmitted by the DTE each time it receives the token. Each row represents one rotation of the token.

All transmissions are assumed to begin after a period of inactivity and hence after the token has been rotating as rapidly as possible. The TRT in DTE 9 is therefore shown as zero to begin with. This assumes that the token passing and propagation delays are negligible compared with the time taken to transmit a normal frame. Also, it is assumed that the high-priority token-hold time is such that a DTE can send up to three high-priority frames on receipt of the token.

During the first rotation of the token, DTE 9 receives the token and sends its maximum of three high-priority frames before passing on the token. When DTE 7 receives the token from DTE 9 its TRT will have incremented to 3, since three frames have been transmitted since it last received the token. This means that DTE 7 can transmit five (TTRT − TRT) lower priority frames before passing on the token. On receipt of the token, the TRT held by DTE 5 will now be 8, as a total of eight frames have been transmitted since it last received the token. It cannot, therefore, transmit any lower priority frames on this pass of the token. DTE 1 then transmits three high-priority frames unconstrained by its computed TRT.

During the second rotation of the token, both DTE 9 and DTE 1 send three high-priority frames unaffected by their computed TRT, but this time DTE 7 is blocked from transmitting any lower priority frames (since its computed TRT exceeds 8 on receipt of the token) and DTE 5 is able to transmit two lower priority frames (TTRT $-$ TRT = 2).

During the third rotation of the token, both DTE 9 and DTE 1 each again send three high-priority frames but this time both DTE 7 and DTE 5 are blocked from sending any lower priority frames, since both their computed TRTs have reached the TTRT limit (8).

During the fourth rotation of the token, a situation similar to that in the second rotation prevails, but notice this time that the computed TRTs are such that DTE 7 has an opportunity to send two lower priority frames instead of DTE 5, which this time cannot send any frames. Similarly, during the fifth rotation of the token, DTE 5 is able to transmit two lower priority frames while DTE 7 is inhibited from sending any lower priority frames. The cycle then repeats itself and it can be readily deduced that, over any three rotations, DTEs 9 and 1 use 18/22nds (82%) of the available capacity and DTEs 7 and 5 share the remaining 4/22nds (18%) equally.

During the eighth rotation of the token, it is assumed that DTE 1 temporarily runs out of high-priority frames to transmit and hence DTEs 7 and 5 are able to transmit more of their waiting lower priority frames. Similarly, during the tenth rotation, DTE 9 runs out of high-priority frames, and so on.

Although this is a simple example, it nevertheless shows how the priority mechanism allows high-priority frames to be transmitted relatively unconstrained and lower priority frames to be transmitted in a fair manner whenever spare capacity is available.

6.4 PROTOCOLS

The various protocol standards for LANs, which deal with the physical and link layers in the context of the ISO Reference Model, are those defined in IEEE Standard 802. This standard defines a family of protocols, each relating to a particular type of medium access control method. The various IEEE standards and their relationship to the ISO Reference Model are shown in Figure 6.23.

The three medium access control (MAC) standards together with their associated physical media specifications are contained in the following IEEE standards documents:

- IEEE 802.3: CSMA/CD bus,
- IEEE 802.4: Token bus,
- IEEE 802.5: Token ring.

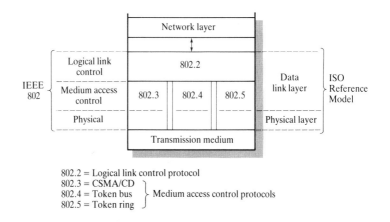

FIGURE 6.23

IEEE 802 protocol set.

The relevant ISO standards are the same except an additional 8 is used: ISO 8802.3, etc.

The descriptions that have been presented so far in this chapter have been concerned with the MAC control and physical layers of these three standards. Although each is different in its internal operation, they all present a standard set of services to the logical link control (LLC) layer, which is intended to be used in conjunction with any of the underlying MAC standards. In general, as mentioned earlier, the various MAC control and physical layers are normally implemented in firmware in special-purpose integrated circuits. This section, therefore, will concentrate only on the LLC and network layers and simply define the interface between the LLC and MAC layers. It should be noted that with a LAN the network, LLC and MAC layers are peer (end-to-end) protocols, since there are no intermediate switching nodes within the network itself similar, for example, to a packet-switching exchange in a PSPDN. The latter will be described in Chapter 8.

As can be seen in Figure 6.23, in the context of the ISO Reference Model the MAC and LLC layers collectively perform the functions of the ISO data link control layer. In this context, therefore, the MAC and LLC layers are referred to as sublayers rather than layers. It may be recalled from the last chapter that the functions of the data link layer are framing (signalling the start and end of each frame) and error detection. Also, for a reliable (connection-oriented) service, error control, flow control and link management. Thus the MAC sublayer performs the framing and error detection components – together with the medium access control operation – while the LLC sublayer performs the remaining functions.

6.4.1 MAC sublayer services

Irrespective of the mode of operation of the underlying MAC sublayer – CSMA/CD, token ring, token bus – a standard set of user services are defined for use by

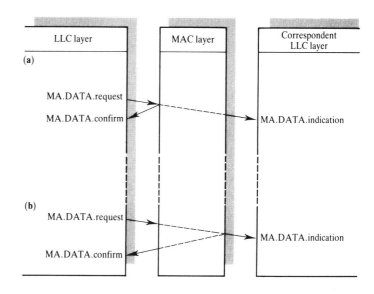

FIGURE 6.24

MAC user service
primitives: (a) CSMA/
CD; (b) token ring bus.

the LLC sublayer to transfer LLC–PDUs to a correspondent layer. The user service primitives supported are:

- MA.DATA.request,
- MA.DATA.indication,
- MA.DATA.confirmation.

A time sequence diagram illustrating their use is shown in Figure 6.24. For a CSMA/CD LAN, the confirm primitive indicates that the request has been successfully (or not) transmitted while for a token LAN it indicates that the request has been successfully (or not) delivered.

Each service primitive has associated parameters. The MA.DATA. request primitive includes: the required destination address (this may be an individual, group or broadcast address), a service data unit (containing the data to be transferred – that is, the LLC–PDU) and the required class of service associated with the PDU. The latter is used with token ring and token bus networks, for example, when a prioritized medium access control protocol is being used.

The MA.DATA.confirm primitive includes a parameter that specifies the success or failure of the associated MA.DATA.request primitive. As can be seen from the figure, however, the confirmation primitive is not generated as a result of a response from the remote LLC sublayer but rather by the local MAC entity. If the parameter is successful, this simply indicates that the MAC protocol entity (layer) was successful in transmitting the service data unit on to the network medium. If unsuccessful, the parameter indicates why the transmission attempt failed. As an example, if the network is a CSMA/CD bus, 'excessive collisions' may be a typical failure parameter.

6.4.2 LLC sublayer

The user services and operation of the LLC sublayer were described in the last chapter when data link control protocols were described. It may be recalled that the LLC protocol is based on the high-level data link control protocol HDLC. Also, that two types of user service and associated protocol are supported: connectionless and connection-oriented. In practice, however, in almost all LAN installations, and especially in the technical and office environment, only a **send-data-with-no-acknowledge (SDN)** connectionless protocol is used. The only user service primitive is thus the L_DATA.request and, because this is a best-try protocol, all data is transferred using the unnumbered information (UI) frame. The interactions between the LLC and MAC sublayers are thus as shown in Figure 6.25.

The L_DATA.request primitive has associated parameters. These are a specification of the source (local) and destination (remote) addresses and the user data (service data unit). The latter will be the **network layer protocol data unit (N-PDU)**. The source and destination addresses are each a concatenation of the MAC sublayer address of the DTE and an additional **service access point (SAP)** interlayer address – the **LLC–SAP**. The latter is used for interlayer routing purposes within the DTE, as will be expanded upon later.

A more detailed illustration of the interactions between the LLC and MAC sublayers is shown in Figure 6.26. The LLC sublayer reads the destination and source LLC service access point addresses (DSAP and SSAP) from the two address parameters associated with the L_DATA.request service primitive and inserts these at the head of an LLC–PDU. It then adds the network layer protocol data unit (N-PDU) to this and passes the resulting LLC–PDU to the MAC sublayer as the user data parameter of a MA.DATA.request MAC

FIGURE 6.25

LLC/MAC sublayer interactions.

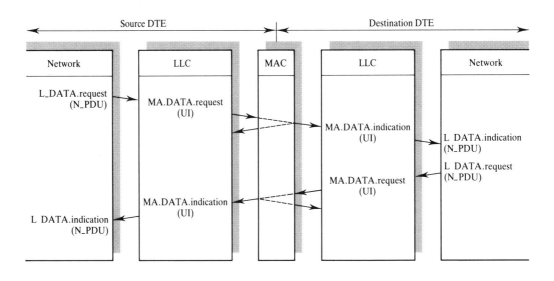

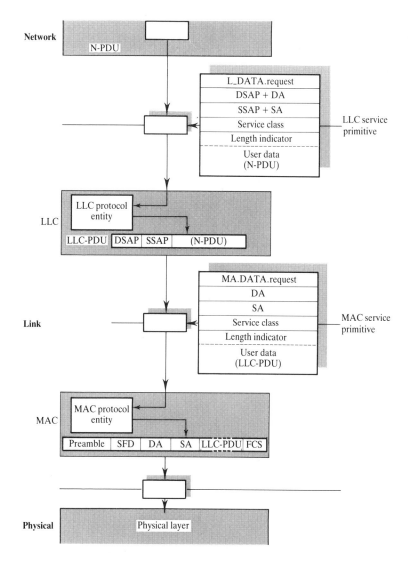

FIGURE 6.26

Interlayer primitives
and parameters.

primitive. Other parameters associated with this primitive include the MAC
sublayer destination and source addresses (DA and SA), the desired service
class, and the number of octets (length indicator) in the user data field. Typically, the service class is used by the MAC sublayer protocol entity to determine
the priority to be associated with the frame if a token network is being used.

On receipt of the request, the MAC protocol entity creates a frame ready
for transmission on the link. Thus, in the case of a CSMA/CD bus network, it
creates a frame containing the preamble and SFD fields, the DA and SA fields,
an I-field and the appropriate FCS field. The complete frame is then transmitted
bit serially on to the cable medium using the appropriate MAC method.

A similar procedure is followed in the destination DTE except that the corresponding fields in each PDU are read and interpreted by each layer. The user data field in each PDU is then passed up to the next layer together with the appropriate address parameters. A further description of layer interactions will be presented in Chapter 13, after the application-oriented protocols have been discussed.

6.4.3 Network layer

The primary role of the network layer is to route the messages associated with the higher protocol layers above it – in the context of the ISO Reference Model – across the network(s) that links the distributed community of DTEs. As with the data link layer, the network layer can operate either in a connectionless mode or a connection-oriented mode. In the case of LANs, however, messages (frames) are addressed and routed between the DTEs that are attached to the same LAN using their **point-of-attachment** (MAC sublayer) **addresses**. Moreover, since LANs utilize high bit rate transmission media that have a very low bit error rate, the DTE-to-DTE **transit delay** associated with each message transfer and the probability of message corruption are both very low. Consequently, a connectionless network layer service and associated protocol is normally used when all the DTEs are connected to a single LAN. Any error and flow control that are needed are then left to the transport layer protocol above it.

Because of its lack of functionality in LANs, the network layer is often known as an **inactive** or **null layer**. The user service primitives associated with the network service and their parameters are shown in Figure 6.27.

The basic message transfer service is N.UNIT_DATA – request and indication – which is a best-try service. The destination and source address parameters associated with this are concatenations of the MAC sublayer point-of-attachement address of the DTE (source or destination) and the LLC–SAP interlayer address extension. A further **network service access point (NSAP)** interlayer address extension is also used. Its role is the same as the LLC–SAP and collectively allow messages to be routed through the various protocol layers to different application processes (programs) within the same DTE. An example is a network server DTE that supports multiple applications such as electronic mail and file transfer.

In general, the **quality of service (QOS)** parameter includes fields to allow the transit delay, message priority and other network parameters to be specified. In the case of a single LAN, however, just the priority field has any significance. Finally, the user data parameter points to the message data to be transmitted.

The N.REPORT.indication primitive is used by the network provider – LLC and MAC sublayers – to report any error conditions that may occur relating to the transfer request. In the case of LANs, examples are excessive collisions if a CSMA/CD LAN is being used.

As may be concluded form the foregoing, the protocol associated with the network layer is minimal. It involves creating a **network protocol data**

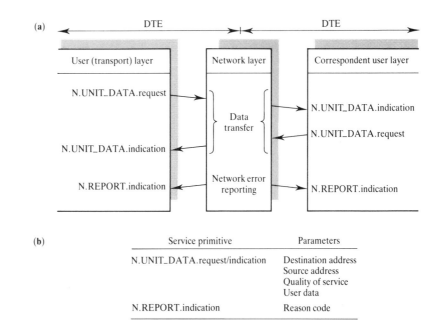

(a)

(b)

FIGURE 6.27

Network layer services:
(a) time sequence
diagram; (b) service
parameters.

unit (N-PDU) from the parameters associated with the incoming N.UNIT_
DATA.request primitive and passing this to the LLC sublayer in the user data
parameter of an L_DATA.request. Similarly, on receipt of an N-PDU from the
LLC sublayer – in the user data parameter associated with an L_DATA.indica-
tion – the protocol takes the source and destination network addresses from the
N-PDU and passes these together with the remaining user data, to the user
(transport) layer using a N.UNIT_DATA.indication primitive.

In conclusion, it should be pointed out that if the network comprises a
number of interconnected networks rather than a single LAN, then the network
layer protocol is far more complex. The total network is then known as an
internetwork or **internet** and the individual networks **subnetworks** or **subnets**.
Further discussion of the network layer will therefore be deferred until Chapter
9 when internetworking is discussed.

6.5 PERFORMANCE

To illustrate the relative performance of the three medium access methods
discussed, a set of simulations have been carried out by the author, the results of
which are presented in Figure 6.28.

In the simulations that were carried out, all LAN segments were assumed
to be of the same length – 2.5 km – and operate at the same bit rate – 10 Mbps.
Also, the number of DTEs/stations that are attached to them is 100 in each case.

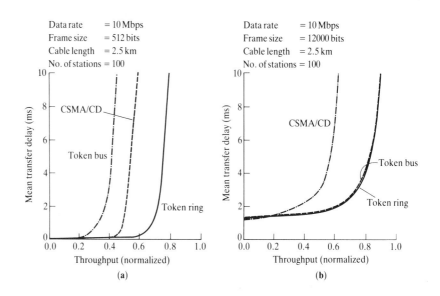

FIGURE 6.28

LAN performance comparisons: (a) 512-bit frames; (b) 12000-bit frames.

The graphs then show the mean time a frame takes to be transferred across the LAN as a function of the offered load. The load is expressed as a fraction of the available bit rate and is referred to as the **normalized throughput**. The graphs in part (a) relate to the case when all frames to be transmitted are 512 bits in length and those in part (b) when all frames are 1200 bits. Also, in the case of the smaller frame size, only a single frame is transmitted on receipt of the token. In practice, this may be higher but, since it is a function of the priority of the frames, then it is not included.

In addition there will, of course, be a mix of short and long frames and hence the mean transfer times will be in between those shown on each set of graphs.

Frames are randomly generated at each station and the **transfer time** is defined as the time from the generation of a frame – and hence when it arrives at that MAC sublayer input queue – to the time it is successfully received at the destination. It thus includes the time the frame is waiting in the MAC sublayer input queue, the delay associated with the particular medium access control method, and the time to transmit the frame.

As can be seen from the graphs, the mean throughput is higher with the larger frame size with each type of LAN. This is because the overheads associated with each frame relative to the frame contents are less with the larger frame size. Notice also, however, that with a token ring LAN, the throughput is less sensitive to the smaller frame size than the token bus LAN. This is because the size of the token is only 24 bits with a token ring, compared with 152 bits with a token bus. Also, the processing overheads associated with a token bus are higher than with a token ring.

With each set of graphs it should be realized that since the throughput is normalized, to achieve a particular throughput, a larger number of frames will be generated with a smaller frame size. Hence with the CSMA/CD access method, the probability of a collision occurring at a particular throughput level is higher with the smaller frame size. In addition, with the smaller frame size the overheads associated with the medium access method increase significantly in terms of the fraction of the time that is lost for collisions and the associated recovery procedure.

In conclusion, it can be said that the differences in throughput are only significant for offered loads in excess of, say, half the total throughput capacity. For offered loads less than this, the mean transit time of all three LANs is similar. In practice, with all but the more advanced applications of the type that will be identified in the next chapter, most LANs operate with only modest offered loads relative to their maximum capacity. In cases where the load is significant, however, the token access method is superior. Moreover, as will be expanded upon in the next chapter, CSMA/CD is inappropriate for higher bit rate LANs.

EXERCISES

6.1 List the four main types of network topology currently in widespread use for LANs and, with the aid of sketches, explain their major operation.

6.2 Use a sketch and associated text to describe how a set of DTEs are interconnected to form a CSMA/CD LAN using the following types of transmission media:

(a)   twisted-pair,
(b)   thin-wire coaxial cable,
(c)   thick-wire coaxial cable and drop cables.

6.3 Explain the meaning of the term broadband working in the context of a coaxial cable LAN. Sketch a typical broadband LAN showing the main networking components required and explain their function. Describe the overall operation of such a network and how multiple data transmission services are derived from a single cable.

6.4 Describe the principle of operation of the following medium access control methods as used in LANs:

(a)   CSMA/CD,
(b)   control token,
(c)   slotted ring.

6.5 Explain the meaning of the following terms associated with a CSMA/CD bus network:

(a)   slot time,
(b)   jam sequence,
(c)   random backoff.

6.6 Describe the principle of operation of the control token medium access control method and, with the aid of diagrams, explain how it may be used with both a bus and a ring network topology. Clearly identify the various control fields associated with each topology.

6.7 Define the structure and contents of a typical frame as used in a slotted ring. Describe the meaning of each field within a frame and the operation of the associated ring protocol. Clearly explain how access to the ring is shared between the stations (DTEs) making up the ring.

6.8 Produce a sketch showing the components necessary to attach a DTE (station) to a thick-wire CSMA/CD bus network. Give an outline of the function of each component in the context of the overall operation of such a network. Define the structure and contents of each frame transmitted and the meaning of each field.

6.9 With the aid of a sketch, explain how a collision can occur with the CSMA/CD medium access control method.

Explain the meaning of the terms interframe gap and jam sequence and hence, with the aid of flowcharts, describe the principle of operation of the transmit and receive sections of the MAC sublayer.

6.10 Explain the operation of the CSMA/CD medium access control method in relation to a hub wiring configuration.

6.11 Produce a schematic diagram showing the components necessary to attach a DTE (station) to a token ring network and give an outline of the function of each component. Include sufficient detail to show how a DTE, once attached to the network, may operate in either the inserted or bypassed mode. Also, the location and function of a wiring concentrator.

6.12 With the aid of a series of sketches, explain the principle of operation of the token medium access control method in relation to a token ring network.

Clearly identify the two alternative token release methods that are used.

6.13 Describe the structure and contents of a token and an information frame as used in a token ring LAN. Explain the meaning of each field within the two frame types and, with the aid of flowcharts, describe the principle of operation of the transmit and receive sections of the MAC sublayer.

6.14 Explain the fault detection method that is used with token ring LANs. Also, how the reliability of the LAN can be enhanced by the introduction of a redundant ring.

6.15 Explain what is understood by the following terms as used in a token ring network:

(a) minimum latency time,
(b) token-holding time,
(c) modified Manchester coding.

6.16 Describe the operation of the priority control scheme used with token ring networks to control the order of transmission of frames of varying priority on to the ring. Include in this description the function of:

(a) the priority and reservation bits contained within each frame,
(b) the priority registers and stacks held in each station,
(c) a stacking station.

6.17 State the aims of the following ring management procedures used with a token ring network and explain their operation:

    (a)   initialization,

    (b)   standby monitor,

    (c)   active monitor,

    (d)   beaconing.

6.18   Define the meaning of the term slot time as used with a token bus network and explain the token-passing procedure used with such networks during both normal and abnormal operation. Include in these descriptions references to the following:

    (a)   to bridge around a faulty DTE,

    (b)   to allow new DTEs to enter an operational logical ring,

    (c)   to create a new token when a ring is first established.

6.19   Explain the function of the following variables held by each DTE to control the order of transmission of frames that have varying priority on a token bus network:

    (a)   high-priority token-hold time,

    (b)   token rotation timer,

    (c)   target token rotation time.

    Produce a sketch, with an accompanying description of an example, to illustrate how the token rotation timer varies as frames are transmitted and the token rotates around the ring. Assume just two priority levels and deduce, from the example, the percentage of the available transmission capacity at each level.

6.20   (a)   Outline the function of the LLC and MAC protocol layers as defined in the IEEE 802 standards documents and indicate their relationship with the lower protocol layers in the ISO Reference Model. Define a typical set of user service primitives for both the LLC and MAC layers and produce a time sequence diagram to illustrate how each LLC primitive is implemented using the defined MAC services.

    (b)   Explain the interlayer interactions that occur when an L_DATA.request service primitive is received by the LLC layer. Clearly identify the parameters associated with each primitive.

6.21   Explain the function of a connectionless network layer. Use a time sequence diagram to show the service primitives provided with the layer and also the parameters associated with each primitive.

6.22   Given the graphs of Figure 6.28(a) and (b), explain the relative performance of a CSMA/CD, token bus, and token ring LAN.

CHAPTER SUMMARY

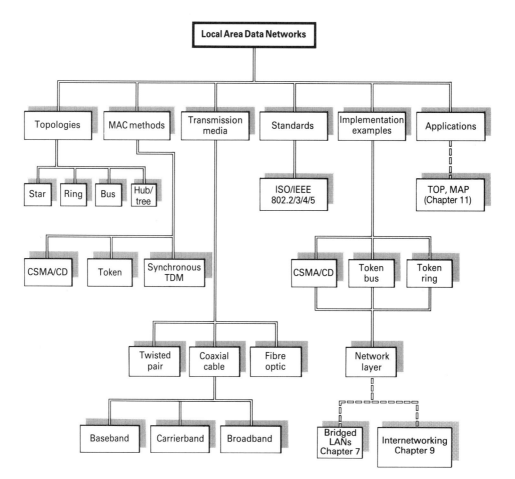

7

High-speed and
bridged local area
networks

CHAPTER CONTENTS

CHAPTER OBJECTIVES

When you have completed studying the material in this chapter you
should be able to:

- describe the operation of FDDI and DQDB LANs;
- understand the function and basic architecture of a bridge;
- know the advantages of a bridge relative to a repeater;
- describe the operation of a transparent bridged LAN and the spanning tree algorithm associated with it;
- describe the operation of a source routing bridged LAN and the route finding procedure associated with it;
- appreciate the differences and advantages and disadvantages of spanning tree and source routing bridged LANs;
- understand the effect on overall LAN performance of various bridge characteristics and interconnection topologies.

7.1 INTRODUCTION

The rapid establishment of standards relating to local area networks (LANs), coupled with the development by the major semiconductor manufacturers of inexpensive chipsets for interfacing computers to them, has resulted in LANs forming the basis of almost all commercial, research, and university data communication networks.

As the application of LANs has grown, so the demands on them in terms of data throughput and reliability have also grown. For example, an early application of LANs was to enable a distributed community of personal workstations (such as PCs) to access an electronic mail server or, say, a laser printer. Such applications involve a relatively small number of transactions, so the resulting demand on the transmission bandwidth of the LAN is only modest. More recently, however, there has been an increase in applications that demand significantly higher bandwidth. For example, the introduction of local communities of diskless workstations that share a common (networked) file system. This means that all file accesses by each of the workstations are via the network thus considerably increasing the demands on network bandwidth. Also, sophisticated applications involving the transmission of documents incorporating images and other media are becoming more common, again considerably increasing the demands on the capacity of the LAN.

Most early LAN installations comprised just a single LAN segment to which the distributed community of workstations and associated peripheral servers were attached. As indicated in the previous chapter, however, the number of stations (systems) that can be attached to a single LAN segment and its physical length are limited. Hence, as the acceptance and applications of LANs has become more widespread, LAN installations comprising multiple linked segments have evolved. This trend has steadily continued and today most large LAN installations are of this type.

7.2 INTERCONNECTION METHODS

A small, but typical, establishment-wide LAN showing some of the different interconnection devices and topologies that are used is shown in Figure 7.1. As was described in the last chapter, the basic means of interconnecting LAN segments is to use physical-layer repeaters. With repeaters, however, the frame transmissions originating from each station propagate (and hence load) the complete network, even though many of these frames may be intended for a station on the same segment as the originating station. This means that the more advanced applications of the type just outlined often result in a substantial load on the total network bandwidth, even though only a small percentage of the traffic on each segment is intended for systems attached to other segments. To overcome this problem, devices known as **bridges** have been introduced as an alternative means of interconnecting LAN segments. A basic bridge interconnects just two

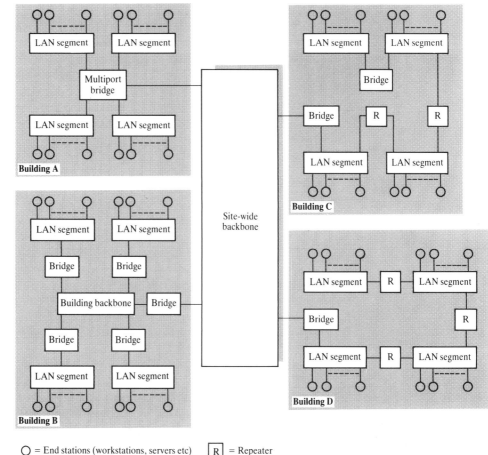

FIGURE 7.1

Typical establishment-wide LAN.

 = End stations (workstations, servers etc)   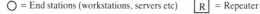 = Repeater

segments, but more sophisticated bridges – known as **multiport bridges** – can be used for the interconnection of a larger number of segments. Normally, the segments have only a relatively small physical separation between them, so multiport bridges are used mainly in a single office complex.

An alternative way of using bridges is to create what is known as a backbone subnetwork. Normally no end systems (workstations, servers etc) are connected to a backbone and they are used solely for inter-segment traffic. For interconnecting only a small number of segments in a single building, backbones of the same type as the interconnected segments (CSMA/CD, token bus or token ring) are used. They are known as **building backbones**.

As the number of interconnected segments increases, there comes a point at which the transmission bandwidth required by the backbone to meet the inter-segment traffic starts to exceed that available with the basic LAN types. To overcome this problem, backbones based on newer high-speed LAN types are used. An example is the **fibre distributed data interface (FDDI)** LAN. This is an optical fibre-based ring network that operates at a bit rate in excess of 100 Mbps. Moreover, it can be used for the interconnection of segments that are spread over a wider geographical area than a single building, such as a university campus or manufacturing plant. The resulting network is then known as an **establishment** or **site backbone**. This chapter includes descriptions of two high-speed LAN types and also two types of bridge that now feature in the standards documents. The chapter concludes with a description of the relative performance of the different LAN topologies that are used.

7.3 HIGH-SPEED LANs AND MANs

The three types of LAN described in the last chapter operate at bit rates ranging from 1 to 16 Mbps. As has just been indicated, although this is adequate for many applications, the interconnection of LANs through intermediate (backbone) networks requires higher-speed LANs to perform the backbone function. Two examples are FDDI and another fibre-based network known as **distributed-queue, dual-bus (DQDB)**. Each has been developed for the interconnection of LANs – FDDI for use in a single establishment such as a university campus and DQDB either for a similar environment or for the interconnection of LANs located in different parts of a town or city. In the latter case they are then known as **metropolitan area networks** or **MANs**.

FDDI can also be used as a basic LAN in applications that demand very high throughputs. An example is the connection of a set of (client) workstations to a server that contains a database of **multimedia information** containing files of data consisting of integrated voice, image and data. The quantity of data in each file can then be very large – several tens of megabytes – so that high-speed LANs are needed to achieve acceptable response times.

7.3.1 Operational modes

The simplest and most widely installed type of LAN is CSMA/CD. As described in the last chapter, this is based on a shared bus network and the stations (DTEs) share the medium by means of the CSMA/CD medium access control algorithm. In general, bus networks work well provided the ratio T_p/T_{ix} is a small fraction. It may be recalled from Chapter 2, that T_p is the signal propagation delay time of the transmission medium and T_{ix} is the time to transmit a frame. Hence if T_p is very much less than T_{ix}, the time wasted when a collision occurs $- 2 \times T_p$ in the worst case – is short compared with the time to transmit a frame. This same time also determines the minimum frame size that can be used.

For example, for a bus with $T_p = 25\,\mu s$ (2.5 km) and a mean frame size of 10 000 bits:

$$- \text{at } 10\,\text{Mbps}, \frac{T_p}{T_{ix}} = \frac{25}{1000} = \frac{1}{40}$$

therefore 500 bits will have been transmitted before a collision is detected;

$$- \text{at } 100\,\text{Mbps, } \frac{T_p}{T_{ix}} = \frac{25}{100} = \frac{1}{4}$$

5000 bits will have been transmitted before a collision is detected;

$$- \text{at } 200\,\text{Mbps, } \frac{T_p}{T_{ix}} = \frac{25}{50} = \frac{1}{2}$$

a complete frame will have been transmitted before a collision is detected.

Above 200 Mbps, the CSMA/CD access method, in addition to being inefficient, requires a minimum frame size in excess of 10 000 bits to work with this length of cable, and higher for longer cable lengths. It is for these reasons that high-speed LANs utilize a control token – FDDI – or a form of slotted bus – DQDB – medium access control method.

7.3.2 FDDI

The fibre distributed data interface (FDDI) LAN standard is defined in ISO 9314. It uses multimode or single mode fibre and operates at a bit rate of 100 Mbps. It uses dual counter-rotating rings in the same way as a token ring LAN to enhance reliability. It also operates with a token medium access control method. There are, however, a number of significant differences between the two LANs and these are now described.

Network configuration

As indicated, FDDI uses two counter rotating rings to enhance reliability: one is referred to as the **primary ring** and the other the **secondary ring**. As described in the last chapter, the secondary ring can be used either as an additional transmission path or purely as a back-up in the event of a break occurring in the primary ring. A typical network configuration is shown in Figure 7.2.

As can be seen, there are two types of station (DTE): a **dual attach station (DAS)** which is connected to both rings and a **single attach station (SAS)** which is attached only to the primary ring. In practice, most user stations are attached to the ring via **wiring concentrators** since then only a single pair of fibres is needed and the connection cost is lower.

If the LAN is being used as a backbone, then most attached stations will be bridges. The protocol used to reconfigure the LAN into a single ring in the event of a ring failure was described in the last chapter and will not be repeated.

The basic fibre cable is **dual core** with **polarized duplex** (two position) **connectors** at each end. This means that each end of the cable has a different physical key so that it can only be connected into a matching socket. This prevents the transmit and receive fibres from becoming inadvertently

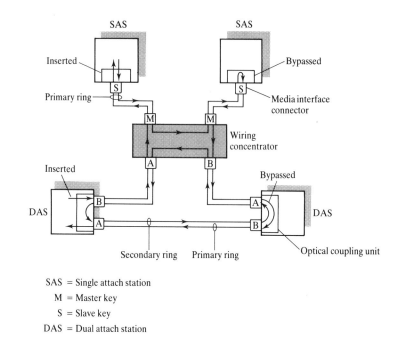

FIGURE 7.2

FDDI networking
components.

SAS = Single attach station
M = Master key
S = Slave key
DAS = Dual attach station

interchanged and bringing down the total network. As a further precaution, different connectors are used to connect each station type – SAS and DAS. In common with the basic token ring, special coupling units are used to isolate (bypass) a station when its power is lost. With FDDI, these are either active or passive fibre devices.

Although the topology is logically a ring, physically it is normally implemented in the from of a hub/tree structure. An example is shown in Figure 7.3(a). To ensure that changes to the wiring are carried out in a controlled way, a combination of **patch panels** and wiring concentrators are used. Typically these are located in the wiring closet (room) associated with either a floor (if a local FDDI ring is being used) or a building (if the ring is a backbone). In the latter case, the patch panels are interconnected as shown in part (b) of the figure to create a tree structure with the root located in, say, the computer centre. Drop cables are used to connect each station – workstations or bridges – to the ring.

Each patch panel has a number of possible attachment points associated with it. In the absence of a connection at a particular point, the ring is maintained using short **patch cables** each with the same type of connector. Adding a new station or concentrator simply involves removing a patch cable and replacing it with a corresponding drop cable. As indicated in the last chapter, this approach is known as **structured wiring**. The ring can exceed 100 km in length and have up to 1000 stations attached to it.

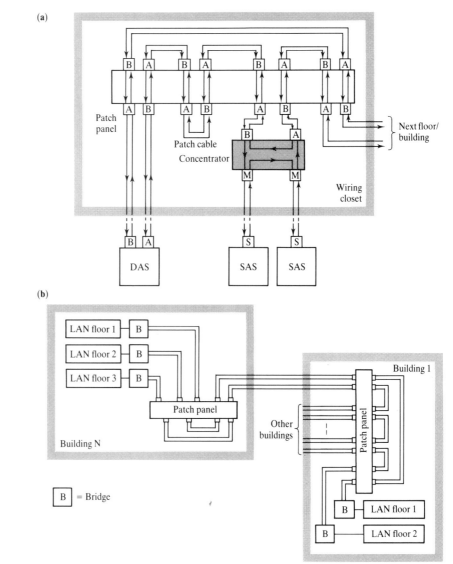

FIGURE 7.3

FDDI wiring schematic:
(a) building;
(b) establishment.

Physical interface

The physical interface to the fibre cable is shown in Figure 7.4. In a basic token ring network, at any instant, there is a single active ring monitor which, amongst other things, supplies the master clock for the ring. Each circulating bit stream is encoded by the active ring monitor using differential Manchester encoding. All the other DTEs (stations) in the ring then frequency and phase lock to the clock extracted from this bit stream. However, such an approach is not suitable at the

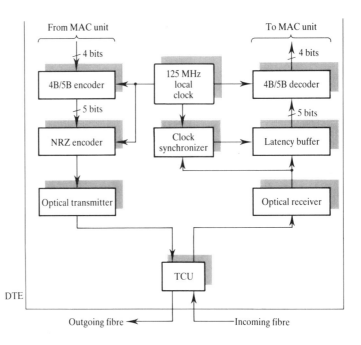

FIGURE 7.4

FDDI physical interface
schematic.

data rates of an FDDI ring since this would require a rate of 200 Mbaud.
Instead, each ring interface has its own local clock. Outgoing data is then
transmitted using this clock while incoming data is received using a clock that is
frequency and phase locked to the transitions in the incoming bit stream. As will
be seen, all data is encoded prior to transmission so that there is a guaranteed
transition in the data stream at least every two bit cell periods, ensuring that the
received data is sampled (clocked) very near to the nominal bit cell centres.

All data to be transmitted is first encoded, prior to transmission, using a
4 of 5 group code. This means that for each four bits of data to be transmitted, a
corresponding five-bit **code word** or **symbol** is generated by the encoder. The
latter is thus known as a **4B/5B encoder**. The five-bit symbols corresponding to
each of the 16 possible four-bit data groups are shown in Figure 7.5(a). As can
be seen, there is a maximum of two consecutive zero bits in each symbol. The
latter are then shifted out through a further NRZI encoder which produces a
signal transition whenever a 1 bit is being transmitted and no transition when a
0 bit is transmitted. In this way, there is a guaranteed signal transition at least
every two bits.

The use of five bits to represent each of the 16 four-bit data groups means
that there are a further 16 unused combinations of the five bits. Some of these
combinations (symbols) are used for other (link) control functions, such as
indicating the start and end of each transmitted frame or token. A list of the link
control symbols is shown in the figure, while Figure 7.5(b) shows the format
used for frames and tokens. In general, the meaning and use of each field is the
same as with the basic token ring but, because of the use of symbols rather than

(a)

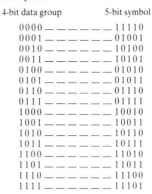

Data symbols

4-bit data group	5-bit symbol
0000	11110
0001	01001
0010	10100
0011	10101
0100	01010
0101	01011
0110	01110
0111	01111
1000	10010
1001	10011
1010	10110
1011	10111
1100	11010
1101	11011
1110	11100
1111	11101

Control symbols

IDLE	11111
J	11000
K	10001
T	01101
R	00111
S	11001
QUIET	00000
HALT	00100

(b)

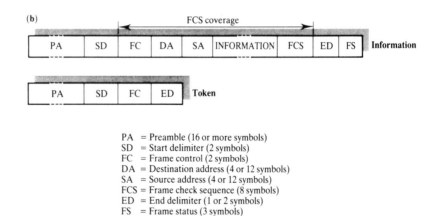

FCS coverage

| PA | SD | FC | DA | SA | INFORMATION | FCS | ED | FS | Information |

| PA | SD | FC | ED | Token |

PA = Preamble (16 or more symbols)
SD = Start delimiter (2 symbols)
FC = Frame control (2 symbols)
DA = Destination address (4 or 12 symbols)
SA = Source address (4 or 12 symbols)
FCS = Frame check sequence (8 symbols)
ED = End delimiter (1 or 2 symbols)
FS = Frame status (3 symbols)

FIGURE 7.5

(a) 4B/5B codes;
(b) frame formats.

bits, there are some differences in the structure of each field, which will now be explained.

The preamble (PA) field is comprised of 16 or more IDLE symbols which, since they each consist of five 1 bits, causes the line signal to change at the maximum frequency. This is thus used for establishing (and maintaining) clock synchronization at the receiver. The start delimiter (SD) field consists of two control symbols (J and K) which enable the receiver to interpret the following frame contents on the correct symbol boundaries. The FC, DA and SA fields have the same meaning as before, but the (decoded) information field in the data frames can be up to 4500 octets with FDDI. The end delimiter (ED) field contains one or two control symbols (T). Finally, the frame status (FS) field, although it has a similar function to the FS field in the basic ring, consists of three symbols that are combinations of the two control symbols R and S.

The local clock used in the physical interface is 125 MHz which, because of the use of 4B/5B encoding, yields a data rate of 100 Mbps. Moreover, since all transmissions are encoded into five-bit symbols, each five-bit symbol must first be buffered at the receiver before it can be decoded. However, the use of two symbols (J and K) for the SD field to establish correct symbol boundaries means that a 10-bit buffer is used at the receiver. This is known as the **latency** (or **elastic**) **buffer**.

Frame transmission and reception

The short latency time (and hence number of bits in circulation) of the basic token ring means that it is necessary for a DTE (station), after initiating the transmission of an information fame, to wait until the FS field at the tail of the frame has been received before transmitting a new token. With an FDDI ring, however, because there is a 10-bit buffer in each ring interface, the latency time is much longer, especially for a large ring containing the maximum of 1000 DTEs. With FDDI, to improve the utilization of the available ring capacity, a station initiates the transmission of a new token immediately after it has transmitted the FS symbol. It then follows the token with IDLE symbols until it receives the SD symbols indicating the start of a new frame or token. This is known as early token release and was shown earlier in Figure 6.12.

As with the basic token ring, the source station removes a frame after it has circulated the ring. Because of the long latency of an FDDI ring, however, more than one frame may be circulating around the ring at one time. The ring interface, therefore, must repeat the SD, FC and DA fields (symbols) of any received frames before it can determine if its own address is in the SA field. This can result, however, in one or more frame fragments – comprising SD, FC and DA fields – circulating around the ring. This means that a DTE, on receipt of a usable token, starts to transmit a frame and concurrently receives and discards any frame fragments that may be circulating around the ring.

Priority operation

Unlike the basic token ring, which is based on the use of priority and reservation bits, the priority operation of an FDDI ring uses the same principle as that used with a token bus network. As may be recalled, this is based on a parameter known as the **token rotation time (TRT)**. The TRT is the time that has expired since a station last received the token. It thus includes the time taken by this station to transmit any waiting frames as well as the time taken by all other stations in the ring for this rotation of the token. Clearly, if the ring is lightly loaded, then the TRT short. As the loading on the ring increases, so the TRT measured by each station increases. Thus the TRT is a measure of the total ring loading. The priority control algorithm then works by only allowing lower priority frames to be transmitted by a station if its measured TRT is lower than a preset maximum limit for each station, known as the **target token rotation time (TTRT)**.

In addition to normal data – known as **asynchronous data** since it is generated at random time intervals – FDDI rings can also support the transmission of **synchronous data**. An example is digitized voice which must be sampled at regular time intervals. Synchronous data is treated as the highest priority data for transmission purposes since late arrival will render it useless. For this type of data, each station is allocated a **synchronous allocation time (SAT)** which defines the maximum length of time that the station can transmit synchronous data each time it receives the token. It is thus analogous to the high-priority token hold time used in token bus LANs.

A further timer, known as the **token hold timer (THT)**, is used for the transmission of normal data. When a station next receives the token, it first transfers the current value in the TRT into the THT and then resets the TRT to zero. Next it transmits any waiting synchronous data, at the same time increasing the TRT and THT contents, and then computes the difference between the TTRT and its current THT. If the difference is positive, the station can transmit any waiting normal data until the TTRT is reached. However, if the difference is zero or negative, the station cannot send any normal data on this pass of the token. An example illustrating the priority mechanism was given in the last chapter when the token bus LAN was described and will not be repeated here.

7.3.3 DQDB

As indicated earlier, distributed-queue, dual-bus (DQDB) is a high-speed, broadcast bus network that has been developed to interconnect LANs either within an establishment or over a public area such as a town or city. In the latter case, they are known as metropolitan area networks or MANs rather than LANs. DQDB is now an international standard defined in IEEE 802.6 (ISO 8802.6).

Access control method

The access control method is based on a distributed queuing algorithm known as **queued-packet, distributed-switch (QPSX)**. The general topology and access control method are shown in Figure 7.6.

DQDB is a multiple access broadcast bus similar in principle to a CSMA/CD bus. However, a slotted access method is used to overcome the access control limitations of the latter. In order to broadcast data, the bus is implemented in the form of two unidirectional buses similar to a ring network. Unlike the ring, however, the two ends are not connected. Each bus is implemented as a series of point-to-point segments, which means that optical fibre can be used to

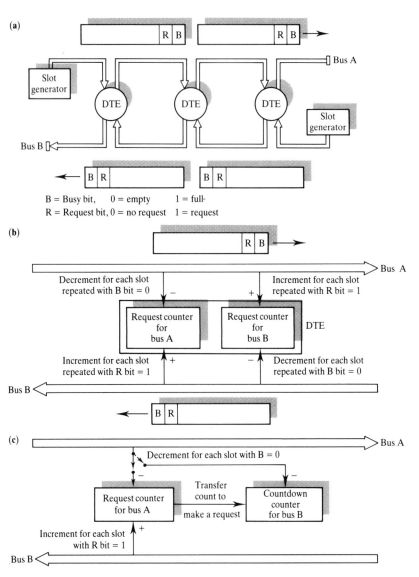

FIGURE 7.6

DQDB access control
method: (a) dual bus
schematic; (b) request
counters; (c) request
mechanism.

implement the bus. As the two buses pass data in opposite directions, broadcasting data involves transmitting it on both buses.

Each bus carries a continuous stream of fixed-sized data **slots** that are generated by the corresponding **slot generator**. Then, as with a slotted ring, each DTE simply reads each bit at each bus input port and repeats it one bit cell later on the corresponding output port. Each slot contains two bits at its head which are used in the distributed queuing algorithm: **busy** or **B bit** and the **request** or **R bit**. Data is then transmitted between two DTEs by the sending DTE writing it into a free slot on each of the two buses.

As can be seen in part (b) of the figure, access to the slots on each bus is controlled by a separate **request counter**, one for each bus. Requests for slots on one bus are made using the R bit in slots on the other bus. Then, for each counter, whenever a slot passes with the R bit set, the contents of the corresponding counter are incremented by one. Similarly, whenever an empty slot is repeated at the interface with the opposite bus, the counter is decremented by one. At any point in time, therefore, the request counter for each bus contains the number of outstanding requests for slots from DTEs that are downstream of the DTE on the particular bus.

To transmit a unit of data – known as a **cell** or sometimes a packet – the sending DTE first sets the R bit in the first slot that is repeated at each bus interface which has a zero R bit. It then transfers the current contents of the request counter for the required bus to a second counter – one for each bus – known as the **countdown counter**, at the same time resetting the contents of the request counter to zero. This has the effect of placing the waiting cell in the **distributed queue** for the two buses.

While a cell is queued for the buses, any slots that are repeated at each bus interface with their R bit set, cause the appropriate request counter to be incremented as before. Slots repeated on the opposite bus with their B bit reset, however, now only cause the countdown counter for that bus to be decremented. The waiting cell is then transmitted on each bus when the related countdown counter becomes zero. The general scheme is shown in part (c) of the figure. The slotted bus structure has the property that it maintains an almost constant (and very low) access delay up to approximately 90% of the total bus capacity. This is significantly better than FDDI.

Priority control scheme

As with FDDI, DQDB networks have been developed to carry both asynchronous and synchronous data. A priority control scheme is used to ensure the synchronous data is transmitted at a higher priority. There are up to four priority levels, each controlled by a separate pair of request and countdown counters. The general arrangement for controlling access to bus A is as shown in Figure 7.7. A similar procedure is used for bus B.

As can be seen, there is a separate R bit for each priority class. These are shown as R1 through R4, where R1 is the highest priority. Assume initially there are no cells awaiting transmission on bus A from this DTE – part (a):

- when an empty slot (B = 0) is repeated at the interface with bus A, the **access control unit** (ACU) associated with bus A decrements all its four request counters by one;

- when a slot is repeated at the interface with bus B with a priority of 2 (for example), then the ACU for bus B increments only request counters 2, 3 and 4 and leaves the higher priority counters (in this case RQ-C (1)) unchanged. This means that lower priority requests will not delay the transmission of higher priority cells.

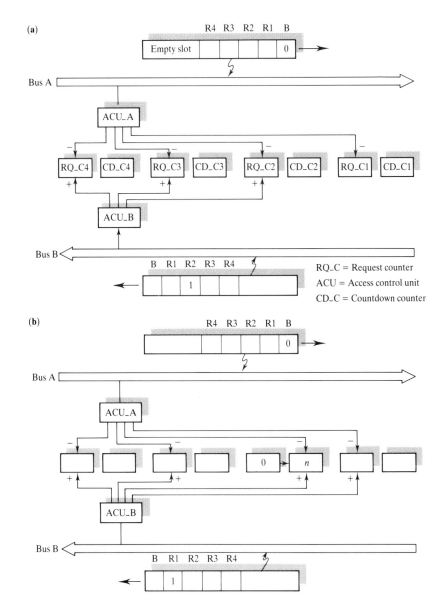

FIGURE 7.7

Priority control method:
(a) no transmission
requests pending;
(b) cell (packet) queued
at priority 2.

Now assume a cell becomes ready to transmit on bus A of priority 2 – part (b):

● the current contents of RQ-C (2), are transferred to CD-C (2) and RQ-C (2) is reset to zero;

● when an empty slot passes, RQ-C (1, 3 and 4) and CD-C (2) are decremented;

● if a slot with an R bit of, say, priority 1 passes, then RQ-C (1, 3 and 4) and CD-C (2) are incremented;

- the segment is transmitted when CD-C (2) becomes zero.

It can be deduced that incrementing any lower priority CD-Cs when a request of higher priority is received, effectively delays the transmission of any waiting cells in that priority class. This again results in a very efficient utilization of the transmission bandwidth which is maintained for both single and multiple priority cells.

Cell structure

DQDB networks have been developed for the interconnection of LANs that are distributed over one or more establishments within a town or city, as illustrated in Figure 7.8. The cell structure used in DQDB networks – LAN or MAN – has

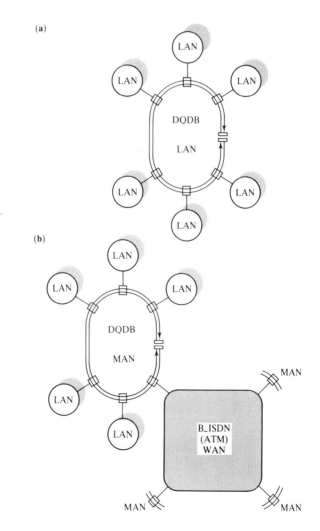

FIGURE 7.8

DQDB applications: (a) as a LAN; (b) as a MAN.

been made compatible with the next generation of public **wide area networks (WANs)**, which are known as **broadband integrated services digital networks** or **B-ISDN**. The B-ISDN has been developed not just to transmit voice (for telephony) and data but also other types of media such as photographic quality images and moving images (video). To cater for this it is proposed that all media – voice, data, image and video – are segmented into small fixed-sized **cells** or **packets** prior to transmission. This has the advantage that the available network transmission bandwidth can be used more efficiently than in the current rigid transmission hierarchy which has been developed for voice. Consequently the next-generation WANs will operate using **cell switching** rather than circuit switching as is currently used.

As will be described in the next chapter when WANs are discussed, a form of cell switching known as packet switching is already widely used for data. Current packet-switching networks use variable length packets so when the term packet is used to describe a cell, the term **fast packet switching** is used to describe the type of switching in the network. Alternatively, the term **asynchronous transfer mode** or **ATM** is used since the cells relating to the same call may arrive at their destination with varying delays between them. All three terms thus refer to the same principle and DQDB networks have been developed to be compatible with such networks.

The cell (packet) structure is shown in Figure 7.9. As can be seen, each cell comprises 53 octets (bytes) and contains a fixed header of 5 octets and a body of 48 octets. The **access control** field contains the request and busy bits. The **virtual channel identifier (VCI)** field is used for switching in MAN applications. When a call is first being set up, each switching exchange within the network assigns a new VCI which is then carried by all the subsequent data-carrying cells associated with that call on the selected outgoing link. This is placed in a routing table together with the VCI that is being used on the

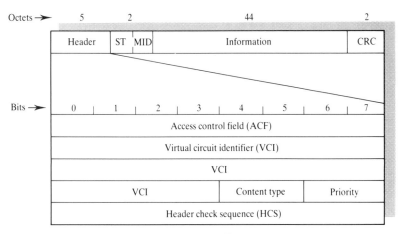

FIGURE 7.9

DQDB cell structure.

ST = Segment type   MID = Message identifier

incoming link. During the subsequent data transfer phase of the call, cell switching involves simply reading the VCI from the cell and replacing it with the new VCI from the routing table to be used on the required outgoing link.

The foregoing relates to calls that are first set up in the normal correction-oriented mode. In contrast, DQDB operates in a connectionless mode in which no route – physical or logical – is set up prior to the data transfer phase. To retain compatibility with the cells used in connection-oriented calls, the VCI in the header is not used. Instead, two additional octets from the information field are used for switching purposes. In private (DQDB LAN) network applications, however, the VCI field can also be used for the same function.

The segments (cells) associated with a call are transmitted in one of four **segment types** as defined in the ST field:

- **single segment:** if the call data can be carried in a single cell;
- **first segment:** if this is the first cell relating to a multiple cell message;
- **intermediate segment:** the intermediate cells relating to the message;
- **last segment**: the last cell of the message.

The **message identifier (MID)** field is assigned by the sending DTE to all cells relating to a multiple cell message. It is a unique identifier which is used by the destination DTE to relate intermediate segments to the same call. Typically it is the physical point-of-attachment address of the DTE on the DQDB bus. The last pair of octets are used as a CRC for the detection of errors in the cell contents.

Frame transmission and reception

Frames can be routed between interconnected LANs using either the destination MAC address in each frame or the network-layer address. In the latter case the interconnection device is known as a **router** rather than a bridge. Since this chapter is concerned with bridges, it only considers the transmission of frames when the DTEs attached to the DQDB bus are bridges. The operation of routers is discussed in Chapter 9 when the subject of internetworking is considered.

As indicated in the last chapter, the MAC address of a DTE (station) connected to a LAN, is a 48-bit globally-unique address. A bridge has knowledge of the stations that are local to each of the links to which it is attached. Thus if the DTE – in practice a bridge – connected to the DQDB bus receives a frame addressed to a station that is not attached to its local LAN, it must broadcast the frame on the bus. All DTEs on the bus therefore receive the frame. The DTE which determines that it is addressed to a station on its local LAN then forwards the frame on the LAN in the normal manner for that LAN.

To broadcast the frame on the bus, the source DTE must first segment the frame into a number of cells ready for transmission. This is shown in Figure 7.10. As can be seen, the complete frame, including the destination and source (MAC) addresses and its CRC, is first segmented into a sequence of 44-octet

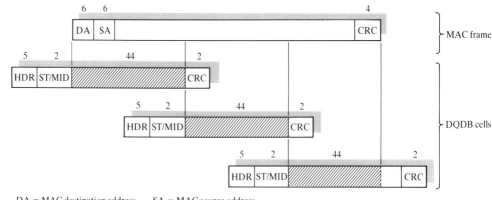

FIGURE 7.10

DQDB
MAC frame
segmentation.

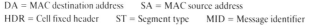

DA = MAC destination address   SA = MAC source address
HDR = Cell fixed header   ST = Segment type   MID = Message identifier

cells, each with a 7-octet header and a 2-octet CRC. The complete set of cells is then broadcast (one after the other) to all the other DTEs attached to the (dual) bus.

Since the sending DTE cannot determine the position of the DTE on the bus from the destination MAC address, it initiates the transmission of the complete set of cells on both buses using the broadcast access control mechanism described earlier. Thus all the cells relating to the frame – first, intermediate and last – carry the same MID field. As each cell is received (and repeated) by a DTE at the appropriate bus interface, it proceeds to reassemble them into a complete frame. It then determines from the destination MAC address at the head of the frame whether it should be forwarded onto its local LAN or discarded.

The actual length of the reassembled frame is determined from the length field. Also, if any of the cells relating to a frame are found to have errors – CRC failure – the frame is simply discarded. It is left to the two communicating LAN stations to determine (and recover from) loss of the frame. As indicated in the last chapter, this is normally done in the transport layer. It should also be noted that the segmentation and reassembly functions performed at each bus interface are carried out purely for transmission purposes. The forwarding (relaying) software associated with the bridge is unaware that this is being done. Instead it views the DQDB bus simply as a broadcast bus similar, in principle, to a high-speed CSMA/CD bus.

7.4 BRIDGES

Before describing the operation of a bridge, it is perhaps helpful to review the basic operation of a repeater. Repeaters are used to ensure that the electrical signals transmitted by the drive electronics within each DTE (station) propagate throughout the network. In the context of the ISO Reference Model, they operate purely at the physical layer, as shown in Figure 7.11(a).

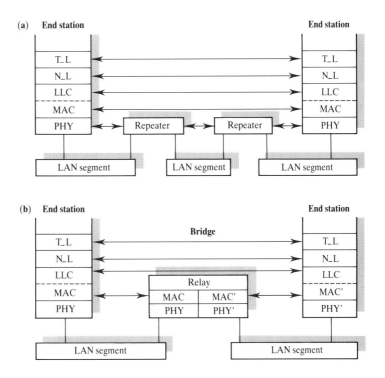

FIGURE 7.11

LAN interconnection
schematic:
(a) repeaters;
(b) bridges.

For any type of LAN segment, a defined maximum limit is set on both the physical length of the segment and on the number of (end) stations that may be attached to it. When interconnecting segments, therefore, a repeater is used to limit the electrical drive requirements of the output circuits associated with the physical interface to that of a single segment. In this way, the presence of multiple segments (and hence repeaters) in a transmission path is transparent to the source station. The repeater simply regenerates all signals received on one segment and forwards (repeats) them onto the next segment.

It may be concluded that there is no *intelligence* (a microprocessor, for example) associated with a repeater. Hence if just repeaters are used for interconnection purposes, all frame transmissions from any station connected to a segment will propagate throughout the network. This means that, in terms of bandwidth, the network behaves like a single segment. Thus as the demands on each LAN segment (in terms of transmission bandwidth) increase, so the loading of the total LAN increases with a corresponding deterioration in overall network response time.

Bridge functions

The function of a bridge is similar to a repeater in so much that it is used for interconnecting LAN segments. When bridges are used, however, all frames received from a segment are buffered (stored) and error checked before they are repeated (forwarded). Moreover, only frames that are free of errors and are addressed to stations on a different segment from the one on which they were received are forwarded. Consequently, all transmissions between stations connected to the same LAN segment are not forwarded and hence do not load the rest of the network. A bridge thus operates at the MAC sublayer in the context of the ISO Reference Model. This is shown in Figure 7.11(b). The resulting LAN is then referred to as a **bridged LAN**.

Buffering frames has advantages and disadvantages relative to a repeater. In general, the advantages far outweigh the disadvantages but it is perhaps helpful to list both.

The advantages of a bridge are:

- Removal of any physical constraints associated with the interconnection function means that both the total number of attached stations and the number of segments making up the LAN can be readily increased. This is particularly important when building large LANs distributed over wide geographical areas.

- The buffering of frames received on a segment before forwarding them on another means that the two interconnected segments can operate with a different medium access control (MAC) protocol. Thus it is easier to create a LAN that is a mix of the different basic LAN types.

- Bridges perform their relaying function based solely on the MAC sub-address in a frame with the effect they are transparent to the protocols being used at higher layers in the protocol stack. This means they can be used with LANs supporting different protocol stacks.

- They allow a large network to be managed more readily and effectively via the LAN itself. For example, by incorporating management-related software into the bridge design, performance data relating to a LAN segment can be readily logged and later accessed. Also, access control mechanisms can be incorporated to improve network security, and the operational configuration of a LAN can be changed dynamically by controlling the status of the individual bridge ports.

- Partitioning a LAN into smaller segments improves the overall reliability, availability and serviceability of the total network.

The disadvantages of bridges are:

- Since a bridge receives and buffers all frames in their entirety before performing the relaying (forwarding) function, they introduce an additional store-and-forward delay compared with repeaters.

- There is no provision for flow control at the MAC sublayer and hence bridges may overload during periods of high traffic; that is, a bridge may need to store more frames (prior to forwarding them on each link) than it has free buffer storage.

- Bridging of segments operating with different MAC protocols means that the contents of frames must be modified prior to forwarding because of the different frame formats. This necessitates a new frame check sequence being generated by each bridge with the effect that any errors introduced while frames are being relayed across a bridge will go undetected.

As has been indicated, bridges are now widely used because the advantages far outweigh the disadvantages. The two most widely adopted types of bridge are transparent (also known as spanning tree) bridges and source routing bridges, the main difference between them being the routing algorithm.

With transparent bridges, the bridges themselves make all routing decisions while with source routing bridges, the end stations perform the major route-finding function. There is now an international standard relating to transparent bridges – IEEE 802.1 (D) – and source routing forms a part of the IEEE 802.5 – token ring – standard for interconnecting token ring segments.

Each will be described separately, but it should be stressed that the descriptions are only intended as technical overviews. Moreover the standards are still evolving, so the reader seeking more details should refer to the relevant standards directly.

7.5 TRANSPARENT BRIDGES

With a **transparent bridge**, as with a repeater, the presence of one (or more) bridges in a route between two communicating stations is transparent to the two stations. All routing decisions are made exclusively by the bridge(s). Moreover, a transparent bridge automatically initializes and configures itself (in terms of its routing information) in a dynamic way after it has been put into service. A schematic of a bridge is shown in Figure 7.12(a) and a simple bridged LAN in part (b).

A LAN segment is physically connected to a bridge through a **bridge port**. A basic bridge has just two ports whereas a **multiport bridge** has a number of connected ports (and hence segments). In practice, each bridge port comprises the MAC integrated circuit chipset associated with the particular type of LAN segment – CSMA/CD, token ring, token bus – together with some associated port management software. The latter is responsible for initializing the chipset at start-up – they are all programmable devices – and for buffer management. Normally, the available memory is logically divided into a number of fixed-size units known as buffers. Buffer management involves passing a free buffer (pointer) to the chipset ready for frame reception and also passing frame buffers (pointers) to the chipset for onward transmission (forwarding).

All bridges operate in the **promiscuous mode** which means they receive and buffer all frames received on each of its ports. When a frame has been received at a port and put into the assigned buffer by the MAC chipset, the port management software prepares the chipset for a new frame and then passes the

(a)

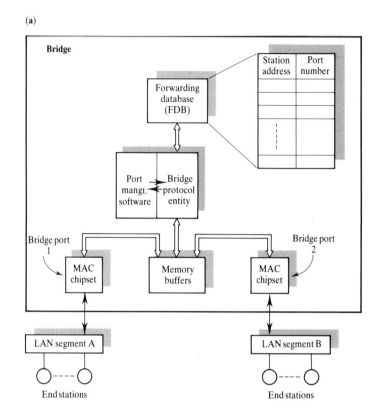

(b)

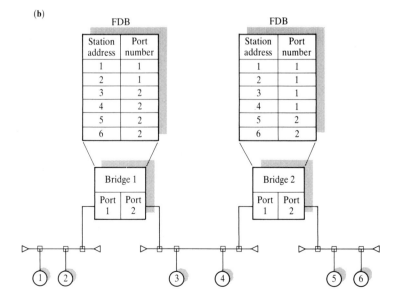

FIGURE 7.12

Bridge schematic:
(a) architecture;
(b) application
example.

pointer of the memory buffer containing the received frame to the **bridge protocol entity** for processing. Normally, since two (or more) frames may arrive concurrently at its ports and two or more frames may need to be forwarded from the same output port, the passing of memory pointers between the port management software and the bridge protocol entity software is carried out via a set of queues.

As will be expanded upon later, each port may be in a number of alternative states and processing of received frames is carried out according to a defined protocol. The function of the bridge protocol entity software, therefore, is to implement the particular bridge protocol being used.

Frame forwarding (filtering)

A bridge maintains a **forwarding database** (also known as a **routing directory**) that indicates, for each port, the outgoing port (if any) to be used for forwarding each frame received at that port. Then, if a frame is received at a port that is addressed to a station on the segment (and hence port) on which it was received, it is discarded; otherwise it is forwarded via the port specified in the forwarding database. The normal routing decision thus involves a simple look-up operation: the destination address in each received frame is first read and is then used to access the corresponding port number from the forwarding database. If this is the same as the port on which it was received, it is discarded, else it is queued for forward transmission on the segment associated with the accessed port. This process is also known as **frame filtering**.

Bridge learning

A major issue with transparent bridges is the creation of the forwarding database. One approach is for the contents of the forwarding database to be created in advance and held in a fixed memory, such as programmable read-only memory (PROM). The disadvantage is that the contents of the forwarding database in all bridges would have to be changed whenever the network topology changed – a new segment added, for example – or a user changed the point of attachment (and hence segment) of his or her station. To avoid this, in most bridged LANs the contents of the forwarding database are not statically set up but rather are dynamically created and maintained during normal operation of the bridge. This is accomplished using a combination of a learning process and a dialogue with other bridges to ascertain the topology of the overall installed LAN. An overview of the learning process works as follows.

When a bridge first comes into service, its forwarding database is initialized to empty. Then, whenever a frame is received, the *source address* within it is read and the incoming port number on which the frame was received is entered into the forwarding database. In addition, since the forwarding port is not known at this time, a copy of the frame is forwarded on all the other output ports of the bridge. As these frames propagate through the network, this procedure is repeated by each bridge. First the incoming port number is entered in the forwarding database against the source (station) address and a copy of the frame is then forwarded on all the other output ports of the bridge. This action is often referred to as **flooding** since it ensures that a copy of each frame transmitted will be received on all segments in the total LAN. During the learning phase this procedure will be repeated for each frame received by the bridge. In this way, all bridges in the LAN rapidly build up the contents of their forwarding databases.

This procedure works satisfactorily as long as stations are not allowed to migrate around the network (change their point of attachment) and the overall LAN topology is a simple tree structure (that is, there are no duplicate paths (routes) between any two segments). Such a tree structure is known as a **spanning tree**. Since in many networks, especially large networks, both these possibilities may occur, the basic learning operation is refined as follows.

The MAC address associated with a station is fixed at the time of its manufacture. Hence, if a user changes the point of attachment to the network of his or her workstation, the contents of the forwarding database in each bridge must be periodically updated to reflect such changes. To accomplish this, an **inactivity timer** is associated with each entry in the database. Whenever a frame is received from a station, the corresponding timer for that entry is reset. If no frames are received from a station within the predefined time interval, the timer expires and the entry is removed. Whenever a frame is received from a station for which the entry has been removed, the learning procedure is again followed to update the entry in each bridge with the (possibly new) port number. In this way the forwarding database in a bridge is continuously being updated to reflect the current LAN topology and the addresses of the stations that are currently attached to the segments it interconnects. It also limits the size of the database since it contains only those stations that are currently active. This is important since the size of the database influences the speed of the forwarding operation.

The learning process will only work if the total bridged LAN has a simple (spanning) tree topology. This means that there is only a single path between any two segments in the network. However, this condition may not always be met since additional bridges may be used to link two segments to improve reliability, for example, or perhaps by mistake when a LAN is being updated.

Multiple paths between two segments cannot exist with the basic learning algorithm outlined since the flooding operation during the learning phase would cause entries in the forwarding database to be continuously overwritten. This can readily be seen by considering the simple LAN topology shown in Figure 7.13. Clearly, if station 10 transmits a frame on segment 1 during the learning phase, then bridges B1 and B2 will both create an entry in their forwarding database and forward a copy of the frame onto segment 2. Each of these frames will in turn be received by the other bridge, an entry will be made (in port 2) and a copy of the frame output at port 1. In turn, each of these will be received by the other bridge, resulting in their corresponding entry for port 1 being updated. The frame will thus continuously circulate in a loop with the entries for each port being continuously updated.

Consequently, for topologies which offer multiple paths between stations, an additional algorithm is needed to select just a single bridge for forwarding

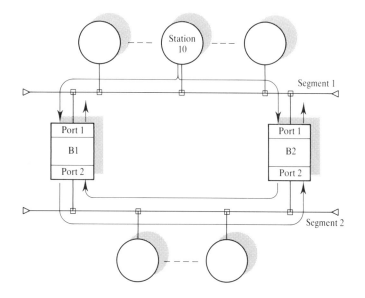

FIGURE 7.13

Effect of dual paths on
learning algorithm.

frames between any two segments. The resulting logical or **active topology** then
behaves as a single spanning tree and the algorithm is known as the spanning
tree algorithm. It should be stressed that although the algorithm selects only a
single bridge for connecting two segments – making redundant any alternative
bridges that may have been introduced to improve reliability, for example – it is
run at regular intervals and will dynamically select a set of bridges from those
currently operational.

7.5.1 Spanning tree algorithm

The **spanning tree algorithm** involves all the bridges regularly exchanging special
frames (messages) – known as **bridge protocol data units** or **BPDUs**. Each bridge
has a priority value and a unique identifier. Then, for the total bridged LAN, a
single bridge is dynamically chosen to be the **root bridge.** This is the bridge with
the highest priority and the smallest identifier. It is determined/confirmed at
regular intervals.

After the root bridge has been established, each bridge then determines
which of its ports forms the least **path cost** to the root bridge. This is known as the
root port since subsequently it will receive all BPDUs sent by the root on this port.

The path cost associated with a port is determined by the bit rate – known
as the **designated cost** – of the segment to which it is attached. The higher the bit
rate, the smaller the designated cost. If there are, say, two alternative paths to
the root comprising two 10 Mbps CSMA/CD segments and the other two 2 Mbps
segments, then the path with the two higher bit rate segments will have the
lowest path cost. In the event of the path cost of two ports within the same
bridge being equal, then the port identifiers are used as tie-breakers.

Once the path costs have been determined, a single bridge (port) is selected for forwarding frames from each segment. This is known as the **designated bridge**. Its choice is based on the least path cost to the root bridge from the segment under consideration. If two bridge ports connected to the segment have the same path cost, the bridge with the smaller identifier is chosen. The bridge port connecting the segment to its designated bridge is known as the **designated port**. In the case of the root bridge, this is always the designated bridge for all the segments to which it is connected. Hence all its ports are designated ports.

When establishing the designated bridge port to be used with a segment, it should be noted that once a bridge port has been selected as a root port, it will not take part in the arbitration procedure to become a designated port. This is so since, once selected, a root port will only receive BPDUs and a bridge will never transmit a BPDU from that port. The choice of designated port is thus between the non-root ports connected to the segment under consideration. The exchange of the configuration BPDUs between the two (or more) bridges involved will allow them to make a joint decision as to the port to be selected.

After the root bridge and the root and designated ports of all other bridges have been established, the state of the bridge ports can be set either to **forwarding** or **blocking**. Initially since all ports of the root bridge are designated ports, they are set into the forwarding state. For all the other bridges, only the root and designated ports are set into the forwarding state and the others into the blocking state. This establishes an active topology equivalent to a spanning tree.

Topology initialization

All the bridges in a LAN have a unique MAC group address which is used for sending all BPDUs between bridges. BPDUs received by a bridge are not directly forwarded; the information they contain can be used by the bridge protocol entity to create the BPDU(s) which it subsequently forwards on its other port(s).

When a bridge is first brought into service, it assumes it is the root bridge. A bridge that believes it is the root (all initially), initiates the transmission of a **configuration BPDU** on all of its ports (and hence the segments connected to it) at regular time intervals known as the **hello time**.

Each configuration BPDU contains a number of fields including:

- the identifier of the bridge which the bridge transmitting the BPDU believes to be the root (itself initially);
- the path cost to the root from the bridge port on which the BPDU was received (zero initially);
- the identifier of the bridge transmitting the BPDU;
- the identifier of the bridge port from which the BPDU was transmitted.

On receipt of a configuration BPDU, each bridge connected to the segment on which it was transmitted can determine, by comparing the root identifier contained within it with its own identifier, whether it has a higher priority or, if equal, whether its own identifier is less than the identifier from the received frame. If this is the case, it will carry on assuming it is the root and simply discard the received frame.

Alternatively, if the root identifier from the received BPDU indicates that it is not the root, it proceeds by adding the path cost associated with the port on which the BPDU was received to that already within the frame. A bridge has knowledge of the designated cost of the segments connected to its ports as a result of earlier network management messages sent to it. It then creates a new configuration BPDU containing this information, together with its own identifiers (bridge and port), and forwards a copy on all its other ports. This procedure is repeated by all bridges in the LAN. In this way the configuration BPDUs flood away from the root to the extremities of the network.

As the configuration BPDUs span out from the root, the path cost associated with each port of all the other bridges will be computed. Thus, in addition to a single root being established, all the other bridges will have determined the path cost associated with each of their ports. They can thus select their root ports and, since at any point in the hierarchy two (or more) bridges connected to the same segment will exchange configuration BPDUs, they can determine from the aggregate root path costs in the BPDU(s) each receives which is to be the designated bridge for that segment. The bridge identifier is again used as a tie-breaker in the event of equal path costs. The designated port will then be selected.

Some basic observations can be made from the foregoing:

- a bridge receives BPDUs on its root port and transmits them on its designated port(s);
- all root and designated ports are in the forwarding state;
- a bridge that has a root port connected to a segment cannot be the designated bridge for that segment;
- there can be only one designated port on each segment.

Topology change

As mentioned earlier, redundant bridges are often introduced to improve the overall reliability of a LAN. Hence, since the foregoing procedure will set some (or all) of the ports associated with such bridges into the blocking state, it is essential that a procedure is incorporated into the algorithm to allow the state of bridges and their associated ports to be dynamically changed in the event of bridge or port failure. This is known as the **topology change procedure**.

Once a single root bridge and associated active topology have been established, only the root bridge will transmit configuration BPDUs. These are sent out at regular intervals on each of its ports every time the hello timer expires. Such BPDUs will propagate throughout the network. Consequently, as each bridge updates the information contained within the BPDUs, the status of each bridge and its associated ports will be confirmed at regular intervals.

To enable other bridges to detect when a failure occurs, a **message age timer** is kept by each bridge for all of its ports. Under error free conditions, this is reset every time a configuration BPDU is received. If a designated bridge or active bridge port fails, the configuration BPDUs will stop being forwarded through this bridge or port. The effect is that the message age timer will expire in bridges that are downstream from the failed bridge or port.

The expiry of a message age timer associated with a port causes the bridge protocol entity to invoke a **become designated port procedure**. Clearly, this will be invoked by all affected bridges. After it has been carried out, one or more new designated bridges and/or ports will have been established. If it was the current root bridge that failed, a new root bridge will have been elected.

In addition, whenever the state of a port is changed from the blocking to the forwarding state, a **topology change notification BPDU** is sent out from the upgraded port in the direction of the root bridge. All designated bridges between it and the root bridge note the change and relay it on towards the root bridge via their root ports. In this way, all bridges affected by the failure are made aware of the topology change. To ensure such BPDUs reach the root reliably, an acknowledgement BPDU and a timer are associated with the sending procedure used to relay them.

Clearly, after the topology has changed, the end stations connected to each LAN segment can be reached by a different port from that currently in the forwarding database of each bridge. Hence, since the timer used by a bridge to timeout entries in its database (that is, the entries relating to end stations that have not transmitted any frames since the timer was started) is relatively long, the next set of configuration BPDUs transmitted by the root after receipt of a topology change notification BPDU have a field (bit) within them to notify bridges to shorten this time. The existing entries in each database will thus timeout and new entries will be established when each station next sends a frame.

Port status

To ensure that no transient loops are created during the period when the active topology is being established, a bridge port is not allowed to go directly from the blocking to the forwarding state. Instead, two intermediate states are defined known as the **listening state** and the **learning state.** A fifth state, the **disabled state**, is also defined to allow a network manager, through special management PBDUs sent via the network, to permanently block specific bridge ports.

While in the various states normal BPDUs and information frames may or may not be forwarded. Frames that are forwarded when in each state are as follows:

- when in the disabled state, only management BPDUs are received and processed;

- when in the blocked state, only configuration and management BPDUs are received and processed;

- when in the listening state, all BPDUs are received and processed;
- when in the learning state, all BPDUs are received and processed; information frames are submitted to the learning process but not forwarded;
- when in the forwarding state, all BPDUs are received and processed; all information frames are received, processed and forwarded.

State transitions

Transitions between port states are effected by the bridge protocol entity and take place as a result either of BPDUs being received relating to a port or timers associated with the bridge protocol expiring. The possible transitions – (1) to (5) – are shown in the state transition diagram of Figure 7.14.

Normally, all bridge ports enter the disabled state when the bridge is first switched on. The transition to the blocking state occurs as a result of a specific network management BPDU being received from a network manager station via the network (1). Similarly, the network manager can disable a specific bridge port at any time by sending a management BPDU via the network (2).

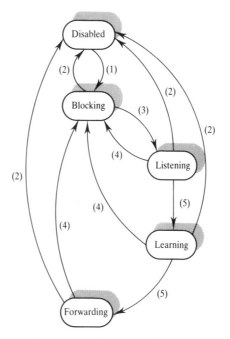

FIGURE 7.14

Port states and transition possibilities.

(1) Port enabled by receipt of a management BPDU
(2) Port disabled either by receipt of a management BPDU or failure
(3) Port selected as a root or designated port
(4) Port ceases to be a root or designated port
(5) Forwarding timer expires

Once a bridge receives an initialization command from the network manager, it will set all its ports into the blocking state and start to send out configuration BPDUs. As indicated earlier, the bridge then takes part in the topology initialization procedure. During this procedure it will start to establish its ports as being root or designated ports. From the earlier discussion, it can be concluded that the state of ports may change during this procedure. For example, bridges lower down in the tree structure (that is, away from the root bridge) may start to assume some of their ports are designated or root ports as a result of local BPDU exchanges. But, as BPDUs start to filter down from the true root, their states may well change. Thus instead of the root and designated ports being transferred directly from the blocking to the forwarding state, they go through the intermediate listening and learning states, each for a fixed time period.

Hence, when a bridge determines that one of its ports is a root or a designated port, it is transferred from the blocking to the listening state (3) and a **forwarding timer** is started. If a port is still a root or designated port when this expires, it will be transferred to the learning state (5). The forwarding timer is then restarted and the same procedure repeated when it expires. This time, however, ports that are still root or designated ports are now set into the forwarding state (5). If a port ceases to be a root or designated port during this period, it will be returned to the blocking state directly (4).

EXAMPLE

To illustrate how the various elements of the spanning tree algorithm work, consider the bridged LAN shown in Figure 7.15(a). The unique identifier of each bridge is shown inside the box representing the bridge together with the port numbers in the inner boxes connecting the bridge to each segment. Typically, the additional bridges on each segment will have been added to improve reliability in the event of a bridge failure. Also, assume that the LAN is just being brought into service.

Determine the active (spanning tree) topology for the following cases:

(a)   All bridges have equal priority and all segments have the same designated cost (bit rate) associated with them.

(b)   As for (a) except bridge B1 fails.

(c)   All bridges are in service but segments S1, S3, S4 and S5 have three times the designated cost of segments S2 and S6; that is, segments S2 and S6 have the higher bit rates.

(d)   The segments have the same designated cost as in (c) but the priority of bridge B4 is set (by network management) to be higher than the other bridges.

(a)   (i)   First the exchange of configuration BPDUs will establish bridge B1 as the root bridge since this has the lowest identifier.

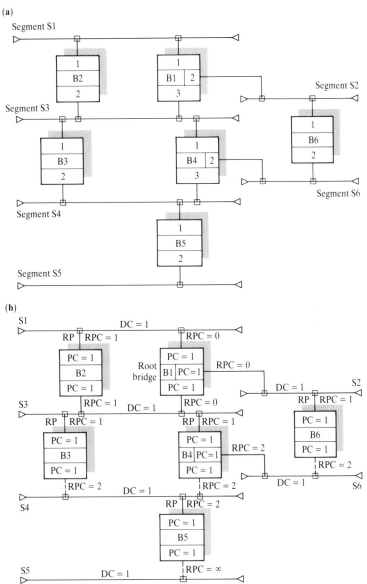

FIGURE 7.15

Active topology
derivation examples:
(a) LAN topology;
(b) root port selection.

(ii) After the exchange of configuration BPDUs, the root path cost (RPC)
      of each port will have been computed. These are shown in part (b)
      of the figure.

(iii) The root port (RP) for each bridge is then chosen as the port with the
      lowest RPC. For example, in the case of bridge B3, port 1 has an RPC
      of 1 and port 2 an RPC of 2, so port 1 is chosen. In the case of B2, both
      ports have the same RPC and hence port 1 is chosen since this has the
      smaller identifier. The selected RPs are also shown in the figure.

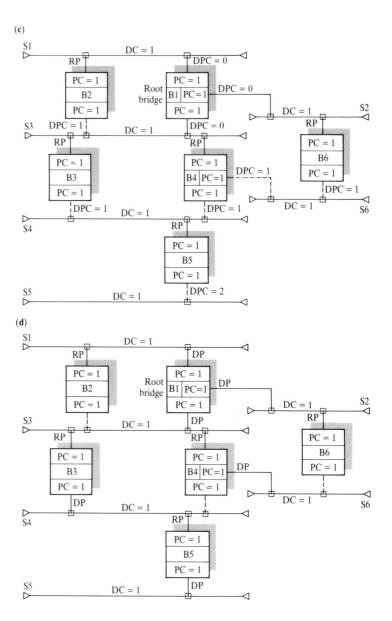

FIGURE 7.15 (cont.)

(c) Designated port selection; (d) active topology example.

(iv)   B1 is the root bridge so all its ports will have a designated port cost (DPC) of 0. Hence they will be the designated ports for segments S1, S2 and S3.

(v)   For S4, port 1 of B5 is a RP and hence will not be involved in selecting the designated port. The two other ports connected to S4 both have a DPC of 1. Hence port 2 of B3 will be selected as the designated port because of its lower identifier.

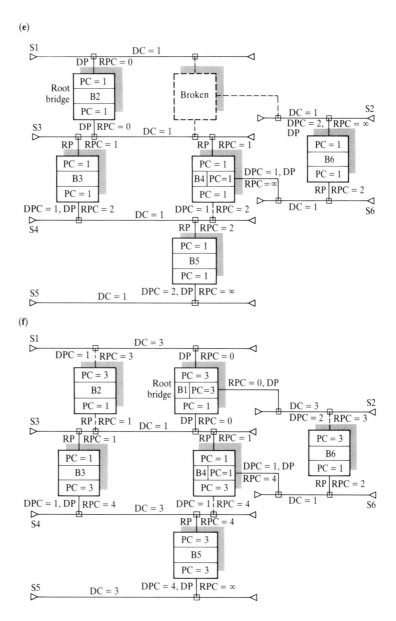

FIGURE 7.15 (cont.)

(e)–(f) Active topology examples.

(vi)   For S5, the only port connected to it is port 2 of B5 and hence this will be selected.

(vii) Finally, for S6 both ports have a DPC of 1, so port 2 of B4 will be selected rather than port 2 of B6.

The designated port costs are shown in part (c) and the resulting active topology is thus as shown in part (d) of the figure.

(b) (i) First the BPDUs exchanged as part of the topology change procedure will establish B2 as the new root bridge since this now has the lowest identifier.

(ii) The new RPCs for each port will then be computed and the RP for each of the bridges established.

(iii) Since B2 is now the root bridge, its ports will be the designated ports for S1 and S3.

(iv) For S2, the only port connected to it is port 1 of B6 and hence this will be selected.

(v) For S4, the two ports in contention again have equal DPCs and hence port 2 of B3 will be selected.

(vi) For S5, port 2 of B5 will be selected.

(vii) Finally, for S6 both ports connected to it have equal DPCs and hence port 2 of B4 is selected.

The modified active topology will thus be as shown in part (e) of the figure.

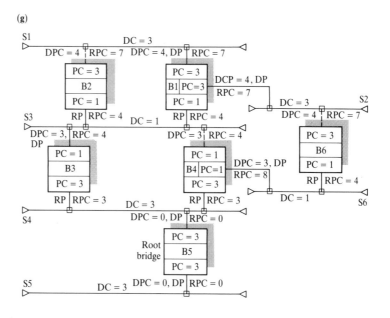

(g)

DPC = Designated port cost
PC = Port cost
DC = Designated cost
RPC = Root path cost
RP = Root port
DP = Designated port
—— = Forwarding state
--- = Blocking state

FIGURE 7.15 (cont.)

(g) Active topology example.

(c)   (i)   The root bridge will again be B1 as this has the lowest identifier.

       (ii)   The RPCs and RPs will be as shown; note that port 2 of B6 is now the RP since it now has a lower RPC than port 1.

       (iii)   B1 is the root bridge and hence its ports will be the designated ports for S1, S2 and S3.

       (iv)   For S4, port 2 of B3 will again be selected.

       (v)   For S5, port 2 of B5 is again selected.

       (vi)   For S6, port 2 of B4 is again selected.

The new active topology is thus as shown in part (f) of the figure.

(d)   (i)   Bridge B5 now has the highest priority and is therefore selected as the new root bridge.

       (ii)   Being the root bridge its ports are the designated ports for S4 and S5.

       (iii)   The new RPCs for each port will be as shown and hence the RPs as indicated.

       (iv)   For S1, port 1 of B1 will be selected.

       (v)   For S2, port 2 of B1 will be selected.

       (vi)   For S3, port 2 of B3 will be selected.

       (vii)   For S6, port 2 of B1 will be selected.

The active topology is thus as shown in part (g) of the figure.

7.5.2 Topology tuning

It may be deduced from the example that if all the bridges in a LAN have the same priority, it is unlikely that the spanning tree algorithm will produce the optimum active topology in terms of its use of the available bandwidth. This can be an important factor in large networks since it then becomes important to maximize the use of any higher bit rate segments that are available.

The inclusion of the priority field in each bridge identifier helps to achieve this goal. Although the unique identifier field of a bridge is fixed at the time of manufacture, the priority field can be set dynamically from a network manager station via the network. Bridges that can respond to network management commands are known as **managed bridges**. By selectively setting the priority of bridges, a network manager is able to optimize or tune the performance of the overall network.

Typically, a computer model of the physical topology is constructed and used to observe the performance of the overall LAN with different active topologies and traffic distributions, thereby identifying potential bottlenecks. Careful selection of the priority of selected bridges then enables the performance of the active topology to be optimized.

7.5.3 Remote bridges

Many large corporations have establishments (and hence LANs) distributed around a country or over many countries. In addition to being able to exchange information between stations connected to the same LAN within a single establishment, many large corporations require to exchange information between stations connected to LANs in different establishments. Clearly, this requires a facility for interconnecting these LANs.

A number of alternatives are possible. One solution is to use a public (or private) packet-switching network for the inter-LAN communication functions. Typically, a limited number of permanent virtual circuits may be used or, alternatively, switched connections established dynamically. However, both these solutions need full network layer addresses for the routing function, making it necessary to use a **router** to connect each LAN to the packet-switching network. This type of solution will be described more fully in a later chapter when internetworking is discussed.

An alternative, and simpler, solution is to interconnect the LANs by dedicated leased (private) lines. Although this approach sacrifices some of the advantages gained by using routers, it will often provide a faster relaying service.

As indicated in Chapter 2, leased lines are hired from a public or private telephone company to create a network of direct (point-to-point) links between, in this instance, the distributed set of LANs. Normally, therefore, no routing is involved across the resulting wide area network. The 48-bit MAC addresses at the head of each frame can be used instead. The MAC addresses used in LANs are normally unique across the total network (that is, across all the LANs). Hence it is possible to use the MAC addresses and bridges to provide the routing function. Such bridges are normally connected directly to the establishment-wide backbone subnetwork on one port and to the leased line(s) on the other. A similar bridge is used at the other end of the leased line. To discriminate between these and the bridges used for the interconnection of LAN segments, they are known as **remote bridges**. An example network based on remote bridges is shown in Figure 7.16.

Many large corporations use leased lines in this way to interconnect the (private) telephone exchanges in each establishment, thereby creating an enterprise-wide private telephone network. The leased lines used for data communication are normally integrated with those used for telephony. The bit rate of the leased lines range from multiples of 56 kbps (64 kbps in Europe) to multiples of 1.54 Mbps (2.048 Mbps in Europe). The possibly long distances spanned by such lines means the propagation delay of the lines must also be considered when determining their transmission delay.

In general, the reliability of a leased line is significantly less than that of a LAN segment, so it is normal to have back-up paths (lines) in the event of failures. Although in principle it is possible to implement the spanning tree algorithm in remote bridges (thus extending the coverage of the spanning tree algorithm across the entire network), in practice this is not always done.

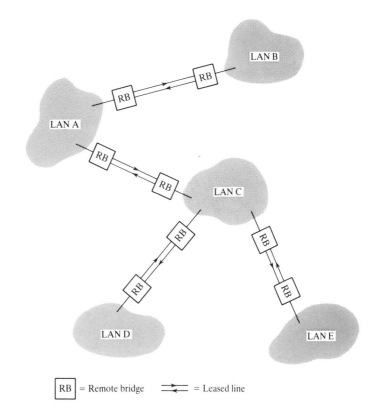

FIGURE 7.16

LAN interconnection through remote bridges.

RB = Remote bridge   = Leased line

As was seen in the earlier example, with the spanning tree algorithm some of the ports associated with selected bridges (which were introduced to enhance reliability, for example) are set into the blocking state to ensure an active spanning tree topology. With leased lines, this means that an available line may not be used since the bridge port to which it is connected is in the blocking state. Unlike the transmission media used with LANs, however, leased lines are expensive, so it is important to maximize their usage.

In many instances the leased lines are part of a much larger, enterprise-wide, voice and data network. Normally, such networks have an integral network management facility, one of the main tasks of which is to reallocate the available bandwidth to the various voice and data services in the event of failure of a leased line.

A common solution is for the network manager (via the network) to dynamically assign an alternative line (channel) for use in the event of a line failure. The remote bridges are not involved in the spanning tree algorithm, but simply perform the basic learning and forwarding (filtering) operations. Although this will lead to a slight degradation in performance during the reconfiguration period, it often leads to a more efficient usage of the available transmission capacity.

7.6 SOURCE ROUTING BRIDGES

Although source routing bridges can be used with any type of LAN segment, they are used primarily for the interconnection of token ring LAN segments. A typical network based on source routing bridges is shown in Figure 7.17(a).

The major difference between a LAN based on source routing bridges and one based on spanning tree bridges is that with the latter the bridges collectively perform the routing operation in a way that is transparent to the end stations. Conversely, with source routing, the end stations perform the routing function. With source routing, a station ascertains the route to be followed by a frame to each destination before any frames are transmitted. This information is inserted at the head of the frame and is used by each bridge to determine whether a received frame is to be forwarded on to another segment or not. The

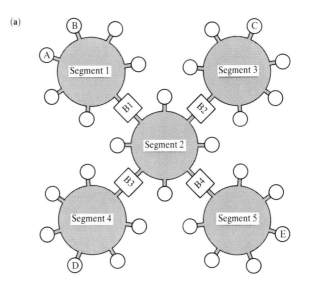

(a)

(b)

Routing table held by A: Destination B = Segment 1 (same segment)

C = Segment 1, B1, Segment 2, B2, Segment 3

E = Segment 1, B1, Segment 2, B4, Segment 5

Routing table held by B: Destination A = Segment 1 (same segment)

D = Segment 1, B1, Segment 2, B3, Segment 4

Routing table held by E: Destination A = Segment 5, B4, Segment 2, B1, Segment 1

C = Segment 5, B4, Segment 2, B2, Segment 3

FIGURE 7.17

An example source routing bridged LAN:
(a) topology;
(b) routing table entries.

routing information comprises a sequence of segment-bridge, segment-bridge identifiers. Routing tables for selected stations in the example network are shown in Figure 7.17(b).

On receipt of each frame, a bridge needs only to search the routing field at the head of the frame for its own identifier. Only if it is present and followed by the identifier of a segment connected to one of its output ports does it forward the frame on the specified LAN segment. Otherwise it is not forwarded. In either event, the frame is repeated at the ring interface by the bridge and, if forwarded, the address-recognized (A) and frame-copied (C) bits in the frame status (FS) field at the tail of the frame are set to indicate to the source station (bridge) that it has been received (forwarded) by the destination station (bridge).

7.6.1 Routing algorithm

The routing information field contained within each frame immediately follows the source address field at the head of the normal (IEEE 802.5) information frame. The modified format is thus as shown in Figure 7.18(a).

Since a routing information field is not always required, for example, if the source and destination stations are on the same segment, the first bit of the *source address* – the individual/group (I/G) address bit – is used to indicate whether routing information is present in the frame (a logical 1) or not (0). This can be done since the source address in a frame must always be an individual address, so the I/G bit is not needed for this purpose.

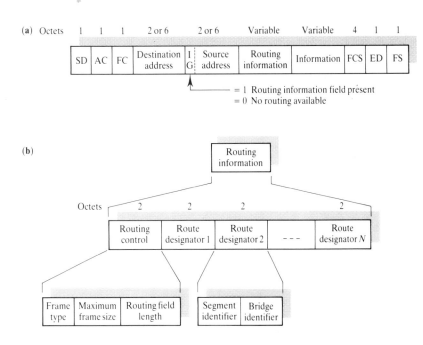

FIGURE 7.18

Token ring frame format: (a) position of routing information field; (b) structure of routing information field.

If routing information is present, its format is as shown in Figure 7.18(b). The routing information field consists of a routing control field and one or more route designator fields. The **routing control field** itself comprises three subfields: frame type, maximum frame size, and routing field length. As will be explained, in addition to normal information frames, two other frame types are associated with the routing algorithm. The **frame type** thus indicates the type of the frame.

Source routing bridges can be used for the interconnection of different types of LAN segments in addition to token rings. Consequently, since there is a different maximum frame size associated with each segment type, the **maximum frame size** field is used to determine the largest frame size that can be used when transmitting a frame between any two stations connected to the LAN.

To achieve this, prior to transmitting a route-finding frame, a station sets the maximum frame size field to the (known) largest frame size that can be used in the total LAN. Before a bridge forwards the frame onto a segment, it checks this field with the (known) maximum frame size of the new segment. If the latter is smaller, it reduces the frame size field to the lower value. In this way, the source station, on receipt of the corresponding route reply frame, can use this information when preparing frames for transmission to that destination.

Finally, since the number of segments (and bridges) traversed by a frame when going from a source to a destination may vary, the **routing field length** indicates the number of route designators present in the rest of the routing information field. Each **route designator** is comprised of a pair of segment and bridge identifiers.

The two additional frame types associated with the route finding algorithm are the single-route broadcast and the all-routes broadcast. To find a route, a station first creates and transmits a **single-route broadcast frame** with a zero routing field length and the maximum frame size set to the known largest value for the total LAN. As with spanning tree bridges, source routing bridges operate in the promiscuous mode and hence will receive and buffer all frames at each of their ports. On receipt of a single-route broadcast frame, a bridge simply broadcasts a copy of the frame on each of the segments connected to its other ports. Since this procedure is repeated by each bridge in the LAN, a copy of the frame will propagate throughout the LAN and thus will be received by the intended destination station irrespective of the segment on which it is attached.

As was indicated in the previous sections, however, if there are redundant bridges (and hence loops) in the LAN topology, multiple copies of the frame will propagate around the LAN. To prevent this, before any route-finding frames are sent, the bridge ports are configured to give a spanning tree active topology. On the surface, this may appear to be the same procedure used with transparent bridges. With source routing bridges, however, the resulting spanning tree active topology is used only for routing the initial single-route broadcast frames. This ensures that only a single copy of the frame propagates through the network. It is not used for routing either normal information frames or the all-routes broadcast frame.

On receipt of a single-route broadcast frame, the destination station returns an **all-routes broadcast frame** to the originating station. Unlike the single route broadcast, however, this frame is not constrained to follow the spanning tree active topology at each intermediate bridge. Instead, on receipt of such frames, the bridge simply adds a new route designator field (comprising the segment identifier on which the frame was received and its own bridge identifier), increments the routing field length, and then broadcasts a copy of the frame on each of its other port segments.

In this way, one or more copies of the frame will be received by the originating source station via all the possible routes between the two stations. By examining the route designators in their routing control fields, the source station can select the best route to be used for transmitting a frame to that destination. This is then entered into its routing table and is subsequently used when transmitting any frames to that station.

Since the all-routes broadcast frame is not constrained to follow the spanning tree active topology, on receipt of such frames additional steps must be taken by each bridge to ensure that no frames are simply circulating in loops. Before transmitting a copy of the all-routes broadcast frame on an output segment, each bridge first searches the existing routing information in the frame to determine if the segment identifiers associated with the incoming and outgoing ports are already present together with its own bridge-identifier. If they are, a copy of the frame has already been along the route, so this copy of the frame is not transmitted on the segment.

It should be stressed that it is not necessary to perform the route finding operation for each frame transmitted. Once a route to an intended destination has been determined and entered (cached) into the routing table of a station, this will be used for the transmission of all subsequent frames to that destination. Moreover, since most stations transmit the majority of their frames to a limited number of destinations, the number of route-finding frames is relatively small compared with normal information frames for modest sized LANs.

EXAMPLE

Assume the bridged LAN shown in Figure 7.19(a) is to operate using source routing. Also assume that all bridges have equal priority and all rings have the same designated cost (bit rate). Derive the following when station A wishes to send a frame to station B:

(a) The active spanning tree for the LAN.
(b) All the paths followed by the single-root broadcast frame(s).
(c) All the paths followed by the all-routes broadcast frame(s).
(d) The route (path) selected by A.

(a)   (i)   Bridge B1 has the lowest identifier and will be selected as the route.
          (ii)   The root ports for each bridge will then be derived as shown.
          (iii)   The designated ports for each segment can now be derived and these are as shown.
          (iv)   The active topology will be as shown in Figure 7.19(b).

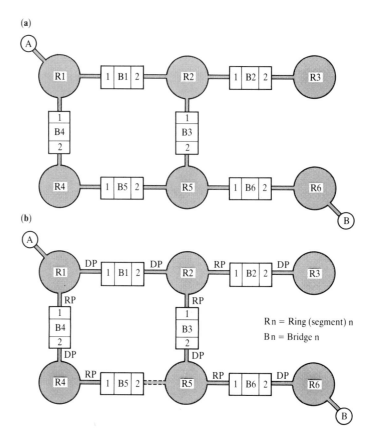

FIGURE 7.19

Source routing
example: (a) topology;
(b) spanning tree.

(b)   Paths of single-route broadcast frames:

R1 ⟶ B1 ⟶ R2 ⟶ B2 ⟶ R3
                    └⟶ B3 ⟶ R5 ⟶ B6 ⟶ R6
       └⟶ B4 ⟶ R4 ⟶ B5

(c)   Paths of all-routes broadcast frames:

R6 ⟶ B6 ⟶ R5 ⟶ B3 ⟶ R2 ⟶ B2 ⟶ R3
                          └⟶ B1 ⟶ R1
                                 └⟶ B4 ⟶ R4 ⟶ B5 ⟶ R5 ⟶ B3

(d)   Since each ring has the same bit rate, the route (path) selected will be
either:

R1 ⟶ B1 ⟶ R2 ⟶ B3 ⟶ R5 ⟶ B6 ⟶ R6

or:

R1 ⟶ B4 ⟶ R4 ⟶ B5 ⟶ R5 ⟶ B6 ⟶ R6

7.6.2 Comparison with transparent bridges

Each of the two bridging schemes – source routing and transparent – has advantages and disadvantages relative to the other. The following sections compare the two schemes based on different criteria.

Routing philosophy

In a LAN based on transparent bridges, the routing of a frame is transparent to the end stations. The latter simply add the MAC address of the destination station to the head of each frame and the bridges then collectively route the frames through the network to their intended destinations. It is thus the bridges that cooperate to perform the route-finding operation.

With a LAN based on source routing bridges, the route to be followed by a frame is inserted at the head of the frame by the source station before transmission. Thus the route to be followed by a frame is determined by the end stations and not by the bridges. A source routing bridge simply forwards each frame from one segment to another based on the routing information in the head of the frame.

Quality of routes

In the case of transparent bridges, the spanning tree algorithm ensures there are no loops in the active topology and the resulting tree is then used as the basis for routing all frames through the network. Although the assignment of bridge priorities and designated costs to segments will help, it is unlikely that the resulting spanning tree topology will yield optimum routes between all stations. Clearly, as has been described, the spanning tree algorithm will inevitably block some segments that ideally should be used when routing frames between two stations.

With source routing bridges, the all-routes broadcast frames will identify all the possible routes between a source and a destination station. Hence the source can select the optimum route to be followed for each destination. It should be noted, however, that this is only true providing the choice of route is based not only on the number of segments (and hence bridges) in the route (the **hop count**) but also the designated cost (bit rate) of each segment. Moreover, with uneven traffic distributions, this may still not give the optimum route. An alternative is simply to select the route from the first all-routes broadcast frame received since this is likely to have experienced the minimum delay.

Use of available bandwidth

To ensure a spanning tree active topology, transparent bridges will block selected ports. Hence the attached segments will not be used for forwarding frames from this bridge, and therefore the full available bandwidth provided by all segments in the LAN will not always be used.

With source routing bridges, all available segments are used during the route-finding process so, in theory, the total available bandwidth will be used. Again, however, this will only be the case if the routes selected by source stations use a strategy that ensures an even loading of all the network segments. In practice, it is unlikely that this will always be the case.

Route forwarding overheads

With a transparent bridge, the processing of each received frame will take longer than with a source routing bridge. This is because a transparent bridge must maintain an entry in its forwarding database for every station in the network that is active and uses routes that pass through that bridge. Thus in large LANs, the forwarding database can have many entries in it with the effect that the time taken to process each frame (that is, to determine the bridge port relating to the destination station of a received frame) can be significant.

To minimize the number of entries in the database, an **inactivity timer** is used for each entry. Then, if a frame is not received from a station while the timer is running, the entry is said to be **aged** and is removed. Clearly, if an entry is removed, when a source station next sends a new frame to the aged entry, the received frame must be broadcast on each of its outport ports that are in the forwarding state. To minimize the number of such broadcasts, the inactivity time is normally selected to be of a reasonable duration with the effect that the forwarding database may still contain a significant number of entries at any point in time.

In contrast, with a source routing bridge, the processing overhead per frame required by the routing function is small since it need only search the routing field at the head of the frame for its own identifier.

The processing overhead is not normally significant with lower bit rate LAN segments (less than, say, 16 Mbps). However, with higher bit rate LAN types like FDDI, which operate at rates in excess of 100 Mbps, it becomes essential to minimize the processing overhead per frame if the use of the available transmission bandwidth is to be maximized.

Route-finding efficiency

With transparent bridges, once an active spanning tree topology has been established, a bridge will rapidly build up entries in its forwarding database as stations start to transmit frames. Entries in the database must be aged to ensure that it only contains entries for stations that regularly transmit frames to stations that have a route through the bridge. The result is that a copy of any new frames that arrive from a station that no longer has an active entry in the database must be broadcast by the bridge on each of its other ports. Because of the active spanning tree topology, the resulting number of frames will be limited to one frame per branch of the tree leading from this bridge node.

In contrast, with source routing bridges, although the initial single-route broadcast frames are constrained to follow a spanning tree, the subsequent all-routes broadcast frames originating from the destination are not. This means that there may be considerable overhead (in terms of their use of transmission bandwidth and bridge processing) associated with these frames, particularly in the case of large LANs comprising many segments and replicated bridges.

Reliability issues

With a transparent bridged LAN, the bridges periodically check for bridge or link failures. This is triggered by the root node transmitting configuration BPDUs at regular time intervals (determined by the hello timer setting). If a failure does occur, the topology change component of the spanning tree algorithm will establish a new active topology to be used by the remaining bridges.

With source routing bridges, the source stations must detect when a failure has occurred since they hold the routing information. Clearly, when a network failure does occur, the routing information held by each station may be incorrect with the effect that wrongly addressed frames (frames with no available route) will be transmitted. Moreover, the absence of a response frame will often trigger a timer, normally in the transport layer of the protocol stack, that will result in another copy of the frame being transmitted by the source station. Assuming the fault is still present, this will unnecessarily load the network. Thus it is necessary for source stations to take corrective action (update their routing tables to reflect the unavailability of a station or a new route) as soon as possible after a fault occurs.

One approach is for each station to have a timer – similar to the inactivity timer used by bridges – associated with each entry in its routing table. Then, if a timer expires – that is, a frame is not sent to that destination station during the period the associated timer is running – a new route will be established before sending any new frames to that station. Clearly, the shorter this time, the less likely it is that frames with incorrect routing information will be generated. Hence a timer setting comparable to that used for the inactivity timer in the bridges should be used. Since this must be carried out by every station and not just by bridges, however, the effect on the network load will be significantly greater.

An alternative approach is to exploit the use of the topology change procedure associated with the spanning tree algorithm. Since the spanning tree algorithm is needed for routing single-route broadcast frames, it will also utilize the associated topology change procedure. It may be recalled that associated with this procedure, the root node transmits a topology change notification BPDU whenever a change in topology is triggered by a link or bridge failure. This is used by each bridge to timeout the entries in its forwarding database so that they will be updated to reflect the new topology. In principle, on receipt of such a BPDU, a bridge could send a corresponding frame to each of the stations on its segments informing them that a topology change has occurred. This would then eliminate the need for stations to maintain timers for the entries in their routing tables, thereby significantly reducing the effect on the network load.

7.6.3 Internetworking with different LAN types

As indicated in Section 7.4.1, because of their store-and-forward mode of operation, bridges can be used to interconnect LAN segments that operate with a different MAC method. In practice, for a number of reasons this is not as straightforward as one might think.

Frame format

Because of the different transmission modes used with the three basic LAN types – broadcast with 802.3 and 802.4 and point-to-point with 802.5 – and their different MAC methods – CSMA/CD with 802.3 and token with 802.4 and 802.5 – they all have different frame formats, as shown in Figure 7.20. For instance, the use of the broadcast mode by 802.3 and 802.4 means that they utilize a preamble at the start of each frame to allow a receiving station to acquire clock (bit) synchronization prior to the start of the frame contents being received. This is not necessary with a token ring, however, since the local clocks in all stations are kept in synchronization by the continuously circulating bit stream.

Similarly, the use of a token for medium access control means that 802.4 and 802.5 have a frame control field preceding the address fields as well as an end delimiter after the FCS. An 802.3 LAN, however, does not use these fields, although it does use a length byte and possibly some additional padding bytes with small frames. To confuse things further, a token ring also uses an additional access control field at the start of the frame to manage the priority and reservation features.

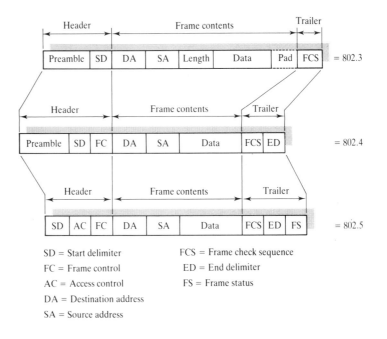

FIGURE 7.20

Comparison of LAN frame formats.

SD = Start delimiter
FC = Frame control
AC = Access control
DA = Destination address
SA = Source address

FCS = Frame check sequence
ED = End delimiter
FS = Frame status

Collectively, these features mean that when a frame passes from one type of LAN segment to another it must be reformatted prior to being forwarded on the new LAN type. In general, this is not a real problem since most of the fields identified are automatically added (and deleted) by the different MAC integrated circuit chipsets at the LAN interfaces before the actual frame contents are transmitted (and stored). However, this is not true of the length and pad fields used with 802.3 LANs, since these are treated as part of the frame contents by the MAC chipsets. This means that when 802.3 LANs are involved, the total frame contents must be reformatted in software by the bridge prior to the frame being forwarded.

The need to reformat a frame increases the processing overheads (and hence delay) within the bridge. In addition, and more importantly, it means that a new FCS field must be used when the frame is being forwarded. Again, this can readily be done since it is computed and added by the MAC chipset. A potential source of errors with bridged LANs is caused by additional bit errors being introduced into frames while they are being stored and retrieved from memory within each bridge. Clearly such errors will go undetected by the new FCS.

A common solution to this problem when all the LAN segments are of the same type, is to use the same FCS field from source to destination. Clearly, this is not possible if a frame is reformatted by a bridge, in which case any bit errors introduced (during processing and storage) will go undetected. These will then be carried forward as residual errors. To minimize this possibility, error correcting memory is often used.

Bit rate

A range of transmission bit rates is used with LANs. These include:

```
802.3  –  1, 2, 10 Mbps
802.4  –  1, 5, 10 Mbps
802.5  –  1, 4, 16 Mbps
```

Clearly, if frames are received on a slow segment and are to be forwarded on a faster segment, there will be no problem. If the reverse is true, and especially if the LAN is heavily loaded, a problem can arise as a result of frames having to be queued at the output port associated with the slower LAN. This will be true even if the two LAN segments are of the same type.

For example, if two token bus LAN segments are bridged, one operating at 10 Mbps and the other at 1 Mbps, a rapid build up of frames will occur during periods of heavy traffic. Since the amount of memory available is limited, the bridge will start to discard frames because insufficient storage is available. Although in practice the transport protocol entities in the source stations affected will initiate the retransmission of another copy of these frames, the long time-out associated with this action means that the transit delay of frames will be increased considerably. Moreover, there is no guarantee that the new copies will not experience a similar fate.

Frame size

The three LAN types each use a different maximum frame size: 802.3 uses 1518 bytes, 802.4 uses 8191 bytes, and that used with 802.5 is determined by the size of the ring. A serious problem can arise if a frame is first transmitted on, say, an 802.4 (token bus) segment but is to be subsequently forwarded on an 802.3 segment. Assuming maximum frame sizes are being used, the only way this can be overcome is for the bridge at the interface with the 802.3 segment to divide the larger frame into smaller subunits, each with the same destination and source addresses, prior to transmission.

Although this can be done, **segmentation** (as it is referred to) is not part of the 802.1(d) standard and so bridges will not normally offer this function. Moreover, it will add overheads within the bridge. Thus, if standard bridges are to be used to perform the interconnection function, the only solution is for each source station to know the range of maximum frame sizes used in the total bridged LAN and to select the minimum size. Clearly, this solution destroys the transparency feature of 802.1 bridged LANs and hence the use of bridges with an additional segmentation capability are often used.

An alternative solution is to use a device known as a **bridge-router** or **brouter** instead of a conventional (transparent or source routing) bridge to perform the interconnection function between segments of different types. As will be expanded upon in Chapter 9, routers perform their relaying function at the network layer rather than at the MAC sublayer. Moreover, they have been designed from the outset to perform a range of harmonizing functions (including segmentation) for going from one network type to another. Thus a brouter can perform its relay function either as a conventional bridge or as a router and are often used for interconnecting different segment types.

7.7 PERFORMANCE ISSUES

As described in Section 2, various interconnection topologies can be used with bridged LANs. Hence, in addition to understanding the operation of bridges, it is important to appreciate the effect on the overall LAN performance of different bridge characteristics and interconnection topologies. This section presents the results of some network simulations that have been carried out to illustrate these effects.

A schematic of the basic LAN topology used for the simulations is shown in Figure 7.21(a). It comprises multiple LAN segments, each supporting a workgroup of client and server systems, which are interconnected using bridges and various network topologies. The results relate mainly to LANs comprising multiple 10 Mbps CSMA/CD segments although in many instances they are also applicable to LANs comprising other types of segments, such as token rings.

The percentage of frame transmissions that is local to a workgroup (and hence a LAN segment) and between workgroups (segments) can be varied. All the results presented relate the total number of client requests per second (that

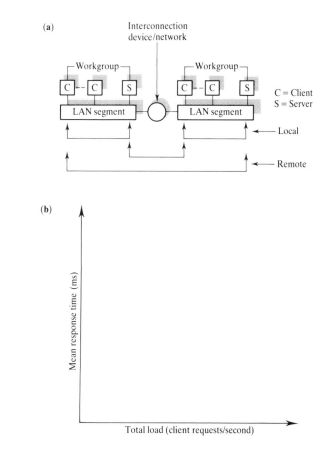

FIGURE 7.21

Simulation
environment:
(a) topology;
(b) performance.

is, for the total LAN) to the mean network response times to these requests.
This is shown in Figure 7.21(b). The mean frame size for each client request is
128 bytes and the mean server response 1250 bytes. The mean response time is
defined as the delay between a client generating a request frame and the client
receiving the corresponding response frame from the server. The simulation
model is based upon the following assumptions:

- Negligible transmission errors are assumed, that is, no frames are discarded as a result of frame check sequence (FCS) errors.
- All stations (including bridges) have equal access to a network segment.
- Requests generated by each client station are exponentially distributed
  and independent of each other.
- The processor in the file server processes all requests with equal priority
  and its service time is assumed to be negligible.
- All workstations and servers have infinite receive and transmit buffer
  capacities and hence no frames are dropped as a result of buffer overflow
  in these systems.

Clearly, the use of a single pair of request-response frames does not take into account the overheads associated with the higher layers in the protocol stack. Hence to obtain actual server-response times would require multiple such exchanges. The aim here, however, is not to quantify the precise server response times but rather to use a typical client server model to investigate the effect of different bridge characteristics and interconnection topologies on the overall performance of the network.

In the absence of faults, the routing scheme associated with the LAN – spanning tree or source routing – will be run relatively infrequently and hence its loading effect on the network, in relation to normal frame transmissions, can be ignored. Similarly, any frame transmissions relating to the network management functions can be ignored. The bridge characteristics considered include the effect of different frame forwarding (processing) rates, available buffer storage capacity and number of bridge ports. The alternative interconnection topologies include cascaded segments and the use of backbone subnetworks.

7.7.1 Repeaters

As indicated in the last chapter, with a single-segment CSMA/CD bus network there is a limit both on the physical length of the bus and on the number of stations that can be attached to it. Also, for a LAN comprising multiple segments interconnected by repeaters, the MAC method limits the number of segments that can be interconnected. The performance of a LAN comprising from one to five segments is presented in Figure 7.22.

In the cases of a single segment and five segments, the mean response time varies according to the well-understood CSMA/CD behaviour described in the last chapter, that is, good response time performance until the total load offered starts to approach the maximum transmission bandwidth of the network. At this point, the increasing number of collisions and deferrals add significant delays to the response time figures. With multiple segments, the total network throughput decreases slightly because the increased length of the medium increases the collision window which in turn causes an earlier degradation in performance.

It can be concluded from these graphs that, with repeaters, all requests generated on any segment will propagate, and hence load, all the other segments in the LAN. This means that the response times shown are independent of the number of segments and the percentage of local and remote traffic that is associated with each segment. They thus form a basis for comparison.

7.7.2 Bridges

With a bridge, only frames that are addressed to a server on a different segment (that is, remote traffic) will be forwarded. Frames addressed to a server on the same segment (local traffic) are not forwarded thus ensuring that local traffic does not load other segments. Clearly, the performance improvements obtained

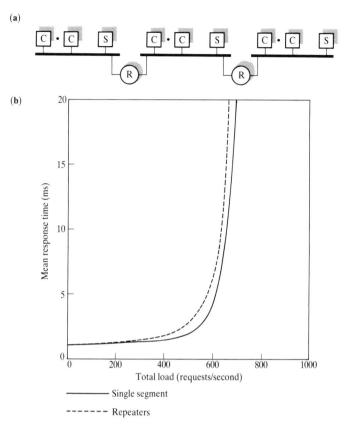

FIGURE 7.22

CSMA/CD (10 Mbps)
segments connected
through repeaters:
(a) topology;
(b) performance.

will be strongly influenced by the ratio of local to remote traffic (load). This can be deduced from the graphs shown in Figure 7.23.

With all local traffic, the full bandwidth of each segment is available to that workgroup. Thus, for a particular response time, the number of requests supported by the total network will increase linearly with the number of segments. As the amount of remote traffic increases, however, so the improvements start to progressively reduce. In the limit, with all remote traffic, the performance will be inferior to that obtained with repeaters because of the increase in load caused by each frame being retransmitted twice.

It can be concluded from these graphs that bridges are ideally suited to environments in which there are a number of workgroups, each operating in a semi-autonomous way, with just occasional accesses to servers outside the group. This is the situation when each workgroup comprises a number of diskless nodes operating with a shared file server. Most of the traffic generated is then for the local server with occasional accesses to servers outside the group for, say, electronic mail.

Conversely, bridges do not give any improvements in performance when the shared resources associated with a LAN are all attached to different segments. It should be remembered, however, that in some instances bridges are

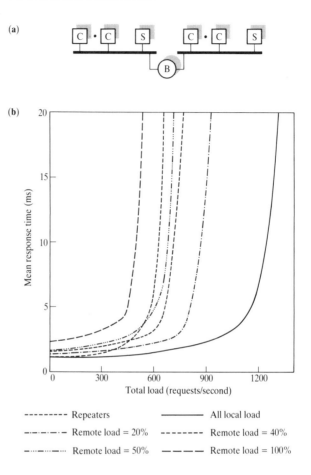

FIGURE 7.23

Ideal bridge – two segments with different local/remote traffic ratios: (a) topology; (b) performance.

utilized for reasons other than performance gains. Examples include protocol transparency and access control.

The results in Figure 7.23 are for an ideal bridge. This means that the bridge has infinite buffer storage capacity for received frames and that it takes negligible time (compared with the transmission delay) to process a frame. To quantify these effects, a set of simulations was carried out which modelled these features.

Forwarding delay

The rate at which frames are filtered (processed) and forwarded for transmission from one port (segment) to another is called the bridge forwarding rate or throughput. To illustrate the effect of this, the same 2-segment network topology was simulated with varying levels of frame forwarding rate. The rate was varied from 1000 to 10000 frames per second, each with a local/remote traffic ratio of 20, 50, and 100%. The results are summarized in Figures 7.24 and 7.25.

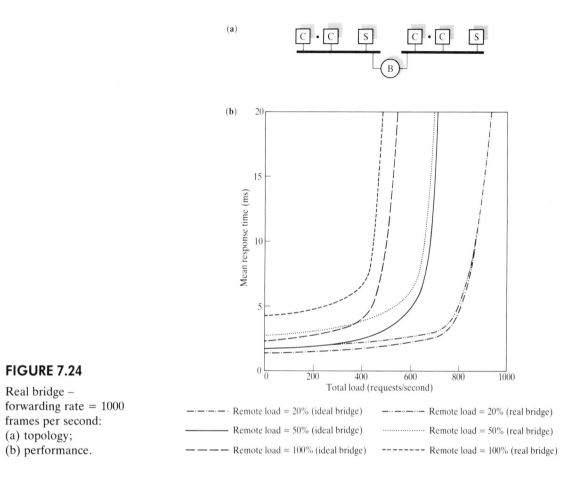

FIGURE 7.24

Real bridge –
forwarding rate = 1000
frames per second:
(a) topology;
(b) performance.

As can be seen, with a 2-port bridge the effect is only noticeable with the lower frame forwarding rate of 1000 frames per second. Essentially, the mean response time increases by the 2 ms each request-reply frame takes to process. Moreover, this only has an observable effect at modest network loads since, with higher network loads, the transmission delays start to dominate.

Buffer capacity

As the loading of a segment (and hence bridge port) increases, so frames must be queued within the bridge while waiting to be forwarded. If there is insufficient buffer storage capacity, frames must be discarded, leading to increased delays as the timeout associated with the end-to-end (transport) protocol within the client/server system is invoked. In practice, the timeout interval used by the transport protocol may be large for bridged LANs. Consequently, an adequate amount of buffer storage capacity should be provided in a bridge to minimize the number frames that are discarded. The results presented in Figure 7.26 quantify the required buffer storage capacity for various network loads and distributions.

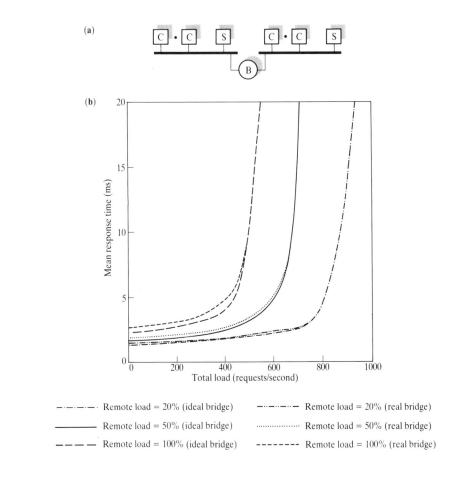

FIGURE 7.25

Real bridge – forwarding rate of 10 000 frames per second: (a) topology; (b) performance.

As can be concluded, with a 2-segment network, the effect is only noticeable at total loads greater than 400 requests per second. Beyond this load, the number of buffers required is then a function of the local/remote traffic ratio; the higher the quantity of remote traffic the more buffers will be required to avoid discarded frames.

7.7.3 Cascaded bridges

The simplest method of expanding a LAN is to cascade segments in the form of a daisy-chain through a series of 2-port bridges. If a LAN is allowed to evolve in this way, however, then the overall improvement in total load will ultimately decrease as the number of segments increase. This is because any remote traffic from or to a workgroup may have to be forwarded over several intermediate segments thus increasing the load on them, as can be seen from the results in Figure 7.27.

All the results relate to a local/remote traffic ratio of 80/20. To demonstrate the effect of the loading of intermediate segments, the number of

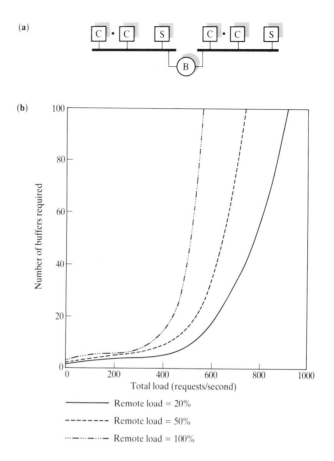

FIGURE 7.26

Required buffer capacity in bridge at different local/remote traffic ratios:
(a) topology;
(b) performance.

segments in the LAN was progressively increased from one to five. As can be seen, as the number of segments increases, so the relative improvement in the total load decreases. The average throughput of an individual segment decreases by nearly 20% for each additional segment added in series. An increase in the amount of remote traffic will accentuate this effect but, in general, a limit of two or possibly three segments should be set when cascading bridges. Beyond this number, either a multiport bridge or a subsidiary backbone segment should be utilized.

7.7.4 Multiport bridges

A multiport bridge, as its name implies, supports multiple ports and hence segments. The maximum number of ports supported ranges from five to ten, so they provide a convenient means of linking segments that are physically distributed around a single office complex.

In practice, producing a bridge that can support multiple ports is technically demanding since its internal architecture needs to support the fast

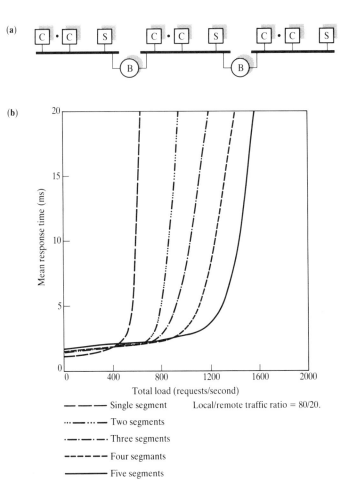

FIGURE 7.27

Cascaded bridges –
segments connected in
series: (a) topology;
(b) performance.

transfer of frames – from one (port) memory to another – while allowing access to the memory for processing and the receipt/transmission of other frames. A major parameter associated with multiport bridges, therefore, is the frame processing rate. Maximum rates from 10 000 to 30 000 frames per second are available. Figures 7.28 and 7.29 illustrate these factors. The graphs in Figure 7.28 compare a cascaded topology with a multiport bridge configuration. The bridge is assumed ideal and a local/remote traffic ratio of 80/20 is used. As can be seen, a multiport bridge gives a much increased total load relative to a simple cascaded topology owing to the presence of just a single bridge between the client and a server for all remote traffic.

The effect of a finite frame processing rate will be a function of the local/remote traffic ratio of course. To illustrate this, the graphs in Figure 7.29 are for a local/remote traffic ratio of 50/50 and a bridge forwarding rate of 1000 and 10 000 frames per second. At this traffic ratio, a bridge forwarding rate of 1000 frames per second, although acceptable for a 2-port bridge, gives unacceptably

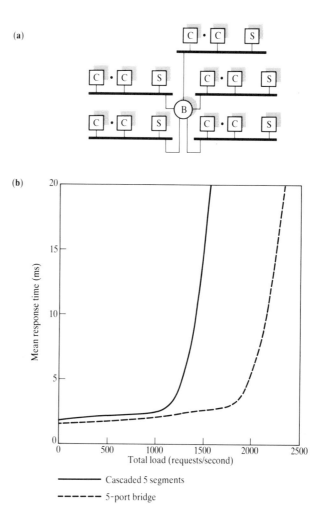

FIGURE 7.28

Multiport bridge
(ideal): (a) topology;
(b) performance.

long delays with five ports. The minimum forwarding rate should thus be greater than 10000 frames per second for a 5-port bridge and higher for bridges with more ports.

7.7.5 Backbones

An alternative way to link multiple segments within a building is to introduce what is known as a building backbone solely for relaying inter-segment traffic. Typically, this operates at the same bit rate as the other segments. The performance gains from utilizing a backbone can be deduced from the results presented in Figure 7.30.

The results are for a CSMA/CD backbone of the same bit rate (10 Mbps) as the five interconnected segments. The improvement in performance over a

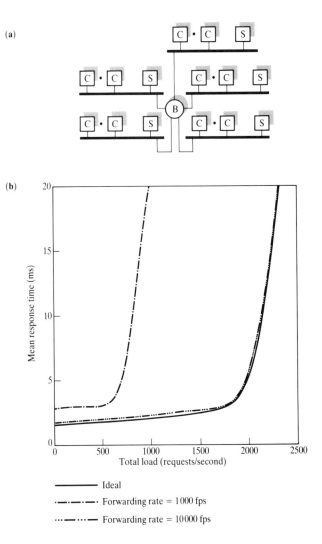

FIGURE 7.29

Real multiport bridge
performance compared
with an ideal bridge:
(a) topology;
(b) performance.

cascaded topology is similar to that obtained with a 5-port bridge. In general, however, the use of a separate backbone allows the segments to be physically distributed over a wider geographical area than with a multiport bridge. If this is not a factor, however, a multiport bridge solution will be more cost effective since the aggregate cost of multiple 2-port bridges will be higher than a single multiport bridge.

As the number of segments attached to the backbone is increased, as is the case with an establishment-wide backbone, the backbone segment will start to saturate and in turn become the limiting factor. In the limit this is true even if each segment is lightly loaded with, for example, 20% of remote traffic. This effect may be alleviated by using a higher bandwidth backbone such as an FDDI (100 Mbps) ring.

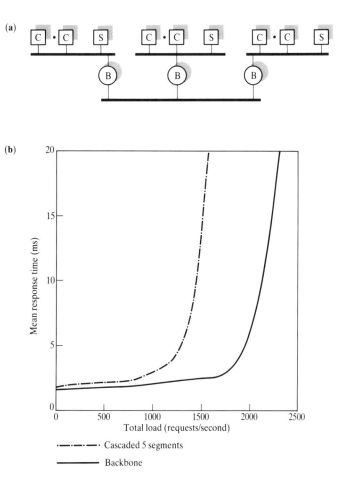

FIGURE 7.30

CSMA/CD (10 Mbps)
backbone: (a) topology;
(b) performance.

The effect of a higher bit rate FDDI backbone can be seen from the
results presented in Figure 7.31. This shows a significant improvement in
response time and an increase in overall throughput as a result of replacing the
CSMA/CD backbone with the higher bit rate FDDI backbone. Performance
results with twenty segments connected through the FDDI backbone are also
shown. Indeed an FDDI backbone can support up to fifty fully loaded 10 Mbps
CSMA/CD segments when each has an 80/20 ratio of local/remote traffic.

7.7.6 Remote bridges

As has been indicated, many large organizations need to provide links between
LANs installed in geographically distributed establishments. In such cases, a
common solution is to use leased lines to link the various sites and remote
bridges. Often the latter are connected directly to each establishment-wide
backbone. The bit rate of the leased lines selected must now be determined by

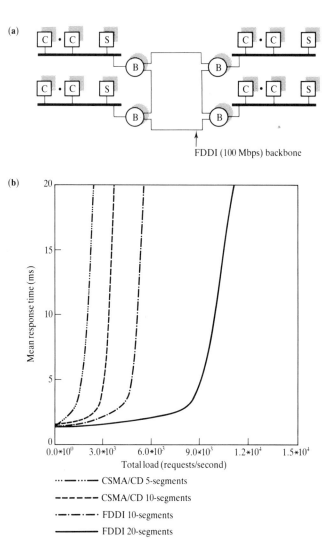

FIGURE 7.31

FDDI (100 Mbps)
backbone: (a) topology;
(b) performance.

considering the level of inter-establishment traffic. Delays associated with this traffic will be made up of the transmission and propagation delays of the leased lines and the buffer delays (the time a frame waits before it is relayed) at each side of the link.

The use of dedicated leased lines means that a first-level estimation of the performance of such networks can be obtained by considering two LANs interconnected by two remote bridges and a duplex leased line. The results presented in Figure 7.32 are for such a topology and illustrate the effect of different types of leased line. The same request/response frame sizes have been used as in the earlier simulations. The mean-response time figures include both the transmission delays of the leased lines and the queuing delays in the remote bridges.

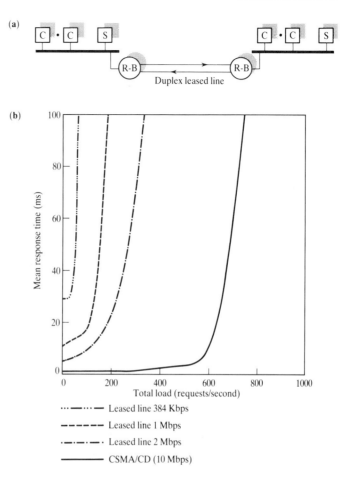

FIGURE 7.32

Remote bridge
connected through
leased lines:
(a) topology;
(b) performance.

They do not include the propagation delays. Thus the mean overall network response time of end stations can be calculated by adding these to the response-time results obtained from the various topologies presented in the earlier sections.

It may be concluded from these graphs that the large disparity between the bit rates of currently available leased lines and those used for LANs means that the overall mean network response times for inter-LAN transactions will be dominated by the delays incurred over the leased lines. Clearly, the effects of this will be determined by the types of transaction involved.

Remote bridges can only be used with dedicated (non-switched) lines. If switched inter-LAN connections are required, a router must be used as outlined earlier. Moreover, as LANs evolve and more sophisticated applications emerge, then the need for more sophisticated interconnection networks arises. An example is a DQDB metropolitan area network (MAN). As described earlier in the chapter, such networks can provide a switched connection at bit rates up to 150 Mbps. Again, however, the internetworking device will be a router.

7.7.7 Summary

It may be concluded from the foregoing that the performance of a bridged LAN depends not only upon the performance of the bridges but also upon the interconnection topology. It has been shown that the use of multiport bridges or backbone segments give a much improved performance compared with simple topologies comprising cascaded segments and 2-port bridges. Multiport bridges are best suited to interconnecting segments within a small geographical area, such as a single floor of an office building, whereas backbone networks provide wider geographical coverage and can support a larger number of segments. It was also shown that the performance of a network using a low bit rate backbone will decrease with increasing inter-segment load. This can be alleviated by employing high-speed backbones such as FDDI. Such backbones, with current technology LANs, can support the interconnection of many segments, the actual number being strongly dependent on the level of inter-segment traffic.

EXERCISES

7.1 With the aid of a diagram, describe the meaning of the following components relating to an FDDI network:

(a)   primary and secondary ring;
(b)   single attach and dual attach station;
(c)   optical coupling unit;
(d)   wiring concentrator;
(e)   polarized duplex connectors.

7.2 Produce a sketch of a wiring plan for an establishment based on a site-wide FDDI backbone network. Assume there are three buildings and that each building patch panel has four ports. Produce a sketch of a single building wiring plan assuming there is a wiring concentrator on each of three floors with two single attach stations per concentrator.

7.3 State why 4B/5B encoding is used in FDDI networks rather than differential Manchester encoding.
Produce a sketch of the physical interface with a single fibre and explain the meaning of the terms latency buffer, 4B/5B encoder/decoder and clock synchronizer.

7.4 Explain the meaning of the following terms relating to the access control method used with DQDB networks:

(a)   request bit,
(b)   busy bit,
(c)   request counter,
(d)   countdown counter.

7.5 With the aid of a diagram, explain the operation of the priority control method used with DQDB networks. Assume four priority levels. Show example cell transmissions on each bus, with varying priority levels, and explain their effect on the contents of the request and countdown counters for each bus.

7.6 Explain why all transmissions on a DQDB bus are carried out in fixed-sized cells.
Produce a sketch showing the various fields present in a cell and explain their functions. Show how a CSMA/CD MAC frame comprising 120 information octets is transmitted on the bus. Indicate the segment types used.

7.7 Explain the meaning of the following terms relating to bridged LANs:
    (a)   bridge,
    (b)   multiport bridge,
    (c)   building backbone,
    (d)   establishment backbone.

7.8 List and discuss the advantages and disadvantages of bridges relative to a repeater.

7.9 Produce a sketch of a typical bridge architecture and, with the aid of an example, describe its principle of operation. Include in your description the terms: promiscuous mode, forwarding database, bridge learning and spanning tree.

7.10 In relation to the spanning tree algorithm, explain the meaning of the following terms:
    (a)   root bridge,
    (b)   root port,
    (c)   designated port,
    (d)   configuration BPDU,
    (e)   topology change BPDU.

7.11 Produce a sketch of a state transition diagram showing the port states and transition possibilities of a bridge and explain the outgoing events and actions relating to each transition.

7.12 For the example bridged LAN shown in Figure 7.15(a), determine the active (spanning tree) topology for the following cases:
    (a)   All segments have the same designated cost but bridge B6 has a higher priority than the other bridges.
    (b)   As for (a) except bridge B4 fails.
    (c)   All bridges are in service but segments S3 and S4 have one half the path cost of the other segments.

7.13 With the aid of sketches, explain the meaning of the terms:
    (a)   topology tuning,
    (b)   remote bridges.

7.14 Produce a sketch of an example bridged LAN based on source routing and, with the help of some example routing table entries, explain how frames are routed across the LAN from one station to another. Include in your description the structure of the routing control information carried in each frame.

7.15 In relation to the routing algorithm used with a source routing bridged LAN, explain the meaning of the terms:
    (a)   single-route broadcast frame,
    (b)   all-routes broadcast frame.

7.16   Assuming the bridged LAN shown in part (a) of Figure 7.19 but with an additional bridge used to link ring segments R3 and R6, derive the following when station A wishes to send a frame to station B:

(a)   the active spanning tree for the LAN,
(b)   all the paths followed by the single-root broadcast frame(s),
(c)   all the roots followed by the all-roots broadcast frame(s),
(d)   the root (path) selected by A.

7.17   Repeat exercise 7.16 assuming that ring R5 operates at twice the bit rate of the other rings; that is, its path cost is one half that of the other rings.

7.18   Compare the operation of a transparent bridged LAN and a source routing bridged LAN in relation to the following:

(a)   routing philosophy,
(b)   quality of roots,
(c)   use of bandwidth,
(d)   routing overheads,
(e)   route finding efficiency,
(f)   reliability.

7.19   With the aid of a sketch showing the format of the different basic LAN types, discuss the issues involved in producing a bridged LAN comprising the different LAN segment types.

7.20   Using example graphs selected from Section 7.7, discuss the following:

(a)   the relative performance improvements of using a bridge over a repeater to link two segments with varying traffic distributions;
(b)   the impact of bridge forwarding rate and buffer storage capacity on the performance of a bridged LAN;
(c)   the advantages of using a multiport bridge over a number of 2-port bridges in a cascaded topology;
(d)   the relative performance of a bridged LAN implemented using either multiport bridges or a backbone segment.

CHAPTER SUMMARY

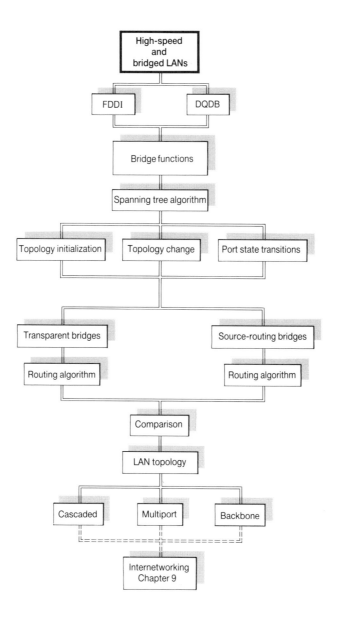

8 Wide area networks

CHAPTER CONTENTS

CHAPTER OBJECTIVES

When you have completed studying the material in this chapter you should be able to:

- describe the different types of public data network;
- understand the difference between a circuit-switched and a packet-switched network and the relative advantages and disadvantages of each type;
- describe the structure of the X.25 protocol as used in packet-switched networks and the operation of the packet (network) layer in the context of the ISO Reference Model;
- describe the function of a packet assembly and disassembly device and the various protocols associated with its use and operation;
- explain how a call is established and cleared using the X.21 protocol and a circuit-switched data network;
- understand the aims of an integrated services digital network and the various user interfaces and protocols associated with these networks;
- understand the main features of a private integrated voice and data network.

8.1 INTRODUCTION

In Chapter 2 and later in Chapter 5, the use of the PSTN for the transmission of data was considered. Indeed, prior to the advent of public data networks, this was the only method available for transmitting data between user equipment located at different establishments. As was indicated, however, a switched connection made through the PSTN currently supports only a modest user data rate, typically less than 9600 bps. Furthermore, as telephone calls are charged on a time and distance basis, a typical transaction can be very expensive owing to the often long distances and times involved, especially when a human user is involved.

It was for these reasons that many large organizations established their own national and international private data networks. Typically, these used dedicated lines leased from the telephone authorities to interconnect a number of privately owned switching nodes or multiplexers of the type described at the end of Chapter 8. Although networks of this type offer the user security, flexibility and ultimate control, they also involve high investment in purchasing or leasing the equipment. Such networks are therefore generally owned and managed by large organizations, such as the major clearing banks, who can both afford the initial capital outlay and also generate sufficient traffic to justify this level of investment. They are then known, therefore, as private **enterprise-wide networks**.

At the time of introduction of many private data networks, the PTT authorities would only lease lines to an organization to enable it to build its own private data network, but would not supply lines to allow such networks to be connected together. The demand and subsequent establishment of public data networks stemmed from the ever-increasing demands from users of private networks for facilities to enable them to communicate with each other.

The generic name given to networks that link DTEs (or indeed establishment-wide LANs) that are physically located in different establishments is **wide area network** or **WAN**. The latter thus include public data networks and also enterprise-wide private data networks. This chapter discusses the operation and protocols associated with such networks.

8.2 CHARACTERISTICS OF PUBLIC DATA NETWORKS

The standards pertaining to WANs are in the main those that have been developed for use by the PTT and public-carrier data networks. A **public data network (PDN)** is a network established and operated by a national network administration authority specifically for the transmission of data. A primary requirement for a PDN is that it should facilitate the interworking of equipment from different manufacturers, which in turn requires agreed standards for access to and use of these networks. After much discussion and experimentation at national and later at international level, a set of internationally agreed standards

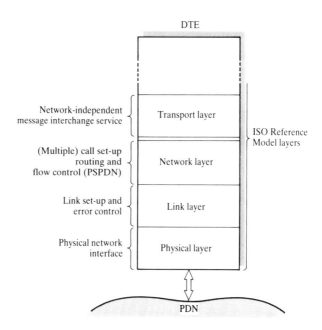

FIGURE 8.1

Network-dependent
protocol layers in PDNs.

have been accepted by CCITT for use with a range of PDNs. These **X-series** and **I-series recommendations** include standards for user data signalling rates and user interfaces with such networks.

There are two main types of PDN: **packet-switched (PSPDNs)** and **circuit-switched (CSPDNs)**. Different standards have been defined for each type. Since the PSTN is still widely used for data transmission, standards have also been established for interfacing to this type of network. In general, the standards for each of these networks refer to the lowest three layers of the **ISO Reference Model** and the functions of each of these layers is as shown in Figure 8.1. It should be remembered that the characteristics of the network-dependent layers in the ISO Reference Model are made transparent to the higher protocol layers by the **transport layer**, which offers the higher layers a network-independent message transport service. This chapter is concerned with the different types of PDN and the various interface protocols that have been defined for use with each type.

8.2.1 Circuit and packet switching

Before describing the various interface standards associated with PDNs, it is necessary to outline the differences between the two types of switching used in these networks. Each connection established through a circuit-switched network results in a physical communication channel being set up through the network from the calling to the called subscriber equipment. This connection is then used exclusively by the two subscribers for the duration of the call. An example of a circuit-switched network is the PSTN; indeed, all connections established through the PSTN are of the circuit-switched type.

In the context of data transmission, a feature of a circuit-switched connection is that it effectively provides a fixed data rate channel and both subscribers must operate at this rate. Also, before any data can be transmitted over such a connection, it is necessary to set up or establish a connection through the network. Currently, the time required to set up a call through the PSTN can be relatively long (tens of seconds), owing to the type of equipment used in each exchange. Normally, therefore, when transmitting data, a connection is established and kept open for the duration of the transaction. However, the widespread introduction of new computer-controlled switching exchanges, coupled with the adoption of digital transmission throughout the network, means that the set-up time of a connection through the PSTN is rapidly becoming much shorter (tens of milliseconds). Furthermore, the extension of digital transmission to the subscriber's equipment will mean that a high bit rate (typically 64 kbps or higher) switched transmission path will be available at each subscriber outlet. It will then be possible to use this path for transmitting data without using modems. The resulting digital PSTN can then also be regarded as a public CSDN or, since such networks can support both digitized voice and data, as an **integrated services digital network (ISDN)**. Further details relating to ISDNs will be presented later in the chapter.

Although the connection set-up time associated with an all-digital circuit-switched network is relatively fast, the resulting connection still only provides a path with a fixed data rate which must be used by both subscribers for transmission and reception. In contrast, with a packet-switched network, it is possible for two communicating subscribers (DTEs) to operate at different data rates, since the rate at which data are passed at the two interfaces to the network is separately regulated by each subscriber's equipment. Also, no physical connections are established through the network with a packet-switched network. Instead, all data to be transmitted is first assembled into one or more message units, called **packets**, by the source DTE. These packets include both the source and destination DTE network addresses. They are then passed bit-serially by the source DTE to its local **packet-switching exchange** (**PSE**). On receipt of each packet, the exchange first stores the packet and then inspects the destination address which it contains. Each PSE contains a **routing directory** specifying the outgoing link(s) (transmission path(s)) to be used for each network address. On receipt of a packet, the PSE forwards the packet on the appropriate link at the maximum available bit rate. This mode of working is often referred to as **packet store-and-forward**.

Similarly, as each packet is received (and stored) at each intermediate PSE along the route, it is forwarded on the appropriate link interspersed with other packets being forwarded on that link. At the destination PSE, determined by the destination address within the packet, the packet is finally passed to the destination DTE.

This procedure is shown in Figure 8.2. As can be seen, each overall transaction occupies only a (random) portion of the available bandwidth on each link, since packets from different sources are interspersed with packets from other

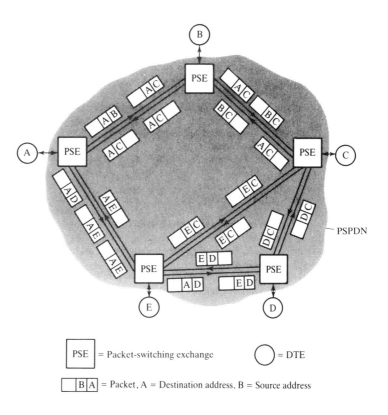

FIGURE 8.2

Packet-switching
schematic.

 = Packet-switching exchange   ◯ = DTE

▢ B A = Packet, A = Destination address, B = Source address

sources on the various network links. In the limit, this will vary from zero when the user is not transmitting any data to the full bandwidth if it is transmitting packets continuously.

It is possible for a number of packets to arrive simultaneously at a PSE on different incoming links and for each to require forwarding on the same outgoing link. Clearly, if a number of particularly long packets are waiting to be transmitted on the same link, other packets may experience unpredictably long delays. To prevent this happening and ensure that the network has a reliably fast transit time, a maximum length is allowed for each packet. It is for this reason that when a packet-switched network is being used, a message submitted to the transport layer within the DTE may first have to be divided by the source transport protocol entity into a number of smaller packet units before transmission. In turn, they will be reassembled into a single message by the correspondent transport protocol entity at the destination DTE. This is transparent to the transport layer user who is instead offered a network-independent message transport.

Another difference between a CSPDN and a PSPDN is that with a CSPDN, the network does not apply any error or flow control on the transmitted data, so this must be performed by the user. With a PSPDN, however, sophisticated error and flow control procedures are applied on each link by the network PSEs.

Consequently, the class of service provided by a PSPDN is normally much higher than that provided by a CSPDN.

It can be concluded that circuit and packet switching offer the user two different types of service. Even with the advent of all-digitial networks, both types of service will still be supported and it will then be up to the user to select a particular service.

8.2.2 Datagrams and virtual circuits

With a PSPDN, two types of service are normally supported: **datagram** and **virtual call (circuit)**. The difference between the two types of service can be explained by the analogy between exchanging messages by letters and by a telephone call. In the first case, the letter containing the message is treated as a self-contained entity by the postal authorities and its delivery is independent of any other letters. In the case of a telephone call, however, a communication path is first established through the network and the message exchange then takes place.

The datagram service is analogous to sending a message by a letter, since each packet entering the network is treated as a self-contained entity with no relationship to other packets. Each packet is simply received and forwarded in the way just outlined. Consequently, the datagram service is primarily used for the transfer of short, single-packet messages.

If a message contains multiple packets, the virtual call service is normally selected. This is analogous to sending a message by a telephone call, since when using this service, before any information (data packets) associated with a call is sent, the source DTE sends a special **call request** packet to its local PSE containing, in addition to the required physical destination DTE network address, a reference number called the **virtual circuit identifier (VCI)**. This is noted by the PSE and the packet is then forwarded through the network as before. At the destination PSE, a second VCI is assigned to the call request packet before it is forwarded on the outgoing link to the required destination DTE. Then, assuming the call is accepted, an appropriate response packet is returned to the calling DTE. At this point, a virtual circuit is said to exist between the two DTEs. The information transfer phase is then entered and all subsequent data packets relating to this call are assigned the same reference numbers on each interface link to the network. In this way, both the source and destination DTEs can readily distinguish between packets arriving on the same link but relating to different calls. The relationship between a logical channel and a virtual circuit is shown in Figure 8.3.

It should be noted that although a virtual circuit might appear to the user to be similar to a connection established through a circuit-switched network, as the name implies, it is purely a logical connection. Moreover, since the PSPDN provides error and flow control procedures at the packet level in addition to those used at the link level, the **class of service** supported by a virtual circuit is very high. This means that there is a very high probability of all the packets relating to a

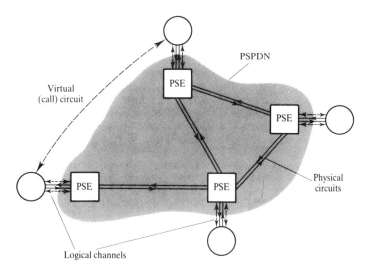

FIGURE 8.3

Logical channels and
virtual calls.

particular call being delivered free of errors and in the correct sequence without
duplicates.

Normally, a virtual circuit is cleared and the appropriate logical channel
identifiers released after all data relating to a call have been exchanged. However,
it is possible for the virtual circuit to be left permanently established, so that a user
who frequently requires to communicate with another user does not have to set up
a new virtual circuit for each call. This is then known as a **permanent virtual
circuit**. Although the user must pay for this facility, the cost of each call is based
only on the quantity of data transferred. As mentioned in relation to a circuit-
switched network, charges are normally made on a distance and call duration
basis.

8.3 PACKET-SWITCHED DATA NETWORKS

The internationally agreed network access protocol that has been defined to
interface a DTE to a PSPDN is X.25. In fact, X.25 is a set of protocols; the various
protocol layers are shown in Figure 8.4. As can be seen, the three protocols
making up X.25 have only **local significance** in contrast to the transport layer
which operates on an **end-to-end** basis.

At the lowest layer, the **X.21 interface** standard is used to define the
physical interface between the DTE and the PTT-supplied local DCE. The link
layer protocol used with X.25 is a version of the HDLC protocol known as LAPB
and its function is to provide the packet layer with an error-free packet transport
facility over the physical link between the DTE and its local PSE. Finally, the
packet layer is concerned with the reliable transfer of transport layer messages –
known as **transport protocol data units** or **TPDUs** – and with the multiplexing of

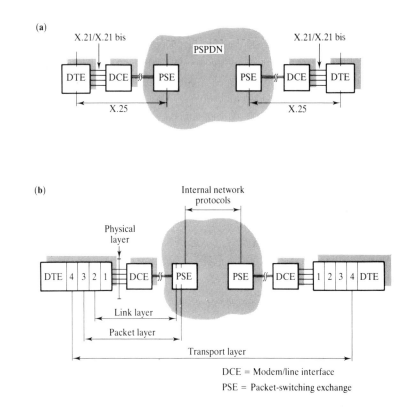

FIGURE 8.4

X.25 network access
protocol:
(a) applicability;
(b) protocol
components.

one or more virtual calls (NSAPs) on to the single physical link controlled by the
link layer. The message units and interactions between the various layers are
shown in Figure 8.5. Each layer will now be considered separately.

8.3.1 Physical interface

The physical interface between the DTE and the local PTT-supplied DCE is
defined in CCITT recommendation X.21. The DCE plays an analogous role to a
synchronous modem since its function is to provide a full-duplex, bit-serial,
synchronous transmission path between the DTE and the local PSE. It can
operate at data rates from 600 bps to 64 kbps. As will be seen in Section 8.4, X.21 is
in fact the same interface as that used with an all-digital circuit-switched network.
Note also that a second standard known as **X.21 (bis)** has been defined for use with
existing (analogue) networks. As it is a subset of RS-232C/V.24, existing user
equipment can be readily interfaced using this standard. The various interchange
circuits associated with X.21 and X.21 (bis) are defined in recommendation X.24
and are shown in Figure 8.6. The use of each line will be described in more detail in
Section 8.4 when CSPDNs are discussed.

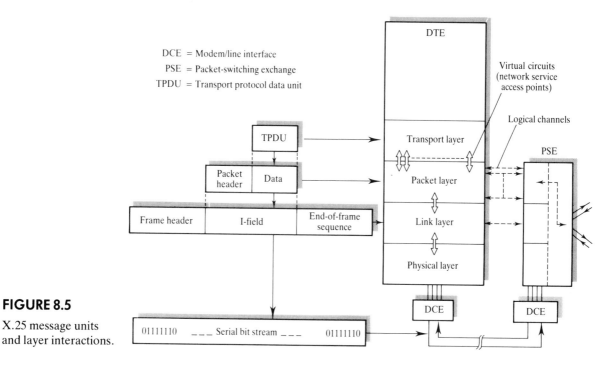

FIGURE 8.5

X.25 message units
and layer interactions.

8.3.2 Link layer

The aim of the link layer, which is often referred to as level 2 because of its position in the ISO Reference Model, is to provide the packet layer with a reliable (error free and no duplicates) packet transport facility across the physical link between the DTE and the local PSE. The link layer has no knowledge of the logical channel to which a packet may belong – this is known only by the packet layer. The error and flow control procedures used by the link layer apply, therefore, to all packets irrespective of the virtual circuits to which they belong.

The frame structure and error and flow control procedures used by the link layer are based on the HDLC protocol. Since the basic operation of HDLC was

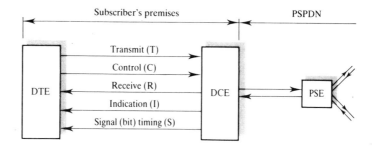

FIGURE 8.6

X.21 physical layer
interface circuits.

described in Chapter 5, it will not be repeated here. It uses the ABM of operation, which is also referred to as **LAPB** in the CCITT X.25 standards documents. This stands for Link Access Procedure Version B since it superseded the earlier Version A link access procedure.

In the context of the ISO Reference Model, the services provided by the link layer to the network (packet) layer above it, together with a list of the PDUs associated with the operation of the link layer protocol entity, are summarized in Figure 8.7(a). The service primitives are shown in the order in which they can be issued with the initiating and corresponding reply primitives on the same line. It should be remembered that either of the packet layers can initiate the three service requests shown.

Using ABM, both the DTE and PSE operate asynchronously, and hence both can initiate the transmission of commands and responses at any time. Also, since the protocol only controls the flow of I-frames across a point-to-point link – that is, across the link between the DTE and its local PSE – the address field in each frame is not used to convey network-wide address information; this is carried in the I-field since network addressing is handled by the packet layer. Instead, the address field contains either the DTE or DCE (PSE) address: if the frame is a command frame, the address specifies the recipient's address; if the frame is a response frame, the address specifies the sender's address. This is shown in Figure 8.7(b).

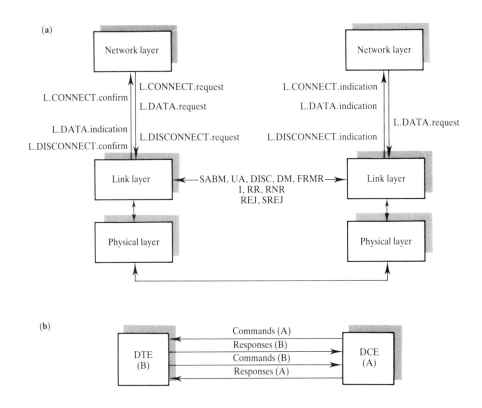

FIGURE 8.7

Link layer:
(a) summary;
(b) address usage.

8.3.3 Packet (network) layer

In the context of the ISO Reference Model, the packet layer is the same as the network layer. Also, because of its position in the reference model, the packet layer is often referred to simply as **level 3**. The transport layer thus uses the services provided by the packet layer to enable it to exchange TPDUs with one or more remote transport layers.

User services

The user services provided by the network (packet) layer are listed in Figure 8.8(a) and their order of usage is shown in the time sequence diagram of Figure 8.8(b). As can be seen, a further service primitive (N.EXPEDITED_DATA) is provided in addition to the normal data transfer service primitive (N.DATA). This, as will be expanded upon later, is an optional service that allows the user to send a single data packet over a connection (logical channel) even though the normal flow of data packets may be stopped by flow control constraints. Another optional service (N.DATA_ACKNOWLEDGE) allows the user to specifically acknowledge receipt of a previously transmitted packet of user data sent using the N.DATA service. Finally, the RESET service allows two users to resynchronize should the flow of packets over a logical channel become out of synchronism while the DISCONNECT service clears the virtual circuit.

FIGURE 8.8

Network layer services: (a) primitives and their parameters.

(a)

Primitive	Parameters
N_CONNECT.request	Called NSAP, Calling NSAP, QDS, Receipt confirmation selection, Expedited data selection, NS_user data
.indication	Called NSAP, Calling NSAP, QDS, Receipt confirmation selection, Expedited data selection, NS_user data
.response	Responding (called) NSAP, QDS, Receipt confirmation selection, Expedited data selection, NS_user data
.confirm	Responding (called) NSAP, QDS, Receipt confirmation selection, Expedited data selection, NS_user data
N_DATA.request	NS_user data
.indication	NS_user data
N_DATA_ACKNOWLEDGE.request	–
.indication	–
N_EXPEDITED_DATA.request	NS_user data
.indication	NS_user data
N_RESET.request	Originator, Reason
.indication	Originator, Reason
.response	–
.confirm	–
N_DISCONNECT.request	Originator, Reason, NS_user data, Responding address
.indicator	Originator, Reason, NS_user data, Responding address

NSAP = Network service access point (address); QDS = Quality of service

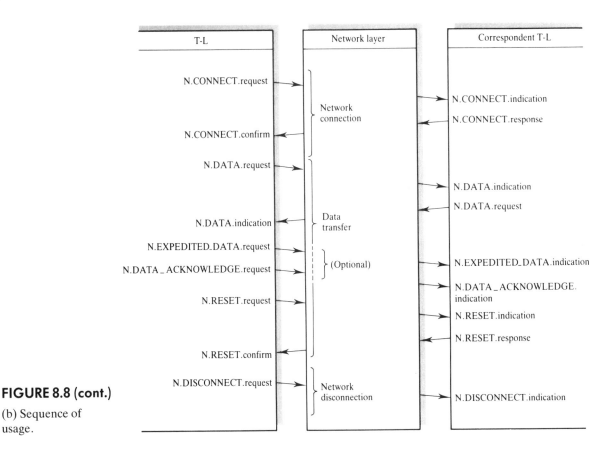

FIGURE 8.8 (cont.)

(b) Sequence of usage.

All of the primitives have parameters associated with them as listed in part (a) of the figure. For example, the parameters associated with the N.CONNECT primitives include the **called (destination) NSAP** and **calling (source) NSAP**. The **NSAP** or **network service access point** is a concatenation of the physical point-of-attachment address and the internal (inter-layer) logical channel (virtual circuit) identifier known as an **address extension**.

The **quality of service (QOS)** parameter comprises two lists of parameters: one the desired and the other the minimum acceptable parameters expected from the network for the connection being set up. These include (packet) transit delay, residual error probability, priority (if applicable), cost (charge for the call) and specified (rather than arbitrary) route. Finally, the two selection parameters allow the two correspondent network service users – transport protocol entities – to negotiate the use of the two optional services which may be used during the subsequent data transfer phase.

As can be deduced from Figure 8.5, the transport layer may have a number of network connections (calls) set up at one time, each call being associated with a single NSAP. The packet layer thus performs a multiplexing function. All connections – virtual circuits (VCs) and permanent virtual circuits (PVCs) – are multiplexed on to a single data link controlled by the link layer. The flow of packets over each virtual circuit is then separately controlled by the packet layer protocol.

NSAP address structure

Most countries have one or more public-carrier PSDNs which are now interconnected globally to form an international PSPDN. Hence the NSAP address associated with each DTE must be a globally-unique network address. Normally, since the total network consists of a number of country-wide PSPDNs, each country network is known as a **subnetwork** or **subnet** in the context of the total network. The structure of the NSAP addresses used in the international PSPDN is defined in CCITT recommendation X.121. In practice, the addresses associated with all the international networks controlled by ISO and CCITT all have a standard format as shown in Figure 8.9.

As can be seen, the addresses are hierarchical and comprised of two parts: the **initial domain part (IDP)** and the **domain specific part (DSP)**. Both parts are defined in the form of either packed binary-coded decimal digits or pure binary; the total NSAP length can be up to 40 decimal digits or 20 binary bytes. The actual length of the addresses used normally precedes the address field so that the recipient DTE can interpret the various fields on their correct byte boundaries.

The IDP is made up of two subfields: the **authority and format identifier (AFI)** and the **initial domain identifier (IDI)**. The AFI specifies the authority responsible for allocating IDIs, the format of IDIs, and the abstract syntax of the DSP. The IDI specifies the particular network addressing scheme to which the actual DSP addresses relate. Thus in the case of the international PSPDN, the IDI will specify X.121.

The DSP is also hierarchical and contains the actual DTE NSAP address. The **subnet identifier (SI)** is the global subnetwork identifier whilst the **point-of-attachment (PA)** field is the physical attachment address in relation to that network. Finally, the **selector (SEL)** subfield has only local meaning and is not used for routing the frame/packet within the network. With an X.25 network, for example, it contains the virtual circuit identifier, whereas with an ISDN it identifies one of eight possible end terminals.

Packet types

The packet types associated with the packet layer protocol (PLP) are known as **packet protocol data units (PPDUs)**. The different PPDU types and their usage are shown in part (a) of Figure 8.10 and their structure in part (b). The pairs of PPDU types across the two interfaces – DTE/DCE and DCE/DTE – have different names but their syntax is the same at both interfaces. Thus the syntax (structure) of the call request is the same as the incoming call and so on.

All PPDUs (packets) have a fixed header comprising the **group format identifier (GFI)**, the **logical group number (LGN)**, and the logical channel number (LCN). The GFI is a 4-bit field consisting of a data qualifier or Q-bit, a delivery

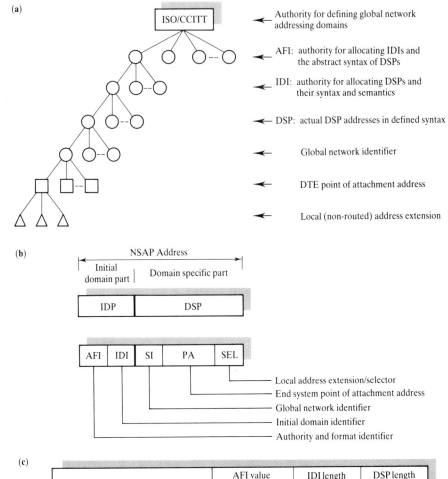

FIGURE 8.9

NSAP address:
(a) hierarchical
structure; (b) contents;
(c) examples.

| | AFI value | | IDI length | DSP length |
	Decimal	Binary	(decimal digits)	(decimal digits)
International PSPDN – X.121	36	37	14	24
International Telex – F.69	40	41	8	30
International PSTN – E.163	42	43	12	26
International ISDN – E.164	44	45	15	23
ISO-assigned country codes – ISO DCC	38	39	3	35
Local (private)	48	49	Null	38

confirmation or D-bit and two additional modulo bits. The use of the Q and D bits will be expanded upon later. The **modulo bits** are used to indicate the modulo (range) of the (packet) sequence numbers used for flow control purposes – 8 or 128. The LGN and LCN collectively form a 12-bit **virtual circuit identifier (VCI)**.

The next octet is the **packet type** field. All control PPDUs have a 1 bit in the least significant bit position while data PPDUs have a 0 bit. It is thus known as the **control bit**. The data and three flow control PPDUs – receive ready (RR), receive not ready (RNR) and reject (REJ) – each have a receive sequence number in the type field. The data PPDU also has a send sequence number and a single **more (M) bit**. The use of these will be expanded upon later. The maximum amount of user data present in a data PPDU is 128 octets although some public carriers use longer lengths up to 4096 octets. The interrupt request PPDU allows the network service user – **NS-user** – to send up to 32 octets of control data outside the normal flow control mechanism. Such PPDUs are acknowledged with an interrupt confirmation.

The **facilities** field in the call request and call accepted PPDUs enable selected operational parameters to be negotiated when a call is being set up. These include the use of fast select, extended sequence numbers, alternative window and packet sizes, reverse charging, and others. Finally, the **diagnostic** PPDU is used by the network to inform a user DTE of any error conditions that may be detected. These include invalid send and receive sequence numbers, invalid packet type received, call set-up problems, and others.

Virtual call establishment and clearing   A time sequence diagram illustrating the various phases of a virtual call is shown in Figure 8.11. A virtual circuit is established (set up) as a result of the user issuing an N.CONNECT.request primitive at a user service access point. The parameters associated with this primitive include the NSAP address of the called DTE and a limited amount of user data. As can be seen, two alternative procedures may be adopted to set up the network connection.

In the first (**normal**) an X.25 virtual circuit is established on receipt of the N.CONNECT.request primitive and the network connect request (N.CR) is then passed over this circuit using an X.25 data packet.

(a)

Packet (PPDU) Types		Protocol usage
DTE → DCE	DCE → DTE	
Call request Call accepted	Incoming call Call confirmation	Call set-up
Clear request DTE clear confirmation	Clear indication DCE clear confirmation	Call clearing
DTE data Interrupt request	DCE data Interrupt confirmation	Data transfer
DTE receiver ready DTE receiver not ready DTE reject Reset request DTE reset confirmation	DCE receiver ready DCE receiver not ready Reset indication DCE reset confirmation	Flow control
Restart request DTE restart confirmation	Restart indication DCE restart confirmation	Resynchronize
Diagnostic	Diagnostic	Network error reporting

FIGURE 8.10

PPDU types:
(a) usage.

(b)

Packet type	Hex						
Call request	0B	Calling addr. length	Called addr. length	Called addr	Calling addr	00	Facilities lgth	Facilities	User data
Call accepted	0F	Calling addr. length	Called addr. length	Called addr	Calling addr	00	Facilities lgth	Facilities
Data	P(R) M P(S) 0	User data: 128/256/512/1024/2048/4096 bytes
Reset request	1B	Reset cause	Diagnostic code (optional)
Reset confirmation	1F
Restart request	FB	Restart cause	Diagnostic code (optional)
Restart confirmation	FF
Diagnostic	F1	Diagnostic code	Explanation
Receive ready	P(R) 00001
Receive not ready	P(R) 00101
Reject	P(R) 01001
Interrupt request	23	User data ≤32 octets
Interrupt confirmation	27
Clear request	13	Clear cause	Diagnostic code (optional)	User data
Clear confirmation	17

GFI = Group format identifier
LCN = Logical channel number
P(R) = Packet receive sequence number
VCI = Virtual circuit identifier

Q = Qualifier bit
D = Delivery confirmation bit
P(S) = Packet send sequence number

FIGURE 8.10 (cont.)

(b) Format.

(a)

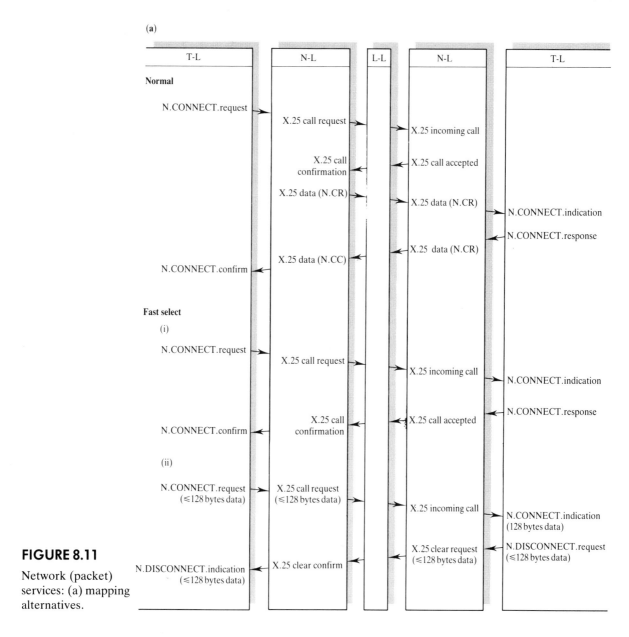

FIGURE 8.11

Network (packet) services: (a) mapping alternatives.

The overheads associated with this method are high and hence the alternative (**fast-select**) mode has been introduced by some carriers. In this case, the network connect request is mapped directly into an X.25 call-request packet, significantly reducing the call set-up overheads. The reset and disconnect services are mapped in a similar way, as shown in part (i). A second application of fast select is to provide a limited **datagram service**; this is shown in part (ii).

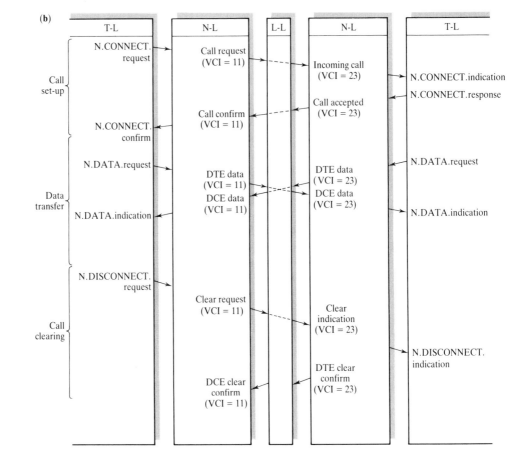

FIGURE 8.11 (cont.)

(b) Example use of VCIs.

Although a connection-oriented service is suitable for applications that involve the transfer of a significant amount of data, many applications involve just a single request/response message exchange. An example is a credit card authorization transaction which simply involves the transfer of the credit card number followed by a short response message. It is unnecessary to set up a virtual circuit for this type of transfer; in a network that supports fast select, this can be carried out using a single message exchange, as shown.

With fast select both the call request and call accepted packets and the clear request and clear accepted packets include a user data field of up to 128 bytes. On receipt of the user data from the incoming N.CONNECT.indication, the destination simply responds with a N.DISCONNECT.request with the response message in the NS-user data parameter. This is then transported back to the sender in a clear request/confirm packet at the same time clearing the virtual circuit.

A time sequence diagram illustrating the use of the virtual circuit identifiers – logical channels – is shown in Figure 8.11(b), assuming the fast-select facility. On receipt of the N.CONNECT.request primitive, the source protocol entity first selects the next free VCI and creates a call-request packet (PPDU) containing the calling and called DTE addresses and the selected VCI. The packet is then passed to the link layer for forwarding to its local PSE.

On receipt of the packet, the local PSE notes the VCI selected and forwards the packet, according to the internal protocol of the network, to the appropriate destination PSE. The latter selects the next free VCI for use on the link to the called DTE, writes this into the packet and changes the packet type into an incoming-call packet. This is then forwarded to the called DTE where its contents are used by the correspondent packet protocol entity to create an N.CONNECT.indication primitive, which is then passed to the correspondent user.

Assuming that the correspondent user is prepared to accept the call, it responds with an N.CONNECT.response primitive which, in turn, is used by the packet protocol entity to create a call-accepted packet. The latter is assigned the same VCI as the one used in the corresponding incoming-call packet. The call-accepted packet is then forwarded to the called DTE's local PSE and the reserved logical channel on this link then enters the data transfer phase. Similarly, the source PSE, on receipt of the call-accepted packet, inserts the previously reserved VCI for use on this part of the circuit into the packet and sets this logical channel into the data transfer state. It then converts the packet into a call-connected packet and forwards it to the calling DTE. Finally, on receipt of the packet, the calling-packet protocol entity issues an N.CONNECT.confirmation primitive to the user and enters the data transfer state.

If the correspondent user does not wish, or is not able, to accept an incoming call, it responds to the N.CONNECT.indication primitive with an N.DISCONNECT.request primitive. This results in the called packet protocol entity returning a clear-request packet to its local PSE, which first releases the previously reserved VCI and then returns a clear-confirmation packet to the called DTE. It then sends a clear-request packet to the source PSE which, in turn, passes the packet to the packet protocol entity in the calling DTE as a clear-indication packet. The DTE first releases the reserved VCI and then passes an N.DISCONNECT.indication primitive to the user. It then returns a clear-confirmation packet to its local PSE to complete the clearance of the virtual circuit. Similarly, either the user or the correspondent user can initiate the clearing of a call at any time by issuing an N.DISCONNECT.request primitive at the corresponding user interface.

Data transfer After a virtual call (network logical connection) has been established, both the user and correspondent user may initiate the transfer of data independently of one another by issuing an N.DATA.request primitive at its network interface with the data to be transferred as a parameter. As has been mentioned, the maximum length of each data packet in a public-carrier packet-switched network is limited, typically to 128 octets of data, to ensure a reliably fast response time. Hence, if a user wishes to transfer a message containing more than this number of octets, the message is first divided into an appropriate number of data packets and each packet sent separately. So that the recipient user knows when each message is complete, each data packet sent through the network contains a single bit in its header known as the **more-data** or **M bit**, which is set whenever further data packets are required to complete a user-level (that is, transport layer) message.

Although the transport layer normally initiates the transfer of its own protocol control messages (TPDUs) to one or more peer transport layers using an N.DATA.request primitive with the TPDU as a data parameter, the X.25 packet layer also allows the user to specify whether the associated parameter contains user-level control or data information. The information type is then embedded into the resulting data packet by the packet layer, which sets a special bit in the packet header known as the **qualifier** or **Q bit**. On receipt of each data packet, this information is passed with the associated data to the correspondent user.

Although the three protocol layers associated with the X.25 protocol set normally have only local significance, a facility is provided to allow acknowledgement information at the packet level to have end-to-end significance. This is implemented by a special bit in each packet header known as the **delivery confirmation** or **D bit**. The D bit in the header of a data packet is set to 1 if the source DTE requires an end-to-end confirmation (acknowledgement) of correct receipt by the remote peer packet layer. As will be seen in Section 8.4, this information is carried in the header of a packet flowing in the reverse direction.

Flow control   All packet layer packets are transferred from a DTE to its local PSE using the services provided by the link layer. The use of the HDLC protocol at the link layer means that the basic packet transport facility supported is relatively reliable. Thus, the emphasis at the packet layer is on flow control rather than error control. The flow control algorithm is based on a **sliding window mechanism** similar to that introduced in Chapter 4. The flow of packets is controlled separately for each logical channel and for each direction of a call; that is, the flow of data packets relating to each call from DTE to PSE is controlled separately from the flow of packets from PSE to DTE.

To implement the window mechanism, all data packets contain a **send sequence number P(S), and a receive sequence number P(R). The** $P(R)$ contained in each data packet relates to the flow of data packets in the reverse direction. Alternatively, if no data packets are awaiting transmission in the reverse direction, the $P(R)$ may be sent by the receiver in a special **receiver-ready (RR)** supervisory packet.

The first data packet in each direction (DTE to PSE and PSE to DTE) of a logical channel is given a $P(S)$ of 0; each subsequent packet in the same direction carries the previous $P(S)$ incremented by 1. The number of packets relating to the same call that may be sent in each direction before a response is received is limited by the agreed window size K for the channel which, for reasons described in Chapter 4, has a maximum value of 7 if eight unique sequence numbers are being used. Thus, once the sender has initiated the transfer of a number of data packets up to the window size, it must cease transmitting further packets until it receives either a data packet or a receiver-ready supervisory packet containing a $P(R)$ that indicates the willingness of the receiver to accept further packets on this channel.

To implement this scheme, the DTE and PSE each maintain three variables for each active logical channel (and hence virtual circuit):

- $V(S)$: This is known as the **send sequence variable** and indicates the $P(S)$ that will be assigned to the next data packet *sent* on this logical channel.

- $V(R)$: This is known as the **receive sequence variable** and indicates the $P(S)$ of the next in-sequence data packet that is expected to be *received* on this logical channel.

- $V(A)$: This is known as the **acknowledgement variable** and is used to determine when the flow of data packets should be stopped.

All three variables are set to 0 when the virtual circuit is first set up or subsequently reset (see later). Then, as each data packet is prepared for sending, it is assigned a send sequence number $P(S)$ equal to the current $V(S)$, which is then incremented modulo-8 or -128 as defined in the GFI field. Similarly, on receipt of each data packet or receiver-ready flow control packet, the receive sequence number, $P(R)$, contained within it is used to update $V(A)$. The sender can continue sending data packets until either the window size is reached (that is, until the incremented $V(A)$ reaches K) or a data or a receiver-ready packet is received containing a $P(R)$ that advances the current $V(A)$. Further data packets may then be sent until the window limit is again reached. A typical packet sequence illustrating this procedure for a window size of 3 is given in Figure 8.12(a). For clarity, a single logical channel is assumed and only a unidirectional flow of data packets is shown.

The use of a window mechanism to control the flow of data packets means that the maximum number of packet buffers required to handle each call is readily determined. In practice, the total number of buffers provided to cater for all the calls that may be currently active is often less than the maximum number required. A facility is provided in the protocol, therefore, to allow the DTE (or PSE) temporarily to suspend the flow of data packets associated with a specific call (virtual circuit). This is achieved by the receiver returning a receiver-not-ready (RNR) packet for this logical channel, instead of a receiver-ready packet. Each RNR packet contains a $P(R)$ that defines the new $V(A)$ for this channel. However, on receipt of an RNR, the sender must cease transmission of further packets until the receiver is ready to continue receiving data packets on this channel. This is normally achieved by the receiver returning an RR packet. A typical packet sequence illustrating the use of the RNR packet is shown in Figure 8.12(b). It can be deduced from the figure that the RNR packet cannot stop the flow of packets immediately, since some packets may be in transit on the link. Any packets received in this way must be accepted, however, because of the lack of any error control associated with the packet layer.

Although the two mechanisms just described are provided to control the flow of data packets over each logical channel, provision is also made in the protocol for a DTE to send a single high-priority data packet to a correspondent DTE independently of the normal flow control procedures. Such a packet is

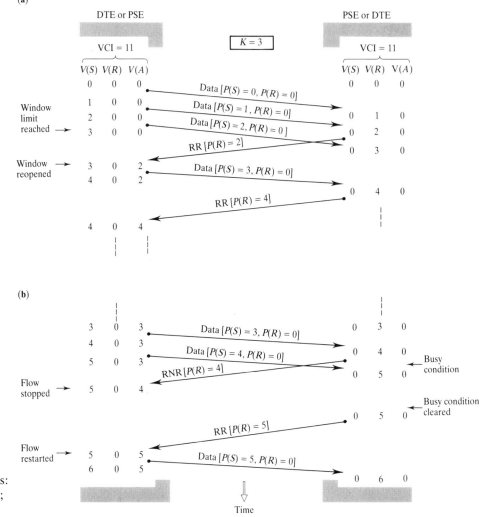

FIGURE 8.12

Flow control examples:
(a) window operation;
(b) RNR operation.

known as an interrupt packet. Since this packet is not affected by the normal flow control mechanisms, it may be received out of sequence from other data packets over this circuit. On receipt of an interrupt packet, the receiving DTE (packet layer) must return an interrupt-confirmation packet, since there can be only one outstanding unacknowledged interrupt packet per virtual circuit at any time. This then allows a further such packet to be sent should this be required, as shown in Figure 8.13(a).

Error recovery The main error recovery mechanisms associated with the packet layer are the reset and restart procedures. The reset procedure is used only during

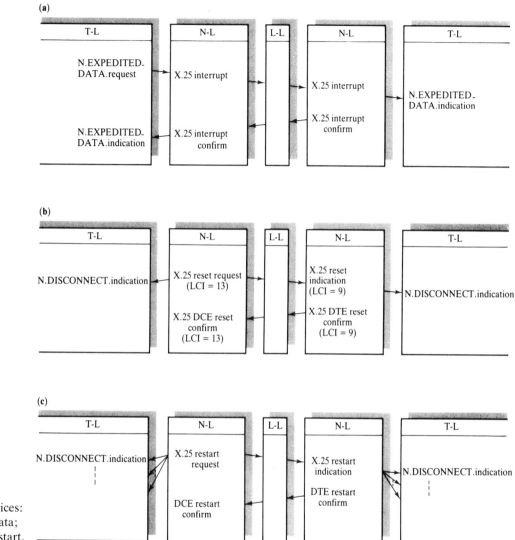

FIGURE 8.13

Additional services:
(a) expedited data;
(b) reset; (c) restart.

the data transfer phase and affects just a single virtual call (circuit). The restart procedure, however, affects all virtual calls currently in progress.

A reset-request packet is sent by either DTE if it receives a data packet that is outside the current window limit. This indicates that the two DTEs have become unsynchronized and hence the flow of data packets must be restarted. A typical packet sequence associated with the reset procedure is shown in Figure 8.13(b). Any data packets associated with the affected virtual circuit are discarded by the packet layer and the user is informed that the network connection has been cleared. The reason for the clearing is passed as a parameter and it is then up to the user (the transport layer, in practice) to recover from any possible loss of data.

The restart procedure is used simultaneously to clear all virtual circuits currently in progress at a DTE. It is utilized when the DTE and PSE become unsynchronized at a level that affects all currently active calls; for example, if an incoming call with a logical channel number that is currently in use is received from the PSE. A typical packet sequence associated with the restart procedure and the effect on a number of active virtual circuits is shown in Figure 8.13(c). The figure only shows the possible effect at a single correspondent packet layer, but clearly a number of other DTEs may be affected in a similar way.

Packet layer summary

Figure 8.14 summarizes the overall operation of the packet layer. The same form of presentation as used for the link layer has been adopted. Three aspects of the operation of the layer can be clearly identified:

- the services it offers to the transport layer above it;
- the PDUs exchanged between two correspondent network (packet) layer protocol entities;
- the link layer services it uses to transport these PDUs.

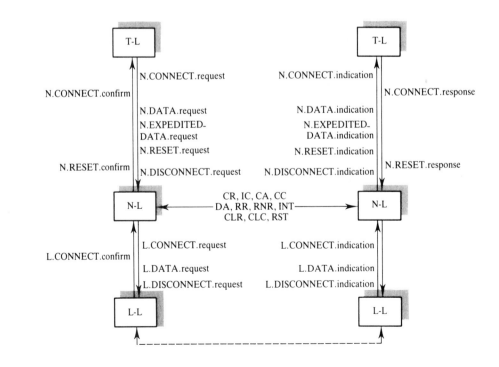

FIGURE 8.14

X.25 packet layer summary.

Protocol specification

To give an insight into the specification of the packet layer protocol, the call establishment phase of the protocol will now be described. The time sequence diagram for this phase was shown in Figure 8.11. For clarity, it is assumed that the fast-select facility is being used and that a data link has already been set up.

In keeping with the style of presentation introduced in Chapter 4, a list of all the incoming events, automaton states, outgoing events, predicates and specific actions related to the call establishment phase of the protocol is given in Figure 8.15. To aid understanding, a state transition diagram of the call establishment phase is shown in Figure 8.16(a). Note that the incoming event and associated outgoing event are shown alongside each transition arc. Figure 8.16(b) gives a more formal definition of the protocol in the form of an event–state table.

(a)

Name	Interface	Meaning
NCONreq	NS-user	N.CONNECT.request received
NCONresp	NS-user	N.CONNECT.response received
CALLconn	Link layer	Call connected packet received
INCcall	Link layer	Incoming call packet received
TCALLconn	Timer	Call connected timer expires

(b)

Name	Meaning
IDLE	No connection established
WFCC	Waiting for a call connected packet
WFNCR	Waiting for an N.CONNECT.response from NS-user
WFCLCF	Waiting for a clear confirm packet
DATA	Connection established and ready for data transfers

(c)

Name	Interface	Meaning
NCONind	NS-user	Send N.CONNECT.indication
NCONconf	NS-user	Send N.CONNECT.confirm
NDISind	NS-user	Send N.DISCONNECT.indication
CALLreq	Link layer	Send call request packet
CALLacc	Link layer	Send call accepted packet
CLRreq	Link layer	Send clear request packet

FIGURE 8.15

Abbreviated names for call establishment phase of network (packet) layer: (a) incoming events; (b) automaton states; (c) outgoing events; (d) predicates; (e) specific actions.

(d)

Name	Meaning
P0	N.CONNECT.request from NS-user unacceptable
P1	N.CONNECT.response from NS-user unacceptable

(e)

Name	Meaning
[1]	Start TCALLconn timer
[2]	Stop TCALLconn timer

(a)

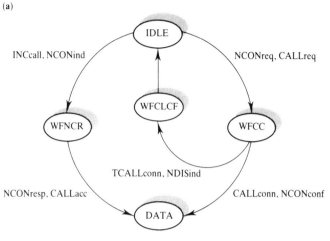

(b)

Event \ State	IDLE	WFCC	WFNCR	WFCLCF	DATA	- - -
NCONreq	1	0	0	0	0	
NCONresp	0	0	3	0	0	
CALLconn	0	2	0	0	0	
INCcall	4	0	0	0	0	
TCALLconn	0	5	0	0	0	
⋮						

FIGURE 8.16

Protocol specification
for call establishment:
(a) state transition
diagram; (b) event–state
table.

0 = NDISind, CLRreq, WFCLCF (Error condition)

1 = PO: NDISind, IDLE;
    NOT PO: CALLreq, [1], WFCC

2 = NCONconf, [2], DATA

3 = NOT P1: CALLacc, DATA

4 = NCONind, WFNCR

5 = NDISind, CLRreq, WFCLCF

It should be stressed, however, that the definitions given are not intended to be complete but rather serve as an introduction to understanding the formal specification of the X.25 packet layer protocol.

8.3.4 Terminal access

The preceding sections relating to the X.25 network access protocol have assumed that the DTE to be connected to the network has sufficient intelligence (or processing capability) to be able to implement the various protocol layers just described. In general, this is true, certainly if the DTE is a computer. In some instances, however, the DTE may not operate in a packet mode nor have sufficient processing capability to implement a protocol like X.25. Hence, to interface this type of DTE to the network it is necessary to provide an additional piece of equipment, which implements the various protocol layers on its behalf and provides a much simpler user-level interface to the DTE. An example of a DTE in this category is a simple asynchronous character-mode terminal like a personal computer or VDU. This normally has only a limited level of intelligence with a simple RS-232C/V.24 physical interface.

To meet this type of requirement, the user may, of course, choose to provide the additional equipment to perform the necessary assembly of character strings from the terminal into network packets and vice versa. Alternatively, because this is not an uncommon requirement, the various PSPDN authorities offer users an alternative network access protocol, known as X.28, which is intended for use with asynchronous character-mode terminals. The additional equipment necessary to provide this type of interface is known as a **packet assembler–disassembler** (**PAD**). Since the PAD is provided by the PSPDN authority, it is normally located with the local PSE. A single PAD is used to support a number of character-mode DTEs. The functions and location of a PAD, together with the additional protocols that have been defined for use with it, are shown in Figure 8.17. As can be seen, protocol X.3 defines the operation and facilities that are provided by the PAD, while X.29 defines the interface between the PAD and a remote packet-mode DTE. Selected aspects of this mode of working will now be considered.

PAD and X.3

Essentially, the function of a PAD is to assemble the individual characters entered by a user at a character-mode asynchronous terminal into meaningful packets that are suitable for transmission through an X.25 PSPDN. Similarly, on receipt of such packets, the PAD disassembles them and passes the individual characters contained within them to the terminal a single character at a time. Thus the PAD must perform all the X.25 protocol functions on behalf of the terminal (such as call establishment, flow control) and in general make the packet mode of working of the network transparent to the user.

The functions and facilities of a PAD are defined in recommendation X.3. In addition to the basic functions just outlined, each terminal connected to a PAD has a number of associated parameters, because character-mode terminals vary widely in their operation and characteristics. These parameters are normally set by commands entered at the terminal or, alternatively, from the remote packet-mode DTE being accessed. They relate to such features as:

- whether local **echo checking** is required;

- selection of **packet terminating** (**data forwarding**) characters, which allow the user of the terminal to signal to the PAD that the transmission of a (partly complete) packet should be initiated;

- specification of alternative control characters for such functions as line feed and carriage return.

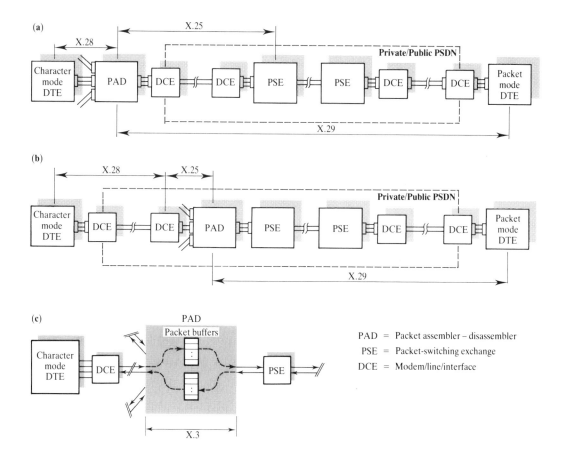

FIGURE 8.17

PAD location and its protocols: (a) with character-mode DTE; (b) with PSE; (c) internal schematic.

To facilitate the use of the PAD, all the parameters associated with a terminal have a **default value**. Only parameters that differ from these need be changed. The initial parameter settings are determined by the **standard profile** selected for use with the terminal. A number of alternative standard profiles have been defined for use with the more popular types of terminal. Both the standard profile to be used and any changes to be made to this are normally selected and entered when a communication link between the terminal and the PAD is first established. The procedure for carrying this out is defined in recommendation X.28.

Recommendation X.28

This recommendation specifies the protocol to be used between an asynchronous character-mode terminal and the PAD. It contains the procedures to be followed to:

- access the PAD;
- set the terminal parameters to the required values;
- establish a virtual call to a destination packet-mode DTE;
- control the exchange of user's data between the terminal and the PAD;
- clear an established call.

Access to the PAD may take several forms. It may be via a switched connection set up using the PSTN or it may be over a leased line. Clearly, if the PSTN uses analogue transmission, modems must be used at each end of the link. Alternatively, if digital data services are provided by the network, a direct digital path can be either set up or leased, and hence a conventional RS-232C/V.24 interface may be used.

Once the terminal has gained access to the PAD, the terminal sends a service request character sequence. This enables the PAD to determine the data rate being used by the terminal and allows the terminal to select an initial standard profile. Procedures are then defined to allow the terminal user to read the parameters associated with the profile and, if required, to change them to other values. The PAD is then ready to establish a virtual call through the PSPDN to a remote packet-mode DTE.

To establish a virtual call, the user first indicates to the PAD the address of the required packet-mode terminal. The PAD then follows the virtual call establishment procedure outlined earlier. Once the call has been established, the PAD enters the data transfer phase.

When in the data transfer phase, the PAD performs the necessary packet assembly and disassembly functions. During the assembly process, the PAD initiates the transfer of a packet either when the user enters an agreed packet termination control character or after an agreed timeout period. Finally, after all information has been exchanged, the user may request the PAD to initiate the clearing of the call.

Recommendation X.29

This recommendation specifies the interaction between the PAD and the remote packet-mode DTE. The basic procedures associated with X.29 for call establishment and data transfer are essentially the same as those used in X.25. However, additional procedures are defined in the recommendation, which reflect the presence of the PAD between the terminal and remote packet-mode DTE. For example, during the call establishment phase, the PAD uses the first four octets of the optional user data field in a call-request packet as a so-called **protocol identifier** field. This allows different types of calling subscriber (terminal) to be identified so that the called packet-mode DTE can utilize alternative protocols should this be necessary.

Similarly, in the reverse direction, when in the data transfer phase, the packet-mode DTE is able to communicate with the PAD directly using the Q bit in the header of each data packet. When the Q bit is set, this indicates that the remaining information in the packet is intended for use by the PAD and should not therefore be disassembled and passed to the user terminal. This procedure allows, for example, the remote packet-mode DTE to read and, if necessary, set the current values of the parameters associated with the calling terminal.

8.3.5 Interconnection of X.25 networks

As has been described, X.25 is the protocol set used for interfacing a DTE to the data circuit terminating equipment (DCE) associated with a packet-switched data network. It is a connection-oriented protocol which means that a virtual circuit (VC) is established between the two communicating DTEs prior to transmitting any data. Associated with this virtual circuit are two logical channel identifiers: one for use over the link connecting the calling DTE to its local DCE/PSE and the other for use over the called DCE/DTE link. These are then used to relate the subsequent data packets associated with the call to that virtual circuit.

Although not part of the X.25 standard, when a virtual circuit is being set up, the virtual circuit must also be established across the network to enable the data packets associated with each call to be routed by the packet-switching exchanges within the network. Some of the routing algorithms that are used with WANs will be discussed in the next chapter when internetworking is discussed. Irrespective of the routing algorithm used to compute routes, however, each exchange contains a number of routing tables to route packets: a **network routing table**, which indicates the outgoing link from this exchange to use for each destination DTE in the network, and an additional set of **link routing tables**, one per link.

On receipt of a call request packet, each exchange involved in a route first uses the destination DTE address within the packet to determine from the network routing table which outgoing link to use to forward the packet. It then obtains the next free VCI to be used on this link – from a list of free VCIs – and makes an entry in the two link routing tables involved. An example is shown in Figure 8.18.

In the example, it is assumed that the call request packet arrived on link 1 with a VCI of 10 and a destination DTE address of 25. Hence the exchange first determines from the network routing table that the required outgoing link is 2. Assuming the next free VCI on link 2 is 15, it makes an entry first in link 1 routing table at location (VCI) 10 of the corresponding outgoing link number (link-out) and VCI (VCI-out) and then in link 2 routing table at location 15 of link 1 and VCI 10. It then initiates the forwarding of the call request packet on link 2 with a VCI of 15 in its header.

This procedure is repeated at each exchange until it reaches the exchange to which the destination DTE is attached. The subsequent call accepted and related data packets are then forwarded along this established route (virtual circuit) by each exchange simply reading, from the incoming link routing table, the outgoing link number and VCI, writing these into the packet header and initiating the forwarding of the packet on the outgoing link.

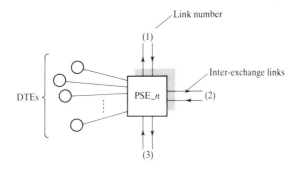

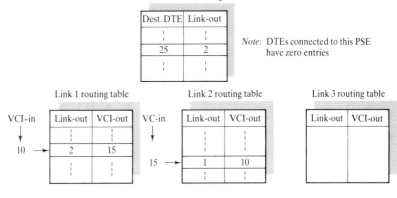

FIGURE 8.18

Intra-network routing example.

It can be concluded that if the total network comprises multiple interconnected networks and the two DTEs are connected to different networks, then a separate virtual circuit must be set up across each intermediate subnetwork. Moreover, in order to relate packets to a particular call, a virtual circuit must also be set up across the links that interconnect these networks together. Thus with a large network that comprises multiple subnetworks, the virtual circuit set up between two DTEs comprises a number of separate virtual circuits (and hence logical channel identifiers), each of use over a particular link. This is shown in Figure 8.19; for clarity, just a single virtual circuit is shown for each subnetwork.

Typically, the individual networks shown in the figure are public-carrier data networks, so many thousands of DTEs may be connected to each network. The interconnecting links between networks are normally multiple 64 or 56 kbps lines or channels. The equipment used to interconnect each network is a special DCE known as a **signalling terminal exchange** or **STE**; the **X.75** protocol is used to establish and release virtual circuits across these links. This protocol is also often used for setting up and releasing virtual circuits across a single network, although this is not specified by CCITT. The figure thus shows the virtual circuits associated with a single call between two DTEs.

The presence of multiple virtual circuits associated with a call is transparent to the two communicating DTEs; each DTE knows only the identity of the virtual

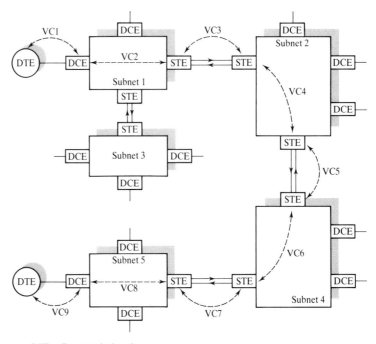

FIGURE 8.19

Virtual circuit structure
across a network that
comprises multiple
subnetworks.

DTE = Data terminal equipment
DCE = Data circuit terminating equipment
STE = Signalling terminating equipment
VC*n* = Virtual circuit *n*

circuit associated with the local link to its DCE/PSE. Flow and error control for all
data packets being carried over these links is then performed in the normal way.
The controlling devices associated with each of the other virtual circuits (DCE–
STE, STE–STE etc) then operate in the same way and impose their own flow and
error control procedures over these circuits. Because the STE between each pair
of networks consists of two halves, each associated with its own network, an STE
is also referred to as a **half gateway**.

Recommendation X.75

The applicability of X.75 is as shown in Figure 8.20. As with X.25, three protocols
are associated with the X.75 standard: the packet layer protocol (PLP), the data
link protocol (DLP) and the physical layer protocol (PHY). Normally, to enhance
reliability and throughput, multiple links are used to interconnect two STEs so the
multilink procedure (MLP) is used as the DLP. It may be recalled from Chapter 5
that with MLP the combined set of links (or subchannels relating to a higher bit
rate circuit) is treated as a single entity when transmitting frames across such links.
Thus when a frame (packet) is to be transmitted, any available link is selected
regardless of the virtual circuit (logical channel identifier) within it. The multilink

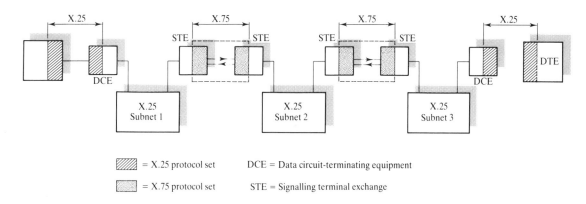

= X.25 protocol set   DCE = Data circuit-terminating equipment

= X.75 protocol set   STE = Signalling terminal exchange

FIGURE 8.20

Applicability of the
X.75 protocol.

FIGURE 8.21

X.75 packets: (a) packet
types and their usage;
(b) packet formats
(i) call request,
(ii) control, (iii) data.

control (MLC) field in each frame is then used by the recipient MLP to resequence frames before they are delivered to the PLP.

The X.75 PLP is simpler than the X.25 PLP in that it requires fewer packet types for its implementation. This is because in X.75 communication is between two directly connected STEs whereas with X.25 two intermediate DCEs are also involved in the communications path between two DTEs. The reduced set of packet types and their general format are shown in Figure 8.21(a) and (b), respectively.

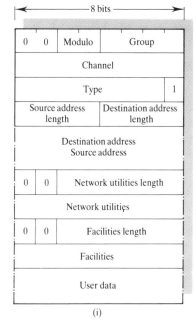

Packet (PPDU) types	Protocol usage
Call request Call connected	Call set-up
Clear request Clear confirmation	Call clearing
Data Interrupt Interrupt confirmation	Data transfer
Receiver ready Receiver not ready Reset confirmation	Flow control
Restart Restart confirmation	Restart

(a)

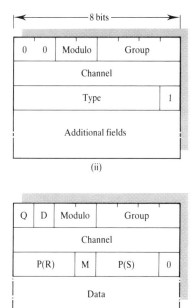

(b)

The various fields and their usage are virtually the same as for X.25. The main additional field is the **network utilities field** in each call request packet. It may be recalled that the same packet in X.25 has a facilities field which is used to request certain operational facilities to be used with this connection, such as selection of the retransmission strategy. In a similar way, the network utilities field is provided to allow an STE to indicate to another STE the utilities associated with the network to which it is attached. These include window and packet size indication, estimated transit delay, and its support (or otherwise) of fast select. Thus it is this field that enables an STE to determine whether the specified minimum facilities required for the connection can be met.

Elements of the operation of the PLP are outlined in Figure 8.22. Part (a) shows the various protocols, while part (b) shows the end-to-end packet sequence used to set up a virtual circuit, then to transfer a single packet of data and finally to clear the circuit. For convenience, the X.75 protocol is assumed to be used for transfers across each subnet as well as across the STE–STE links. The relay function within each STE is used to perform any packet format conversions.

Each STE has a specific X.121 address. Since this is hierarchical, on receipt of a packet, the receiving STE (and each intermediate packet switching exchange within the network) can use the highest order part of the destination address to determine the route to be followed either to the next STE or to the destination DCE/DTE.

On receipt of a call request packet, the source PSE determines from the (DTE) destination address within it that it is for a different network. The PSE uses its **routing table** to determine the outgoing link to be used to forward the packet to the appropriate STE. On receipt of the packet, the relay layer within the STE first makes a record of the virtual circuit identifier (VCI) associated with this call and then reformats the packet with a new VCI and the appropriate network utilities parameters. It then initiates the transfer of the packet across the STE–STE link using the appropriate protocol stack.

The relay layer within the receiving STE then makes a record of the network utilities and VCI within it, enters a new VCI and again uses the DTE destination address contained within the packet to forward the packet through the second subnetwork to the destination PSE. The relay layer within the destination PSE then reformats the packet into an incoming call packet, changes the VCI and forwards the packet to the destination DTE using the X.25 PLP.

A similar procedure is used with call accepted/call connected packets except that in this case the utilities associated with the second network are made known to the other STE. Finally, data packets can be transferred over the established virtual circuits on receipt of the call connected packet by the source DTE.

As indicated earlier, the normal X.25 flow and error control procedures are applied over each virtual circuit in turn. Thus if the flow is stopped at any point in a network, this will be reflected back to the neighbouring network virtual circuit and so on back to the source DTE. This type of flow control is known as **back pressure**.

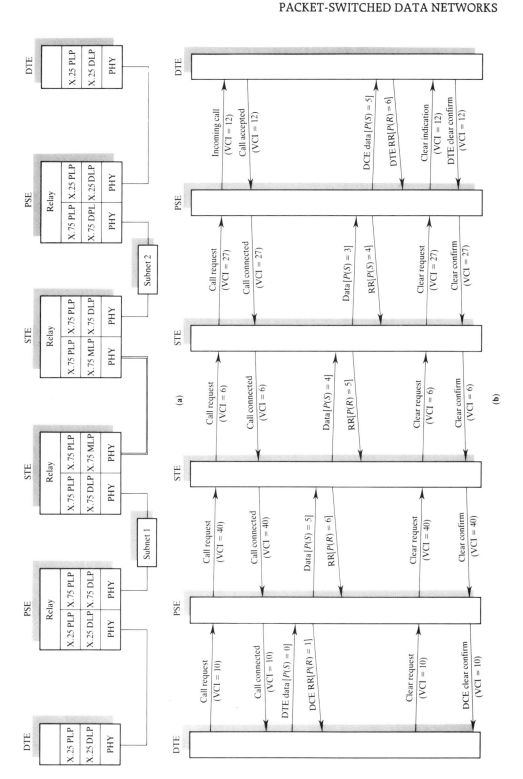

FIGURE 8.22   End-to-end packet flow: (a) protocol stacks; (b) packet sequence diagram.

The figure shows a single data packet being transferred with a separate (non-piggybacked) acknowledgement being used on each virtual circuit. Alternatively, if the D bit is set in a data packet then this bit remains set throughout its transfer across the total network. The resulting acknowledgement is treated in the same way and hence has end-to-end significance. Finally, the call clearing procedure is similar to that used with X.25 except that it is extended across the complete network.

8.3.6 X.25 PLP over LANs

Although the DTEs (stations) connected to many LANs operate with a best-try connectionless network layer protocol, it is also possible for them to operate with an X.25 packet layer protocol. This is done, for example, when the DTEs (stations) connected to the LAN require to communicate with a remote system through an X.25-based WAN. All the networks are then of the same type and

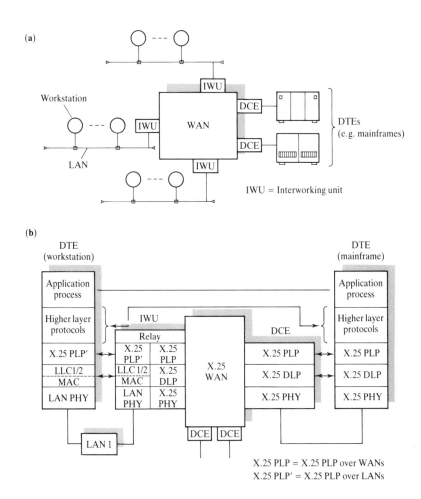

FIGURE 8.23

X.25 PLP over LANs:
(a) example application;
(b) possible protocol
hierarchy.

hence the internetworking issues are much simplified. A simple interconnected network of this type is shown in Figure 8.23.

In the example, it is assumed that the total network comprises a distributed community of LANs each connected to an X.25-based WAN. The aim is for all stations connected to each LAN either to communicate with another station on the same LAN directly or to access, say, a mainframe computer connected to the X.25 WAN.

To meet such a requirement, a special node on each LAN acts as the interface point to the X.25 WAN. Because of its role, it is known (in CCITT terminology) as an **internetworking unit** or **IWU**. It has a known X.25 WAN address. If the X.25 PLP in a station determines that the required destination network address is different from its own, then it sends the call request packet to the IWU using the latter's (known) MAC address. The relay function in the IWU then sends a separate call request packet across the X.25 WAN in the normal way.

Two problems with this type of interworking are the selection of virtual circuit (logical channel) identifiers and the disparity in frame (packet) sizes. Clearly, the IWU associated with each LAN essentially has a number of independent DTEs connected to it each of which could initiate the sending of a call request packet. To overcome the (high) probability of a collision occurring in the selection of virtual circuit identifiers, one (or more) identifiers is (are) assigned to each DTE in advance; this is known by the DTE. In the case of different packet sizes, the normal approach is to adopt the maximum packet size of the X.25 WAN for all communications involving the WAN.

The LLC sublayer can be either LLC1 or LLC2, both of which were described in Chapter 5. Since this type of network is commonly used, the use of the X.25 PLP over a LAN is now an international standard defined in ISO 8881.

8.4 CIRCUIT-SWITCHED DATA NETWORKS

The various protocols associated with the lowest three network-dependent layers in the ISO Reference Model for use with a CSPDN are as shown in Figure 8.24(a). The operational characteristics of the physical interface to a circuit-switched network are defined in recommendation X.21. The aim is to provide the user with a full-duplex synchronous data transmission path, which is available for the duration of the call. The various interchange circuits associated with X.21 were shown in Figure 8.6 and hence the remainder of this section will concentrate on the operation of the X.21 interface protocol.

8.4.1 X.21 interface protocol

With a circuit-switched network, a physical communication path exists between the calling and called DTEs once a call has been established. The X.21 interface protocol is concerned, therefore, only with the set-up and clearing operations associated with each call. The control of the ensuing data transfer is the

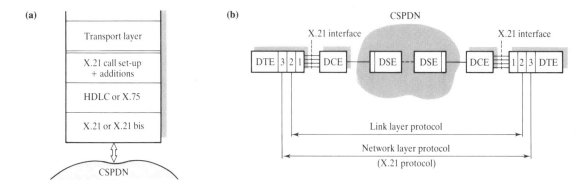

FIGURE 8.24

CSPDNs: (a) network-dependent protocols; (b) applicability.

responsibility of the link layer which, because of the operation of a circuit-switched network, operates on an end-to-end basis. This is shown in Figure 8.24(b).

A typical interchange sequence to set up a call, exchange data and then clear the call using the various interchange circuits associated with X.21 is shown in Figure 8.25. Part (a) shows the interchange sequence across the calling DTE/DCE interface and (b) shows the interchange sequence across the called DTE/DCE interface. Initially, the transmit (T) circuits from both the calling and called DTEs are set at logical 1, indicating that they are both ready to either initiate a call or receive a call. Similarly, the receive (R) circuits from each DCE are also at logical 1, indicating their availability.

The calling DTE first indicates that it wishes to make a call by setting its control (C) circuit to the on state and simultaneously setting its transmit circuit to the logical 0 state (Figure 8.25(a)). When the DCE is ready to accept the call, it responds by transmitting two (or more) SYN characters on the receive circuit followed by a series of '+' IA5 (ASCII) characters. On receipt of the '+' characters, the calling DTE proceeds by transmitting two (or more) SYN characters followed by the network address of the required destination DTE, again in the form of IA5 characters each with a single parity bit. The address is terminated by a single '+' character. The DTE then enters a wait state and the DCE responds by transmitting idle (call progress) characters while it attempts to set up the call.

When the call request reaches the required destination DCE, the latter informs the called DTE by first transmitting two SYN characters followed by a series of BEL characters (Figure 8.25(b)). The called DTE then accepts the call by setting its control circuit to on and the DCE, in turn, passes other call set-up information in the form of a series of IA5 characters on the receive circuit. This information includes reverse charging and similar information. Finally, the call set-up phase is completed by both the calling and called DCEs setting their indication (I) control circuits to indicate that a circuit has been set up and the network is ready for data.

After the connection has been established, a data transparent, full-duplex communication path is available to both the calling and called DTEs for the

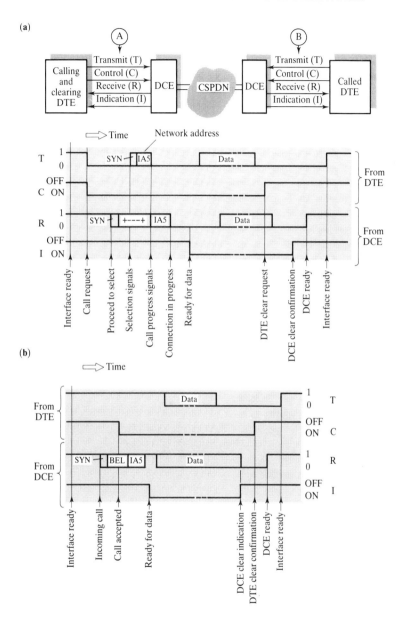

FIGURE 8.25

Successful call and clear interchange sequences: (a) calling DTE/DCE interface (A); (b) called DTE/DCE interface (B).

transfer of link layer data. (Typically, this involves the exchange of frames according to the HDLC protocol.) Each DTE initiates the transmission of a data frame on its transmit circuit. This is then sent through the network and passed to the recipient DTE on the incoming receive circuit from its local DCE. Finally, after one of the DTEs has finished transmitting all its data, it initiates the clearing of the call (circuit) by switching its control circuit to off (DTE clear-request)

(Figure 8.25(a)). As can be seen, however, since the circuit is full-duplex, the clearing DTE must be prepared to accept further data on the incoming receive circuit.

The clear-request signal is passed through the network to the remote DCE which informs its local DTE by setting the indication control circuit to the off state (DCE clear-indication) (Figure 8.25(b)). The local DTE responds by setting its control circuit to the off state (DTE clear-confirmation). This is then passed through the network to the clearing DCE which informs the DTE by setting its indication circuit to off (DCE clear-confirmation) (Figure 8.25(a)). Finally, both sides of the connection return to the 'interface ready' state.

8.4.2 X.21 bis

The X.21 interface protocol is intended for use with an all-digital CSPDN. However, before such networks become widely available, and to ease the transition from existing RS-232C/V.24-based equipment to the newer equipment needed with X.21, an alternative interface protocol has been defined known as X.21 bis, the bis indicating that it is the alternative protocol. This is the same interface as that described in Chapter 2 for use with a synchronous modem – that is, one that supplies a bit-timing clock signal – since it must perform digital-to-analogue conversion for transmitting data through the network and analogue-to-digital conversion on receipt of data from the network.

8.4.3 Link and network layers

As was indicated in Figure 8.24, in a circuit-switched network both the link layer and network layer protocols are end-to-end protocols. However, with an all-digital network, the link layer protocol can be the same as that used in X.25 since a full-duplex circuit is set up, that is, HDLC with LAPB. However, with older analogue access circuits and networks, only a two-wire, half-duplex circuit is set up so recommendation X.75 must be used. The link set-up procedure with X.75 is a derivative of LAPB known as LAPX. This again is intended for the set-up of a logical data link over a half-duplex physical circuit.

If no flow control functions are supported, the CSPDN network layer (level 3) can be relatively simple, since, after setting up the connection, each network data transfer service primitive issued by the transport layer can be mapped directly into a similar request to the intermediate link layer. The transport layer would then perform its own flow control functions. Alternatively, to ease interworking with other types of network, it is possible to have a network layer similar to that used with X.25. If this is done, however, the various virtual circuit identifiers discussed would have an end-to-end significance rather than local significance, as with an X.25 packet-switched network. Also, in a CSPDN each call would, of course, be a separate circuit

8.5 INTEGRATED SERVICES DIGITAL NETWORKS

As indicated earlier, the PTT authorities in most countries are rapidly upgrading their existing PSTNs to all-digital operation. When this is complete, a high bit rate, all-digital interface will be available at each subscriber outlet. Also, since the new networks will employ all-digital transmission and switching, a very fast connection (call) set-up time will be provided for local, national and international calls. It is intended that the new subscriber interface will have sufficient capacity not only to handle voice communications but also data communications directly, the two services operating concurrently if this is desired. These new networks are referred to therefore as **integrated services digital networks (ISDNs)**.

Because of the far-reaching consequences of such networks CCITT has already defined a set of standards for interfacing equipment to such networks; these are referred to as the I-series recommendations. The remainder of this chapter gives an overview of the different types of user interface proposed for ISDNs and of some of the I-series recommendations.

8.5.1 User interfaces

A limited set of standard, multi-purpose user (subscriber) interfaces has been proposed for ISDNs, as summarized in Figure 8.26. As can be seen, the basic service offered will be for voice communications, as is the case for existing telephone networks. It should be noted, however, that since the subscriber outlet is digital, voice traffic will have to be digitized in the subscriber (telephone) handset prior to transmission and converted back to analogue form on reception. As a bit rate of 64 kbps is required to transmit digitized voice, the user interface will offer multiples of this basic rate.

In the second example in the figure, the same outlet (but with a different user terminal, of course) is used to provide a circuit-switched connection for data communications. The basic data rate will be 64 kbps. And because digital transmission and switching are used, a very fast call set-up time will be available. Also, as in the third example, the user may use the outlet as an integrated voice and data facility, both operating concurrently.

The fourth example shows that, with an appropriate terminal, the basic outlet may also be used to provide access to a packet-switching service. This, as will be seen, may be at 64 kbps or, optionally, at a lower bit rate of 16 kbps.

These four examples utilize the ISDN simply for providing a switched transmission path and are referred to as **bearer services**. However, it is intended that PTT authorities will provide additional, more sophisticated, equipment to allow the ISDN to be used as a fast Teletex, Facsimile or Videotex network. These are referred to as **teleservices** and are illustrated in Figure 8.26(b). Essentially, a **Teletex** network provides a general-purpose facility for exchanging messages (comprising alphanumeric and graphical characters) between similar terminals. A **Facsimile** network is a general-purpose facility for transmitting scanned images of

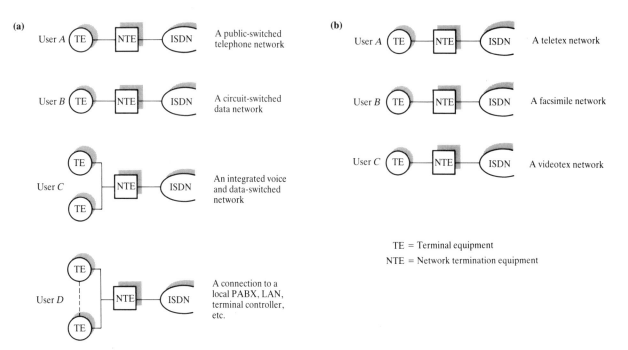

FIGURE 8.26

ISDN user services:
(a) bearer services;
(b) teleservices.

documents electronically between similar terminals. And a **Videotex** network is a general-purpose facility for gaining access to a remote database storing various types of information such as stocks and share prices.

8.5.2 Network access points

To allow for this wide range of uses, the **network termination equipment** (**NTE**) provided by the PTT authorities will have a number of alternative access points associated with it. These are shown in Figure 8.27.

Clearly, by the time ISDN networks are fully operational, many users will have invested heavily in equipment that conforms to existing standards, such as the V- and X-series. To cater for this, the NTE associated with ISDNs will support not only the newer generation of equipment but also existing equipment and interfaces. This will be achieved by providing a range of **terminal adapters** which will perform the necessary mapping function.

The alternative access points (R, S and T) illustrated in the figure clearly imply a varying level of intelligence in the NTE. In relation to the ISO Reference Model, these access points require a varying number of protocol layers. Figure 8.28 summarizes the layers required to support each service. As can be seen, these range from layer 1 to support a basic transmission service, layers 1–3 to support such services as a switched voice and/or data terminal, to layers 1–7 to support various teleservices.

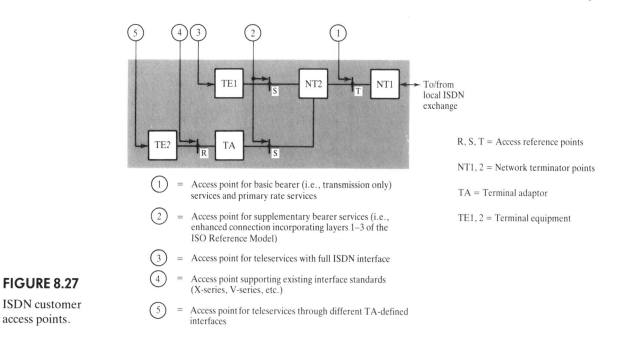

1 = Access point for basic bearer (i.e., transmission only) services and primary rate services

2 = Access point for supplementary bearer services (i.e., enhanced connection incorporating layers 1–3 of the ISO Reference Model)

3 = Access point for teleservices with full ISDN interface

4 = Access point supporting existing interface standards (X-series, V-series, etc.)

5 = Access point for teleservices through different TA-defined interfaces

R, S, T = Access reference points

NT1, 2 = Network terminator points

TA = Terminal adaptor

TE1, 2 = Terminal equipment

FIGURE 8.27

ISDN customer access points.

8.5.3 Channel types

The basic subscriber interface to an ISDN will provide two 64 kbps channels, known as **B channels**, and an additional 16 kbps channel, known as the **D channel**. The basic use of the D channel is for signalling; the NTE uses it to inform the local ISDN exchange of the address of the destination NTE. The use of a separate channel for signalling results in a significantly faster call set-up time. In addition, because new calls are set up relatively infrequently, it is proposed that the D channel should also be available to the subscriber when signalling is not in progress. For example, it is proposed that the D channel should be used for packet-switching albeit with a reduced packet size. The total available bit rate to the subscriber at the basic interface is thus 144 kbps – (2B + D).

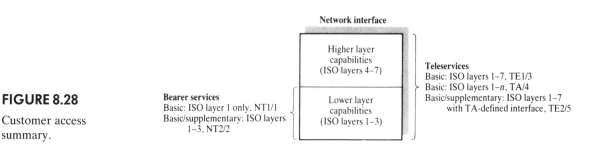

FIGURE 8.28

Customer access summary.

It is also proposed that higher bit rate channels should be available on request. These are referred to as **primary rate** or **H channels**. Currently, the bit rates associated with these channels are being discussed, but include:

- H0 : 384 kbps,
- H11: 1536 kbps,
- H12: 1920 kbps.

The proposed uses of these channels include video telephone (view phone), high bit rate dedicated communication channels (as are currently available) and switched channels for high-speed teleservices. These will be accessed at reference point 1, the T interface. The structure of a primary rate interface

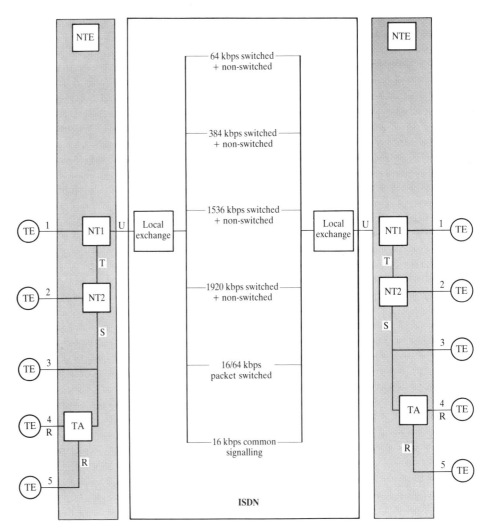

FIGURE 8.29

User network interface summary.

including the location of the signalling channel was shown earlier in Figure 2.21 of Chapter 2. The various interfaces and the proposed range of alternative bit rates are summarized in Figure 8.29.

8.5.4 User–network interface

A schematic of the user-network physical (layer 1) interface is shown in Figure 8.30. The circuit between the local exchange and the customer premises is a single twisted-pair wire. Thus for the basic access service this must support duplex (2-way simultaneous) transmission for the 2B + D channels. As described in Chapter 2, the transmission line code used on this circuit is 2B1Q; a hybrid transformer is used to achieve duplex transmission. In principle, the transformer should allow only the received signal to be passed to the receiver section but, owing to imperfections, a portion of the (much stronger) transmitted signal also feeds back to the receiver section. To overcome this, an **adaptive hybrid** or **echo cancellor** is used to cancel the (known) transmitted signal from the composite received signal. For the echo cancellor to operate correctly, there must be no correlation between the transmitted and received signals. To achieve this, two **scrambler circuits** are used, one for transmit and one for receive. Such circuits randomize the bit sequence in a pseudo-random (and hence repeatable) way.

In North America the equipment that performs the network termination function (NT1) technically belongs to the customer. In other countries, however, it belongs to the network provider and the user interface thus starts at the customer side of the NT equipment. This is a 4-wire (2-pair) interface with one pair for transmit and the other for receive. Each pair of wires carries the 2B + D

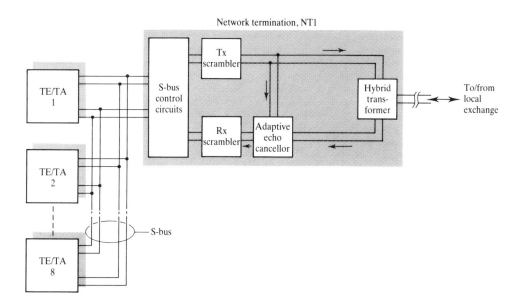

FIGURE 8.30

User-network physical interface schematic.

bit stream using a standard frame structure to allow the bit periods associated with each B and D channel to be identified.

Since the customer side of the NT is the S interface, the 4-wire circuit is known as the S-bus. It allows up to eight independent terminal equipments or terminal adaptors to be connected to it. A contention control scheme is incorporated to allow the various items of equipment to time-share the use of the two B and one D channel in a fair way. Consequently, the NT equipment is a relatively sophisticated box owing to its rich functionality.

8.5.5 User interface protocols

A key feature of the ISDN is the logical separation of the signalling channel from the normal voice and/or data channels. The signalling channel, because it is used for call set-up, is said to be part of the control or **C plane**, while the user channels are said to belong to the user or **U plane**. As has been indicated, the ISDN supports both circuit-switched and packet-switched services. Two new frame-level services, one known as **frame relay** and the other as **frame switching**, are also supported. The different service types are shown in Figure 8.31.

Irrespective of the type of service, a circuit/virtual path must first be set up through the network before any user data is transferred. With a switched connection this is done at the time of the call, although **semi-permanent connections** (similar to leased circuits) can also be provided. To set up a circuit or virtual path, signalling messages are exchanged over the D channel between a TE/TA and its local exchange using a 3-layer protocol stack. Within the network itself, a separate **signalling network** which involves a full 7-layer protocol stack is used to set up the necessary circuits or virtual paths through the network. This is known as **common channel signalling number 7** or **CCS-7**. The use of a separate signalling network allows the network operator to provide a wide range of advanced services more readily since a path is simply set up to the required service on demand.

In the case of a circuit-switched service, a circuit is set up in the same way as with the PSTN, as shown in part (a) of the figure. The set-up circuit then provides a transparent 64 kbps transmission path.

In the case of the two frame-based services, a virtual circuit – known as a **virtual path** – is set up in an analogous way to a virtual circuit through a PSPDN. Additional routing information is retained at each intermediate exchange that allows the subsequent frames of user data to be routed (relayed) across the set-up virtual path, as shown in part (b). In the case of frame relay, a simple best-try service is supported. With frame switching, on the other hand, error and flow control are performed on each frame. In comparison with packet switching, the routing of frames is much simpler and hence can be carried out at much higher bit rates. A user may have a number of virtual paths to different destinations set up at the same time and the network will route frames to their intended destination using addressing information contained within each frame. Semi-permanent virtual paths can also be requested.

The packet-switched service uses a full 3-layer user stack similar to that used in an X.25 PSPDN, as can be seen in part (c). In practice, since PSPDNs are

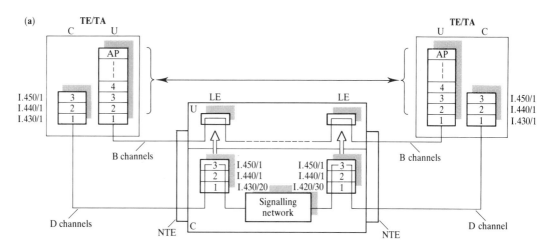

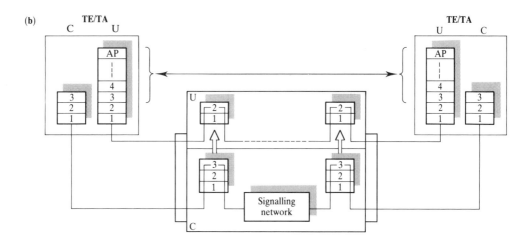

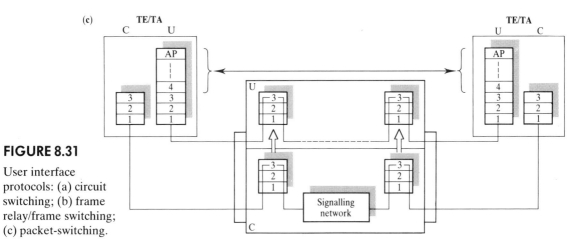

FIGURE 8.31

User interface protocols: (a) circuit switching; (b) frame relay/frame switching; (c) packet-switching.

now widely available, an alternative arrangement to that shown has also been proposed which provides internetworking between an ISDN and a PSPDN. This is defined in CCITT recommendations **X.31** and **I.462**. With this scheme, a basic circuit-switched connection is set up through the ISDN – as in part (a) – to a gateway device associated with the PSPDN. This gateway device operates in a similar way to a STE; the ISDN simply provides a transparent 64 kbps switched or semi-permanent circuit between the packet-mode terminal equipment and the PSPDN gateway. The user protocol stack uses the X.25 PLP at layer 3 and the link layer protocol defined in I.420.

It is also proposed to allow the D channel to be used in a similar way. In this case, however, X.25 packets will be routed across the ISDN to the gateway using the signalling network rather than over a B channel circuit. Although this will avoid setting up a circuit, the use of the D channel limits the packet size to 260 octets compared with 1024 octets for the other service. The 16 kbps rate of the D channel is also lower.

8.5.6 Signalling protocols

The three protocols associated with the signalling (D) channel are identified in Figure 8.31(a). The two layer 1 protocols I.430/20 collectively define the physical interface from the user TE to the local exchange. As may be recalled, they include, in addition to the definition of the proposed interface arrangement, the mechanisms to be used for bit, octet and frame synchronization, as well as for power feeding. The last of these is necessary to enable (telephone) calls to be made in the event of a local power failure. The conversion from 4-wire to 2-wire and different transmission formats and the presence of other TEs on the bus are thus transparent to the layer 2 (and 3) protocol which sees just a duplex transmission path for 2B + D channels.

The layer 2 protocol is defined in I.440/1 which is the same as Q.920/1. Known as LAPD, it is used to transfer the level 3 call set-up messages. The basic operation of LAPD was described in Chapter 5 and hence only its relationship with respect to the signalling procedure will be discussed here.

As may be recalled from the earlier discussion of the physical interface, since up to eight different items of equipment may be sharing the user and signalling channels, a way of identifying specific items of equipment must be incorporated. This is achieved by using the address field in the header of each layer 2 (LAPD) frame. The address contains two subaddresses (identifiers): the **service access point identifier (SAPI)** and a **terminal endpoint identifier (TEI)**. The SAPI allows different terminals to belong to a different **service class** (voice or data, for example), while the TEI is used to identify a specific terminal associated with that class. It is also possible to use a **broadcast address** to allow the exchange to send a frame to multiple terminals. This may be used, for example, for an incoming voice (telephone) call to be received by all voice TEs.

It should be noted, however, that this address has only local significance on the user access line and plays no part in the routing of signalling messages within the network signalling system. As shown in Figure 8.9 when the structure of

NSAP address was discussed, the final part of the address has only local significance and this will be passed transparently by the network signalling system. Hence, in the case of ISDN addresses, a typical scheme is to use part of this address to identify the specific TE/TA required. Then, if the user data is also being carried on the D channel (packet switching), the remainder can be used for interlayer address selectors (SAPs). Alternatively, if the user data is to be carried on a B channel then the addresses selectors will not be required. In the latter case, this will be a function of the application protocol that is associated with the U plane.

The layer 3 protocol is defined in I.450/1, which is the same as Q.931. It is concerned with the sequence of messages (packets) that are exchanged over the D channel to set up a call. An abbreviated list of the message types used is as follows:

- Call establishment: ALERTing
                         CONNECT
                         CONnect ACKnowledge
                         SETUP
                         Others
- Information transfer: USER INFOrmation
                         Others
- Call clearing: DISConnect
                         RELEASE
                         RELease COMPlete
                         Others

Some of these messages have local significance (TE/NTE) while others have end-to-end significance (TE/TE). All the messages, however, are transferred within layer 1 I-frames. An example illustrating the use of these messages is shown in Figure 8.32; it assumes a circuit-switched call which may be used for voice and/or data over the B channel(s).

8.5.7 Frame relay service

As indicated earlier, there are two new frame-mode services associated with the ISDN: frame relay and frame switching. The same signalling procedures are used for both services. The major difference is that the network performs error and flow control procedures with frame switching. The procedures associated with the frame services are defined in CCITT recommendation I.122/Q.922. In practice, frame relay is by far the dominant service, owing to its minimal overheads, and is therefore discussed in more detail.

It may be recalled that with X.25, the multiplexing of multiple virtual circuits (calls) is handled by the packet layer, while the link (frame) layer is concerned only with error control of the resulting frames over the local DTE/DCE link. This has the effect that the combined link/packet layer protocol is relatively complex, hence the corresponding packet throughput of each network exchange is limited by the high processing overheads per packet.

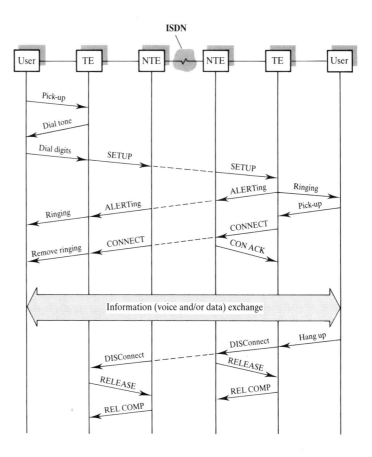

FIGURE 8.32

Example message
sequence – circuit-
switched call.

TE = Terminal equipment

NTE = Network termination equipment

In contrast, with frame relay, multiplexing and routing are performed at the link (frame) layer. Moreover, the routing of frames is very straightforward with the effect that the combined link bit rates can be much higher than with packet switching. This has had the effect that, although defined for use with ISDN, frame relay is also finding widespread use in private networks.

Frame relay allows multiple calls to different destinations to be in progress concurrently. Hence, when each call (virtual path) is first set up – using the D channel in response to an L-CONNECT.request service primitive – it is allocated a unique connection identifier known as the **data link connection identifier** or **DLCI**. All subsequent data transfer requests relating to this call then include the allocated DLCI as a parameter. The DLCI is embedded into the header of the resulting frames and is used to route (relay) the frames to their intended destination. In the case of semi-permanent virtual paths, the DLCIs are allocated at registration time.

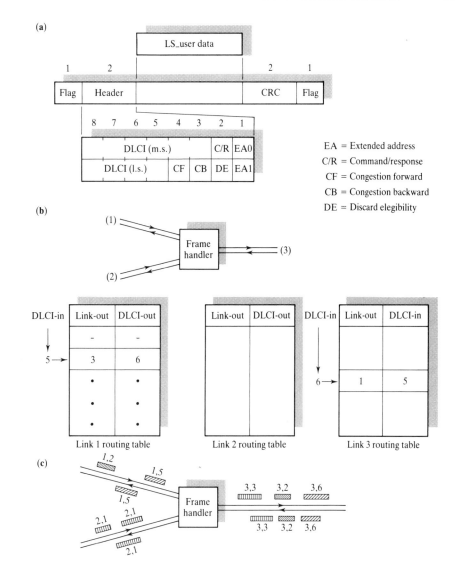

FIGURE 8.33

Frame relay principles:
(a) frame format;
(b) frame routing;
(c) frame relay
schematic.

The format of each frame transmitted on the user B channel is shown in Figure 8.33(a). It comprises a 2-byte (extended) address header with no control field owing to the lack of any error control. In addition to the DLCI, the header contains the **congestion forward notification (CF) bit**, the **congestion backward notification (CB) bit** and the **discard eligibility (DE) bit**. These are used for controlling congestion within the network and will be discussed later.

The DLCI, like the VCI in packet-switched networks, has only local significance on a specific network link and therefore changes as a frame traverses the links associated with a virtual path. When the virtual path is being set up, on receipt of a call request packet – on the D channel – each exchange along the path (route) determines the outgoing link to be used for the required (ISDN) destination address, obtains a free DLCI for the link and then makes an entry in that links **routing table** of the incoming link/DLCI and the corresponding outgoing link/DLCI, as shown in part (b) of the figure. Again, for semi-permanent virtual paths, entries are made at subscription time.

When a frame is received during the subsequent data transfer – frame relay – phase, the frame handler within each exchange simply reads the DLCI from within the frame and combines this with the incoming link number to determine the corresponding outgoing link and DLCI. The new DLCI is then written into the frame header and the frame is queued for forwarding on the appropriate link. The order of relayed frames is thus preserved and their routing is very fast.

Since multiple calls can be in progress concurrently over each link within the network and frames relating to each call are generated at random intervals, during periods of heavy traffic it is possible for an outgoing link to become temporarily overloaded resulting in its queue starting to build up. This is known as **congestion**: the additional congestion control bits in each frame are used to alleviate this condition should it arise.

Whenever the frame handler relays a frame to a link output queue, it checks the size of the queue. If this exceeds a defined limit, the frame handler signals this condition to the two end users involved in the call. This is done in the forward direction by setting the CF bit in the frame header. In the backward direction, it is done by setting the CB bit in the header of all frames which are received on this link. In addition, if the condition persists, it also returns a special frame known as a **consolidated link layer management (CLLM)** frame to all user devices that have routes (paths) involving the affected link. Such frames are simply relayed by each intermediate exchange in the normal way.

When the frame handler in an end user device receives an indication of network congestion, it temporarily reduces its frame forwarding rate until there are no further indications of congestion. In the event of the overload increasing, however, the exchange must start to discard frames. In an attempt to achieve fairness, the DE bit in the frame header is used since this is set by the frame handler in each user system whenever a user exceeds its negotiated throughput rate.

To minimize the possibility of wrongly delivered frames, the CRC in each frame trailer is used to detect bit errors in the frame header (and information) fields. Then, if an error is detected, the frame is discarded. In the case of the frame relay service, error recovery is left to the higher protocol layers in the end user devices.

8.6 PRIVATE NETWORKS

As indicated in the introduction at the start of the chapter, as an alternative to using PTT or public-carrier networks many large corporations install (and manage) their own enterprise-wide private integrated voice and data networks.

Telephone (voice) calls made through a public switched telephone network (PSTN) or public ISDN are charged on a time and distance basis. If the networks are used for the transmission of data – using a modem with the PSTN – such calls are charged on the same basis. Similarly, calls made using a public data network are normally charged either on the same basis or on the basis of the quantity of data transferred.

In most establishments (companies, universities, hospitals etc) the major-ity of communications (voice and data) are local to the establishment with only a small percentage of the calls for outside the establishment. Hence, to avoid public network charges, all establishments install their own private automatic branch exchange (PABX) for telephony and a (private) local area network (LAN) for data communication.

Clearly, for an enterprise operating on a single site (establishment), all external calls must then be made using a PTT or public-carrier network. For an enterprise operating at multiple sites, however, an alternative is to extend the private facilities associated with each site to embrace all sites, since again there is often a significant proportion of inter-site calls. In practice, the choice is based on a number of factors, the major one being the level of inter-site traffic. This is because the creation of an enterprise-wide private network normally involves the leasing of transmission circuits from the PTTs or public-carriers. Clearly, these are charged for on the basis that they are used 24 hours per day rather than on a per call basis.

For many small to medium sized enterprises the number of inter-site calls does not justify linking the sites with leased lines. Instead external calls are made using public-carrier networks, certainly for voice. For data, if an (analogue) PSTN is to be used, an additional factor is the relatively long call set-up time with a switched call. Also, the level of security with public facilities is often cited as a factor.

For many large enterprises, however, the level of inter-site traffic – both voice and data – can be considerable. Consequently, many such enterprises install and manage their own private integrated voice and data networks. An added benefit is that more sophisticated services can be more readily offered and, since the network is private – apart from the transmission lines, of course – more secure. Such networks are known simply as **private networks** or **enterprise-wide networks**. If they span multiple countries, they are known as **global networks**.

8.6.1 Architecture

A schematic of a typical private network configuration is shown in Figure 8.34(a). Generally a private network consists of a linked set of **intelligent multiplexers (IMUX)** – one per site – interconnected by leased lines which form an **enterprise-wide backbone** transmission network. Typically, the network uses high-speed digital leased lines of the type described at the end of Chapter 3. These operate at multiples of 64 kbps; 1.544 Mbps (DS1/T1) and 2.048 Mbps (E1) are common.

Each IMUX has a range of voice and data interfaces to meet the require-ments at that site. In the case of voice, these can involve direct links to telephone

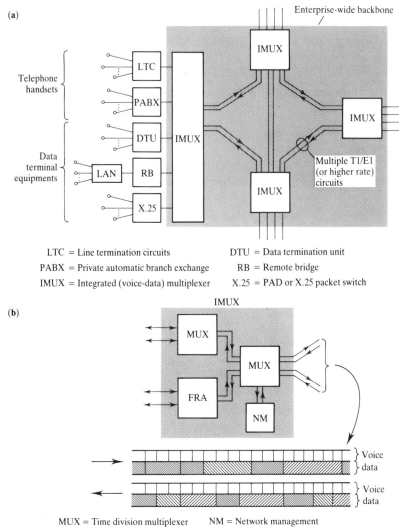

LTC = Line termination circuits   DTU = Data termination unit
PABX = Private automatic branch exchange   RB = Remote bridge
IMUX = Integrated (voice-data) multiplexer   X.25 = PAD or X.25 packet switch

FIGURE 8.34

Private WAN:
(a) network schematic;
(b) node schematic.

MUX = Time division multiplexer   NM = Network management
FRA = Frame relay adapter

handsets or, more usually, a high bit rate link to a PABX. As indicated in Chapter 3, normally 64 kbps is used for each voice circuit but some multiplexer manufacturers incorporate sophisticated compression algorithms to provide good-quality voice communication using 32, 16 or even 8 kbps. This means that two, four or eight voice circuits can then be multiplexed onto a single 64 kbps time slot giving a substantial saving in the number of circuits required between sites. This technique is known as **subrate multiplexing**.

As described in Chapter 3, a similar technique is used for connecting asynchronous or synchronous terminals, such as PCs. In this case a 64 kbps channel can be used to support multiple terminals. Examples include

20×2.4 kbps and 5×9.6 kbps. The technique is known as **rate adaption**. Such links are often used to connect a distributed community of data terminals to a central computer holding, for example, an enterprise-wide electronic mail server or database.

The increasing use of LANs in many establishments means that it is now common practice to provide a means of linking such LANs. As described in the last chapter, this is normally done using **remote bridges**. Private X.25 packet switching exchanges are also sometimes incorporated. Alternatively, as can be seen in part (b) of the figure, private **frame relay adapters (FRAs)** are now being incorporated to achieve added levels of (statistical) multiplexing. Since in private networks circuits are normally set up throughout the network on a semi-permanent basis using network management, each FRA needs only to packetize data. This is done only when data is to be transmitted, thus eliminating the need to allocate permanent channels.

Although many private networks are run and managed by the enterprises to which they belong, a number of PTTs and public-carrier operators are now cooperating to provide a facility that enables an equivalent private network to be set up within the public network. Known as **virtual private networks** or **VPNs**, they offer similar services to a private network but are managed and operated by the PTT or public carrier.

EXERCISES

8.1 Describe the differences between a circuit-switched data network and a packet-switched data network. Clearly identify the effects on the users of these networks.

8.2 Explain what is understood by the following terms used in relation to packet-switched data networks:

(a) datagram,
(b) virtual call (circuit),
(c) logical channel.

8.3 Use sketches to illustrate the applicability and components of the X.25 network access protocol and write explanatory notes describing the function of each component.

8.4 Define the set of user service primitives associated with the packet (network) layer of the X.25 protocol. Explain the use of the following additional facilities:

(a) more-data,
(b) qualifier,
(c) delivery confirmation.

8.5 Tabulate the main PDUs (packet types) used by the packet layer of protocol X.25 to perform the following operations:

(a) establish a virtual call (circuit),
(b) exchange a message unit over this circuit,
(c) clear the call.

Sketch a time sequence diagram to illustrate the sequence in which the PDUs are exchanged to implement these operations.

8.6   Explain the structure and meaning of the various fields that make up an X.121 address as used at the interface to an X.25 PSPDN.

8.7   Explain the meaning of the term fast-select in relation to the X.25 packet layer protocol.

With the aid of a time sequence diagram, describe how a datagram service is obtained with the fast-select facility.

8.8   (a)   Describe the flow control method used by the packet layer protocol of X.25 and list the packet layer PDUs (packet types) that are used to implement it.

(b)   Sketch diagrams to illustrate how the flow of data packets relating to a single logical channel is controlled by:

(i)   the window mechanism,

(ii)   the use of additional supervisory packets.

Include in the diagrams the state of the send and receive variables ($V(S)$ and $V(R)$) and the acknowledgement variable ($V(A)$) at both sides of the logical channel as each data packet is transmitted.

8.9   Discriminate between the reset and restart error recovery procedures used in the packet layer of X.25 and explain their operation.

8.10   (a)   Describe the function of a PAD as used in X.25-based networks and identify on a diagram the various protocols that have been defined for use with it.

(b)   Outline the essential features of the following protocols used with PADs:

(i)   X.3,

(ii)   X.28,

(iii)   X.29.

8.11   Describe how a packet-switching exchange in an X.25 network routes packets. Include in your description the structure and use of the network and link routing tables.

8.12   Explain the role of a signalling terminal exchange – half gateway – for the interconnection of X.25 networks.

8.13   Use a sketch of an X.25-based internetwork to identify the applicability of the X.75 protocol.

Explain the use of the following fields in an X.75 PPDU:

(a)   network utilities,

(b)   D bit.

8.14   (a)   Outline the function of the three lowest network-dependent protocol layers used with a circuit-switched data network.

(b)   Sketch a diagram showing the various interchange circuits associated with X.21 and outline their functions.

(c)   With the aid of a time sequence diagram, describe the operation of the X.21 interface protocol. Clearly show the transitions on each interchange circuit at both the calling DTE/DCE interface and the called DTE/DCE interface. Identify on this diagram the call set-up, data transfer and call clearing phases.

8.15 (a) Explain the meaning of the term ISDN.
       (b) Give examples of the following user services related to an ISDN:
            (i) bearer services,
           (ii) teleservices.

8.16 Produce a sketch and associated descriptions of an ISDN NTE and indicate on the sketch the following customer access points:

    (a) basic bearer services,
    (b) supplementary bearer services,
    (c) teleservices,
    (d) existing X-series services.

8.17 Produce a sketch showing the outline structure of the network termination equipment associated with the customer interface to an ISDN and explain the main features associated with it.

8.18 Explain the meaning of the terms control (C) plane and user (U) plane in relation to the customer access to an ISDN network.
       Use sketches to identify the role of the C and U planes for the following cell types:

    (a) circuit-switched,
    (b) frame relay,
    (c) packet-switched.

8.19 Use the setting up of an ISDN circuit-switched call to explain the function of the various signalling protocols that operate over the D channel.

8.20 Explain the principle of operation of frame relay and how it differs from X.25 packet-switching. Include in your description how frames are routed.

CHAPTER SUMMARY

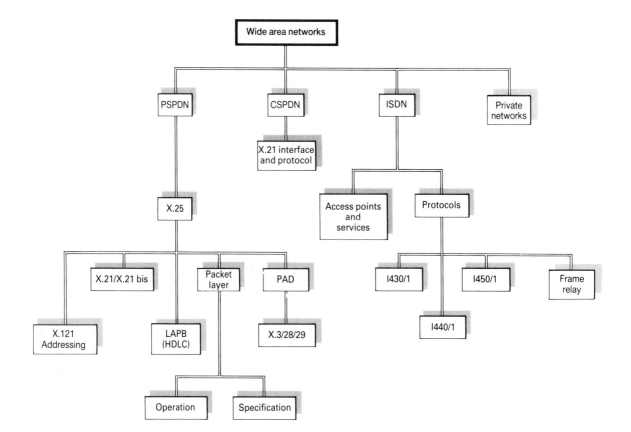

9

Internetworking

CHAPTER CONTENTS

CHAPTER OBJECTIVES

When you have completed studying the material in this chapter you should be able to:

- know the terminology used and the issues involved in creating an open system networking environment comprising multiple inter-connected networks;
- understand the function of the three sublayer protocols associated with the network layer that are needed to create an open networking environment;
- describe different harmonizing functions that are needed for the interconnection of different network types;
- explain the operation of some of the different protocols that make up the internetworking protocol associated with the TCP/IP protocol suite;
- describe the operation of the ISO internetworking protocol;
- understand how routing is carried out in a large open networking environment and the operation of the two major routing protocols that are used.

9.1 INTRODUCTION

In the earlier chapters on local area networks (LANs) and wide area networks (WANs) it was assumed that stations/DTEs – normally referred to as **end systems** (ESs) or **hosts** – were all attached to the one network type; that is, either all the systems were attached to a single LAN (or bridged LAN) or to a single WAN. This was done to defer discussion of the additional issues that must be addressed when considering two systems communicating through networks consisting of two or more different network types.

Clearly, in addition to open system networking environments comprising just a single type of network (LAN or WAN), there are networking environments that comprise an interconnected set of networks. An example is a distributed community of LANs, each located in a different university and interconnected through a country-wide WAN, that has been established to allow end systems attached to different LANs to exchange electronic mail or computer files. Another is an interconnected set of WANs that enables programs in a distributed community of bank computers to carry out funds transfers and other transactions. Clearly, there are many such applications.

When two or more networks are involved in an application, the mode of working between systems is normally referred to as **internetworking**. The term **internetwork** (or **internet**) is also used to refer to the composite network (LAN/WAN/LAN, for example) being used. Each constituent network (LAN or WAN) of the internetwork is then sometimes referred to as a **subnetwork** (or **subnet**).

The device that interconnects the two networks is known in ISO terminology either as an **intermediate system (IS)** or an **interworking unit (IWU)**. Alternatively, since one of the major functions performed by an intermediate system is that of routing, it is sometimes referred to as a **router** or, since it provides the link between two networks, a **gateway**. The term **protocol converter** is used to refer to an IS that links two networks which operate with completely different protocol stacks; for example, an ISO stack and a proprietary stack relating to a specific manufacturer. As will be described, a router performs its routing (and other) functions at the network layer. In an open system environment, the upper layer protocols – transport through application – are the same in all end systems. The difference between a router and a protocol converter is shown in Figure 9.1

In part (a) it is assumed that each network is of a different type and hence that the router will have a different set of network protocols associated with each network port. Packets (NPDUs) received from one network will thus be processed and passed up through the set of protocols relating to that network then, after the relaying function, down through the different set of protocols relating to the other network.

In contrast, as can be seen in part (b), a protocol converter performs its relaying function above the application layer. This is because, in addition to the network protocols being different for the two network types, the higher network-independent protocol layers are also different. Moreover, the network protocols used in different proprietary protocol stacks are different. This means that a

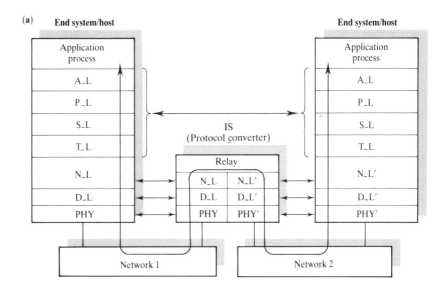

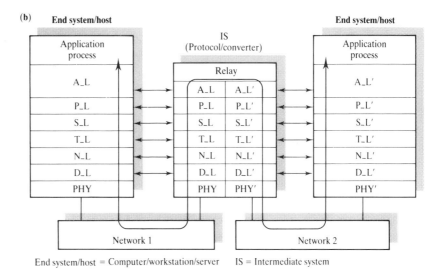

FIGURE 9.1

Example intermediate systems: (a) router/ gateway; (b) protocol converter.

protocol converter must also be used for the interconnection of two proprietary systems that are connected to the same network. This requirement highlights the advantages to be gained by moving towards an open systems approach: firstly, systems connected to the same network can communicate directly and secondly, although a router may be required to perform the relaying functions if two different networks are involved, the higher-layer protocols are the same in all systems.

9.2 INTERNETWORK ARCHITECTURES

Before discussing the issues to be addressed with internetworking, it is helpful to first consider some typical internetwork architectures. Some example architectures are shown in Figure 9.2

Part (a) shows two examples of single network types. The first is a site-wide LAN which, typically, as discussed in Chapter 7, comprises a set of LANs, one per office or building, interconnected by a backbone network. The devices connecting

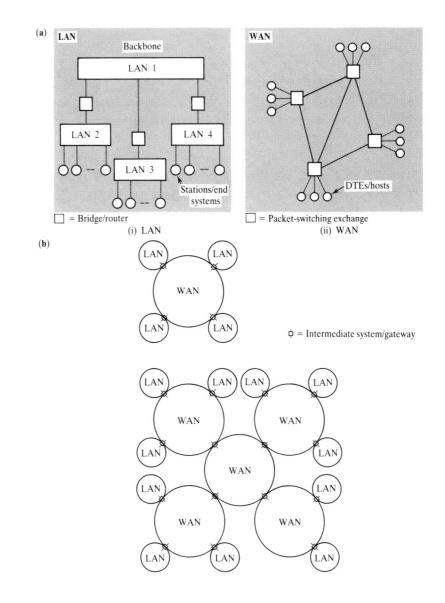

FIGURE 9.2

Internetwork architectures: (a) single LAN and WAN; (b) interconnected LAN/WAN examples.

each LAN to the backbone are then either bridges, if all the LANs are the same type, or routers if they are different.

The second example is a single WAN, such as an X.25 network. In this case, as discussed in the last chapter, each packet-switching exchange (DCE/PSE) services its own set of DTEs, either directly or through a PAD, and the PSEs are then interconnected by a mesh topology switching network.

Irrespective of the type of network – LAN or WAN – from the point of view of internetworking, each is considered as a single network with its own internal routing protocols. Two internetworks are shown in part (b) of the figure; each consists of a linked set of such networks. This chapter is concerned with the additional issues that must be considered when creating networking environments of the types shown and, in particular, those comprising multiple network types. It is also concerned with with the alternative solutions and associated network protocols.

9.3 INTERNETWORKING ISSUES

From the point of view of an internet user, a transport protocol entity in practice, the internet should provide a defined network service at the user network service access point (NSAP) address which enables it to communicate with similar users in remote systems. The possible presence of multiple networks (and possibly network types) should be transparent to the users who simply view the internet as providing a defined network service as though it were a single LAN or WAN. This is shown in Figure 9.3(a).

Before discussing the alternative solutions that are used to achieve this goal, it is perhaps helpful to first identify the major issues that must be considered. These include:

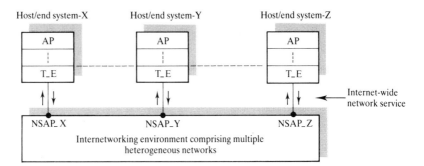

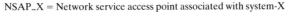

NSAP_X = Network service access point associated with system-X
⇌ = Network service primitives
AP = Application process
T_E = Transport protocol entity

FIGURE 9.3

Internet network service schematic.

- network service;
- addressing;
- routing;
- quality of service;
- maximum packet size;
- flow and congestion control;
- error reporting.

Network service

It may be recalled that within a LAN, MAC sublayer addresses are used to identify end systems (stations/DTEs) and, with transparent bridges, to route frames between systems. Moreover, because of the short transit delays and low bit error rate of LANs, a simple (best-try) connectionless network protocol is normally used. This means that many LAN-based networks have a **connectionless network service (CL-NS)** associated with them.

In contrast to LANs, link layer addresses in most WANs have only local significance; network layer addresses are used to identify end systems and to route packets across the network. Also, because of the relatively long transit delays and inferior bit error rate of WANs, a more sophisticated connection-oriented protocol is normally used. This means that most WANs have a **connection-oriented network service (CO-NS)** associated with them.

Clearly, since NS-users may be connected to different networks in an internet, one of the first issues that must be addressed is the type of network service (CL or CO) that is to be used at the internet interface in each end system. Moreover, in internetworks that consist of multiple subnet types, it is necessary to consider how the selected service is married or **harmonized** with the varying services associated with the different networks that make up the internet.

Addressing

It may be recalled that the NSAP (network service access point) address used to identify an NS-user in an end system is a unique network-wide address which allows that user to be uniquely identified within the total network. Thus within a single LAN or WAN, it is only necessary for NSAP addresses to be unique within that limited, single-network addressing domain. Hence, since within a single network the point of attachment (PA) address of an end system is unique within that network, the NSAP address of an NS-user is made up of the PA address of the system concatenated with the LSAP and NSAP interlayer address selectors within the system.

For an internet comprising multiple networks each of a different type – for example, LANs and X.25 WANs – the format (structure) and syntax of the PA addresses of end systems (and hence intermediate systems) will differ from one

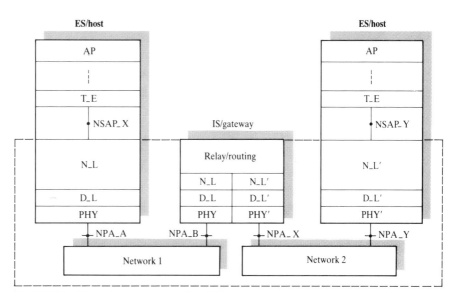

FIGURE 9.4

Relationship between
NSAP and NPA
addresses.

NSAP_X/Y = Network service access point of NS-user

NPA = Network point of attachment address of ES/host

(e.g. NPA_A/B = LAN MAC addresses; NPA_X/Y = X.25 WAN X.121 addresses)

network to another. As many such networks are already in existence and have addresses assigned to them, it is not possible to use the **network point of attachment (NPA)** address of each system as the basis of the NS-user NSAP address in the combined internet. Instead, when creating an **open system internetworking environment (OSIE)**, a completely different set of NSAP addresses must be used to identify each NS-user uniquely. These addresses are independent of the NPA addresses of the systems in which the NS-users (transport entities) reside. The relationship between NSAP and NPA addresses is shown in Figure 9.4.

It can be concluded from the figure, that two completely different addresses are associated with each end system connected to an internet: the NPA and the NSAP. The NPA address enables a system to send and receive NPDUs over its local network and hence only has meaning within that network. Its NSAP address, however, is an internet-wide identifier which uniquely identifies NS-users within the total OSIE. Also, since an IS is attached to more than one network, it will have an associated NPA address for each network to which it is attached.

Routing

A service request primitive received at an NSAP in an end system, will have only a specification of the required destination NSAP. For a single network, the PA subaddress within the NSAP will be sufficient to route the resulting NPDU to the required destination. For example, if the network is a LAN, the NPDU will be broadcast within a frame with the required destination MAC address at its head.

Alternatively, if the network is an X.25 packet-switching network, then the NPDU will be transferred to the X.25 PLP within its local DCE/PSE. From there the destination NSAP will be used directly to route it through the network to the destination DCE (and hence DTE).

For internetworks comprising multiple networks interconnected by intermediate systems, the destination NSAP address will not necessarily refer to an end system attached to the same network as the originating ES. Rather, it may refer to an ES attached to any of the other networks in the internet. Clearly, therefore, the routing of NPDUs is more difficult with internets.

To identify the routing requirements, consider the hypothetical internet shown in Figure 9.5. First it must be remembered that since the NPA address of a system and the NS-user NSAP address are different, it is not possible to use the destination NSAP address directly to route an NPDU to its destination. Also, the NPA addresses of an IS will each have a similar format to that of any other ES on each of the interconnected networks. It can be assumed, therefore, that an ES can send an NPDU directly to an IS on the same network providing it knows the latter's NPA address. In addition, since an IS has an NPA address for each network to which is is attached, it can send an NPDU to another IS that is attached to that same network as long as it knows the NPA address of the other IS.

Assuming these basic capabilities, consider the sending of an NPDU from ES1.1 on network 1 to ES5.1 on network 5. A number of alternative routes are

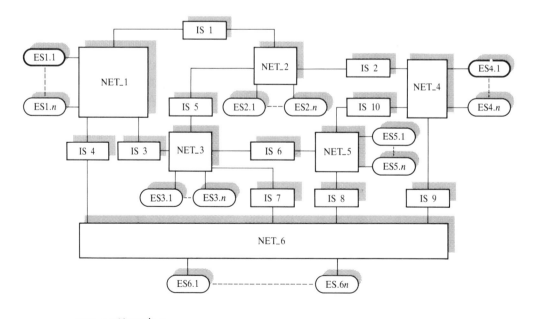

FIGURE 9.5

Hypothetical internet.

NET_*n* = Network_*n*
IS *n* = Intermediate system/gateway *n*
ES.*n* = End system/host.*n*

possible but perhaps the most obvious (assuming all networks have the same operational parameters) is:

ES1.1 → IS 1 → IS 2 → ES5.1

Others include:

ES1.1 → IS 3 → IS 6 → IS 10 → ES5.1
ES1.1 → IS 4 → IS 9 → ES5.1
ES1.1 → IS 4 → IS 7 → IS 6 → IS 8 → IS 9 → ES5.1.

Although this can be deduced simply by looking at the internet topology, a number of questions must be answered before this can be carried out in practice. These include:

- How does an ES determine the NPA address(es) of the IS(s) attached to its network?

- How does an IS determine the NPA addresses of ESs attached to its networks?

- How does an ES select a specific IS when sending an NPDU?

- How does an IS determine the NPA addresses of other ISs that are attached to the same network?

- How does an IS select a specific IS to route an NPDU to a given destination ES?

These are some of the questions relating to internet routing that must be resolved.

Quality of service

A quality of service (QOS) parameter is associated with each service request primitive received at an NSAP. In practice this is a set of parameters that collectively specify the performance of the network service that the NS-user expects from the NS-provider in relation to this request. In addition, it is also used to specify the optional services to be used with this request.

QOS parameters include: the transit delay expected of the network (NS-provider) to deliver an NSDU to the specified destination; the level of protection required from unauthorized monitoring or modification of the NSDU; cost limits to be associated with this request; expected residual error probability; and the relative priority to be associated with the NSDU.

With a connection-oriented network service, a peer-to-peer negotiation takes place between the two NS-users when a call is being established. The originating NS-user specifies the QOS parameters expected and the responder, if necessary, modifies selected parameters. In contrast, with a connectionless network service, since no virtual call is established, the NS-user initiating a request must know about the QOS expected from the NS-provider.

Thus when internetworking between different network types, since the QOS may vary from one network to another, a means must be provided to enable the network entity in each end system to build up a knowledge of the internet-wide QOS to be expected when going to any specified destination NSAP.

Maximum packet size

The maximum packet size used in different networks varies and is determined by such factors as:

- Bit error rate: the higher the bit error rate of the network links, the smaller the maximum packet size must be to ensure a significant number of packets are received error-free with a high probability.

- Transit delay: the longer the maximum packet size, the longer other packets must wait at each link before being forwarded, with a consequential increase in the packet transit delay.

- Buffer storage requirements: the smaller the maximum packet size, the smaller the size of memory buffers required for storage.

- Processing overheads: the smaller the maximum packet size, the larger the number of packets required to send each message (NSDU), with a consequential increase in processing overheads per message.

Typical maximum packet sizes vary from 128 bytes for some public-carrier networks to 8000 bytes (and higher) for some LANs.

With a single network, the maximum packet size is normally known and so the transport layer protocol entity can itself divide – **segment** or **fragment** – larger messages into smaller units for transfer across the network. In the case of internets comprising networks with varying maximum packet sizes, however, either the minimum packet size must be known and used, or the network layer in each end and intermediate system must perform the necessary segmentation (fragmentation) and reassembly operations. The first alternative will result in some networks being used inefficiently, while the second requires an additional function to be performed by the network layer.

Flow and congestion control

Flow control is implemented to control the flow of packets relating to a single call in order to overcome the difference between the rate at which a source system sends packets and the rate at which a destination can accept packets. If the destination can accept packets faster than the source can send them, clearly there is no problem. However, if the reverse is true a harmonization (flow control) function must be provided.

Congestion control is concerned with a similar function within the network itself. If the composite rate at which packets enter the network exceeds the rate at which packets leave, then the network will become congested. Similarly, at a more local level, if packets arrive at a network node – an intermediate system, for example – faster than they can be processed and forwarded, then the node will become congested thus affecting the flow of packets relating to all calls through that node.

With a connection-oriented network such as X.25, flow control is performed on a virtual circuit basis across the local DTE/DCE and DCE/DTE interfaces. A send window is defined and when this number of packets have been sent (typically two), the sender must wait until an acknowledgement relating to either of them is received. Since this function is being performed at the periphery of the network on a per call basis, in addition to regulating the flow of packets into the network, it helps to control congestion. However, it will not prevent it completely.

In contrast, with a connectionless network no flow control is applied to the packets associated with a call within the network. Instead it is left to the transport protocol entity within each end system to perform flow control on an end-to-end basis. Thus if congestion starts to occur within the network, flow control information will be delayed and the source transport protocol entities will stop sending new data into the network. Again, although this will help to relieve network congestion, as with a connection-oriented network, it will not always avoid it. With both schemes, therefore, it is also necessary to incorporate a congestion control algorithm within the network. Moreover, for internets comprising multiple network types, the congestion control algorithm must harmonize between the different network algorithms.

Error reporting

The way in which errors are reported varies from one network type to another. Consequently, a means of error reporting across multiple networks must be established.

All these issues must be addressed with any internetworking solution.

9.4 NETWORK LAYER STRUCTURE

It is the role of the network layer in each end system to provide an end-to-end, internet-wide network service to its local NS-user(s). This can be either a connection-oriented service or a connectionless service. In both cases the NS-users should be unaware of the presence of multiple, possibly different, network types. Hence the routing and all other functions relating to the relaying of NSDUs must be carried out in a transparent way by the network layer entities in each of the end and intermediate systems.

To achieve this goal, in the context of the ISO Reference Model the network layer in each end and intermediate system consists not just of a single protocol but rather three (sublayer) protocols, each performing a complementary role in providing the network layer service. In the ISO terminology, each network that makes up an internet is known as a **subnet** and hence the three protocols are known as:

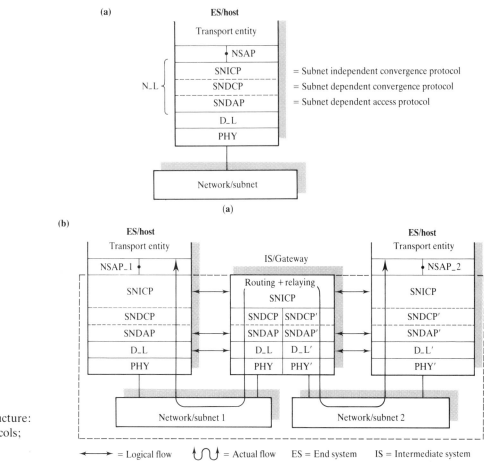

FIGURE 9.6

Network layer structure:
(a) sublayer protocols;
(b) IS structure.

- subnetwork independent convergence protocol (SNICP),
- subnetwork dependent convergence protocol (SNDCP),
- subnetwork dependent access protocol (SNDAP).

The relative position of the three protocols in an end system is given in Figure 9.6(a); part (b) shows the protocols in relation to an intermediate system.

The SNICP supports the network service to be provided to NS-users at the interface with the internet. Its role is to carry out the various harmonizing (convergence) functions which may be necessary to route and relay user data (transport protocol data units) across the internet. Its operation is independent of the characteristics of the specific subnets (networks) to be used in the internet and it assumes a standard network service from them.

The SNDAP is the access protocol associated with a specific subnet (network) in the internet. Examples are the X.25 packet layer protocol for an

X.25 network and the connectionless network protocol that is often used for LANs. Because the service and operational characteristics associated with the SNDAPs will differ from one network type to another, it is necessary to provide an intermediate sublayer between the SNICP and the SNDAP to allow for this possibility. This is the role of the SNDCP. As can be deduced from the foregoing, the detailed mapping operation that it performs will vary for different subnet/ network types.

9.5 INTERNET PROTOCOL STANDARDS

As discussed in the last chapter, multiple X.25 WANs can be interconnected by X.75-based gateways. Also, the introduction of a standard specifying the operation of the X.25 packet-layer protocol for use with LANs means that one approach to internetworking is to adopt X.25 as an internet-wide protocol. The latter can be operated in either a connection-oriented mode or in a pseudo-connectionless mode by using fast select.

Such a solution has the appeal that the various internetworking functions are much reduced. The disadvantage is that the overheads associated with X.25 packet-switching are high and hence the packet throughput of these networks is relatively low. This is also true with fast-select, since the same virtual-circuit/error control functions are still used. Moreover, the much improved bit error rate performance of the next generation of wide area networks, such as ISDN, means that frame relay and cell (fast-packet) switching will be the preferred operational modes rather than conventional packet switching.

The solution adopted by ISO is based on a connectionless internet service and an associated connectionless SNICP. The SNICP is defined in ISO 8475. In practice, it is based on the internet protocol that has been developed as part of research into internetworking funded by the **U.S. Defense Advanced Research Projects Agency (DARPA).** The early DARPA internet – ARPANET – was used to interconnect the computer networks associated with a small number of research and university sites with those of DARPA. When it came into being in the early 1970s, ARPANET involved just a small number of networks and associated host computers. Since that time, the internet has grown steadily. Instead of just a small number of mainframe computers at each site, there are now large numbers of workstations. Moreover, the introduction of LANs means that there are now several thousand networks/subnets. ARPANET is now linked to other internets. The combined internet, which is jointly funded by a number of agencies, is thus known simply as **the Internet**.

The internet protocol is only one protocol associated with the complete protocol suite (stack) used with the Internet. The complete suite, known as **TCP/ IP**, includes transport and application protocols which are now used as the basis of many other commercial and research networks. All the TCP/IP protocols specifications are publicly available, as a result of which the Internet is by far the largest currently operational internet based on open standards. The two protocols discussed in this chapter are the internet protocol associated with the Internet –

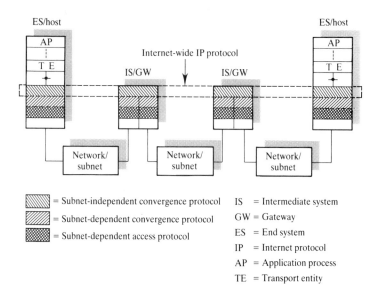

FIGURE 9.7

Internet-wide IP
protocol schematic.

known as the **Internet IP** or simply **IP** – and the ISO internet protocol known as
ISO-IP, which is intended for use with ISO stacks. The general approach of both
standards is illustrated in Figure 9.7.

IP is an internet-wide protocol that enables two transport protocol entities
resident in different end systems/hosts to exchange message units (NSDUs) in a
transparent way. This means that the presence of multiple, possibly different,
networks/subnets and intermediate systems/gateways is completely transparent to
both communicating transport entities. As the IP is a connectionless protocol,
message units are transferred using an unacknowledged best-try approach.

Although the operational features associated with ISO-IP are based on
experience gained from the evolution and use of IP, there are differences both in
terms of terminology and operational detail. Hence each protocol will be discussed separately.

9.6 INTERNET IP

TCP/IP is now widely used in many commercial and research internets in addition
to the Internet. Nevertheless, almost all the protocols associated with the TCP/IP
suite have been researched and developed as part of the Internet. Indeed, new
protocols are introduced relatively frequently as research associated with the
combined Internet continues. There is, however, a core set of protocols that forms
an integral part of all TCP/IP implementations. Other optional protocols are
intended for open systems of varying size and complexity. Only the core protocols
will be considered in the discussion that follows.

9.6.1 Address structure

As may be recalled, there are two network addresses associated with a host/end system attached to an internet. In ISO terminology, these are the network service access point (NSAP) address and the subnet point of attachment (SNPA) address. With TCP/IP, these are the IP address and the network point of attachment (NPA) address, respectively. The NPA address is different for each network/subnet type, whereas the IP address is a unique internet-wide identifier. The structure of an IP address is shown in Figure 9.8. In order to give the authority establishing the internet some flexibility in assigning addresses, the address structure shown in part (a) has been defined.

To ensure that all hosts have a unique identifier, a 32-bit integer is used for each IP address. Then three different address formats are defined, to allow for the different sizes of network to which a host may be attached. Each format is known by an **address class**; a single internet may use addresses from all classes. The three primary classes are A, B and C; each is intended for use with a different size of

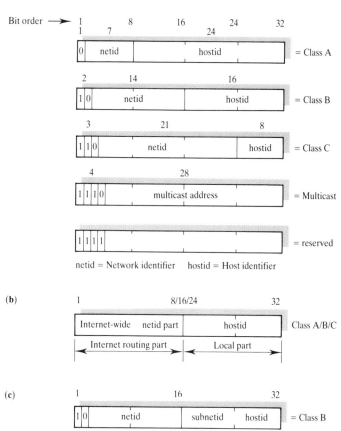

FIGURE 9.8

IP address formats:
(a) frame; (b) subnet addressing; (c) modified class B address.

network. The class to which an address belongs can be determined from the position of the first zero bit in the first four bits. The remaining bits specify two subfields – a **network identifier (netid)** and a **host identifier (hostid)**. The subfield boundaries are located on byte boundaries to simplify decoding.

Class A addresses have 7 bits for the netid and 24 bits for the hostid; class B addresses have 14 bits for the netid and 16 bits for the hostid and class C addresses 21 bits for the netid and 8 bits for the hostid. Thus class A addresses are intended for use with networks that have a large number of attached hosts (up to 2^{24}) while class C addresses allow for a large number of networks each with a small number of attached hosts (up to 256). An example of a class A network is ARPANET; an example of a class C network is a single site-wide LAN.

An address with a hostid of zero is used to refer to the network in the netid field rather than a host. Similarly, an address with a hostid of all 1s refers to all hosts attached to the network in the netid field or, if the latter is all 1s also, then all hosts in the internet. Such addresses are used for broadcast purposes.

To make it easier to communicate IP addresses, the 32 bits are broken into four bytes. These are converted into their equivalent decimal form with a dot (period) between each. This is known as **dotted decimal**. Example addresses are as follows:

00001010 00000000 00000000 00000000	= 10.0.0.0. = Class A
	= netid_10 (ARPANET)
10000000 00000011 00000010 00000011	= 128.3.2.3 = class B
	= netid_128.3, hostid 2.3
11000000 00000000 00000001 11111111	= 192.0.1.255 = class C
	= all hosts broadcast on netid_ 192.0.1

Class D addresses are reserved for **multicasting**. In a LAN, a frame may be sent to an individual, broadcast or **group address**. The last one is used to allow a group of hosts – workstations, for example – that are cooperating in some way, to arrange for network transmissions to be sent to all members of the group. This is often referred to as **computer-supported co-operative working** or **CSCW**; class D addresses allow this mode of working to be extended across an internet.

Although this basic structure is adequate for most addressing purposes, the introduction of multiple LANs at each site means that it can give rise to unacceptably high overheads in terms of routing. As described in Chapter 7, MAC bridges are normally used to interconnect LANs of the same type. This solution is attractive for routing purposes, since the combined LAN then behaves like a single network. When interconnecting dissimilar LAN types, the differences in frame format and, more importantly, frame length, mean that routers are normally used since the fragmentation and reassembly of packets/frames is a function of the network layer rather than the MAC sublayer. However, the use of routers means that each LAN must have its own netid. In the case of large sites, there may be a significant number of such LANs.

This means that with the basic addressing scheme, all the routers relating to a site would need to take part in the overall internet routing function. The efficiency of any routing scheme is strongly influenced by the number of routing nodes that make up the internet. Hence the concept of subnets has been introduced to decouple the routers – and hence routing – associated with a single site from the overall internet routing function. Essentially, instead of each LAN associated with a site having its own netid, only the site is allocated an internet netid. The identity of each LAN then forms part of the hostid field. This refined address format is shown in Figure 9.8(b).

The same address classes and associated structure are used, but the netid now relates to a complete site rather than a single network. Hence, since only a single gateway attached to a local-site network performs internet-wide routing, the netid is now considered as the **internet part**. Then, to allow for a single netid having a number of associated subnetworks the hostid part consists of two subfields: a **subnetid part** and a **local hostid part**. Because these have only local significance, they are known collectively as the **local part**.

Because of the possibly wide range of subnets associated with different site networks, no attempt has been made to define rigid subaddress boundaries for the local address part. Instead, an **address mask** is used to define the subaddress boundaries for a particular network (and hence netid). The address mask is kept by the internet gateway for the site. It consists of binary 1s in those bit positions that contain a network address – including the netid and subnetid – and binary 0s in positions that contain the hostid. Hence an address mask of

11111111   11111111   11111111   00000000

would mean that the first three bytes (octets) contain a network/subnet identifier and the fourth octet the host identifier.

If, for example, the address is a class B address – a zero bit in the second bit position – this is readily interpreted as: the first two octets the internet-wide netid, the next octet the subnetid and the last octet the hostid on this subnet. An example of such an address is shown in part (c) of the figure.

Dotted decimal is normally used to define address masks, in which case the above mask would be written:

255.   255.   255.   0

Again, byte boundaries are normally chosen to simplify address decoding. Hence with this mask, and assuming the netid was, say, 128.10, then all the hosts attached to this network would have this same internet routing part. The presence of a possibly large number of subnets and associated routers is thus transparent to the internet gateways for routing purposes.

To ensure IP addresses are unique, it is necessary for them to be assigned by the central authority that is setting up the open system environment. For a small internet, this is relatively straightforward. However, in the case of large internets, such as the Internet, this is normally done at two levels. First a central authority is set up to allocate netid's and multicast addresses. Second there is an authority associated with each network which assigns hostids on that network. The central authority for the Internet is known as the **Network Information Centre** or **NIC**.

9.6.2 Datagrams

Before describing the various functions and protocols associated with the IP, it is helpful to describe the format of an IP protocol data unit. This is known as a **datagram**; the format and contents of a datagram are shown in Figure 9.9.

The **version** field contains the version of the IP protocol used to create the datagram and ensures that all other systems – gateways and hosts – that process the datagram during its transit across the internet interpret the various fields correctly.

The header can be of variable length. The **header length** specifies the actual length of the datagram in multiples of 32-bit words. The minimum length –

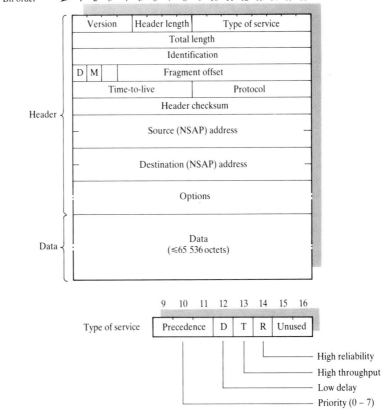

FIGURE 9.9

Internet datagram
format and contents.

without options – is five. If the datagram contains options, these must be in multiples of 32 bits. Any unused bytes must be filled with **padding** bytes.

The **type of service** plays the same role as the quality of service parameter used in ISO networks. It allows an application process to specify the preferred attributes associated with the route and is, therefore, used by each gateway during route selection. For example, if a reliable delivery service is preferred to a best-try transfer, then given a choice the gateway should choose a connection-oriented network rather than a connectionless network. The **total length** defines the total length of the datagram including the header and user data parts. The maximum length is 65 536 bytes.

As will be explained later, user messages may be transferred across the internet in multiple datagrams, with the **identification** field being used to allow a destination host to relate different datagrams to the same user message.

The next three bits are known as **flag bits** of which two are currently used. The first, known as the **don't fragment** or **D bit**, is again intended for use by intermediate gateways. If the D bit is set this indicates that a network should be chosen that can handle the datagram as a single entity rather than as multiple smaller datagrams – known as **fragments**. Hence if the destination host is connected to that network (or subnet) it will receive the user data in a single datagram or not at all. The transit delay of the user data can therefore be more accurately quantified.

The second flag bit, known as the **more fragments** or **M bit**, is also used during the reassembly procedure associated with user data transfers involving multiple datagrams. The **fragment offset** is also used by the same procedure since it indicates the position of the (data) contents of the datagram in relation to the initial user data message. The reassembly procedure will be described later.

The **time-to-live** value defines the maximum time for which a datagram is allowed to be in transit across the internet. The value, in seconds, is set by the source IP. It is then decremented by each gateway by a defined amount. Should it become zero, the datagram is discarded. This allows the destination IP to wait a known maximum time for a datagram fragment during the reassembly procedure. It also enables datagrams that are looping to be discarded.

More than one protocol is associated with the TCP/IP protocol suite. Consequently, the **protocol** field is used to enable the destination IP to pass the datagram to the required protocol.

The **header checksum**, which applies just to the header part of the datagram, is a safeguard against corrupted datagrams being routed to incorrect destinations. It is computed by treating each 16-bit field as an integer and adding them all together using 1's complement (end-around-carry) arithmetic. The checksum is then the 1's complement (inverse) of the sum.

The **source address** and **destination address** are the internet-wide IP (NSAP) addresses of the source and destination hosts.

Finally, the **options** field is used in some datagrams for functions such as error reporting, debugging and route redirection. If present, the contents must be in multiples of 32 bits.

9.6.3 Protocol functions

The IP protocol provides a number of core functions and associated procedures to carry out the various harmonizing functions that are necessary when interworking across dissimilar networks. These include:

- Fragmentation and reassembly: this is concerned with issues relating to the transfer of user messages across networks/subnets which support smaller packet sizes than the user data.

- Routing: to perform the routing function, the IP in each source host must know of the location of the internet gateway or local router that is attached to the same network or subnet. Also, the IP in each gateway must know the route to be followed to reach other networks or subnets.

- Error reporting: when routing or reassembling datagrams within a host or gateway, the IP may discard some datagrams. This function is concerned with reporting such occurrences back to the IP in the source host and with a number of other reporting functions.

Each will be discussed separately.

9.6.4 Fragmentation and reassembly

The size of the user data associated with an NS-user request – normally referred to as an NSDU – can be up to 64K or 65536 octets (bytes). The maximum packet sizes associated with different types of network are much less than this, ranging from 128 octets for some X.25 packet-switching networks to over 8000 octets for some LANs. The fragmentation and reassembly functions associated with the IP fragment the NSDU associated with an NS-user request into smaller fragments – segments in ISO terminology – so that they can be transferred across a particular network in appropriately sized datagrams. On receipt of the fragments of data relating to the same NSDU contained in each IP datagram, it reassembles the NSDU before passing it on to the destination NS-user.

One of two approaches may be adopted since the maximum packet size may vary from one network to another. Either the fragmentation and reassembly functions can be performed on a per network basis – **intranet fragmentation** – or on an end-to-end (internet-wide) basis – **internet fragmentation**. The two approaches are shown in Figure 9.10(a) and (b), respectively.

In general, the IP in a host only knows the maximum packet size associated with its local network. Similarly, the IP in each gateway will only know the maximum packet sizes associated with the two networks to which it is connected. Hence with intranet segmentation, the IP in the source host first fragments the NS-user data – the NSDU – into a number of individually-addressed datagrams as dictated by the network to which it is attached. It then initiates the sending of these either to the destination host or to the first IS (gateway) in the route using the SNDCP. It is the latter that obtains the NPA address of the host or gateway.

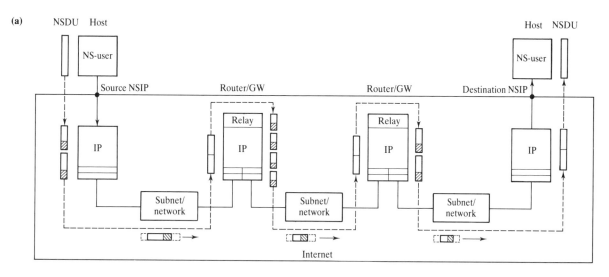

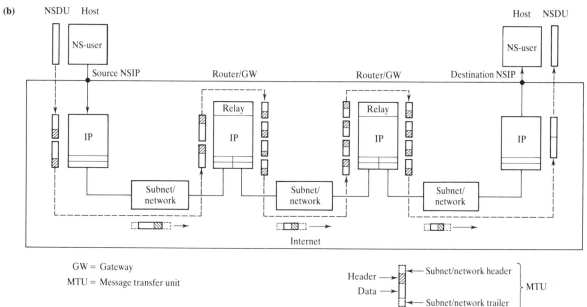

FIGURE 9.10

Fragmentation
alternatives:
(a) intranet;
(b) internet.

The way in which it obtains the NPA address will be described later. On receipt of each datagram, the IP in the host or gateway proceeds to reassemble the NSDU. Next it refragments the reassembled NSDU into a possibly different set of individually-addressed datagrams as dictated by the maximum packet size of the second network.

This procedure is repeated by each gateway until it reaches the IP in the destination host, where the NSDU is again reassembled and passed to the destination NS-user.

In the case of internet fragmentation, the IP in the source host carries out the same fragmentation procedure as before and sends the resulting datagrams to the IP in the first gateway. This time, however, the IP does not reassemble the NSDU. Instead it either modifies the appropriate fields and sends the received datagrams directly onto the second network (if the latter can support this size of datagram), or refragments the datagram into smaller fragments (datagrams) if it cannot. In the example, the maximum packet size associated with the second network/subnet is assumed to be smaller than that used by the first. Consequently, the IP will segment each datagram it receives into a number of smaller datagrams each with the same source and destination addresses.

This procedure is repeated at the next gateway. However, since in the example the last network/subnet can support a larger packet size than the datagrams it receives, these are transmitted directly with only selected modifications to some header fields. As before, the IP in the destination host reassembles the user data from each datagram it receives and passes the resulting NSDU to the destination NS-user.

It can be deduced from the foregoing, and especially from the packet flows associated with the third network, that intranet fragmentation allows the maximum packet size of each network to be utilized, since the individual fragments are reassembled by each gateway in the route. With internet fragmentation this will not necessarily be the case, but it has the advantage that the reassembly processing is not needed at each gateway.

The IP does in fact use internet fragmentation. This may at first appear surprising but it is used because of the problem of lost datagrams. Some networks will operate with a best-try connectionless protocol with the possibility that one or more datagrams relating to a single NSDU may be corrupted while being transmitted. As has been shown, with intranet fragmentation the receiving IP in each gateway reassembles the complete NSDU before relaying it to the next network. If any fragments are missing (for example, a datagram is discarded because it has been corrupted), the receiving IP must decide at what point to abort the reassembly function.

This is determined by the IP in the source host defining a maximum time limit that a gateway should wait for any datagrams relating to an NSDU during each reassembly operation. Known as the **time-to-live**, this limit is carried in the header of all datagrams relating to the NSDU. It is set by the IP in the source host and is then decremented by each IP that processes the datagram. If a datagram is fragmented, the current value is copied into the header of the new datagrams. Then, if it reaches zero at any point during the reassembly processing in a gateway (or host), the reassembly function is aborted and all fragments relating to that NSDU are discarded.

The time-to-live field in each datagram is in multiples of 1 second, so the amount it is decremented by each IP will vary depending on the (known) mean transit delay of the associated network. In the case of internet fragmentation, the IP in each gateway still decrements the time-to-live lifetime field in each datagram it receives and discards any datagrams for which the value reaches zero. Similarly, the IP in the destination host aborts its reassembly operation in the same way. In both cases, if fragments are missing and the reassembly operation aborted, a **time exceeded** error message is generated and returned to the IP in the source host.

EXAMPLE

An NSDU of 1000 octets is to be transmitted over a network which supports a maximum NS-user data size of 256 octets. Assuming the header in each IP datagram requires 20 octets, derive the number of datagrams (fragments) required and the contents of the following fields in each datagram header:

- identification,
- total length,
- fragment offset,
- more fragments flag.

Maximum usable data per datagram = 256 − 20 = 236 octets
Use, say, 29 × 8 = 232 octets
Hence five datagrams will be required, four with 232 octets of user data and one with 72 octets
The fields are as follows:

identification	20 (say)	20	20	20	20
total length	252	252	252	252	92
fragment offset	0	29	58	87	116
more fragments flag	1	1	1	1	0

9.6.5 Routing

As each network (or subnet) making up an internet may use different point-of-attachment addresses, a system – host or gateway – attached to a network can only send a datagram directly to another system if it is attached to the same network. To route datagrams across multiple networks, therefore, the IP in each inter-network gateway must know the point-of-attachment address of the destination host – if it is attached to a network to which the gateway is attached – or the next gateway along the route to the required destination network if it is not. Again, the latter must be attached to a network to which the gateway is attached. The major issue with routing, therefore, is how the hosts and gateways within the internet obtain and maintain their routing information.

Two basic approaches are used for routing within an internet: centralized and distributed. With a **centralized routing** scheme, the routing information associated with each gateway is downloaded from a central site using the network and special network management messages. The network management system endeavours to maintain their contents up-to-date as networks and hosts are added

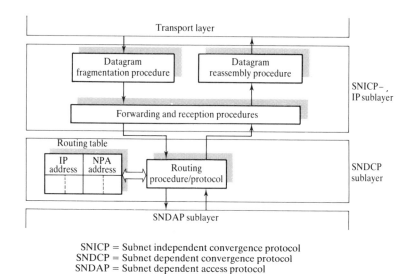

FIGURE 9.11

General routing scheme
within a host.

SNICP = Subnet independent convergence protocol
SNDCP = Subnet dependent convergence protocol
SNDAP = Subnet dependent access protocol
NPA = (Sub)net point of attachment (address)

or removed and faults are diagnosed and repaired. In general, for all but the
smallest internets, this is only a viable solution as long as each individual network
has its own network management system which incorporates sophisticated configuration and fault management procedures.

With a **distributed routing** scheme, all the hosts and gateways cooperate in
a distributed way to ensure that the routing information held by each system –
hosts and gateways – is up-to-date and consistent. Routing information is retained
by each system in the form of a **routing table** which contains the network point of
attachment (NPA) address to be used to forward each datagram. The Internet
uses such a scheme.

The routing procedure associated with the IP first reads the destination IP
(NSAP) address from within a datagram and then uses this to find the correspond-
ing point of attachment address – of a host or a gateway – from the routing table.
In addition, a set of routing protocols are used to create and maintain the contents
of each routing table in a distributed way. The general scheme used within a host
IP is shown in Figure 9.11.

Autonomous systems

Before discussing the various routing protocols relating to the Internet, it is
helpful to describe its architecture and the associated terminology. To reflect the
fact that the Internet is made up of a number of separately managed and run
internets, each internet is treated as being an **autonomous system** with its own
internal routing algorithms and management authority. The combined Internet,
therefore, is considered as being made up of a **core backbone network** to which a
number of autonomous systems are attached. The general architecture is shown in

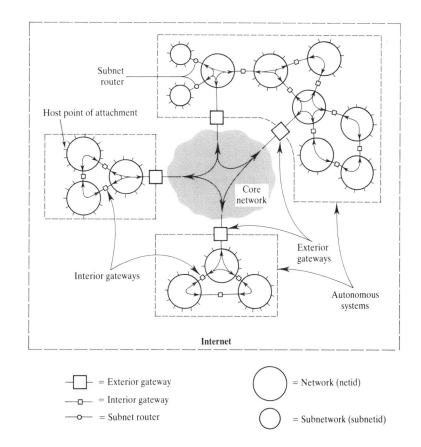

Subnet router

Host point of attachment

Core network

Exterior gateways

Interior gateways

Autonomous systems

Internet

FIGURE 9.12

General internet architecture and terminology.

☐— = Exterior gateway
—□— = Interior gateway
—○— = Subnet router

◯ = Network (netid)

◯ = Subnetwork (subnetid)

Figure 9.12 together with some (very much simplified) autonomous system topologies.

To discriminate between the gateways which are used within an autonomous system and those used to connect an autonomous system to the core network, the terms **interior gateway** and **exterior gateway** are used, respectively. The corresponding routing protocols are the **interior gateway protocol (IGP)** and the **exterior gateway protocol (EGP)**. Since the Internet consists of an interconnected set of internets, each of which has evolved over a relatively long period of time, each autonomous system has its own IGP. The Internet EGP, however, is, as indeed it must be, an internet wide standard.

Although each autonomous system within the Internet comprises a large number of networks/subnets, in a more general application, an autonomous system might consist of just one network managed and run by a single corporation. Others might consist of a set of subnets connected to a site-wide backbone network with a single exterior gateway. An example would be a site with multiple LANs interconnected by routers. To simplify the discussion, only autonomous systems that consist of multiple networks will be considered since the presence of subnets just adds another level of routing between an interior gateway and the hosts.

If every gateway and host system in an internet contained a separate entry in its routing table for all other systems, the size of the routing tables and the amount of processing and transmission capacity needed to maintain the tables would be excessive and, for the Internet, unmanageable. Instead, the total routing information is organized hierarchically:

- hosts maintain sufficient routing information to enable them to forward datagrams to other hosts or an interior gateway(s) that is (are) attached to the same network;
- interior gateways maintain sufficient routing information to enable them to forward datagrams to hosts or other interior gateways within the same autonomous system;
- exterior gateways maintain sufficient routing information to enable them to forward datagrams either to an interior gateway, if the datagram is for the same autonomous system, or to another exterior gateway if it is not.

A number of routing protocols have been developed to implement this scheme. These include an intranet protocol known as the **address resolution protocol (ARP)**, a number of **interior gateway protocols (IGP)** and an **exterior gateway protocol (EGP)**. The scope of each protocol and the routing tables associated with them are shown in Figure 9.13. Each will be discussed separately.

Address resolution protocol

To enable an interior gateway to forward any datagrams it receives for hosts that are attached to one of its local networks, it must keep a record of the hostid and corresponding network point of attachment (NPA) address – known as an **address pair** – for all the hosts attached to each of these networks. To obtain this information, each host simply informs the local gateway of its existence by sending it its IP/NPA address pair. Typically, this is stored at the host in permanent storage (such as the hard disk) and is then broadcast. In the case of non-broadcast networks, the address pair of its local gateway(s) is (are) also stored and used directly. As a result, each interior gateway builds up a **local routing table** with the IP/NPA address pairs of all hosts that are attached to each of the networks to which it is itself attached.

When a host wishes to send a datagram to another host on the same network, the IP simply sends the datagram to its local gateway for forwarding. Although this must be done for datagrams addressed to hosts on other networks, for hosts attached to the same network it can lead to excessively high overheads, especially if a large number of hosts are attached to the network. To overcome this, the IP in each host endeavours to obtain the hostid/NPA address pair of all hosts on the same network with which it communicates. This enables a host to send a datagram to such hosts directly without involving the gateway.

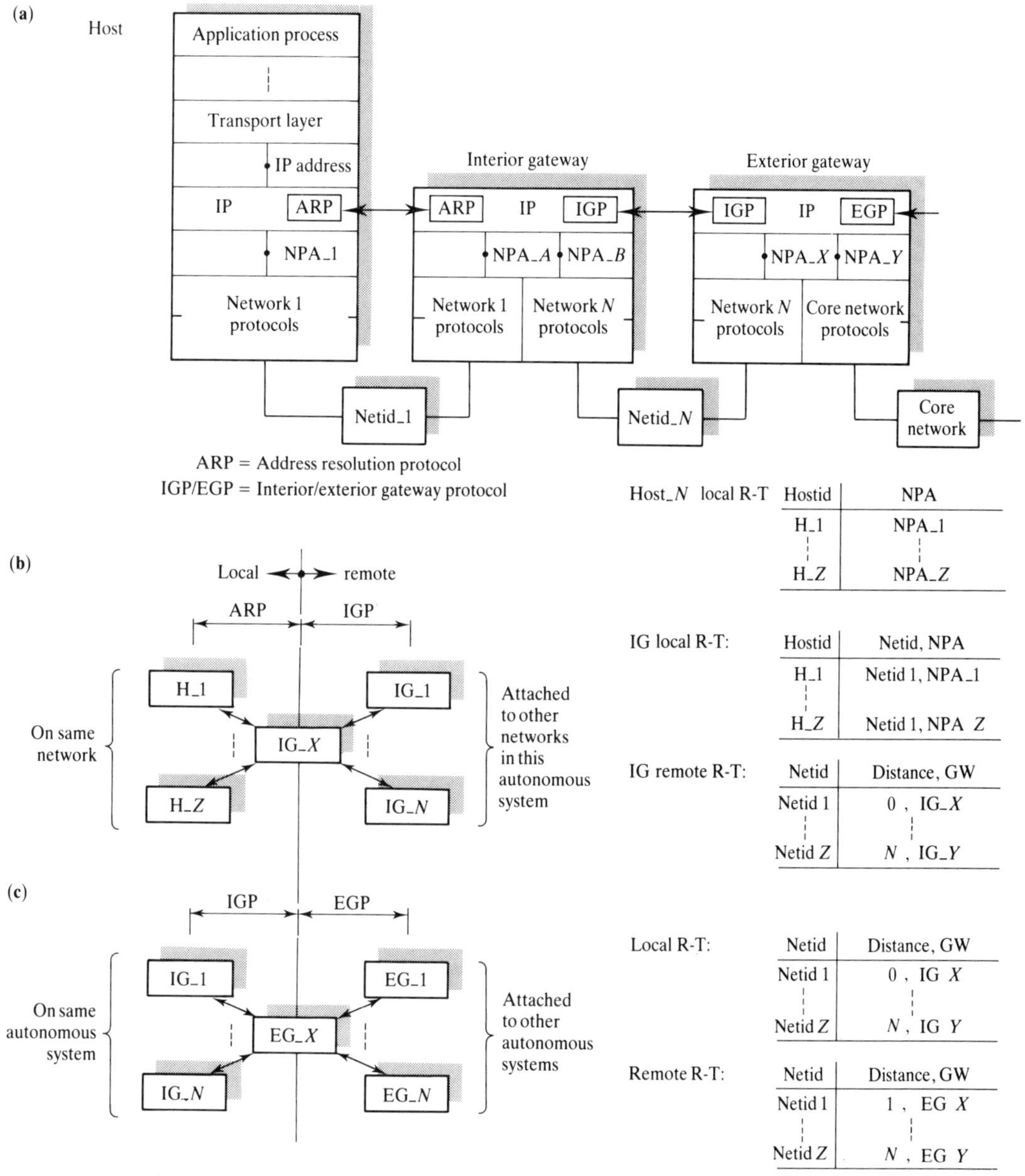

FIGURE 9.13

Routing protocols:
(a) general architecture;
(b) ARP/IGP scope and
routing tables; (c) IGP/
EGP scope and routing
protocols.

The protocol that performs this function is known as the **address resolution protocol (ARP)**. ARP forms an integral part of the IP in each host; there is a peer ARP in each interior gateway, as shown in Figure 9.13(a).

Whenever the **fragmentation procedure** associated with the IP creates a datagram for forwarding, it first passes the address pointer of the memory buffer in which the datagram is stored to the ARP. The latter maintains a local routing table which contains the hostid, NPA address pairs of all the hosts connected to this network with which the host communicates. Hence, if the destination IP address in the datagram is present in the table, then the ARP simply passes the datagram address pointer with the corresponding NPA address on to the SNDAP protocol, with the netid field of the IP address set to zero to indicate this network. The SNDAP then initiates the sending of the datagram either by broadcast or directly.

If the NPA address is not present, the ARP endeavours to find it by creating and sending an **ARP request message** and waiting for a reply. The request message contains both its own IP/NPA address pair and the required (target) IP address. Again, this can either be broadcast – in which case it is received by the ARP in all hosts – or sent directly to the ARP in the gateway using the latter's (known) NPA address. In the second case, the ARP in the gateway simply relays the message to the required host using its own local routing table and the required destination IP address in the request message.

The ARP in the required destination host recognizes its own IP address in the request message and proceeds to process it. It first checks to see whether the source hostid, NPA address pair is within its own routing table; if not, it enters them. It then responds by returning an **ARP reply message** containing its own NPA address to the ARP in the requesting host – using the latter's NPA address from the request message. On receipt of the reply message, the ARP in the source host first makes an entry of the requested hostid, NPA pair in its own routing table and then passes the waiting datagram address pointer on to the SNDAP protocol together with the corresponding NPA address which indicates where it should be sent. The hostid, NPA pair is recorded by the destination since it is highly probable that the destination host will require it later when the higher layer protocol responds to the datagram.

As was indicated earlier, the IP/NPA address pair of a host is normally held in permanent storage and read by the computer operating system at startup. In the case of diskless hosts, this is not possible, so an associated protocol known as the **reverse address resolution protocol** or **RARP** is used. The server associated with each set of diskless hosts has a copy of the IP/NPA address pair of all the hosts it serves. When a diskless host first comes into service, it broadcasts an RARP request message to the server containing its own physical hardware network address, that is, its NPA. On receipt of such messages, the RARP in the server responds with a reply message containing both the IP address of the requestor and its own IP/NPA address pair. In practice, the format of the request and reply messages associated with ARP and RARP are the same, as shown in Figure 9.14.

The **operation** field specifies the particular message type: ARP request/reply, RARP request/reply. When making an ARP request, the sender writes its own **hardware address (HA)** and IP address in the appropriate fields together with the destination IP address in the **target IP** field. In the case of a RARP, the sender simply includes its own HA address. To ensure that the HA address is interpreted correctly, the **hardware type** field identifies the type of LAN; CSMA/CD, for example, is 1. The **protocol type** field indicates the type of protocol being used: ARP, RARP and others to be defined.

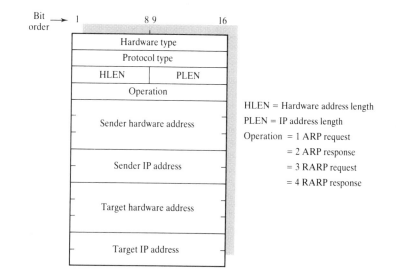

Bit order

| 1 | 8 9 | 16 |

Hardware type

Protocol type

HLEN | PLEN

Operation

Sender hardware address

Sender IP address

Target hardware address

Target IP address

HLEN = Hardware address length
PLEN = IP address length
Operation = 1 ARP request
= 2 ARP response
= 3 RARP request
= 4 RARP response

FIGURE 9.14

ARP and reverse ARP message formats.

Interior gateway protocol

As indicated earlier, the interior gateway routing protocol can vary from one autonomous system to another. The most widely used protocol is the IP **routing information protocol (RIP)**. It is a **distributed routing protocol**, which is based on a technique known as the **distance-vector algorithm (DVA)**. A more recently introduced protocol is based on two algorithms known as the **link-state** and **shortest-path-first algorithms (LSA** and **SPE)**. Known as the **link-state open shortest path first (link-state OSPF)** protocol, it has been adopted as the international standard for use with the ISO-IP. Since the DVA is specific to the TCP/IP it will be discussed here. The link-state OSPF will be discussed later in the context of the ISO-IP.

The term **distance** is used as a **routing metric** between two gateways. For example, if the metric is **hops**, then this is the number of intermediate networks between two gateways. If the metric is delay, then this is the mean transit delay between the two gateways, and so on. Whichever metric is used, the DVA uses a distributed algorithm to enable each interior gateway in an autonomous system to build up a table containing the distance between itself and all the other networks in that system.

Initially, each gateway knows only the netid of each network to which it is attached as well as the IP/NPA address pair of each gateway attached to these networks. Typically this information is entered by management when the gateway is initialized; the netid in the **remote routing table** and the IP/NPA address pairs in the **adjacency table** for the gateway. The format of the remote routing table associated with an interior gateway was shown in Figure 9.13(b). If the metric is hops, the remote routing table will contain simply the netid of each of its local networks, a distance of zero, and its own IP address as the gateway from which the distance applies. Similarly, if the metric is delay, this would have been determined

FIGURE 9.15

Distance vector
algorithm example:
(a) topology; (b) build
up of routing tables
assuming hop-count
metric; (c) reachability
table for GW.

by a gateway sending a message (datagram) to each of the gateways attached to its
own networks and measuring the time delay before receiving the responses. The
distance would then be set to, say, half of these values.

Periodically, each gateway sends the current contents of its (remote)
routing table to each of its neighbours. Based on the contents of its neighbours'
tables which it receives, it proceeds to update, or add to, the contents of its own
routing table. The receiving gateway simply adds the known distances to each of
its immediate neighbours to the distances contained in the received tables. Since
this procedure repeats, after each iteration the routing table will start to build up

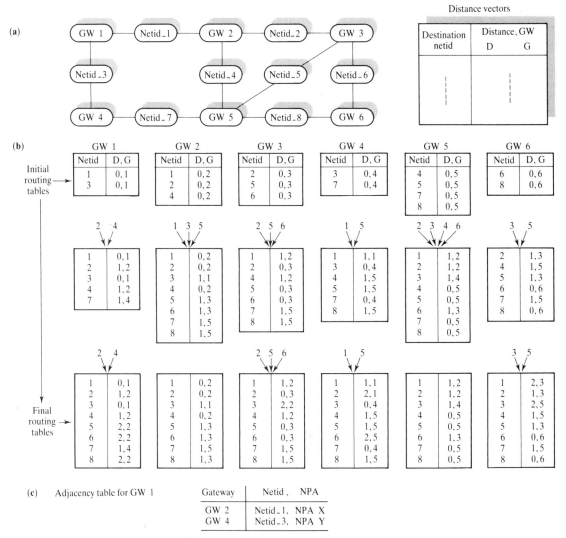

(c)   Adjacency table for GW 1

Gateway	Netid , NPA
GW 2	Netid_1, NPA X
GW 4	Netid_3, NPA Y

NPA = Network point of attachment address

as new distances are reported. If a reported distance to a network is less than a current entry, the entry is updated. After a number of iterations, each gateway will have an entry for each of the networks in the autonomous system. The time taken to achieve this will be a function of the size of the system and the frequency with which routing information is exchanged. The latter is known as the **route propagation delay**.

As an example, consider the simple network shown in Figure 9.15(a) and assume the metric is hops. The way in which the routing tables build up are shown in part (b) of the figure. The initial contents of each gateway simply contain the netid of its local networks. For this network, the contents of each routing table will be complete after just two exchanges of routing tables. The final routing table for each gateway then contains the distances to each network in the system and the immediate neighbour gateway to be used to reach it. Thus from gateway 1, the distance to netid_6 is two hops – that is, two intermediate networks – via gateway 2. At gateway 2, netid_6 is a distance of one hop via gateway 3 to which netid_6 is attached.

It can readily be deduced that a metric of hops can lead to inferior routes being selected. For example, if the delay metric associated with each network is the same as its netid, it would be quicker to go from gateway 4 to netid_6 via gateways 1, 2 and 3 in three hops rather than 5 and 6 with two hops. The delay metric, therefore, will often give a better performance. A protocol that uses delay is **HELLO**. As its name implies, the delay is determined by periodically sending **hello messages** to each of its neighbours and timing their responses.

To ensure that table entries reflect the current topology of the network when faults develop, each entry has an associated timer. If the entry is not confirmed within a defined time, then it is timed-out. This means that each gateway transmits its complete routing table at regular intervals, typically 30 seconds. For a small network this is not necessarily a problem, but for large networks the overheads associated with the distance vector algorithm can be very high. Also, it is possible for gateways to have dissimilar routes to the same destination since entries will be made in the order in which they are received and equal distance routes are discarded. As a result, datagrams between certain routes may loop rather than going directly to the desired gateway. Also, only a single route is held in the routing tables so alternative routes are not used. It is for these reasons that OSPF is becoming the preferred IGP for large internets.

Exterior gateway protocol

The management authority associated with each autonomous system nominates one or more gateways to function as exterior gateways for that system. Within the autonomous system, these communicate with the other interior gateways using the IGP for that system. Hence each exterior gateway, through its local routing table, knows about the netids within that system and their distances from that gateway. This is built up in the way just described.

When each exterior gateway is first initialized, it is given the unique identity of the autonomous system to which it is attached. It also receives the contents of a routing table, known as the **reachability table**, which enables it to communicate with all the other exterior gateways via the core network. The exterior gateway protocol (EGP) then involves each exterior gateway making contact with selected exterior gateways, as required, and exchanging routing information with them. This routing information consists of the list of netids within the corresponding autonomous system together with their distances and routes from the reporting exterior gateway. The latter is used by a sending gateway to select the best exterior gateway to use when forwarding datagrams to a particular autonomous system.

The three main functions associated with the EGP are:

- neighbour acquisition,
- neighbour reachability,
- routing update.

Each function operates using a request-response message exchange. The messages associated with each function are shown in Table 9.1.

Since each autonomous system is managed and run by a different authority, before any routing information is exchanged, two exterior gateways attached to different systems must first agree to exchange such information. This is the role of

Table 9.1   EGP message types and their meaning.

Function	EGP message	Meaning
Neighbour acquisition	Acquisition request	Requests a gateway to become a neighbour
	Acquisition confirm	Gateway agrees to become a neighbour
	Acquisition refuse	Gateway refuses
	Cease request	Requests termination of a neighbour relationship
	Cease confirm	Confirms break-up of relationship
Neighbour reachability	Hello	Requests neighbour to confirm a previously established relationship
	I-heard-you	Confirms relationship
Routing update	Poll request	Requests network reachability update
	Routing update	Network reachability information
Error response	Error	Response to any incorrect request message

the **neighbour acquisition and termination** procedure. When two gateways agree to such an exchange, they are said to have become **neighbours**. When a gateway first wants to exchange routing information, it sends an **acquisition request** message to the EGP in the appropriate gateway which then returns either an **acquisition confirm** message or, if it does not want to accept the request, an **acquisition refuse** message which includes a reason code.

Once a neighbour relationship has been established between two gateways – and hence autonomous systems – they periodically confirm their relationship. This is done either by exchanging specific messages – **hello** and **I-heard-you** – or by embedding confirmation information into the header of normal routing information messages.

The actual exchange of routing information is carried out by one of the gateways sending a **poll request** message to the other gateway asking it for the list of networks (netids) that are reachable via that gateway and their distances from it. The response is a **routing update** message which contains the requested information. Finally, if any request message is incorrect, an **error message** is returned as a response with an appropriate reason code.

As with the other IP protocols, all the messages (PDUs) associated with the EGP are carried in the user data field of an IP datagram. All EGP messages have the same fixed header; the format is shown in Figure 9.16.

The **version** field defines the version number of the EGP. The **type** and **code** fields collectively define the type of message while the **status** field contains message-dependent status information. The **checksum**, which is used as a safeguard against erroneous messages being processed, is the same as that used with IP. The **autonomous system number** is the assigned number of the autonomous system to which the sending gateway is attached; the **sequence number** is used to synchronize responses to their corresponding request message.

Neighbour reachability messages only contain a header with a type field of 5, a code of 0 = hello and a 1 = I-heard-you.

Neighbour acquisition messages have a type field of 3; the code number defines the specific message type. The **hello interval** specifies the frequency with which hello messages should be sent; the **poll interval** performs the same function for poll messages.

A poll message has a type field of 2. The code field is used to piggyback the neighbour reachability information: a code of 0 = hello and a code of 1 = I-heard-you. The **source network IP address** in both the poll and the routing update response messages indicates the network linking the two exterior gateways. This allows the core network itself to consist of multiple networks.

The routing update message contains the list of networks (netids) that are reachable via each gateway within the autonomous system arranged in distance order from the responding exterior gateway. As indicated, this enables the requesting gateway to select the best exterior gateway through which to send a datagram for forwarding within an autonomous system. Notice that to conserve space, each netid address is sent in three bytes (24 bits) only with the most significant 8-bit hostid field missing. Clearly, the latter is redundant for all class types.

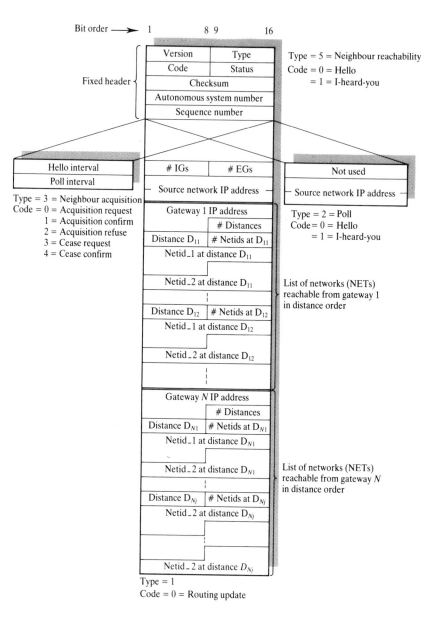

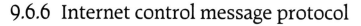

FIGURE 9.16

EGP message formats.

9.6.6 Internet control message protocol

The **internet control message protocol (ICMP)** forms an integral part of all IP implementations. It is used by both hosts and gateways for a variety of functions, and especially by network management. The main functions associated with the ICMP are:

- error reporting,
- reachability testing,
- congestion control,
- route-change notification,
- performance measuring,
- subnet addressing.

The message types associated with each of these functions are shown in Table 9.2. Each is transmitted in a standard IP datagram.

Since the IP is a best-try (unacknowledged) protocol, datagrams may be discarded while they are in transit across the internet. Transmission errors are one cause, of course, but datagrams can be discarded by a host or gateway for a variety of reasons. Clearly, in the absence of any error reporting functions, a host would not know whether the repeated failure to send a datagram to a given destination was the result of a poor transmission line (or other fault within a network) or simply the destination host being switched off. The various messages associated with the **error reporting** function are used for this purpose.

If a datagram is corrupted by transmission errors, it is simply discarded. However, if a datagram is discarded for any other reason, the ICMP in the host or gateway that discards the datagram generates a **destination unreachable** error

Table 9.2 ICMP message types and their use.

Function	ICMP message(s)	Use
Error reporting	Destination unreachable	A datagram has been discarded due to the reason specified in the message
	Time exceeded	Time-to-live parameter in a datagram expired and hence discarded
	Parameter error	A parameter in the header of a datagram is unrecognizable
Reachability testing	Echo request/ reply	Used to check the reachability of a specified host or gateway
Congestion control	Source quench	Used to request a host to reduce the rate at which datagrams are sent
Route exchange	Redirect	Used by a gateway to inform a host attached to one of its networks to use an alternative gateway on the same network for forwarding datagrams to a specific destination
Performance measuring	Timestamp request/reply	Used to determine the transit delay between two hosts
Submit addressing	Address mask request/reply	Used by a host to determine the address mask associated with a subnet

ICMP = Internet control message protocol

report message and returns it to the ICMP in the source host with a reason code. Reasons include:

- destination network unreachable,
- destination host unreachable,
- specified protocol not present at destination,
- fragmentation needed but don't fragment (DF) flag set in datagram header,
- communication with the destination network is not allowed for administrative reasons,
- communication with the destination host is not allowed for administrative reasons.

Other error report messages include **time exceeded** – which indicates that the time-to-live parameter in a discarded datagram has expired – and **parameter error** which indicates that a parameter in the header of the discarded datagram was not recognized.

If a network manager receives reports from a user that a specified destination is not responding, it is necessary to determine the reason. The **reachability testing** function is used for this purpose. Typically, on receipt of such a report, the network manager initiates the sending of an **echo request** message to the suspect host to determine whether it is switched on and responding to requests. On receipt of an echo request message, the ICMP in the destination simply changes this to an **echo reply** message which it returns to the source. A similar test can then be performed on selected gateways should this be necessary.

In the event of a datagram being discarded because no free memory buffers are available as a result of a temporary overload condition, a **source quench** message is returned to the ICMP in the source host. Such messages can be generated either by a host or a gateway. They request the source host to reduce the rate at which it sends datagrams. When a host receives such a message, it should reduce the sending rate by an agreed amount. A new source quench message is generated each time a datagram is discarded with the result that the source host incrementally reduces the sending rate. Such messages thus help to alleviate congestion control within the internet. Congestion will be discussed further in the context of the ISO-IP.

When a network has multiple gateways attached to it, it is possible for a gateway to receive datagrams from a host even though it determines from its routing table that they would be better sent via a different gateway attached to the same network. To inform the source host of this, the ICMP in the gateway returns a **redirect** message to the ICMP in the source indicating which is the better gateway to the specified destination. The ICMP in the source then makes an entry in its routing table for this destination.

An important operational parameter for an internet is the mean transit delay of datagrams. This is a measure of the time a datagram takes to traverse the internet from a specified source to a specified destination. To ascertain this, a host or a network manager can send a **timestamp request** message to a specific destination. Each such message contains three time-related parameters (known as **timestamps**):

- the time the datagram was sent by the source,
- the time the datagram was received by the destination,
- the time the datagram was returned by the destination.

On receipt of a timestamp request message, the ICMP in the destination simply fills in the appropriate timestamp fields and returns the datagram to the source. On receipt of the reply, the source can quantify the curent round-trip delay to that destination and from this determine the datagram transit delay.

Finally, when subnet addressing is being used, the **address mask request** and corresponding reply messages are used by a host to ascertain the address mask associated with a local subnet. This is needed by a host to determine, for example, whether a specified destination is attached to the same subnet. The address mask is held by the local router associated with the subnet. The ICMP in a host can obtain it sending a request message and reading the mask from the reply.

9.7 THE ISO INTERNET PROTOCOL

The ISO approach to internetworking is based on an internet-wide, connection-less, subnetwork-independent convergence protocol known as the **ISO Internet Protocol** or **ISO-IP**. It is defined in ISO 8473 and has many of the features of the IP protocol just described on which it is based.

In addition to the full internetworking protocol, there are two subsets: the **inactive network layer protocol** and the **non-segmenting protocol**. The former is the connectionless network protocol often used with LANs and is intended for applications involving a single network. Thus the source and destination end systems (stations) are both connected to the same network so none of the harmonizing functions identified earlier are required.

The non-segmenting protocol (non-fragmenting in IP terminology) is intended for use in internets that consist of subnets – networks in IP terminology – which have maximum packet sizes all less than or equal to that required to transfer the NS-user data (NSDU) in a single internet protocol data unit. Clearly, the segmentation function associated with the protocol is not required in this case.

9.7.1 User services

The user service primitives associated with the protocol and their parameters, are shown in Figure 9.17. They are the same as those used with the inactive network layer protocol – shown in Chapter 6 – except that the QOS and service characteristics relate to the complete internet rather than a single network. Normally, the N.FACILITY service is used by an NS-user to determine the QOS and service

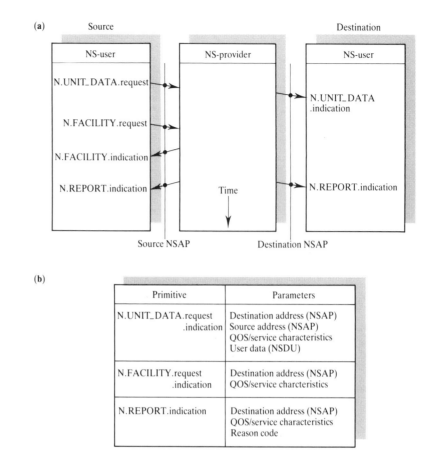

FIGURE 9.17

Internet service
primitives:
(a) sequence;
(b) parameters.

QOS = Quality of service

characteristics to be expected from the internet when communicating with the specified destination NSAP address. This information is then used by the source NS-user when specifying the QOS associated with each N.UNIT_DATA.request primitive.

The source and destination addresses are the internet-wide NSAP addresses of the two communicating NS-users. Their format is shown in Figure 9.18 it is the same as that defined in the last chapter by ISO and CCITT for use with public-carrier WANs and other networks. As may be recalled, these are hierarchical and are 20 octets in length (40 binary-coded decimal digits). The AFI specifies the authority responsible for allocating IDIs, the format of IDIs and the abstract syntax of the DSP. The IDI specifies the particular network addressing scheme to which the DSP addresses relate. The DSP is itself hierarchichal and comprises: an optional address domain part, an area part, a subnet identifier part and a system identifier (ID) part. The length (number of digits) used for each part may differ from one open system environment to another. However, once defined for an environment, all systems (ES and IS) will have the same NSAP format. The

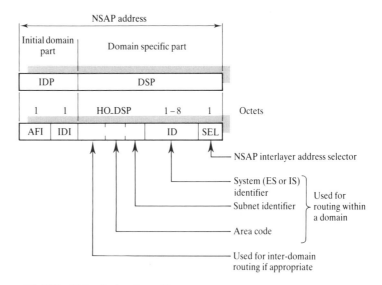

FIGURE 9.18

ISO-IP NSAP address
structure.

HO_DSP = High order domain specific part

final SEL octet at the end of each NSAP is used at the NS-user interface to allow
multiple (up to 256) transport entities within a single ES to be identified. This is
needed, for example, in ESs that support multiple application layer entities.

As will be expanded upon later when routing is discussed, with large
internets it is possible to divide a single addressing domain into a number of areas.
Typically, the least significant two octets of the **high-order domain specific part
(HO_DSP)** are then used to identify each area/subnet within a domain. The
remainder of the HO_DSP field is then set to all zeros. Alternatively, if there is a
real need to interconnect domains – analogous to autonomous sysems within the
Internet – it is used for interdomain routing. In small open system environments
an area may relate to a single site, in which case each area address will identify,
say, a single site-wide LAN. With larger environments, however, the area address
may itself be hierarchical to allow for an area to contain multiple sites. In both
cases, the ID field uniquely identifies an NS-user within that area/subnet hierarchy.

The user data parameter is a (NS-user) transport protocol data unit which
can be up to 64512 octets in length. In practice, since the protocol provides only a
best-try connectionless service, the NS-user (the transport protocol entity) will
normally perform additonal end-to-end error control and is therefore unlikely to
use such a large user data length because of the possibly long transit delays
associated with retransmitted NSDUs. The latter is related to the QOS expected
of the internet and can be used by the transport entity when selecting the length of
the user data field to be adopted.

The QOS parameter is in fact a list of parameters that collectively express
the service performance of the internet in relation to the specified destination
(NSAP) address. These include:

- *Transit delay:* the mean time to successfully transmit an NSDU across the internet from the source NSAP to the specified destination NSAP. This is used by the local source transport protocol entity to determine the timeout interval to be used with its retransmission protocol.

- *Cost determinants:* this optional field consists of a set of costs and options that allow an NS-user to influence the choice of route selected by the intermediate systems for this NSDU.

- *Residual error probability:* defines the number of lost, duplicated or incorrectly delivered NSDUs as a percentage of the total number of NSDUs transmitted. This information influences the choice of maximum user data field selected by the source transport entity.

- *Priority:* this optional parameter allows the NS-user to specify the relative priority of an NSDU in relation to others it transmits. It might be used, for example, to send expedited data.

- *Source routing:* this optional parameter consists of a set of sub-parameters that allow an NS-user to specify the route through the internet – a sequential list of intermediate systems, in practice – to be followed by this NSDU. Normally, this is not known in a large internet and so the parameter will not be present.

The list of internet characteristics associated with the N.FACILITY service include:

- *Congestion control:* this specifies whether flow control will be exercised by the internet (NS-provider) at the NS-user interface. With a connectionless service, this is done by the local ISO-IP returning an N.REPORT. indication primitive in response to a N.UNIT_DATA.request with the reason code set to NS-provider congestion.

- *Sequence preservation probability:* this is the result of a measurement made by the local ISO-IP indicating the ratio of sequence-preserved transmissions to total transmissions and is again used by the local transport entity in relation to its error and flow control functions.

- *Maximum NSDU lifetime:* this indicates the maximum time the internet is allowed to take to deliver the NSDU before discarding it. This allows the transport protocol entity to quantify the maximum time it must wait for receipt of acknowledgement information before retransmitting an NSDU.

9.7.2 Used service

As previously indicated, the internet protocol (the SNICP) offers the same set of user service primitives to all NS-users irrespective of the service offered by the underlying subnet to which the end system is attached. In an internet comprising multiple subnet (network) types, these subnets can be connection-oriented or connectionless. Since the ISO-IP is subnet independent, a choice must be made as to the assumed service provided by each subnet. With the ISO-IP, it is assumed that all subnets provide a connectionless service. Because this is the same as that offered at its own NS-user interface, the prefix SN instead of N is used to indicate the service assumed from each constituent subnet to transfer its protocol data units. Clearly, in some end systems this will be the same as that provided by the underlying subnet, while in others it will be different. To allow for this difference, the SNDCP is used to perform any necessary mapping operations. Two examples are given in Figure 9.19 to illustrate this.

In part (a), it is assumed that the end system is attached to an X.25 packet-switching subnet, so the actual subnet service will be connection-oriented. The interactions shown thus relate to those that occur at the source DTE/DCE interface. In part (b), however, it is assumed that the end system is attached to a LAN which provides a connectionless service. Typically, the interactions shown take place between the ISO-IP in the ES and the ISO-IP in an intermediate system attached to the same LAN.

On receipt of an N.UNIT_DATA.request primitive, the ISO-IP will create a **data protocol data unit** (data PDU) using the parameters associated with the primitive. It then initiates the sending of the PDU (to a peer IP) via the SNDCP using a SN.UNIT_DATA.request primitive with the PDU as the user data parameter. Since in part (a) the subnet is connection-oriented, the SNDCP must set up a virtual call (circuit) using the N.CONNECT service before sending the PDU. It thus waits for the N.CONNECT.confirm primitive and then sends the PDU using an N.DATA.request primitive with the PDU as the user data parameter. Subsequent PDUs can then be sent directly using the N.DATA service.

Since the IP provides a connectionless user service, the question arises as to what triggers the clearing of this virtual circuit. In the absence of a specific disconnection request from the IP (the SNICP), the SNDCP must itself initiate the clearing of the virtual call. To do this, the SNDCP has a timer – the **inactivity timer** – which is restarted every time a primitive is received relating to this virtual call from either the IP or the the SNDAP (X.25 PLP). If the timer expires, the SNDCP assumes that the dialogue associated with the call is finished and initiates the clearing of the call by issuing an N.DISCONNECT.request primitive.

In part (b), since the subnet is connectionless, the SNDCP only needs to perform a simple one-to-one mapping. It thus initiates the sending of the PDU using an N.UNIT_DATA.request primitive directly to the SNDAP with the PDU as the user data parameter. Transfers in the reverse direction are treated in the same way.

9.7.3 Protocol functions

The ISO-IP includes a number of separate functions to carry out the various harmonizing operations identified in Section 9.3. These include functions to perform:

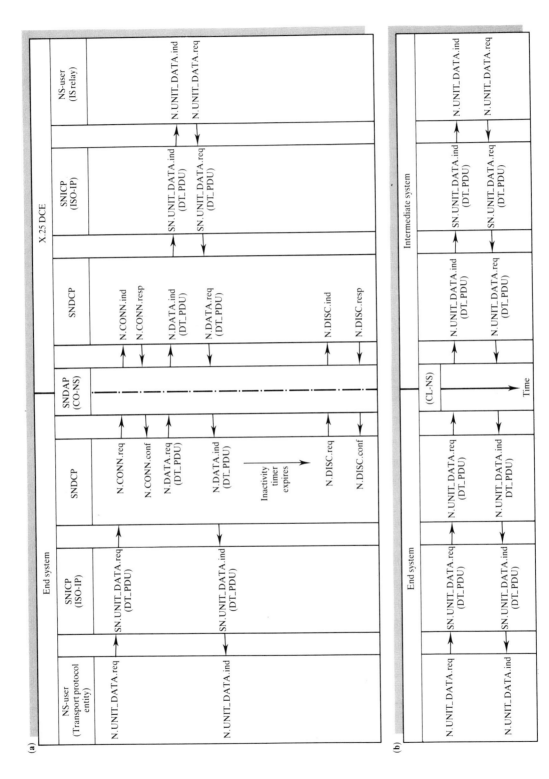

FIGURE 9.19 SNDCP function: (a) CO-SNDAP; (b) CL-SNDAP.

- segmentation and reassembly,
- routing,
- flow and congestion control,
- error reporting.

Various fields in each data PDU relate to each of the above functions. The structure of each data PDU is shown in Figure 9.20; the meaning and use of each field will be described as the various functions are discussed.

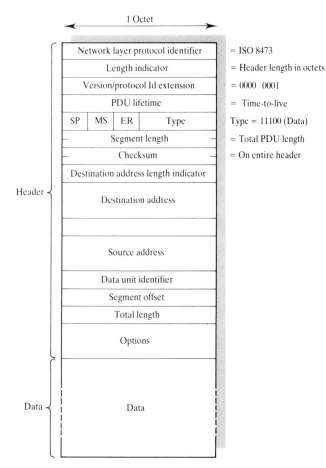

FIGURE 9.20

ISO Internet Protocol – data PDU structure.

Segmentation and reassembly

The segmentation and reassembly functions associated with the ISO-IP are basically the same as the fragmentation and reassembly functions associated with the Internet IP. In fact the ISO-IP supports both intranet and internet segmentation (fragmentation), although the latter is the default. When a PDU (or an NSDU) is segmented into a number of smaller PDUs – datagrams in IP terminology – the latter are known as **derived PDUs** while the former is known as the **initial PDU**. Also, with the ISO-IP the time-to-live field is known as the **PDU lifetime** and is in multiples of 500 milliseconds.

The fields in each data PDU (datagram) relating to the segmentation and reassembly functions are:

*   *segment length:* the number of octets (bytes) in the PDU including both header and data;

*   *segment offset:* the offset from the start of the first octet in the initial NSDU that the data in the segment begins;

*   *more segments flag:* set to one if this is not the last PDU relating to the initial PDU from which it was derived;

*   *total length:* specifies the entire length of the initial NSDU.

Derived PDUs are related to their initial NSDU by the source and destination NSAP addresses and an additional unique **data unit identifier** (DUI) that is assigned by the IP in the source ES when it is created. It is thus the same as the identification field in an IP datagram. Also, a **segmentation permitted flag** is used to indicate to the IP in each IS whether or not further segmentation is permitted. This is used during the routing of PDUs since, if segmentation is not permitted (flag = 0), a route (subnet) must be selected that can support the current size of the PDU. In the event of a suitable route not being available, the PDU is discarded and an error report is generated with the reason code set to destination unreachable. An example illustrates the use of each field.

EXAMPLE

Assume two NS-users are communicating over the internet shown earlier in Figure 9.10 and that the NSDU to be transferred is 1024 octets in length. Also, the SNDAPs associated with the three subnets are all connectionless with a maximum user data length of 512 octets for SN 1, 128 octets for SN 2 and 256 octets for SN 3. The header associated with each data PDU is fixed and is equal to 24 octets.

Assuming internet segmentation, derive the contents of the following fields in the header of each PDU as it is transferred across the three subnets:

*   total length,
*   segment length,
*   segment offset,

- more segment flag,
- data unit identifier.

(a)   *SN 1*
The user data field of SN 1 = 512 octets
Header = 24 octets and hence actual data = 488 octets
There are, therefore, three initial PDUs for SN 1: the first two with 488 data
octets and the third with 48 octets of data.
The contents of the various fields for each PDU are thus:

total length:	1024	1024	1024
segment length:	512	512	72
segment offset:	0	488	976
more segments flag:	1	1	0
data unit identifier, say,	20	20	20

(b)   *SN 2*
The user data field of SN 2 = 128 octets
Header = 24 octets and hence actual data = 104 octets
Hence the first two initial PDUs from SN 1 will each require five derived
PDUs for SN 2. The third can be transmitted without change.
The contents of the various fields in each derived PDU are thus:

total length:
1024 1024 1024 1024 1024 | 1024 1024 1024 1024 1024 | 1024
segment length:
 128 128 128 128   96 | 128 128 128 128 128 | 72
segment offset:
   0 104 208 316 424 | 488 592 696 800 904 | 976
DUI:
  20   20   20   20   20 | 20   20   20   20   20 | 20

(c)   *SN 3*
The data field with SN 3 = 256 octets and hence, with internet segmenta-
tion, all the incoming PDUs will be transmitted without change over SN 3.
   At the receiving IP in the destination ES:

(i)   from the total length it can proceed to reassemble a 1024-octet
       NSDU;
(ii)   the DUI with the source and destination addresses is used to relate all
       derived PDUs to the initial NSDU;
(iii) the segment offset relative to the NSDU total length can be used to
       reassemble all the segments in the correct sequence.

9.7.4 Routing

Again, the basic routing operation associated with the ISO-IP is similar to that
used with the IP except that different terminology is used. To enable each ES and
IS to build up the local routing information associated with a single subnet

(network), a protocol known as the **end system-to-intermediate system (ES-to-IS)** is used. This is defined in ISO 9542 and performs a similar function to the address resolution protocol (ARP) used with the IP. The protocol used for routing between intermediate systems (gateways) is known as the **intermediate system-to-intermediate system (IS-to-IS)** protocol. It is defined in ISO 10589 and performs a similar function to the internal gateway protocols (IGPs) used with the IP. Currently, there is no equivalent in the ISO-IP protocol set to the exterior gateway protocol (EGP) used with the IP.

Since routing is the major function associated with an SNICP and the terminology used with the ISO-IP is different, then it is helpful to describe the two routing protocols associated with the ISO-IP in some detail. Two routing protocols and their associated routing information databases are shown in Figure 9.21(a) and (b).

As the ES-to-IS and IS-to-IS routing protocols are both part of the SNICP sublayer, their PDUs are exchanged between systems using the same SNDCP/SNDAP sublayers as are used by the ISO-IP. The routing database in each ES – known as the **ES routing information base** or **ES-RIB** – is maintained solely by the ES-to-IS protocol, whereas that in each IS – known as the **IS routing information base** or **IS-RIB** – is maintained jointly by the ES-to-IS and IS-to-IS protocols.

A more detailed description of both protocols is given later in Section 9.8. Essentially, however, the PDUs relating to each protocol, containing the routing information, are created and exchanged periodically. Hence the information contained within each routing database is continuously being updated. At any point in time, however, the current contents of the two databases are used to route the data PDUs.

The scope of each protocol in relation to an example internet is shown in Figure 9.22(a); example entries in the two routing information bases for this internet are shown in parts (b) and (c). As can be seen, each RIB comprises a number of tables. For ease of identification, the SNPA addresses show only the identity of the particular subnet to which they relate. In practice, they may be ISO 8802 MAC addresses, CCITT X.121 addresses or even privately assigned addresses.

It should be remembered that the NSAP address is hierarchical and comprises an internet-wide subnet (plus area) identifier and a system identifier (ID) which uniquely identifies the NS-user/IS within the total internet. Also, that each IS has multiple SNPA addresses, one for each subnet to which it is attached, but a single system identifier. The latter is known as its **network entity title** or **NET** in ISO terminology.

Initially, the ESs attached to a subnet will not know the SNPA addresses of their local ISs; that is, the ISs attached to the same subnet. Similarly, ISs will not know the SNPA addresses of the ESs that are attached to its subnets. Thus, as part of the ES-to-IS protocol, each ES broadcasts its identity – NSAP, SNPA – over its local subnet, and each IS broadcasts its identity – NET, SNPA – over each of the subnets to which it is attached. Normally, ESs record only the NET, SNPA pairs of its local ISs while ISs record the NSAP, SNPA pairs of all the ESs attached to their subnets.

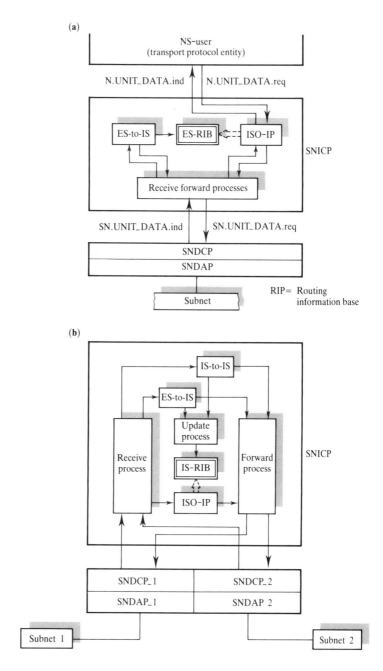

FIGURE 9.21

SNICP outline
structure: (a) ES; (b) IS.

Hence the minimum routing information in each ES comprises a list of
NET, SNPA pairs, one for each IS connected to the same subnet as the ES. These
are shown in part (b) of the figure and are used by an ES to forward each PDU to
an appropriate IS attached to the same subnet that will relay it to the necessary
destination. On receipt of a PDU, the IS will then either forward it to the

(a)

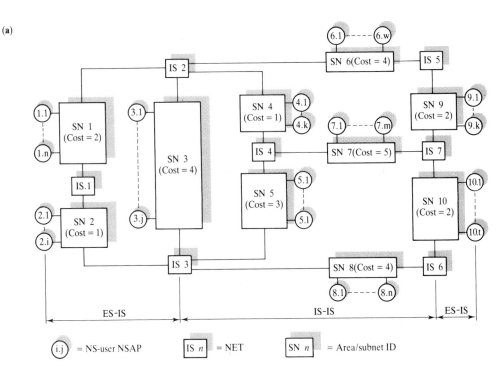

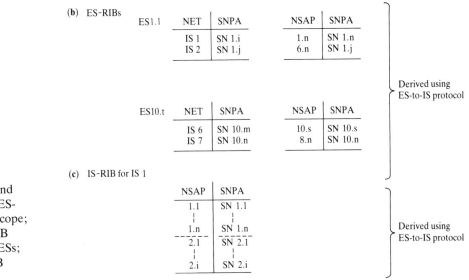

FIGURE 9.22

Example internet and routing tables: (a) ES-to-IS and IS-to-IS scope; (b) example ES-RIB tables for selected ESs; (c) example IS-RIB tables for IS 1.

Circuits database:

SN ID	Costs
SN 1	2, X, Y, Z
SN 2	1, X', Y', Z'

Adjacency database:

NET	SNPA
IS 2	SN 1.j
IS 3	SN 2.i

Entered by network management

Link-state database:

IS 1: SN 1, 2/SN 2, 1
IS 2: SN 1, 2/SN 3, 4/SN 4, 1/SN 6, 4
IS 3: SN 2, 1/SN 3, 4/SN 5, 3/SN 8, 4
IS 4: SN 4, 1/SN 5, 3/SN 7, 5
IS 5: SN 6, 4/SN 9, 2
IS 6: SN 8, 4/SN 10, 2
IS 7: SN 7, 5/SN 9, 2/SN 10, 2

Forwarding information base:

SN ID	Attached NETs
SN 1	IS 1, IS 2
SN 2	IS 1, IS 3
SN 3	IS 2, IS 3
SN 4	IS 2, IS 4
SN 5	IS 3, IS 4
SN 6	IS 2, IS 5
SN 7	IS 4, IS 7
SN 8	IS 3, IS 6
SN 9	IS 5, IS 7
SN 10	IS 6, IS 7

NET	Path , Cost
IS 1	Load, 0
IS 2	IS 2 , 2
IS 3	IS 3 , 1
IS 4	IS 2 , 3
IS 5	IS 2 , 6
IS 6	IS 3 , 5
IS 7	IS 3 , 7

Derived using IS-to-IS protocol

FIGURE 9.22 (cont.)

(c) Example IS-RIB tables for IS 1.

destination ES directly if it is attached to one of its local subnets or to a **neighbour IS** if the PDU is to be routed to a remote subnet. Two ISs are said to be neighbours if they are both attached to the same subnet.

The list of subnets that are attached to an IS, together with their path costs, are entered by network management and kept in a table known as the **circuits database**. Another table known as the **adjacency database** is used to hold the NETs of the neighbours of an IS together with their SNPA addresses.

Concurrently with PDUs being exchanged as part of the ES-to-IS protocol, neighbour ISs exchange routing information with one another as part of the IS-to-IS protocol. This is contained within IS-to-IS PDUs known as **link state PDUs**. Each PDU contains a list of the subnets (links) that are currently attached (and hence are reachable) via the IS that sends the PDU, together with their corresponding path cost values (one for each metric being used). Thus, on receipt of a link state PDU, the IS-to-IS protocol first initiates entry/confirmation of the NET of the sending IS in its adjacency database and recording of the information contained within the PDU – using the **update process** – in another table known as the **link state database**. It then forwards a copy of the PDU to each of its neighbours except for the one that sent the PDU. In this way, all the ISs in the internet build up the same connectivity matrix (graph) of the internet with the ISs as nodes, the current direct links (subnets) that exist between them and the costs associated with each link.

A new set of link state PDUs is initiated at regular intervals. After each new set has been received, each IS performs an algorithm, known as the **shortest path first (SPF)**, on the updated connectivity matrix. The actual operation of the SPF will be described later in Section 9.8. Essentially, however, it computes the shortest path between a specified source IS and all the other ISs – and hence subnets – in the internet. The output of the SPF is then entered into one of two tables that are collectively known as the **forwarding information base** or **FIB**. The other table is derived directly from the link state database and contains the list of ISs (NETs) that are attached to each subnet in the internet.

After both procedures have been carried out, the internet is ready to route data PDUs between any pair of NS-users (ESs). The ISO-IP in the source ES simply sends each data PDU to one of its local ISs using the latter's SNPA address obtained from its RIB. The ISO-IP in the receiving IS first determines the subnet identifier from the destination NSAP address in the PDU and then consults its FIB to determine where it should be forwarded to. If it is for an ES attached to one of its own subnets, it sends it directly to that ES. If it is for an ES attached to a remote subnet, however, then it sends it to the neighbour IS (adjacency) which is on the shortest path to its intended destination. For example, for the internet in part (b) of Figure 9.22, if the destination ES is attached to subnet 5 then it can be reached via either IS 3 or IS 4. The path costs to reach each of these are one and three units, respectively, hence IS 3 is chosen.

In addition, after forwarding the PDU, if it was addressed to an ES that is attached to the same subnet as the source ES, as part of the ES-to-IS protocol, the IS sends another PDU to the source ES containing the NSAP, SNPA pair of the destination ES. This informs the source ES of the SNPA of the destination ES just requested. The source ES can then (optionally) make an entry in its RIB to enable it to send future PDUs directly to the destination ES.

In the same way, the IS may inform the ES if a better IS connected to the same subnet – that is, one with a more direct path – should be used for routing PDUs to the destination NSAP contained within the earlier PDU. Thus the NSAP entries shown in the ES-RIBs in part (b) of Figure 9.22 are intended to be arbitrary ESs that the NS-user in the ES has called.

It may be deduced from the foregoing that for large internets comprising many hundreds of subnets, each with a large number of attached ESs, the FIB in each IS will be very large. It is for this reason that large addressing domains are divided into a number of **areas**. Also, although only a single FIB is shown in the figure for each IS, in practice there may be a number of FIBs, one for each routing metric. Again this will be expanded upon in Section 9.8.

The interactions between the various sublayers during the forwarding process are shown in Figure 9.23. On receipt of an NS-user request, the IP in the source ES first creates a data PDU (DT_PDU) using the parameters associated

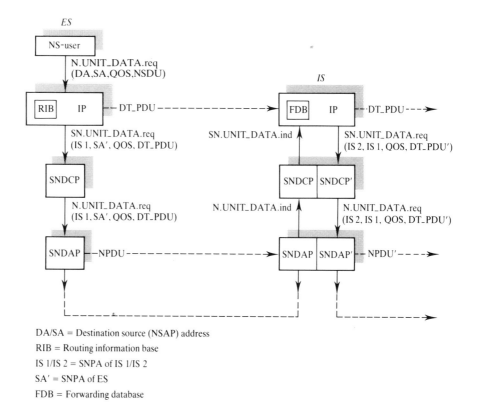

FIGURE 9.23

Sublayer interactions.

DA/SA = Destination source (NSAP) address
RIB = Routing information base
IS 1/IS 2 = SNPA of IS 1/IS 2
SA' = SNPA of ES
FDB = Forwarding database

with the request. It then consults its RIB and initiates the sending of the PDU using the subnet request service with the SNPA address of the IS obtained from the RIB as the destination address parameter and the created PDU as user data. In the figure, it is assumed that both subnets are connectionless. Hence, on receipt of the network request, each SNDAP in turn creates a new NPDU with the DT_PDU in the data field and the IS SNPA from the RIB in the destination address field. It then forwards this in the normal way.

A similar procedure is then followed in the IS. The PDU is first passed up through the sublayers of the subnet as user data to the IP. The IP then consults the FIB – using the destination NSAP address from the PDU – to determine the SNPA address either of the ES, if it is attached to a local subnet, or of the IS attached to an adjacent subnet, if it is for a remote subnet. Assuming no segmentation is necessary, the PDU will then be forwarded unchanged on the adjacent subnet using the SNDCP service with the address of the next IS obtained from the FIB as a parameter.

The foregoing assumed that, for PDUs addressed to remote subnets, the RIB in each ES contained only the SNPA address of the first (local) IS involved in the route. In some instances, however, the RIB may contain not just a single entry but rather the complete (or partial) list of IS identifiers (NETs) involved in a route. This information is obtained by the IP in a source ES selecting the **record route** parameter in the PDU options field. When this is set, the IP in each IS that processes the PDU, in addition to routing the PDU, records the NET of the IS in the options field. In this way the route followed by the PDU is built up as it traverses the internet. This information can then be stored in the RIB at the destination ES and subsequently used for forwarding PDUs in the reverse direction. A similar procedure is followed in the reverse direction. Thus, after the first exchange of PDUs, a route between the two ESs will be known.

When using this feature, the IP in the ES receiving requests for an ES whose route is known, simply loads the complete list of IS identifiers into the options field and selects the **source routing** parameter code. Associated with this field is an offset which is incremented as the PDU is forwarded from one IS to the next. Hence, on receipt of a PDU for which the source routing parameter is selected, the IP simply accesses the identity of the next IS in the list, increments the offset, and then initiates the forwarding of the PDU to that IS.

The IS-to-IS protocol, as will be explained, endeavours to maintain the entries in all routing tables up-to-date so that they reflect current traffic distributions and IS failures. As a result, in the event of an IS failure, all recorded routes involving that IS will only be partially valid. If this is the case, then only the partial list will be loaded and the **partial source routing** parameter selected. After reaching the last entry in the list, the remaining part of the route will be derived dynamically from the entries in the FIBs of the ISs involved.

In addition to being used for routing, the record route option can be used for network management functions. By analysing routes followed by PDUs, a knowledge of the behaviour of the internet can be obtained and potential problems/bottlenecks identified. Indeed, this is the principal function of the record route option as the normal dynamic routing method will, in general, yield the optimum route to be followed by each PDU.

9.7.5 Flow and congestion control

Since the ISO-IP is a connectionless protocol, flow control is not applied on a per call basis within the internet. It is thus left to the transport protocol entities in each ES to control the flow of data relating to each call on an end-to-end basis. As will be described in the next chapter, the flow control algorithm used with a connection-oriented (reliable) transport protocol is based on a modified sliding-window mechanism similar to that used with the X.25 packet layer protocol described in the last chapter. Hence, as congestion within the internet starts to build up, the flow control information relating to calls that pass through the congested region(s) will be delayed and consequently the transport entities will slow down the entry of new NSDUs. The internet thus introduces an additional form of **implicit flow control** on affected calls. Although this will help to alleviate congestion within the internet, it will not necessarily stop new calls being set up. In the limit, if the number of calls continues to build up, then the flow of PDUs relating to all calls will be affected.

As indicated earlier, congestion arises when the number of NSDUs (and hence data PDUs) entering the internet starts to approach the total resources available within the internet to handle them. Or, at a more local level, an individual IS will become congested if the number of PDUs entering the IS starts to approach its total available resources. Since all subnets operate in a store-and-forward mode, the resources include the processing capacity within each IS which is used to process received PDUs and the number of memory buffers that are available to store PDUs waiting to be forwarded on a particular outgoing link.

Normally, ISs are designed to be able to process received PDUs faster than the combined maximum rate at which they can arrive. Thus only a single input buffer is required for each input link. However, since two or more PDUs received on different input links may need to be forwarded on the same output link after processing, a separate (output) queue is needed for each output link. As the internet load increases and the rate of arrival of PDUs increases, so the size of the output queues will build up and increasing delays will be experienced in each IS. This signals the start of congestion and, in the limit, if all the buffers become full, the available resources are exceeded. The IS is then said to be overloaded and delays experienced by PDUs will increase rapidly. The effect of congestion on the performance of an internet (or an IS) is shown in Figure 9.24.

Part (a) shows that although in the ideal case the maximum mean throughput rate of PDUs will be maintained when overload occurs, without a congestion control algorithm this will not necessarily happen in practice. This is so because the segmentation and reassembly function carried out within the internet

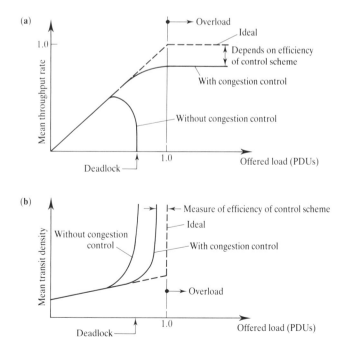

FIGURE 9.24

Effect of congestion on:
(a) throughput;
(b) transit delay.

can cause a phenomenon known as **deadlock** to occur. It is thus necessary to incorporate a congestion control scheme in each IS to avoid deadlock. However, as such schemes are not perfect, the actual throughput will be less than that in the ideal case. The difference between the two is thus a measure of the efficiency of the congestion control scheme being used. The effect of congestion and overload on the mean transit delay experienced by PDUs is shown in part (b) of the figure. This is directly related to the mean throughput graph.

The feature incorporated into the protocol to help control congestion on an internet-wide basis is for the IP in the source ES to monitor the performance of the internet and, if congestion is suspected, to start to reject new N.UNIT_ DATA.requests. This is done by returning an N.REPORT.indication to the source NS-user with the reason code set to internet congestion. The IP in ESs monitor the performance of the internet by maintaining counts of selected parameters in internet-generated **error report PDUs**. If the number of such PDUs received with internet congestion as the reason code is above a defined threshold, the IP will start to reject new requests. This has a similar effect to using flow control at the DTE/DCE interface in an X.25 packet switching network.

Another feature in the protocol that helps to alleviate (rather than control) congestion on an internet-wide basis is the inclusion of the PDU lifetime field in each initial and derived PDU. As indicated earlier, this is first set by the IP in the source ES and then decremented by each IP that processes the PDU. If it reaches zero at any point during its transit across the internet, it is discarded. Hence, in the event of one or more ISs becoming congested, the PDU lifetime associated with affected PDUs will expire on processing and they will be discarded. This means that as long as the timeout interval used by transport entities in ESs exceeds twice the PDU lifetime value – to allow related acknowledgement information to be returned – unnecessary duplicate copies of NSDUs should not be sent. The inclusion of the PDU lifetime field thus provides a form of **implicit congestion control** by avoiding multiple copies of PDUs being sent by ESs into the internet.

Although such schemes endeavour to control congestion on an internet-wide basis, uneven traffic distributions mean that they will not necessarily stop individual ISs from becoming overloaded. Consequently, additional procedures must be incorporated into the basic operation of each IS to minimize the possibility of this occurring.

Before describing the types of congestion that can occur within an IS, it is perhaps helpful to describe the distribution and use of the memory buffers associated with the SNICP sublayer. A typical layout is shown in Figure 9.25(a). In this example it is assumed that 12 buffers are available and that intranet segmentation is being used. Thus all (derived) PDUs received must be re-assembled before they can be processed.

At any point in time, the 12 buffers will be distributed between input buffers (one per subnet), reassembly buffers and output queues. In practice, once a PDU has been received and stored in a (memory) buffer, all references to the PDU are made relative to the start address of the buffer, which is known as the **buffer pointer**. When buffers (PDUs) are being transferred from one place to another, it is the buffer pointers that are transferred and not the buffer contents.

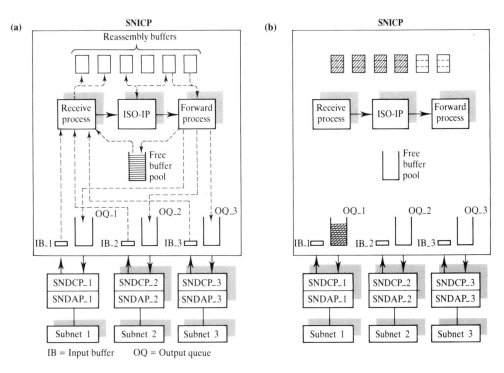

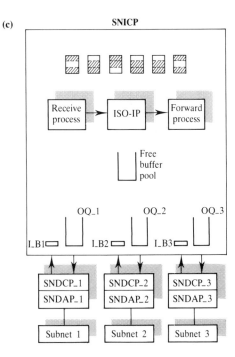

FIGURE 9.25

Congestion possibilities:
(a) buffer usage;
(b) direct store-and-forward deadlock;
(c) reassembly deadlock.

On receipt of a (derived) PDU in an input buffer (from the SNDCP), the receive process transfers it to the appropriate reassembly buffer, obtains a new buffer from the free buffer pool and transfers it to the input buffer ready for receipt of the next PDU. If the received PDU completes an initial PDU, this is transferred by the receive process to the ISO-IP for processing.

In the example, it is assumed that the packet sizes associated with the three subnets are the same. Thus the ISO-IP simply changes the appropriate fields in each derived PDU and passes these to the forward process for forwarding. The forward process reads the destination NSAP address from each PDU, consults the FIB for the output link (subnet) to be used and transfers the buffer to the tail of the appropriate output queue. The SNDCP associated with this output queue then initiates the sending of the PDU and the freed buffer is returned to the free buffer pool by the forward process.

The most basic cause of congestion can be deduced by considering the buffer distribution shown in part (b) of Figure 9.25. It is assumed that the three subnet inputs are operating near their maximum capacity and that all received PDUs from these links, after reassembly, require to be forwarded on the same output link. Hence, if the three links operate at the same rate, the output queue associated with link (subnet) 1 will start to build up, thereby increasing the transit delays experienced by PDUs using that link. Moreover, if this condition continues, in the limit all the buffers will become full and queued for output link 1. Any new PDUs will then be discarded as there are no free buffers to store them, even though they may require a different output link.

It should be noted that increasing the number of buffers will not necessarily help the problem since this may simply allow a single output queue to become even longer. The increased delays experienced by PDUs waiting to be forwarded in those queues, therefore, is likely to result in the timers being used by the transport protocol entities in ESs to expire. The latter will thus start to retransmit the affected NSDUs – and hence PDUs – which, in turn, will simply increase the load on the affected links.

A more subtle type of congestion can be deduced by considering the buffer distribution shown in part (c) of Figure 9.25. In this example it is assumed that intranet segmentation is being used and hence all received (derived) PDUs must be reassembled before being forwarded. If we assume that 12 memory buffers are available and that each initial PDU comprises three derived PDUs, then none of the six initial PDUs being reassembled is complete and can be forwarded. However, the absence of any further memory buffers means that no new PDUs can be received to complete any of them. Deadlock is then said to have occurred since the flow of all PDUs through the IS will come to a halt. This type of congestion is known as **reassembly deadlock** or **reassembly lockup**. A similar condition can arise at an ES with internet segmentation.

Congestion of the type shown in part (b) of Figure 9.25 can be controlled by limiting the number of PDUs that are allowed to be queued for a single output link. Allowing all the buffers to be queued for a single link causes PDUs using that link to experience unacceptable delays and affects the flow of PDUs on all other links since no free buffers are available to receive them. To avoid this happening, a limit is set on the number of buffers that can be queued on each output link. Normally, the limit is set so that a free buffer is always available for each input link in addition to a minimum number of buffers available for each of the other output links. Firstly, this ensures a flow of PDUs on all links in the presence of congestion. Secondly, it sets a maximum limit on the delays experienced within each IS. The latter can be particularly helpful when determining the value to be assigned to the PDU lifetime value carried in each PDU. This is important with large internets comprising many subnets.

In practice, determining the optimum number of buffers to allow to be queued for a single output link – as a percentage of the total number of buffers available – is a complex issue and depends on the number of output links and the routing scheme being used. Also, the optimum value is not static since it varies with the loading of the IS, thus implying some form of dynamic allocation.

Although many schemes have been researched, the scheme that has been shown to give a good (not optimum) level of performance in a large internet – ARPANET – is based on an empirical formula that defines the maximum number of buffers per link as a function of the number of links and the number of free buffers being used. Known as the **square root limiter**, it is the scheme that is currently proposed for use with the ISO-IP. The formula is as follows:

$$U_d = \frac{N_b}{\sqrt{N_c}}$$

where: U_d = the maximum buffer limit in a link output queue; N_b = the number of free buffers available (excluding input buffers); N_c = the number of (active) output links.

In addition, a minimum number of buffers is dedicated to each output link to ensure that flow is not stopped on these links when one (or more) other links are overloaded. An example is shown in Figure 9.26(a).

In the example, it is assumed that internet segmentation is being used so no reassembly of PDUs is required, and that the three subnets all use the same maximum packet size. It also assumes that there are 12 free buffers available plus an additional three buffers for use with the input links. The maximum number of entries in each output queue is thus 6 $(12/\sqrt{3})$. Hence sufficient buffers are available to ensure that there is a single buffer for each input link and a minimum of two buffers for each output link. Thus if a new PDU is received for forwarding on link 3, it will be discarded and the freed buffer returned to the buffer pool. If a new PDU is received for forwarding on either link 1 or link 2, however, then these can be forwarded as they are unaffected by the overload on link 3. Similarly, if the situation arises in which, say, OQ_2 and OQ_3 contain four and six entries, respectively, and a PDU is to be forwarded on either of these links, then it will be discarded to ensure that at least two buffers are available for OQ_1.

If intranet segmentation is being used, it is also necessary to control the allocation of buffers for reassembly purposes to prevent reassembly deadlock. One scheme is to set a limit on the number of initial PDUs that can be in the

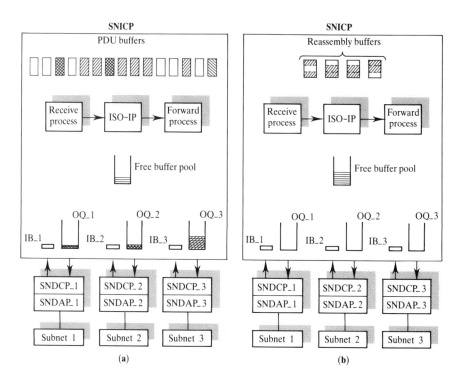

FIGURE 9.26

Congestion control:
(a) square root limiting
(internet segmentation);
(b) reassembly deadlock
control (intranet
segmentation).

process of reassembly at any point in time and, when this limit is reached, discard any derived PDUs that are received relating to new PDUs. In this way, since the maximum size of PDUs being used with each subnet connected to the IS is known, the IS can ensure that it will always have enough free buffers available to complete the reassembly processing.

An example is shown in part (b) of Figure 9.26. Again, intranet segmentation is assumed and each initial PDU comprises three derived PDUs. By setting a limit of four initial PDUs being reassembled at any point in time, no reassembly deadlock will occur with 12 buffers with three additional buffers for the input buffers.

It should be noted that these congestion control schemes are not part of the protocol as such but rather examples of **buffer management**. A number of variations of these basic schemes are possible. The aim of all such schemes, however, is to ensure that a flow of PDUs is maintained even in the presence of temporary overload conditions.

In conclusion, it should be said that discarding PDUs is not an ideal solution since it will inevitably lead to an increase in the transit delay associated with the internet. It is, however, necessary if congestion and deadlock are to be controlled. The subject of congestion control in large internets, together with the allied subject of routing, are still active areas of research.

9.7.6 Error reporting

As shown earlier in Figure 9.20, each data PDU contains an **error report (ER) flag** in its header. This flag enables the IP in a source ES to request that it is informed if another IP, either in an IS or the destination ES, discards the PDU during its transit across the internet. Then, if it is set and the PDU is discarded by an IS, the latter generates an **error report PDU** with a reason code indicating why the PDU was discarded, the identity of the PDU and where in the internet the error was detected. It then replaces the destination (NSAP) address with the source address from the data PDU and initiates the return of the PDU to the source IP in the normal way.

The IP in each ES is thus able to build up knowledge of the performance of the internet by maintaining counts of the various reason codes during a particular monitoring period. The use of a flag means that such PDUs are only generated when an ES wishes to update its knowledge of the internet performance.

A PDU may be discarded for a number of reasons, including:

- IS congestion,
- PDU lifetime expired,
- destination address unreachable.

By maintaining counts of the error report PDUs received either with a reason code of IS congestion or PDU lifetime expired, the IP in a source ES can detect the onset of congestion and, if necessary, start to reject new NS-user service requests. Similarly, counts of the reason codes PDU lifetime expired and destination address unreachable can help to determine the efficiency of the routing protocol being used.

Finally, the checksum field in the header of each data (and error report) PDU is included to minimize the probability of a PDU being processed with erroneous fields. It is normally software generated and comprises two octets. The algorithm used is the same as that used with transport protocol data units. The latter is described in the next chapter and will not be discussed here. The checksum is verified each time fields in the PDU are processed and before processing takes place. If the fields in the PDU are changed by the processing, then a new checksum for the PDU is computed. In the event of a checksum error being detected with the ER flag set, an error report PDU will be generated with a reason code set to checksum error.

9.8 ISO ROUTING PROTOCOLS

An outline structure of the SNICP sublayer showing the two ISO routing protocols in each end and intermediate system and their relationship with the ISO-IP was shown in Figure 9.21. The routing information contained within the ES-RIB in each ES and the IS-RIB in each IS is created from the routing information exchanged as part of the ES-to-IS and IS-to-IS protocols. The PDUs relating to both protocols are periodically created and exchanged. Consequently, the information contained within each database is continuously being updated and thus reflects the current active topology of the internet. At any instant, however, the current contents of the two databases are used to route a data PDU to the next IS involved in the route to the destination NSAP address contained within it. As the routing procedure was described in Section 9.7.4, this section is concerned only with how this information is built-up using the two routing protocols.

9.8.1 ES-to-IS protocol

It may be recalled that a PDU relating to the ISO-IP cannot be routed directly by inspecting the destination NSAP address contained within it. Normally, all routing information is held at ISs. Hence, to send a PDU, a source ES must first send it to one of the ISs attached to the same subnet. To be able to do this, all the ESs on each subnet must know the SNPA addresses of their local ISs. Also, for an IS to be able to route PDUs received from other subnets, it must know the NSAP, SNPA address pairs of all the ESs attached to its local subnets. This is the basic role of the ES-to-IS protocol.

The protocol operates by each ES and IS broadcasting its identity over its local subnet(s). It is intended, therefore, for use with broadcast subnetworks such as LANs since the overheads of a system broadcasting to all other systems are low. Clearly, to carry out the same function with a general (mesh) topology subnet would involve prohibitively high overheads, especially if a large number of ESs are involved. With such subnets, the equivalent routing information must be loaded into each system (ES and IS) by other means, such as by network management.

There are three PDU types associated with the ES-to-IS protocol. Namely:

- End system hello, ESH – this is used by an ES to inform all ISs on the subnet of the NS-user NSAP(s) in that ES.

- Intermediate system hello, ISH – this is used by an IS to inform all ESs on each of its subnets of its NET.

- Redirect, RD – this is used by an IS to inform an ES of the SNPA address on its own subnet either of the destination NSAP just requested or the NET of another (better) IS to route PDUs to that NSAP.

Each of the PDUs comprises a common header part, an address part and an options part. The general structure of each PDU type is shown in Figure 9.27. All the fields in the header part have the same meaning as those used with ISO-IP data (and error) PDUs except that the **holding time** field replaces the segment length. Since no data is associated with these PDUs, the segment length is not required. The holding time is used to specify the maximum time for which the receiving protocol entity should retain the address (routing) information contained within

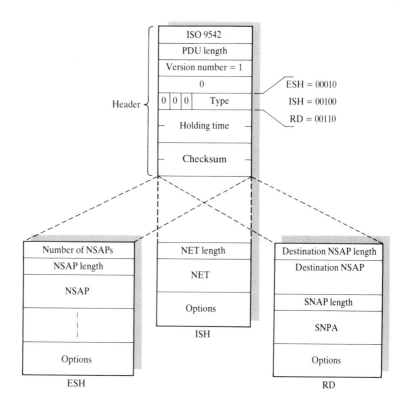

FIGURE 9.27

ES-to-IS PDU
structure.

the PDU. To ensure that address information relating to each ES and IS is kept up-to-date, new information is exchanged at regular intervals by each system. Thus the holding time essentially ages the current address information and, if an ES is switched off, its routing entry will automatically be removed from the RIB in each IS until it is switched on again and makes a new network request.

The address part of each PDU contains the NSAP, NET and/or SNPA addresses, depending on the particular PDU type. Finally, the contents of the options part are similar to those used with the ISO-IP.

Two broadcast (group) addresses are associated with the protocol for broadcasting PDUs: the **all ES** and the **all IS**. Then, in order for an ES to inform its local ISs of its presence on the subnet (and its SNPA address), it creates an ESH PDU containing the NSAP address(es) currently present in this ES and issues an SN.UNIT_DATA.request primitive to its SNDCP with the PDU as user data and the all IS as the destination address.

The broadcast address used on a particular subnet to reach all ISs may vary for different subnets, with any translation being carried out by the SNDCP. When the local SNDAP broadcasts the PDU, it includes the SNPA of the ES as the source address in the particular subnet NPDU. On receipt of the NPDU, the peer SNDAP in the IS passes the SNPA up as a parameter (with the ESH PDU) to the

ES-to-IS protocol. The latter then makes an entry – NSAP, SNPA – in its RIB which is retained until the specified holding time expires.

Similarly, in order for the ESs attached to a subnet to learn the SNPA addresses of its local ISs, each IS broadcasts an ISH PDU at regular intervals with its NET in the address field. The corresponding SNPA is again received as a parameter with the PDU by all active ESs. The ES-to-IS protocol in the latter then make an entry – NET, SNPA – in their RIBs.

Finally, the RD PDU is used by an IS to inform an ES attached to one of its local subnets of the SNPA address either of another local NS-user NSAP or of a better IS which can be used to reach the destination NSAP specified in an earlier data PDU. It may be recalled that this information – NSAP, SNPA – may be (optionally) retained in its RIB to speed up the routing process.

9.8.2 Routing algorithm

Before describing the operation of the IS-to-IS protocol, it is helpful to describe the routing algorithm used by ISs to route PDUs across the internet. It is known as the **shortest path first algorithm**. There are a number of such algorithms but the one used by ISO is the **Dijkstra algorithm**. This algorithm is already used in a number of large networks, including ARPANET.

Since all routing is carried out by ISs, for routing purposes an internet is considered simply as a distributed community of ISs that are interconnected by (logical) links. In practice, the links may be a path through a LAN or WAN or a direct point-to-point link. Associated with each link are a number of **routing metrics** each of which has a **cost value** associated with it. These are:

- Capacity – this is a measure of the throughput of the circuit in bits per second, a higher value indicating a lower capacity. This is the default metric that is used in practice.

- Delay – this relates to the mean transit delay associated with a link (subnet) and thus includes the queuing delays in bridges and exchanges. Again a higher value indicates a longer transit delay.

- Expense – this is a measure of the monetary cost of using a link, a high value indicating a larger monetary cost. Clearly, if a private subnet can be used then this will be preferable to using, say, a link through a switched public carrier subnet.

- Error – this is a measure of the mean residual error probability associated with the circuit, higher values indicating a larger probability of undetected error.

It may be recalled that all the above relate to parameters of the QOS which is therefore used when selecting the routing metric.

The term **path cost** is used to indicate the aggregate total cost of the links used in a particular path (route) through the internet between any pair of ESs. The path cost associated with a route may thus differ from one metric to another. The term shortest path cost therefore refers to a path (route) using a single routing metric.

The shortest path first algorithm can best be described by considering a specific internet, such as the one shown in Figure 9.22 which was used to describe the ISO-IP routing procedure. A simplified representation of this is shown in Figure 9.28(a).

The links between each IS are shown as point-to-point circuits each with an associated cost value which may vary for different metrics. For each metric, however, the task is to find the path (route) through the internet from a signal source IS to each of the other ISs in the internet that has the minimum aggregate cost associated with it. The various steps in the algorithm are shown in parts (b) through (h) of the figure. The example assumes that IS 1 is the source.

Associated with each of the other ISs is a measure (shown in parentheses) of the aggregate distance from that IS back to the source IS via the IS indicated. Thus an entry of (2, IS 4) means that the cost of the path back to IS 1 is two units via IS 4. Initially, the path costs to all ISs not directly connected to the source are unknown and are therefore marked with an infinite path cost figure; that is, the largest possible cost. Also, until a cost value is known to be the minimum cost, it is said to be **tentative** and the IS box is shown unshaded. When the shortest path cost from an IS to the source is known, it is then said to be **permanent** and the IS box is shaded.

Initially, since IS 1 is the source it is shown shaded. Also, the path costs to the two directly-connected (neighbour) ISs – IS 2 and IS 3 – are shown equal to their respective link path costs. Thus IS 2 has an entry (2, IS 1), indicating the cost is two units to get back to IS 1 directly, while IS 3 has an entry of (1, IS 3). All the other costs remain at their maximum value. The IS with the minimum cost value is then chosen from *all* the ISs that are still tentative. Clearly this is IS 3 with a cost of 1. Hence this is now marked as permanent and the new set of aggregate path cost values from IS 3 computed. These are shown in part (c) of the figure.

For example, the entry for IS 4 of (4, IS 3) indicates that the aggregate path cost back to the source via IS 3 is four units – three to get back to IS 3 and a further one to return to IS 1. In the case of IS 2, since the path cost via IS 3 would be five units – four plus one – then the existing smaller tentative value is left unchanged. The IS with the minimum cost value is again chosen from all those that remain tentative; this is IS 2 with a cost value of 2. This is therefore marked permanent and the new path costs computed from this IS, as shown in part (d).

As can be seen, the new path cost for IS 4 via IS 2 is only three units, so the existing entry is replaced by (3, IS 2). Once all the other distances have been computed, the minimum is again chosen – IS 4 – and the procedure repeated. The remaining steps are thus as shown in parts (e) through (h).

Finally, having determined the minimum path cost value from IS 1 to all other ISs – that is, they are all now permanent – the shortest (minimum) path cost routes from IS 1 to each of the other ISs can be determined. These are shown in part (i) of the figure. Thus to get to, say, IS 5 from IS 1, the route is IS 1 → IS 2 → IS 5.

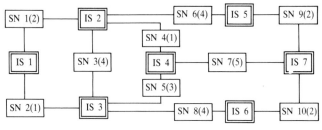

(a) Internet topology

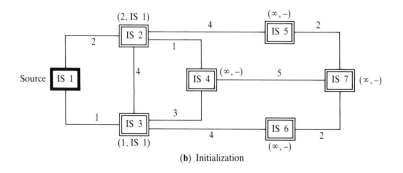

(b) Initialization

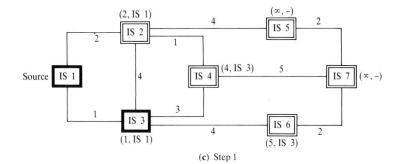

(c) Step 1

FIGURE 9.28

Shortest path-cost route
calculations.

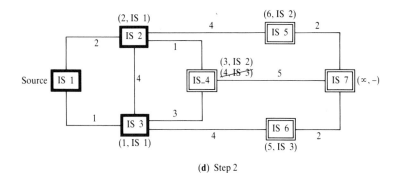

(d) Step 2

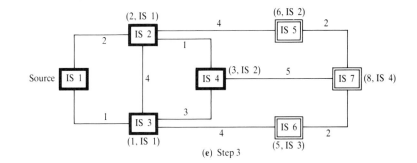

(e) Step 3

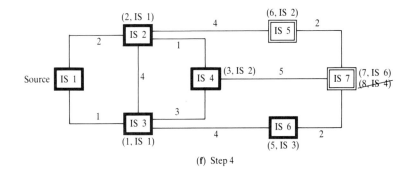

(f) Step 4

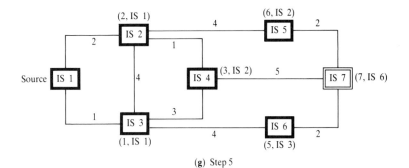

(g) Step 5

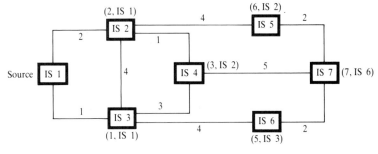

FIGURE 9.28 (cont.)

Shortest path-cost route calculations.

(h) Final path costs from IS 1

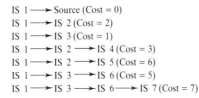

IS 1 ⟶ Source (Cost = 0)
IS 1 ⟶ IS 2 (Cost = 2)
IS 1 ⟶ IS 3 (Cost = 1)
IS 1 ⟶ IS 2 ⟶ IS 4 (Cost = 3)
IS 1 ⟶ IS 2 ⟶ IS 5 (Cost = 6)
IS 1 ⟶ IS 3 ⟶ IS 6 (Cost = 5)
IS 1 ⟶ IS 3 ⟶ IS 6 ⟶ IS 7 (Cost = 7)

(i) Shortest path cost routes from IS 1

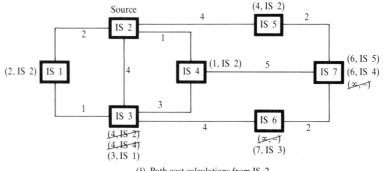

(j) Path cost calculations from IS 2

IS 2 ⟶ IS 1 (Cost = 2)
IS 2 ⟶ Source (Cost = 0)
IS 2 ⟶ IS 1 ⟶ IS 3 (Cost = 3)
IS 2 ⟶ IS 4 (Cost = 1)
IS 2 ⟶ IS 5 (Cost = 4)
IS 2 ⟶ IS 1 ⟶ IS 3 ⟶ IS 6 (Cost = 7)
IS 2 ┬⟶ IS 4 ⟶ IS 7 (Cost = 6)
     └⟶ IS 5 ⟶ IS 7 (Cost = 6)

(k) Shortest path cost routes from IS 2

FIGURE 9.28 (cont.)

Shortest path-cost route
calculations.

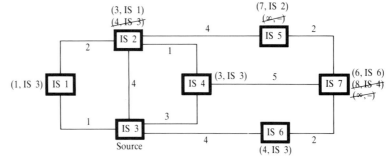

(l) Path cost calculations from IS 3

IS 3 ⟶ IS 1 (Cost = 1)
IS 3 ⟶ IS 1 ⟶ IS 2 (Cost = 3)
IS 3 ⟶ Source (Cost = 0)
IS 3 ⟶ IS 4 (Cost = 3)
IS 3 ⟶ IS 1 ⟶ IS 2 ⟶ IS 5 (Cost = 7)
IS 3 ⟶ IS 6 (Cost = 4)
IS 3 ⟶ IS 6 ⟶ IS 7 (Cost = 6)

(**m**) Shortest path cost routes from IS 3

IS 1: Destination	Path, Cost	IS 2: Destination	Path, Cost	IS 3: Destination	Path, Cost
IS 1	–	IS 1	IS 1,2	IS 1	IS 1,1
IS 2	IS 2,2	IS 2	–	IS 2	IS 1,3
IS 3	IS 3,1	IS 3	IS 1,3	IS 3	–
IS 4	IS 2,3	IS 4	IS 4,1	IS 4	IS 4,3
IS 5	IS 2,6	IS 5	IS 5,4	IS 5	IS 1,7
IS 6	IS 3,5	IS 6	IS 1,7	IS 6	IS 6,4
IS 7	IS 3,7	IS 7	IS 4/IS 5,6	IS 7	IS 6,6

FIGURE 9.28 (cont.)

Shortest path-cost route
calculations.

(**n**) Routing table examples

Now consider the same procedure applied first with IS 2 as the source and then with IS 3. The final path cost values associated with each IS together with their corresponding shortest path cost routes are shown in parts (j) through (m). Some observations can now be made about the algorithm:

● If two ISs have the same computed path cost associated with them, then an arbitrary selection can be made as to which is made permanent.

● If a new computed path cost for a tentative IS via a different route (IS) is the same as that already shown, both can be retained since load sharing then becomes possible.

● If an IS is on the shortest path cost route from IS 1 to another destination IS, then it is also the shortest path from that IS to the same destination. For example, the shortest route from IS 1 to IS 7 is IS 1 → IS 3 → IS 6 → IS 7 and the route from IS 3 is IS 3 → IS 6 → IS 7.

● The computed shortest path cost routes are reversible; for example, IS 2 → IS 1 → IS 3 → and IS 3 → IS 1 → IS 2.

The combined effect of this is that if each IS computes its own set of shortest paths from itself to all other ISs, then the paths computed for each IS will coincide one with another. This means, that it is only necessary for an IS to retain routing information to allow it to route a PDU to the first (neighbour) IS on the route; that is, routing can be carried out on a **hop-by-hop** basis. The routing tables for IS 1, IS 2 and IS 3 are thus as shown in part (n) of the figure.

9.8.3 IS-to-IS protocol

The aim of the IS-to-IS protocol is to determine the contents of the FIB in each IS; that is, the neighbour ISs (adjacencies) to be used when routing ISO-IP data PDUs. Before the route-finding algorithm can be started, however, each IS must first establish the NET, SNPA pair of each of its neighbours.

In the case of broadcast subnets, this is done by each IS broadcasting an **IS-to-IS (II) PDU** on each of its subnets using the All IS destination address. This contains the NET of the source IS within it and each receiving SNDAP passes the corresponding SNPA address (on this subnet) up to the IS-to-IS protocol as a parameter using the intermediate SNDCP. For non-broadcast subnets, this must again be entered by network management. In either event, this information is stored in a separate database known as the **adjacency database**. Once this has been carried out, the IS-to-IS protocol can take part in the shortest path cost derivation procedure.

It may be recalled that the identities of the subnets that are attached to an IS, together with their cost metrics, are entered into a table (known as the **circuit database**) by network management. At regular intervals, therefore, each IS (the IS-to-IS protocol, in practice) sends to each of its neighbours a **link state (LS) PDU** containing the NET of the IS, and a list of the identifiers of the subnets to which the IS is attached together with the cost values (one for each metric) associated with each subnet. In this way, an IS receives an LS PDU from each of its neighbours informing it of the subnets (links) that are attached to it and their cost values. This information is stored in the **link state database** by the update process in the SNICP.

When it has done this, the update process in each IS sends a copy of the LS PDU to each of its neighbours (except the one that sent the PDU). As a result, each IS receives a further set of LS PDUs which have effectively originated from its neighbours' neighbours. This procedure then continues. As can be deduced, over a period of time each IS will receive a complete set of LS PDUs containing the identities of the subnets – and their path cost values (one for each metric) – which are attached to all other ISs in the internet. This type of routing procedure is known as **flooding**.

Whenever a new set of LS PDUs is entered into the link state database, **decision process** is run. Its role is first to perform the SPF algorithm on the link state database, and second to determine, from all the entries in the various databases, which neighbour IS should be used to reach each of the other ISs based on their corresponding path cost values. This is done for each routing metric in turn. A separate forwarding information base is created for each metric.

To illustrate this procedure, consider its application to the example subnet shown in Figure 9.28. This is repeated in Figure 9.29(a), again using a single routing metric for illustrative purposes. The initialized adjacency and circuit databases are shown in part (b) and the first set of LS PDUs that are received by each IS are shown in part (c) of the figure. For example, IS 1 will receive two LS PDUs, one from IS 2 and the other from IS 3. Similarly, IS 2 will receive four LS PDUs, one each from IS 1, 3, 4 and 5.

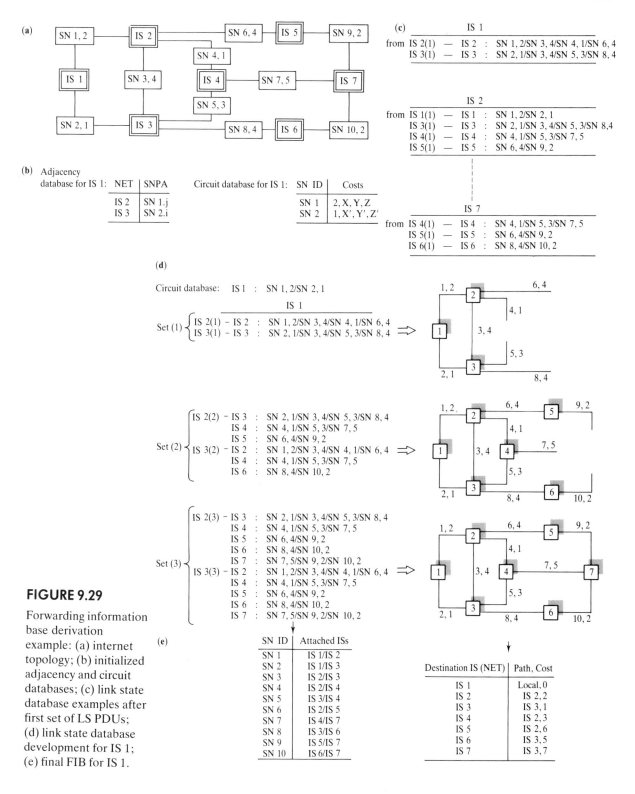

FIGURE 9.29

Forwarding information base derivation example: (a) internet topology; (b) initialized adjacency and circuit databases; (c) link state database examples after first set of LS PDUs; (d) link state database development for IS 1; (e) final FIB for IS 1.

As described earlier, on receipt of each of these PDUs, each IS will then generate another set of LS PDUs, and pass them on to each of its neighbours. This procedure then repeats. The first, second and third sets of LS PDUs that will be received by IS 1 are as shown in part (d).

Finally, part (e) shows the output of the decision process for IS 1. This is the FIB and is computed by the decision process performing the SPF algorithm on the contents of the link state database to determine the shortest (minimum) path cost to each destination IS. As can be seen, the contents of the FIB are the same as those shown in part (n) of Figure 9.28. Also, it can readily be deduced how an IS performs the redirect function. For example, if an ES attached to, say, SN 2 sends a PDU to IS 1 addressed to an ES on SN 5, then IS 1 can readily deduce that the shortest route is via IS 3 which is in fact one of its adjacencies on SN 2 and hence should be used in preference to itself.

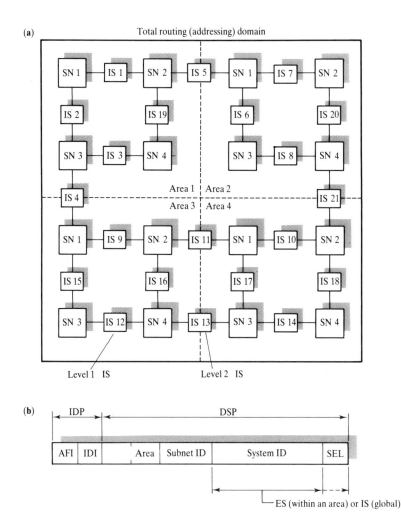

FIGURE 9.30

Hierarchical routing:
(a) example topology;
(b) address structure.

In the foregoing, it has been assumed that the transmission of LS PDUs is reliable and none are lost as a result of transmission errors. To allow for the possibility that errors will occur each LS PDU contains a sequence number. This is retained with the PDU when it is placed in the link state and forwarding databases. At regular intervals, ISs exchange other PDUs known as **sequence number PDUs** which contain the sequence numbers of the LS PDUs in the FIB of the transmitting IS. This information is used to ensure the FIBs in all ISs are consistent.

With very large internets the number of entries in each database can become unacceptably large. To overcome this, the protocol allows **hierarchical routing** to be used. Using this technique, the total routing (addressing) domain is divided into a number of **areas** each containing a number of subnets and first level (level 1) ISs. Then, if a required destination ES is attached to a subnet in this area (determined by the area address in the high-order part of the DSP address), it is routed directly using the foregoing procedure.

Alternatively, if the required destination is in a different area, the PDU is first sent to a second, higher level (level 2) IS. This IS then routes the PDU using other level 2 ISs until it reaches a (level 2) IS attached to the required destination area. From there it will then be routed within the area using level 1 ISs. In this case, each database is much smaller and hence the routing overheads are significantly reduced. Figure 9.30 illustrates this general approach.

Finally, it should be stressed that the IS-to-IS protocol is complex, especially when hierarchical routing is included. The foregoing provides only an overview of the protocol. For a more detailed description, the reader should refer to the ISO 10589 document directly.

EXERCISES

9.1   Explain the meaning of the following terms relating to internetworking:

    (a)   internet,
    (b)   subnet,
    (c)   intermediate system/gateway/router,
    (d)   protocol converter.

9.2   With the aid of sketches, describe the structure of:

    (a)   IP addresses,
    (b)   IP datagrams.

Clearly identify each field and explain its function in the context of the IP protocol.

9.3   An NSDU of 200 octets is to be transmitted over a network, using the IP protocol, that supports a maximum NS-user data size of 512 octets. Assuming a minimum IP header size, derive the following fields in each of the datagram headers:

    (a)   identification,
    (b)   total length,
    (c)   fragment offset,
    (d)   more fragments flag.

9.4 (a) Produce a sketch of an internet to illustrate the role of a subnet router, interior gateway and exterior gateway.

(b) In relation to the internet produced for part (a), identify the scope of the following routing protocols and produce example entries in the routing tables associated with each protocol:

(i) ARP,
(ii) IGP,
(iii) EGP.

9.5 With the aid of an example internet, explain the operation of the distance vector algorithm.

Use your internet to show how the routing tables in each gateway are derived assuming a routing metric of hop-count.

9.6 List the message types associated with the internet control message protocol (ICMP) and hence explain the various functions associated with the protocol.

9.7 Explain the meaning of the following terms in relation to the ISO-IP:

(a) NS-user,
(b) NS-provider,
(c) NSAP,
(d) CO-NS and CL-NS.

9.8 With the aid of sketches, describe the structure of an ISO internet NSAP address and the relationship between an NSAP address and an SNPA address.

9.9 List the names of the three sublayers that make up the network layer and describe their function in both an end system and an intermediate system.

9.10 Assuming an ISO-IP based internet, produce a time sequence diagram showing the service primitives that are exchanged between the three network sublayers, to transfer an NSDU between two NS-users in both directions assuming:

(a) a connection-oriented subnet,
(b) a connectionless subnet.

9.11 Produce a sketch of the structure of an ISO-IP data PDU and explain the meaning of each field.

9.12 Discriminate between the terms intranet segmentation and internet segmentation in relation to the ISO internet protocol.

Assuming the internet shown in Figure 9.10, produce a sketch showing the segmentation and reassembly operations at each ES and IS if the NSDU = 512 octets, the three subnets are all connectionless and operate with maximum user data lengths of 128 octets, 256 octets, and 512 octets, and intranet segmentation is being used.

9.13 If now internet segmentation is used, derive the content of the following fields in the header of each PDU as it is transferred across the three subnets:

(a) total length,
(b) segment length,
(c) segment offset,
(d) more segment flag.

9.14 Assuming ISO internetworking, produce a sketch showing the outline structure of the SNICP sublayer in both an ES and an IS. Include in your sketch the ISO-IP and the two routing protocols ES-to-IS and IS-to-IS.

Write an outline description of the operation of each system and the interactions between each protocol.

9.15 Assuming the internet structure and the table contents shown in Figure 9.22, describe the routing of an ISO-IP data PDU from NSAP 1.1 to:

(a)   NSAP 1.10,
(b)   NSAP 3.5,
(c)   NSAP 10.3.

9.16 With the aid of a sketch, explain the meaning of the terms overload, congestion control and congestion control efficiency in relation to an IS in an internet.

9.17 Describe the operation of the two functions in the ISO-IP that are provided to help avoid congestion in the internet.

Assuming the memory buffer structure shown in part (a) of Figure 9.25, derive an example worst-case buffer distribution assuming square root limiting, 15 free buffers available and internet segmentation.

9.18 Using the sketch in part (b) of Figure 9.25, explain the meaning of the term reassembly deadlock assuming intranet segmentation is being used.

9.19 Assume for a different routing metric the path cost values of the ten subnets shown in part (a) of Figure 9.28 are 1, 2, 3, 2, 2, 3, 4, 1, 2, and 2 units, respectively. Use Dijsktra's algorithm to derive the shortest path-cost routes from IS 1 to each of the nine other ISs.

9.20 Describe the routing of an ISO-IP data PDU, using the forwarding information base tables shown in part (e) of Figure 9.29, between NSAP 1.1 and the following NSAPs:

(a)   1.5,
(b)   3.4,
(c)   9.3.

9.21 Assuming an ES attached to SN 1 sends a PDU to IS 2 addressed to an NSAP on SN 2, describe the steps taken by IS 2 to route the PDU and the subsequent redirect operation. Explain clearly how IS 2 can determine the redirection that is possible.

9.22 Assuming the internet shown in part (a) of Figure 9.29 and the path cost values in question 9.18, derive the first set of link-state PDUs received by each IS.

CHAPTER SUMMARY

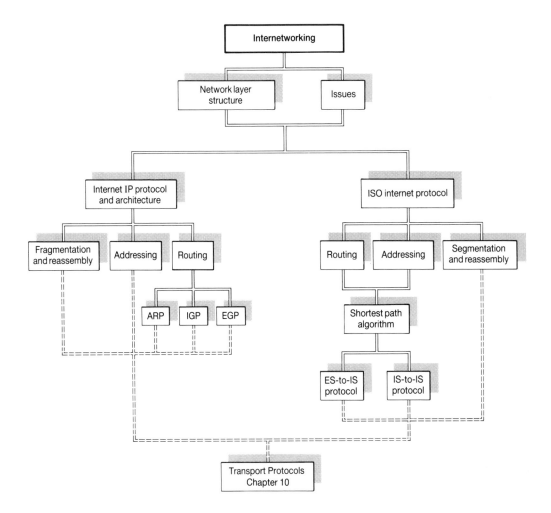

PART THREE

OPEN SYSTEMS

Part Three of the book describes the function and operation of the additional protocols that are needed to enable a set of application programs – running in computers from different manufacturers and interconnected by different types of computer network – to communicate with one another to perform specific distributed application functions. The protocols are known as application-oriented protocols and the resulting communication environment is known as an open system interconnection environment. There are two sets of protocols that are available to achieve this: TCP/IP and OSI, both of which are discussed.

Chapter 10 presents an overview of the function of the application-oriented protocols associated with both the TCP/IP and the OSI suites. A detailed description of the two protocols that convert the variable service provided by the different network types into a network-independent message transport service are also discussed.

Chapter 11 introduces and describes the protocols in the OSI suite that provide general, application-support services. These include the protocols needed to establish a session connection, to provide syntax conversions if the representation of data in the two communicating computers is different, and other support services.

Chapter 12 discusses the functionality and operation of the more specific application protocols in both protocol suites. These include protocols to support the transfer of electronic mail and files between dissimilar mail or file systems.

The additional system aspects that must be addressed to achieve open system interconnection are discussed in Chapter 13. These include name-to-address mapping, known as directory services, and how the protocols in a complete protocol suite co-operate and exchange information with a similar protocol suite.

10

Transport protocols

CHAPTER CONTENTS

CHAPTER OBJECTIVES

When you have completed studying the material in this chapter you should be able to:

- know the various transport protocols associated with the TCP/IP protocol suite and the OSI protocol suite;
- know the interlayer address selectors associated with the TCP/IP protocol suite;
- understand the role of the UDP protocol and describe the format and meaning of each field in the header of a UDP datagram;
- understand the role of the TCP protocol and the service primitives associated with the reliable stream service;
- explain the format of the PDU (segment) associated with the TCP protocol and the meaning of each field in its header;
- describe the connection establishment, data transfer and connection termination phases of the TCP protocol;
- understand the terminology used in the ISO standards documents to describe the services provided by a protocol layer and the operation and specification of a protocol entity;
- describe the services and operation of the ISO connectionless and connection-oriented transport protocols;
- understand the formal specification of the ISO transport protocol and a methodology for its implementation in structured program code.

10.1 INTRODUCTION

The position of the transport layer in the context of both a TCP/IP protocol suite and an OSI protocol suite is shown in parts (a) and (b) of Figure 10.1, respectively.

In the case of the TCP/IP suite, irrespective of whether the underlying data communications network is a single network – LAN or WAN – or an internetwork, the internet protocol (IP) is always present in the network layer. Thus there is a close coupling between the protocols in the transport layer and the IP protocol. Also, all the protocol data units associated with the transport layer protocols are transferred across the underlying network in IP datagrams.

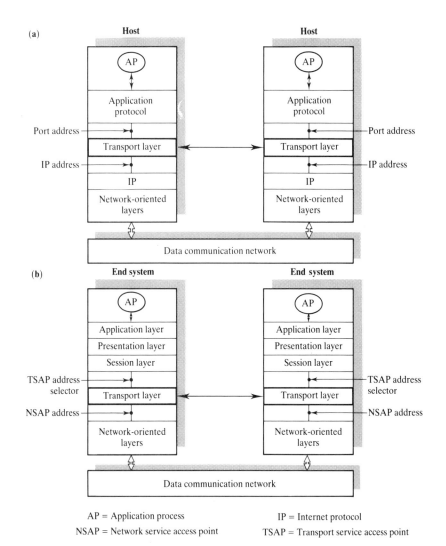

FIGURE 10.1

Position of transport layer: (a) in a TCP/IP protocol suite; (b) in an ISO protocol suite.

AP = Application process   IP = Internet protocol
NSAP = Network service access point   TSAP = Transport service access point

In contrast, in the case of an OSI suite, the network-oriented protocols normally reflect the type of underlying network that is being used. This means that the network layer interface may be connection-oriented, if the underlying network is based on X.25, or connectionless, if the underlying network utilizes the ISO-IP protocol. Moreover, in the case of the TCP/IP suite, the transport layer serves the application protocols directly, whereas in the case of the OSI suite it serves the application protocols through the intermediate session and presentation layers.

Despite these differences, both transport layers perform a similar set of functions. Thus there is a best-try (connectionless) protocol associated with both suites as well as a reliable (connection-oriented) protocol. Clearly, not all applications require a reliable service. For example, if files of data containing digitized images are being transferred, occasional errors are relatively less important than speed of transfer. A similar requirement applies to digitized voice messages. It is important to realize, however, that although the bit error rate probability may be low with networks such as LANs, it is non-zero and hence the connectionless transport protocol should only be utilized for applications in which occasional errors are acceptable. For all other applications, the connection-oriented protocol should be used.

The two transport protocols associated with both protocol suites will be described, starting with the two protocols associated with TCP/IP.

10.2 USER DATAGRAM PROTOCOL

The transport layer in TCP/IP always operates with the IP protocol. As may be recalled, this protocol provides a best-try (connectionless) service for the transfer of individually-addressed message units known as datagrams.

This mode of operation minimizes the overheads associated with each message transfer since no network connection is established prior to sending a message (datagram). Also, the IP protocol does not perform any error control. To enable an application protocol to exploit this property, TCP/IP provides a connectionless transport protocol known as the **user datagram protocol (UDP)**.

The TCP/IP protocol that provides a user application process with a reliable service is known as the **transmission control protocol (TCP)**. The position of the two protocols in relation to the other protocols, together with the protocol data units associated with each protocol and the interlayer addresses are shown in Figure 10.2. This section describes UDP; TCP is described in the next section.

The figure shows the outline structure of an information frame that is transmitted/received by a host. At the network interface it comprises the LAN/WAN frame header, the information (user data) field and an associated trailer (end-of-frame marker plus CRC). As may be recalled, the IP address – comprising the netid and hostid addresses – is used to route datagrams to a specific host. Also, the protocol field in the datagram header indicates the attached protocol within that host to which the user data part of the datagram should be

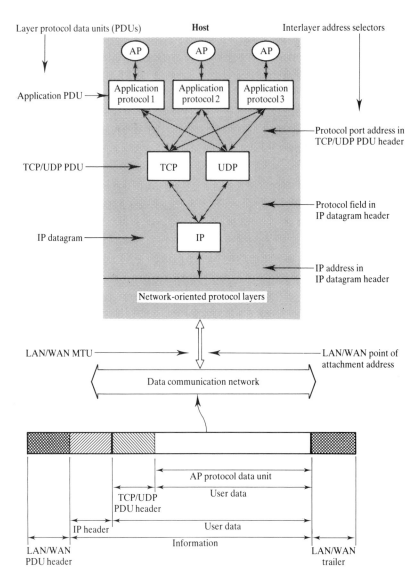

FIGURE 10.2

TCP/IP protocols with associated protocol data units and interlayer address selectors.

sent. This may be a protocol associated with IP – ICMP, for example – or one of the two transport protocols, UDP or TCP.

As can be seen in the figure, UDP and TCP can both serve multiple applications. Hence in order for the UDP (or TCP) to relay the user data part of their respective protocol data units (PDU) to the appropriate application protocol, it is necessary to incorporate an additional address field in the header of each PDU. In an OSI protocol suite this is the role of the interlayer **transport service access point** (or **address selector**), while in TCP/IP it is known as the **(protocol) port address**.

With TCP/IP, the composite address of an application protocol is the internet-wide IP address of the host plus the additional protocol port address. In dotted notation, an example address of an application protocol is:

128.3.2.3, 53

the first part being the IP address – netid = 128.3 and hostid = 2.3 – and the part after the comma the port address (53). In ISO terminology, the composite address is known as the **fully-qualified address**. It comprises the internet-wide NSAP address plus the interlayer address selectors between the transport layer and each of the higher protocol layers.

As indicated earlier, as UDP is a connectionless protocol only a single PDU – also known as a datagram – associated with the protocol is transmitted in the user data field of an IP datagram. To distinguish between an IP datagram and the datagram in the user data field associated with UDP, the term **user datagram** is used to refer to the latter. The format of the header part of a user datagram – the UDP PDU – is shown in Figure 10.3.

The **source port** is the port address of the source (sending) application protocol; the **destination port** is the port address of the intended recipient application protocol. Both are 16-bit integers. The source port is optional in a UDP datagram and is included only if a reply is expected. If it is not required, it is set to zero.

The **length** field is a count of the total number of octets in the complete (UDP) datagram, including the header. The checksum in the IP header applies only to the fields in the IP header and not the user data field. Hence the **checksum** field in the UDP header relates to the complete UDP datagram. In view of the various applications for the UDP, the checksum is also optional; if not used, it is set to zero. Note that with 1's complement number representation, zero can be all 0s or all 1s. Hence if a checksum is being used and the computed sum is zero, then all 1s is utilized.

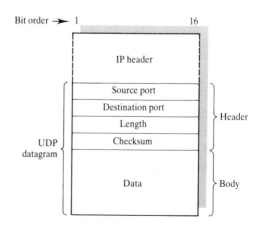

FIGURE 10.3

UDP datagram header format.

As may be deduced from the foregoing, before an application protocol can send a user datagram to another application protocol in a remote host, it is necessary to know the IP and port addresses of the destination process. This is a function of the application, not of the UDP (or TCP), as will be discussed later.

10.3 TRANSMISSION CONTROL PROTOCOL

The UDP is used either when error correction is not needed or for a single short request/response message exchange between two application protocols. In most open distributed applications, however, a reliable (connection-oriented) message transport service is required. An example is the transfer of the contents of a file containing a customer's bank record. Clearly, in such applications, the corruption of a single binary bit is all-important.

In the TCP/IP suite, the connection-oriented transport protocol is known as the **transmission control protocol (TCP)** and the service it offers to users – through application protocols – as the **reliable stream transport service**.

10.3.1 The reliable stream service

The reliable stream service is similar to the user services associated with the class 4 transport protocol in the ISO suite to be discussed later. Service primitives are provided to enable an application protocol – through the presentation and session layers in the case of an ISO suite – to establish a logical connection with a similar (peer) application protocol in a remote host, to exchange messages over this connection in a duplex (two-way simultaneous) way, and to clear the connection. The TCP protocol endeavours to transfer the data associated with these exchanges in a reliable way, that is, error free, with no losses or duplicates and in the same order as it was submitted.

The term **stream** is used with TCP since it treats all the user data associated with a connection – a sequence of request/response messages, for example – as two separate data streams, one in each direction, each comprising a string (stream) of octets/bytes. To achieve a reliable service, the TCP protocol transmits all data in units known as **segments**. Normally the TCP protocol decides when a new segment is transmitted. At the destination side, the receiving TCP protocol buffers the data received in a segment in a memory buffer associated with the application and delivers it when the buffer is full. Thus a segment may consist of multiple user messages if short message units are being exchanged, or part of a single large message if, say, the contents of a large file are being transferred. The maximum length of each segment is a function of the TCP protocol which simply endeavours to ensure that the total submitted octet stream associated with each direction is delivered to the other side in a reliable way.

In addition, to allow a user to force a message unit to be transferred and delivered immediately – for example, a short request message for some data – then the user can indicate in a parameter associated with the data transfer request primitive that data should be sent (and delivered) directly. Also, a user can

Table 10.1 TCP user service primitives and their parameters.

Primitive	Type	Client/ server	Parameters
UNSPECIFIED_PASSIVE_OPEN	Request	S	Source port, *timeout, timeout-action, precedence, security range*
FULL_PASSIVE_OPEN	Request	S	Source port, destination port, destination address, *timeout, timeout-action, precedence, security range*
ACTIVE_OPEN	Request	C	Source port, destination port, destination address, *timeout, timeout-action, precedence, security range*
ACTIVE_OPEN_WITH_DATA	Request	C	Source port, destination port, destination address, data, data length, push flag, urgent flag, *timeout, timeout-action, precedence, security range*
OPEN_ID	Local response	C	Local connection name, source port, destination port, destination address
OPEN_SUCCESS	Confirm	C	Local connection name
OPEN_FAILURE	Confirm	C	Local connection name
SEND	Request	C/S	Local connection name, data, data length, push flag, urgent flag, *timeout, timeout-action*
DELIVER	Indication	C/S	Local connection name, data, data length, urgent flag
ALLOCATE	Request	C/S	Local connection name, data length
CLOSE	Request	C/S	Local connection name
CLOSING	Indication	C/S	Local connection name
TERMINATE	Confirm	C/S	Local connection name, reason code
ABORT	Request	C/S	Local connection name
STATUS	Request	C/S	Local connection name
STATUS_RESPONSE	Local response	C/S	Local connection name, source port, source address, destination port, destination address, connection state, receive window, send windows, waiting ack, waiting receipt, urgent, precedence, security, timeout
ERROR	Indicator	C/S	Local connection name, reason code

indicate that the data to be transferred is **urgent** which means that it should be sent outside of the flow control mechanism used by the TCP protocol for normal data. This provides a similar function to the expedited data service associated with an OSI suite.

A list of the user service primitives associated with TCP, together with their parameters, is given in Table 10.1. The majority of open distributed applications are based on the **client–server model**. This is best understood by considering an application program (process) accessing and using a remote file system (application process). The file system is thus the server, since it only responds to requests for file services, and the user application program is the client, since it always initiates requests. Note also that a single server process must normally be able to support access requests from a distributed community of clients concurrently. Many of the user service primitives reflect this mode of interaction. Those that relate to each type of user – client/server – are indicated in the table.

The **destination address parameter** is the IP address of the destination host and the **source** and **destination ports** are then the interlayer port addresses associated with the source and destination protocols, respectively.

The **timeout** parameter allows a user application protocol to specify a maximum time interval that the source TCP protocol should wait for an acknowledgement relating to a segment that it sends. As may be recalled, since IP provides a best-try service a segment may be discarded during transfer. The timeout value, therefore, is normally set to be greater than twice the time-to-live value carried in each IP datagram. The **timeout-action** parameter specifies the action that should be taken if a timeout occurs. Normally this is to close the connection.

The **precedence** parameter is a collection of parameters that allow a user to specify the contents of the service type field in the IP datagram header that is used to transport the TCP segment. The contents of this field were identified in Figure 9.9 when the IP protocol was discussed. As may be recalled, it performs the same function as the quality of service parameter associated with the corresponding ISO primitives. Note that this parameter is used by the IP protocol and not TCP. It is thus an example of a **pass-through parameter**, that is, it is simply passed down from one protocol layer to another without modification.

The **security range** parameter allows a server application protocol to specify a level of security that should be applied to potential users. The **push flag** and **urgent flag** enable a user to indicate to the TCP how it should treat the data in the **data** parameter: push, transmit immediately, and urgent outside the normal flow. Finally, the **local connection name** is allocated by the local TCP protocol entity when a connection is first established. Although the port address enables the TCP to relate a received segment to a particular application protocol, in the case of a server, multiple transactions – and hence logical connections – may be in progress concurrently. The **local connection name** is thus used to enable the TCP to relate primitives to the same connection. The connection endpoint identifier parameter in an OSI suite performs the same function. Most of the parameters associated with the STATUS primitive relate to the TCP protocol entity and hence will be identified later.

As may be deduced from the foregoing, many of the parameters are concerned with the (relatively) low-level operation of the transport protocols TCP and IP. Moreover, in many cases the same parameter values will be used with different primitives. To allow for this, the parameters shown in italics have default values. If a value is not explicitly stated, the default values will be assumed. To illustrate the interrelationship of the various primitives, they are shown in the form of a time sequence diagram in Figure 10.4.

The UNSPECIFIED_PASSIVE_OPEN and FULL_PASSIVE_OPEN primitives are used by a server to indicate its readiness to accept a connection(s) request. The term **passive** is thus used to indicate that it is ready to receive a connection request rather than (actively) initiating the setting up of a connection. Unspecified open indicates that it is prepared to accept a request from any process that meets the specified security level (if present). Full open, however, also includes a destination port and IP address parameter which indicates a specific

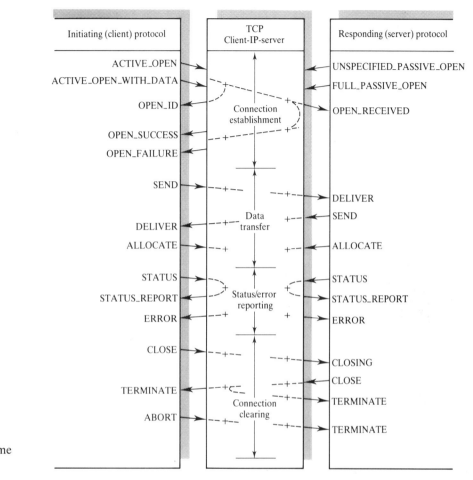

FIGURE 10.4

TCP user services: time sequence diagram.

application protocol/process from which it is awaiting a request. Normally, a server is opened when it is first run and remains open until the machine on which it is running is switched off.

At the client side, a user – through the application protocol – can initiate the establishment of a connection in two ways. With the first, the client protocol simply issues an ACTIVE_OPEN request specifying the port and IP addresses of the destination. The local TCP responds by returning an OPEN_ID which informs the application protocol of the identifier – connection name – it has assigned to this connection (request). It then initiates the setting up of a connection. If successful, both users can start to exchange data messages using the SEND and DELIVER primitives.

With the second way, the client issues an ACTIVE_OPEN_WITH_DATA request primitive which, as the name implies, contains a user data message in a parameter. The local TCP responds as before by returning a connection name. However, it then initiates the setting up of a connection concurrently with transferring the submitted data message. This mode is useful if a single short (reliable) request/response message exchange is involved since the overheads associated with the call are reduced.

As indicated, data is transferred in each direction using the SEND/ DELIVER primitives together with the push and urgent flags as required. The ALLOCATE primitive is used by a user to increase the amount of message buffer storage for this connection at the local side. Also, while in the data transfer phase, the user can request the status of the connection using the STATUS primitive. The local TCP responds using the STATUS_RESPONSE primitive. Should an error condition arise – for example, the two TCP protocol entities become unsynchronized – the user is informed by the ERROR primitive.

Finally, the connection can also be cleared in two ways. Since the flow of message data in each direction is controlled separately, it is usual to clear the connection in each direction separately. This is known as **graceful disconnection** and requires both users to issue a separate CLEAR request primitive after all data has been submitted to the local TCP. The alternative mode is for a user to issue an ABORT primitive which results in both sides discarding any outstanding data and terminating the connection.

10.3.2 Protocol operation

The TCP protocol incorporates many of the features of the HDLC protocol discussed in Chapter 5. It supports duplex message transfers and incorporates a go-back-N error control procedure with a type of sliding window flow control mechanism.

All the protocol data units that the TCP protocol uses to set up a connection, transfer data and clear a connection have a standard format and are known as **segments**. All segments are transferred between two TCP entities in the user data field of IP datagrams. Their format is shown in part (a) of Figure 10.5.

As with a UDP datagram, the first two fields in the header are the **source port** and **destination port** addresses. They have the same meaning as in a UDP datagram except that with TCP the two addresses indicate the end-points of the logical connection between the two application protocols.

The **sequence number** has the same role as the send sequence number in the HDLC protocol, and the **acknowledgement number** the same role as the **receive sequence number**. The former thus relates to the flow of data in the direction of the sending TCP entity and the latter to the flow in the reverse direction. With TCP, however, although data is submitted for delivery in blocks, the flow of data in each direction is treated simply as a stream of octets for error and flow control purposes. Thus the sequence and acknowledgement numbers relate to the position of an octet in the complete message stream rather than the position of a message block in the sequence. Consequently, the sequence number indicates the position of the first octet in the data field of the segment relative to the start of the complete message, while the acknowledgement number indicates the octet in the data stream flowing in the reverse direction that the sending TCP expects to receive next.

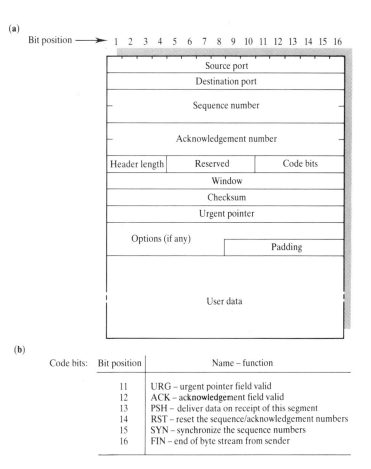

FIGURE 10.5

TCP protocol:
(a) segment (PDU)
format; (b) code bit
definitions.

The presence of an options field in the segment header means that the header can (in theory) be of variable length. The **header length** therefore indicates the number of 32-bit words in the header. The **reserved field**, as its name implies, is reserved for future use.

All segments (and hence PDU types) have the same header format and the validity of selected fields in the segment header is indicated by the setting of bits in the 6-bit **code field**; if a bit is set (= 1), the corresponding field is valid. Note that multiple bits can be set in a single segment. The bits have the meaning shown in part (b) of Figure 10.5.

The **window field** relates to the sliding window flow control scheme. It indicates the number of data octets relative to the octet number in the acknowledgement field that the source is prepared to accept. Thus it is determined by the amount of buffer storage the source has available for this connection.

As with a UDP datagram, the checksum relates to the complete segment, header plus contents. It is the complement of the sum of all the 16-bit words in the segment added together using 1's complement arithmetic.

When the URG flag is set in the code field, the **urgent pointer** indicates the amount of urgent (expedited) data in the segment. Normally this is delivered by the receiving TCP entity immediately it is received.

The default maximum number of octets in the data field of a segment is 536. This has been chosen on the assumption that wide area networks are present in the route since, in general, they have an inferior bit error rate probability. When the two communicating application protocols are running in hosts that are both attached to a network that has a low bit error rate – a LAN, for example – a larger segment size can be used. Hence the **options field** is used to enable the sending TCP entity to indicate to the receiver the maximum number of octets in the user data field of a segment it is prepared to receive.

Connection establishment

FIGURE 10.6

TCP connection establishment:
(a) client-server;
(b) collision possibility.

Although in a client-server interaction the client always initiates the setting up of a connection, in more general applications not based on the client-server model it is possible for both parties to try to set up a connection at the same time. To allow for this possibility, a connection is established using a three-way message (segment) exchange. It is thus known as a **three-way handshake** procedure. Also, as has been described, the flow of data in each direction of a connection is controlled independently. To avoid any ambiguity with the initial sequence number settings at both sides of a connection, each side informs the other of the initial sequence number it proposes to use. These are in turn acknowledged as part of the handshake procedure. Two example segment exchanges are shown in Figure 10.6.

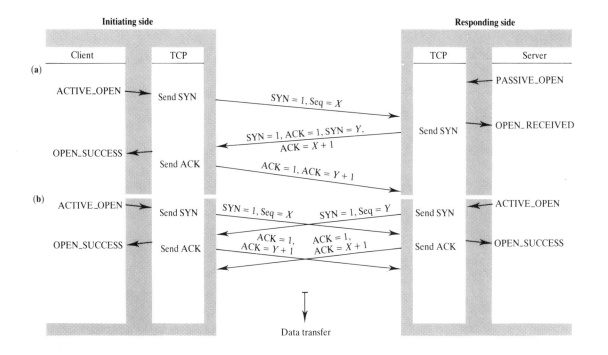

A connection is set up by the initiating side sending a segment with the SYN flag set and the proposed initial sequence number in the sequence number field (seq = X). On receipt of this, the responding side first makes a note of the sequence number setting for the incoming direction. It then returns a segment with both the SYN and ACK flags set with the sequence number field set to its own assigned value for the reverse direction (seq = Y) and an acknowledgement field of X + 1 (Ack = X + 1) to acknowledge it has noted the initial value for its incoming direction. On receipt of this, the initiating side makes a note of Y and returns a segment with just the ACK flag set and an acknowledgement field of Y + 1. In the event of both sides sending a SYN segment at the same time – part (b) – each side simply returns an ACK segment acknowledging the appropriate sequence number. Both sides of the connection are now set up and can start to send data independently.

Data transfer

FIGURE 10.7

TCP data transfer example.

As indicated earlier, the error and flow control procedures associated with the data transfer phase are based on a go-back-N error control strategy and a sliding window flow control mechanism. Since these were discussed in some detail in Chapter 4, and again in Chapter 5 when the HDLC protocol was described, they are not discussed here. To illustrate the use of the push flag, however, an example of a typical segment exchange relating to a client-server request/response message exchange is shown in Figure 10.7.

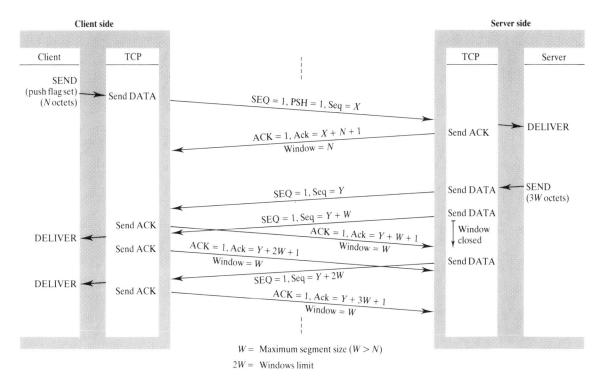

In the example, it is assumed that the client issues a short request message of N octets and, to force delivery, sets the push flag parameter. The sending TCP sends this directly in a segment with the SEQ and PSH flags set and a sequence number set to its current value – assumed to be X. On receipt of the segment, the receiving side detects the PSH flag is set and hence delivers this directly and returns a segment with the ACK flag set and an acknowledgement number of X + N + 1 – indicating the next octet it expects to receive – and a window value of N to return the window to its original setting.

The server then returns a response message which is assumed to be equal to three times the maximum segment size W. The local TCP must therefore send the message in three segments. To illustrate the window mechanism, it is assumed that the send window is equal to 2W, that is, sufficient for two maximum segments to be sent. After sending two segments, the server must wait until it receives an acknowledgement with a further credit allocation in its window field.

On receipt of each segment, the client TCP returns a segment for these with the ACK flag set; on receipt of the second segment, it delivers the current contents of its buffer – containing the two segments – to the client AP. At the server, on receipt of the first ACK segment, the server TCP increments its credit value and proceeds to send the third segment. In the example it is assumed that this third segment is delivered to the client application directly by the recipient TCP.

Although not shown, if a segment is received with an incorrect sequence or acknowledgement field, then a segment is returned with the RST and SEQ/ACK flags set and the expected value(s) in the appropriate field(s).

Connection termination

The actions of each TCP entity in response to the two alternative connection termination methods are shown in Figure 10.8. The first relates to a graceful disconnection and the second to the abort sequence.

In the first example, it is assumed that the client protocol has finished sending all its data and simply wants to terminate the connection. Hence, on receipt of the CLOSE primitive, it sends a segment with the FIN flag set. On receipt of this segment, the server issues a CLOSING primitive to the server protocol and returns an ACK segment to the client acknowledging receipt of the FIN segment.

It is assumed that the server protocol has also finished submitting data and hence issues a CLOSE primitive in response to the CLOSING primitive. In the example, however, it is assumed that the server TCP still has outstanding data to send, which it sends in a segment together with the SEQ and FIN flags set. On receipt of this segment, the client TCP issues a TERMINATE primitive and returns an ACK for the data just received. When it receives the ACK, the server TCP issues its own TERMINATE to the server protocol. Alternatively, if an ACK is not received within a time of twice the time-to-live period, it assumes the ACK has been corrupted and issues a TERMINATE to the server.

In the case of the abort sequence, the client side immediately terminates both sides of the connection and sends a segment with the RST flag set. On receipt

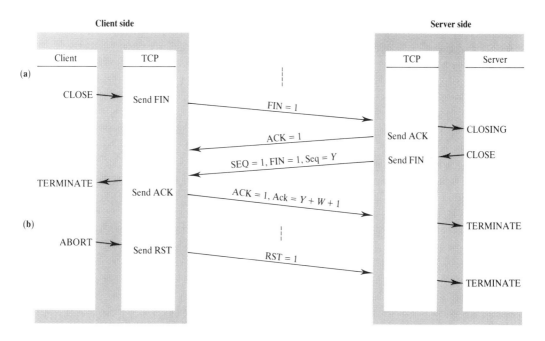

FIGURE 10.8

TCP connection termination: (a) normal; (b) abort.

of this segment, the server terminates both sides of the connection abruptly and issues a TERMINATE primitive with a reason code set to connection aborted.

To reinforce understanding of the connection establishment and termination phases of two TCP protocol entities, one a server and the other a client, a state transition diagram of each is shown in parts (a) and (b) of Figure 10.9, respectively.

As may be recalled from Chapter 4 when state transition diagrams were introduced, the various states associated with each automaton (finite state machine) are shown in circles with directional lines (known as arcs) indicating the transitions between states. Alongside each arc is the incoming event that initiates the transition – a service primitive or the arrival of a TCP segment (PDU) – followed by the resulting outgoing event(s). Hence the reader should be able to relate the various transitions at each side to the segment exchanges associated with the connection establishment and termination phases shown earlier in Figures 10.6 and 10.7.

10.4 OSI PROTOCOLS

When describing the operation of any of the OSI protocol layers, it is important from the outset to discriminate between the services provided by the layer, the internal operation (that is, the protocol) of the layer and the services used by the layer. This is important because only then can the function of each layer be

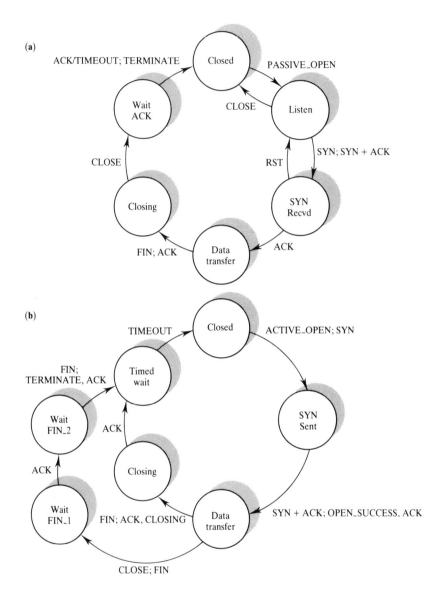

FIGURE 10.9

TCP state transition diagram: (a) server; (b) client.

defined in the context of the other layers. This also has the effect that a person (programmer) who is implementing a single protocol layer only needs to know which services the layer is to provide to the layer above, the internal protocol of the layer, and the services that are provided by the layer below to transfer the appropriate items of information associated with the protocol to the similar layer in a remote system. It should not be necessary for the implementor to have any further knowledge of the other layers.

For example, to describe the function of the transport layer, it is necessary only to consider:

(1) The defined set of services the transport layer is to provide to the session layer (for the purpose of transporting session layer message units to a peer session layer in a remote system).

(2) The internal operation (protocol) of the transport layer. (This is concerned with such functions as establishing and managing logical connections with a similar peer transport layer in a remote system, and the error and flow control of transport layer message units across established connections.)

(3) The services provided by the (lower) network layer to transfer these message units to a peer transport layer.

When describing the functions of each protocol layer, therefore, these three aspects will be treated separately.

The specification of each protocol layer comprises two sets of documents: a **service definition document** and a **protocol specification document**. The service definition document contains a specification of the services provided by the layer to the layer above it – that is, the **user services**. Normally, these take the form of a defined set of **service primitives** each with an associated set of **service parameters**. As will be seen, it is through the service parameters that the layer above initiates the transfer of information to a similar **correspondent layer** in a remote system.

The protocol specification document contains:

(1) A precise definition of the **protocol data units (PDUs)** used by the **protocol entity** of that layer to communicate with a similar (peer) protocol entity in a remote system.

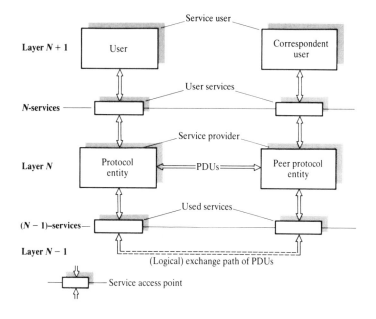

FIGURE 10.10

Protocol layer model.

(2)   A specification of the services used by the layer (that is, the services provided by the layer immediately below it) to transfer each PDU type.

(3)   A precise definition of the operation of the protocol entity presented in one of the formal specification methods.

Some of the terms just introduced are summarized in Figure 10.10.

10.5 SERVICE DEFINITION

In any networking system it is important to discriminate between the *identity* of a user application process and the *location* in the network where the process currently resides. The identity of a user application process is normally in the form of a symbolic *name* or *title* while the location in the network is in the form of an *address*. This is similar to the use of names and addresses when sending a letter via the postal system: a name is used to identify the recipient of the letter while the address indicates where the recipient is currently resident. Also, because a number of application processes may be resident in the same computer, the address must contain not only the physical address of the computer within the network, but also addressing information for use within the computer itself. This is analogous to, say, the floor and room numbers within a block of flats or apartments.

10.5.1 Names

As symbolic names are used for identification purposes at the user level, it is necessary for the names utilized for each user application process (AP) to be unique within a specific OSI environment. Normally, the actual physical location of other APs in the network is not known by an AP and so an AP communicates with another AP simply by specifying the name or title of the intended correspondent. To ensure that names are unique within a particular (OSI) environment, some means of managing the allocation of names to APs (user processes and service provider processes) must be provided. The system that provides this function is known as a **name server**. It is normally maintained by the authority administering the environment.

For a relatively small environment comprising, say, a distributed community of computer-based systems connected to a single LAN, it is usually sufficient to maintain a single name server for the complete system. However, for larger environments comprising perhaps several thousand systems interconnected by a number of LANs and WANs, a single name server often becomes unmanageable. In this case, a separate name server is used for each subnetwork. Then, to ensure that each name is unique within the complete environment, the name associated with a user on one subnetwork is prefaced by the identity of the subnetwork within the complete OSI environment.

10.5.2 Addresses

Although names are used at the user level, addresses are used within the OSI environment itself to ascertain, firstly, the physical location of the computer within the network in which the required AP currently resides and, secondly, the identity of the application layer protocol entity to which the AP is currently said to be attached. It is, thus, the responsibility of the OSI environment to relate the required correspondent symbolic name specified by a user AP into a specific network-wide address. The list of relationships or mappings between symbolic names and addresses is contained in a **system directory**. In principle, the actual physical location of an AP may vary simply by changing its entry in the system directory.

The addresses used in the OSI environment comprise a concatenation of a number of subaddresses known as **service access points** (**SAPs**) or, because of their function, **interlayer address selectors**. They are used at the interface between each protocol layer in the system to which the AP is currently attached. Thus, the address of an AP is made up as follows:

$$AP\ address = PSAP + SSAP + TSAP + NSAP$$

where PSAP is the service access point subaddress between the application layer protocol entity (to which the AP is attached) and the presentation layer, SSAP is the service access point subaddress between the presentation layer and the session layer, and so on. It is the NSAP that contains the network-wide address of the system in which the AP is resident. The P/SSAP and TSAP addresses are then used within the system to determine the specific application layer protocol entity to which the user AP is currently attached. This is shown in Figure 10.11.

An AP address is known as a **presentation address** or, because of its structure, a **fully-qualified address**. As can be seen, the PSAP and SSAP selectors can be used in a number of ways. In A the PSAP and SSAP are not used for multiplexing/demultiplexing purposes; it is the TSAP address selector that selects a specific application entity/process within the system. This is similar to the scheme used in a TCP/IP suite. In B and C, however, a further level of selection is provided by the PSAP and SSAP.

In B a further level of selection is provided by the SSAP address selector thus allowing multiple application/presentation entities to use the same session connection. Alternatively, in C the PSAP is being used to allow multiple application entities/processes to use the same presentation connection. The topic of addresses will be expanded upon in Chapters 12 and 13.

In the event of multiple transactions involving the same application entity being in progress concurrently – for example, multiple transactions involving an AP acting as a server such as a file server – it is an implementation-dependent (local) matter for each protocol layer within that system to know the identity of the particular transaction to which messages relate. That is, this is not part of the SAP address structure. To allow for this, a **connection (endpoint) identifier** or **instance number** is associated with the appropriate PDUs exchanged. This will be expanded upon later when the transport layer is described.

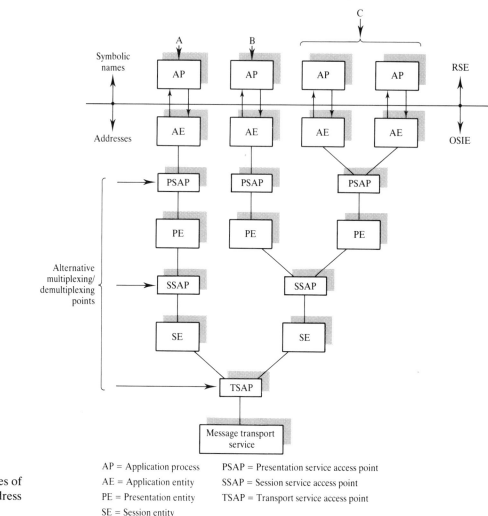

FIGURE 10.11

Some alternative uses of
the PSAP/SSAP address
selectors.

AP = Application process	PSAP = Presentation service access point
AE = Application entity	SSAP = Session service access point
PE = Presentation entity	TSAP = Transport service access point
SE = Session entity	

Finally, although in the figure the AP is shown separate from the AE, this is
simply to identify the dividing line between the OSI environment and the real
system environment. In practice, as will be expanded upon in Chapter 12, the
application entity(s) involved in an application is (are) closely bound to the
application processes. For this reason an AE is said to be **attached** to an AP.

10.5.3 Service primitives

The user services provided by a layer are specified by a set of service primitives.
The services associated with a layer can be of two types: confirmed or uncon-
firmed. A diagram illustrating the difference between the two types is shown in
Figure 10.12(a) and (b).

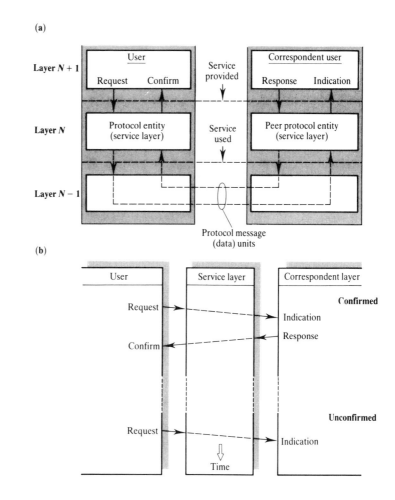

FIGURE 10.12

Service primitives:
(a) space
representation;
(b) time sequence
representation.

Normally, a particular transfer starts by the user of the layer passing a **request primitive** across the layer interface. This, in turn, results in an associated PDU being generated by the local protocol entity within the layer and this being passed, using the services provided by the underlying layer, to a correspondent (peer) protocol entity in a remote system. Then, on receipt of the PDU, the peer protocol entity in the remote system creates an associated **indication primitive** and passes this up to the correspondent user. In the case of an unconfirmed service this completes the transfer, but with a confirmed service this is followed by the correspondent user issuing a **response primitive**. Again, this results in an associated PDU being generated by the local protocol entity which is then sent back to the originating protocol entity, using the services provided by the underlying layer. On receipt of this, the originating protocol entity then creates a **confirmation primitive** and passes it up to the user to complete the transfer.

It can be concluded that there is a logical relationship between the various service primitives and that these relationships are related in time. The interrelationship between the service primitives within a layer are often illustrated in the form of a **time sequence diagram**. As an example, Figure 10.12(b) shows the interrelationship of the four primitives just described. It should be apparent from this figure that a time sequence diagram is only an abstract way of representing the logical relationships between the service primitives of a layer and does not indicate how the specified services are implemented by the layer.

Normally, the type of primitive and the identity of the layer providing the service are included with the primitive name. Thus:

- T.CONNECT.request is a request primitive, issued by the transport service user (TS-user) – that is, the session layer – to set up a (logical) transport connection with a remote TS-user (session layer).

- S.DATA.indication is an indication primitive issued by a peer (correspondent) session layer to the presentation layer above it and is concerned with the transfer of data received from a remote presentation layer.

10.5.4 Service parameters and layer interactions

Associated with each service primitive is a defined set of parameters. As will be seen, it is through these parameters that adjacent layers within the same system pass information and also how two correspondent user layers in different systems exchange PDUs. For example, the parameters associated with the previous service primitives may include:

T.CONNECT.request (called address, calling address, . . . , user data)

S.DATA.indication (connection identifier, user data)

In the first example, the called address and calling address parameters are concatenations of the relevant service access point subaddresses associated with the particular logical connection being established. Normally, the user data field parameter is an address pointer to a memory buffer containing a PDU generated by the protocol entity in the user layer above to be passed to a correspondent protocol entity in the user layer in the remote system. Thus, although the term 'user data' is used, this does not necessarily imply it is data as generated by a user application process. Rather, it means that it is data with meaning only to the user layer above and, as will be seen, it may contain protocol control information being exchanged between two correspondent user layers.

The user data parameter associated with a service primitive is known as a **service data unit** (**SDU**) by the recipient layer. Since this contains a PDU relating to the layer above, a $(N + 1)$-PDU is the same as a (N)-SDU. Typically, on receipt of a service primitive, the protocol entity of the layer reads selected parameters associated with the primitive and combines them with additional **protocol control information** (**PCI**) to form a PDU for that layer. The resulting PDU is then passed to the layer below in the user data field of a suitable primitive with additional parameters as appropriate. This is shown in Figure 10.13(a).

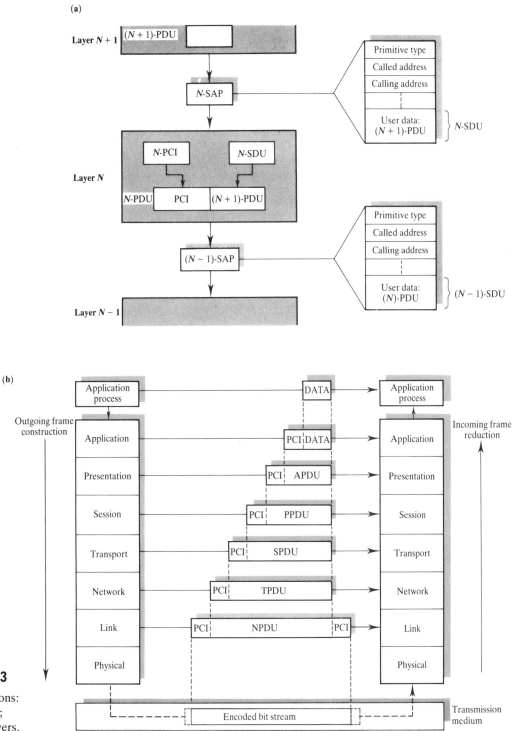

FIGURE 10.13

Layer interactions:
(a) single layer;
(b) multiple layers.

It may be concluded from this discussion that the user data field (para-meter) associated with the service primitive at each layer interface grows as it passes down through the layers, with each layer adding its own PCI. Also, once the link layer protocol entity has added its own PCI, it is this that is encoded and transmitted to the remote system. Conversely, at the remote system, the user data field reduces at each layer interface as it passes up through the layers and the protocol entity in each layer reads and interprets the PCI relating to it. This is shown in Figure 10.13(b) and will be expanded upon in Chapter 13 after the detailed operation of each layer has been described.

10.5.5 Sequencing of primitives

Each layer has an associated range of primitives to provide such services as connection establishment and data transfer. On receipt of a service primitive at the interface of a layer, it is necessary to determine whether the primitive is in the correct sequence. For example, it is not normally possible to issue a data transfer request primitive before a connection has been established. Within the standards documents, therefore, the acceptable sequence of service primitives associated with a layer is illustrated in the form of either a state transition diagram or a **sequence table**. An example of each is shown in Figure 10.14.

FIGURE 10.14

Service primitives: (a) state transition diagram; (b) sequence table.

In the example, the user services supported are intended to allow a user first to establish a logical connection with a remote (correspondent) user, then to transfer data across this connection and finally to disconnect (clear) the connection. For clarity, only the connect and data transfer primitives are included. Normally, the state transition diagram is used simply to show the correct

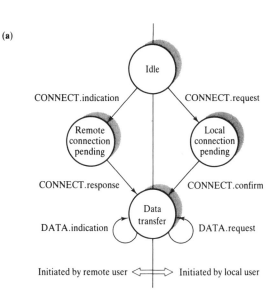

(a)

(b)

May be followed by: \ This: →	CONNECT.request	CONNECT.indication	CONNECT.response	CONNECT.confirm	DATA.request	DATA.indication	---
CONNECT.request							
CONNECT.indication							
CONNECT.response		+					
CONNECT.confirm	+						
DATA.request			+	+	+	+	
DATA.indication			+	+	+	+	

+ = Permissible   Blank = Error

sequence of primitives that are allowed at the user interface. The sequence table, in contrast, is a more precise definition as it shows all possible sequences, both valid and invalid. The sequence diagram is used, therefore, for implementation purposes to ascertain whether a received primitive is in the permitted sequence. Normally, receipt of an out-of-sequence primitive is a protocol violation and results in the associated connection being cleared (disconnected).

10.6 PROTOCOL SPECIFICATION

The protocol specification document for a layer comprises:

- A qualitative description of the types of PDU associated with the protocol entity and their purpose, together with a description of the fields present in each PDU and their use.

- A description of the procedures followed during the various phases of operation of the protocol entity and the services it uses to transfer each PDU type.

- A formal definition of the structure of each PDU type.

- A precise definition of the operation of the protocol entity in one of the formal specification methods.

10.6.1 PDU definition

Two peer protocol entities communicate with each other by exchanging PDUs. Typically, a PDU contains user data and a PCI generated by the layer (protocol entity) itself. Since the parameters associated with a service primitive have only local significance (meaning), they are normally defined in terms of abstract data types, such as *INTEGER*, *BOOLEAN*. In contrast, PDUs generated by a protocol entity are passed *between* systems. To avoid ambiguity, these must be defined in a precise way so that they have a common meaning in both systems.

To achieve this, the PDUs associated with a protocol entity are defined in the standards documents in a precise way using either a specific bit string form or in an abstract data type form (known as Abstract Syntax Notation Number One or ASN.1) coupled with an associated set of **encoding rules**. An example of a PDU defined in each form is given in Figure 10.15. The example shown in Figure 10.15(a) is a PDU used by a transport layer protocol entity. It is a connect-request TPDU (transport protocol data unit). This, as will be described later in the chapter, is generated by a transport layer protocol entity to initiate the establishment of a logical connection with a peer transport entity as a result of a T.CONNECT.request service primitive at its user interface. The PDU in Figure 10.15(b) is associated with the application protocol entity FTAM, which will be described in Chapter 12.

As can be seen from Figure 10.15(a), the bit string form of each PDU is made up of a number of octets and the intended use and format of each octet are

(a)

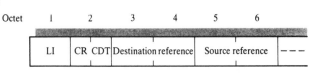

LI = Length indication = number of octets in PDU

CR = PDU type; CONNECT request = 1110 (bits 8–5)

CDT = Credit allocation; initial credit = 0000 (bits 4–1)

Destination reference = Connection endpoint identifier used by the destination
for this connection; set initially to zero

Source reference = Connection endpoint identifier used by the source for this connection

(b)

FINITIALIZErequest ::= *SEQUENCE* {
    protocolId [*0*] *INTEGER* { *isoFTAM* (*0*) },
    versionNumber [*1*] *IMPLICIT SEQUENCE* {
      major INTEGER, minor INTEGER },
    – – initially { *major 0, minor 0* }
    serviceType [*2*] *INTEGER* {
      reliable (*0*), *user correctable* (*1*) },
    serviceClass [*3*] *INTEGER* { *transfer* (*0*),
      access (*1*), *management* (*2*) },
    functionalUnits [*4*] *BITSTRING* {
      read (*0*),
      write (*1*),
      fileAccess (*2*),
      limitedFileManagement (*3*),
      enhancedFileManagement (*4*),
      grouping (*5*),
      recovery (*6*),
      restartDataTransfer (*7*) }
    attributeGroups [*5*] *BITSTRING* {
      storage (*0*),
      security (*1*) }
    rollbackAvailability [*6*] *BOOLEAN DEFAULT FALSE*,
    presentationContextName, [*7*] *IMPLICIT ISO8822String* { "*ISO8822*"},
    identityOfInitiator [*8*] *ISO646String OPTIONAL*,
    currentAccount [*9*] *ISO646String OPTIONAL*,
    filestorePassword [*10*] *OCTETSTRING OPTIONAL*,
    checkpointWindow [*11*] *INTEGER OPTIONAL*}

FIGURE 10.15

Example PDU
definition: (a) bit string
form; (b) ASN.1 form.

precisely defined. Although this form of definition has been used with all the lower network-dependent layers, ASN.1 has been adopted for use with most of the application-oriented layers. Essentially, as can be deduced from Figure 10.15(b), ASN.1 is based on data typing as is used with most high-level programming languages. Thus, a PDU defined using ASN.1 is comprised of a number of typed data elements. Both simple (primitive) types (*INTEGER* and *BOOLEAN*) and structured types (*SET* and *SEQUENCE*) are used, the latter being similar to the **record** type in Pascal.

As the name implies, ASN.1 is an abstract syntax, which means that although a data element may be of a defined type (*INTEGER*, for example), its absolute syntax in terms of the number of bits and the order of the bits used is not implied. Thus, a set of encoding rules must be used to produce the absolute or concrete syntax for a PDU defined in ASN.1. The resulting PDUs are then simply strings of octets which are interpreted in the same (fixed) way in each system. A more complete description of ASN.1 will be given in Chapter 11 when the application-support protocols are discussed.

10.6.2 Protocol operation – overview

The operation of a protocol entity was first introduced in Chapter 4 when link-level protocols were described. A protocol entity is modelled in the form of a finite-state machine or automaton. This means that a protocol entity can only be in one of a finite number of states at any one time. The current operational state of the automaton, together with other related protocol state information, is retained in a set of state variables maintained by the automaton.

A transition from one state to another is prompted by a valid incoming event occurring at one of the automaton interfaces; for example:

- receipt of a service primitive from the interface with the layer above;
- receipt of a service primitive from the interface with the layer below;
- receipt of a service primitive from the interface with a **local entity** such as a **timer** or **management sublayer**.

This is shown in Figure 10.16. Normally, the occurrence of a valid incoming event results in a PDU being generated by the protocol entity, which is output in the form of an outgoing event (action) at one of the layer interfaces. Typically, this is associated with a change of state of the automaton and, possibly, a specific internal action, such as the starting of a timer, with an associated change to one or more of the automaton state variables.

All incoming events are assumed to be **atomic**, that is, a protocol entity (automaton) carries out all the operations associated with an event (outgoing

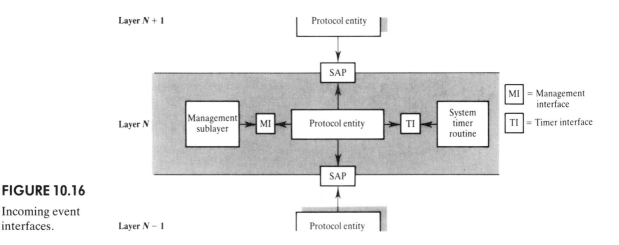

FIGURE 10.16

Incoming event interfaces.

event, specific actions, change of state) before another incoming event is processed. To ensure that each incoming event is processed in an atomic way, local events such as the occurrence of timeouts are passed to the protocol entity in the same way as other incoming events. Normally, the various interfaces shown in Figure 10.16 are each implemented in the form of a pair of queues (mailboxes): one for input to the protocol entity and the other for output. The queues are then serviced by the protocol entity in a prescribed way. This will be expanded upon later in the chapter.

In some instances, the operations performed by a protocol entity and the new state (if any) assumed by it depend on the current state of one or more **enabling conditions** or **predicates**. A predicate is a Boolean variable that depends on a combination of the values of the parameters associated with an incoming event and the current values of one or more of the automaton state variables. Normally, predicates are given the symbol P with an additional numeric qualifier. For example:

P0: T.CONNECT.request is acceptable;

P2: Retransmission count = Maximum.

Typical examples of their use are:

P5& (Not P1): Outgoing event *A*
New state *X*;

P0: Outgoing event *B*
New state *Y*.

If a predicate condition is not satisfied and the alternative state is not defined, a protocol error condition is said to have occurred and a predefined outgoing event and new automaton state are generated.

10.6.3 Protocol specification method

The ISO standards documents present the formal specification of a protocol entity as follows:

- a definition of all the possible incoming events at each interface;
- a definition of the possible automaton states;
- a definition of all the possible outgoing events generated by the protocol entity together with a list of any specific actions to be carried out;
- a definition of the state variables and predicates (enabling conditions) associated with the operation of the automaton;
- an event–state table defining, for all possible incoming event and present state combinations, the outgoing event (and any specific actions) and the new automaton state together with any alternative event and new state combinations that depend on predicates.

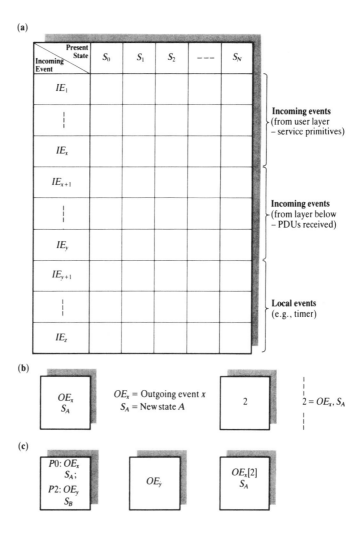

FIGURE 10.17

Event–state tables:
(a) table format;
(b), (c) alternative entry
formats.

The format of the event–state table used by the ISO is similar to that described in Chapter 4; an example is shown in Figure 10.17(a). Each entry in the table specifies the appropriate outgoing event (together with any specific actions) and the new state of the automaton for that particular (incoming) event–(present) state combination. Normally, only valid event–state combinations have an entry in the table, all other combinations being left blank. A blank entry is a protocol error and will always be treated in a defined way.

Each entry in the table is specified in one of two ways, as shown in Figure 10.17(b). The entry either contains a specification of the actual outgoing event and the new state in the cell itself, or it contains a reference number that refers to an entry in a separate list of outgoing event/new state specifications.

If the outgoing event and the new state are determined by predicates, these are included in the entry. An example is shown in Figure 10.17(c). Again, if none of the predicates are satisfied, a protocol error is assumed. Furthermore, if there is no state transition associated with an entry (that is, the automaton remains in the same state), only an outgoing event is specified. Similarly, if there is a specific action associated with an entry, a reference to the action in the list of actions is given. In the last example shown in Figure 10.17(c), the specific action [2] may mean, say, stop the associated timer.

10.7 TRANSPORT LAYER

The aims of this section are two-fold: firstly, to give an example of the application of the specification methodology introduced in the previous sections and, secondly, to describe the operation and specification of the transport layer in the context of the ISO Reference Model.

10.7.1 Overview

In keeping with the methodology outlined, a model of the transport layer is shown in Figure 10.18. A user of the transport service (the TS-user) communicates with its underlying transport entity (or service provider) through a **transport service access point** (**TSAP**) using a defined set of user service primitives. The TSAP used is that associated with the initiating application entity. Service primitives cause, or are the result of, the exchange of **transport protocol data units** (**TPDUs**) between the two correspondent (peer) transport entities involved in a **transport connection** (**TC**). The resulting TPDUs are exchanged using the services provided by the underlying network layer through an associated **network service access point** (**NSAP**). Collectively, it is the TSAP and NSAP addresses that help to identify, uniquely, the application entity (and hence the attached AP) involved in the connection.

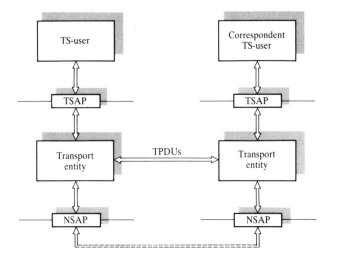

FIGURE 10.18

Model of transport layer.

As already mentioned, the function of the transport layer is to provide the session layer with a reliable (error-free, in-sequence, with no loss or duplication) message transport facility that is independent of the quality of service provided by the underlying network. To cater for the different types of network, five classes of service are provided to the user:

- Class 0: Simple class (normally used with a network offering a high QOS such as the Telex network or a PSDN).
- Class 1: Basic error recovery class.
- Class 2: Multiplexing class.
- Class 3: Error recovery and multiplexing class.
- Class 4: Error detection and recovery class. This contains the maximum control functions, such as error detection and retransmission and flow control. It is intended for low-quality networks such as a PSTN or a WAN or a LAN operating with a connectionless network layer.

All the classes of service assume a connection-oriented mode of operation; that is, a logical TC is established between the two correspondent transport entities prior to any data transfers being made. Although this is the preferred mode of working in most applications, it inevitably involves a certain level of protocol overheads in connection with the setting up and clearing of the TC. For certain selected application environments in which overheads are important, a more efficient (but less reliable) class of service based on a connectionless mode of working has been proposed. In this mode, data may be transferred between two correspondent entities without a TC first being established.

It should be noted that it is not necessary for the transport layer to support all the different classes of service available. Normally, for a particular OSIE, the controlling authority of the environment specifies which class of service is to be used. All systems would then be expected to utilize that class, which would be chosen to best suit the QOS provided by the underlying network(s).

10.7.2 User services

The services provided by the transport layer can be divided into two categories: connection oriented and connectionless. In turn, the connection-oriented services can be divided into two subsets: those concerned with connection management and those concerned with data transfer. Connection management services allow a TS-user to establish and maintain a logical connection to a correspondent TS-user in a remote system. The data transfer services provide the means for exchanging data (messages) between the two correspondent users over this connection. A list of the service primitives associated with the transport layer, together with their parameters, is given in Figure 10.19 and a time sequence diagram showing the order of their use is given in Figure 10.20.

The called and calling address parameters associated with the T.CON-NECT service are concatenations of the TSAP and NSAP addresses associated

(a)

Primitive	Parameters
T.CONNECT.request .indication	Calling address Called address Expedited data option Quality of service TS user data
T.CONNECT.response .confirm	Responding address Quality of service Expedited data option TS user data
T.DATA.request .indication	TS user data
T.EXPEDITED_DATA.request .indication	TS user data
T.DISCONNECT.request	TS user data
T.DISCONNECT.indication	Disconnect reason TS user data

(b)

Primitive	Parameters
T.UNIT_DATA.request .indication	Calling address Called address Quality of service TS user data

FIGURE 10.19

User service primitives and associated parameters:
(a) connection oriented;
(b) connectionless.

with the called and calling application entities involved in the connection. The QOS parameter refers to certain characteristics expected from the TC, such as throughput and error rates. Normally, these are defined for a particular network type.

The additional T.EXPEDITED_DATA service can only be used during the data transfer phase after a connection has been established and on the proviso that the two correspondent TS-users agreed on the use of this service when the TC was first established. It is provided to allow a TS-user to send an item of data that bypasses the flow control procedure associated with the T.DATA service of class 4. An example of its use will be identified when the application-support layers are described in Chapter 11.

The sequence of primitives shown in Figure 10.20 assumes a successful connection establishment phase. However, should the request for a connection be unacceptable by the correspondent TS-user, then the latter issues a T.DISCONNECT.request primitive, instead of a T.CONNECT.response primitive, with the reason for the rejection given as a parameter. Once a TC has been established, either user can initiate its release at any time by issuing a T.DISCONNECT.request at the user interface with the reason as a parameter. Also, should the underlying network connection become disconnected, the transport entity initiates the release of the TC using a T.DISCONNECT.indication primitive.

The two primitives associated with the connectionless mode of working, T.UNIT_DATA.request and T.UNIT_DATA.indication, enable a TS-user to initiate the transfer of an item of user data without first establishing a TC. With this service, however, there is no guarantee that the transfer has been successful and it is left to the higher application-oriented layers to recover from such

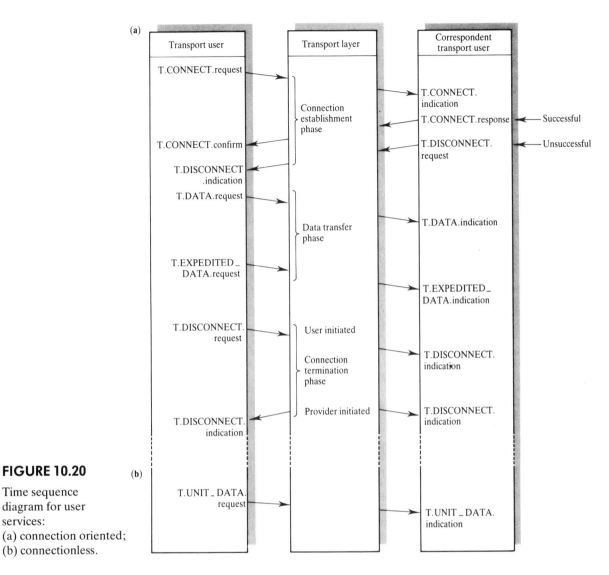

FIGURE 10.20

Time sequence
diagram for user
services:
(a) connection oriented;
(b) connectionless.

eventualities. Inevitably, the protocol associated with the connection-oriented services is more complex than that associated with the connectionless mode. Hence the remainder of this chapter will concentrate on the connection-oriented mode of operation.

A state transition diagram and an associated sequence table relating to the user services with the connection-oriented mode are shown in Figure 10.21. As can be seen, the sequence table gives a more complete specification of the acceptable sequence of primitives by each user.

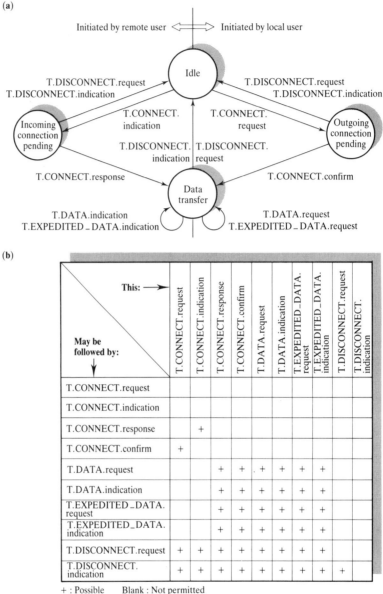

FIGURE 10.21

User services: (a) state
transition diagram;
(b) sequence table.

+ : Possible   Blank : Not permitted

10.7.3 Protocol operation

On receipt of a valid incoming service primitive (either from the TS-user or the
network provider), the transport protocol entity generates an associated TPDU.
Typically, assuming the incoming primitive is from the TS-user, the TPDU
comprises the user data associated with the primitive together with additional

protocol control information added by the transport entity. The generated TPDU is then transferred to the correspondent transport entity using the services provided by the underlying network layer.

The TPDUs associated with the transport protocol are as follows:

- CR: connect request,
- CC: connect confirm,
- DR: disconnect request,
- DC: disconnect confirm,
- DT: data,
- AK: data acknowledge,
- ED: expedited data,
- EA: expedited acknowledge,
- RJ: reject,
- ER: error.

Each of these TPDU types has a number of associated fields; the precise format and contents of each field are shown in Figure 10.22. The **LI (length indicator)** field indicates the number of octets in the header, excluding the LI octet; the **class field** specifies the protocol class to be used with this connection (0–4); and the **option field** specifies whether normal (7-bit sequence number and 4-bit credit values) or extended (31-bit sequence and 16-bit credit) sequence and credit (CDT) fields are to be used.

The fields shown constitute what is known as the **fixed header** part of each PDU. In addition, most PDUs contain a **variable header** part and a **user data** part. The variable part also consists of a number of fields each represented in the form of an 8-bit field type, an 8-bit field length and the field value. The fields and PDUs in which they are present are as follows:

- calling TSAP address (CR and CC),
- called TSAP address (CR and CC),
- TPDU size (CR and CC),
- protocol version number (CR and CC),
- user security parameter (CR and CC),
- checksum (all PDUs with class 4 – explained later),
- additional options (CR and CC),
- alternative protocol class acceptable (CR and CC),
- estimated acknowledgement delay time (CR and CC),
- throughput requirement – eight values (CR and CC),
- residual error rate (CR and CC),
- connection priority (CR and CC),

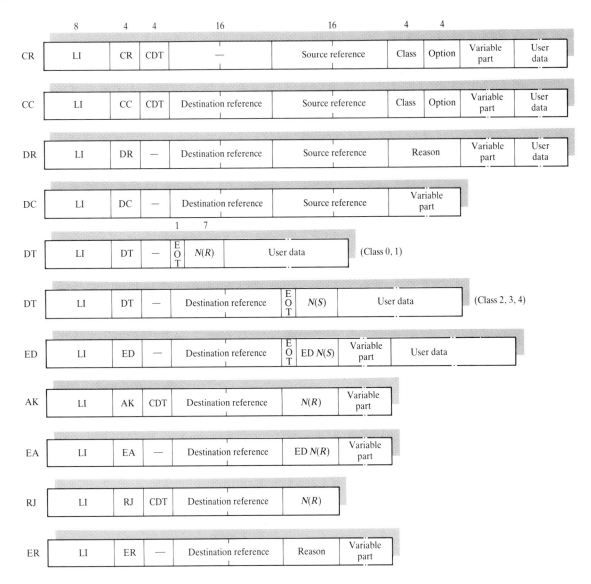

FIGURE 10.22

TPDU types and
header fields.

- transit delay requirement (CR and CC),
- network reassignment (reconnection) attempts (CR and CC classes 1 and 3),
- user defined additional information (DR),
- AK number (AK),
- flow control confirmation (AK),
- invalid TPDU (ER).

As can be seen, most are used in CR and CC TPDUs to negotiate the operational characteristics of the transport connection. The additional **user data** part associated with most PDUs allows a user to send up to 32 bytes of data with these PDUs.

Connection establishment

The establishment of a transport connection begins when a TS-user issues a T.CONNECT.request primitive. The local transport protocol entity responds by creating a CR-TPDU and sends this to its peer transport protocol entity in the called system. On receipt of this, the latter notifies the designated user in its own system of the connection request by means of a T.CONNECT.indication primitive. Then, providing the correspondent user is prepared to accept the call, it responds by issuing a T.CONNECT.response primitive. Alternatively, if the correspondent user does not wish to accept the call, it issues a T.DISCONNECT.request primitive with the reason for the rejection as a parameter. The peer transport protocol entity then relays the appropriate response in either a CC-TPDU or a DR-TPDU, respectively. Finally, the response is relayed by the initiating protocol entity to the user by means of the T.CONNECT.confirm primitive or the T.DISCONNECT.indication primitive, respectively, the latter containing the reason for the rejection as a parameter. Notice that since only a two-way exchange is used, in the event of two users trying to establish a connection with the other concurrently, two independent connections will be established. In practice, however, this is unlikely since all current ISO applications are based on the client-server model.

The parameters contained in the CR- and CC-TPDUs relay information relating to the connection being established which both transport protocol entities must know in order to manage subsequent data transfers across the established connection. This includes such information as the connection (endpoint) identifiers (references) to be associated with the TC by both the calling (source) and called (destination) transport entity, the class of service required and the maximum length of subsequent DT-TPDUs. Typically, the latter is determined by the type of underlying network(s) being used and may range from 128 octets to 8192 octets increasing in powers of 2. Once the transport connection has been established, data can be accepted by the transport entities for transfer across the established logical connection in either direction.

Data transfer

A TS-user initiates the transfer of data to a correspondent user across a previously established connection using the T.DATA.request primitive. The local transport entity then transfers the user data (TSDU) in one or more DT-TPDUs, depending on the amount of user data in the TSDU and the maximum size of the TPDU specified for the connection. Each DT-TPDU contains a marker (EOT) which, when set, indicates that this is the last TPDU in a sequence making up a single TSDU. Also, each DT-TPDU contains a send sequence number $N(S)$ which is used both to indicate the order of the TPDU in a sequence and, in conjunction with the AK-TPDU, for acknowledgement and flow control. When the destination transport entity has received, and acknowledged, all the DT-TPDUs making up a TSDU, it then passes the reassembled block of data (that is, the TSDU) to the correspondent user using a T.DATA.indication primitive.

The acknowledgement and flow control mechanisms used vary for different classes of service, which in turn are determined by the quality of service of the underlying data network being used to transport the TPDUs. With an X.25 PSPDN, for example, the integrity and order of transmitted TPDUs is maintained by the network layer. Hence, only minimal acknowledgement and flow control mechanisms are needed in the transport protocol. With other types of network, however, this is not the case, so more sophisticated mechanisms, similar to those described in Chapter 4, must be used.

The acknowledgement procedure with class 4 is based on a go-back-N strategy (see Chapter 4) which works as follows. The receiver, on receipt of the next in-sequence DT-TPDU or, if the TPDU completes a contiguous sequence of TPDUs, returns an AK-TPDU which contains a receive sequence number $N(R)$ that positively acknowledges correct receipt of those DT-TPDUs up to and including that with a send sequence number of $N(R) - 1$. On receipt of an out-of-sequence DT-TPDU (that is, with an $N(S)$ exceeding the next in-sequence DT-TPDU expected), the receiving transport entity returns an RJ (negative acknowledgement) TPDU with an $N(R)$ indicating the $N(S)$ of the next in-sequence DT-TPDU expected. Also, a timeout mechanism is employed for both these TPDUs to overcome the loss of an AK- or RJ-TPDU.

If the network layer does not ensure that DT-TPDUs always arrive in sequence, the receiving transport entity uses the sequence numbers contained in each DT-TPDU to reassemble them into the correct order. In such cases, therefore, it is only when a DT-TPDU arrives in sequence or completes a contiguous sequence of outstanding TPDUs that the receiver returns an AK-TPDU indicating their correct receipt. A typical sequence of TPDUs to implement a user data transfer request is shown in Figure 10.23.

Another factor that must be considered is that if the service provided by the network layer is of a low quality, it may lose TPDUs without notifying the sender or intended receiver. It may also pass on TPDUs containing transmission errors. To allow for these possibilities, at connection establishment the user may specify a class of service which invokes a timeout and retransmission procedure, to allow for the possibility of lost TPDUs, as well as computed checksums and error-detection mechanisms to ensure the integrity of each transmitted TPDU.

The protocol mechanism used to implement the timeout and retransmission scheme works as follows. When a transport entity sends a TPDU that requires a response, it sets a timer. Then, if the timer expires before the appropriate response is received, the TPDU is retransmitted and the timer reset. This cycle is repeated a number of times. If the appropriate response is still not received, the transport entity assumes that communication with its peer has been lost. It then notifies the user by means of a T.DISCONNECT.indication primitive with the reason for the disconnection being passed as a parameter. The use of

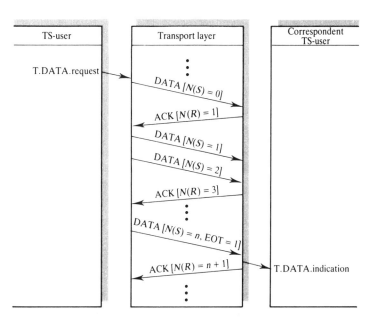

FIGURE 10.23

Data transfer example.

timeouts means that duplicates may be generated – for example, TPDU received correctly but acknowledgement lost. If a DT-TPDU is found to be a duplicate of a previously received TPDU, which is determined by its sequence number, an AK-TPDU is returned but the duplicate is discarded.

Data integrity is accomplished by generating and including a 16-bit checksum as a parameter in the header of each TPDU transmitted. The receiver then uses a similar algorithm to compute a checksum for the complete TPDU including the checksum parameter. This checksum should be zero if the TPDU does not contain any errors. If the computed checksum is not zero, the TPDU is discarded, but the timeout and retransmission schemes ensure that a new copy of the TPDU is sent.

A checksum is used with all CC- and CR-TPDUs and also with all other TPDUs if class 4 is selected. The checksum is intended to detect any TPDUs with residual (undetected) errors after their transfer across the network. The algorithm in the standards document has been chosen to minimize the amount of processing required per TPDU. The algorithm calculates two checksum octets, X and Y, such that:

$$X = -C1 + C0; \qquad Y = C1 - 2C0$$

where:

$$C0 = \sum_{i=1}^{L} a_i \qquad \text{(modulo-255)}$$

$$C1 = \sum_{i=1}^{L} (L + 1 - i)a_i \quad \text{(modulo-255)}$$

Assume TPDU contents are:

$$i = \begin{array}{|c|c|c|c|c|} \hline 5 & 9 & 6 & X & Y \\ \hline \end{array} \quad L = 5$$

$$\begin{array}{ccccc} & 1 & 2 & 3 & 4 & 5 \end{array}$$

Check sum generation:

$$
\begin{array}{llll}
i = 0 & C0 = C1 = 0 & X = Y = 0 \\
i = 1 & C0 := 0 + 5 = 5 & C1 := 0 + 5 = 5 \\
i = 2 & C0 := 5 + 9 = 14 & C1 := 5 + 14 = 19 \\
i = 3 & C0 := 14 + 6 = 20 & C1 := 19 + 20 = 39 \\
i = 4 & C0 := 20 + 0 = 20 & C1 := 39 + 20 = 59 \\
i = 5 & C0 := 20 + 0 = 20 & C1 := 59 + 20 = 79 \\
\multicolumn{3}{l}{X = -79 + 1.20 = -59 \,(196)} \\
\multicolumn{3}{l}{Y = +79 - 2.20 = +39 \,(\; 39)} \\
\end{array}
$$

Check sum checking:

$$
\begin{array}{llll}
i = 0 & C0 = C1 = 0 & X = -59\,(196) \quad Y = +39\,(39) \\
i = 1 & C0 := 0 + 5 = 5 & C1 := 0 + 5 = 5 \\
i = 2 & C0 := 5 + 9 = 14 & C1 := 5 + 14 = 19 \\
i = 3 & C0 := 14 + 6 = 20 & C1 := 19 + 20 = 39 \\
i = 4 & C0 := 20 - 59 = -\;39\,(216) & C1 := 39 - 39 = 0\,(255) \\
i = 5 & C0 := -39 + 39 = 0\,(255) & C1 := 0 + 0 = 0\,(255) \\
\end{array}
$$

FIGURE 10.24

Transport protocol
checksum example.

n is the position of the first checksum octet, L is the number of octets in the complete TPDU and a is the value of the ith octet in the TPDU.

An example showing the checksum generation and checking procedures is shown in Figure 10.24. The contents of the TPDU are assumed to be comprised of a string of unsigned 8-bit integers with the two checksum octets (X and Y) initially zero. The two checksum octets are then computed as follows:

(1) Initialize C0 and C1 to zero.

(2) Process each octet sequentially from $i = 1$ to L.

(3) At each stage:

   (a) add the value of the octet to C0,
   (b) add the new C0 to C1.

(4) Calculate X and Y such that:

$$X = -C1 + C0; \qquad Y = C1 - 2C0$$

It should be noted that this procedure produces the same C1 as that produced by summing $X(L + 1 - i)a_i$. Once computed, the two checksum octets (X and Y) are inserted into the TPDU prior to transmission, and a similar sequence of steps is followed at the receiver during the checking phase. Then, if *either* C0 or C1 is zero, no error is assumed. If C0 and C1 are *both* non-zero, however, an error is assumed and the TPDU is ignored. It is for this reason that a timeout is incorporated into the protocol.

During the computation of C0 and C1, modulo 255 arithmetic is used, that is, unsigned arithmetic (no overflow and carry ignored), and the results are assumed to be in the range $[0..255]$. Also, to compute the two checksum octets (X and Y), one's complement arithmetic is used. This implies the use of an end-around-carry and a result of 255 is regarded as being zero.

The objective of a flow control mechanism is to limit the amount of data (or DT-TPDUs) transmitted by the sending transport entity to a level that the receiver can accommodate. Clearly, therefore, if the transport entity is only servicing a single user, the appropriate amount of buffer storage required to process the subsequent user TSDUs may be reserved in advance. Consequently, when the transport connection is being established no flow control mechanism need be provided. If the transport entity is servicing multiple users, however, and buffer storage is reserved on a statistical basis, then a flow control mechanism must be supported by the protocol. This again is determined by the class of service provided by the transport entity.

The flow control mechanism used with class 4 is based on a variation of the **sliding window protocol**. An initial credit value, equal to the number of outstanding (unacknowledged) DT-TPDUs, for each direction of transmission is specified in the CDT field of each CR-TPDU and the CC-TPDU exchanged during connection establishment. The initial sequence number for each direction of transmission is set to zero when the connection is first established and this becomes the **lower window edge (LWE)**. The sender can continuously compute the **upper window edge (UWE)** by adding, modulo the size of the receive sequence field, the credit value for the connection to the LWE. The flow of DT-TPDUs is then stopped if $N(S)$ becomes equal to the UWE value. The LWE is continuously incremented as AK-TPDUs for outstanding DT-TPDUs are received. This is shown in Figure 10.25.

The actual number of new DT-TPDUs that can be transmitted by the sender may vary during the lifetime of a connection since this is completely under the control of the receiver. Each AK-TPDU contains, in addition to a receive sequence number, a new credit value which specifies the number of new TPDUs that the receiver is prepared to accept after the one being acknowledged. If this is zero, the sender must cease transmission of DT-TPDUs over the connection.

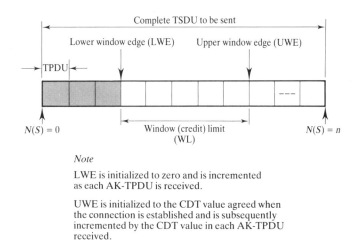

FIGURE 10.25

Flow control mechanism.

Note

LWE is initialized to zero and is incremented as each AK-TPDU is received.

UWE is initialized to the CDT value agreed when the connection is established and is subsequently incremented by the CDT value in each AK-TPDU received.

Flow is stopped if $N(S)$ reaches UWE.

Normally, however, the credit value is used in the situation where the receiver allocates a fixed number of buffers for the connection. Then, as each TPDU is received, this progressively reduces the number of new TPDUs it is prepared to accept (the UWE) as the transfer proceeds and buffers start to be used up.

Connection termination

Connection termination (or release) is initiated by either of the TS-users issuing a T.DISCONNECT.request primitive to its local transport entity with the reason for the clearing as a parameter. With class 0, termination of the TC also implies termination of the associated network connection (NC), while with the other classes the TC may be terminated independently of the NC. On receipt of the T.DISCONNECT primitive, the transport entity sends a DR-TPDU. It then ignores all subsequently received TPDUs until it receives a DC-TPDU. The peer entity, on receipt of the DR-TPDU, returns a DC-TPDU and issues a T.DIS-CONNECT.indication to the correspondent TS-user. The TC is then assumed closed.

10.7.4 Network services

The transport layer uses the services provided by the network layer to exchange TPDUs with a correspondent transport layer in a remote system. The network layer can operate in either a connectionless or a connection-oriented mode. As will be described in subsequent chapters, LANs normally operate with a connectionless network layer while WANs normally operate with a connection-oriented network layer. The set of service primitives associated with each mode are shown in Figure 10.26. As can be seen from Figure 10.26(b), a single (unconfirmed) service primitive (N.UNIT_DATA) is provided for the transfer of all information with a connectionless mode.

(a)

```
N.CONNECT.request
         .indication
         .response
         .confirm

N.DATA.request
       .indication

N.EXPEDITED_DATA.request
                 .indication

N.RESET.request
        .indication
        .response
        .confirm

N.DISCONNECT.request
             .indication
```

(b)

```
N.UNIT_DATA.request
           .indication
N.FACILITY.request
          .indication
N.REPORT.indication
```

FIGURE 10.26

Network services:
(a) connection oriented;
(b) connectionless.

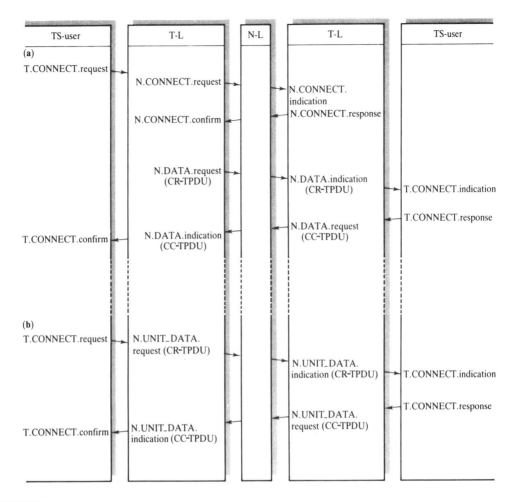

FIGURE 10.27

Network services for
connection
establishment:
(a) connection oriented;
(b) connectionless.

To illustrate the added overheads associated with a connection-oriented service, Figure 10.27 shows the network layer primitives necessary to establish a transport connection using (a) a connection-oriented service and (b) a connectionless service. As can be seen, the CR-TPDU is transferred directly using the N.UNIT_DATA service in the connectionless service. In contrast, with a connection-oriented service a (network) connection must first be established before the CR-TPDU can be transferred as NS-user data. Clearly, however, the quality of service associated with a connectionless service is normally lower than that with a connection-oriented service.

A summary of the various services provided and the services used by the transport layer is given in Figure 10.28 together with a list of the various TPDU types exchanged between two correspondent (peer) layers. This style of presentation will also be used with the other protocol layers to be discussed.

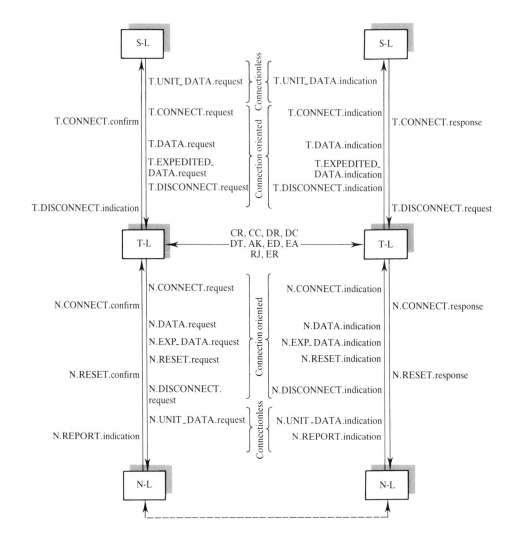

FIGURE 10.28

Transport layer summary.

10.7.5 Protocol specification

As was described earlier, in the ISO standards documents the formal specification of a protocol entity is specified in the form of an event–state table. This defines, for all possible incoming event–present state combinations, the appropriate outgoing event (together with any specific actions) and the new state. Furthermore, if predicates are involved, all the alternative outgoing event–new state possibilities are defined.

Normally, the event–state table(s) associated with a protocol are preceded by lists of the (abbreviated) names used for the possible:

- incoming events,
- automaton states,

- outgoing events,
- predicates,
- specific actions.

To illustrate the protocol specification technique used by ISO, a list of these names for the connection establishment phase of the transport entity are given in Figure 10.29. Since the network service primitives used to transfer the different TPDU types differ for both the type of network service and the type of TPDU being exchanged, only N-provider is normally specified in the various

(a)

Name	Interface	Meaning
TCONreq	TS-user	T.CONNECT.request received
TCONresp	TS-user	T.CONNECT.response received
NCONconf	N-provider	N.CONNECT.confirm received
CR	N-provider	CONNECT.request TPDU received
CC	N-provider	CONNECT.confirm TPDU received

(b)

Name	Meaning
CLOSED	Transport connection is closed
WFNC	Waiting for a network connection
WFCC	Waiting for the CC-TPDU
OPEN	Transport connection is open and ready for data transfer
WFTRESP	Waiting for the T.CONNECT.response from the TS-user

(c)

Name	Interface	Meaning
TCONind	TS-user	Send T.CONNECT.indication
TCONconf	TS-user	Send T.CONNECT.confirm
TDISind	TS-user	Send T.DISCONNECT.indication
NCONreq	N-provider	Send N.CONNECT.request
CR	N-provider	Send CONNECT.request TPDU
CC	N-provider	Send CONNECT.confirm TPDU
DR	N-provider	Send DISCONNECT.request TPDU
NDISreq	N-provider	Send N.DISCONNECT.request

(d)

Name	Meaning
P0	T.CONNECT.request from TS-user unacceptable
P1	Unacceptable CR-TPDU received
P2	No network connection available
P3	Network connection available and open
P4	Network connection available and open and in progress
P5	Unacceptable CC-TPDU received

FIGURE 10.29

Abbreviated names for connection establishment of the transport entity:
(a) incoming events;
(b) automaton states;
(c) outgoing events;
(d) predicates.

(a)

State \ Event	CLOSED	WFTRESP	WFNC	WFCC	OPEN ---
TCONreq	P0: TDISind CLOSED; P2: NCONreq WFNC; P3: CR WFCC; P4: WFNC				
TCONresp		CC OPEN			
NCONconf			CR WFCC		
CR	P1: DR CLOSED; NOT P1: TCONind WFTRESP				
CC	DR CLOSED			NOT P5: TCONconf OPEN; P5: TDISind NDISreq CLOSED	

(b)

State \ Event	CLOSED	WFTRESP	WFNC	WFCC	OPEN ---
TCONreq	1	0	0	0	
TCONresp	0	2	0	0	
NCONconf	0	0	3	0	
CR	4	0	0	0	
CC	5	0	0	6	

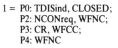

0 = TDISind, NDISreq, CLOSED
(Error condition)

1 = P0: TDISind, CLOSED;
P2: NCONreq, WFNC;
P3: CR, WFCC;
P4: WFNC

2 = CC, OPEN

3 = CR, WFCC

4 = P1: DR, CLOSED;
NOT P1: TCONind, WFTRESP

5 = DR, CLOSED

6 = NOT P5: TCONconf, OPEN;
P5: TDISind, NDISreq, CLOSED

FIGURE 10.30

Event–state table formats for connection establishment.

tables. The specific service to be used is then specified as the different TPDUs are defined.

Two alternative forms of the event–state table definition associated with the connection establishment phase are shown in Figure 10.30. In Figure 10.30(a) each entry in the table specifies the actual outgoing event and the new state combination(s), whereas in Figure 10.30(b) the entry is simply an offset in a table that contains the list of event–state combinations. All blanks in the table in (a) are error conditions and are the same as the zero entries in (b). If none of the predicates associated with an entry are satisfied, this also constitutes an error condition. The latter are all treated in the defined way.

10.7.6 Protocol implementation

A basic methodology for implementing a protocol entity was introduced in Chapter 4 when link-level protocols were first discussed. The aim here, therefore, is simply to illustrate how the basic methodology can be extended to allow for the fact that the transport layer is one of a number of such layers.

It was stressed in the earlier sections of this chapter that when describing the operation of a communication subsystem which has been structured according to the ISO Reference Model, it is essential to treat each protocol layer as an autonomous entity. This means that it provides a defined set of (user) services to the layer above it and, in turn, uses the services provided by the layer below it to transport the protocol data units generated by the layer to a similar peer layer in a remote system. In the same way, when implementing the various protocol layers in the software, it is essential to retain the same approach, otherwise the benefits gained by the adoption of a layered architecture are lost.

Normally a complete communication subsystem is implemented as a suite of task (process) modules, one per protocol layer, with additional tasks to perform local management and timer functions. Tasks communicate with each other through a set of **FIFO queues** or **mailboxes** as shown in Figure 10.31. As will be expanded upon in Chapter 13, a communication subsystem is normally implemented using a separate processing subsystem because of the relatively high processing overheads associated with a complete communication subsystem. Intertask communication is then managed by the local (real-time) kernel associated with the processing subsystem. The kernel also handles such functions as task scheduling and interrupt handling – for the timers associated with each protocol entity, for example.

As has been described, a protocol layer communicates with an adjacent layer by means of the service primitives associated with that layer. Each service primitive, together with its associated parameters, is first created in the defined (local) format in a **memory buffer** known as an **event control block (ECB)**. Unlike

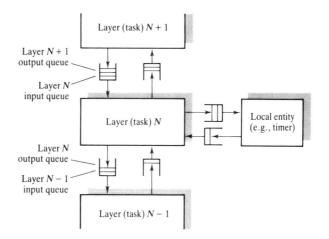

FIGURE 10.31

Intertask queue structure.

the rigid structure (syntax) associated with PDUs, many of the parameters associated with each service primitive are in the form of a list of abstract data types. Hence, assuming a high-level language is being used for the implementation of each protocol entity (and hence task), a language-dependent typed data structure is used when passing parameters between tasks.

In general, the number and type of parameters associated with each primitive varies but, to avoid the need for a different data structure for each primitive type, there is normally just a single-typed data structure (the ECB) associated with each protocol layer. At the head of the ECB is a primitive type field. This is followed by an additional (typed) field for all the possible parameters associated with the complete set of service primitives of that layer. When passing primitives between layers, the sending task indicates the type of primitive being passed at the head of the ECB. As will be seen later, the receiving task then uses this to determine the particular outgoing event procedure to be invoked. The latter reads only those parameters related to it and hence those having meaningful values assigned to them.

The structure of a typical ECB is shown in Figure 10.32(a). The example selected relates to the transport layer and is thus used for all communications between the session and transport layers; that is, for all transport request, indication, response and confirm service primitives. The complete ECB is a **record** structure and the type of the service primitive is assigned to *EventType*. The use of the *UDBpointer* and its associated *UDBlength* will be expanded upon later. The calling and called SSAP, TSAP and NSAP fields are used with the T.CONNECT primitives while the *DestinationID* and *SourceId* are used with subsequent T.DATA primitives to relate the user data associated with the primitive to a specific TC.

```
(a)   const  octet      = 0..255;
             maxSSAP = 2;
             maxTSAP = 2;
             maxNSAP = 11;

      type   SSAPaddrtype  = array [1..maxSSAP ] of octet;
             TSAPaddrtype  = array [1..maxTSAP ] of octet;
             NSAPaddrtype  = array [1..maxNSAP] of octet;
             TransportECBtype =

             record  EventType:       integer;
                     UDBpointer:      ↑ UDB;
                     UDBlength:       integer;
                     CallingSSAP:     SSAPaddrtype;
                     CallingTSAP:     TSAPaddrtype;
                     CallingNSAP:     NSAPaddrtype;
                     CalledSSAP:      SSAPaddrtype;
                     CalledTSAP:      TSAPaddrtype;
                     CalledNSAP:      NSAPaddrtype;
                     DestinationId:   integer;
                     SourceId:        integer;
                     QOS:             integer
             end;

      var    TransportECB : TransportECBtype;
```

FIGURE 10.32

Interlayer communication schematic: (a) transport ECB structure.

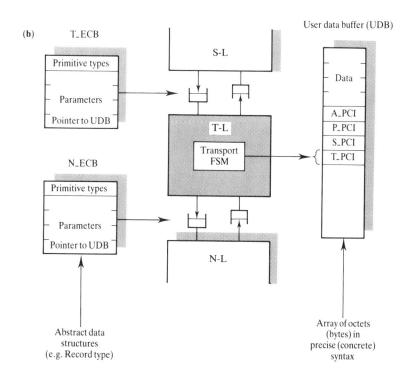

FIGURE 10.32 (cont.)

(b) Relationship
between ECB and UDB.

Service primitives are passed between layers (tasks) by the initiating task simply invoking an intertask communication primitive (to the local kernel) with the address pointer of the ECB as a parameter. This results in the pointer being inserted by the kernel at the tail of the appropriate interlayer queue. Then, when a task is scheduled to run, it examines each of its input queues – with the layers above and below and with the timer and management tasks – to determine if an ECB is awaiting processing. If it is, it first reads the pointer from the head of the appropriate queue and proceeds to process the incoming event. Typically, this results in a PDU being generated and a suitably formatted message (ECB) being created and passed to one of its output queues.

The mechanism just outlined is suitable as long as only a single application layer activity, and hence service request, is being processed at one time. In many instances, however, a number of different activities (service requests) may be processed concurrently. In such cases, either all interlayer messages are passed using a single set of queues or there is a separate set of queues associated with each active service access point (channel). The problem with the former approach is that, since conditions are often associated with the state of a protocol entity (layer) which must be met before a particular action can be carried out (for example, the send window associated with a flow control mechanism being closed), it is sometimes necessary to suspend the processing of a message until the inhibiting condition is cleared. Normally, of course, the latter only affects a single channel so other active channels should not be affected.

The management of such issues can become quite complicated (especially when expedited data is present, for example). To alleviate this, it is common practice to have a set of queues associated with each access point. Then, if a channel becomes temporarily closed, this is readily controlled simply by suspending the processing of entries in the affected queue until the inhibiting condition is cleared. In this way, the flow of messages through the other channels (queues) is unaffected.

As described earlier, each service primitive normally has user data associated with it which, in general, is a concatenation of the PCI relating to the higher protocol layers. On receipt of a service primitive (ECB), the protocol entity uses the parameters associated with the primitive, together with the current protocol state information associated with the connection, to create the PCI for the layer. This PCI is then added to the user data associated with the incoming primitive to form the layer PDU which is then passed down to the next lower layer in the user data field associated with a suitable primitive. The general scheme is shown in Figure 10.13(b).

The user data associated with a primitive is held in a separate **user data buffer (UDB)**. As can be deduced from the preceding paragraph, it is the UDB that contains the accumulated PCI (PDUs) for each of the higher layers. Hence, it is the contents of the UDB that are eventually transmitted by the physical layer. As indicated in Section 10.6.1, the PCI associated with each layer is defined in a rigid or concrete syntax, since it must be interpreted in the same way by two, possibly different, systems. Irrespective of the way the PDUs are defined, this takes the form of a string of octets, so each UDB is declared simply as an array of octets. The UDB-pointer field in each ECB is the address pointer to the UDB containing the user data associated with the primitive. The UDB-length is used to indicate the number of octets currently in the buffer. As each layer adds its own PCI to the existing contents, it increments the UDB-length by the appropriate amount. Then, on receiving the UDB at the physical layer, the specified number of octets are transmitted from the UDB.

The outline structure of a single protocol layer in the context of a complete communication package is as shown in Figure 10.33. Since the ECBs and associated UDBs must be accessible by each layer, they are each declared as global data structures. Normally, a pool of ECBs (for each layer) and UDBs is created when the system is first initialized and the pointers to these buffers are linked in the form of a free list. Hence, whenever a new buffer is required, a free buffer pointer is obtained from the free list. Whenever a buffer is finished with, it is returned to the free list.

Although there is a single *EventStateTable* array associated with each layer (task), there will be a separate set of state variables associated with each active channel if the layer can handle multiple service requests concurrently. For clarity, however, only a single set is shown in the figure. The example layer relates to the transport layer. Hence, the various event types, automaton states, outgoing event procedures and predicates are as shown in the event–state table of Figure 10.30.

The scheduling of tasks is normally managed by the local real-time kernel. If a task is idle (waiting for an incoming event to occur) and an ECB pointer is

```
program  Communications_Subsystem;
global   Intertask queues (mailboxes);
         Event Control Blocks;
         User Data Buffers;
              ⋮

    task  Transport_Layer;
    local type  Events = (TCONreq, TCONresp, NCONconf, CR, CC, ---);
                States = (CLOSED, WFNC, WFCC, OPEN, WFTRESP, ---);
                     ⋮

        var  EventStateTable = array [Events, States] of 0..N;
             PresentState:  States;
             EventType:  Events;
             ECB: ↑  ECB Buffer;
             UDB: ↑  UDB Buffer;

                     ⋮

        procedure  Initialize; {Initialize EventStateTable contents and state variables}
        procedure  TCONind;    ⎫
        procedure  TCONconf;   ⎬ List of outgoing event procedures
        procedure  TDISind;    ⎭

                     ⋮

        function P0: boolean;  ⎫ List of predicate functions
        function P1: boolean;  ⎭

        begin  Initialize;
            repeat   Wait for an ECB to arrive at an input interface queue;
                     EventType := type of event in ECB;
                     case  EventStateTable [PresentState, EventType] of
                         0: begin TDISind, NDISreq, PresentState := CLOSED end;
                         1: begin if P0 then begin TDISind; PresentState := CLOSED end
                            else if P2 then begin NCONreq; PresentState := WFNC end
                            else if P3 then begin CR; PresentState := WFCC end
                            else if P4 then PresentState := WFNC
                            else begin TDISind; NDISreq; PresentState := CLOSED end
                            end;
                         2:
                              ⋮

            until Forever
    end.

              ⋮
```

FIGURE 10.33

Outline program structure of a protocol layer.

transferred to one of its input queues, the kernel automatically schedules the task to be run. The type of event (from the ECB) is first assigned to *EventType* and this, coupled with the current *PresentState*, is used to access the *EventStateTable* array. The entry in the table then defines the appropriate outgoing event procedure to be invoked and the new *PresentState*. Alternatively, if predicates are involved, the list of alternative outgoing event–new state combinations is defined.

Normally, the predicates relate to a number of different conditions. Hence, they are set/reset either at the appropriate points during the processing of each event or by invoking specially written Boolean functions that compute the predicate state.

EXERCISES

10.1 With the aid of a sketch showing the protocols associated with the TCP/IP protocol suite, identify in which layer protocol data unit the following fields are present and explain their functions:

(a) IP address,
(b) protocol port address.

10.2 Produce a sketch of a frame transmitted on a LAN that shows the relative position of the MAC, IP, TCP/UDP and application protocol control information.

10.3 Explain the intended applications of the UDP protocol.
With the aid of a sketch, identify the fields that make up a user datagram header and explain their role.

10.4 Explain the meaning of the term reliable stream service and how it differs from a basic message transfer service.

10.5 With the aid of time sequence diagrams showing typical user service primitive exchanges, explain how two transport users perform the following:

(a) client-server connection establishment,
(b) normal data transfer,
(c) forced data transfer,
(d) status interrogation,
(e) graceful connection termination,
(f) aborted termination.

10.6 Produce a sketch showing the fields that make up the header of a TCP segment and explain the function of each field.

10.7 Show typical segment exchanges between two TCP protocols, together with descriptive text, to explain the following parts of the TCP protocol:

(a) client-server connection establishment,
(b) connection collision,

Clearly identify the segment types being exchanged and typical sequence number values.

10.8 With the aid of a sketch showing typical segment exchanges between two TCP protocols, explain the normal and forced data transfer modes of the TCP protocol.
Assuming a maximum segment size of W octets, a window of 2W and a round-trip delay of 3W, sketch an example segment exchange relating to the transfer of a message of 3W octets. Include example sequence, acknowledgement and window values for each segment.

10.9 With the aid of a sketch showing typical segment exchanges between two TCP protocols, explain the normal and abnormal (abort) connection termination alternatives.
Include in your descriptions the use of the FIN, SEQ and ACK flags.

10.10 Starting with the state transition diagram shown in Figure 10.9, develop a specification for a client and server TCP protocol entity that is based on an event–stable table. Clearly identify the incoming event initiating each transition and any local (specific) actions involved.

10.11 With the aid of a sketch, explain the meaning of the following terms relating to an ISO protocol layer:

(a) service user,
(b) user services,
(c) service provider,
(d) layer protocol entity,
(e) used services.

10.12 In the context of the ISO Reference Model for open systems interconnection, explain briefly, with the aid of sketches where appropriate:

(a) The meaning and interrelationship of the terms network environment, open systems environment and real systems environment.
(b) The difference between a user name (title) and a fully qualified address.
(c) How the overheads associated with a user message increase as the message passes down through each protocol layer prior to transmission and decrease as it passes up through the layers on reception.

10.13 Explain the aim of the ISO Reference Model for open systems interconnection and outline the function of each layer.

10.14 Make a sketch summarizing the structure of the ISO Reference Model and indicate where the following services are provided:

(a) distributed information services,
(b) syntax-independent message interchange service,
(c) network-independent message interchange service.

10.15 Make a sketch of a model of a protocol layer, together with additional descriptions, where appropriate, to explain the meaning of the following terms:

(a) The services provided by the layer.
(b) The service access points associated with the layer.
(c) The PDUs exchanged between two peer protocol entities.
(d) The services used by the layer.

10.16 Outline the structure of the event–state table used in the methodology adopted by the ISO to specify a protocol entity with particular emphasis on the meaning of each row and column. Give an example in such a table that has:

(a) A single outgoing event and new state combination.
(b) A number of alternative outgoing event and new state combinations determined by predicates.
(c) A specific action associated with the outgoing event.

10.17 (a) Use a time sequence diagram to illustrate a typical set of user services for the transport layer and describe their functions.

(b) Define a set of TPDUs to implement these services and hence derive a time sequence diagram showing a typical sequence of TPDUs exchanged to implement the services in (a).

(c)   Define a set of network service primitives and hence derive a time sequence diagram showing how the TPDUs defined in (b) are transferred using these services.

10.18   Describe the following in relation to the data transfer phase of the ISO transport protocol:

(a)   The acknowledgement procedure.
(b)   The error-detection method used and an example of its use.
(c)   The flow control mechanism.

10.19   The connection establishment phase of the ISO transport protocol is to be implemented.

(a)   Produce a list of the incoming events, automaton states, outgoing events and predicates associated with this phase.
(b)   Derive an event–state table for the protocol entity showing clearly the outgoing event–new state possibilities for each incoming event–present state combination.

10.20   Outline a methodology for the implementation of an ISO protocol entity. Include in the description:

(a)   The structure and use of an ECB.
(b)   The structure and use of a UDB.

CHAPTER SUMMARY

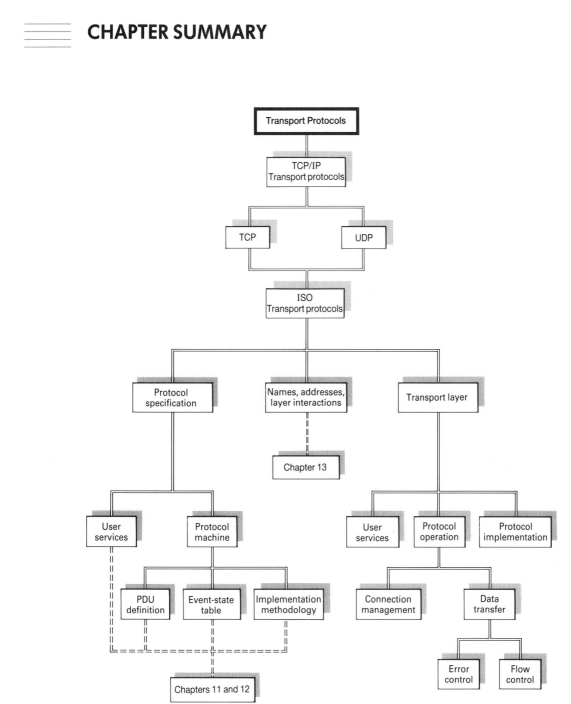

11

Application support protocols

CHAPTER CONTENTS

CHAPTER OBJECTIVES

When you have completed studying the material in this chapter you should be able to:

- appreciate that an OSI protocol stack has a number of intermediate application-support protocols between the application and transport layers;
- know the functionality of these protocols;
- describe the services and operation of the session layer and how the session protocol entity is specified in the ISO standard;
- know the various functions associated with the presentation layer;
- know the roles and operation of abstract syntax notation number one (ASN.1);
- know the terminology and principles involved in selected data encryption standards;
- describe the services and operation of the presentation protocol and how it is specified in the ISO standard;

- understand the role of the association control service element (ACSE) and the remote operations service element (ROSE);
- appreciate the problems associated with concurrency control and multiple copy update and explain the services and operation of the commitment, concurrency and recovery (CCR) protocol.

11.1 INTRODUCTION

As may be recalled from the last chapter, although in the TCP/IP protocol suite application protocols (or application processes) interact directly with the transport layer protocols (UDP and TCP), in an OSI stack they interact through the protocol entities associated with the intermediate session and presentation layers. Also, as shown in Figure 11.1, the application layer consists of two sets of protocols, each of which is known as an **application service element** or **ASE**. The term ASE is used to refer to the combined service and protocol specification of a protocol. One set performs specific application functions while the other performs more general support functions which are also known as **common application service elements** or **CASE elements**. Thus in the TCP/IP protocol suite, the functionality of the CASE elements and the functionality provided by the session and presentation layers are embedded into each application protocol as appropriate.

The session layer is included in the OSI stack primarily to minimize the effects of network failures during an application transaction. In many networking applications, a transaction may occupy a considerable time and involve a substantial amount of data being transferred. An example is a database containing a set of customer accounts or employee details being transferred from a server application process to a client process. Clearly, if a network failure occurs towards the end of such a transfer, then the complete transfer – or multiple such transfers – may have to be repeated. The session layer provides services to reduce the effect of such failures.

If you were asked to write an application program to process records from a set of files relating to an open system application involving, say, a number of computers each belonging to a different bank or other financial institution, you would, of course, want to use a suitable high-level programming language. Each record would then be declared in the form of, say, a record structure with the various fields in each record declared as being of suitable types. However, although the data types used may be the same as those used by the programmer who created the files, the actual machine representation of each field after compilation may be quite different in the two machines. For example, in one computer an integer type may be represented by a 16-bit value while in another it may be represented by 32 bits. Even if the two computers both use 16 bits to represent an integer type, the position of the sign bit or the order of the two bytes that make up each integer may still be different. Similarly, the character types used in different computers also differ. For example, EBCDIC may be used in one and ASCII/IA5 in another. The representation of the different types are thus said to be in an **abstract syntax** form.

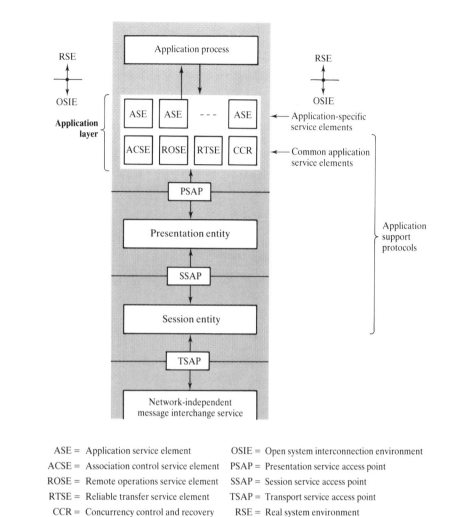

FIGURE 11.1

Application support protocols in the context of the ISO Reference Model.

ASE =	Application service element	OSIE =	Open system interconnection environment
ACSE =	Association control service element	PSAP =	Presentation service access point
ROSE =	Remote operations service element	SSAP =	Session service access point
RTSE =	Reliable transfer service element	TSAP =	Transport service access point
CCR =	Concurrency control and recovery	RSE =	Real system environment

The effect of this is that when a block of data – holding a set of records, for example – is passed from one computer to another, it is not sufficient simply to transfer the block of data from one computer memory to the other since the program in the receiving computer may then interpret the data on the wrong byte boundaries. Consequently, when transferring data between computers, it is essential to ensure that the syntax of the data is known by the receiving machine and, if this is different from its local syntax, to convert the data into this syntax prior to processing.

One approach to this problem is to define what is known as a **data dictionary** for the complete (distributed) application which contains an application-wide definition of the representation of all the data types used in the application. Then, if this is different from the local representation used by a machine, it must convert all data received into its local syntax prior to processing and convert it back into the standard form if it is to be sent to another machine. The form used in the data dictionary is thus known as the **concrete** or **transfer syntax** for the application.

This is a common requirement in many distributed applications, especially in open systems that involve interworking between computers from different manufacturers. The approach adopted by ISO, therefore, is to integrate this function into the protocol stack; this is one of the main roles of the presentation layer. Others include data compression and encryption, both of which are concerned with the representation of transferred data.

Similarly, a number of other functions are common to many applications. The ISO approach is to separate these from the actual application-specific functions and to implement them as a set of support protocols. Then, if a particular support function is required in an application, an instance of the appropriate support protocol(s) is (are) linked with the particular application-specific protocol. As indicated earlier, all the protocols associated with the application layer are known as **application service elements** or **ASEs**. The ASEs that perform general support functions include the **association control service element (ACSE)**, the **remote operations service element (ROSE)**, the **reliable transfer service element (RTSE)** and the **concurrency control and recovery (CCR)** service element.

As may be recalled from the last chapter, two application processes/ protocols can communicate in one of two ways. Either a logical connection – known as an **association** when it relates to an application – can be set up between the two processes before transferring any data (messages) associated with the application, or an application process can simply send the message directly and, if appropriate, wait for a response. The first approach is appropriate for the transfer of large volumes of data to ensure the receiver is prepared for the data before it is sent. The second may be more appropriate for a short request–response exchange. The services provided by ACSE have been defined for the first case and those associated with ROSE the second. In addition, RTSE includes the services of both the ACSE and selected session services.

The functions provided by the CCR service element are also required in many applications. They are concerned with controlling access to a shared resource; for example, a file containing seat reservations in an airline reservation system or a file containing a customer account in a banking application. In this type of application, the files must be accessible from many sites concurrently. Consequently, steps must be taken when changing the contents of such files to ensure this is done in a way that ensures their contents always reflect the operations that have been performed. Similarly, in an application that involves multiple copies of the same file being available at different sites, care must be taken to ensure that the contents of all copies remain consistent when changes are being made. The CCR ASE has been defined to help perform these functions.

This chapter discusses all the protocols identified and the functions and operation of each.

11.2 SESSION LAYER

Figure 11.2 shows the position of the session layer in relation to an OSI suite. Although the session and presentation layers are treated separately for specification purposes, they operate in close cooperation with the various protocols in the application layer to provide a particular application-support function. Hence, even if the PSAP and SSAP address selectors are used to provide additional multiplexing/demultiplexing above the transport layer, most of the service primitives associated with the application layer translate directly into equivalent presentation/session primitives. Indeed, in many instances the presentation layer passes selected service primitives directly to the session layer without modification. Alternatively, if a primitive relates to both the presentation and session layers, then the presentation entity simply adds its own protocol control information to the head of the message (PDU) it receives and passes this on to the session layer in the user data parameter of a matching session service primitive.

Also, as may be recalled, connection-oriented and connectionless communication modes may be used by application entities. These two modes are supported by a connection-oriented and a connectionless presentation and session

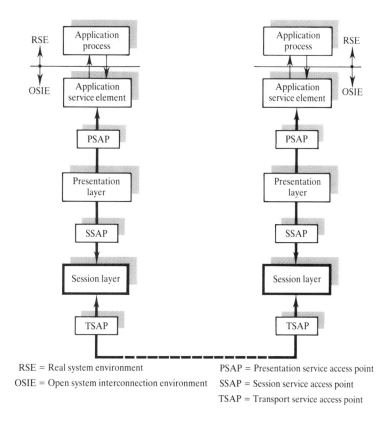

FIGURE 11.2

Session layer schematic.

RSE = Real system environment   PSAP = Presentation service access point
OSIE = Open system interconnection environment   SSAP = Session service access point
                                     TSAP = Transport service access point

protocol. In practice, however, all the OSI profiles defined to date utilize only the two connection-oriented protocols. To achieve a fast response it is possible to transfer a quantity of user data – 512 octets or greater – with the initial connect PDU and, if required, with a returned connect confirm PDU. The connection would then be cleared. Alternatively, it is possible to establish a presentation/session connection and leave this in place. Data transfer (in both directions) is then carried out using this connection as required. Also, as will be expanded upon later, a subset of the full session service known as the **basic combined subset (BCS)** is normally used as a way of minimizing the overheads associated with each message transfer.

The main features of both connection-oriented protocols will be discussed. The two connectionless protocols, because of their minimum functionality, are much simpler.

The session layer provides the means for an application protocol entity, through the services offered by the presentation layer, to:

- establish a logical communication path (session connection) with another application entity, to use it to exchange data (**dialogue units**) and to release the connection in an orderly way;
- establish synchronization points during a dialogue and, in the event of errors, to resume the dialogue from an agreed synchronization point;
- interrupt (suspend) a dialogue and resume it later at a prearranged point;
- be informed of certain exceptions that may arise from the underlying network during a session.

11.2.1 Token concept

For two application entities to manage a dialogue over an established (session) connection, a set of tokens is defined:

- the data token,
- the release token,
- the synchronization-minor token, and
- the major/activity token.

Each of these tokens is assigned dynamically to one session-service (SS) user (that is, application entity through its related presentation entity) at a time to allow that user to carry out the corresponding service. The current owner of a token gives that user the exclusive use of the related service. Thus, the **data token**, for example, is used to enforce a half-duplex data exchange between the two users and the **release token** to negotiate the release (termination) of a connection in a controlled way.

The **synchronization-minor** and **major/activity** tokens are associated with the synchronization process that may be used during a session. When two SS-users are exchanging large quantities of data, it is advisable to structure the data into a number of identifiable units so that, should a (network) fault develop during the session, only the most recently transferred data is affected. To allow a user to perform this function, a number of **synchronization points** may be inserted into sequential blocks of data before transmission. Each synchronization point is identified by a serial number which is maintained by the session protocol entity. Two types of synchronization points are provided:

- **Major**: Normally, these are associated with complete units of data (dialogue units) being exchanged between two users.
- **Minor**: Normally, these are associated with parts of a dialogue unit.

These two types of synchronization token are provided to allow two users to implement the associated synchronization process. Typical synchronization points established during a complete session connection are shown in Figure 11.3(a).

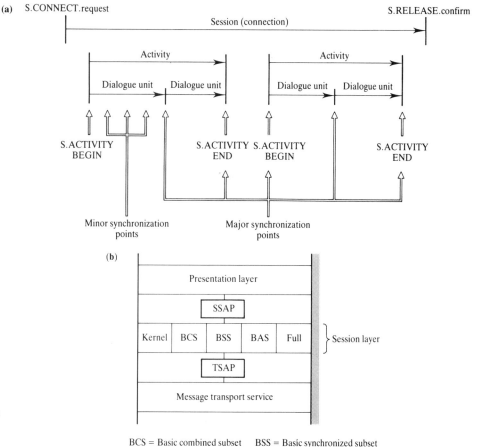

FIGURE 11.3

Session layer detail:
(a) activity and dialogue unit synchronization concepts; (b) protocol subsets.

BCS = Basic combined subset   BSS = Basic synchronized subset
BAS = Basic activity subset

The concept of an **activity** is used to allow two SS-users to distinguish between different logical pieces of work associated with a session. Although a complete session may comprise a number of activities, only one activity may be in progress at a time. In this way, an activity can be interrupted and then resumed either on the same session connection or on a different connection. Each activity is therefore made up of a number of **dialogue units**. For example, an activity may relate to a number of files. A dialogue unit would then relate to a single file which is in turn made up of a number of records.

11.2.2 User services

The services offered by the session layer to a user are extremely varied and hence are grouped into a number of **functional units** to allow two SS-users to negotiate the precise services required when the session connection is first established. The functional units available include:

- **Kernel**: provides the basic (and minimal) functions of connection management and duplex data transfer.
- **Negotiated release**: provides an orderly release service.
- **Half-duplex**: provides for one-way alternate data exchange.
- **Synchronization**: provides for (re)synchronization during a session connection.
- **Activity management**: provides for identifying, starting, ending, suspending and restarting activities.
- **Exception reporting**: provides for reporting an exception during a session connection.

To avoid the need for the user to specify each required functional unit when a session connection is first established, a number of **subsets**, comprising different combinations of units, have been defined. These are summarized in Figure 11.3(b) and are:

- **Basic combined subset**: includes the kernel and half-duplex units.
- **Basic synchronized subset**: includes the synchronization units.
- **Basic activity subset**: includes the activity management and exception reporting units.

User service primitives are also available to implement all the foregoing functions. As an example, the services provided to implement the basic combined subset (BCS) are shown in the time sequence diagram in Figure 11.4(a).

In addition, parameters are associated with each service. For example, the parameters associated with the S.CONNECT.primitives allow two SS-users to negotiate such things as the services (functional units) to be used during the session connection, initial token ownership and (when selected) sync-point serial

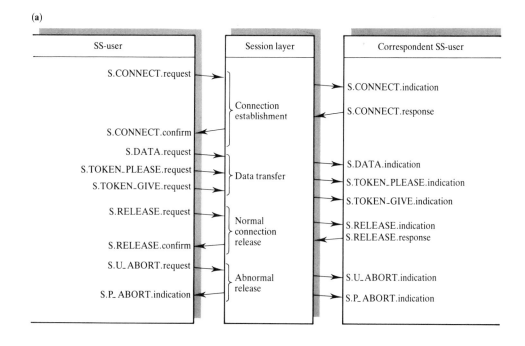

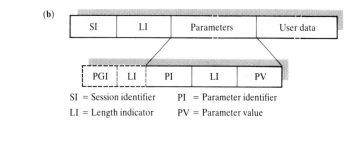

SI = Session identifier   PI = Parameter identifier

LI = Length indicator   PV = Parameter value

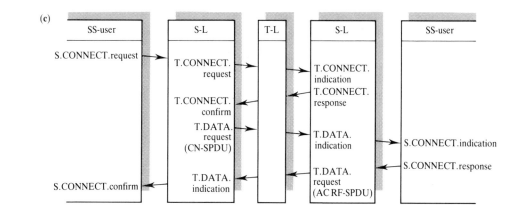

FIGURE 11.4

Session services:
(a) user services;
(b) SPDU format;
(c) used services.

number settings. These are in addition to the normal calling and called addresses and a (session) connection identifier to be used during the subsequent data exchange phase. The parameters associated with the two TOKEN primitives include the type of the token – data, release etc. The S.TOKEN_PLEASE service is used to request the specified token(s) and the S.TOKEN_GIVE service to transfer the specified token(s).

11.2.3 Session protocol

Most of the service primitives previously described result in a corresponding session protocol data unit (SPDU) being created and sent by the session protocol entity. For example, the SPDUs associated with the BSC service primitives are:

SPDU	*Sent in response to:*
CONNECTION.CN	S.CONNECT.request
ACCEPT. AC	S.CONNECT.response (if successful)
REFUSE.RF	S.CONNECT.response
DATA.DT	S.DATA.request
GIVE TOKEN.GT	S.GIVE_TOKEN.request
GIVE TOKEN ACK. GTA	GT received
PLEASE TOKEN, PT	S.PLEASE_TOKEN.request
FINISH.FN	S.RELEASE.request
DISCONNECT.DN	S.RELEASE.response
ABORT.AB	S.U_ABORT.request
ABORT ACCEPT.AA	AB received

The general point of a SPDU is shown in Figure 11.4(b). The first two fields in all SPDUs are the **SPDU type identifier (SI)** and the **SPDU length identifier (LI)** in octets. The different SPDUs each have a number of fields – known as parameters – associated with them. Each parameter is in a standard form comprising a **parameter identifier (PI)**, a **parameter length identifier (LI)** and a **parameter value (PV)**. In some instances, parameters are grouped together; the parameter string is then preceded by a **parameter group identifier (PGI)** and a **parameter count (LI)**.

The user data associated with a service primitive can be segmented into a number of SPDUs for transfer across a transport connection. It should be noted, however, that this is a function of the session protocol entity and is nothing to do with the segmentation procedure in the transport layer.

Before any SPDUs can be sent, a transport connection must first be established over which all SPDUs are then sent – including the CONNECT SPDU – using the T.DATA service. This is shown in Figure 11.4(c).

To illustrate the use of some of the other SPDUs, Figure 11.5 shows those that are transferred to set up a connection, to transfer data using both full duplex and half duplex, and to release the connection both normally and abnormally.

It is possible to send up to 512 bytes of data in a CONNECT (CN) SPDU. In addition, if the user data associated with the S.CONNECT.request primitive

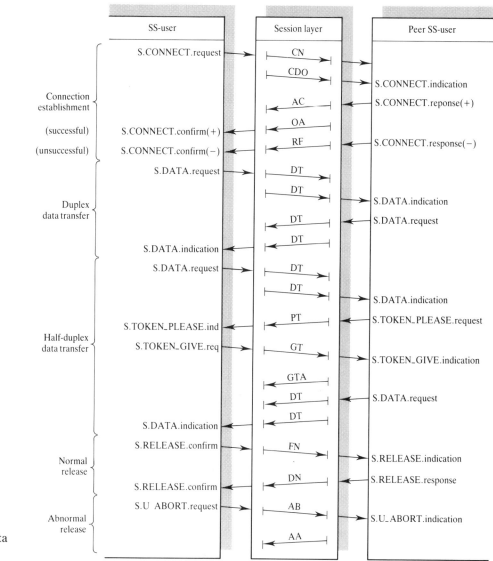

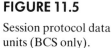

FIGURE 11.5

Session protocol data units (BCS only).

exceeds 512 bytes, the source session protocol entity can send the extra data immediately using a second SPDU known as a CONNECT DATA OVERFLOW (CDO). Similarly, if the user data associated with the resulting S.CON-NECT.response primitive exceeds 512 bytes this also can be sent immediately using the additional ACCEPT DATA OVERFLOW (OA) SPDU.

With duplex data transfer, both sides of the connection can send data at any time. When half duplex is being used, however, only the current owner of the data token can send data. Hence, when the responding entity wants to return data, it

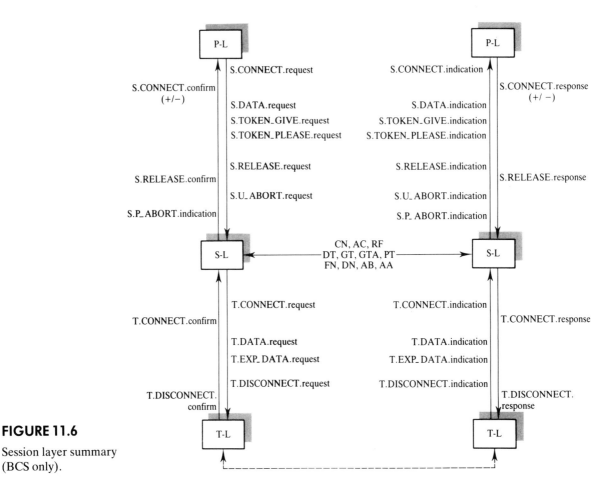

FIGURE 11.6

Session layer summary
(BCS only).

must request the token from the other side before sending the data. In the figure, it is assumed that the submitted data in both directions requires two DATA (DT) SPDUs to send.

Finally, the figure shows the two alternative release methods, normal and abnormal. A summary of the various SS-user services, together with the SPDUs exchanged and the used services, associated with the BCS is given in Figure 11.6.

11.2.4 Protocol specification

The formal specification of the session protocol entity is presented in the standards documents in the form outlined in the last chapter. The aim here, therefore, is to present just an introduction; the reader is referred to the relevant standards for a more complete description. The connection establishment phase for the BCS subset has been selected as an example.

(a)

Name	Interface	Meaning
SCONreq	SS-user	S.CONNECT.request received
SCONresp(+)	SS-user	S.CONNECT.response (accept) received
SCONresp(−)	SS-user	S.CONNECT.response (reject) received
TCONind	TS-provider	T.CONNECT.indication received
TCONconf	TS-provider	T.CONNECT.confirm received
CN	TS-provider	Connect SPDU received
AC	TS-provider	Accept SPDU received
RF	TS-provider	Refuse SPDU received
STIM	Timer	Timer STIM expires

(b)

Name	Meaning
STA 01	Idle, no transport connection
STA 01B	Wait for T.CONNECT.confirm
STA 01C	Idle, transport connection in place
STA 02	Wait for AC-SPDU
STA 08	Wait for S.CONNECT.response
STA 16	Wait for T.DISCONNECT.indication
STA 713	Data transfer

(c)

Name	Interface	Meaning
SCONind	SS-user	S.CONNECT.indication issued
SCONconf(+)	SS-user	S.CONNECT.confirm (accept) issued
SCONconf(−)	SS-user	S.CONNECT.confirm (reject) issued
SPABTind	SS-user	S.P_ABORT.indication issued
TCONreq	TS-provider	T.CONNECT.request issued
TCONresp	TS-provider	T.CONNECT.response issued
TDISreq	TS-provider	T.DISCONNECT.request issued
CN	TS-provider	Connect SPDU sent
AC	TS-provider	Accept SPDU sent
RF	TS-provider	Refuse SPDU sent
AB	TS-provider	Abort SPDU sent

(d)

Name	Meaning
P1	This SPM initiated TC

(e)

Name	Meaning
[1]	Set P1 false
[2]	Set P1 true
[3]	Stop timer STIM
[4]	Start timer STIM

FIGURE 11.7

Abbreviated names for session protocol specification:
(a) incoming events;
(b) automaton states;
(c) outgoing events;
(d) predicates;
(e) specific actions.

First, a list of the various incoming events, automaton states, outgoing events, predicates and specific actions are given, as shown in Figure 11.7. The abbreviated names used for each incoming and outgoing event, together with the layer interface to which they relate, are presented and the same names are then used in the event–state table, shown in Figure 11.8.

The underlying transport connection to be used can be initiated by either session entity. The latter is normally referred to as the **session protocol machine (SPM)**. Also, a timeout mechanism is associated with the RF-(REFUSE) SPDU: if the timer (STIM) expires before a T.DISCONNECT.indication is received (signalling that the transport connection has been disconnected), the RF-SPDU is retransmitted. In practice, if a different subset is used, there are a number of additional state variables associated with the SPM for retaining such information

State / Event	STA 01	STA 01B	STA 01C	STA 02	STA 08	STA 16	---	STA 713
SCONreq	1	0	2	0	0	0		
SCONresp (+)	0	0	0	0	3	0		
SCONresp (−)	0	0	0	0	4	0		
TCONind	5	0	0	0	0	0		
TCONconf	0	6	0	0	0	0		
CN	0	0	8	0	0	7		
AC	0	0	7	9	0	12		
RF	0	0	7	10	0	12		
¦								
STIM	0	0	0	0	0	11		

0 = SPABTind, AB, STA 01

1 = TCONreq, [2], STA 01B

2 = P1: CN, STA 02A

3 = AC, STA 713

4 = RF, [4], STA 16

5 = TCONresp, [1], STA 01C

6 = CN, STA 02A

7 = TDISreq, [3], STA 01

8 = P1: TDISreq, STA 01;
    NOT P1: SCONind, STA 08

9 = SCONconf(+), STA 713

10 = SCONconf(−), TDISreq, STA 01

11 = RF, [4], STA 16

12 = STA 16

FIGURE 11.8

SPM event–state table.

as the types of token in use with the session connection, the current assignment of tokens, the current synchronization point serial number and so on. Nevertheless, the specification follows the same form as that discussed in the last chapter and hence the same methodology can be used for its implementation.

11.3 PRESENTATION LAYER

The presentation layer is concerned with the representation (syntax) of the data in the messages associated with an application during its transfer between two application processes. The aim is to ensure that the messages exchanged between two application processes have a common meaning – known as **shared semantics** – to both processes. The general scheme is shown in Figure 11.9.

With any distributed application it is necessary for all application processes involved to know the syntax of the messages associated with the application. If the application involves customer accounts, for example, the application processes in all systems that process these must be written to interpret each field in an account

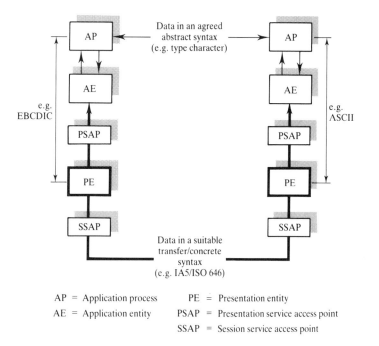

FIGURE 11.9

Presentation layer
schematic.

AP = Application process   PE = Presentation entity
AE = Application entity   PSAP = Presentation service access point
SSAP = Session service access point

in the same way. As indicated earlier, however, the representation of data types associated with a high-level programming language may differ from one computer to another. To ensure that data is interpreted in the same way, therefore, before any data is transferred between two processes it must be converted from its local (abstract) syntax into an application-wide transfer or concrete syntax. Similarly, before any received data is processed, it must be converted into the local syntax if this is different from the transfer syntax.

Two questions arise from this: first, what abstract syntax should be used, and second, what representation should be adopted for the transfer syntax. One solution to the first question is to assume that all programming will be done in the same high-level programming language and then declare all data types relating to the application using this language. However, different programmers may prefer to use different languages. Also, the question of the transfer syntax is still unanswered.

As this is a common requirement, ISO (in cooperation with CCITT) has defined a general abstract syntax that is suitable for the definition of data types associated with most distributed applications. It is known as **abstract syntax notation number one** or **ASN.1**. Most new applications now use ASN.1. As the name implies, the data types associated with ASN.1 are abstract types. Hence, in addition to the abstract syntax definition, an associated transfer syntax has also been defined.

As an aid to the use of ASN.1, a number of companies now sell **ASN.1 compilers** for a range of programming languages. There is thus an ASN.1 compiler

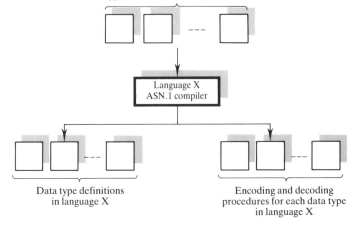

FIGURE 11.10

ASN.1 shared
semantics.

for Pascal and another for C. The general approach for using such compilers is
shown in Figure 11.10.

First the data types associated with an application are defined using ASN.1.
If, for example, two application processes are to be written, one in Pascal and the
other in C, the ASN.1 type definitions are first processed by each compiler. Their
output is the equivalent data type definitions in the appropriate language together
with a set of **encoding** and **decoding procedures/functions** for each data type. The
data type definitions are linked and used with the corresponding application
software whilst the encoding and decoding procedures/functions are used by the
presentation entity in each system to perform the encoding and decoding operations associated with each data type.

As will be described later, each data type associated with an application has
a **tag** assigned to it for identification. This tag is passed with the data type to the
presentation entity which uses it to call the appropriate encoding procedure
before transferring the message. The output of the encoding procedure is an octet
string, the first octet of which identifies the data type. Hence this string is used by
the receiving presentation entity to invoke the corresponding decoding procedure. The output of the decoding procedure – in abstract syntax form – is then
passed to the application for processing.

Although syntax conversion is the major role of the presentation layer,
since it performs processing operations on all data prior to transfer and on all data
that is received, it is also the best place to perform such functions as **data
encryption** and, if required, **data compression**. Thus the source presentation
entity, after encoding the data in each message from its local abstract syntax into
the corresponding transfer syntax, first encrypts the data – using a previously
negotiated and agreed encryption algorithm/key – and then compresses the
encrypted data using an appropriate (agreed) compression algorithm. The reverse
functions are carried out by the receiving protocol entity prior to decoding the
received data into its local abstract syntax ready for delivery to the recipient

application entity. Before describing the operation of the presentation protocol entity, therefore, a discussion of ASN.1 and data encryption are presented. The subject of data compression was discussed earlier in Chapter 3.

11.4 ASN.1

ASN.1 has been defined for use both as an application syntax (for example, for defining the structure of electronic mail) and as a means of defining the structure of PDUs associated with a protocol entity. Although it is not possible to give a complete definition of ASN.1 in a book of this type, the following should be sufficient to enable the reader to interpret the meaning of a set of PDUs relating to a particular protocol entity defined in ASN.1. The principle is the same as that adopted with most high-level programming languages for defining the data types associated with the variables used in a program: as each variable is declared, the data type associated with it is also defined. Then, when a value is assigned to the variable, its syntax is of the defined type.

ASN.1 supports a number of type identifiers, which may be members of four classes:

- UNIVERSAL: these are the generalized types such as integer.
- CONTEXT-SPECIFIC: these are related to the specific context in which they are used.
- APPLICATION: these are common to a complete application entity.
- PRIVATE: these are user definable.

The data types associated with the UNIVERSAL class may be either primitive (simple) or constructed (structured). A primitive type is either a basic data type that cannot be decomposed – for example, a BOOLEAN or an INTEGER – or, in selected cases, a string of one or more basic data elements all of the same type – for example, a string of one or more bits, octets or IA5/graphical characters. The keywords used with ASN.1 are always in upper case letters and the primitive types available include:

UNIVERSAL (primitive):   BOOLEAN
INTEGER
BITSTRING
OCTETSTRING
IA5String/GraphString
NULL
ANY

Some examples of simple types are shown in Figure 11.11(a).

As with a program listing, comments may be inserted at any point in a line; the comments start with a pair of adjacent hyphens and end either with another pair of hyphens or the end of a line. The assignment symbol is ::= and the

(a)
```
              married ::= BOOLEAN -- true or false
      yrsWithCompany ::= INTEGER
          accessRights ::= BITSTRING{read(0), write(1)}
        PDUContents ::= OCTETSTRING
                  name ::= IA5String
```

(b)
```
personnelRECORD ::= SEQUENCE{
                      empNumber INTEGER,
                      name IA5String,
                      yrsWithCompany INTEGER
                      married BOOLEAN}
```

```
c.f. personnelRecord =  record
                          empNumber = integer;
                          name = array [1..20] of char;
                          yrsWithCompany = integer;
                          married = boolean
                        end;
```

(c)
```
personnelRecord ::= SEQUENCE{
                      empNumber [APPLICATION1] INTEGER,
                      name [1] IA5String,
                      yrsWithCompany [2] INTEGER,
                      married [3] BOOLEAN}
```

(d)
```
personnelRecord ::= SEQUENCE{
                      empNumber [APPLICATION1] INTEGER,
                      name [1] IMPLICIT IA5String,
                      yrsWithCompany [2] IMPLICIT INTEGER,
                      married [3] IMPLICIT BOOLEAN}
```

FIGURE 11.11

Some example ASN.1
type definitions:
(a) simple types;
(b) constructed type;
(c) tagging; (d) implicit
typing.

individual bit assignments associated with a BITSTRING type are given in braces
with the bit position in parentheses.

A NULL type relates to a single variable and is commonly used when a
component variable associated with a constructed type has no type assignment.
Similarly, the ANY type is used to indicate that the type of the variable is defined
elsewhere.

A constructed type is a type defined by reference to one or more other
types, which may be primitive or constructed. The constructed types used with
ASN.1 include:

- UNIVERSAL (constructed) SEQUENCE – This is a fixed (bounded),
  ordered list of types, some of which may be declared optional; that is, the
  associated typed value may be omitted by the entity constructing the
  sequence.

- SEQUENCEOF – This is a fixed or unbounded, ordered list of elements,
  all of the same type.

- SET – This is a fixed, unordered list of types, some of which may be
  declared optional.

- SETOF – This is a fixed or unbounded, unordered list of elements, all of
  the same type.

- CHOICE – This is a fixed, unordered list of types, selected from a
  previously specified set of types.

An example of a constructed type is shown in Figure 11.11(b), together with the equivalent type definition in Pascal for comparison purposes.

To allow the individual elements within a structured type to be referenced, ASN.1 supports the concept of **tagging**. This involves assigning a **tag** or **identifier** to each element and is analogous to the index used with the array type in most high level languages.

The tag may be declared to be either

CONTEXT-SPECIFIC:	the tag has meaning only within the scope of the present structured type.
APPLICATION:	the tag has meaning in the context of the complete application (collection of types).
PRIVATE:	the tag has meaning only to the user.

An example of the use of tags in relation to the type definition used in Figure 11.11(b) is given in part (c). In the example, it is assumed that empNumber is used in other type definitions and hence is given a unique application-wide tag. The other three variables need only be referenced within the context of this sequence type.

Another facility supported in ASN.1 is to declare a variable to be of an **implied type**. This is done using the keyword IMPLICIT which is written immediately after the variable name and, if present, the tag number.

Normally, the type of a variable is explicitly defined, but if a variable has been declared to be of an IMPLICIT type, then the type of the variable can be implied by, say, its order in relation to other variables. It is thus used mainly with tagged types since the type of the variable can then be implied from the tag number. An example is shown in part (d) of Figure 11.11. In this, the types of the last three variables can be implied – rather than explicitly defined – from their tag number. The benefit of this will become more apparent when the encoding and decoding rules associated with ASN.1 are described.

To illustrate the use of some of the other types associated with ASN.1, the use of ASN.1 for the definitions of the protocol data units (PDUs) associated with a protocol will be considered. The PDU type definitions discussed so far are all defined in the form of an ordered bit string with the number of bits required for each field and the order of bits in the string defined unambiguously. This is necessary to ensure that the fields in each PDU are interpreted in the same way in all systems.

To minimize the length of each PDU, many of the fields have only a few bits associated with them. With this type of definition, it is not easy to use a high-level programming language to implement the protocol since isolating each field in a received octet string – and subsequent encoding – can involve complex bit manipulations.

To overcome this problem, the PDU definitions of all the higher protocol layers – presentation and application – are now defined using ASN.1. By passing each PDU definition through an appropriate ASN.1 compiler, the type definitions of all the fields in each PDU are automatically produced in a suitable high-level language compatible form. The protocol can then be written in the selected language using these type definitions. Again, however, since the fields are now in an abstract syntax, the corresponding encoding and decoding procedures produced by the ASN.1 compiler must be used to convert each field into/from its concrete syntax when transferring PDUs between two peer protocol entities.

The application service element that enables a file server process to be accessed and used in an open way is known as FTAM for file transfer access and management. Its operation will be discussed in the next chapter. However, as an example of the use of ASN.1, the definition of a PDU relating to FTAM is given in Figure 11.12 – this is the same as that used for example purposes in Figure 10.16(b).

```
ISO8571-FTAM DEFINITIONS ::=

BEGIN

PDU ::= CHOICE {
                    InitializePDU,
                    FilePDU,
                    BulkdataPDU
                    }
InitializePDU ::= CHOICE {
                    [APPLICATION 1]     IMPLICIT FINITIALIZErequest,
                    [1]                 IMPLICIT FINITIALIZEresponse,
                    [2]                 IMPLICIT FTERMINATErequest,
                    [3]                 IMPLICIT FTERMINATEresponse,
                    [4]                 IMPLICIT FUABORTrequest,
                    [5]                 IMPLICIT FPABORTresponse
                    }

FINITIALIZErequest  ::= SEQUENCE {
                    protocolId [0] INTEGER { isoFTAM (0) },
                    versionNumber [1] IMPLICIT
                                    SEQUENCE { major INTEGER,
                                              minor INTEGER },
                                    – – initially { major 0, minor 0}
                    serviceType [2] INTEGER { reliable (0),
                                              user correctable (1)}
                    serviceClass [3] INTEGER  { transfer (0),
                                                access (1),
                                                management (2)}
                    functionalUnits [4] BITSTRING   {read (0),
                                                     write (1),
                                                     fileAccess (2),
                                                     limitedFileManagement (3),
                                                     enhancedFileManagement (4),
                                                     grouping (5),
                                                     recovery (6),
                                                     restartDataTransfer (7) }
                    attributeGroups [5] BITSTRING  { storage (0),
                                                     security (1)   }

                    rollbackAvailability [6] BOOLEAN DEFAULT FALSE,
                    presentationContextName [7] IMPLICIT ISO646String {"ISO8822"},
                    identityOfInitiator [8] ISO646String OPTIONAL,
                    currentAccount [9] ISO646String OPTIONAL,
                    filestorePassword [10] OCTETSTRING OPTIONAL,
                    checkpointWindow [11] INTEGER OPTIONAL}
```

FIGURE 11.12

ASN.1 PDU definition
example.

```
FINITIALIZEresponse ::= SEQUENCE {


END
```

The complete set of PDUs relating to a particular protocol entity is defined as a **module**. The name of a module is known as the **module definition**. In the example of Figure 11.12, this is given as ISOFTAM-FTAM DEFINITIONS. It is followed by the assignment symbol (::=); the module body is then defined between the BEGIN and END keywords.

Following BEGIN, the CHOICE type is used to indicate that the PDUs used with FTAM belong to one of three types: InitializePDU, File PDU or BulkdataPDU. A further CHOICE type is then used to indicate that there are six different types of PDU associated with the InitializePDU type: FINITIALIZE-request, FINITIALIZEresponse and so on. Note that these are tagged so that they can be distinguished from one another. Also, since the tags are followed by IMPLICIT, the type of PDU can be implied from the tag field; that is, no further definition is needed, such as a PDU type. Note that since the FINITIALIZE-request PDU will always be the first PDU received in relation to FTAM, it is assigned an application-specific tag number of 1. The remaining PDU types then have a context-specific tag; note that the word CONTEXT is not needed as they will have meaning in the context of FTAM. The definition of each PDU is then given and, in the example, the FINITIALIZErequest PDU is defined.

The SEQUENCE structured type (similar to the **record** type in Pascal) is used in this definition to indicate that the PDU consists of a number of typed data elements, which may be primitive or constructed. Although with the SEQUENCE type the list of variable types are in a set order, normally the individual elements are (context specifically) tagged since, as will be seen later, this can lead to a more efficient encoded version of the PDU. The first element, protocolId, is of type INTEGER and is set to zero, which indicates it is ISO FTAM (isoFTAM). The second element, versionNumber, is then defined as a SEQUENCE of two INTEGER types – major and minor. As before, the use of the word IMPLICIT means that the type (SEQUENCE) can be implied from the preceding tag field and need not be encoded. A comment field is used to indicate the initial setting of the two variables. The next two elements are both of type INTEGER; the possible values of each are shown in the curly brackets.

The next element, functionalUnits, is of type BITSTRING; the eight bits in the string are set to 1 or 0 depending on whether the particular unit is (1) or is not (0) required. Finally, some of the later elements in the sequence are declared OPTIONAL, which means that they may or may not be present in an encoded PDU. Since the individual elements in the PDU have been tagged, the receiver of the PDU can determine if the element is present or not. The keyword DEFAULT has a similar meaning except that if the element is not present in a PDU, it is assigned the default value.

Encoding

It should be stressed that ASN.1 is an abstract syntax, which means that although a data element is defined to be of a specified type, does not necessarily have a fixed syntax. Thus even though the various data elements making up a PDU are of the same (abstract) type, their structure (syntax) may be different. Consequently,

ASN.1 has an associated encoding method which converts each field in a PDU, which has been defined in ASN.1 form, into a corresponding concrete syntax form. It is this conrete syntax that is transferred between two application entities so that the exchanged PDU has a common meaning to both entities.

The standard representation for a value of each type is a data element comprising three fields:

- Identifier, which defines the ASN.1 type,
- Length, which defines the number of octets in the contents field,
- Contents, which defines the contents (which may be other data elements for a structured type).

Each field comprises one or more octets. The structure of the identifier octet is as shown in Figure 11.13. Example encodings of different typed values are given in Figure 11.14. To help readability, the content of each octet is represented as two hexadecimal digits and the final encoded value (as a string of octets) is given at the end of each example. If the number of octets in the contents field exceeds 127, the most significant bit of the first length octet is set to 1 and the length is then defined in two (or more) octets.

In the first example, the identifier 01 (hex) indicates that the class is UNIVERSAL (bits 8 and 7 = 00), it is a primitive type (bit 6 = 0) and the tag

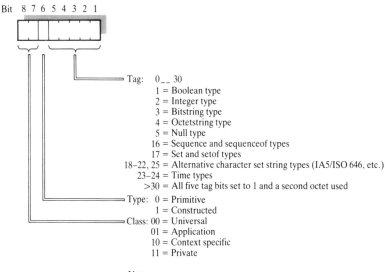

FIGURE 11.13

ASN.1 identifier bit definition.

(bits 1 through 5) is 1, thus indicating it is Universal 1 and hence BOOLEAN. The length is 01 (hex) indicating that the content is a single octet. TRUE is then encoded as FF (hex) and FALSE as 00 (hex).

Integer values are encoded in two's complement form with the most significant bit used as the sign bit. Thus, a single octet can be used to represent a value in the range −128 to +127. More octets must be used for larger values. It should be stressed, however, that only sufficient octets are used to represent the actual value, irrespective of the number of bits used in the original form That is, even if the value 29 shown in the example is represented as a 16-bit or 32-bit integer locally, only a single octet would be used to represent it in its encoded form. Similarly, if the type is BITSTRING, the individual bits are assigned starting at the most significant bit with any unused bits set to zero.

With a variable of type SEQUENCE (or SEQUENCEOF), the identifier is 30 (= 0011 0000 binary). This indicates that the class is UNIVERSAL (bits 8 and 7 = 00), it is a constructed type (bit 6 = 1) and the tag equals 16 (bit 5 = 1 and bits 4

(a) BOOLEAN – UNIVERSAL 1

e.g., *Employed* ::= *BOOLEAN*
– – assume true

Identifier = 01 (Hex)   – – Universal 1
Length   = 01
Contents = FF

i.e., 01   01   FF

INTEGER – UNIVERSAL 2

e.g., *RetxCount* ::= *INTEGER*
– – assume = 29 (decimal)

Identifier = 02   – – Universal 2
Length   = 01
Contents = 1D   – – 29 decimal

i.e., 02   01   1D

BITSTRING – UNIVERSAL 3

e.g., *FunctionalUnits* ::= *BITSTRING* {read (0), write (1), fileAccess (2)}
– – assume read only is required

Identifier = 03
Length   = 01
Contents = 80   – – read only = 1000   0000

i.e., 03   01   80

UTCTime – UNIVERSAL 23

e.g., *UCTTime* ::= [*UNIVERSAL 23*] *IMPLICIT ISO646String*
– – assume 2.58 p.m. on 5th November 1989 = 89   11   05   14   58

Identifier = 17 (Hex)   – – Universal 23
Length   = 0A
Contents = 38 39 31 31 30 35 31 34 35 38

i.e., 17   0A   38 39 31 31 30 35 31 34 35 38

FIGURE 11.14

ASN.1 encoding
examples: (a) primitive.

(b) SEQUENCE/SEQUENCEOF – UNIVERSAL 16

e.g., *File* ::= *SEQUENCE* {*userName IA5String, contents OCTETSTRING*}
– – assume userName = "FRED" and contents = 0F 27 E4 Hex

```
Identifier = 30 (Hex)                          – – Constructed, Universal 16
Length    = 0B                                 – – Decimal 11
Contents  = Identifier = 16                    – – Universal 22
            Length   = 04
            Contents = 46  52  45  44
            Identifier = 04                    – – Universal 4
            Length   = 03
            Contents = 0F  27  E4
```

i.e., 30 0B 16 04 46 52 45 44 04 03 0F 27 E4

Tagging/IMPLICIT

e.g., *UserName* ::= *SET* {*surname* [*0*] *IMPLICIT ISO646String, password* [*1*] *ISO646String* }
– – assume surname = "BULL" and password = "KING"

```
Identifier = 31                                – – Constructed, Universal 17
Length    = 0E                                 – – Decimal 14
Contents  = Identifier = 80                    – – Context-specific 0 = surname
            Length   = 04
            Contents = 42  55  4C  4C
            Identifier = A1                    – – Context-specific 1 = password
            Length   = 06
            Contents = Identifier = 16         – – Universal 22
                      Length   = 04
                      Contents = 4B  49  4E  47
```

FIGURE 11.14 (cont.)

(b) Constructed.

i.e., 31 0E 80 04 42 55 4C 4C A1 06 16 04 4B 49 4E 47

through 1 = 0). Similarly, the identifier with a SET (or SETOF) type is 31, indicating it is UNIVERSAL, constructed with tag 17.

Note also that the two fields in the type UserName have been context specifically tagged −[0] and [1]. The two identifiers associated with these fields are 80 (= 1000 0000 binary) and A1 (= 1010 0001 binary), respectively. The first indicates that the class is context specific (bits 8 and 7 = 10), it is a simple type (bit 6 = 0) and the tag is 0. The second, however, is context specific, constructed and the tag is 1. This is the case because the first context specific tag has been declared IMPLICIT, in which case the type field can be implied from the tag. With the second, however, the type field must also be defined so two additional octets are required.

An example FTAM PDU encoding is given in Figure 11.15. The PDU selected is FINITIALIZErequest, as defined earlier in its ASN.1 form in Figure 11.12. The actual values associated with the PDU are defined in Figure 11.15(a) while Figure 11.15(b) shows how the selected values are encoded. Typically, as will be expanded upon in the next chapter, the various fields in the PDU are abstract data types associated with a data structure in a program. After encoding, however, the PDU is comprised of a precisely defined string of octets which, for readability, are shown in hexadecimal form. The complete octet string is then transferred to the correspondent (peer) FTAM protocol entity where it is decoded back into its (local) abstract form.

(a)

FINITIALIZErequest = {protocolId = 0,
    versionNumber {major = 0, minor = 0}
    serviceType = 1,
    serviceClass = 1,
    functionalUnits {read = 1, write = 1, fileAccess = 1,
           limitedFileManagement = 0,
           enhancedFileManagement = 0,
           grouping = 0, recovery = 0,
           restartDataTransfer = 0}
    attributeGroups {storage = 0, security = 1}
    rollbackAvailability = T,
    PresentationContextName = "ISO8822"}

(b)

```
Identifier = 61                              -- Application-specific 1 = FINITIALIZErequest
Length    = 31                              -- Decimal 49
Contents = Identifier = A0                  -- Context-specific 0 = protocolId
            Length    = 03
            Contents = Identifier = 02       -- Universal 2 - INTEGER
                        Length    = 01
                        Contents = 00        -- isoFTAM
           Identifier = A1                  -- Context-specific 1 = versionNumber
           Length    = 06
           Contents = Identifier = 02        -- Universal 2
                       Length    = 01
                       Contents = 00         -- major
                      Identifier = 02        -- Universal 2
                      Length    = 01
                      Contents = 00          -- minor
                      Identifier = A2
                      Length    = 03
                      Contents = Identifier = 02
                                  Length    = 01
                                  Contents  = 01         -- serviceType = user correctable
                     Identifier = A3
                     Length    = 03
                     Contents = Identifier = 02
                                 Length    = 01
                                 Contents  = 01          -- serviceClass = access
                    Identifier = A4                  -- Context-specific 4 = functionalUnits
                    Length    = 03
                    Contents = Identifier = 03        -- Universal 3 = BITSTRING
                                Length    = 01
                                Contents  = E0         -- read, write, fileAccess = 1110  000
                   Identifier = A5                  -- Context-specific 5 = attributeGroups
                   Length    = 03
                   Contents = Identifier = 03
                               Length    = 01
                               Contents  = 40          -- security = 0100  000
                  Identifier = A6                  -- Context-specific 6 = rollbackAvailability
                  Length    = 03
                  Contents = Identifier = 01        -- Universal 1 = BOOLEAN
                              Length    = 01
                              Contents  = FF          -- true
                 Identifier = A7                  -- Context-specific 7 = PresentationContextName
                 Length    = 07
                 Contents  = 49   53   4F   38   38   32   32          -- "ISO8822"
```

FIGURE 11.15

Example FTAM PDU
encoding: (a) PDU
contents; (b) encoded
form.

Concrete syntax of the above PDU is thus:

```
61   2F   A0   03   02   01   00   A1   06   02   01   00   02   01   00 A2
03   02   01   01   A3   03   02   01   01   A4   03   03   01   E0   A5   03
03   01   40   A6   03   01   01   FF   A7   07   49   53   32   38   38   32
32
```

Decoding

On receipt of the encoded string, the correspondent entity performs an associated decoding operation. For example, the leading octet in the string is first used to determine the type of PDU received – Application-specific 1 = FINITIALIZE-request. Clearly, since each PDU has a unique structure, it is necessary to have a separate decoding procedure for each PDU type. Hence, on determining the type of PDU received, the corresponding decoding procedure is invoked. Once this has been done, the various fields (data elements) making up the PDU will be in their local (abstract) syntax form and processing of the PDU can start.

11.5 DATA ENCRYPTION

As the knowledge of computer networking and protocols has become more widespread, so the threat of intercepting and decoding message data during its transfer across a network has increased. For example, the end systems (stations) associated with most applications are now attached to a LAN. The application may involve a single LAN or, in an internetworking environment, one or more intermediate wide area networks. However, with most LANs transmissions on the shared transmission medium can readily be intercepted by any system by setting the appropriate MAC chipset into the promiscuous mode and recording all transmissions on the medium. Then, with a knowledge of the LAN protocols being used, the protocol control information at the head of each message can be identified and removed thus leaving the message contents. It is then possible to start to interpret the message contents including passwords and other sensitive information.

This is known as **listening** or **eavesdropping** and its effects are all too obvious. In addition, and perhaps more sinister, it is then possible for an intruder to use a recorded message sequence to generate a new sequence. This is known as **masquerading** and again the effects are all too apparent. It is for this reason that encryption should be applied to all data transfers that involve a network. In the context of the ISO Reference Model, the most appropriate layer to perform such operations is the presentation layer. Hence, this section provides an introduction to the subject of data encryption.

11.5.1 Terminology

Data encryption (or **data encipherment**) involves the sending party – presentation protocol entity, for example – processing all data prior to transmission so that if it is accidentally or deliberately intercepted while it is being transferred it will be incomprehensible to the intercepting party. Of course, the data must be readily interpreted – **decrypted** or **deciphered** – by the intended recipient. Consequently, most encryption methods involve the use of an **encryption key** which is hopefully known only by the two correspondents. The key then features in both the encryption and decryption processing. Prior to encryption, message data is

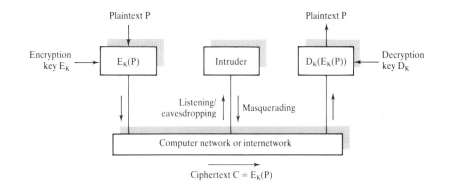

FIGURE 11.16

Data encryption
terminology.

normally referred to as **plaintext** and after encryption as **ciphertext**. The general
scheme is thus as shown in Figure 11.16.

When deciding on a particular encryption algorithm to use, it must always
be assumed that a transmitted message can be intercepted and recorded by an
intruder. Also, that the intruder knows the context in which the messages are
being used; that is, the intruder knows the type of information being exchanged.
The aim is then to choose an encryption method such that an intruder, even with
access to a powerful computer, cannot decipher the recorded ciphertext in a
realistic time period. In practice, there are two widely used algorithms but before
these are discussed, some of the more fundamental techniques on which they are
based are described first.

11.5.2 Basic techniques

The simplest encryption technique involves **substituting** the plaintext alphabet
(codeword) with a new alphabet which is then known as the **ciphertext alphabet**.
For example, a ciphertext alphabet could be defined which is the plaintext
alphabet simply shifted by n places where n is then the key. Hence, if the key is 3,
the resulting alphabet would be:

plaintext alphabet:	a	b	c	d	e	f	g ...
ciphertext alphabet:	d	e	f	g	h	i	j ...

The ciphertext is then obtained by substituting each character in the
plaintext message by the equivalent letter in the ciphertext alphabet.

A more powerful variation is to define a ciphertext alphabet that is a
random mix of the plaintext alphabet. For example:

plaintext alphabet:	a	b	c	d	e	f	g ...
ciphertext alphabet:	n	z	q	a	i	y	m ...

The key is then determined by the number of letters in the alphabet; for
example, 26 if just lower-case alphabetic characters are to be transmitted or 128 if,
say, the ASCII alphabet is being used. There are therefore $26! = 4 \times 10^{26}$ possible

keys with the first alphabet or many times this with the larger alphabet. Notice that in general, the larger the key the more time it will take to break the code.

Although this may seem to be a powerful technique, in practice there are a number of shortcuts that can be used to break such codes. The intruder is likely to know the context in which the message data is being used and hence the type of data involved. For example, if the messages involve textual information, then the statistical properties of text can be exploited: the frequency of occurrence of individual letters (e, t, o, a, etc), of two letter combinations (th, in, er, etc) and of three letter combinations (the, ing, and, etc) are all well documented. By performing statistical analyses on the letters in the ciphertext such codes can be broken relatively quickly.

Substitution involves each character being replaced by a different character, so the order of the characters in the plaintext is preserved in the ciphertext. An alternative approach is to reorder (**transpose**) the characters in the plaintext. For example, if a key of 4 is used, the complete message could first be divided into a set of 4-character groups. The message would then be transmitted starting with all the first characters in each group, then the second, and so on. As an example, assuming a plaintext message of 'this is a lovely day', the ciphertext would be derived as follows:

```
1   2   3   4      ← key
t   h   i   s
–   i   s   –
a   –   l   o
v   e   l   y
–   d   a   y
```

ciphertext = t–av–hi–edisllas–oyy

Clearly more sophisticated transpositions can be performed but, in general, when used alone transposition ciphers suffer from the same shortcomings as substitution ciphers. Most practical encryption algorithms, therefore, tend to use a combination of the two techniques. They are then known as **product ciphers**.

Product ciphers

Product ciphers use a combination of substitutions and transpositions. Also, instead of substituting/transposing the characters in a message, the individual bits in each character (codeword) are operated upon. The three alternative transposition (also known as **permutation**) operations that are used are shown in Figure 11.17(a). Each is normally referred to as a **P-box**.

The first involves transposing each 8-bit input into an 8-bit output by cross-coupling each input line to a different output line as defined by the key. It is thus known as a **straight permutation**. The second has a larger number of output bits than input bits; they are derived by reordering the input bits and passing selected input bits to more than one output. It is thus known as an **expanded permutation**. And the third has fewer output bits than inputs; it is formed by transposing only selected input bits. It is thus known as a **compressed** or **choice permutation**.

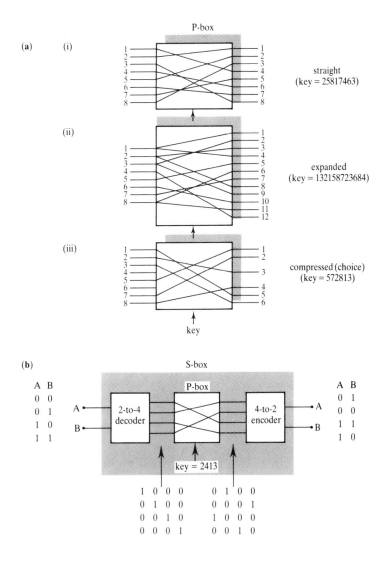

FIGURE 11.17

Product cipher components: (a) P-box examples; (b) S-box example.

To perform a straight substitution of eight bits would require a new set (and hence key) of 2^8 ($= 256$) 8-bit bytes to be defined. This means the key for a single substitution would be 2048 bits. To reduce this, a substitution is formed by encapsulating a P-box between a decoder and a corresponding encoder, as shown in part (b) of the figure. The resulting unit is then known as an S-box. The example would perform a 2-bit substitution operation using the key associated with the P-box. An 8-bit substitution would thus require four such units.

Product ciphers are then formed by having multiple combinations of these two basic units, as shown in Figure 11.18. Each P-box and S-box is the same as that shown in Figure 11.17. In general, the larger the number of stages the more powerful the cipher. A practical example of product ciphers is the **data encryption**

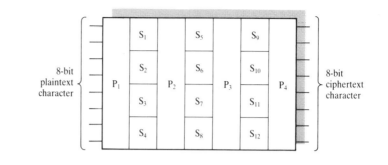

FIGURE 11.18

Example of a product cipher.

standard (DES) defined by the US National Bureau of Standards. This is now widely used. Consequently, various integrated circuits are available to perform the encryption operation in hardware thereby speeding up the encryption and decryption operations.

11.5.3 The data encryption standard

The DES algorithm is a **block cipher**, which means that it works on fixed-sized blocks of data. Thus, a complete message is first split (segmented) into blocks of plaintext, each comprising 64 bits. A (hopefully) unique 56-bit key is then used to encrypt each block of plaintext into a 64-bit block of ciphertext, which is subsequently transmitted through the network. The receiver uses the same key to perform the inverse (decryption) operation on each 64-bit data block it receives, thereby reassembling the blocks into complete messages.

The larger the number of bits used for the key, the more likely it is that the key will be unique. Also, the larger the key, the more difficult it is for someone to decipher it. The use of a 56-bit key in the DES means that there are in the order of 10^{17} possible keys to choose from. Consequently, DES is regarded as providing sufficient security for most commercial applications.

A diagram of the DES algorithm is shown in Figure 11.19. The 56-bit key selected by the two correspondents is first used to derive 16 different subkeys, each of 48 bits, which are used in the subsequent substitution operations. The algorithm comprises 19 distinct steps. The first step is a simple transposition of the 64-bit block of plaintext using a fixed transposition rule. The resulting 64 bits of transposed text then go through 16 identical iterations of substitution processing, except that at each iteration a different subkey is used in the substitution operation. The most significant 32 bits of the 64-bit output of the last iteration are then exchanged with the least significant 32 bits. Finally, the same transposition as was performed in step 1 is repeated to produce the 64-bit block of ciphertext to be transmitted. The DES algorithm is designed so that the received block is deciphered by the receiver using the same steps as for encryption, but in the reverse order.

The 16 subkeys used at each substitution step are produced as follows. First, a fixed transposition is performed on the 56-bit key. The resulting

(a)

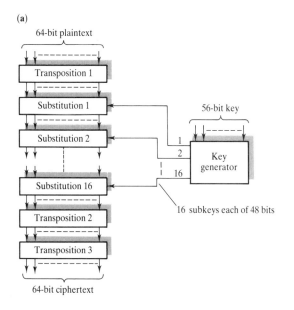

(b)

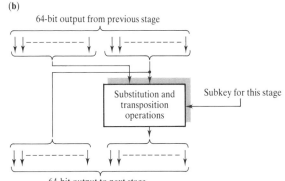

FIGURE 11.19

DES algorithm:
(a) overall operation;
(b) substitution
schematic.

transposed key is then split into two separate 28-bit halves. Next, these two halves are rotated left independently and the combined 56 bits are transposed once again. Each subkey comprises 48 bits of transposed data. The other subkeys are produced in a similar way except that the number of rotations performed is determined by the number of the subkey.

The processing performed at each of the 16 intermediate steps in the encryption process is relatively complex as it is this that ensures the effectiveness of the DES algorithm. This processing is outlined in Figure 11.19(b). The 64-bit output from the previous iteration is first split into two 32-bit halves. However, the least significant 32-bit output is derived by performing a sequence of transposition and substitution operations on the most significant input half, the precise operations being a function of the subkey for this stage.

This mode of working of DES is known as **electronic code book (ECB)** since each block of ciphertext is independent of any other block. Thus each block of ciphertext has a unique matching block of plaintext, which is analogous to entries in a code book. The ECB mode of working is shown in Figure 11.20(a).

Although the ECB mode of operation of DES gives good protection against errors or changes that may occur in a single block of enciphered text, it does not protect against errors arising in a stream of blocks. Since each block is treated separately in ECB mode, the insertion of a correctly enciphered block into a transmitted stream of blocks would not be detected by the receiver; it would simply decipher the inserted block and treat it as a valid block. Consequently, the stream of enciphered blocks could be intercepted and altered by someone who knows the key without the recipient being aware that any modifications had occurred. Also, this mode of operation has the weakness that repetitive blocks of

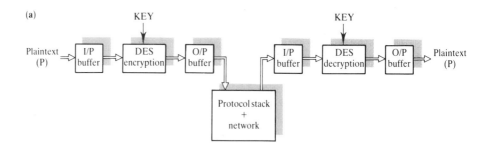

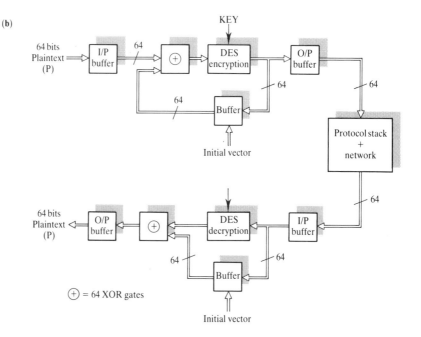

FIGURE 11.20

DES operational
modes: (a) ECB;
(b) CBC.

$\oplus$ = 64 XOR gates

plaintext generate a string of identical blocks of ciphertext, a factor that can be of great benefit to someone trying to break the code (key). Hence, an alternative mode of operation is to use the notion of **chaining**. This mode of operation of DES is known as **chain block cipher**, or simply **CBC**.

Although the chaining mode uses the same block encryption method as previously described, each 64-bit block of plaintext is first exclusive-ORed with the enciphered output of the previous block before it is enciphered, as shown in Figure 11.20(b). The first 64-bit bock of plaintext is exclusive-ORed with a 64-bit random number called the **initial vector**, after which subsequent blocks operate in a chained sequence as shown. Thus, since the output of a block is a function both of the block contents and the output of the previous block, any alterations to the transmitted sequence can be detected by the receiver. Also, identical blocks of plaintext yield different blocks of ciphertext. For these reasons, this is the mode of operation normally used for data communication.

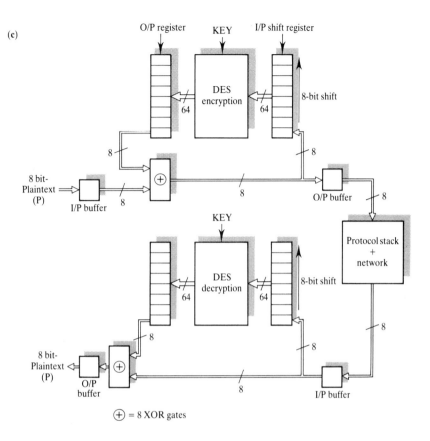

FIGURE 11.20 (cont.)

(c) CFM.

$\oplus$ = 8 XOR gates

Since the basic CBC mode operates with 64-bit blocks, all messages must be multiples of 64 bits. Otherwise padding bits must be added. As described earlier, however, the contents of all messages are comprised of strings of octets, so the basic unit of all messages is eight bits rather than 64. An alternative mode of DES known as the **cipher feedback mode (CFM)** has also been defined which operates on 8-bit boundaries. A schematic of the scheme is shown in Figure 11.20(c).

With this mode, a new DES encryption operation is performed after every eight bits of input rather than 64 with the CBC mode. A new 8-bit output is also produced which is the least significant eight bits of the DES output exclusive-ORed with the eight input bits. Then, after each 8-bit output has been loaded into the output buffer, the 64-bit contents of the input shift register are shifted by eight places. The eight most significant bits are thus lost and the new 8-bit input is loaded into the least significant eight bits of the input shift register. The DES operation is then performed on this new 64 bits and the resulting 64-bit output loaded into the output register. The least significant eight bits of the latter are then exclusive-ORed with the eight input bits and the process repeats.

CFM mode is particularly useful when the encryption operation is being performed at the interface with the serial transmission line. This mode of operation is thus used with the DES integrated circuits; each new 8-bit output is loaded directly into the serial interface circuit.

Both the DES modes rely, of course, on the same key being used for both encryption and decryption. An obvious disadvantage is that some form of key notification must be used before any encrypted data is transferred between two correspondents. This is perfectly acceptable as long as the key does not change very often, but in some instances, this is not the case. In fact it is common practice to change the key on a daily, if not more frequent, basis. Clearly, the new key cannot reliably be sent via the network, so an alternative means, such as a courier, must be used. Thus the distribution of keys is a major issue with private key encryption systems. An alternative method, based on a public rather than a private key, is sometimes used to overcome this problem. The best known public key method is known as the RSA algorithm named after its three inventors: Rivest, Shamir and Adelman.

11.5.4 The RSA algorithm

The fundamental difference between a private key system and a public key system is that the latter uses a different key to decrypt the ciphertext from the key that was used to encrypt it. Thus a public key system uses a pair of keys: one for the sender and the other for the recipient.

Although this may not seem to help, the inventors of the RSA algorithm used number theory to develop a method of generating a pair of numbers – the keys – in such a way that a message encrypted using the first number of the pair can only be decrypted by the second number. Furthermore, the second number cannot be derived from the first. This second property means that the first number of the pair can be made available to anyone who wishes to send an encrypted message to the holder of the second number since only that person can decrypt the resulting ciphertext message. The first number of the pair is thus known as the **public key** and the second the private or **secret key**. The principle of the method is shown in Figure 11.21.

As indicated, the derivation of the two keys is based on number theory and is therefore outside the scope of this book. However, the basic algorithm used to compute the two keys is simple and is summarized below together with a much simplified example.

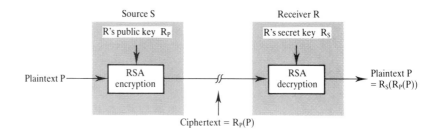

FIGURE 11.21

RSA schematic.

To create the public key Kp:	Example:
• select two large positive prime numbers P and Q	$P = 7, Q = 17$
• compute $X = (P - 1)*(Q - 1)$	$X = 96$
• choose an integer E which is prime relative to X	$E = 5$
• compute $N = P*Q$	$N = 119$
• Kp is then N concatenated with E	$Kp = 119, 5$

To create the secret key Ks:

- compute D such that $MOD (D*E, X) = 1$

$$D*5/96 = 1$$
$$D = 77$$

- Ks is then N concatenated with D

$$Ks = 119, 77$$

To compute the ciphertext C of plaintext P:

- treat P as a numerical value

$$P = 19$$

- $C = MOD (P^E, N)$

$$C = MOD(19^5, 119)$$
$$C = 66$$

To compute the plaintext P of ciphertext C:

- $P = MOD (C^D, N)$

$$P = MOD(66^{77}, 119)$$
$$P = 19$$

As can be deduced from this example, the crucial numbers associated with the algorithm are the two prime numbers P and Q, which must always be kept secret. The aim is to choose a sufficiently large N so that it is impossible to factorize it in a realistic time. Some example (computer) factorizing times are:

$N = 100$ digits ≈ 1 week
$N = 150$ digits ≈ 1000 years
$N > 200$ digits ≈ 1 million years

As can be deduced from the example, the RSA algorithm requires considerable computation time to compute the exponentiation for both the encryption and decryption operations. There is, however, a simple way of avoiding the exponention operation by performing instead the following algorithm which only uses repeated multiplication and division operations:

```
        C := 1
        begin for i = 1 to E do
                C := MOD (C*P, N)
end
```

Decryption is performed in the same way by replacing E with D and P with C in the above expression; this yields the plaintext P. For example, to compute $C = MOD (19^5, 119)$:

Step 1: $C = MOD (1*19, 119) = 19$
    2: $C = MOD (19*19, 119) = 4$
    3: $C = MOD (4*19, 119) = 76$
    4: $C = MOD (76*19, 119) = 16$
    5: $C = MOD (16*19, 119) = 66$

Note also that the value of N determines the maximum message that can be encoded. In the example this is 119 and is numerically equivalent to a single ASCII-encoded character. A message comprising a string of ASCII characters, therefore, would have to be encoded one character at a time.

Although a public key system offers an alternative to a private key system to overcome the threat of eavesdropping, if the public key is readily available it can be used by a masquerader to send a forged message. The question then arises as to how the recipient of a correctly ciphered message can be sure that it was sent by a legitimate source. There are a number of solutions to this problem of **message authentication**.

11.5.5 Message authentication

One solution is to exploit the dual property of public key systems; namely, that not only is a receiver able to decipher all messages it receives (which have been encrypted with its own public key) using its own private key, but any receiver can decipher a message encrypted with the sender's private key, using the sender's public key.

Figure 11.22 shows how this property may be exploited to achieve message authentication. Encryption and decryption operations are performed at two levels. The inner level of encryption and decryption is as already described. At the outer level, however, the sender uses its own private key to encrypt the original (plaintext) message. Thus, if the receiver can decrypt this message using that sender's public key, this is treated as proof that the sender did in fact initiate the sending of the message.

Although this is an elegant solution, it has a number of limitations. Firstly, the processing overheads associated with the RSA algorithm are high. As can be deduced from the earlier (much simplified) example, even with a small message (value), the numbers involved can be very large. It is thus necessary to divide a complete message into a number of smaller units, the size of which is a function of

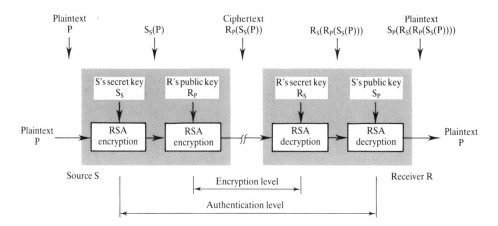

FIGURE 11.22

Message authentication using RSA.

the computer being used. Hence, even though integrated circuits are available to help with these computations, the total message throughput with RSA is still relatively low. Secondly, the method requires two levels of encryption even though it may not be necessary to encrypt the actual message; that is, although only message authentication is required, the actual message contents must still be encrypted.

One solution is to compute a much shorter version of the message based on its contents. This is then encrypted using the sender's private key and sent at the tail of the message which is sent in plaintext. The encrypted trailer to the message is analogous to a signature at the end of a letter since, when decrypted using the sender's public key, it verifies that the person did in fact send the message. The trailer is thus known as a **digital signature**; an example is the CRC for the message. Clearly, however, the generator polynomial used to compute the CRC must be secret and known only by the source and receiver.

11.6 PRESENTATION PROTOCOL

Although the subject of data encryption is often discussed in the context of the presentation layer, the actual presentation protocol entity is concerned only with the syntax of messages during their transfer across the network. As may be recalled, the syntax of a message during its transfer across the network is known as the concrete (or transfer) syntax and that used by application processes, its local or abstract syntax.

The association of an abstract syntax with a compatible transfer syntax constitutes a **presentation context**. Hence, one of the functions associated with the presentation layer is to negotiate a suitable presentation context for use with this session/presentation connection. Also, since an application entity must use many of the services provided by the session layer through the services provided by the presentation layer, another function of the presentation layer is to map such services directly into the corresponding service provided by the session layer. The functions performed by the presentation layer can be summarized, therefore, as:

- negotiation of an appropriate transfer syntax(es) which is (are) suitable for conveying the type of (presentation) PS-user data messages to be exchanged;

- transformation of PS-user data from its local abstract syntax into the selected transfer syntax;

- transformation of received message data in its transfer syntax into the local abstract syntax for use by the PS-user;

- mapping application layer service requests for such functions as dialogue control (token management) and synchronization control into the corresponding session service primitives.

It can be deduced that if the PS-user data to be exchanged during an application session consists of a variety of abstract types, then a number of different presentation contexts may be selected. The proposed presentation context(s) to be used during a session is (are) negotiated during the connection establishment phase. They are collectively referred to as the **presentation context set**. Alternatively, the two PS-users may adopt an existing **default context** for the transfer, such as IA5/ISO 646.

PS-user data, and hence application layer user data, are passed to the presentation layer in the form of **tagged data elements**, where the **tag** or name associated with an element identifies the presentation context associated with it. The presentation entity then applies, if necessary, the corresponding transformation on each element before forwarding it to the session layer.

11.6.1 Presentation services

A time sequence diagram showing the basic (kernel) services supported by the presentation layer is given in Figure 11.23(a). As can be seen, each primitive has associated parameters. For example, the P.CONNECT parameters include the called and calling presentation (session) addresses, the session connection identifier and other session-related parameters such as token requirements. Because the presentation and session layers form an integrated function on behalf of the application layer, most of the presentation service primitives shown result in a corresponding presentation protocol data unit (PPDU) being generated using the parameters associated with the primitives. Thus:

Service primitive	*Generates PPDU*
P.CONNECT.request	Connect presentation CP
P.CONNECT.response (+)	Connect presentation accept CPA
P.CONNECT.response (−)	Connect presentation reject CPR
P.DATA.request	Presentation data transfer TD
P.U_ABORT.request	Abnormal release (user) ARU
P.P_ABORT.indication	Abnormal release (provider) ARP

This is shown in Figure 11.23(b).

In addition, a number of presentation service primitives map directly into a corresponding SS primitive without modification, that is, without a PPDU being generated. Normally, the parameters associated with such primitives are passed in the user data field of the associated SS primitive. These include the P.RELEASE service primitives and the primitives provided for the (optional) functions of:

- synchronization control,
- token control,

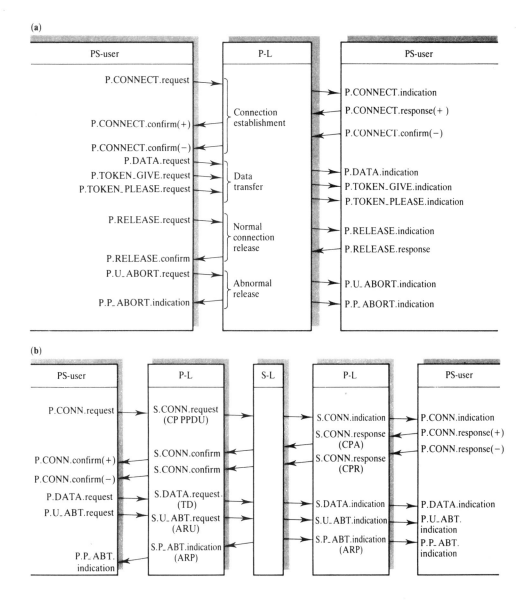

FIGURE 11.23

Presentation services:
(a) basic services;
(b) related session
services.

- exception reporting,
- activity management.

Finally, although there is always an agreed default presentation context for a connection, service primitives exist to allow two PS-users to negotiate a presentation context set for use with a connection. A summary of the various presentation services associated with the basic subset, together with the PPDUs and the used session services, is given in Figure 11.24.

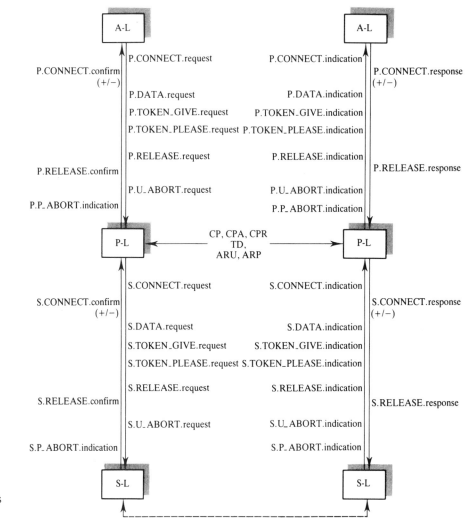

FIGURE 11.24

Presentation layer
summary (basic services
only).

11.6.2 Protocol specification

To re-inforce understanding of the various functions and the interrelationships
between the presentation services and associated PPDUs, the connection establishment phase of the specification of the presentation protocol is summarized in
Figure 11.25. As in the previous examples, the abbreviated names used in the
event–state table for the **presentation protocol machine (PPM)** are given first
followed by the event–state table. The procedure outlined in the last chapter can
be followed for its subsequent implementation.

(a)

Name	Interface	Meaning
PCONreq	PS-user	P.CONNECT.request received
PCONresp(+)	PS-user	P.CONNECT.response (accept) received
PCONresp(−)	PS-user	P.CONNECT.response (reject) received
CP	SS-provider	CONNECT PRESENTATION PPDU received
CPA	SS-provider	CONN.PRESENT.ACCEPT PPDU received
CPR	SS-provider	CONN.PRESENT.REJECT PPDU received
⋮		

(b)

Name	Meaning
STA 10	Idle, no presentation connection (PC)
STA 11	Wait for CPA-PPDU
STA 12	Wait for P.CONNECT.response
⋮	⋮
STA CO	Data transfer

(c)

Name	Interface	Meaning
PCONind	PS-user	P.CONNECT.indication issued
PCONconf(+)	PS-user	P.CONNECT.confirm (accept) issued
PCONconf(−)	PS-user	P.CONNECT.confirm (reject) issued
PPABTind	PS-user	P.P_ABORT.indication issued
CP	SS-provider	CONNECT PRESENTATION PPDU sent
CPA	SS-provider	CONN.PRESENT.ACCEPT PPDU sent
CPR	SS-provider	CONN.PRESENT.REJECT PPDU sent
⋮		

(d)

Name	Meaning
P1	CN-PPDU acceptable
P5	Presentation contexts acceptable
⋮	

(e)

Name	Meaning
[1]	Record abstract and transfer syntaxes for the defined and default context sets
[2]	Select a transfer syntax for each context set
[3]	Propose a transfer syntax for each context set
⋮	⋮

(f)

State \ Event	STA 10	STA 11	STA 12	- - -	STA CO
PCONrequest	1	0	0		
PCONresp(+)	0	0	2		
PCONresp(−)	0	0	3		
CP	4	0	0		
CPA	0	5	0		
CPR	0	6	0		
⋮					

0 = PPABTind, ARU, STA 10

1 = P5: CP, [3], STA 11

2 = CPA, [1], [2], STA CO

3 = CPR, STA 10

4 = P1: PCONDind, STA 12;
   NOT P1: CPR, STA 10

5 = PCONconf(+), [1], STA CO

6 = PCONconf(−), STA 10

FIGURE 11.25

Presentation protocol specification:
(a) incoming events;
(b) automaton states;
(c) outgoing events;
(d) predicates;
(e) specific actions;
(f) event–state table.

11.7 ASSOCIATION CONTROL SERVICE ELEMENT

As may be recalled, the application layer consists of multiple protocol entities, each known as an application service element or ASE. Since a number of functions are common to many applications, the approach adopted by ISO is to implement such functions as separate ASEs (protocols) which are then linked with selected application-specific ASEs when the appropriate support service is required. The combined entity, known as an **application entity**, is linked with the user application process.

To discriminate between ASEs that perform common application-support services and those that perform specific application-support services, the term **common application service element** or **CASE** is sometimes used to refer to the first, and the term **specific application service element** or **SASE** to refer to the second. The remainder of this chapter describes three CASE elements; various SASEs are discussed in the next chapter.

Communication between two user application processes – and hence application entities – is carried out using either a (logical) communication channel that is set up between the two application entities before any data is exchanged, or using a simple request/response message exchange. A logical connection between two application entities is known as an association. The ASE that initiates the setting up and clearing of an association between two application-specific ASEs – SASEs – is thus known as the association control service element or ACSE.

Normally, an association is established in response to a request from a client user application process for access to a particular networked service, such as a file server. As will be described in the next chapter, to perform such services in an open way, a separate SASE is associated with each service present in the application layer in each networked system (computer). At one side it is known as the client ASE (SASE) and at the other as the server ASE.

Normally, on receipt of the initial service request from the client user application process, the client SASE first creates its own initialize (connection-receipt) PDU and then uses the services provided by the ACSE to establish an association with the correspondent (called) SASE. The initialize PDU, together with other information such as the addresses of the calling and called SASEs, are passed as parameters with the ACSE associate request service primitive.

Once an association has been established, ACSE does not feature in the subsequent SASE dialogue until the latter requests that the association be released (disconnected). The service primitives associated with ACSE are thus:

- A.ASSOCIATE.request/indication/response/confirm,
- A.RELEASE.request/indication/response/confirm,
- A.ABORT.request/indication,
- A.P_ABORT.indication.

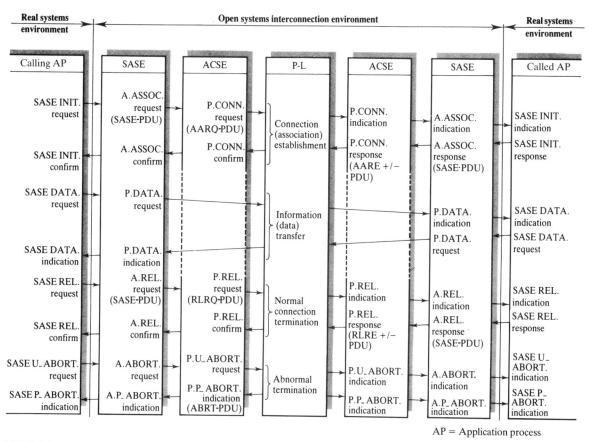

AP = Application process

FIGURE 11.26

Interrelationship of service primitives.

A time sequence diagram showing the interrelationship between the various application and presentation service primitives is shown in Figure 11.26. Each service primitive maps directly from one layer to the other including (but not shown) from the presentation layer to the session layer. Also, there is a single connection identifier common to all the application-oriented layers.

The parameters associated with the A.ASSOCIATE service include:

- Calling and called application entity titles: These are the unique (system-wide) names used to identify each user AP (and hence the application entity (AE) to which the user AP is attached) in the OSI environment.

- Calling and called presentation addresses: These are the corresponding fully qualified addresses (P/SAP + TSAP + NSAP) associated with each AE.

- Application context name: FTAM, JTM, etc.

- Presentation context information.

- Communication quality of service (QOS).

- Connection identifier.

(a)

Name	Interface	Meaning
AASCreq	CS-user	A.ASSOCIATE.request received
AASCresp(+)	CS-user	A.ASSOCIATE.response (accept) received
AASCresp(−)	CS-user	A.ASSOCIATE.response (reject) received
AARQ	PS-provider	AARQ-PDU received
AARE(+)	PS-provider	AARE + PDU received
AARE(−)	PS-provider	AARE − PDU received
PCONconf(−)	PS-provider	P.CONNECT.confirm (reject) received

(b)

Name	Meaning
STA 0	Idle (unassociated)
STA 1	Awaiting AARE-APDU
STA 2	Awaiting A.ASSOCIATE.response
STA 5	Associated

(c)

Name	Meaning
P1	CPM can support connection

(d)

Name	Interface	Meaning
AASCind	CS-user	A.ASSOCIATE.indication issued
AASCconf(+)	CS-user	A.ASSOCIATE.confirm (accept) issued
AASCconf(−)	CS-user	A.ASSOCIATE.confirm (reject) issued
AARQ	PS-provider	AARQ-PDU sent
AARE(+)	PS-provider	AARE + PDU sent
AARE(−)	PS-provider	AARE − PDU sent
AABRind	CS-user	A.ABORT.indication issued
ABRT	PS-provider	ABRT-PDU sent

(e)

State / Event	STA 0	STA 1	STA 2	
AASCreq	1	0	0	
AASCresp(+)	0	0	2	
AASCresp(−)	0	0	3	
AARQ	4	0	0	
AARE(+)	0	5	0	
AARE(−)	0	6	0	
PCONconf(−)	0	6	0	

0 = AABRind, ABRT, STA 0

1 = P1: AARQ, STA 1

2 = AARE(+), STA 5

3 = AARE(−), STA 0

4 = P1: AASCind, STA 2;
    NOT P1: AARE(−), STA 0

5 = AASCconf(+), STA 5

6 = AASCconf(−), STA 0

FIGURE 11.27

Abbreviated names for ACSE protocol machine: (a) incoming events; (b) automaton states; (c) outgoing events; (d) predicates; (e) event–state table.

- Session requirements: Subset, token assignment, etc.
- User data: Typically, the SASE initialize-PDU.

On receipt of each service primitive from the SASE, the ACSE protocol machine (entity) creates a corresponding PDU. This, together with other parameters from the service primitive, is then passed to the correspondent ACSE entity in the user data parameter of the corresponding presentation service primitive. The PDUs associated with the ACSE protocol machine, together with the appropriate presentation service primitives, are also shown in Figure 11.26.

User APs communicate using names or titles. Consequently, before initiating a particular service, the user AP must obtain the corresponding fully qualified addresses of the two correspondent AEs (to which the user APs are attached). These are obtained from the local directory service agent (DSA), as will be described in Chapter 13. Subsequent service calls to other SASEs then normally have both the names and corresponding addresses of the two AEs as parameters.

Finally, to re-inforce understanding of the operation of ACSE, the formal specification of the ACSE protocol machine for the association establishment phase is given in Figure 11.27. As in the previous examples, a list of the abbreviated names and meanings of the incoming events, states, outgoing events and predicates is given first followed by the event–state table. The procedure outlined in the last chapter can then be used for its implementation.

11.8 REMOTE OPERATIONS SERVICE ELEMENT

As will be described in the next chapter, most application-specific ASEs operate in a connection-oriented mode: an association is set up and, after the appropriate transaction has been carried out, cleared. Considerable state information (variables) is thus retained by both ASEs for each association. In addition, however, a small number of ASEs operate using a short request/response message exchange with a minimum of state information being retained by each ASE. An associated support ASE, known as the **remote operations service element** or **ROSE** has been defined to support this type of application.

The semantics associated with this type of communication are clearly different from those involving a connection-oriented mode of communication. The latter is equivalent to two programs communicating with one another whilst the other is equivalent to the calling process invoking a (remote) procedure to perform a specific function or operation. This mode of communication is thus known as a **remote procedure call** or, in the ISO terminology, a **remote operation**. Input parameters/arguments are, therefore, associated with each invocation request and result parameters are possibly returned. No state information is retained after the operation has been performed, and each new request is treated as a separate entity.

The user service primitives associated with ROSE are shown in Figure 11.28 together with the PDUs that are exchanged between two ROSE protocol entities.

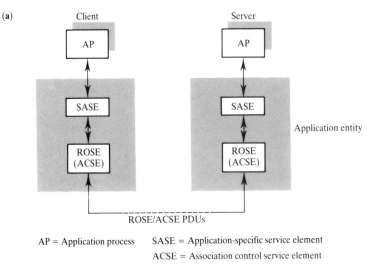

(a)

AP = Application process   SASE = Application-specific service element
                            ACSE = Association control service element
                            ROSE = Remote operations service element

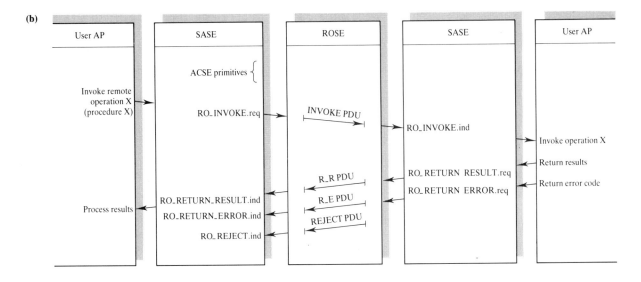

FIGURE 11.28

ROSE schematic and associated service primitives/PDUs.

The RO_INVOKE service primitive is used by an AP through a related SASE to invoke a remote operation on a peer AP. It contains the arguments associated with the operation (procedure) as parameters. Although just a single INVOKE request is shown, in practice a number of requests can be issued before a response is received. Indeed, in some instances, there may not be a result associated with an operation.

The RO_RETURN_RESULT reports the successful completion of an operation and normally has result arguments associated with it. As indicated, however, not all operations return a result. If a result is expected but the operation was unsuccessful, a RO_RETURN_ERROR primitive (and associated PDU) is returned together with a defined error code number. The REJECT is returned by a ROSE protocol entity if it receives a PDU containing unrecognizable fields.

Since ROSE is a general support ASE intended for use by many ASEs, the operations to be performed and the meaning of the input and output arguments associated with these operations, must be defined in the APs that use it and hence outside of ROSE. Similarly, any error messages that may be returned must have meaning only to the APs. The parameters associated with the four primitives are as follows:

> RO_INVOKE.request/indication – InvokeID, OpCode, input argument list
> RO_RETURN_RESULT.request/indication – InvokeID, output argument list
> RO_RETURN_ERROR.request/indication – InvokeID, ErrorCode
> RO_REJECT.indication – InvokeID, ProblemCode

The list of possible operations to be performed, together with the list of input arguments associated with each operation, are defined using ASN.1. ROSE is concerned only with the syntax of these, however, and their meaning – semantics – is known only to the two communicating APs. The list of result (output) arguments, if any, are defined in the same way.

To ensure generality, each operation is assigned an **operation code number** OpCode. OpCode and the list of input arguments together form the parameters associated with the INVOKE service primitive. In addition, since more than one invocation can be issued before a result is returned, an additional parameter known as the **invocation number** InvokeID is used with each INVOKE primitive. Similarly, the RO_RETURN_RESULT primitive, in addition to any result arguments, also has an invocation number as a parameter to enable the sending AP to relate any results to the corresponding invocation request. The RO_RETURN_ERROR and RO_REJECT primitives also have an invocation number parameter in addition to an **error code number** or a **problem code number**. Again it is the AP that relates these to a specific error or problem definition.

As an example, if the AP is a (client) directory user agent AP, then OpCode 1 with, say, a single input argument, may be intepreted by the receiving (server) directory service agent AP as *perform an address resolution operation on the name in the input argument*. This, as will be described in Chapter 13, involves consulting the directory information base to obtain the fully-qualified address corresponding to the given name. Each invocation request would then have a different InvokeID which would be returned either with the result or the ErrorCode/ProblemCode number. The latter would be intepreted by the client in the defined way.

Normally, all ROSE PDUs are transferred using services provided by the presentation layer. To reflect the semantics associated with remote operations, the connectionless presentation and session protocols should be used. As indicated at the start of the chapter, however, currently defined OSI profiles only use connection-oriented protocols. Hence, before any invocation requests are issued, a presentation/session connection must first be in place. This is the role of ACSE, of course. Thus a typical application entity comprises a SASE and the ACSE and ROSE service elements. To minimize overheads, however, if a connectionless network service is being used, then a connection can be set up at the start of a session and simply left open. This is appropriate, for example, if the application involves many/frequent operations. Irrespective of this, all ROSE PDUs are transferred using the P.DATA service of the presentation layer.

11.9 COMMITMENT CONCURRENCY AND RECOVERY

Many distributed applications involve a number of application processes requiring access to a single shared resource. An example is a file system in a banking application that contains customer accounts. Typically, these are accessed concurrently by a number of client systems to perform credit and debit operations on the various accounts. To illustrate the problems that can arise in such applications, consider the sequence of operations performed by two client systems as shown in Figure 11.29.

In the example it is assumed that client A is involved in transferring 10 K (pounds, dollars, whatever) from account (a) to account (b) concurrently with client B transferring 20 K from account (b) to account (c). Each client simply reads the appropriate two accounts from the server, performs the corresponding

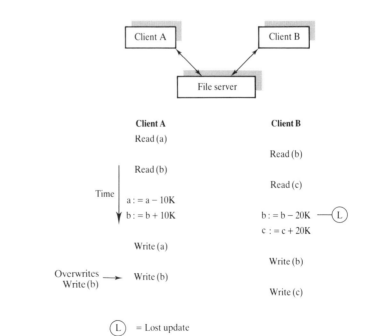

FIGURE 11.29

Lost update schematic.

transfers and returns the updated accounts to the server. As can readily be deduced, however, client A overwrites the update performed by client B on account (b). This is known, therefore, as a **lost update**. Without an appropriate (concurrency) control mechanism, such losses can occur in all applications that involve concurrent access to a single shared resource.

A related problem can occur when multiple copies of a file are being kept in different locations. If not all copies of a file are the same (consistent), in a similar banking application it is possible for a customer to be allowed to complete a withdrawal even though there is no money left as a result of an earlier withdrawal. This is known as the **multiple-copy update problem**. Both problems are common to many distributed applications. The **commitment, concurrency and recovery (CCR)** ASE has been defined to help control such operations.

CCR is a support ASE, the services of which are available to application processes (APs) either directly or as pass-through services of a related SASE. The user services of the ASE known as distributed transaction processing, for example, include additional primitives that are mapped directly into CCR primitives of the same name.

CCR is based on the concept of an atomic action with a **two-phase commit protocol** and **rollback error recovery**. Essentially, an **atomic action** is a sequence of operations that is performed by two or more cooperating APs such that:

- the sequence of operations is carried out without interference from an AP that is not part of the atomic action;
- the operations being carried out by each AP involved in the atomic action are either all completed successfully or are all terminated; any data modified during the preceding operations is restored to the state prior to the commencement of the atomic action.

The AP initiating an atomic action is referred to as the **master** or **superior**, since it directly or indirectly controls the entire activity associated with the atomic action. Similarly, all other APs involved in the atomic action are known as **slaves** or **subordinates**, since they are all controlled (using the CCR protocol) by the single master that initiated the atomic action.

All data affected by the operations within an atomic action is known as **bound data**. The values of all bound data at the commencement of an atomic action are known as their **initial state** and their values after the atomic action as their **final state**. On completion of an atomic action, the bound data associated with it is either committed to its final state if all operations have been carried out successfully, or is recovered to its initial state if one or more of the operations failed. This is accomplished using a form of **handshake procedure**: after all the operations associated with an atomic action have been carried out, the superior first asks all subordinates whether they have successfully completed their processing; hence they are said to be 'prepared to commit'. Then, if all subordinates respond positively, the order to commit all bound data to its final state is given. Alternatively, if one or more of the subordinates responds negatively (or fails to

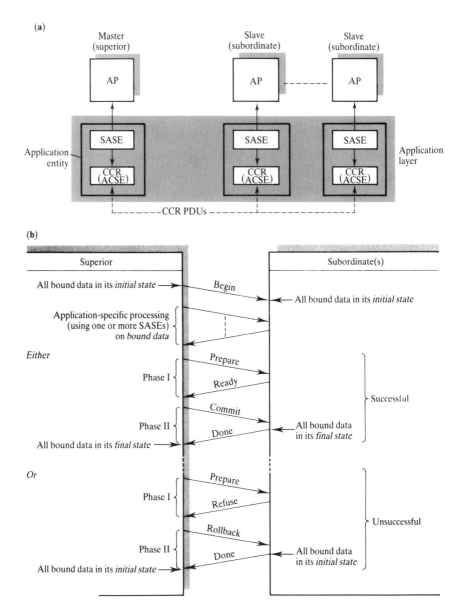

FIGURE 11.30

Atomic action principles: (a) CCR schematic; (b) two-phase commit sequence.

respond) the order is given to recover all bound data to its initial stage. The various terms are shown in Figure 11.30.

It should be stressed that the nature of the atomic action being controlled is determined by the APs, and associated SASEs, that manipulate the bound data involved, and that the CCR protocol provides only the means whereby an AP may initiate and control the atomic action. That is, it is a purely local matter for the APs involved in the atomic action to take steps to ensure that the rules of an atomic action are adhered to. Thus, once an AP has indicated its willingness to take part in an atomic action, it is a local matter for the AP to ensure that an AP which is not involved in this atomic action is not allowed to access or manipulate any of the bound data associated with the atomic action. Normally, this is accomplished using a **locking mechanism** such as **a semaphore**. This is a form of token since, once a semaphore has been set, all other accesses to the data controlled by the semaphore are excluded until the semaphore has been reset. It is similar to the various forms of mutual exclusion mechanisms associated with concurrent programming languages such as Ada.

User service

The service primitives provided with CCR have been designed so that the atomic action that it is controlling is subjected to the following constraints:

- After the order to commit has been given by a superior, the bound data held by the superior and the subordinate(s) will be in its final (permanent) state and no recovery capability is supported to allow any data to be returned to its initial (or an intermediate) state.

- A superior may order rollback to the initial state at any time prior to ordering commitment.

- A superior may not order a subordinate to commit unless it has received an offer to commit from that subordinate.

- Once a subordinate has returned an offer to commit to the superior, it may not then refuse an order to commit.

- Before returning an offer to commit, a subordinate may abort the atomic action (and hence return all bound data to its initial state) at any time.

- The superior may order rollback if any of the subordinates refuse the offer to commit.

The service primitives associated with CCR are shown in the time sequence diagram of Figure 11.31. More than one subordinate can be involved in an atomic action. Also, before an atomic action can be initiated, there must be an existing association between the superior AP (and hence SASE) and each of the subordinate APs. Normally, these are established using the ACSE. An atomic action is then started by the superior AP informing each of the subordinates using the C_BEGIN service. Thus, on receipt of the C_BEGIN.indication primitive, each subordinate must create a new instance (working copy) of all bound data values to be involved – for example, to read a copy of a file from disk – and initiate the locking mechanism. In practice, the C_BEGIN primitives have the effect of establishing a session layer major synchronization point for this association.

The application-specific processing associated with the atomic action, using SASE primitives, is then carried out. Figure 11.31(b) shows the two possible termination phases. In the first, all subordinates return a positive offer to commit, using the C_READY service. In the second, one or more of the subordinates

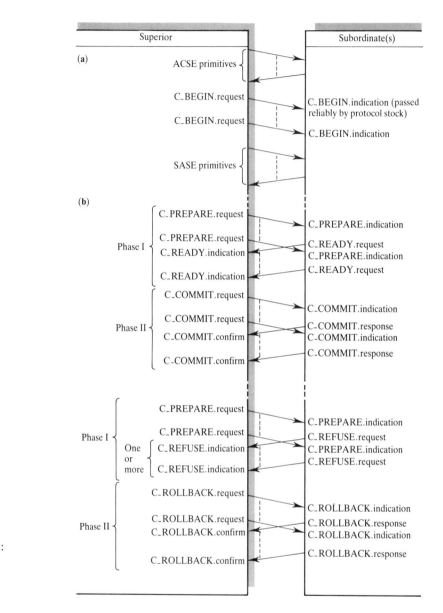

FIGURE 11.31

CCR service primitives:
(a) establishment;
(b) successful;
(c) unsuccessful.

returns a negative reply using the C_REFUSE service. In practice, the C_PREPARE service is optional. If it is not used, the subordinate(s) indicate their readiness (or otherwise) to commit with a C_READY or C_REFUSE immediately after the relevant application processing has finished. In addition, there is a confirmed service, the C_RESTART service, which may be used by either a superior or a subordinate if it becomes necessary to return all bound data involved in an atomic action to an earlier known state. It can only be used by a subordinate, however, provided it has not signalled its readiness to commit. Typically, it is used by a superior if a response from a subordinate times out, indicating a possible application or communication failure.

Some of the occasions when the RESTART service may be used are best illustrated by considering several possible failures that may occur during an atomic action. Some examples are shown in the time sequence diagrams in Figure 11.32. Although the failure in the examples relates to the COMMIT service, it may equally arise with a failure with the ROLLBACK service. It can be deduced from these examples, however, that after a failure has occurred, the precise state of a subordinate may not be known. For example, in Figure 11.32(a) did the communication failure occur before the C_COMMIT request was received or after? The RESTART service is provided to allow a superior, for whatever reason, to return the state of an atomic action to an earlier known state. It is a confirmed service and may be used at any time, provided the atomic action is intact.

A superior determines the current state of a subordinate by issuing a C_RESTART.request primitive with a defined **resumption point** as a parameter. The resumption point in the request (and hence indication) primitive is one of the following:

- ACTION: This is used to request the subordinate to restart the atomic action at the beginning.

- COMMIT: This is used to request the subordinate to restart the atomic action after the last COMMIT point.

- ROLLBACK: This is used to request the subordinate to restart the atomic action after the last ROLLBACK point.

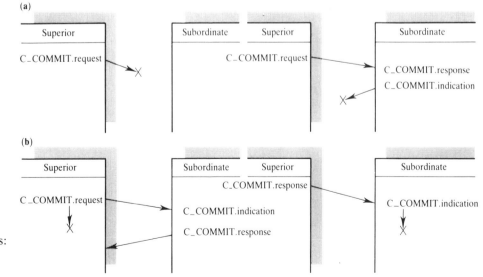

FIGURE 11.32

Some example failures:
(a) communications;
(b) applications.

Similarly, the resumption point in the response (and hence confirmation) primitive is one the following:

- DONE: This indicates that the subordinate has in fact done the last commit or rollback request.

- REFUSE: This indicates that the subordinate has not done the last commit request and hence the superior should issue a rollback request.

- ACTION: This indicates that the superior should restart the atomic action from the beginning.

- RETRY-LATER: This indicates that the subordinate cannot proceed with a restart at this time and therefore the superior should retry at a later time.

When an order to commit is received (C_COMMIT.indication), it is necessary for the subordinate(s) to update the bound data from its initial to its final state; that is, with the contents of the current working copy. Typically, this involves writing the latter to disk. A check is often carried out to ensure that the final write operation is successful before returning a positive C_COMMIT. response. The data is then said to be **secure** or **stable**. One way of achieving this is first to write two copies of the data to disk and then to read and compare them; only if the two copies are equal is the data said to be secure.

Parameters are associated with the various CCR primitives. For example, the parameters associated with the two C_BEGIN primitives include:

- Atomic action identifier: This includes the name (title) of the master AP and a suffix to allow for the possibility of more than one atomic action being in progress concurrently.

- Atomic action timer: This (if present) indicates the time interval the master waits before issuing a rollback request.

It is also possible with the CCR protocol for a subordinate of one atomic action to act as a superior for another atomic action, thus creating a form of tree structure. A further parameter, branch identifier, is then used to identify a specific branch in the hierarchy, and hence atomic action, in relation to the atomic action identifier assigned by the (single) master. The branch identifier is the name of the superior, for a particular (sub)atomic action in the tree, together with a branch suffix. A typical CCR tree is shown in Figure 11.33.

When creating atomic action trees of the type shown, care must be taken to avoid the possibility of **deadlock** occurring. This occurs when an AP forms an atomic action with several other APs and makes a request to one of them. If, however, it is waiting for a response from another AP that cannot respond because it in turn is waiting for a response from an AP that itself is locked into the first atomic action, then a deadlock has occurred. A simple explanation is as follows.

Three APs (A, B and C) are involved in a distributed information processing task. First assume that A creates an atomic action with B and C as subordinates

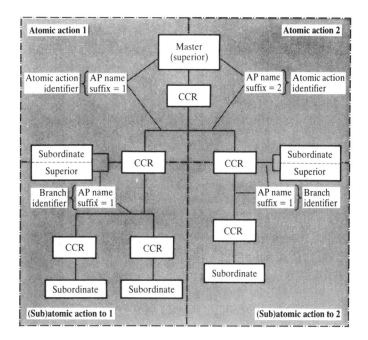

FIGURE 11.33

Example CCR atomic action tree.

and requests data from B. Before B can respond to a request from A, however, assume that B must first form an atomic action with C to request data from it. The system is now deadlocked since A is waiting on B and B is waiting on C, whose resources are locked (bound) to A. Although it will not overcome the deadlock, the timer parameter associated with an atomic action is useful in such circumstances since it will ensure that an AP does not wait indefinitely for a response from another AP.

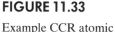

11.10 RELIABLE TRANSFER SERVICE ELEMENT

As will be described in the next chapter when the application service elements are considered, some applications often use two or more of the service elements described (ACSE, ROSE and CCR) in a single application entity. In addition, a fourth application-support service element, known as the **reliable transfer service element (RTSE)**, has been defined which is effectively a combination of two separate service elements. The aim of the RTSE is to provide the user – an application specific service element – with a reliable means of transferring a single message (APDU), or a series of messages.

The history of the RTSE is that, at the time such a service was needed, the full set of presentation services was not complete. Thus the RTSE uses a combination of the ACSE services with a small subset of the session layer services. The latter are accessed as pass-through services of the presentation layer. The

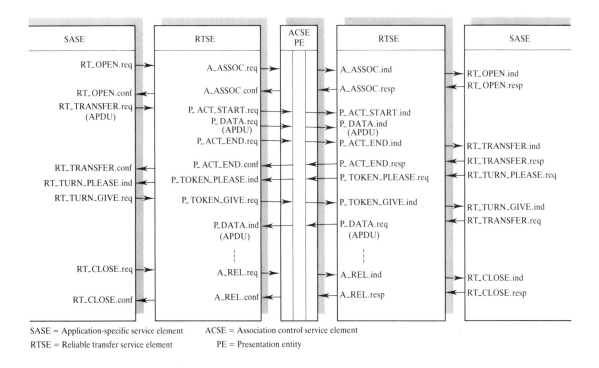

FIGURE 11.34

RTSE service primitive and mapping operations.

service primitives associated with the RTSE, together with the ACSE/ presentation service(s) to which each is mapped, are shown in Figure 11.34.

To send each message reliably, the RTSE operates using a form of send (stop)-and-wait protocol by using a combination of the activity and data token services of the session layer. Once an association has been established, a single message (APDU) is sent by the user issuing an RT_TRANSFER.request primitive. The RTSE then uses the activity service of the session layer to ensure this is transferred reliably. Thus, prior to sending the APDU it signals the start of an activity. Since it is an unconfirmed service, it follows this immediately with a P_DATA.request with the APDU as the user data parameter. Then, to ensure this has been transferred reliably, it follows immediately by setting a synchronization point and ending the activity. Receipt of the confirm primitive indicates that the data was indeed received reliably and hence it issues an RT_TRANSFER.confirm to the user.

If the user wished to send a series of APDUs, instead of closing the activity each time it would send a P_SYNC_MINOR to checkpoint each APDU. Only when all APDUs have been transferred does it signal the end of the activity. Then, if a reply is expected, it can initiate the sending of the data token to the other side using the RT_TURN_PLEASE/GIVE primitive. These in turn map into the P_TOKEN_PLEASE/GIVE primitives. The association is then released using the RT_CLOSE service.

EXERCISES

11.1   Produce a sketch showing the relationship between the various application-support protocols discussed in this chapter and explain the functions of each protocol.

11.2   Describe the meaning of the following terms relating to the session layer:

(a)   token concept,
(b)   activity,
(c)   dialogue unit,
(d)   synchronization points,
(e)   basic combined subset.

11.3   With the aid of a time sequence diagram, illustrate the user service primitives in the basic combined subset of the session layer.

Show on your diagram the SPDUs that are generated by each session protocol entity to implement each of the user services shown in your diagram.

11.4   Use the implementation methodology introduced in the last chapter to show how the connection component of the session protocol machine can be specified in the form of structured program code. Use the specification given in Figure 11.8 and the same variable names in your program as are used in the figure.

11.5   Describe the meaning of the following terms relating to the presentation layer:

(a)   abstract syntax,
(b)   concrete/transfer syntax,
(c)   presentation context.

Give an example of each.

11.6   Give an example ASN.1 abstract type definition for each of the following data types:

(a)   boolean,
(b)   integer,
(c)   bitstring,
(d)   character string.

11.7   Explain the meaning of the terms implicit, explicit and tag in relation to ASN.1.

Give an example sequence type definition that uses each of the types you defined in 11.6.

Modify your definition to include a context-specific tag and an application-specific tag.

11.8   Define the meaning of the class, type and tag that make up the identifier octet associated with an ASN.1 encoded type.

Use example value assignments to the data types you declared in 11.6 to illustrate how each type is encoded.

11.9   Use the two sequence type definitions derived in 11.7 to show the encoding of the sequence type and the added overheads associated with the use of tags. Clearly identify the context-specific tag in your encoding example.

11.10 With the aid of a sketch, explain the meaning of the following terms relating to data encryption:

   (a)   plaintext,
   (b)   ciphertext,
   (c)   listening,
   (d)   masquerading,
   (e)   encryption and decryption keys.

11.11 Use a short sentence to illustrate the difference between a substitution cipher and a transposition cipher. Define the key you use in each case.

11.12 Design an S-box that comprises a 3-to-8 decoder, a straight 8-bit permutation (P-box) and an 8-to-3 encoder. Define the key associated with your design.

11.13 Design an encryption unit for 6-bit values based on a product cipher. Use three stages in your design including the S-box design you derived in 11.12. Specify the key for your design.

11.14 With the aid of schematic logic diagrams, describe the following operational modes of the DES algorithm:

   (a)   ECB,
   (b)   CBC,
   (c)   CFM.

11.15 With the aid of an example, explain the principle of operation of the RSA algorithm and how the public and secret keys are derived. Use the prime numbers 3 and 11 in your example and an E of 7.

11.16 Explain the meaning of the terms message authentication and digital signature.

     Show how the RSA algorithm can be used to obtain message authentication.

11.17 Discriminate between the terms application service element and application entity.

     Use a time sequence diagram to show the interrelationships between the user service primitives of the ACSE and presentation layers.

11.18 Explain the meaning of the term remote operation.

     List the service primitives associated with the remote operations service element (ROSE) and explain the meanings and use of the parameters associated with each primitive.

11.19 With the aid of examples, explain the meaning of the terms lost update and multiple copy update.

     Explain the principle of operation of a two-phase commit protocol with error recovery. Include in your description the meanings of the terms:

   (a)   master (superior) and slave (subordinate),
   (b)   bound and secure data,
   (c)   initial and final state,
   (d)   two-phase commit,
   (e)   rollback recovery.

11.20 Assume an application process wishes to carry out an atomic action on a remote file. Derive a time sequence diagram showing the sequence of the CCR primitives associated with a successful and an unsuccessful atomic action.

CHAPTER SUMMARY

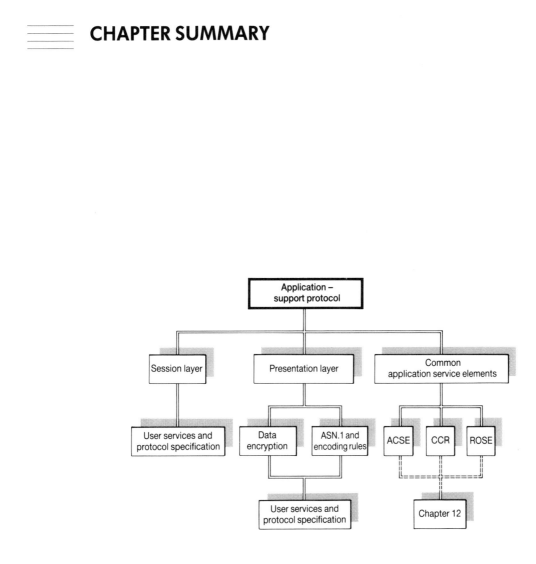

Application-specific
protocols

CHAPTER CONTENTS

CHAPTER OBJECTIVES

When you have completed studying the material in this chapter you should be able to to:

- know the functions of the main application-specific protocols that have been defined for use with the TCP/IP and OSI protocol suites;
- describe the services and operation of the following TCP/IP application protocols:
  - TELNET,
  - FTP,
  - SMTP,
  - SNMP;
- describe the services and operation of the equivalent ISO application protocols:
  - VT,
  - FTAM,
  - MOTIS,
  - CMISE;
- describe the services and operation of the following additional ISO application protocols:
  - MMS,
  - JTM,
  - DTP.

12.1 INTRODUCTION

The last chapter described a selection of the ISO protocols that provide general support services to the protocols that perform specific application functions. The latter include protocols associated with remote file access, electronic mail and so on. As indicated, the TCP/IP protocol suite does not have support protocols. Instead, when a particular service is needed, it is integrated directly with the application-specific protocol. Thus in a TCP/IP suite, the latter communicate directly with the transport protocols.

The term application process is used to refer to the programs/software that perform the actual processing functions associated with a (distributed) application. For example, a client application process (AP) may be a program running in one computer that requires access to a file server AP that is running in another computer. The application-specific protocols then provide the necessary support to enable a client to access the various server APs in an open way as if the client were running on the same machine as the server. A schematic showing the general approach with both suites is shown in Figure 12.1.

In the case of an OSI suite, the approach is to define, for each distributed application service, a **virtual device** together with a defined set of user service-primitives for use with it. Thus there is a virtual file store/server, a virtual mail server and so on. The application protocol associated with a particular service is then implemented on the assumption that the client and server application processes communicate using primitives that are the same as those associated with the defined virtual device. In this way, all request and response primitives at the interface with each application protocol – and hence at the interface with the open system interconnection environment – are in a standard form. Also, each application protocol operates in a defined way that is independent of any differences that might exist in the mode of operation of the related real application processes. Then, if the services associated with the latter are different from these associated with the virtual device, an additional device-dependent software layer is used between each application process and the related application protocol to perform any mapping functions that may be necessary to convert the service primitives associated with the virtual device to and from those used with the real device. In this way, existing application and server software can be used without modification. The mapping software is known as the **user element (UE)** or **user agent (UA)**. The general scheme is shown in part (a) of the figure.

In practice, the UE is implemented either as a separate process or in the form of a set of library procedures (or functions) that are linked to the user application process. With most services, there is an initiator AP (and hence application entity to which it is said to be attached) and a responder AP. The former acts as the initiator (or originator) of virtual device requests while the latter acts as the responder (or recipient) of virtual device requests. Also, as described in the last chapter, if the syntax of the data being exchanged between two user APs is different, the presentation entity performs the mapping from the agreed transfer (concrete) syntax to the local syntax as appropriate. The

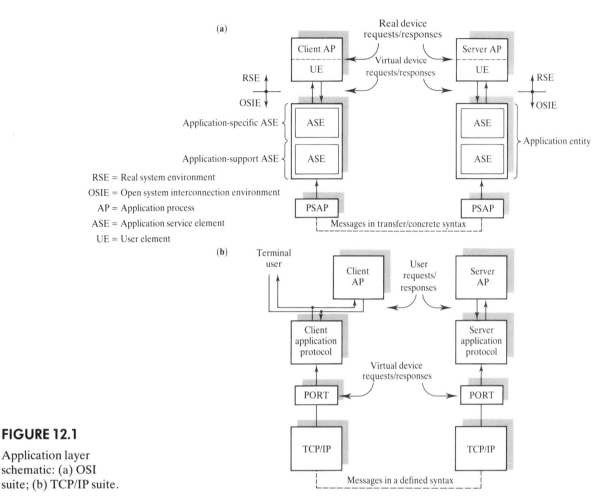

(a)

Real device
requests/responses

Client AP

Virtual device
requests/responses

Server AP

UE

UE

RSE

RSE

OSIE

OSIE

Application-specific ASE { ASE

ASE

Application entity

Application-support ASE { ASE

ASE

RSE = Real system environment

OSIE = Open system interconnection environment

AP = Application process

ASE = Application service element

UE = User element

PSAP

PSAP

Messages in transfer/concrete syntax

(b)

Terminal
user

Client
AP

User
requests/
responses

Server
AP

Client
application
protocol

Server
application
protocol

Virtual device
requests/responses

PORT

PORT

TCP/IP

TCP/IP

Messages in a defined syntax

FIGURE 12.1

Application layer
schematic: (a) OSI
suite; (b) TCP/IP suite.

particular presentation context(s) to be used are negotiated when the association (connection) is first established.

In contrast, in the case of the TCP/IP protocol suite, in addition to implementing the protocol associated with the defined application service, each application protocol performs all the other support functions including any mapping operations that may be necessary. Also, as can be seen in part (b) of the figure, most protocols provide a (user) terminal interface as well as a user AP interface. In general, therefore, the TCP/IP application protocols are relatively sophisticated compared with the ISO application protocols. Selected TCP/IP application protocols are described first and this is followed by a description of several ISO application protocols.

12.2 TCP/IP APPLICATION PROTOCOLS

A selection of the application protocols in the TCP/IP protocol suite is shown in Figure 12.2. These are:

- TELNET – this enables a user at a terminal (or a user application process) on one machine to communicate interactively with an application process, such as a text editor running on a remote machine, as if the user terminal was connected directly to it;
- FTP – this enables a user at a terminal (or a user application process) to access and interact with a remote file system;
- SMTP – this provides a network-wide mail transfer service between the mail systems associated with different machines;
- SNMP – this enables a user (a network manager, for example), to gather performance data or control the operation of a network element (such as a bridge or gateway) via the network itself.

FIGURE 12.2

TCP/IP application protocol summary.

A common requirement with all client server interactions is that of establishing a communications path between the two application protocols/ processes involved. Before describing the different application protocols, therefore, a brief discussion of how a communications path is established is presented.

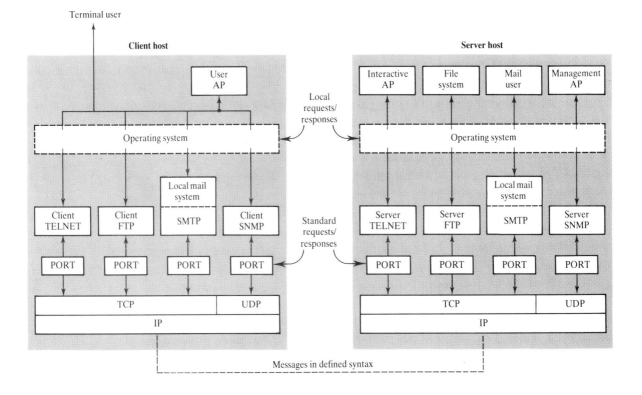

12.2.1 Establishing a transport connection

As may be recalled from Chapter 10, all server application processes have an associated name which translates into a corresponding network-wide address. The translation procedure is carried out by a process known as the **domain name server**. The operation of the latter will be discussed in the next chapter, together with other system aspects. The resulting network-wide address of a server process consists of two parts: the network-wide IP address of the host in which the process is running and a local port number. The IP address is used by the IP protocol in each internet gateway to route datagrams across the internet to the required destination host. The port number is then used by the TCP protocol within the host – or UDP, if this is being used – to identify the specific process within that host to which a received message should be sent.

An open system will include multiple clients and servers both of different types (FTP, SMTP etc) and of the same type (multiple file servers, mail servers etc). All servers of the same type, however, are assigned the same system-wide port number; a specific server is then identified by the IP address of the host in which it runs. The port numbers associated with the different server types are known as **well-known ports** and include:

> 21 – FTP,
> 22 – TELNET,
> 25 – SMTP.

Hence, when a client process initiates a call to a correspondent server process, it uses as a destination address the IP address of the host in which the server is running coupled with the appropriate well-known port number of that server. As a source address it uses the IP address of its own host together with the next free (unused) port number on that host. If TCP is being used, the local TCP protocol entity will then establish a transport connection between the client and server processes – using these addresses – over which the appropriate message exchanges can take place.

12.2.2 TELNET

As can be seen in Figure 12.3, the client TELNET protocol/process is accessed through the local operating system either by a user application process or, more usually, by a user at a terminal. It provides services to enable a user to log on to the operating system of a remote machine, to initiate the running of a program/process on that machine – for example, a text editor – and then to interact with it as if the user terminal/process were connected/running on the same machine. All commands (control characters) and data entered at the user terminal – or submitted by the user AP – are passed by the local operating system to the client TELNET process which then passes them, using the reliable stream service provided by TCP, to the correspondent server TELNET. The latter then issues the commands on behalf of the user, through the local operating system, to the interactive process. The server TELNET is thus also known as a **pseudo terminal**.

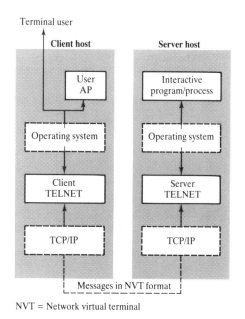

FIGURE 12.3

TELNET client/server
interaction schematic.

Any data output by the interactive process is returned in the same way for display
on the client terminal or for interpretation by the user application process.

The two TELNET protocols communicate with each other using commands – comprising single characters or strings of characters – that are encoded in
a standard format known as **network virtual terminal (NVT)**. The character set
used for commands is ASCII. Also, all input and output data relating to an
interaction is transferred as ASCII strings. If this is different from the local
character set being used, the corresponding TELNET will carry out any necessary
mapping functions. Thus, the two TELNET protocol entities also perform the
role of the presentation layer in an OSI stack.

As may be recalled from Chapter 3, the ASCII character set uses seven bits
per character. All commands and data in the NVT format, however, are encoded
using 8-bit bytes. Then, if the most significant (eighth) bit is a 0, all the characters
have their normal meaning, including the ASCII control characters. Also,
selected pairs of these are defined, such as CR-LF to signal a new line. In addition,
an extra set of command characters is defined by setting the most significant bit to
1. Since such characters have their most significant bit set, they can be readily
distinguished from the standard ASCII set. Hence, if required, they can be
interspersed with a data stream that is flowing in a particular direction. A selection
of the command bytes that have been defined, together with their meanings, is
given in Table 12.1.

All commands are preceded by the all 1s (255) IAC byte. If a command
consists of more than one byte, then the byte string must start with an SB
command and terminate with an SE command. As can be deduced, some of the

Table 12.1 NVT command bytes and their meaning.

Command	Decimal	Meaning
IAC	255	Interpret the following byte as a command byte
NOP	241	No operation
EC	247	Erase character
EL	248	Erase line
GA	249	Go ahead
AYT	246	Are you there
IP	244	Interrupt process
AO	245	Abort output
BRK	243	Break (stop) output
DMARK	242	Resume output
SB	250	Start option negotiation string
SE	240	End option negotiation string
WILL	251	Agreement/request option
WON'T	252	Refuse option request
DO	253	Accept request option
DON'T	254	Refuse to accept option request

commands have the same meaning as those used with most interactive software. Others are needed because the interactive software (process) is running in a remote machine. For example, most interactive programs allow a user to control the output of long strings of characters to the terminal screen by entering defined control characters or pairs of characters. The BRK and DMARK command bytes are thus used to signal the same function: BRK to stop outputting and DMARK to resume. Also the AO command is used to request that the current output is aborted. In addition, if the output process continues outputting data after being requested to stop – for example, as a result of the command bytes being held up by network congestion – the user would normally enter a character sequence to terminate the (remote) process. If this occurs, it is signalled by the client TELNET sending an IP command byte using the TCP service primitive URGENT. As may be recalled, data associated with this primitive is sent outside of the normal flow control window which is operating for the current connection. Hence the IP command should always be received by the server.

As indicated, all data is normally transferred as 7-bit ASCII character strings. In addition, it is possible to send strings of 8-bit bytes should this be required. This may be needed to transfer special display characters or, if an application process is the client rather than a user at a terminal, the client and server processes may wish to exchange blocks of binary data. To achieve this, one side enters a command known as **option negotiation**. Other operational functions can also be requested in the same way. The option codes used are listed in Table 12.2.

Option requests can be initiated by either side of a connection using the WILL, WON'T, DO and DON'T command bytes followed by the particular code

Table 12.2 NVT option codes and their meaning.

Name	Code	Meaning
Transmit binary	0	Request/accept change to 8-bit binary
Echo	1	Echo characters received back to sender
Status	5	Request/reply status of receiving TELNET
Timing mark	6	Insert timing mark in returned stream
Terminal type	24	Request/response type of remote terminal
Line mode	34	Send complete lines instead of individual characters

number from the table. Typical option commands are thus:

IAC, SB, WILL, '0', SE

to request the receiver to accept 8-bit binary. The receiving TELNET would then return either

IAC, SB, DO, '0', SE

if it is prepared to accept, or

IAC, SB, DON'T, '0', SE

if it is not. Alternatively, the receiver could initiate the switch by sending

IAC, SB, DO, '0', SE.

The sender would then return either

IAC, SB, WILL, '0', SE

to indicate it is going to switch or

IAC, SB, WON'T, '0', SE

to refuse. In binary mode, any all 1s (IAC) bytes are sent twice to signal to the receiver to interpret the byte as data and not the start of a command.

The **timing mark** command performs a similar function to the synchronization function in the session layer of an OSI stack. The use of the other commands can be deduced from their meanings.

12.2.3 FTP

Access to a remote file server is a fundamental requirement in many distributed applications. In some instances a single file server may be accessed by multiple clients, while in others multiple copies of the same file may be held in a number of servers. An example application is shown in Figure 12.4.

A client FTP can be accessed either by a user at a terminal or by a user application process. Normally, a single client can support multiple such users concurrently. It provides each user with a similar set of services to those that are available with most file systems. Thus a user can list directories, create new files,

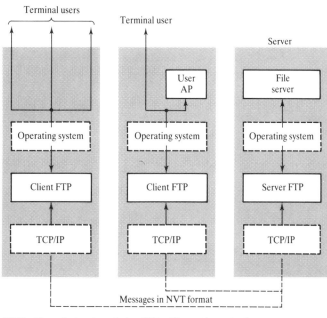

FIGURE 12.4

FTP client/server
interaction schematic.

NVT = Network virtual terminal   FTP = File transfer protocol

obtain (read) the contents of existing files, perform update operations on them, delete files and so on. Similarly, a server FTP can respond to requests from multiple clients concurrently. On receipt of each request, the server FTP interacts with its local file system to carry out the request as if it had been generated locally.

The client FTP allows a user to specify the structure of the file involved and the type of data in the file. Again these reflect those used with most file systems. Three file structures are supported (unstructured, structured and random access) as well as four data types (8-bit binary, text (ASCII and EBCDIC) and variable length binary). The FTP server then accesses each file from its local file system and transfers it to the client FTP in an appropriate way according to its defined structure.

As an **unstructured file** can contain any type of data – binary or text – it is transferred between the two FTP protocol entities as a transparent bit stream. The user then interprets the bit stream according to the data types within it.

Structured files consist of a sequence of fixed-sized records of a defined type. Hence the contents of such files are normally transferred as a string of fixed-sized blocks. Alternatively, the contents may be transferred in compressed form. This is appropriate with text files as they often contain long strings of the same character, such as space characters. This, and other types of redundancy, can be exploited by each FTP protocol entity applying an agreed compression algorithm to the field contents prior to transmission. In the case of an OSI stack, this would be performed by the presentation layer.

Random access files are comprised of records of variable-size. Normally, such records are referred to as **pages** and the file a **paged file**. Each record/page has an associated header which includes a length and type field and positional information which indicates the position of the record/page relative to the total file contents. Each page is then transferred between the two protocol entities in this same form.

In the case of compressed and block-mode transfers, the two FTP protocol entities perform checkpointing to allow large files to be transferred in a controlled way. This is similar to the synchronization services provided by the session layer in an OSI stack.

To handle multiple requests concurrently, each server FTP – and client, if it also supports multiple requests – creates (spawns) a new instance of the FTP protocol/process for each new request received. Normally, there is a single master process – with its well-known port number – to which all new requests are passed. This master process proceeds to create a new process for this connection. This **control process**, as it is known, performs the various control functions associated with the session, including the log on (with password) procedure and the definition of the structure and data types associated with the file(s) to be transferred. It also defines whether compression is to be used and, if so, the type of compression algorithm. Many implementations then proceed to create another process to handle the actual data transfers associated with the session. In such cases, therefore, a single FTP session involves two transport connections, one for exchanging control messages and the other for transferring file contents. This, of course, is all transparent to the user and server software.

The format of the messages associated with the file contents is determined by the defined structure of the file. The format of the messages exchanged between the two FTP control processes – the FTP protocol data units – must also be in an agreed syntax to ensure they have the same meaning (and are interpreted in the same way) in both computers. To achieve this, the NVT format described in the last section is used, except that option negotiation is not required with FTP.

TFTP

The FTP protocol is relatively complex since it contains all the features that are needed for use with a variety of file types and, if required, compression algorithms. Although these are often required in applications involving internetworks, this level of functionality is not normally required in more local applications. An example is the file transfer protocol between a networked file server and a local community of diskless workstations.

In this case, since each file transfer request issued by a client must go via the network, the server and client workstations are all connected to the same LAN segment. Also, such transfers do not require many of the functions associated with FTP. Consequently, an additional file protocol, known as the **trivial file transfer protocol (TFTP)**, is available with the TCP/IP protocol suite.

As indicated, TFTP is intended for use primarily in LAN applications. As may be recalled from Chapter 6, the bit error rate probability of LANs is normally very low, so TFTP uses UDP rather than TCP for all message transfers. Then, to overcome the possibility of corrupted messages (datagrams), a simple idle RQ (stop-and-wait) error control procedure is incorporated into the protocol. With idle RQ only a single message (block) may be sent until either an acknowledgement for the block is received or a timeout occurs. In the latter event, the waiting block will be retransmitted. This is adequate because of the short transit delay associated with LANs.

The TFTP protocol uses just four message – PDU – types which are also encoded in ASCII. They are:

read request:	this is sent by a client to initiate a file read operation;
write request:	this is sent by a client to perform a file write operation;
data block:	this is used to convey the file contents;
acknowledgement:	this is sent by either a client or the server to inform the other of an error condition.

To initiate a file transfer operation, the client sends either a read or write message containing the file name and file type. The data associated with the file request is then transferred in fixed-sized blocks, each of which contains up to 512 bytes. Each data block has a sequence number in its header; the same number is returned in the associated acknowledgement. This is used by the receiver – client for read, server for write – to detect duplicates in the event of an acknowledgement being lost. The end of a file is detected by the receipt of a data block containing less than 512 bytes.

In common with FTP, a TFTP server can support multiple client transfer requests concurrently. Hence, after the initial read or write request message has been received, the server relates subsequent data blocks or acknowledgements to the correct file transfer by means of the client port/IP addresses. This information is passed up to the TFTP by the IP/UDP protocols on receipt of the datagram in which the data block/acknowledgement message was carried.

12.2.4 SMTP

Electronic mail – normally referred to as **e-mail** – is probably the most widely used service associated with computer networks. Local mail systems have been available with most large interactive computer systems for many years. Hence, it was a natural evolution to extend this service across the network when these were networked together.

The **simple mail transfer protocol (SMTP)** manages the transfer of mail from one host computer mail system to another. It is not responsible for accepting mail from local users nor for distributing received mail to its intended recipient(s). These are the responsibility of the local mail system. The interrelationship between SMTP and the local mail system is shown in Figure 12.5.

Since SMTP interacts with the local mail system and not the user, it is masked from any mail transfers that are local to that machine. Only when an item of mail is to be sent to a different machine or is received from a remote machine is

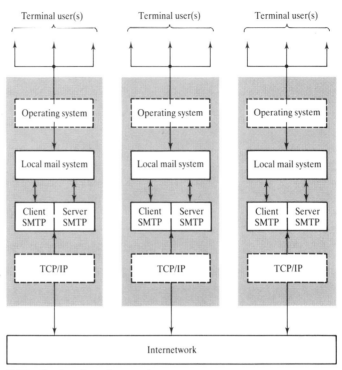

FIGURE 12.5

SMTP – local mail
system schematic.

SMTP = Simple mail transfer protocol

the SMTP scheduled to run. Normally, there is an input queue and an output queue at the interface between the local mail system – often referred to as the **native mail system** – and the client and server parts of the SMTP. The client is concerned with initiating the transfer of mail to another system while the server is concerned with receiving mail. Also, although multiple users are shown in the figure, it is possible for a single user at, say, a personal computer to be involved.

The local mail system will retain a **mailbox** for each user into which the user can deposit or retrieve mail. Each mailbox has a unique name which consists of two parts: a **local port** and a **global port**. The first is the name of the user and is unique only within that local mail system. The second, the identity of the host, must be unique within the total internet. It normally comprises a number of fields and the precise format varies for different types of establishment – education, government, military etc. Some examples will be given in the next chapter when directory services and name-to-address mapping are discussed.

Two issues are involved in the transfer of mail: the format of the mail – to ensure that it is interpreted in the same way in each system – and the SMTP protocol used to transfer it from one machine to another. The mail format consists of a header and a body which themselves consist of a number of lines of ASCII text with a blank line separating the header from the body. Only ASCII text is accepted.

Each line in the header comprises a **keyword** followed by a text string with a colon separating the two. Some keywords are compulsory whilst others are optional. The minimum header is:

TO: name of recipient
FROM: name of sender

Others include:

TO: name of recipient
REPLY TO: name to send reply to

and:

TO: name of recipient
FROM: name of sender
CC: copies to
SUBJECT:
DATE:
ENCRYPTED: encryption pointer

The ENCRYPTED keyword indicates that the body part – the contents – have been encrypted using a key which the recipient can deduce from the encryption pointer. The header, including the SUBJECT and the names of the intended recipient(s), is always in plaintext. Although in some instances the two communicating machines may be connected to the same network, if internet gateways are involved in the route, additional lines of the form:

RECEIVED FROM: identity of a gateway that forwarded the mail

may be added to the header by each gateway. This provides a means of determining the route taken by the mail through the internet.

After an item of mail has been created in the standard format, the local mail system determines from the name of the recipient whether it should be deposited into a local mailbox or in the output queue ready for forwarding. To send the mail, the client SMTP first ascertains the IP address of the destination host from the directory service – known as the **domain name system** – and then uses this, together with the well-known port address of SMTP (25), to initiate the setting up of a transport connection with the server SMTP in the destination host. Once a connection has been established, the client initiates the transfer of the waiting mail to the server.

Transferring the mail involves the exchange of SMTP PDUs known as **commands**. All commands are encoded as ASCII character strings and comprise either a 3-digit number or a textual command or sometimes both. They are transferred over the established transport connection using the TCP SEND/ DELIVER user primitives. The sequence of commands exchanged is shown in Figure 12.6.

Once a TCP connection has been established, the server SMTP returns command 220 back to the client to indicate it is now ready to receive the mail. The client responds by returning a HELO command together with the identity of the

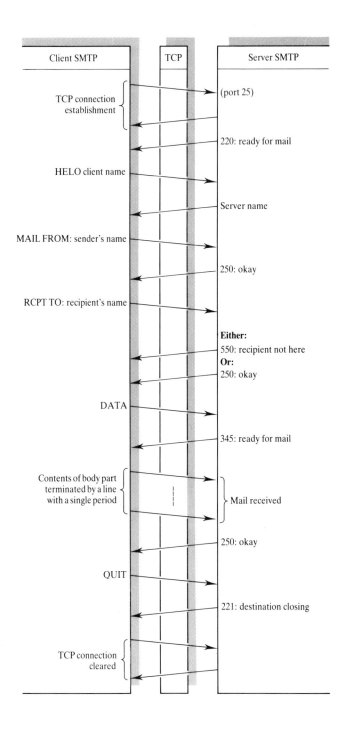

FIGURE 12.6

SMTP protocol command exchange sequence.

client machine. On receiving this, the server responds with the identity of the server machine which is used as a record of the mail transaction. The client then initiates the sending of the mail header by issuing a MAIL command followed by the FROM: line from the mail header. The general acknowledgement command 250 is returned by the server. The client continues by sending a RCPT command followed by the TO: line from the mail header. This is again acknowledged by a 250 command; any further header lines are sent in the same way.

The start of the contents of the mail body are then signalled by the client sending a DATA command. The server responds with a 354 command and the client then proceeds to send the mail contents as a sequence of lines terminated by a line with a single period. The server acknowledges receipt of the latter by returning a 250 command. The mail transfer phase is then terminated by the client sending a QUIT command and the server returning a 221 command, following which the transport connection is cleared.

The foregoing describes the basic functions associated with the SMTP protocol but a number of additional functions are available with some implementations. For example, if the intended recipient no longer has a mailbox at the server it may return a forwarding address. Also, after a client SMTP has sent its mail, it may invite the server to send mail in the reverse direction – if any is waiting – before clearing the transport connection.

So far it has been assumed that all the intended recipient hosts utilized the SMTP protocol. In practice, many other mail protocols are used in other networks. To enable mail to be exchanged with other mail systems, therefore, a **mail gateway** must be used. An example is a TCP/IP-to-OSI gateway. As the name implies, it acts as a mail transfer point between the two dissimilar mail systems/ network protocols. Thus mail received using SMTP at one network port is then forwarded using MOTIS – the ISO mail protocol – at the other network port. A number of other gateway services can be performed in the same way.

12.2.5 SNMP

The three application protocols discussed so far – TELNET, FTP and SMTP – are all concerned with providing network-wide user application services. In contrast, the **simple network management protocol (SNMP)** is concerned not with user services but rather with management of all the communication protocols within each host and the various items of networking equipment that provide these services. In other words, the total networking environment.

As may be recalled from the last section on computer networks, a typical open system networking environment comprises a range of different items of networking equipment. These include bridges for the interconnection of similar LAN segments, routers for the interconnection of dissimilar LANs, packet switches for use in packet-switching networks, various types of internetwork gateways for the interconnection of networks, the communication links that connect these and so on.

Clearly, in any networking environment, if a fault develops and service is interrupted, users will expect the fault to be corrected and normal service resumed with a minimum of delay. This is often referred to as **fault management**. Similarly, if the performance of the network – for example, its response time or throughput – starts to deteriorate as a result of, say, increased levels of traffic in selected parts of the network, users will expect these to be identified and additional equipment/ transmission capacity introduced to alleviate the problem. This is an example of **performance management**. In addition, most of the protocols associated with the TCP/IP suite have associated operational parameters, such as the time-to-live parameter associated with the IP protocol and the retransmission timer associated with TCP. As a network expands, such parameters may need to be changed while the network is still operational. This type of operation is known as **layer management**. Others include **name management**, **security management** and **accounting management**. The SNMP has been defined to help a network manager to carry out the fault and performance management functions.

The standard approach to network management is to view all the network elements that are to be managed – a protocol, a bridge, a gateway etc – as **managed objects**. Associated with each managed object is a defined set of management-related information. This includes variables – also known as attributes – that can either be read or written to by the network manager via the network. It also includes, when appropriate, a set of **fault reports** that are sent by a managed object should a related fault occur. In the case of the IP protocol, for example, a read variable may relate to, say, the number of IP datagrams discarded as a result of the time-to-live parameter expiring, while a write variable may be the actual time-to-live timeout value. Similarly, in the case of a gateway, if a neighbour gateway ceases to respond to hello messages, in addition to modifying its routing table to reflect the loss of the link, the gateway may create and send a fault report – via the network – to alert the management system of the problem. Then, if the management system receives a number of such reports from other neighbours, it can conclude that the gateway is probably faulty, not just a communications link.

SNMP is an application protocol so a standard communication platform must be used to enable associated messages – protocol data units – to be transferred concurrently with the messages relating to user services. To achieve this, SNMP normally uses the same TCP/IP protocols as the other three protocols discussed. The general scheme is thus as shown in Figure 12.7.

The role of the SNMP is to provide a way for the **manager process** in the manager station to exchange management-related messages with the management processes running in the various managed elements; hosts, gateways etc. The management process in these elements will have been written to perform the defined management functions associated with that element. Examples include responding to requests for specified variables (counts), receiving updated operational variables and generating and sending fault reports.

Management information associated with a network/internet is kept at the network manager station (host) in a **management information base (MIB)**. A network manager is provided with a range of services to interrogate the information in the MIB, to initiate the entry and collection of additional information and to initiate network configuration changes. Clearly, the manager station is the nerve centre of the complete network, so strict security and authentication

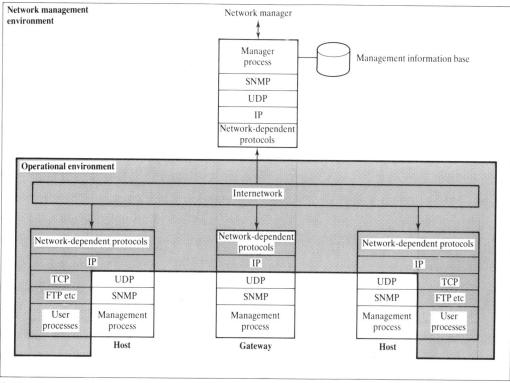

SNMP = Simple network management protocol   UDP = User datagram protocol

FIGURE 12.7

SNMP network
management software.

mechanisms are implemented. Normally, there are various levels of authority depending on the operation to be performed. Also, in large internetworks, multiple manager stations may be used, each responsible for a particular part of the internet.

To reflect the wide range of objects to be managed, management information is often stored in a **relational database** since the information held for a single managed object is often used in several parts of the database. A simple hierarchical structure is shown in Figure 12.8.

At the top of the hierarchy is the internet which consists of a number of major entities, including directory services, network elements and security services. Network elements include networks, interior and exterior gateways and, if subnets are involved, routers and bridges. At the leaves of the branches are the managed objects, each of which will have a unique name. In addition a defined set of variables/fault reports will be associated with each object. Hence a major role of the authority responsible for managing and running an internet, is to define the structure – known as the management information tree – and contents of the MIB. All equipment suppliers must then be informed of the management information that will be required for that equipment and how it will be gathered.

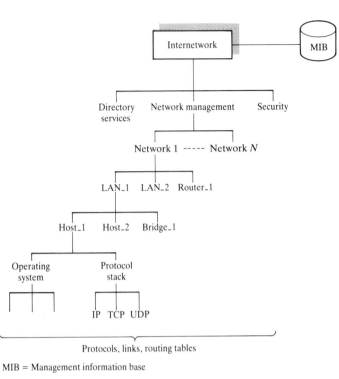

FIGURE 12.8

Management object
hierarchy (information
tree).

The actual managed objects – and hence management information – associated with an internet may differ from one open system to another. Consequently, the SNMP protocol has been defined to enable it to gather management information in a variety of networking environments. Thus the meaning of the management information being transferred is transparent to the SNMP which simply offers a defined set of services, each with an associated set of parameters (in a defined syntax). It is the various management processes that interpret the transferred information/commands in a defined way. This is more in line with the mode of operation of the ISO protocols than the three protocols already discussed, reflecting the fact that SNMP is a more recently introduced protocol. As may be recalled, these three protocols integrate many application-dependent function into their normal operation.

The user services/commands – and matching PDUs – associated with the SNMP are of the remote procedure/operation type and are thus very simple. Three primitives are available to the manager process:

- *get request:* used to request the current value(s) associated with a declared variable (or list of variables) relating to a managed object;

- *get-next-request:* used to request the next value associated with a variable, such as a table, that comprises a list of elements;

- *set-request:* used to transfer a value to be assigned to a specified variable associated with a managed object such as an operational parameter associated with a protocol layer;

and two primitives which are available to the (agent) management process:

- *get-response:* used to return the value(s) associated with an earlier get-request;

- *trap:* used to report the occurrence of a fault condition, such as the loss of communication with a neighbour.

The resulting messages – PDUs – generated by the SNMP protocol in response to these primitives are all exchanged using UDP and are defined in ASN.1. A simplified definition to illustrate the approach is given in Figure 12.9.

The two SNMP protocol entities do not retain state information, which means that the manager process can have a number of outstanding requests awaiting responses. Hence, each GETrequest PDU contains a request identifier – requestID – which is also present in the subsequent response and enables the network manager process to relate it to a specific request. The varBindList is then a sequence containing a variable number of object name, value pairs. In a GETrequest PDU, the value associated with each object name is NULL but in the associated GETresponse PDU the actual value will be returned. Since the object name is an IA5String, however, its meaning is transparent to SNMP.

Finally, as will be described in the next section when the ISO application protocols are discussed, an ISO management protocol known as the **common management information protocol, CMIP**, is now available. This has more sophisticated features than SNMP and may be more suitable for larger networks/internets. Because of this, it is likely to be the preferred network management

FIGURE 12.9

Simplified ASN.1 definition of SNMP PDUs.

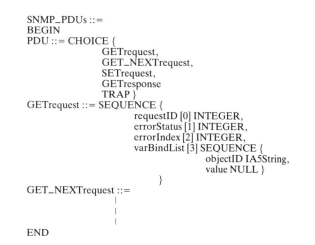

protocol for some networks that nevertheless use TCP/IP rather than the equivalent ISO protocols. When used with a TCP/IP suite, the CMIP is thus known as **CMOT** which is an acronym for CMIP over TCP/IP.

12.3 ISO APPLICATION PROTOCOLS

In addition to the various application-support protocols described in the last chapter, a complete suite of application-specific protocols (application service elements or ASEs) have now been defined. Most are now full international standards (ISs) while others are still in draft form (DIS). Some provide similar services to the TCP/IP application protocols described in the last section while others provide additional services. The current list of ISO application protocols includes:

- *Virtual terminal (VT):* this IS provides similar services to the TELNET protocol.

- *File transfer access and management (FTAM):* this IS provides similar services to the FTP protocol.

- *Message oriented text interchange standard (MOTIS):* this IS provides similar services to the SMTP protocol.

- *Common management information protocol (CMIP):* this IS provides similar services to the SNMP protocol.

- *Job transfer and manipulation (JTM):* this IS provides a facility for a user application process (AP) to submit a job (work specification) to a remote AP for processing.

- *Manufacturing messaging service (MMS):* this IS provides a standard means whereby an AP running in a supervisory computer associated with an automated manufacturing plant can send manufacturing-related messages to a distributed community of other APs controlling a numerical machine tool, programmable controller, robot and so on.

- *Remote database access (RDA):* this DIS provides a facility to enable an AP to access a remote database management system (DBMS).

- *Distributed transaction processing (DTB):* this DIS provides the necessary support services to enable two APs to communicate according to the rules that were defined in the last chapter for the CCR protocol.

As with the TCP/IP application protocols, the aim of the various ISO protocols is to enable two application processes running in different computer systems to communicate with each other to carry out a particular distributed application function. Thus in the case of FTAM, for example, the aim is to enable a client process running in one computer to interact with a file server process running in a remote (and possibly different) computer, as if the client process were running in the same computer as the server.

To achieve this goal, the ISO approach is to define a virtual device model for each distributed application function – a virtual terminal, virtual file store, virtual manufacturing device and so on. The two communicating application service elements (and hence protocols) are implemented as if the two communicating application processes both operate according to this model. In this way, all (user) services associated with each ASE have a standard form and the protocol associated with the ASE can be implemented independently of any variations that might exist between the two communicating processes. Any differences that do exist are resolved outside of the open system interconnection environment by the user element that is linked with the application process. The services associated with the presentation layer then ensure that data that is exchanged between the two communicating processes has a common meaning to both processes. A description of the main ISO protocols is now given.

12.3.1 VT

The **virtual terminal (VT)** ASE enables a user at a terminal to interact with an application process running in a remote computer as if the terminal were connected directly to that computer. In practice, a wide variety of terminals exist, each with different operational characteristics. For example, there are **scroll mode terminals** that operate with single characters, **screen** or **page mode terminals** that operate with a complete screen of characters, and **form mode terminals** that are normally used in applications involving selected character/word positions to be entered against a fixed (form) template. There are many variations in each category. Moreover, a considerable amount of existing application software has been written for use with such terminals. The aim of the VT ASE, therefore, is to enable such applications to be accessed in an open way using a variety of terminals.

Unlike the TELNET protocol, the client VT ASE (protocol) does not provide a direct terminal interface. Instead, a local application process – user element – must always be used to manage the interaction with the terminal. It is this user element that interacts with the client VT ASE according to the defined virtual terminal characteristics. If necessary, it also performs any mapping operations between the characteristics of the two terminals. The general scheme is shown in Figure 12.10.

Because of the wide variety of terminals, there is not just one virtual terminal. Rather, the VT ASE provides the means for two users to negotiate the specific virtual terminal characteristics that are required for an application. Before any interactions can take place, both users must agree on what is known as the **virtual terminal environment (VTE)** that will apply for the application. In some instances only a small number of operational parameters need to be negotiated, while others involve a much larger number.

A number of **standard profiles** have been defined to help the two users to negotiate the operational parameters (characteristics). The two users can adopt the parameters relating to a specific profile or negotiate selected parameter changes.

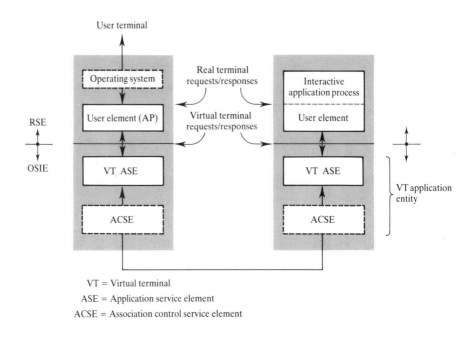

FIGURE 12.10

VT interaction
schematic.

VT = Virtual terminal
ASE = Application service element
ACSE = Association control service element

The two VT users communicate with one another through a shared data structure known as the **conceptual communication area (CCA)**. A separate copy of the CCA is maintained by each VT protocol entity. Changes to the contents of the CCA held by each entity are initiated by the local user element/process issuing a defined VT request service primitive at the interface. The resulting changes are carried out on the local CCA and then relayed to the peer VT entity in the remote system using the VT protocol and associated PDUs. The transferred changes are then carried out and relayed to the peer user process by means of a matching indication primitive. The general scheme is shown in Figure 12.11(a).

Each CCA contains a number of data structures that collectively describe the characteristics of the virtual terminal being used. These are shown in part (b) of the figure.

Associated with each terminal input and output device – keyboard, mouse, display, printer etc – are three objects, each comprised of a number of parameters. These are:

- **Display objects**: these allow events relating to the associated real device to be represented by corresponding events associated with the virtual device. It consists of an array of elements each holding a single character from the character set associated with the virtual terminal.

- **Control objects**: these are used to model terminal features that are not normally triggered by the user, such as a bell.

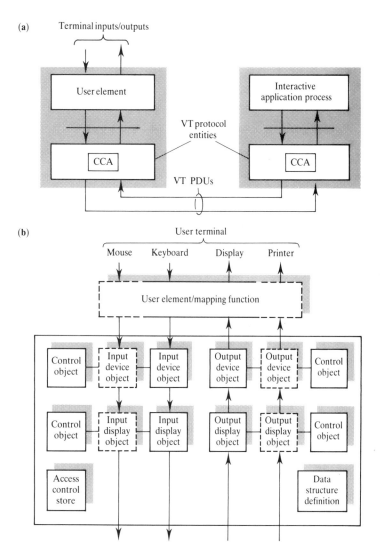

FIGURE 12.11

VT protocol data
structures:
(a) conceptual
communication area;
(b) object definitions.

- **Device objects**: these model characteristics of the associated real device. A set of boolean variables associated with each device object indicates the state of such items as the on-off switch.

Synchronous and asynchronous modes of operation are supported. In the **synchronous mode**, the input and output functions at each side of a connection/association are combined. Hence it is necessary to use a number of tokens to control the order of interaction between the user and the remote process. In the **asynchronous mode**, the input and output functions are separate, enabling each side to initiate an event concurrently. The **access control store (ACS)** holds the current assignment of the tokens being used when the synchronous mode has been selected. In practice, tokens are transferred using the token control service provided by the session (through presentation) layer. The **data structure definition (DSD)** contains the type definitions of the parameters associated with the display, control and device objects being used with this association.

User services

The VT ASE is used in conjunction with the ACSE support protocol. Consequently, primitives exist to establish an association:

> VT_ASSOCIATE.request/indiction/response/confirm,

to negotiate the terminal characteristics to be used with this association:

> VT_START_NEG.request/indication/response/confirm,
> VT_NEG_INVITE.request/indication,
> VT_NEG_OFFER.request/indication,
> VT_NEG_ACCEPT.request/indication,
> VT_NEG_REJECT.request/indication,
> VT_END_NEG.request/indication/response/confirm,

to initiate the transfer of the changes associated with the CCA:

> VT_DATA.request/indication,

to control any token(s) that may be in use (synchronous mode):

> VT_REQUEST_TOKEN.request/indication,
> VT_GIVE_TOKEN.request/indication,

and finally to terminate an association:

> VT_RELEASE.request/indication/response/confirm,
> VT_U_ABORT.request/indication,
> VT_P_ABORT.indication.

The VT protocol entity generates a PDU in response to each of the service primitives. These are then transferred to the peer entity as shown in Figure 12.12. Thus the PDUs generated by the VT_ASSOCIATE, RELEASE and ABORT primitives are transferred as user data with the equivalent A_ASSOCIATE primitives of ACSE. The PDUs relating to the remainder are then transferred using P_DATA except for the two token control PDUs which are sent using the P_TOKEN_PLEASE and P_TOKEN_GIVE services.

12.3.2 FTAM

It should be stressed that the various application service elements (ASEs) are not concerned with providing a specific application service but rather with creating the means by which a related service provided by a user AP in the real system environment (RSE) can be accessed and used in an open way. As an example, the **file transfer, access and management (FTAM)** ASE provides the means whereby a

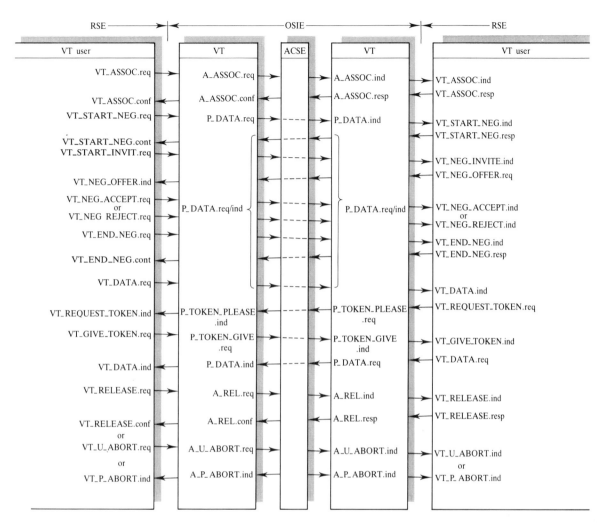

FIGURE 12.12

VT user services and ACSE interaction.

distributed community of client processes (APs) can access and manage a remote file server implemented as a user AP running on a computer, possibly from a different manufacturer from the client system. Each client process (and hence the AE to which it is attached) is referred to as an **initiator AP** and the server process as the **responder AP** as shown in Figure 12.13.

The primitives used by the client APs to access and manage the remote file store, as well as the primitives used to access and manage the real file store, are local (that is, machine-dependent) matters. In this way, existing file systems and associated access software can be used. All the user needs to provide (assuming the OSI software is in place) is the associated user element to perform the necessary mapping functions.

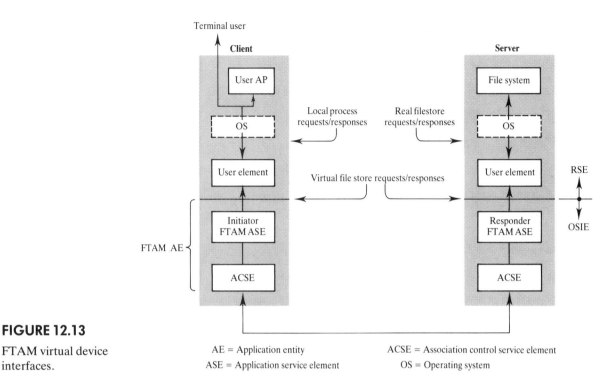

FIGURE 12.13

FTAM virtual device interfaces.

AE = Application entity   ACSE = Association control service element
ASE = Application service element   OS = Operating system

Virtual file store model

Before describing the user service primitives associated with FTAM, it is necessary to describe the (virtual) file store model to which the primitives relate. Clearly, the aim is to adopt a model that is sufficiently flexible to allow any real file system to be readily accessed and managed with a minimum set of mapping functions.

The virtual file store is modelled as an addressable entity with which a remote user (initiator) may communicate (have an association). An arbitrary number of initiators may have an association with the (responder) file store at any one time. The file store may comprise an arbitrary number of files, each of which has a number of associated attributes. These include:

- a filename: this allows the file to be referenced unambiguously,
- permitted actions: these indicate the range of actions (read, insert, replace, etc) that can be performed on the file,
- access control: read-only, read-write, etc,
- file size,
- presentation context of file contents,
- identity of creator,

- data and time of creation,
- identity of last modifier/reader,
- data and time of last access,
- content type,
- encryption key.

There are three commonly used file structures: unstructured, flat and hierarchical. As the name implies, there is no apparent structure to an **unstructured file**. An example is a text file. Although this has structure to the user, it is transparent to the file system and hence only complete files can be read or written.

A **flat file** consists of an ordered sequence of records (data units), which may be of variable length and type. Normally, each record has an identifier (label) associated with it that enables individual records to be read or written. Note, however, that even though a record may comprise a number of (user identifiable) data elements, these are not identifiable by the file system.

A **hierarchical file**, in addition to having identifiable records, has an associated structure. This is a tree structure with a number of branch nodes. Typically, each branch node has an identifier and a data record associated with it. The nodes are normally identified in a known order so that it is possible to identify a node by its position relative to other nodes. Alternatively, if each node has an associated identifier, a node can be identified by giving a path name from the root. As can be concluded, the other two structures are special cases of the hierarchical structure. The virtual file store selected by ISO is based on a hierarchical structure. The related structure and terminology are shown in Figure 12.14.

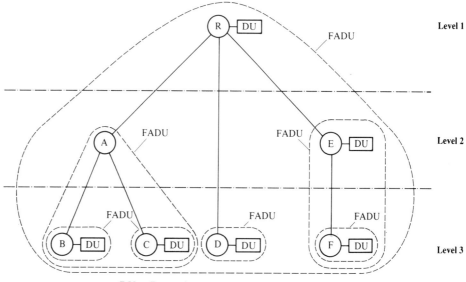

FIGURE 12.14

Virtual file store access structure.

DU = Data unit
FADU = File access data unit
R, A, B, C, D, E, F = Identifiers

The structure of the tree consists of a **single root node** with **internal nodes** and **leaves** connected by directed **arcs**. A node can belong to only one level. Each node, in turn, gives access to its **subtree**, which is known as a **file access data unit (FADU)**. The contents of a file in the file store are held in one or more **data units (DUs)**. At most, there can be only one DU assigned to a node, which means that a DU may be accessed by the identification of the node FADU. Access to each node within the FADU is in the assumed order: R, A, B, C, D, E, F.

A DU is a typed data object (scalar, vector, set) and contains elements of atomic data called **data elements**. Associated with each data element is an abstract syntax (character, octet, integer, etc); all the elements within a DU are related. The normal relationship of elements is in the form of a tree, although alternative relationships, such as a single data element or a vector, may be used. The tree is traversed in the order just outlined; the accessed DUs are passed to the presentation entity in the same sequence. The presentation entity treats each element as independent and uses the corresponding (negotiated) transfer syntax to transfer the elements while maintaining their relative order.

The actions relating to the file store are invoked by corresponding service primitives. These include create, open, close and delete on complete files, and locate, read, insert, replace, extend and erase on the DUs within a file.

Service primitives

Having given a brief overview of the virtual file store model, it is now possible to define the user service primitives associated with FTAM. These services are grouped into a nested set of **regimes**, as shown in Figure 12.15(a). A corresponding regime is entered as progressively more contextual details are established.

Associated with each regime is a defined set of service primitives, as shown in the simplified event–state diagram in Figure 12.15(b). A summary of the services associated with each regime is as follows:

- **Application connection (association)**: This is not specific to FTAM but rather relates to ACSE. In relation to FTAM, however, it establishes the authorization and accounting information necessary for the ensuing operations on the file store.

- **File selection**: This identifies (or creates) a unique file (FADU) to which operations in subsequent phases relate. The selection (identification) process is in terms of a file name; operations performed in subsequent phases relate to this file.

- **File access**: This establishes a regime in which file data transfer can take place. It includes the establishment of the capabilities required for the transfer and of a suitable access context.

- **Data transfer**: This includes commands (read, write, etc) that relate to actions on the DU within the accessed (identified) FADU. Smaller data elements may be identified for presentation purposes but they cannot be accessed individually.

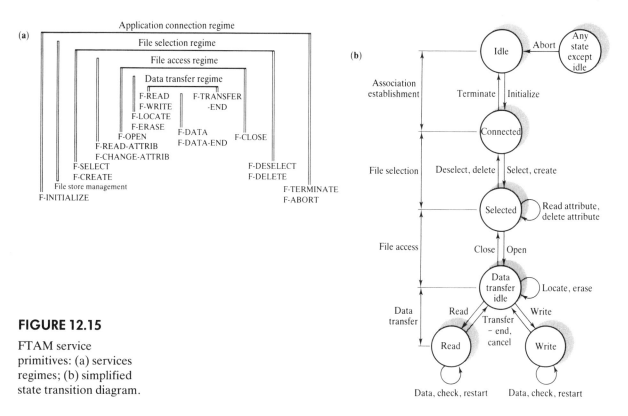

FIGURE 12.15

FTAM service primitives: (a) services regimes; (b) simplified state transition diagram.

As with some of the other protocol layers, the service primitives associated with FTAM are grouped into a number of functional units (FUs). FUs required during a specific (dialogue) session are specified during the association establishment phase. Supported FUs include:

- **Kernel**: This provides facilities for application association and termination, file selection (deselection) and file opening (closing).

- **Read**: This provides facilities for reading files (bulk data) and individual DU.

- **Write**: This provides facilities for writing files (bulk data) and individual DU.

- **File access**: This provides facilities for locating and erasing FADUs.

- **Limited file management**: This provides facilities for file creation and deletion and for reading attributes.

Some of the primitives associated with each FU are shown in the time sequence diagram of Figure 12.16. It should be noted that for brevity only the request primitives are shown in Figure 12.16(c). In practice, they are each confirmed services.

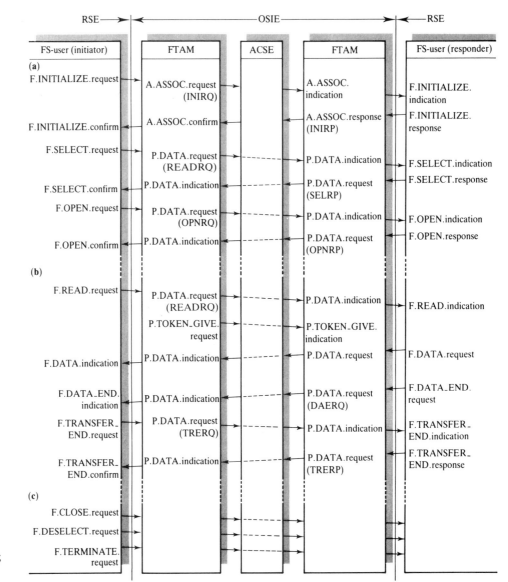

FIGURE 12.16

FTAM service
primitive:
(a), (c) kernel FU;
(b) read FU.

All the services shown in the figure relate to the **normal transfer mode** since they are used primarily when a server maintains a separate set of files for each client. An alternative mode, known as the **reliable transfer mode**, is used in applications such as transaction processing. In such applications it is common for a single file to be accessed and updated by a number of clients concurrently. It is thus necessary to ensure that all changes to the contents of the file are carried out in a controlled way. The CCR ASE has been defined for this function; the additional FTAM primitives that are used in the reliable mode map directly into

Table 12.3   FTAM to CCR mappings for reliable file service.

FTAM	CCR	Use
F_BEGIN_GROUP	C_BEGIN	Signal the start of an atomic transaction
F_END_GROUP	C_COMMIT	Signal the end of the atomic transaction
F_RECOVER	C_ROLLBACK	Return to start of atomic transaction
F_RESTART	C_RESTART	Indicates current state of the sending side

an equivalent CCR primitive. The mappings are listed in Table 12.3. The reader is referred back to Section 11.9 for further descriptions of these.

To operate in the reliable mode, the FTAM application entity would consist of the FTAM ASE and an instance of both the ACSE and CCR application-support ASEs.

Protocol

As can be seen from Figure 12.16, on receipt of each service primitive, the FTAM protocol entity creates a corresponding PDU based on the service primitive type and the parameters associated with the primitive. The PDUs are then passed in the user data field of the appropriate ACSE/presentation primitive. In the sequence shown, it is assumed that the data token is used; hence, prior to the data transfer phase, the token is passed from the initiating FTAM entity to the responding FTAM entity using the P.TOKEN_GIVE service. It should be noted that in the data phase there is no PDU corresponding to the F.DATA service. This is because the file data is passed directly to the presentation entity as a string of tagged data elements – in their abstract syntax – using the P.DATA service.

Finally, to illustrate how the ISO application protocols are specified and to formalize some of the sequences shown in Figure 12.16, a part of the formal specification of the FTAM protocol machine is given in Figures 12.17 and 12.18. The parts considered relate to the association establishment and file selection regimes. First, the abbreviated names and meanings of the incoming events, states, outgoing events and predicates are given in Figure 12.17 followed by the event–state tables in Figure 12.18. The two tables in Figure 12.18 relate to the initiating protocol entity (that is, the entity linked to the client process) and the responding entity (that is, the entity linked to the server process). This mode of specification is used for all ISO application protocols.

12.3.3 MOTIS

MOTIS, the ISO electronic mail system, plays a similar role to the SMTP protocol in the TCP/IP suite. In practice, MOTIS is a complete message (mail) transfer system rather than a single protocol. It is thus also known as the ISO **message handling system (MHS)** and is based on the public X.400 message handling service which has been defined by CCITT.

(a)

Name	Interface	Meaning
F_INIRQ	FS-user	F.INITIALIZE.request received
F_INIRP	FS-user	F.INITIALIZE.response received
F_SELRQ	FS-user	F.SELECT.request received
F_SELRP	FS-user	F.SELECT.response received
INIRQ	CS-provider	Initialize request PDU received
INIRP	CS-provider	Initialize response PDU received
SELRQ	PS-provider	Select request PDU received
SELRP	PS-provider	Select response PDU received
┆		

(b)

Name	Meaning
STA 0	Application connection closed
STA 1	Association pending
STA 2	Application connection open
STA 3	Select pending
STA 4	Selected
┆	

(c)

Name	Interface	Meaning
F_INIIN	FS-user	F.INITIALIZE.indication issued
F_INICF	FS-user	F.INITIALIZE.confirm issued
F_SELIN	FS-user	F.SELECT.indication issued
F_SELCF	FS-user	F.SELECT.confirm issued
INIRQ	CS-provider	Initialize request PDU issued
INIRP	CS-provider	Initialize response PDU received
SELRQ	PS-provider	Select request PDU issued
SELRP	PS-provider	Select response PDU issued
F_ABTIN	FS-user	F.ABORT.indication issued
ABTRQ	CS-provider	Abort request PDU issued
┆		

(d)

Name	Meaning
P1	F.INITIALIZE.request acceptable
P2	INIRP-PDU acceptable
P3	INIRQ-PDU acceptable
P4	SELRP-PDU acceptable
P5	F.SELECT.response acceptable
┆	

(e)

Name	Meaning
[1]	Initialize all state variables
[2]	Set rejection parameter accordingly
┆	

FIGURE 12.17

Abbreviated names for
FTAM protocol
machine: (a) incoming
events; (b) automaton
states; (c) outgoing
events; (d) predicates;
(e) specific actions.

CCITT recommendation X.400 been defined to provide an international
electronic messaging service that is similar in principle to the current (hand-
delivered) mail system. It consists of a suite of protocols each of which performs a
specific function in relation to the complete message handling system. The various
entities (and their associated protocols) that make up the set of X.400 recommendations are identified in Figure 12.19.

The user interface to the system is assumed to be a terminal (such as a
personal computer) that has sufficient processing and memory capabilities to
enable the user to interactively create a message (mail) and to read and browse
through messages that have been received. This is one of the functions of the **user
agent (UA)**. Also, since it is intended that the MHS should be used for a variety of
message types, the UA must be able to communicate with a similar peer UA in a
remote terminal so that a transferred message has the same meaning in both
terminals. This is the role of the **P2 protocol**. Clearly, the structure and meaning of
messages will differ from one application to another so a suite of protocols is
defined, each intended for use in a particular application domain. For example,

(a)

State Event	STA 0	STA 1	STA 2	STA 3	---
F_INIRQ	1	0	0	0	
INIRP	0	2	0	0	
F_SELRQ	0	0	3	0	
SELRP	0	0	0	4	

0 = F_ABTIN, ABTRQ, STA 0

1 = P1: INIRQ, [1], STA 1;
    NOT P1: F_INICF, [2], STA 0

2 = P2: F_INICF, STA 2;
    NOT P2: F_INICF, [2], STA 0

3 = SELRQ, STA 3

4 = P4: F_SELCF, STA 4;
    NOT P4: F_SELCF, [2], STA 2

(b)

State Event	STA 0	STA 1	STA 2	STA 3	---
INIRQ	1	0	0	0	
F_INIRP	0	2	0	0	
SELRQ	0	0	3	0	
F_SELRP	0	0	0	4	

0 = F_ABTIN, ABTRQ, STA 0

1 = P3: F_INIIN, [1], STA 1;
    NOT P3: INIRP, [2], STA 0

2 = INIRP, STA 2

3 = F_SELIN, STA 3

4 = P5: SELRP, STA 4;
    NOT P5: SELRP, [2], STA 2

FIGURE 12.18

Event–state table for FTAM protocol machine: (a) initiating entity; (b) responder entity.

the standard relating to simple person-to-person messaging is known as the **interpersonal messaging (IPM) protocol**.

Once a message has been prepared and the UA has added its own protocol information, it is passed to a companion service element known as the **submission and delivery service element (SDSE)**. The role of SDSE is to control the submission and reception of messages to and from the equivalent of the local post office. The latter is known as the **message transfer agent (MTA)**. A defined protocol is used for controlling the transfer of messages between the SDSE and its local MTA. Known simply as the **P3 protocol**, it covers the submission and delivery procedures together with related functions such as charging.

UAs communicate with one another using globally-unique names. Within the MTS, however, fully-qualified addresses are used; that is, PSAP addresses. Thus on receipt of a message, the local MTA must first perform a name-to-address translation. The structures of the names and addresses are defined in CCITT recommendation X.500. Associated with the MTA is a directory service agent which performs this translation function. This will be described in the next chapter. Essentially, if the two user terminals are both connected to, say, the international X.25 network, then the addresses will be the X.121 addresses of the

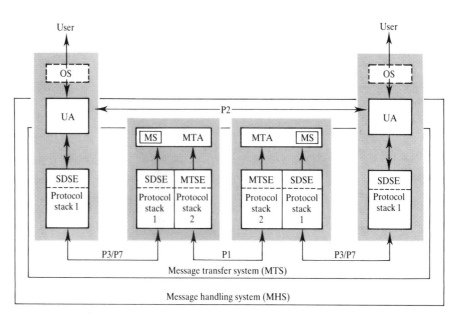

FIGURE 12.19

X.400 functional model.

OS = Operating system   SDSE = Submit/deliver service element
UA = User agent   MTSE = Message transfer service element
MTA = Message transfer agent   MS = Message store

terminals and will have the structure described in Chapter 8. Alternatively, if an internetwork is being used, then addresses of the type described in Chapter 9 will be used.

Once the MTA has obtained the addresses, it proceeds to create the equivalent of an electronic envelope by adding the address of both the originator (sender) and recipient (receiver) – together with other information specific to the MTS – to the head of the message received from the UA. It then sends the message using the appropriate protocol stack under the control of a third protocol known as the **P1 protocol**.

On receipt of a message addressed to one of its UAs (terminals), an MTA will try to deliver it to the SDSE in the terminal using the P3 protocol. Since the user terminal will normally be located remotely from the MTA, however, there is the possibility that it may be switched off or out of service. To allow for this, an MTA has a **message store (MS)** associated with it. In the event of a UA not being available, the message will be deposited into the MS for later delivery. A fourth protocol, known as the **P7 protocol**, is then used to control the interaction between a user, through its UA, and the local MS to retrieve any waiting messages.

Although the foregoing relates to the X.400 public messaging service the ISO MHS is based on this to ensure compatibility. A typical private system for use with a large site is shown in Figure 12.20.

A site-wide messaging system must be able to support both local messaging and inter-site messaging. Thus, in the example, each user terminal (workstation,

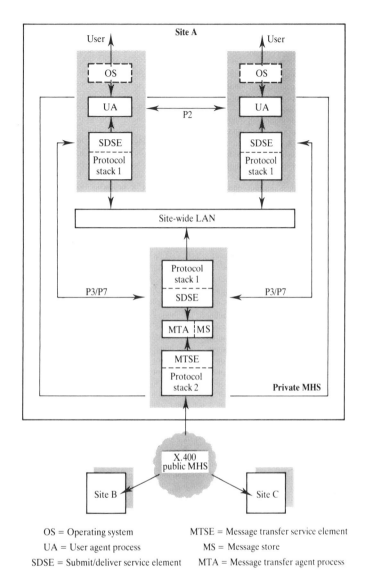

FIGURE 12.20

MOTIS functional model.

OS = Operating system   MTSE = Message transfer service element

UA = User agent process   MS = Message store

SDSE = Submit/deliver service element   MTA = Message transfer agent process

personal computer etc) communicates with a site-wide message server. If a received message is addressed to a user at the same site, the MTA in the server either relays it directly to the recipient or places it in the local message store for later delivery. Alternatively, if the message is addressed to a user off-site, since it is a private system, it must initiate the submission of the message to the public X.400 system. Typically, the message server will have a direct connection to the same public network as is used by the X.400 MTS. Hence, in the example, it is assumed that the server has an MTA associated with it. If this is not the case, an SDSE would be used.

Message format

As indicated earlier, there is a range of different message types, each with its own P2 protocol. Irrespective of the message type, however, all messages consist of an MTS header – the envelope – and the message contents. The addresses and other fields in the header are used by the MTS to transfer the message to its intended destination. Hence these are in a standard form for all message types. In the same way as the contents of an envelope in normal hand-delivered mail (a letter, invoice etc) has an additional heading for use by the recipient, so the message contents has an additional heading for use by the UA. It is this heading that changes for different messaging applications – personal (letters, memos etc), business (invoices, orders etc) and so on. As an example, the structure and contents of a message relating to the interpersonal messaging (IPM) protocol are shown in Figure 12.21.

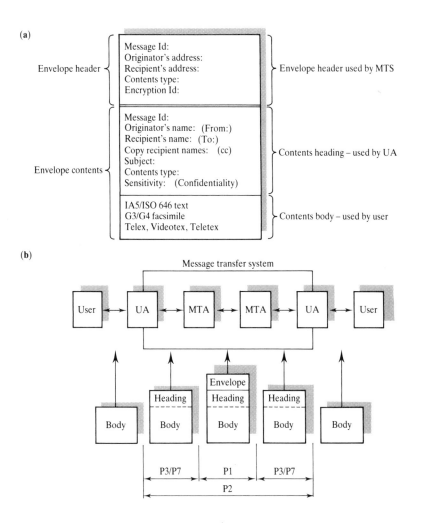

FIGURE 12.21

Message formats:
(a) interpersonnel
message format;
(b) message
construction.

In practice, both the MTS header and the contents heading can have many more fields than are shown in the figure. Also, the MHS allows different types of user terminal to be used. Hence, should the recipient terminal be different from the originator's terminal, then the MTA will endeavour to perform the necessary conversion. If it cannot do this, the message will be discarded and an appropriate reason code returned to the originator's MTA and from there to the UA. An example conversion might be from an X.400 terminal – and hence character set – to a teletext or telex terminal.

The **encryption identifier** field in the MTS header, in common with the other fields, is just an example from a group of fields that collectively enable the initiator MTA to specify the type of security level being used with the message contents during its transfer across the MTS. If the message contents are being encrypted, the encryption identifier will be present to enable the destination MTA to select the appropriate key for decryption. Other fields include a check sum on the contents – or encrypted contents – or the digital signature of the originator and/or recipient. The reader is referred back to Section 11.5 for further descriptions of these. Also, note that unlike the SMTP protocol, the complete message contents, including the heading, are treated as a single entity for encryption purposes.

MHS protocols

As was shown earlier in the functional models of the X.400 and MOTIS messaging systems, the application service elements and associated protocol stack differ with each protocol. Also, in practice, the SDSE is made up of three separate service elements, as can be seen in Figure 12.22.

The two ASEs associated with the P3 protocol are the **message submission service element (MSSE)** and the **message delivery service element (MDSE)**, while the ASE associated with the P7 protocol is the **message retrieval service element (MRSE)**. The MSSE controls the submission of messages by the UA to its local MTA. Similarly, the MDSE controls the delivery of the received messages from the MTA to the recipient UA. The MSRE is then used by a UA to retrieve stored messages from the message store (MS).

Both protocols use the ACSE and ROSE application-support protocols. As may be recalled, ACSE provides the means to establish an association between the two message handling ASEs, whereas ROSE provides a general remote invocation-request/reply-message transfer service. Thus, in this application, the message would be carried in either the request (MSSE) or the reply (MDSE/MRSE).

The **message transfer service element (MTSE)** used with the P1 protocol is used with the RTSE and ACSE service elements. As may be recalled, RTSE is an early protocol that uses ACSE and the session activity service. It enables a single message – or series of messages – to be transferred reliably between two (MTSE) ASEs using a basic stop-and-wait protocol. The remainder of the protocol stack used with each application entity will depend on the type of network/link being

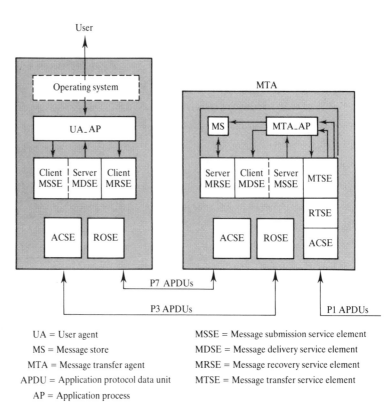

FIGURE 12.22

MHS protocols.

UA = User agent
MS = Message store
MTA = Message transfer agent
APDU = Application protocol data unit
AP = Application process

MSSE = Message submission service element
MDSE = Message delivery service element
MRSE = Message recovery service element
MTSE = Message transfer service element

used. In the case of the P3 and P7 protocols, this could be a LAN or a dial-up circuit. Similarly, for the P1 protocol it could be an X.25-based PSPDN, a frame relay ISDN or a private internetwork.

12.3.4 SMAE

The ISO network management protocol that is equivalent to the SNMP in a TCP/IP suite, is known as the **common management information service element (CMISE)**. In practice, this is only one component of the complete OSI **system management application entity (SMAE)**. One function of the SMAE is to allow a network manager to remotely manage the various (managed) objects associated with an open system networking environment – protocols, bridges, routers, packet switches etc. It also provides a general facility for managing any networking system such as the various systems and subsystems that make up a complete telecommunications network. The CMISE, therefore, only provides a basic service for sending and receiving management-related messages. Additional functionality is provided by a second ASE known as the **system management application service element (SMASE)**. The structure of the complete SMAE is thus as shown in Figure 12.23.

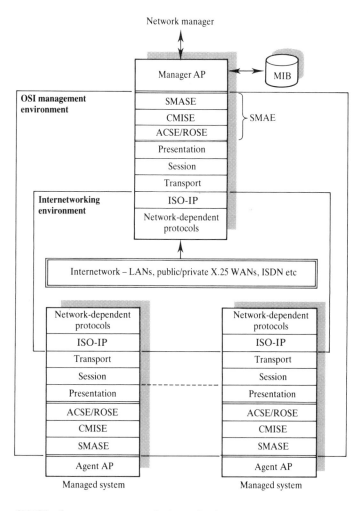

FIGURE 12.23

OSI system
management
components.

SMASE = System management application service element

CMISE = Common management information service element

SMAE = System management application entity

MIB = Management information base

All systems that contain one or more managed objects – that is, network elements that are to be managed by the network manager – must contain the complete SMAE. Also, although not shown in the figure, in some cases management processes may use the file transfer services of the FTAM/ACSE application entity. This is used, for example, to download object code after an object has been initialized. The manager, through the manager application process and the associated management information base (MIB), then interacts with the agent application process associated with a particular system to manage the various (managed) objects associated with that system. As with a TCP/IP suite, the MIB at the manager station contains configuration, performance, fault and other information relating to the complete network. The various software components associated with the manager AP provide the manager with the necessary facilities to manage the complete network.

Terminology

Before describing the operation of the two management service elements, it is necessary to define some of the relevant terminology.

The term **managed object (MO)** originates from the object-oriented design methodology on which the overall structure is based. It refers to any network element that is to be managed. Also, all elements to be managed must be logically represented by a managed object in the MIB. Thus, a managed object is a logical representation of a real item of hardware, software, data structure etc. It is defined by:

- the **attributes** associated with it;
- the **management operations** that can be applied to it;
- the **behaviour** it exhibits in response to applied operations;
- the **notifications** (events) that it can generate.

Although in practice a managed object may be the logical representation of a complicated item of equipment – a bridge, router, computer etc – as far as the network management system is concerned, only those attributes, operations, behaviour and notifications that have been defined for use with it in the MIB are visible to the network management system. This feature is based on the object-oriented design feature of **encapsulation** (or **information hiding**) which means that all implementation and other related details are hidden from the network management system.

An attribute – normally referred to as a variable in the SNMP – is a property of a managed object that reflects its current state. An attribute can have one or more values associated with it, such as a bridge port, a retransmission counter, a timer setting or the contents of a routing table. Any operations to be performed on an attribute are directed to the managed object to which the attribute relates rather than to the attribute directly. It is then a local matter how the managed object (procedure/program) carries out the specified operation.

Operations that can be performed on the attributes of a managed object are:

- **get attribute value**: returns the attribute value(s);
- **set attribute value**: sets the specified attributes to the values supplied with the operation;
- **derive attribute value**: sets the specified attributes to their default (or other previously specified) values;

- **add attribute value**: adds additional values to an attribute comprising a set of values;
- **remove attribute value**: removes values from a set of attribute values.

In addition, there are three operations that relate to a complete managed object rather than an attribute:

- **create**: creates a new managed object;
- **delete**: deletes an existing managed object;
- **action**: performs an action relating to this type of object.

A notification is emitted by a managed object when an internal or external event occurs. An example of an external event is the loss of communication with a neighbouring element. An internal notification might be a retransmission count exceeding a defined limit. Notifications are also known, therefore, as **event reports.**

The behaviour of a managed object relates to the effect of operations on it. It also covers the rules under which selected operations can be performed and the consequences of performing such operations. Examples include the rules relating to the creation or deletion of a managed object and the consequences of performing these functions.

All managed objects belong to a **managed object class** which defines the type of the managed object. There can be many instances of managed objects from this class, all of which have the same attributes, operations, behaviour and notifications associated with them. Each instance, however, is allocated a unique name and all operations then relate to that specific instance of the managed object class. An example of a class is the ISO-TP4 transport protocol of which there can be many instances.

Managed object classes must be specified in a standard way so that the attribute values associated with them have the same meaning to both the manager AP and the agent AP. Typically, the manager AP may run on an advanced workstation while the agent may be running on a microprocessor-based item of equipment such as a modem or router. Hence all classes are defined using ASN.1 and a library of all classes is maintained for the total system. All attribute values relating to a managed object are then transferred in their concrete syntax form to ensure they have the same meaning in all systems.

Managed-object classes are arranged in a hierarchy known as an **inheritance tree**. Each class is then a subclass of its parent in the tree. The term **inheritance** is another feature of object-oriented design and is used to indicate that a subclass inherits all the characteristics – attributes etc – of its parent. Thus, when a new class is defined, it is only necessary to define the additional characteristics that are to be associated with the new class. For example, a class **managed bridge** could be defined as a subclass of bridge. An instance of the managed bridge would then have the same characteristics as an instance of bridge but, in addition, would have network management software.

Managed object classes and instances of classes have specified **relationships** with one another. For example, if two object instances are bridge-1 and LAN 2, then a relationship might be 'bridge-1 is **connected to** LAN 2'. Another relationship is that of **containment** which has the same meaning as the term *is part of*. An example of the latter, therefore, might be 'port-2 is **part of** bridge-3'. Other relationships are possible. Also, higher-level relationships such as 'MO_A is managed by NM-2' or 'NM-1 is managed NM-8'; MO means managed object and NM network manager. A schematic showing the use and interrelationship of some of these terms is given in Figure 12.24.

As can be seen, the operations and notifications that are exchanged between the manager AP and an agent AP relate to a specific managed object. The intermediate SMAEs then ensure that the information exchanged and the mode of interaction is carried out in an open way. It is then a local matter how an agent AP carries out specified operations or generates defined notifications.

CMISE

The common management information service element (CMISE) provides the manager/agent AP above it – through the SMASE – with a generalized set of services to remotely invoke management procedures relating to operations, notifications and other data manipulation functions. The services are thus of the remote operation (procedure) type; in some instances a request/reply (confirmed) message exchange is involved, while in others a unidirectional (unconfirmed) message transfer occurs. It thus uses the ACSE and ROSE application-support service elements. ACSE provides the means to establish an association with a peer CMISE and ROSE to relay the remote operation and notification invocation requests and, if required, responses. A list of the services provided is given in Table 12.4.

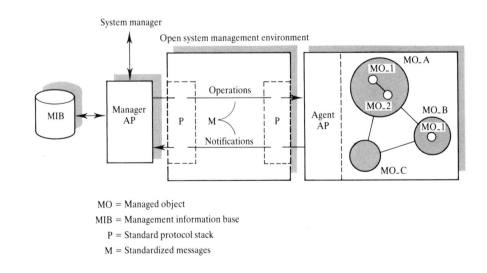

FIGURE 12.24

Manager-agent
interaction schematic.

MO = Managed object
MIB = Management information base
P = Standard protocol stack
M = Standardized messages

Table 12.4 CMIS service primitives.

Service	Type	Support ASE
M_INITIALIZE	C	ACSE
M_TERMINATE	C	ACSE
M_ABORT	U	ACSE
M_EVENT_REPORT	C/U	ROSE
M_GET	C	ROSE
M_SET	C/U	ROSE
M_ACTION	C/U	ROSE
M_CREATE	C	ROSE
M_DELETE	C	ROSE
M_CANCEL_GET	C	ROSE

C = Confirmed   U = Unconfirmed

It should be remembered that the services provided by the CMISE – known as **common management information services (CMIS)** – are general management services. Their effect is a function of the way the managed objects interpret the information associated with each service. The M_INITIALIZE, TERMINATE, and ABORT services are used to establish an association with a specified agent AP. Hence, all the resulting APDUs map directly into the equivalent ACSE primitives. Similarly, the APDUs relating to the other services are all transferred using an appropriate ROSE primitive. The various services have a direct relationship with the operations listed earlier.

The **M_GET** service is a general service that enables a manager AP to request the retrieval of mangement information from a specified agent AP. It is a confirmed service since there are results associated with it. An example is the retrieval of the current status of a managed object.

The **M_SET** service is a general service that enables a manager AP to request the modification of some mangement information relating to a managed object. It can be unconfirmed or confirmed if a result is expected. An example is to set a timeout value and, if required, obtain an acknowledgement.

The **M_EVENT_REPORT** service enables an agent AP to notify the manager AP of the occurrence of an event relating to a managed object. This can also be confirmed or unconfirmed.

The M_CREATE, DELETE and ACTION services all relate to a complete managed object rather than an attribute. An example is to create a new instance of, say, a protocol entity – CREATE – and then initialize it – ACTION.

The M_CANCEL_GET is used to cancel an earlier M_GET operation. It is useful, for example, if there is a long string of result values associated with the earlier M_GET since it allows a manager to interrupt the transfer operation.

As indicated, the services are general services. Each service primitive includes an **invoke identifier** that is used by the recipient to carry out a related – previously defined – management operation. The other parameters are then interpreted by the recipient in relation to this. For example, the parameters associated with the M_EVENT_REPORT primitive include:

- *Invoke identifier:* used to specify the notification involved and allow the recipient to relate the other parameters to this;
- *Mode:* confirmed or unconfirmed;
- *Object class:* the class of the managed object;
- *Object instance:* the specific managed object that has generated the notification;
- *Event type:* the type of event;
- *Event time:* the time it occurred;
- *Event information:* details relating to the event.

The protocol associated with CMISE is known as the **common management information protocol (CMIP)**. It generates an equivalent APDU for each of the service primitives listed. Also, each parameter associated with a primitive has an equivalent field in the APDU. Thus, on receipt of a service primitive, a CMIP creates an equivalent APDU and sends this using the services of either ACSE or ROSE. Similarly, on receipt of an APDU it performs the reverse function.

Most of the parameters associated with CMIS services that relate to the ACSE are mapped directly into the equivalent parameters of the corresponding ACSE service. A small number of parameters of each primitive, however, form the APDU of CMIP and the latter is then passed in the user data parameter of the appropriate ACSE primitive. Because of the close relationship between the CMISE remote operations and notifications and the equivalent ROSE services, they are normally defined together. To illustrate this a small section of the CMIP definitions after they have been included with the ROSE operations is shown in Figure 12.25.

It should be remembered that there are no real parameters/arguments associated with the ROSE. These are generated by the application-specific ASE to which it is linked. First the APDU types associated with the ROSE protocol are defined and then linked with the CMIP APDU definitions. Thus the m-Event-Report CMIP APDU is carried in a ROIV PDU of ROSE. The value of the **invoke identifier** parameter associated with the M_EVENT_REPORT primitive is then assigned to the invokeID field of the ROSE ROIVapdu. Each APDU associated with CMIP has a different **operation-value**; it is zero for **m-EventReport**. The argument field of the ROIVapdu is then that associated with, in this case, CMIP. Hence it is that defined in the figure relating to **EventReportArgument**. All the other CMIP APDUs are defined in a similar way. Other ASEs that use ROSE are all defined in a similar way.

SMASE

CMISE is now an international standard that is being used by many of the major suppliers of telecommunications and computer networking equipment in various network management applications. As has been indicated, however, the

FIGURE 12.25

CMISE PDU definition
schematic in relation to
the ROSE PDUs.

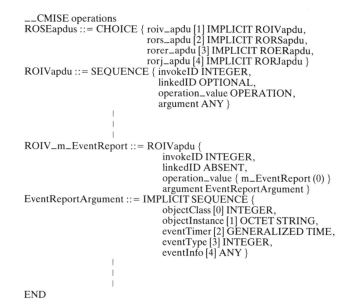

```
__CMISE operations
ROSEapdus ::= CHOICE { roiv_apdu [1] IMPLICIT ROIVapdu,
                       rors_apdu [2] IMPLICIT RORSapdu,
                       rorer_apdu [3] IMPLICIT ROERapdu,
                       rorj_apdu [4] IMPLICIT RORJapdu }
ROIVapdu ::= SEQUENCE { invokeID INTEGER,
                        linkedID OPTIONAL,
                        operation_value OPERATION,
                        argument ANY }
                        |
                        |
                        |
ROIV_m_EventReport ::= ROIVapdu {
                        invokeID INTEGER,
                        linkedID ABSENT,
                        operation_value { m_EventReport (0) }
                        argument EventReportArgument }
EventReportArgument ::= IMPLICIT SEQUENCE {
                        objectClass [0] INTEGER,
                        objectInstance [1] OCTET STRING,
                        eventTimer [2] GENERALIZED TIME,
                        eventType [3] INTEGER,
                        eventInfo [4] ANY }
                        |
                        |
                        |
END
```

management services it offers are general services. Consequently, it is left to the implementor of the manager and agent application processes to define the contents and structure of the MIB and the operations and notifications that can be performed on the attributes relating to each managed object. This is perfectly adequate for modest applications, such as the management of a single network. However, for the management of all aspects of a large global internetwork or telecommunications system, it means that many of the management-related functions have to be defined outside of the open system management environment. Additional issues include accounting management – charges for access or use of a managed object – and security management – access control and authentication procedures to be applied to users trying to gain access to a managed object. All these issues must be addressed by any system management facility.

As may be recalled, the aim of the combined system management application entity (SMAE) is not just to provide services to manage the various networking elements that make up an internetwork – communication lines, packet switches, intermediate systems/gateways, routers, bridges, protocol stacks etc – but rather to provide the services that are necessary to provide a total **integrated network management system (INMS)**. To achieve this goal, therefore, as was shown earlier in Figure 12.23, the SMAE contains an additional service element on top of the CMISE known as the **system management application service element (SMASE)**. Its function is to provide a higher-level of management services on top of those provided by CMISE yet still within the open system management environment.

SMASE is comprised of a set of **system management functions (SMFs)**. Each SMF then utilizes the underlying generalized services provided by CMISE to perform in own system management function. The total SMAE can be viewed, therefore, as consisting of a set of **network management profiles**, each performing a specific management function in the context of the total integrated network management system. SMFs are also known, therefore, as **management application services (MASs)**.

Each SMF provides a defined set of services that can be performed on the managed objects that relate to a particular management function. Associated with each SMF is a set of generic managed objects that relate to that function together with a definition of their attributes and the related operations and notifications. Associated with each of the managed objects in a set is the ASN.1 definition – a template – of all the parameters that are associated with each of the corresponding CMISE primitives. In this way, a management application is provided with a higher-level of abstraction since it need only specify the name of a managed object, together with the list of parameters that are to be associated with the operation/notification to be performed. SMASE then uses the corresponding ASN.1 template to create the corresponding service primitive that is compatible with those associated with CMISE.

Unlike SMISE, SMASE is still in the process of being developed. It is planned, however, that over a period of time, a range of SMFs/MASs will be defined as the OSI SMAE is used in various applications. Already a number of SMFs have been defined. Some are listed in Table 12.5 together with their use.

Table 12.5   A selection of system management functions and their use.

SMF	Use
Alarm reporting	Defines the syntax and semantics of events generated by managed objects
Event-management reporting	Defines the mechanism for controlling and filtering the reporting of events
Log control	Defines the mechanism for establishing, controlling the operation of, and selecting the contents of the event report logs (records)
Security alarm reporting	Defines the syntax and semantics for generating alarm notifications in the event of security violations
Accounting metering	Defines the mechanism for recording and reporting the use of network resources for accounting purposes
Workload monitoring	Defines the mechanism for monitoring the use of network resources for the purpose of evaluating performance
Measurement summary	Defines the mechanism for obtaining statistical summaries of the operating characteristics of network resources
Object management	Defines the mechanism to create and delete objects and to manage the attributes associated with objects
State management	Defines object states and the mechanisms to detect and modify states
Relationship management	Defines the mechanisms for establishing and maintaining relationships between objects

MIB

The naming principles associated with the objects in an OSI environment are fully compatible with those described earlier in the context of the SNMP protocol associated with a TCP/IP suite. Thus there is a management information tree (MIT) that defines the names of all the managed objects that are present in the MIB. The tree structure then reflects the containment rules associated with each instance of a managed object. The name of an instance of a managed object is then a combination of:

- the name of the next higher-order managed object to which it is linked – its superior;
- an additional name that uniquely identifies it within the scope of its superior.

In this way, the name of a managed object consists of a sequence of names starting at the root and working out to that object in the tree. The total name of an object is thus known as its **distinguished name (DN)**, and each constituent part as its **relative distinguished name (RDN)**. Clearly, the distinguished name allows a managed object to be uniquely identified within the total management system. In many instances, however, it is only necessary to define a name within the scope of a managed object other than the root. This is then known as a **partial distinguished name (PDN)**. An example is an internetwork comprising multiple networks and a local manager referring to the names of objects within the scope of a single network.

In addition to the MIT, two other trees are defined in the MIB. One is known as the **inheritance tree** and the other as the **registration tree**. The inheritance tree is used to show the superclass-subclass relationships between managed object classes. Thus, in the inheritance tree a particular class appears only once, whereas in the MIT multiple instances of the same class can be present at different locations within the tree. The registration tree is then used to manage the assignment of identifiers to managed objects. As may be recalled, these must be unique within the context of the total management system since they are used in CMIP APDUs.

12.3.5 MMS

The **manufacturing message service (MMS)** is an ASE that has been developed for use in fully automated manufacturing environments. Within such environments, there is a requirement for a facility to enable all the computer-based equipment to exchange messages in an open way. Normally, each manufacturing cell has an associated cell controller (control computer) which, in addition to communicating on a factory-wide basis with other systems using, say, FTAM, controls the computer-based equipment associated with the cell. Typically, these include robot controllers (RCs), numerical machine tool controllers (NCs), automatic guided vehicle controllers (AGVs), programmable logic controllers (PLCs) and so on. MMS has been defined to allow the cell controller to exchange messages with all this automated equipment in an open way.

A typical sequence of events might be as follows. First, at a factory-wide level, FTAM is used to pass information about a part or component to a cell controller. The controller then uses MMS to send appropriate commands to the automated equipment associated with the cell to cause the part (component) to be manufactured and/or assembled. Typically, commands such as:

- select and load a specific set of tools in an NC,
- request an RC to select an item of raw material and place it on an AGV,
- instruct the AGV to transport the material to the NC,

would be issued by the cell controller (CC). Status messages would be returned to the CC as tasks are completed.

Service primitives

As the specific MMS primitives associated with each device (CC, RC, NC etc) vary, subsets of the total service are defined for use with each type of device. For example, the services associated with a CC include:

- establish an association with a specific controller (context management);
- cause a controller to read a data file from the CC containing, say, tool data or operating instructions (obtain file);
- download a program to a controller (program load) from the CC;
- remotely control the operation of a controller (job control);
- read and change (write) selected variables associated with a controller program (variable access);
- request a controller to identify the MMS services that it supports (identity).

As with FTAM, the service primitives are grouped into a number of functional units (FUs); a list of some of the primitives associated with each FU is given in Table 12.6. It should be stressed that these are only examples and, of course, there are parameters associated with each primitive. As can be seen, MMS also supports a limited file service for local use within a cell; for example, to transfer a file containing the parts list associated with a controlled device. Of necessity, therefore, it is far less sophisticated than FTAM.

12.3.6 Job transfer and manipulation

The **job transfer and manipulation (JTM)** service is a collection of JTM SASEs located on different open systems. Collectively, the JTM elements (entities) form what is referred to as the **JTM service provider**. In the same way that FTAM does not actually implement a file service (that is, it only provides an environment

Table 12.6 A selection of the services associated with MMS.

Functional unit	Service primitive	Confirmed
Context management	Initiate	Yes
	Release (Conclude)	Yes
	Abort	No
Obtain file	ObtainFile	Yes
File transfer	FileOpen	Yes
	FileClose	Yes
	FileRead	Yes
Program load	LoadFromFile	No
	StoreToFile	No
Job control	Start	No
	Stop	No
Variable access	Read	Yes
	Write	Yes
Device status	Status	No
	UnsolicitedStatus	No
General services	Reject	No
	Cancel	Yes
	Identify	No

whereby a real file system may be accessed and managed in an open way), so JTM provides an environment whereby documents relating to jobs, referred to as **job specifications**, may be transferred between real (open) systems and the jobs executed by them. Indeed, the type of job transferred is transparent to the JTM service provider.

The AP that submits a specification of an OSI job, through an associated UE, is known as the **initiating agency**. A job specification completely specifies the job to be carried out. For example, with a simple application of JTM, it may relate to the specification of a program together with the data to be run by an AP on a remote computer system, or a document to be printed by a remote print server application process. With a more sophisticated application, it may relate to, say, an order for an item of equipment from a remote supplier's computer, or to an invoice or statement relating to an order. Clearly, the type of processing associated with a job may vary. In its simplest form it may involve the processing of the document, resulting from the job specification, while in others the initial job specification may spawn other associated job specifications (subjobs).

The AP that actually executes a job is known as the **execution agency** while the AP that receives the requests from the JTM service provider for information/ data relating to a job is known as the **source agency** – for example, a local file store. Also, as the time between submitting a job specification and the job being completed may be long in some instances, the initiating agency may specify an AP to follow the progress of the job when it submits a job specification. This AP is known as the **job monitor**. Thus, whenever a significant event occurs in the lifetime of the job, the JTM service provider creates a **report document** and sends

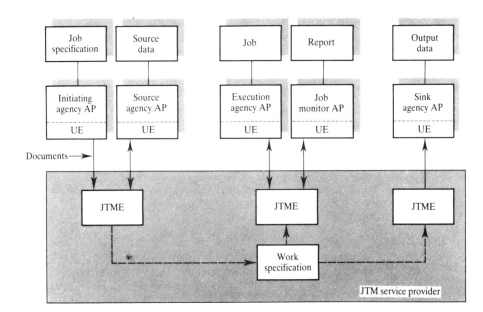

FIGURE 12.26

Model of JTM service.

this to the associated job monitor. The initiating agency may then make enquiries as to the current status of the job. Finally, after an execution agency has completed all the work associated with a job specification, the JTM service provider submits a document to a nominated AP – the **sink agency**.

It may be concluded from the foregoing that JTM is concerned mainly with the movement of documents (which relate to jobs) between APs. The latter are known as agencies to the JTM service provider. The various agencies associated with JTM are shown in Figure 12.26. Although each AP (agency) is shown as a separate entity, one or more of the APs may be associated with the same system. For example, the initiating and sink agencies may be in the same system, or the sink and monitor agencies, and so on.

JTM services

The full range of services associated with JTM are too extensive to describe here; hence, only the user services associated with what is known as the **basic class** will be described. This class only supports a restricted form of job specification – a single job. Thus, it does not result in any subjobs being spawned. Also, as there is no secondary monitor agency, the only events reported are those related to an abnormal operation.

The user service primitives associated with the basic class are shown in the time sequence diagram of Figure 12.27. The initiating agency (AP) is known as the **JTM service requestor** and the various agencies (APs) that receive requests from the JTM service provider are known as **JTM service responders.** The use of the various services shown are as follows:

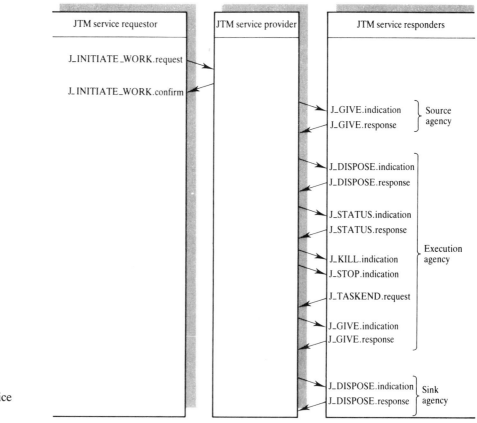

FIGURE 12.27

JTM basic class service primitives.

- J_INITIATE_WORK: This allows an initiation agency to submit an OSI job specification document to its local JTM entity.
- J_GIVE: This allows a JTM entity associated with the JTM service provider to request a document from a source or an execution agency.
- J_DISPOSE: This allows a JTM entity to pass a document to an execution or sink agency.
- J_TASKEND: This allows an execution agency to signal completion of an activity associated with a job to its local JTM entity.
- J_STATUS: This allows a JTM entity to obtain information about the progress of an activity associated with a job.
- J_KILL: This allows a JTM entity abruptly to terminate all activity associated with a job.
- J_STOP: This allows a JTM entity temporarily to stop all activity associated with a job.

Again, parameters are associated with each primitive. For example, the parameters associated with the J_INITIATE_WORK.request primitive include the following:

- name of initiating agency AP,

- local identifier,

- OSI job name,

- authorization,

- name of source agency AP,

- name of execution agency AP,

- name of sink agency AP,

- pointer to document containing job specification,

- JTM action parameter.

A JTM action parameter is present with all primitives and indicates the type of action associated with this primitive. This may be either document movement or work manipulation; the latter would be associated with a J_DISPOSE primitive passed to an execution agency, for example. In general, the response and confirm primitives only have the local identifier used with the corresponding indication and request primitives.

12.3.7 DTP

The **distributed transaction processing (DTP)** application service element is being developed to control the operations associated with transaction processing systems that involve multiple open systems. As may be recalled from the last chapter, many distributed applications involve multiple users (clients) requiring to access a single shared resource concurrently.

An example is a database or a file system in a banking application containing customer accounts to which a distributed community of client systems require access for both reading and update operations. As may be recalled, the CCR ASE has been defined to help control such applications to ensure the contents of the database/file store remain consistent and reflect all the operations that have been initiated. An application of the CCR that involves just a single resource was described earlier in relation to the reliable service associated with the FTAM ASE.

In addition to such uses, however, CCR supports the control of multiple (nested) transactions that involve several operating systems. Such requirements are typical of many distributed transaction processing applications. The DTP ASE has been defined for use in such applications together with the nested services of CCR.

A transaction involves multiple operations that are performed according to the following rules:

- **atomicity**: the operations are either all performed or none of them are performed;
- **consistency**: the operations associated with a successful transaction will transform any data involved from one consistent state to another consistent state;
- **isolation**: intermediate results associated with the operations are not accessible from outside and, if several transactions are running concurrently, they are controlled as if they were performed sequentially;
- **durability**: should faults occur while the operations are being performed, then they are recovered to a consistent state.

These are often referred to, therefore, as **acid rules**. The DTP ASE provides services to control the exchange of information between the APs that are involved in distributed transactions according to these rules.

Typical DTP systems involve multiple APs that are carrying out interrelated transactions between them. An example is a distributed community of client systems accessing the reservation systems of multiple airlines. Clearly, many booking operations will involve multiple interrelated transactions on several systems. These must be controlled in such a way that it is equivalent to a single client accessing each system sequentially. Also, should a client system crash during a series of transactions, then it is necessary to be able to detect this and return each server to a known consistent state.

Services

A complete DTP application entity comprises the DTP ASE and the support services provided by the ACSE and CCR ASEs. A typical distributed transaction processing application is shown in Figure 12.28.

Each client AP may wish to initiate a transaction that involves multiple servers and hence multiple subtransactions. The aim of the DTP service, therefore, is to provide each client with services that enable it to carry out such transactions concurrently with other clients. For each (distributed) transaction the user APs involved are organized in the form of a tree structure with the client initiating the original transaction at the root. The root AP, known as the master (superior), will then initiate a transaction with multiple servers each of which is known as a subordinate or slave. Also, in more sophisticated applications, while the operations associated with a transaction are being performed, a subordinate may wish to initiate a subtransaction. An example is if there are multiple copies of, say, a file held by a server. Hence, before responding to a commit request it may wish to initiate the updating of each copy thus creating what is known as a **transaction tree**.

Clearly, there are various levels of complexity associated with transaction processing systems: in some instances access to just a single resource may need to

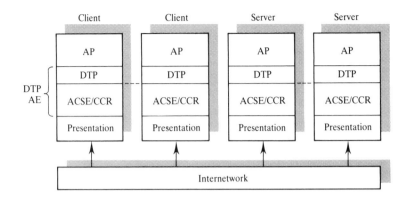

FIGURE 12.28

DTP application schematic.

DTP = Distributed transaction processing

AE = Application entity

be controlled while in others multiple concurrent transactions each involving transaction trees may need to be controlled. The user services associated with the DTP, therefore, are divided into a number of functional units (FU) each of which provides a defined control function. The services associated with the various FUs are:

The **kernel** FU provides the services to enable a user to establish an association with a server and initiate a transaction (begin a dialogue), perform any operations (data transfers) associated with this, signal an error back to the initiator, and close the transaction and association (end dialogue).

The **commit** FU provides the additional services that are necessary to enable a client to carry out a transaction according to the acid rules and hence involves the two-phase commit with rollback error recovery services of CCR.

The **polarized control** FU provides services to enable a single server to be accessed by only one user at a time.

The **unchained transaction** FU allows a superior to block the creation of a transaction subtree and then to allow it at a later time.

The **handshake** FU allows two clients to synchronize the processing function associated with a transaction.

EXERCISES

12.1 Produce a sketch, together with descriptive text, to explain the meaning of the following terms relating to a TCP/IP suite and an OSI stack:

(a) user requests/responses,

(b) virtual device requests/responses,

(c) real device requests/responses.

Hence identify the differences in terms of implementation and structure between the two.

12.2 Explain the meaning of the following terms in relation to the TELNET protocol:

(a) virtual terminal,
(b) network virtual terminal,
(c) pseudo terminal.

Using the commands listed in Table 12.1, produce a sequence of commands that would be exchanged between a client and server TELNET protocol to negotiate the following options:

(a) change from 7-bit ASCII to 8-bit binary,
(b) echo any characters you receive.

Assume first the client is making the request and then the server.

How are FF (hex) bytes transferred in the 8-bit binary mode?

12.3 Explain the meaning of the following terms relating to a file store:

(a) unstructured,
(b) structured,
(c) random access,
(d) flat,
(e) hierarchical.

Explain how the FTP in a TC/IP suite handles the first three structures.

12.4 List the four message types associated with the trivial FTP protocol and explain their meanings.

Assuming an unstructured file containing 1 K characters, use a time sequence diagram to show how this could be transferred between a client and server TFTP using the message types just described.

12.5 Explain the meaning of the following terms relating to an e-mail system:

(a) mailbox,
(b) native mail,
(c) mailbox name,
(d) mail header and keywords.

12.6 Use a time sequence diagram to illustrate a typical command message exchange sequence relating to the SMTP protocol to send an item of mail from one mail system to another with a copy to a third system.

12.7 Produce a sketch, together with descriptive text, to show the interrelationship between the terms 'operational environment' and 'network environment'. Include in your sketch a typical protocol suite relating to a host and a gateway.

12.8 Produce a sketch of a typical – but simplified – management information tree (MIT) for a campus network comprising a number of LANs interconnected by routers.

List the five user service primitives associated with the SNMP protocol and explain their use in relation to your MIT.

Define the PDU names corresponding to each service primitive and an example definition of one such PDU in ASN.1.

12.9 In the context of an OSI stack, explain the meaning and interrelationship between the following terms:

(a) service element,
(b) application-specific service element,

(c)   application-support service element,

(d)   application entity.

Give an example of the latter and identify the other terms in relation to this.

12.10 With the aid of a sketch, explain the meaning of the following terms relating to the ISO VT protocol:

(a)   virtual terminal,

(b)   user element,

(c)   conceptual communication area.

Identify the data structures that make up the latter and explain their functions.

12.11 With the aid of a sketch, describe the structure and how the elements of a filer are identified in the virtual file store model used with the ISO FTAM protocol. Include the meaning of the terms:

(a)   FADU,

(b)   DU,

(c)   data element.

12.12 With the aid of a state transition diagram, explain the four service regimes associated with the FTAM user services. Outline a typical sequence to read a data unit from a named file.

Clearly explain the operation of the F_READ/WRITE services.

12.13 Discriminate between the terms 'normal' and 'reliable transfer' modes in relation to FTAM.

List the additional services associated with the reliable transfer mode and explain how they relate to the services of the CCR application-support protocol.

12.14 With the aid of a sketch, explain the meaning of the following terms relating to the ISO mail standard MOTIS:

(a)   UA,

(b)   IPM protocol,

(c)   SDSE,

(d)   MTA,

(e)   MS.

Identify the various protocols associated with MOTIS and how they relate to your sketch. Give a brief explanation of the functions of each.

12.15 Explain the format of messages associated with the ISO MHS and how each component part is interpreted by the various protocols identified in 12.14.

12.16 Identify the protocols associated with the various elements that might be used for a campus e-mail system that is compatible with the public X.400 standard. In relation to this, explain how mail (messages) is sent

(a)   internally,

(b)   externally.

12.17 Produce a sketch showing the ASEs that make up a SMAE in an OSI management system and explain the function of each service element. Include in your descriptions the meaning of the term SMF.

12.18 Explain how the ISO management protocol differs from the SNMP used in a TCP/IP suite.

12.19 In relation to the OSI management framework, explain the meaning of the terms:
- (a) managed object,
- (b) attributes,
- (c) operations,
- (d) behaviour,
- (e) notifications.

Give examples of the operations that can be performed on the attributes of a managed object and how a managed object generates notifications.

12.20 Explain the meaning of the following terms used in relation to a managed object:
- (a) information hiding,
- (b) managed object class,
- (c) inheritance tree,
- (d) containment,
- (e) managed object instance,
- (f) management information tree,
- (g) distinguished name,
- (h) relative and partial distinguished name.

12.21 Outline the function and services associated with each of the following ISO ASEs:
- (a) MMS,
- (b) JTM,
- (c) DTP.

CHAPTER SUMMARY

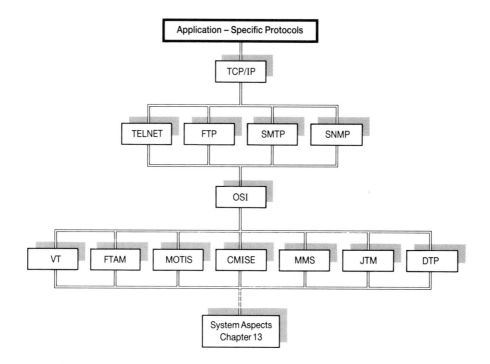

13

System aspects

CHAPTER CONTENTS

CHAPTER OBJECTIVES

When you have completed studying the material in this chapter you should be able to:

- explain the structure and operation of the domain name system used in a TCP/IP suite and how the names associated with an open system environment are managed;
- explain the structure and operation of the X.500 directory system and the protocols associated with it;
- know the architecture of the MAP and TOP protocol suites and their intended applications;
- understand how the various protocols that make up both a TCP/IP suite and an OSI suite interact one with another to implement a specific user application service;
- understand how a protocol suite is structured in relation to its local operating system;
- explain the main issues that are involved in relation to the implementation of the various components that make up a protocol suite.

13.1 INTRODUCTION

The previous chapters have been concerned primarily with describing the function, operation and specification of the different protocol entities that have been defined to enable open systems to be established in a range of application environments. The aim of this chapter is to discuss some of the issues relating to the operation and implementation of a complete communication subsystem based on these open standards.

As may be recalled, user applications use symbolic names for communication purposes whereas numerical addresses are used within the open system interconnection environment. Thus, it is necessary first to discuss how the protocol suite associated with an open application performs the name-to-address mapping function as well as how the assignment of names to users is managed. This is known as directory services.

Some examples of open system environments based on the TCP/IP and ISO protocols are then considered. This is followed by a more detailed look at how the various protocols that make up an open system suite cooperate and interact with one another to perform the required communication support function. Some issues relating to the implementation of the two complete protocol suites are then considered. The chapter concludes with a short discussion of the standards work that is going on in addition to the communication standards.

13.2 DIRECTORY SERVICES

As has been described, addresses are used within the open system interconnection environment to identify the source and destination application processes involved in a network session. An address consists of two parts: one for use by the network/internetwork to route messages to the required host/end system and the other for use within the host/end system to route a received message to the required application process.

The network-related part is analogous to a telephone number. If all calls involve just a single site – a PABX or a private network – then the numbers can be relatively short since they only need to identify a telephone outlet within that limited environment. In the case of a computer network this is analogous to the point-of-attachment address associated with a single network such as a LAN. If, however, the telephone is connected to a PTT or public-carrier network, the numbers must be longer to be able to identify and route calls across many national and possibly international exchanges. International telephone numbers are analogous, therefore, to the X.121 addresses used with the X.25 PSPDN or to an IP or ISO-IP address if multiple network types are involved. In both cases, the address is used to ensure that a host/end system address is unique within the total network/internetwork.

The second part of the address, which identifies a specific application process within a host, takes different forms with the two suites. In the case of

(a)

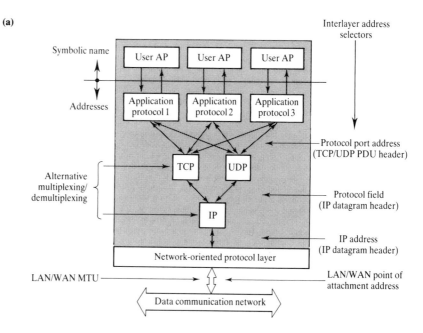

(b)

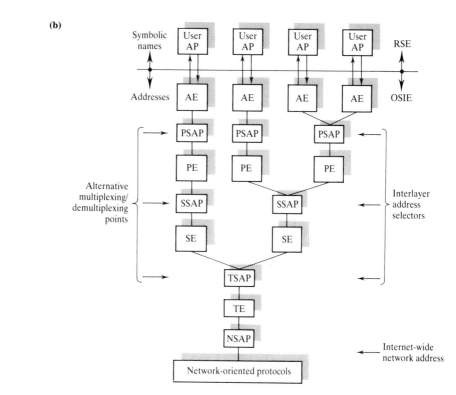

FIGURE 13.1

Address composition
(a) TCP/IP; (b) OSI.

TCP/IP, this is the role of the port address, while in an OSI suite, because multiple intermediate layers exist between the transport and application protocols, this is the role of the interlayer address selectors/service access points: TSAP, SSAP and PSAP. The addresses used with each protocol suite are shown in Figure 13.1

The addresses used in both suites are comprised of a significant number of digits. In the case of a TCP/IP suite, the IP address is a 32-bit integer which, in dotted decimal, can be up to 12 decimal digits. The port number is then a further three digits (eight bits). In an OSI suite, the network-related address can be as long as 40 decimal digits with additional digits for interlayer multiplexing/demultiplexing. Consequently, it is not feasible to use addresses – even in decimal form – outside of the open system interconnection environment (OSIE).

Within the real system environment, therefore, users – people and application processes (APs) – are known by **symbolic names** rather than addresses. Thus, in the same way that users of the telephone system use directory services to find the telephone number of a called party, so the **directory services** associated with an OSIE are used to find the address of a named destination user/AP. This **address resolution service** is the most frequently used of the directory services.

Although the use of names is essential if long addresses are to be provided, it is also necessary for other reasons. For example, the use of names isolates the users/APs from any knowledge of the network configuration which may, of course, change. For example, a subnetwork (LAN) may be added or removed or a different public data service used to interconnect subnetworks. Also, in some applications, a user AP should be able to migrate from one location on a network to another without, ideally, other APs being aware of this. To allow for such eventualities, the directory service must provide not only an address resolution service, but also services to allow the contents of the directory, containing the list of symbolic names and their corresponding addresses, to be changed and updated in a controlled way. The **binding** between the symbolic name of an AP and its address – location – is therefore said to be dynamic.

The total directory system in a TCP/IP suite is known as the **domain name system** while in an OSI suite it is the **X.500 directory**. Although the latter is a CCITT recommendation, it has been jointly developed with ISO. The directory system used by ISO is thus based on this standard. Each will be considered separately.

13.2.1 Domain name system

Two interrelated issues must be considered with any directory system. The first is the structure of the names and how their assignment is to be administered; the second is how the various directory services are to be implemented.

Name structure and administration

With any internet, the structure of the names is important since it strongly influences the efficiency of the directory services. There are basically two approaches that can be used. One is to adopt a **flat structure** and the other a

hierarchical structure. Although a flat structure will, in general, use the overall name space more efficiently, the resulting directory must be administered centrally. Also, as in large internets (and hence directories) it is normal to maintain multiple copies of the directory to speed up the directory services, the use of a flat address space means that all copies of the directory must be updated when changes occur. For these reasons, the directory systems associated with all but the smallest networks use a hierarchical naming structure.

Again an analogy can be drawn with the structure and assignment of subscriber numbers in the telephone system. At the highest level there is a country code, followed by an area code within that country, and so on. Thus the assignment of numbers can then be administered in a distributed rather than a centralized way. The assignment of country codes is administered at international level, the assignment of area codes within each country at national level and so on down to the point where the assignment of numbers within a local area can be administered within that area. This can then be done knowing that as long as each higher-level number is unique within the corresponding level in the address hierarchy, then the combined number will be unique within the total address space.

The adoption of a hierarchical structure also means that the various directory services can be carried out more efficiently since it is possible to partition the directory in such way that most address resolution operations – and other services – can be carried out locally. For example, if names are assigned according to the geographical distribution of hosts, then the directory can be partitioned in a similar way. Since most network transactions, and hence directory service requests, are between hosts situated in the same local area – for example, between a community of workstations and a local server or e-mail system – then the majority of service requests can be resolved locally. Relatively few transactions have to be referred to another site; these are known as **referrals**.

As an example we will consider the hierarchical address structure used with the Internet. As may be recalled from Chapter 9, the Internet is comprised of a number of interconnected internets. Because these internets have been interconnected relatively recently, each had its own naming hierarchy in place before the Internet was created. To accommodate this, there are a number of alternative partitioning possibilities, known as **organizations** or **domains**, at the highest level in the hierarchy (tree). The names of these domains are listed in Table 13.1.

All hosts that are to be attached to a network or subnet of the Internet must be registered with one of these organizational domains. The overall directory for the Internet is partioned according to these domains. Consequently, the choice of domain to be registered under is made in such a way as to minimize the number of referrals. Hence, if a host is to be attached to a network that belongs to an educational institution, since it is likely that most network transactions will involve hosts that are attached to its own network or those of other educational institutions, it would be registered within the EDU domain. Similarly, if a host is attached to a network belonging to a military research establishment it would be registered within the MIL domain, and so on.

Table 13.1 Domain names used in the Internet.

Domain name	Meaning
COM	Commercial organizations
EDU	Educational institutions
GOV	Government institutions
MIL	Military groups
NET	(Internet) network support centres
ORG	Other organizations
INT	Internal organizations
USA	
UK	} Country codes for geographical assignments

Each domain uses an appropriate naming hierarchy. Thus in the EDU domain the next level in the hierarchy is the names of the different educational institutions, while in the COM domain it is each (registered) commercial organization. The general scheme and naming convention are thus as shown in Figure 13.2.

Each component of a domain name is known as a **label**. As the example shows, labels are written with the local label on the left and the top domain on the right, each separated by a period.

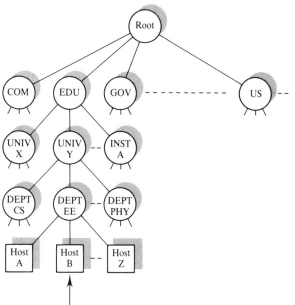

FIGURE 13.2

Domain name hierarchy.

HOST_B . DEPT_EE . UNIV_Y . EDU

Although prefixes are given to each label in the example, this is only done to illustrate a typical hierarchical breakdown. In practice, each label would simply be the registered domain name for that level in the hierarchy.

As indicated earlier, the adoption of a hierarchical structure means that names can be assigned locally rather than centrally. Thus in the case of an educational institution, as long as the institution – and hence name – is registered with the EDU domain name authority, it is possible for the authorized computer manager at that institution, to assign names as well as IP addresses to hosts that are to be attached to that institution network.

Domain name server

Associated with each institution network is a host (computer) that runs an application protocol/process known as the **domain name server (DNS)**. Associated with this is a database known as the **directory information base (DIB)** which contains all the directory related information for that institution. Thus when a new host is to be registered, the manager interactively enters the name and IP address – and other information – that have been assigned to that host into the DIB of the local domain name server. A user can then initiate transactions that involve the Internet.

As indicated earlier, when initiating a network transaction involving a particular application protocol, a terminal user or an application process will use the name of the host machine on which the server is running when communicating with its local client protocol. Hence, before this protocol can initiate the setting up of a transport connection with the server, it must ascertain the IP address of the host in which the server runs. In a TCP/IP suite all server protocols/processes are allocated a fixed port number – the well-known port – so it is not necessary to maintain port numbers in the DIB.

To obtain the IP address of a named server, each host has a client protocol/process known as the **name resolver**. Its position is shown in Figure 13.3 together with the outlined sequence of events that is followed by the client protocol to carry out the name-to-address mapping.

On receipt of the name, the client application protocol passes it to the name resolver using the standard interprocess communication primitive supported by the local operating system. On receipt of the name, the resolver creates a resolution request message in the standard message format of the domain name server protocol. This format is shown in Figure 13.4

A resolver can have multiple requests outstanding at any time. Hence the IDENTIFICATION field is used to relate a subsequent response message to an earlier request message. The type of message – request/response – and additional qualifiers relating to responses – format error, server failure etc – are given in the PARAMETER field. Responses also contain information about the server(s) – its AUTHORITY and IP address. In addition, each request and response message can contain multiple requests/responses.

The name resolver passes the request message – using the standard TCP/IP protocols and messages – to its local domain name server. Then, if the request is

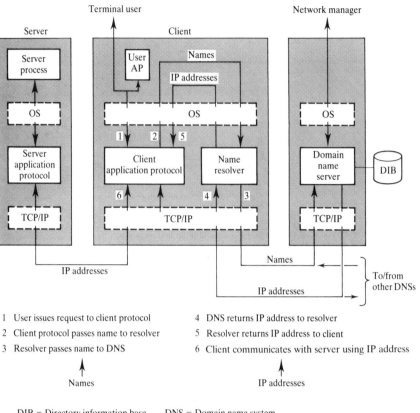

FIGURE 13.3

Name-to-address resolution protocols and sequence.

1   User issues request to client protocol
2   Client protocol passes name to resolver
3   Resolver passes name to DNS
4   DNS returns IP address to resolver
5   Resolver returns IP address to client
6   Client communicates with server using IP address

DIB = Directory information base   DNS = Domain name system

FIGURE 13.4

Domain server protocol: (a) message format; (b) parameter bit definition.

(a)

Identification
Parameter
Number of questions
Number of answers
Number of authority fields
Number of additional fields
Domain name(s)
Responses
Authority fields
Additional information fields

(b)

Bit position	Meaning
1	0 = request
	1 = response
2 – 5	0000 = standard
	0001 = inverse
6	1 = answer authoritative
7	1 = message truncated
8	1 = recursion desired (query)
9	1 = resursion available (response)
13 – 16	0000 = no error
	0001 = format error
	0010 = server failure } (response)
	0011 = name unknown

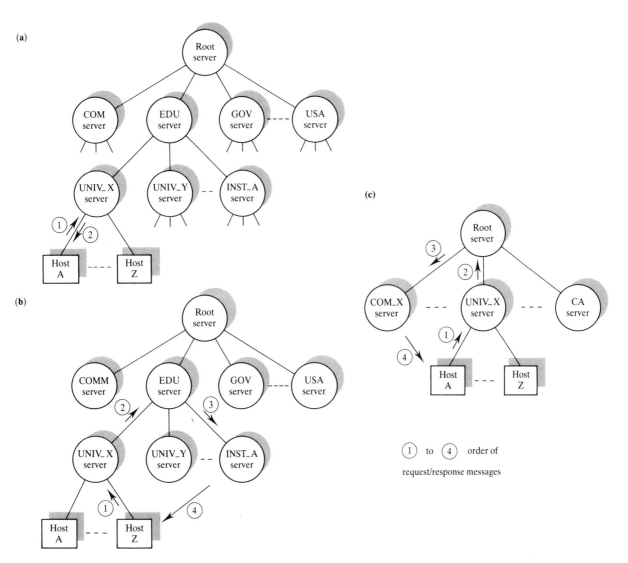

FIGURE 13.5

Domain server hierarchy: (a) local request; (b) higher-level request; (c) collapsed hierarchy.

for a server (host) on this network, the local domain name server obtains the corresponding IP address from its DIB and returns it in a reply message. If it does not contain the required address, however, then it must seek help from another server by creating a request message. This is known as a referral and the aim is to minimize the number of referrals that are needed. To achieve this, the servers are organized in a hierarchical structure as shown in Figure 13.5(a).

As can be seen, a higher-level server associated with each organization tree incorporates a table containing the names and IP addresses of all the name servers associated with the organizations/institution registered with that domain hierarchy. Hence, on receipt of a request that it cannot resolve, the local domain name server creates and sends a referral request to the higher-level server. The latter first checks the domain name associated with the request and, assuming it is for another server within the same domain, uses the name to access the IP address from its own name table. It then returns this in a response message to the local server which then makes a direct request to the indicated server for the required IP address. The sequence of the messages exchanged is thus as shown in part (b) of the figure.

Similarly, a further level of referral must be initiated by the higher-level server to resolve a request that involves an organization in another domain. Thus in the scheme shown, the root server would have a table containing the names and IP addresses of all the higher-level domain servers and, on receipt of a request involving another domain, it would relay the request via the root server. The required domain server would then respond directly as before.

In practice, the amount of information associated with the intermediate domain name servers is only modest since the number of entries in its referral table is determined by the number of institutions/organizations and not the number of hosts at each site. Hence to reduce the number of message exchanges, the alternative structure shown in part (c) of the figure is also used. With this approach, the root server contains the IP address of all the servers in all registered organizations. Hence each referral request can then be answered with a maximum of four message exchanges.

Although this scheme reduces the number of message exchanges, like the other scheme it still leads to a significant load on the internet because many messages may need to be transmitted over several networks to resolve each query. To minimize this, therefore, each local server maintains a record of the most recently referred names – together with their IP addresses – together with the names and IP addresses of the servers that provided the addresses. This information is retained in a table known as the **name cache**. On receipt of a request for which it does not have a local entry, the local server searches its name cache and, if an entry is present, responds with it. In the response message, however, it resets the authoritative flag to zero and puts the answer in the authority field together with the name and IP address of the server that provided the answer. This allows for the possibility that the information may be out-of-date as a result of a network reconfiguration, for example. Thus on receipt of the reply, the client can either accept the information or make a new request directly to the name server.

To ensure that the list of cached entries is reasonably up-to-date, a timeout period is associated with each entry. The value of this period is that given by the server that provided the information. Hence the timeout for each entry may vary one from another. Once an entry timeout expires, it is removed and any new requests for that entry will have to be referred.

13.2.2 X.500 directory

The directory services associated with an OSI suite are those used with the X.500 standard. This is a CCITT recommendation but, because of their common goal, it has been jointly developed with ISO. The standard consists of several parts, each concerned with a different aspect of the overall directory function. The complete system is known simply as the **Directory**. The structure and services associated with the directory have been defined so that it can be used not only to provide directory services to the application processes in an OSI suite, but also to provide services to other applications, such as management processes in system management applications, and to message transfer agents within an X.400 message transfer system.

Information and directory model

The structure and naming convention associated with the Directory is based on the object-oriented design principles that were described in Section 12.3.3 of the last chapter. The terminology, which is thus similar to that used with the X.400/MOTIS message message handling service, is summarized in Figure 13.6(a).

All entries in the directory information base are known as **objects** which are **instances** of a particular **object class**. Objects are then organized in a tree structure known as the **directory information tree (DIT)**. All objects at a particular level in a branch hierarchy belong to the same object class. Objects at the next higher level of the tree from a class of objects are members of the superclass of those objects while those at the next lower level are members of their subclass.

Associated with each object class (and hence object) is a set of **attributes** each of which has a **type** and one or more **values**. The attribute type identifies the

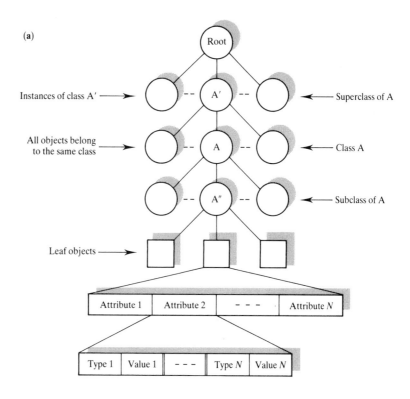

FIGURE 13.6

DIT structure:
(a) terminology.

(b) -- attribute data type --
```
      Attribute ::= SEQUENCE {
                          type AttributeType
                          values SET OF AttributeValue
                          -- at least one value is required -- }
      AttributeType ::= ObjectType
      AttributeValue ::= ANY
      AttributeValueAssertion ::= SEQUENCE {
                                      AttributeType, AttributeValue }
   -- naming data types --
      Name ::= RDNSequence
      RDNSequence ::= SEQUENCE OF RelativeDistinguishedName
      DistinguishedName ::= RDNSequence
      RelativeDistinguishedName ::= SET OF AttributeValueAssertion
```

FIGURE 13.6 (cont.)

(b) Attribute definition
in ASN.1.

class of the object – for example, the country code, C. At least one of the values must be the name of the object – for example, UK. The attribute structure of each object is shown relative to a leaf object although all objects in the tree have the same structure. A more formal definition of the attribute structure is given in part (b) of the figure together with a definition of the terminology associated with object names. Both are expressed in ASN.1.

The naming convention is similar in principle to that used in the domain name system. With X.500, however, each label is referred to as a **relative distinguished name (RDN)** – as with X.400 – and the complete list of labels associated with an entry (object) in the tree as the **distinguished name (DN)**. As with the domain name system, however, the RDNs used must be unique at any level in a branch hierarchy. Consequently, they are assigned by the administrative authority responsible for that level. A (simplified) portion of a DIT is shown in Figure 13.7(a). The names used may relate, for example, to an X.400 mail system.

In the example, the Country (C), Organization (O), Organizational Unit (OU) and Common Name (CN) are all class (attribute) types; UK, UNIV, SWAN etc are the corresponding attribute values. Note that the object class Organizational Unit has an additional attribute of type DEPT, the value of which is EE. The RDN and DN for each object name in the tree are then as given at the side of the tree.

Entries with **alias names** can be included at the leaves of the DIT, in addition to entries with object names. An alias (name) entry in the DIT, in addition to having a distinguished name, always points to (gives the distinguished name of) an object in a different part of the DIT. This object need not be a leaf entry. Hence an alias name allows an object to belong to more than one branch of the DIT and therefore have more than one name. An example is shown in part (b) of the figure.

The tree is an extension of the tree in part (a). An object COM – company – is defined as of class Organization (O = COM). This has a subclass Company Name (CN = IT, L = SWAN) which in turn has a subclass Name (N = HALS). The last one is a leaf node and is an alias name for HALS in the other organizational branch. It thus has an additional alias name attribute giving the distinguished name (DN) of the other entry in the tree.

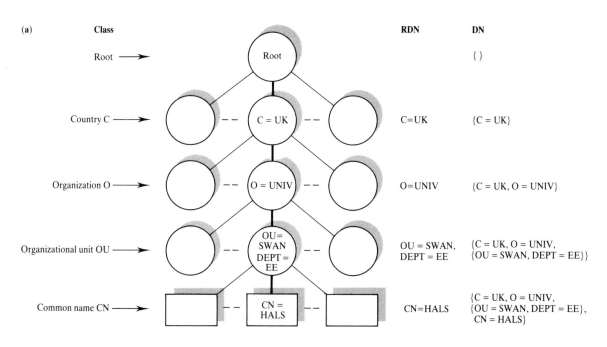

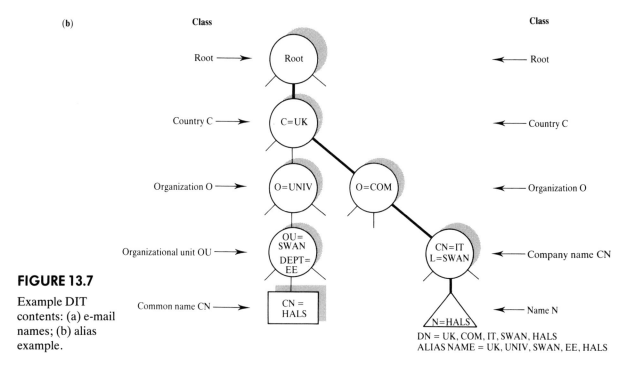

FIGURE 13.7

Example DIT contents: (a) e-mail names; (b) alias example.

Directory services

The model of the directory service is shown in Figure 13.8. All users access the directory through an application process known as the **directory user agent (DUA)**. As indicated earlier, the directory should meet the needs of a range of different applications. Thus the user can either be a person at a terminal or an application process. To resolve each request, a DUA interacts with the directory through an application process known as the directory service agent (DSA). The DUA thus plays a similar role to the name resolver in a TCP/IP suite and the DSA in the domain name server.

Services provided by a DUA to a user are classified as either **directory interrogations** or **directory modifications**. These are listed, together with their meanings, in Table 13.2.

Most of the requests shown have a number of associated **qualifiers**. For example, the user can set a limit on the length of time, the scope of a search and the priority to be associated with a request – **control qualifiers**. In addition, a directory entry may have an associated security mechanism, such as a digital signature, that has to be given before a request will be initiated – **security qualifiers**. And if a request involves a number of entries, a **filter qualifier** can be included with the request. This qualifier specifies one or more conditions that an

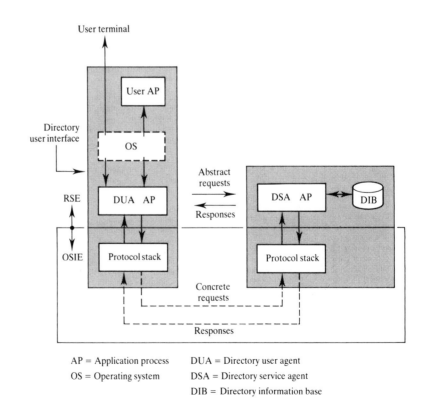

FIGURE 13.8

Directory services model.

AP = Application process   DUA = Directory user agent
OS = Operating system   DSA = Directory service agent
                                        DIB = Directory information base

Table 13.2 Directory services: request types.

Directory interrogation requests

READ	Requests the values of some or all of the attributes associated with an object entry; the user throughout DUA supplies the attribute types that are required.
COMPARE	Requests the directory to compare a given value – for example, a password – with that associated with a given attribute of a given entry.
LIST	Requests the list of immediate subordinates of a given entry.
SEARCH	Requests the values of all attributes within a defined portion of the DIT that satisfy a given filter.
ABANDON	Informs the directory that the user is no longer interested in the result of an earlier request.

Directory modification requests

ADD_ENTRY	Requests that a given object name or alias name – with attributes – is added to a specified location of the DIT as a real entry.
REMOVE_ENTRY	Requests that a given object name or alias name – which must be leaf entities – be removed from the DIT.
MODIFY_ENTRY	Requests a sequence of changes to be made to a given entry. The changes are either all carried out successfully or none of them are carried out. The changes include: addition, removal or replacement of given attributes or attribute values.
MODIFY_RDN	Requests the relative distinguished name associated with an object or alias leaf entry is changed to that given.

entry must satisfy before it can become part of the response. An example is a request in an X.400 messaging system for, say, all company names of a given type in a specified town or city. Similarly, a user can browse through the contents of the directory by using a combination of the LIST and SEARCH services.

The READ service performs the basic address resolution (look-up) service. It results in the DUA supplying the distinguished name of an object together with the attribute type of the result that is required. The local DSA will then return any value(s) corresponding to that attribute type. Thus in an OSI internet application, the distinguished name would be that of a server and the attribute type the (fully-qualified) PSAP address. Similarly, in an OSI messaging system, the distinguished name(s) would be the originator/recipient name(s) and the attribute type their O/R address(es) in the total messaging system. Alternatively, an alias name can be provided instead of a distinguished name. Also, the values of a number of attribute types can be requested with a single request.

The directory always reports the outcome of each request that is made of it. Clearly, any of the requests may fail for reasons such as violations of the security mechanism associated with an entry or problems with the parameters provided – invalid name or attribute value, for example. In such cases an error message is returned with an appropriate error type.

In applications that require user authentication before access is granted to an entry in the directory an **authentication attribute**, such as a password, can be included with the entry. The directory would then only return a positive response to a request if the correct password were submitted, otherwise an error message would be returned. This is necessary with a network manager station, for example. The manager – through an appropriate interactive application process – would have to provide the correct password before being allowed to add/remove/ modify entries in the directory. Similarly, with a networked resource such as a file server that contains confidential information, a set of attributes could be used containing the passwords of only those users who are allowed access to the server. Any other users would simply receive an error message.

The foregoing are examples of **simple authentication**. In more demanding applications, the authentication attribute could be the password of the user that has been encrypted using that user's public key. In this case an authenticated password is only obtained if the user provides the password encrypted using its private key. This is an example of **strong authentication**. It requires the DSA process to perform additional security processing.

Directory structure

As was discussed in the last section, for all but the smallest of directories, it is necessary to structure the directory in a distributed way. The physical distribution normally reflects the logical distribution of the directory information tree. The total DIB is thus divided into a number of partitions that relate to the structure of the DIT. A DSA is then associated with each partition that provides access to it. The general scheme is shown in Figure 13.9(a).

On receipt of a request from one of its local DUAs, a DSA first searches its DIT partition for the required information. If this information is present, it

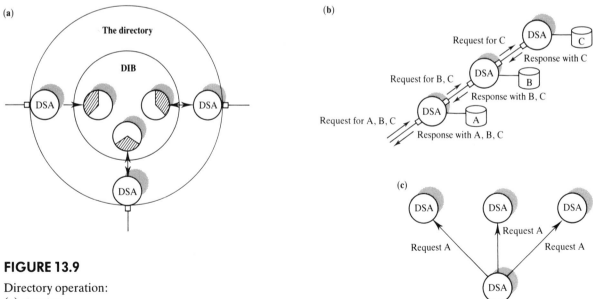

FIGURE 13.9

Directory operation:
(a) structure;
(b) chaining;
(c) multicasting.

responds directly to the DUA. If it is not, then it must refer the request to another, higher-level, DSA – a referral. As can be deduced from this, the procedure is the same as that used in the domain name system. In addition to referrals, however, the DSA supports two search procedures: chaining and multicosting.

With **chaining**, if a DSA receives a request for which it only has part of the required information, it creates a request for the remainder of the information and sends this to the DSA which it thinks should have the information. This type of request is known as a **chained request** since, if the recipient DSA does not have all the required information either, then it too will create a new (chained) request, and so on. The response to a chained request must always return along the path taken by the matching request. The recipient DSA then combines the received information with its own contribution and returns this to the next DSA in the chain or to the DUA if the end of the chain has been reached. The general scheme is shown in part (b) of the figure.

Multicasting is similar to flooding. If a DSA does not have the required information relating to a request in its DIB partition, it forwards a copy of the request to all the other DSAs it has knowledge of. Then, assuming one of them has the information, it returns this to the requesting DSA and from there to the user. This is shown in part (c) of the figure.

As with the domain name system, a DSS maintains a cache of the network addresses of all the other DSAs in the system with which it communicates to minimize the number of referrals. Hence, on receipt of a request for which it has to generate a referral it can normally send the request directly to the appropriate DSA or inform the DUA of the address of the DSA that should be used to answer the request. The DUA would then issue a new request directly to that DSA.

Directory protocols

It should be remembered that the DUA and DSA are application processes and not protocols. Hence, in terms of the ISO Reference Model they are in the real system environment and not the open system interconnection environment. All communications between a DUA and a DSA take place using standard request-response (remote operations) messages that are in an abstract syntax. Similarly, all messages that are exchanged between DSAs are in an abstract syntax and of the same request-response type. All messages relating to both exchanges are defined using ASN.1. Thus in addition to the definition of these messages, supporting protocols must be utilized to ensure these message exchanges are carried out in an open way; that is, the messages exchanged will have the same meaning in the two communicating systems.

To achieve this, two supporting protocols have been defined, each of which uses the ACSE and ROSE application-support service elements and, of course, the services provided by the presentation layer. The protocol associated with the DUA-to-DSA message exchanges is known as the **directory access protocol (DAP)** and that associated with the DSA-to-DSA message exchanges as the **directory system protocol (DSP)**. An example arrangement is shown in Figure 13.10.

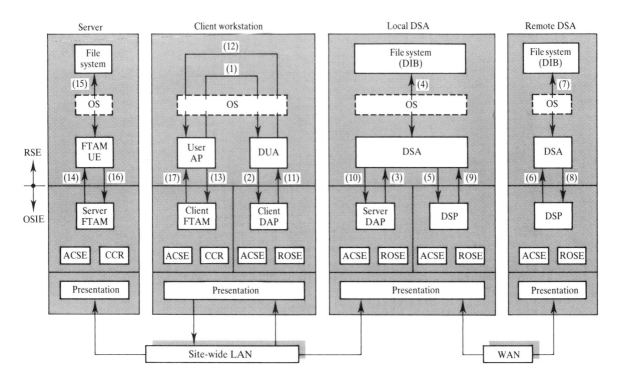

| Server | Client workstation | Local DSA | Remote DSA |

DUA = Directory access protocol   DUA = Directory user agent process

DSP = Directory system protocol   DSA = Directory service agent process

UE = User element   AP = Application process

(1) User AP sends name of FTAM server to DUA AP
(2) DUA sends request message to client DAP
(3) Server DAP passes request to local DSA
(4) Local DSA checks its DIB for object
(5) Local DSA sends referral request to DSP
(6) Remote DSP passes request to its DSA
(7) Remote DSA obtains attribute from its DIB
(8) Remote DSA returns response to its DSP
(9) DSP passes response to the local DSA

(10) DSA relays response to its DAP
(11) Client DAP passes response to its DUA
(12) Response returned to user AP
(13) User AP issues FTAM request
(14) Server FTAM issues request to UE
(15) Local file access carried out
(16) Data returned to server FTAM
(17) Data passed to user AP

FIGURE 13.10

X.500 directory protocols and example message/APDU exchange.

The arrangement shown assumes that the user AP running in the client workstation wants to obtain a file from a file server that is connected to the same site-wide LAN. Thus before initiating the (remote) file request to its local FTAM application entity – assumed to be comprised of the FTAM client ASE and the ACSE and CCR service elements – it must first obtain the fully-qualified PSAP address of the server which it knows only by its application title (name). Numbers (1) through (12) thus indicate the sequence of the messages that are exchanged to obtain this address.

As indicated, both the DAP and DSP use remote operations – remote procedure call – for communications and hence these are supported by

DAP/ROSE. Thus after an association has been established between the DUA and it local DSA – using the services of ACSE – all requests from the DUA are implemented by invoking a suitable remote operation/procedure in the local DSA using the services of DAP/ROSE. The server name and PSAP-address attribute type are passed as arguments in a RO_INVOKE primitive and the result is returned in an argument of the RO_RESULT primitive.

In the sequence shown, it is assumed that the local DSA associated with the site does not have the required address in its DIB – in practice, unlikely – and must refer the request to a remote DSA. Steps (5) through (9) indicate the message exchanges that take place to obtain the address from the remote DSA. After the local DSA receives the requested attribute – PSAP address – it relays this address back to the requesting DUA and from there to the user AP – steps (10) through (12).

The remote AP can then initiate the file access request to the remote file server/system using the services provided by the local (client) FTAM application entity. The sequence of messages resulting from this are thus (13) through (17). In practice, more messages are exchanged than are shown since and association must first be established between the client and server APs – using the services of ACSE – and messages relating to the file selection and open procedures must be exchanged before any file data is transferred. The sequences, however, are intended to illustrate the operation of X.500 and not FTAM.

13.3 EXAMPLE OSI ENVIRONMENTS

As may be recalled from Chapter 9, the Internet is by far the largest open system interconnection environment currently in existence. Moreover, as well as providing communications support for a wide range of internet-wide applications to many thousands of users, it is still being used as a testbed for investigating many issues relating to internetworking and the associated network protocols.

In contrast, there are currently relatively few networks based on the OSI suite. Until relatively recently this has been primarily because of the lack of firm standards for the higher application-oriented layers. However, a full set of standards is now available and as a result many new open system environments are being defined based on the OSI suite.

In the public sector, a number of OSI environments are currently being established by the PTTs and public carriers. These include X.400 public messaging networks as well as Teletex, Videotex and Facsimile networks. All of the equipment used to provide access to such networks utilizes a full OSI suite. Normally, the protocols used at each layer are CCITT X-series recommendations but these are fully compatible with the equivalent ISO standards. As has been described, the X.500 Directory is now also a full international standard and will therefore further promote the use of OSI suites in such applications. Collectively, the services provided by such networks are referred to by the PTTs as **teleservices**. Those just listed were first introduced in Chapter 8 when wide area networks were discussed.

In the private sector, two examples of OSIEs are MAP and TOP. In the manufacturing industry, an initiative by General Motors of the United States has resulted in a set of protocols, all based on ISO standards, being selected to achieve open systems interconnection within an automated manufacturing plant. The resulting set of protocols are known as **manufacturing automation protocols** (**MAPs**). A typical MAP network, together with the protocols selected for use with it, is shown in Figure 13.11.

As can be seen from the figure, MAP is based on a factory-wide, backbone cable distribution network. This is coaxial cable and operates at 10 Mbps. Because of the wide range of communication requirements within a factory, the broadband mode of working has been selected. The MAC sublayer is ISO 8802.4, the token bus standard, which has been selected because of its deterministic access time. Both the network layer and the LLC sublayer operate in a connectionless mode and the transport layer operates using the class 4 connection-oriented protocol known as TP-4. The distributed information services currently selected include FTAM and MMS, each of which operates through an ACSE application-support service element.

For communications within a manufacturing cell (that is, for exchanging messages between, say, a cell controller and a distributed set of robots and other computer-controlled machines), the simpler and less costly carrierband transmission method is used. Since most communications within a cell are local, a reduced set of protocols has been selected. Clearly, the time overheads associated with the full seven-layer model are significant and, in some instances, unacceptable for communications between the cell controller and the automated equipment. The reduced set of protocols selected, therefore, comprises MMS (which also includes a basic file service) interfaced directly to the LLC sublayer, which then operates in a connection-oriented mode. In this way, the time overheads associated with intra-cell communications are much reduced. The resulting system is then known as the **enhanced performance architecture** (**EPA**). Normally, a cell controller supports both the full seven-layer MAP architecture and the EPA; hence, in addition to performing a local supervisory or control function, the cell controller can also communicate on a factory-wide basis over the backbone network.

In a similar way, an initiative by the Boeing Corporation (also from the United States) has resulted in a set of ISO standards being selected to achieve open systems interconnection in a technical and office environment. The selected set of protocols is known as **technical and office protocols** (**TOPs**). A typical establishment-wide TOP network, together with the protocols selected for use with it, is shown in Figure 13.12.

The transmission medium used with a TOP network is also coaxial cable operating at 10 Mbps. In general, the communication requirements in such environments are limited to voice (which is normally already provided by the existing telephone system) and data, the latter being primarily concerned with communications between a distributed community of advanced workstations (performing computer-aided design, for example). The cable, therefore, is operated in a baseband mode and the MAC protocol is ISO 8802.3 (CSMA/CD). As

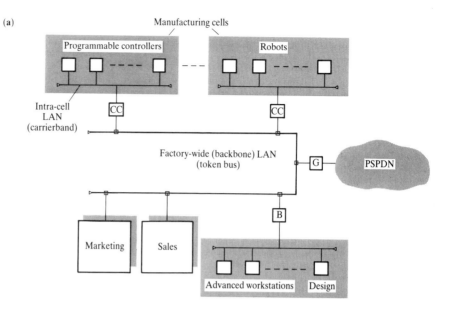

FIGURE 13.11

MAP network:
(a) schematic;
(b) protocol.

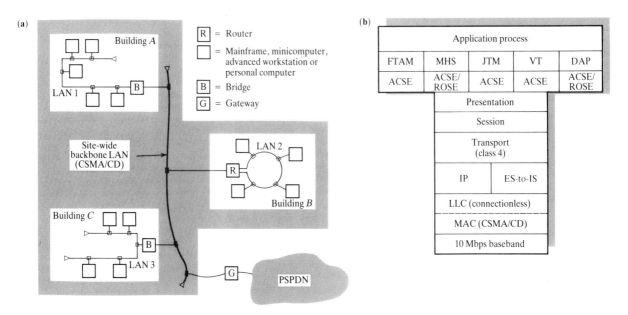

FIGURE 13.12

TOP network:
(a) schematic;
(b) protocols.

with MAP, the network layer and LLC sublayer operate in a connectionless mode while the transport layer operates using the class 4 service. The distributed information services selected include FTAM, MHS, JTM and VT.

These are just some examples of currently established OSIEs. As the administrative authorities in other application domains move towards open systems, however, many others will evolve.

13.4 LAYER INTERACTIONS

To gain an understanding of the operation of complete communication suites, it is necessary to understand how the various protocols – protocol entities – that make up each suite interact to carry out a particular network operation. To achieve this, consider an application domain that consists of a number of client workstations that communicate with a networked file server. Assume that the network is a single LAN. First we will consider the message (PDU) exchanges relating to a TCP/IP suite and then those involving an OSI suite.

13.4.1 TCP/IP

A typical sequence of frame transmissions on the LAN cable between a single (client) user AP and the file server, together with the layer interactions that take place relating to each transmission, is given in parts (a)–(f) of Figure 13.13. For clarity, it is assumed that the client FTP has already obtained the IP address of the server from its local name resolver and that all the messages exchanged are

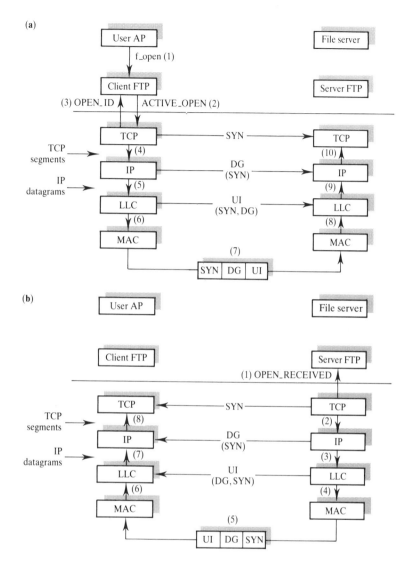

FIGURE 13.13

TCP/IP layer
interactions to
implement a remote file
open.

correctly formed and no transmission errors occur. The sequence shown relates
only to opening a (remote) file ready for reading or writing.

The server would first have issued a PASSIVE_OPEN to its local TCP to
inform it that it is active and waiting to receive new file transfer requests. The
sequence starts with the client user AP – it could be a user at a terminal – initiating
a file operation by issuing an f_open request to its local client FTP. This would
include all the additional information that is necessary such as the name of the
server and the file name. The client FTP would first obtain the IP address of the
server – not shown – and then initiate the setting of a transport connection (TC)
between the client and server FTPs using the IP address of the server and the well-
known port address of the FTP (21).

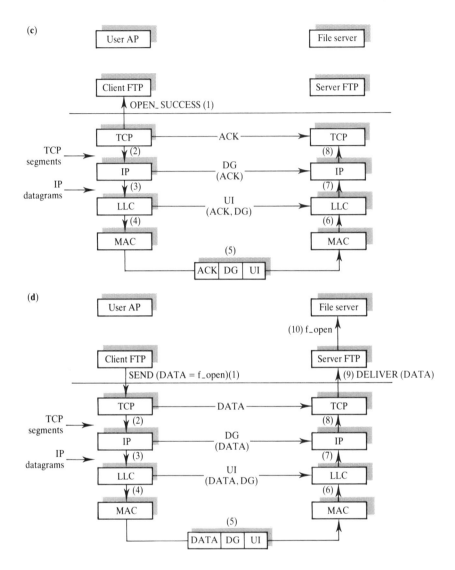

FIGURE 13.13 (cont.)

The sequence starts with the client FTP issuing an ACTIVE_OPEN request. The layer interactions that result from this are shown in part (a) of the figure where the numbers in parentheses indicate the sequence in which the interactions occur. The local TCP first responds by returning an OPEN_ID to the client FTP to enable it to relate subsequent messages to this port address and hence TC. It then creates and sends a SYN segment – as described in Chapter 10 – containing the well-known port address of the server. It passes the SYN segment to the IP for transmission together with the IP address of the server. The IP, in turn, creates an IP datagram with this address in its header and the SYN segment in the user data area. This is sent using the LLC and MAC sublayers associated with the LAN. Each will add its own protocol control information (PCI) at the

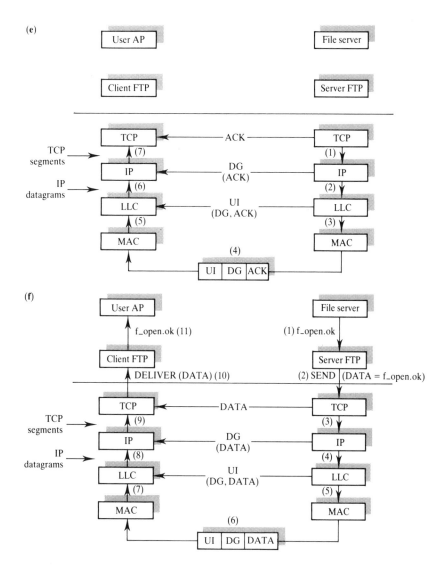

FIGURE 13.13 (cont.)

head of the IP datagram and hence the composition of the actual frame that is transmitted on the cable medium is as shown at the bottom of the figure. On receipt of the frame, the MAC, LLC and IP layers each interpret their own PCI at the head of the frame and pass on the remaining data to the next higher layer. Thus only the SYN segment remains when it arrives at the TCP layer.

On receipt of the SYN, the TCP responds as in part (b). It first informs the local FTP server that a new connection request has been received and then establishes the return path of the TC by returning its own SYN segment. This is transferred in the same way as before. The TCP at the client side then proceeds as shown in part (c) of the figure.

The TCP first issues an OPEN_SUCCESS to the client FTP – indicating that a TC is now in place – and returns an ACK segment to the server TCP to complete the connection establishment procedure. At the same time, the client FTP responds as shown in part (d). It first sends an f_open request message to the server FTP over the established TC as user data. This is transferred to the server side in a DATA segment. On receipt, the TCP passes the f_open request to the server using a DELIVER primitive. The server then issues an f_open to its local file system in the normal way as if it were a local call.

Since the f_open is passed in a DATA segment, the TCP at the server returns an ACK. The sequence is as shown in part (e) of the figure. Part (f) then shows the file system responding positively to the open request to its local server FTP; again this is passed back in a DATA segment. The client FTP then relays the open acknowledgement to the user AP which proceeds to initiate subsequent read and write operations on the opened file.

In practice, the sequences shown have been simplified for descriptive purposes. However, they illustrate how each layer performs its own functionality within the context of the complete protocol suite.

13.4.2 OSI

Before describing the equivalent sequence with an OSI suite, it is necessary to define the **applicaton profile** of the suite being used. We will assume the following:

- the selected OSIE is based on TOP;
- the application entity comprises just FTAM and the ACSE application service elements;
- the network-dependent protocol layers (network, LLC and MAC) all operate using the connectionless mode;
- the transport layer provides a class-4 connection-oriented service.

A typical sequence of frame transmissions on the LAN cable medium between a client (initiator) AP and the server (responder) AP, together with the layer interactions that take place relating to each transmission, is given in Figure 13.14. For clarity, it is assumed that all service primitives and associated PDUs are of the correct structure (and hence accepted) and that no transmission errors occur.

To initiate a remote file operation, the client user AP (through its linked UE) first issues an F.INITIALIZE.request primitive. This results in the layer interactions depicted in Figure 13.14(a), where the numbers in parentheses indicate the sequence in which the interactions occur. Thus, as can be seen, on receipt of the request primitive (1), the initiator FTAM entity generates an INIRQ-PDU, using the parameters associated with the service request, and writes the ASN.1 encoded version of the PDU into the user data buffer (UDB). This buffer is simply an array of octets (bytes); it is the contents of the UDB that are eventually transmitted on the cable medium.

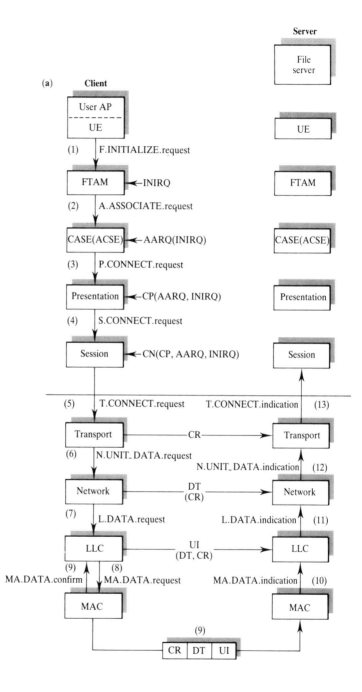

FIGURE 13.14

(a) OSI layer
interactions.

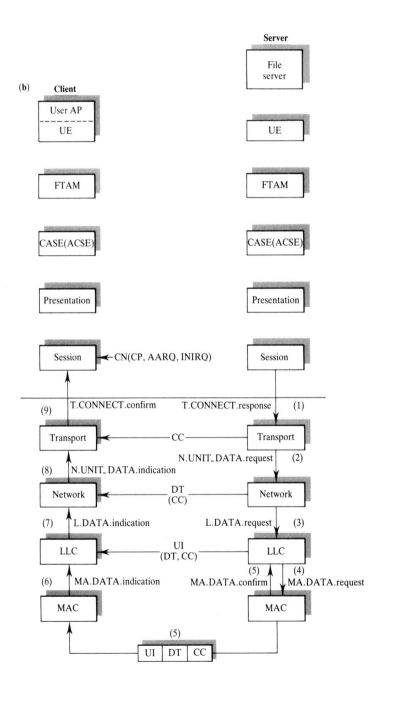

FIGURE 13.14 (cont.)

(b) OSI layer
interactions.

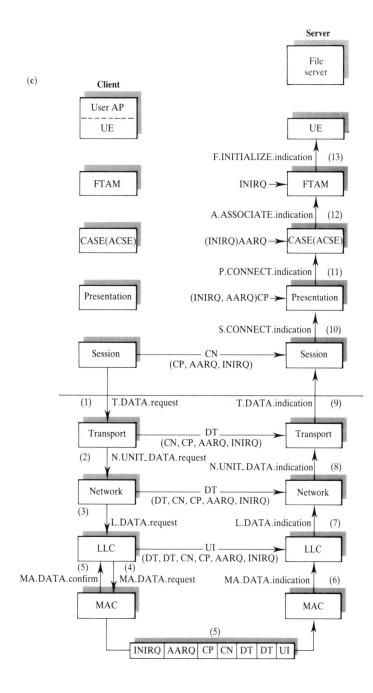

FIGURE 13.14 (cont.)

(c) OSI layer
interactions.

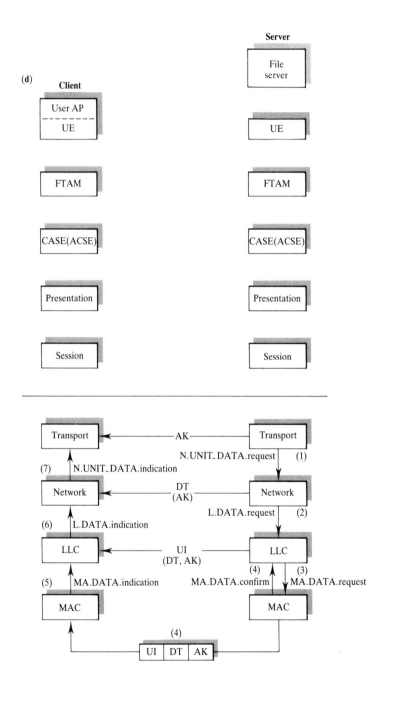

FIGURE 13.14 (cont.)

(d) OSI layer interactions.

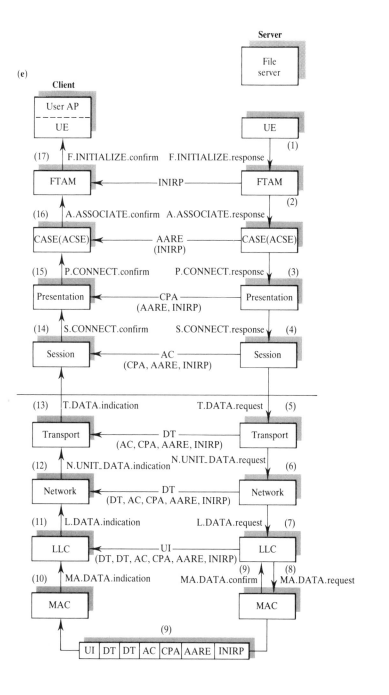

FIGURE 13.14 (cont.)

(e) OSI layer
interactions.

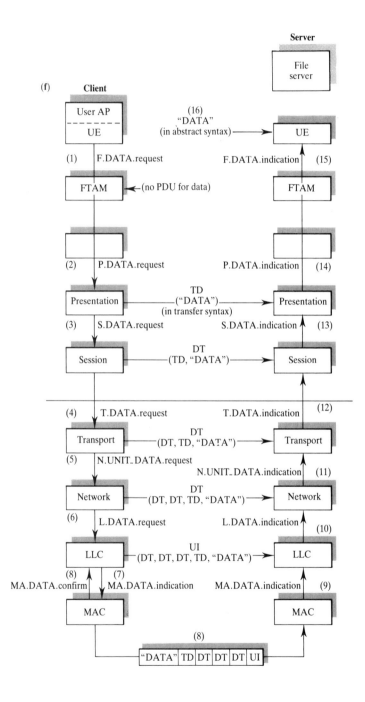

FIGURE 13.14 (cont.)

(f) OSI layer
interactions.

The address pointer of the UDB is then passed to the ACSE in the user data parameter of an A.ASSOCIATE.request primitive (2) together with additional parameters as defined for use with this primitive. The ACSE entity, in turn, generates its own protocol control information (PCI) and adds this at the tail of the existing INIRQ-PDU in the UDB. Collectively, the two parts form an AARQ-PDU. The address pointer of the UDB is then passed in the user data parameter of a P.CONNECT.request primitive, again with additional parameters as defined for use with this primitive (3).

The same procedure is followed by the presentation entity: it first generates its own PCI, adds this to the UDB (to form a CP-PDU) and finally issues an S.CONNECT.request primitive (4). Similarly, the session entity generates its own PCI and adds this to the UDB to form a CN-PDU. The various PDUs relating to the ACSE, presentation and session layers were described in Chapter 11. At this point, however, it is assumed that a transport connection (TC) is not currently established with the remote system. Hence, before the session entity can transfer the composite PDU to the peer session entity, it must establish a TC.

The session entity uses the address information (and the specified communication QOS) associated with the parameters of the S.CONNECT.request primitive and issues a T.CONNECT.request primitive (5). On receipt of this, the transport entity creates a CR-PDU, using the parameters associated with the service request, and writes this into a new UDB. As has been indicated, it is assumed that the network and link layers operate in a connectionless mode. Hence the transport entity then issues an N.UNIT_DATA.request primitive with the address pointer of the UDB containing the CR-PDU as a parameter (6).

On receipt of this, the network entity uses the parameters to generate its own PCI and adds this at the tail of the CR in the UDB to form a DT-PDU. It then issues an L.DATA.request primitive with the address pointer of the UDB as a parameter (7). Similarly, the LLC sublayer adds its own PCI to the UDB to form a UI-PDU, and then issues an MA.DATA.request to the MAC sublayer (8). Finally, the MAC sublayer first adds its own PCI (which includes the destination and source LAN addresses) and adds this to the UDB. At this point, the UDB contains the PCI relating to the four layers in the order transport, network, LLC and MAC. The various PDUs relating to the network, LLC and MAC layers were described in Chapter 6.

The MAC sublayer now initiates the transmission of the complete UDB contents. It first gains access to the shared cable medium (according to the CSMA/CD medium access control method) and, as the preassembled frame contents are being transmitted, it generates the FCS field and adds this at the tail of the frame. It then issues an MA.DATA.confirm primitive to the LLC sublayer to inform the latter that the frame has been transmitted successfully (9). It should be noted that since the MAC PCI is the same for each frame transmitted – that is, the same source and destination addresses – it is not shown in any of the figures for reasons of clarity.

On receipt of the frame, the MAC sublayer in the server station stores the complete frame in a UDB so that the UDB contents are in the same order as they were transmitted. It should be stressed at this point that, although the frame (and hence UDB contents) comprises PCI relating to a number of protocol layers, since the PCI for each layer (and hence PDU) is in a precisely defined (fixed) format, each layer can readily access and interpret just its own PCI. Hence, on receipt of the complete frame, the MAC sublayer first interprets its own PCI and then passes the address pointer of the UDB up to the LLC sublayer using an MA.DATA.indication primitive (10).

In practice, as will be described later, the UDB also contains an address offset which indicates the start address of the next PCI to be processed. On receipt of the UDB pointer, the LLC sublayer uses the address offset to determine the start address of its own PCI. Having established the type of PDU received (UI), it then processes the remaining PCI pertaining to it according to the standard format and issues an L.DATA.indication primitive, with appropriate parameters, to the network layer (11). In turn, the network layer processes its own PCI in the UDB and issues an N.UNIT_DATA.indication primitive to the transport layer (12). Finally, the transport entity processes its own PCI and issues a T.CONNECT.indication primitive to the session layer (13).

Assuming it is prepared to establish a TC, the recipient session entity responds by issuing a T.CONNECT.response primitive. The resulting layer interactions are shown in Figure 13.14(b). On receipt of the T.CON-NECT.response primitive (1), the transport entity first creates a CC-PDU, writes this into a (new) UDB and issues an N.UNIT_DATA.request primitive to the network layer (2). The same procedure is then followed as in the previous example, finishing when the transport entity issues a T.CONNECT.confirm to the originating session layer to confirm that a TC has been established (9).

The originating session entity is now able to transfer the waiting CN-PDU (which includes the CP-, AARQ- and INIRQ-PCI in its user data field) across the TC. It does this by issuing a T.DATA.request primitive with the address pointer of the UDB containing the waiting CN-PDU as a parameter. The resulting interlayer interactions are as shown in Figure 13.14(c). As can be seen, a similar sequence ensues as in the earlier examples except that this time the lower network-dependent layers simply add their own PCIs after the CN-PDU in the UDB.

On receipt of the UDB at the server station (5), each protocol layer proceeds to process its own PCI and passes the remaining contents up to the next higher protocol layer. Finally, on receipt of the UDB by the FTAM entity (12), the latter issues an F.INITIALIZE.indication primitive to the responder UE with parameters constructed from the INIRQ-PDU (l3). In addition, since the PCI relating to the application-oriented layers is passed as user data in a DT-TPDU by the calling transport entity, the called transport entity, after passing the UDB to the session layer (containing the CN-PDU), initiates the sending of an acknowledgement for the DT-TPDU. The sequence shown in Figure 13.14(d) traces the resulting interactions. As can be seen, the interactions are similar to those shown in Figure 13.14(b) except that in this case the TPDU is an AK.

On receipt of the F.INITIALIZE.indication primitive, the server AP (through its linked UE) responds by issuing an F.INITIALIZE.response primitive to its attached FTAM entity. The interactions that follow are outlined in

Figure 13.14(e). As can be seen, since a TC has now been established, the UDB contents eventually transmitted (9) contain PCIs relating to all the protocol layers. Hence, as the received UDB is passed up through the layers in the client system, each layer reads and interprets the PCI relating to it. Finally, the initiating FTAM entity issues a F.INITIALIZE.confirm primitive to the client UE (17).

As described in the previous chapter, the normal sequence with FTAM would then involve the required file being selected and opened before any specific action was carried out on the file. Each of these steps would result in a sequence similar to that just followed. The sequence shown in Figure 13.14(f), however, traces the layer interactions that occur when the client AP is sending data to the server. Clearly, this would have been preceded by an additional F.WRITE.request primitive. The data being transferred may be in an abstract syntax but the data transferred between the two presentation entities – that is, the TD-PDU – must be in an agreed transfer (concrete) syntax. Also, the ACSE entity is shown blanked out since it does not feature in the data transfer phase.

UDB decoding

To enforce understanding of the layer interactions shown in Figure 13.14, the contents of a typical transmitted frame are shown in Figure 13.15(a). This frame is intended to correspond to that shown earlier in Figure 13.14(a). The contents of the frame, and hence the UDB, are shown as a string of octets with each octet represented as two hexadecimal digits. The frame is also assumed to contain a destination and a source MAC address.

To illustrate how the received frame is interpreted by the various protocol layers, the decoded version of the frame is shown in Figure 13.15(b). In the example, it is assumed that 16-bit MAC addresses are used; hence, the MAC protocol entity first reads and interprets the first four octets in the UDB – the destination and source addresses. The UDB pointer is then passed to the LLC sublayer as the user data parameter of an MA.DATA.indication primitive with an address offset of 4.

On receipt of the UDB pointer, the LLC protocol entity reads and interprets its own PCI from the UDB; first the DSAP and SSAP octets and then the control field octet. From the latter, it determines that the frame is a UI (unnumbered information) frame and hence interprets it as the end of its own PCI. Thus, it increments the address offset to 7 and passes the UDB pointer to the network layer as the user data parameter of an L.DATA.indication primitive.

A similar procedure is then followed by the network and transport layers. First, the network protocol entity reads and interprets the appropriate number of octets, according to the network protocol. It then passes the UDB pointer to the transport layer, with the address offset suitably incremented, as the user data parameter of an N.UNIT_DATA.indication primitive. Similarly, the transport protocol entity reads and interprets its own PCI. At this point, however, the UDB would be exhausted, so the transport entity simply issues a T.CONNECT.indication primitive to the session layer using some of the fields from the received UDB to form the necessary parameters.

(a) 00 2E 36 39 FE 0E 03 81 21 01 09 1C 00 21 00 00 0B

49 00 02 02 00 00 00 00 2E FE 00 0B 49 00 03 08 00

00 00 36 39 0E 00 08 E0 00 00 70 00 40 97 B7

(b) MAC PCI

00 2E = Destination address
36 39 = Source address

LLC PCI

FE = DSAP
0E = SSAP
03 = UI (unnumbered information)

Network PCI

81   = Network protocol identifier
21   = Header length
01   = Version number
09   = PDU life time
1C   = 0001 1100 = no segmentation, DT PDU
00 21 = PDU segment length
00 00 = Check sum (ignored)
0B   = Destination address length
49 00 02 02 00 00 00 00 2E FE 00 = Destination address
                                49   = AFI (local)
                                00 02 = IDI
                                02 00 = SI
                                00 00 2E = PA
                                FE   = LSAP ⎫ SEL
                                00   = NSAP ⎭
0B   = Source address length
49 00 03 08 00 00 00 36 39 0E 00 = Source address

Transport PCI

08   = Length indicator
E0   = 1110 = CR TPDU, 0000 = CDT
00 00 = Destination reference
70 00 = Source reference
40   = Class 4 service
70 00 = Check sum

FIGURE 13.15

Example UDB
decoding: (a) UDB
(frame) contents;
(b) decoded fields.

Address parameters

The parameters associated with each service primitive include address information. For example, the calling and called addresses associated with the F.INITIALIZE.request primitive are fully qualified addresses obtained from, say, the local directory server. They include, therefore, the P/SSAP, TSAP and NSAP, with the latter including the NSAP and LSAP extensions (or suffixes) relating to the interlayer interfaces, and also the physical network address. As the service primitives resulting from the F.INITIALIZE.request pass down through the protocol layers, each protocol entity reads and embeds its own SAP into the PCI associated with that layer. Hence, as the primitives pass down through the layers, the size of the address parameters diminishes until, at the MAC sublayer, only the physical network address remains. Similarly, as the service primitives pass up through the protocol layers at the server, the address parameters are reconstructed as each protocol entity reads its SAP from the PCI and adds this to the existing addresses. This is shown in Figure 13.16(a).

Session and transport connection identifiers are assigned to the application association and transport connections as they are established. Subsequent service primitives then include only the relevant connection identifier as a parameter. When implementing each protocol entity, therefore, it is necessary to retain a record of the calling and called addresses in addition to the protocol state information relating to each connection. This is shown in Figure 13.16(b).

Once each TPDU associated with a connection is passed to the network layer, the network entity can access the corresponding stored NSAPs, which include the physical network address and the NSAP and LSAP extensions. In this way, the complete address information will have been inserted when the complete PDU is transmitted by the MAC layer. In the chosen example, the network-oriented layers are assumed to operate in the connectionless mode. However, if a connection-oriented mode is used, it would be necessary to utilize a separate network connection identifier.

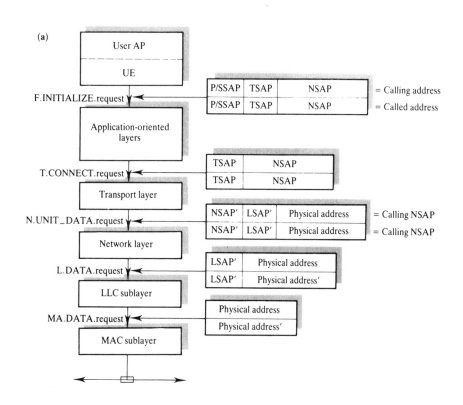

FIGURE 13.16

Address parameters:
(a) connection request.

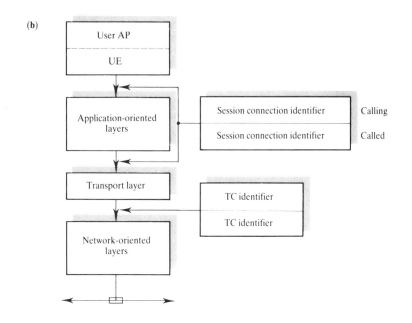

FIGURE 13.16 (cont.)

(b) Data transfer.

13.5 IMPLEMENTATION ISSUES

Associated with any computer operating system there is a set of primitives (calls), each with a defined set of parameters, that allow a user program/process to access the various peripherals that are attached to the computer in a high-level, user-friendly way. Thus there are primitives to interact with a printer, a terminal and so on. Primitives are also provided to interact with the local file system to create/delete/modify/read and write files. The issue here, therefore, is what primitives should be provided to a user application program/process to interact with a networked resource such as file server.

Clearly, the user must be isolated from the detailed implementation of the protocol suite and instead should be provided with a similar set of primitives to those used to access and use a similar facility. To achieve this, the overall communications software is divided into two parts: one concerned with the implementation of the protocol suite and the other with the implementation of the user interface.

In the case of a TCP/IP suite, the user interface at the client side is normally an integral part of the client application protocol such as the client FTP. Hence this is normally implemented as a separate application process that can communicate with either a user at a terminal or with a user application process through primitives supported by the local operating system. The remainder of the suite – TCP, IP etc – is then implemented as a separate entity that is accessed by the client protocol/process in a standard way, again through primitives provided by the operating system.

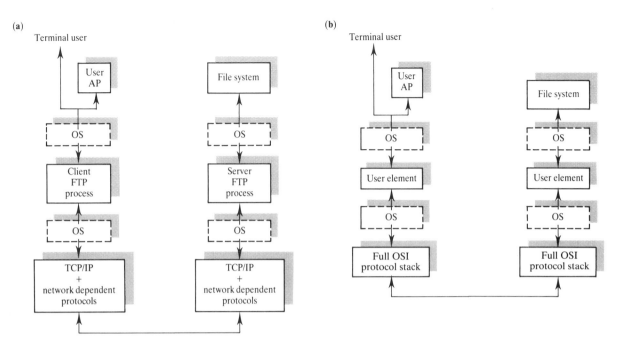

FIGURE 13.17

Protocol architectures:
(a) TCP/IP suite;
(b) OSI suite.

A similar structure is used at the server side; the server application protocol/process communicates with the local file system using the standard user primitives provided by the operating system. It is thus transparent to the file system whether the service requests are coming from a local application process or from a remote process. The general scheme is shown in Figure 13.17(a). For example purposes, the figure assumes the application protocol is FTP.

In the case of an OSI suite, the application protocol (entity) and the user interface are normally separated into two quite separate entities. Hence the application protocol is normally linked with the remainder of the protocol stack. The general scheme is as shown in part (b) of Figure 13.17.

Normally, the interface with the protocol software is through a set of high-level primitives provided by the operating system. In the case of TCP/IP, these are similar to those shown earlier in Figure 10.5 of Chapter 10, while with an OSI suite they are the same as those associated with the particular application entity being accessed.

The protocol software itself can be implemented in one of two ways. In the case of TCP/IP, it is normally implemented as part of the basic input-output system (BIOS) of the local operating system and hence forms an integral part of the operating system. However, with an OSI suite the processing overheads associated with the full protocol stack are high, as can be deduced form the earlier figures. To minimize the processing load on the host main processor, the protocol software is therefore often implemented on a separate plug-in board which includes the network interface chipset, some memory and a local processor. This latter scheme is shown in Figure 13.18(a).

(a)

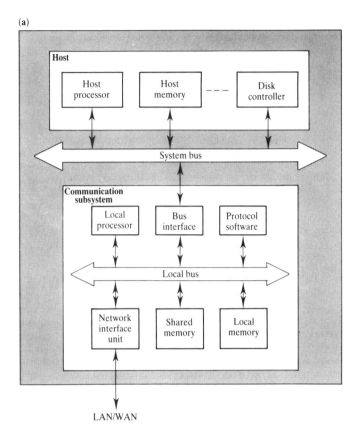

FIGURE 13.18

Overall architecture:
(a) hardware.

Typically, the complete communication subsystem is implemented on a separate printed circuit board that plugs into the internal bus – interconnection mechanism – of the host system. This board contains, in addition to the local (communication) processor, memory for the protocol software, additional memory for storing protocol state information relating to each layer (local) and message buffers being passed between layers (shared), and also the circuitry that is required to perform the physical interface to the communication network. As has been mentioned, the latter may be a public WAN or a LAN, the only differences being the type of interface circuitry required and, as described in Section 2 of the book, slightly different network protocol software.

Normally, the shared memory is **multi-ported**; that is, it may be accessed directly by the network interface unit, the local processor and, via the system bus in the system, the host processor. In this way, all memory buffers (containing interlayer messages and user data) are directly accessible to each. Hence, when information is passed between the buffers (and between layers), only the address pointer to the buffer is utilized, thereby avoiding the added overheads associated with physically transferring blocks of data from one layer or device (and hence part of memory) to another.

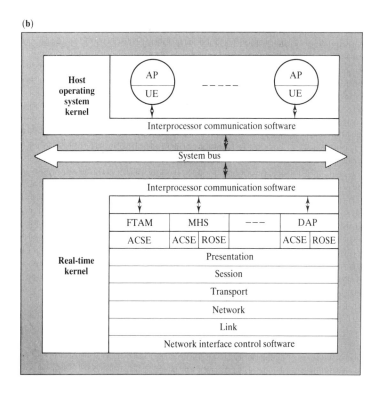

FIGURE 13.18 (cont.)

(b) Software.

An associated software structure for use with this architecture is shown in Figure 13.18(b). It has been stressed in earlier chapters that when describing the operation of a communication subsystem structured according to the ISO Reference Model, it is essential to treat each protocol layer as an autonomous entity which provides a defined set of user services to the layer above it and, in turn, uses the services provided by the layer below it to transport the PDUs generated by the layer to a similar peer layer in a remote system. In the same way, when implementing the various protocol layers in software, it is essential to retain the same approach otherwise the benefits gained by the adoption of a layered architecture will be lost.

The communication subsystem, therefore, is implemented as a suite of task (process) modules (one per protocol entity) with additional tasks for management (see later) and timer functions. Tasks communicate with each other through a set of FIFO queues or mailboxes as shown in Figure 13.19. Intertask communication is managed by the local real-time kernel which is also responsible for such functions as task scheduling and interrupt handling. The latter are generated by the timer task, for example, and the network interface unit. Communication between the subsystem and the host is through the interprocessor communication software, a copy of which is in both systems. Typically, the latter is interrupt driven to ensure a synchronized transfer of information between the two systems. Thus, whenever the host processor wishes to transfer information to the

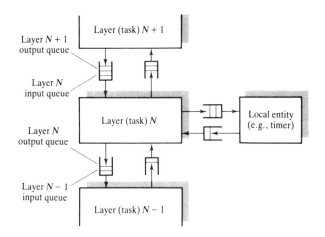

FIGURE 13.19

Interlayer
communication
schematic.

communication processor, it first writes the information into a free memory buffer associated with the application entity and then generates an interrupt to the communication processor. The interrupt service routine in the latter first reads the address pointer of the buffer, determines the SASE involved and then places the pointer at the tail of the appropriate input queue to await processing. A similar procedure is followed for passing information in the reverse direction.

13.5.1 Interlayer communication

A user AP gains access to the distributed information services supported by the communications subsystem through the defined set of primitives associated with its local user element (UE). This can be either a separate process or a set of library procedures (or functions) that is linked to the user AP prior to running.

As described in Section 10.7.6, interlayer primitives and their associated parameters are passed between layers using a typed data structure known as an **event control block (ECB)**. Since the number and types of the parameters associated with the primitives for each layer are usually different, there is a separate ECB data structure for each layer, which is used for passing all service primitives from a higher layer to that layer; that is, for all request, indication, response and confirm primitives received and issued by the layer from and to the higher layer. As as example, a typical ECB relating to the transport layer was shown in Figure 10.34.

Thus, to communicate with an SASE, the UE first obtains a free ECB relating to it (in practice, the address pointer to a buffer in shared memory), writes the necessary parameters associated with the primitive into the ECB and initiates the transfer of the address pointer of the ECB to the SASE using the inter-processor communication software. Any user data associated with the primitive is written into a separate buffer, the user data buffer (UDB). The address pointer of the UDB associated with the primitive is then written into the ECB together with an indication of the amount of data it contains.

On receipt of the service primitive (ECB), the selected SASE entity uses the parameters associated with the primitive, together with any protocol state information associated with the connection (association), to create the PCI for the layer. This is added to any user data already in the UDB to form, collectively, an SASE-APDU. The SASE then obtains a free ECB associated with the presentation entity (task), writes the appropriate primitive type and parameter information into it (including the address pointer of the UDB containing the APDU and the updated length of its contents) and issues a send message request to the local real-time kernel. The latter, in turn, transfers the ECB address pointer to the input queue of the presentation task and, if it is idle (waiting for an incoming event), schedules the task to be run.

Each layer task performs a similar function, first adding its own PCI to the UDB and then passing an appropriate primitive and associated parameters to the next lower layer using a free ECB of that layer. This is shown in Figure 13.20(a). It should be remembered that the PCI associated with each layer is in a concrete syntax comprising a string of octets. Thus, each UDB is simply an array of octets. It is the contents of the UDB that are eventually transmitted under the control of the network interface hardware and software.

Clearly, the amount of user data contained within a UDB, after it has passed through all the protocol layers, will vary from, say, a few hundred octets if only PCI is involved to, possibly, several thousand octets if, say, the contents of a

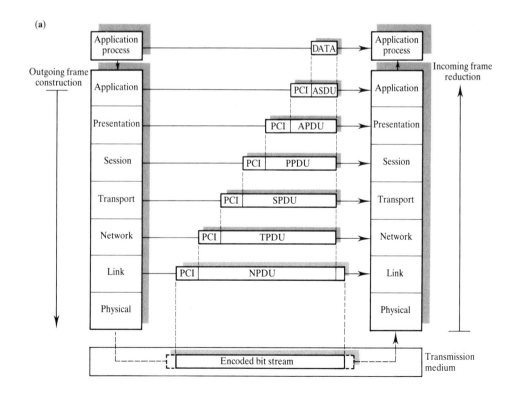

FIGURE 13.20

Layer interactions:
(a) schematic.

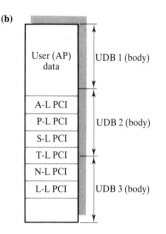

(b)

User (AP) data — UDB 1 (body)

A-L PCI
P-L PCI — UDB 2 (body)
S-L PCI
T-L PCI
N-L PCI
L-L PCI — UDB 3 (body)

FIGURE 13.20 (cont.)

(b) UDB structure and contents.

file are being transferred. To allow for this, each UDB is of a fixed length and a linked-list strategy is used to handle composite dialogue units (PDUs) exceeding this length. Thus, if a UDB becomes full, a new UDB pointer is obtained from the free list, and this is then linked to the UDB that is now full. This is shown in a schematic form in Figure 13.20(b).

13.5.2 User element implementation

It may be concluded from the previous section that the primitives received by the UE are from two sources: those received from the user AP and those received from the interface with an SASE via the interprocessor communication software. Clearly, the primitives in each case may be of different types. For example, the primitives from the user AP may relate either to a confirmed service (that is, a request primitive that will subsequently generate a confirm primitive) or to an unconfirmed service (that is, a request primitive with no confirm). Similarly, the primitives from the SASE interface may also be of different types. For example, they may be either a confirm primitive returned in response to an earlier request primitive, an indication primitive that requires no response or an indication primitive that requires a response.

Hence, for the UE to respond to each incoming primitive in the correct way, it is necessary for the UE to retain a record of the last received primitive relating to this SASE session. In practice, this is best accomplished by using an event–state table similar to that defined for each protocol machine. Then, as with the implementation strategy for each protocol machine, the UE retains a state variable for each active session, which indicates the current status of the interface; that is, the previous primitive received. On receipt of an incoming primitive (event), this is used to determine the processing to be carried out, from the event–state table.

As an example, assume that a user AP has a UE linked to it and is accessing a remote file server AP through an OSIE-supporting FTAM and that the set of user primitives provided is:

- f_open (input_file, status),
- f_read (input_file, message_buffer, status),
- f_write (input_file, message_buffer, status),
- f_close (input_file, status).

The parameter **input_file** is the full path name (title) of the file to be manipulated; thus it includes the unique OSIE-wide name of the server system together with the name of the FTAM entity within that system and the name of the file to be operated on. The parameter **status** is an indication of the success or failure of the network request and, in the event of a failure, the reason for the failure. The **message_buffer** parameter is a pointer that indicates where the data relating to the transfer request (read or write) is to be put or found.

As has been outlined, each of these primitives has an associated library procedure, and the complete set of procedures – the FTAM UE – is linked to the user AP. A suitable event–state table for the UE is thus as shown in Figure 13.21.

It can be readily deduced from the short list of user primitives provided that each primitive results in multiple FTAM primitives. For example, the library procedure f_open generates a sequence of FTAM primitives associated with the services: F.INITIALIZE, F.SELECT and F.OPEN. Similarly, the f_read procedure generates a sequence related to the services: F.READ, F.DATA and F.TRANSER_END. Thus, the f_open procedure, after first obtaining the fully qualified address of the remote (called) FTAM entity from the directory service, creates an F.INITIALIZE.request primitive and initiates its transfer, together with its associated parameters, to the local FTAM entity in an FTAM ECB. Typically, this is accomplished using an appropriate interprocess communication primitive through the ICP software. The user AP, through the linked f_open procedure, is then suspended while waiting for an F.INITIALIZE.confirm primitive (ECB). The interface thus enters the WTINICF state.

The F.INITIALIZE.confirm primitive, together with its associated parameters, is now transferred by the local FTAM entity (in an FTAM ECB), again using an interprocess communication primitive and the ICP software. The user AP is then rescheduled at the point of suspension in the f_open procedure. The latter, as can be deduced from the event–state table, then issues an F.SELECT.request primitive, again with parameters deduced from the initial call, and enters the WTSELCF state. Similarly, on receipt of the F.SELECT.confirm primitive, it issues an F.OPEN.request. Finally, on receipt of the F.OPEN.confirm primitive, the interface enters the OPEN state and returns to the initiating user AP at the statement immediately following the f_open procedure call, the status parameter indicating the success or failure of the call.

Assuming that the f_open procedure was successful, this is typically followed by an f_read or f_write call, which again results in a sequence of FTAM primitives. Finally, when all transfers are complete, the user AP initiates the termination of the association – and hence FTAM transaction – using the f_close procedure.

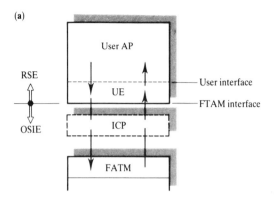

(a)

(b)

State \\ Primitive	CLOSED	WTINICF	WTSELCF	WTOPNCF	OPEN	---
f_open	1					
f_read					5	
f_write						
f_close						
F_INICF		2				
F_SELCF			3			
F_OPNCF				4		
⋮						

From user interface

From FTAM interface

1: F_INIRQ,
    WTINICF

2: F_SELRQ,
    WTSELCF

3: F_OPNRQ,
    WTOPNCF

4: OPEN (return)

FIGURE 13.21

FTAM UE structure:
(a) interfaces;
(b) event–state table.

F_INIRQ/CF = F_INITIALIZE.request/confirm
F_SELRQ/CF = F_SELECT.request/confirm
F_OPNRQ/CF = F_OPEN.request/confirm
WTINICF   = Wait for F_INITIALIZE.confirm
WTSELCF   = Wait for F_SELECT.confirm
WTOPNCF   = Wait for F_OPEN.confirm

It may be deduced from the foregoing that, if a piece of software exists with these same user primitives, then to change to an open system it is only necessary to change or rewrite the existing library procedures required to interface with the FTAM. It should be remembered, however, that, in addition to generating the appropriate FTAM primitives, it may be necessary to convert the file contents into or from the agreed transfer syntax. Also, the UE at the server converts the incoming FTAM primitives into those used by the particular server (file system) being used, if necessary.

13.5.3 Layer management

In addition to the tasks (protocol entities) associated with each layer, a complete communication subsystem has two other tasks: a timer task, which performs the necessary timeout functions associated with the various protocol entities (state machines), and a system management task which, as its name implies, is responsible for both layer and system management functions. These include such functions as the gathering of protocol error statistics and the setting of operational parameters associated with each protocol layer (entity). A complete communication subsystem is thus as shown in Figure 13.22.

Timer task

As indicated in Chapter 10, to ensure that incoming events associated with each protocol machine are atomic, the interface between the timer task and each of the protocol entities (tasks) using its services is through a separate intertask mailbox or queue. Since there is a single timer task for the complete subsystem, there is normally only a single input queue associated with it. Also, as with other intertask communication, there is a single type of ECB associated with the timer task, which is then used for all communications with it.

A suitable set of user service primitives associated with the timer task are:

- TIMER.start (layer ID, timer ID, time),
- TIMER.cancel (layer ID, timer ID),
- TIMER.expired (timer ID).

Since there is a single input queue associated with the timer task, the two input primitives (start and cancel) each have a layer ID parameter associated with them to identify the protocol layer issuing the primitive. Also, since with each layer a number of timers may be running (active) concurrently, the timer ID parameter is used to identify with which timer the primitive is associated. Typically, the connection identifier is used for this purpose. The time parameter then indicates the time interval, in terms of system clock ticks, that must elapse before the timer task informs the appropriate protocol entity that the named timer has expired.

To initiate a timeout operation (for example, to limit the time a protocol entity will wait for a suitable response to an outgoing event), the protocol entity first obtains a free (timer) ECB and writes the layer and timer identities together with the required time interval as parameters within it. It then initiates the transfer of the ECB pointer to the timer task input queue (mailbox) by issuing a suitable intertask communication primitive – send message, for example – to the local real-time kernel. On receipt of the request, the timer task creates an entry in a table

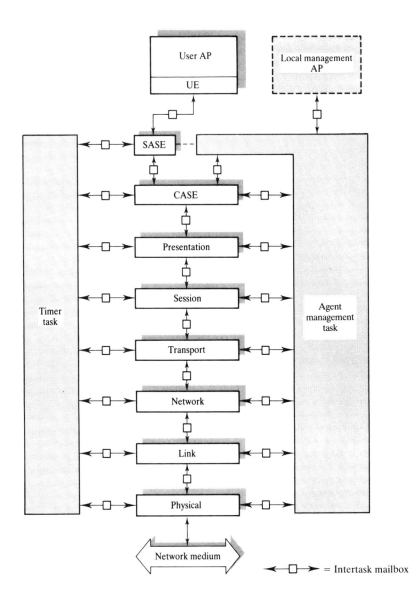

FIGURE 13.22

Complete
communication
susbystem schematic.

indicating the identity of the timer and the time duration associated with it. The
latter is simply a counter variable.

Normally, the timer task is interrupt driven from a system clock. This
means that a signal (the interrupt) is generated at preprogrammed time intervals,
equal to the minimum clock tick time of, say, one second, and the timer task is
then scheduled to run. First, it determines whether there are any ECBs in its input
queue awaiting processing and, if so, processes them. The outstanding time
interval associated with any currently active timers are each decremented by one
(tick). Then, if any of the timers become zero, indicating that the timeout interval

for the timer has expired, a TIMER.expired primitive is generated (in an ECB) and the ECB pointer is transferred to the appropriate layer (timer) input queue using an intertask communication primitive. Thus, when the layer task is next scheduled to run, it examines not only its input queues with the layers (protocol entities) above and below it but also its input queue from the timer task. Any entries in each queue are then processed in an atomic way, including any actions resulting from a timeout occurring if the entry is from the input queue with the timer task.

If, after initiating a timer for a particular outgoing event, the protocol entity receives a suitable response (incoming event), it initiates the cancellation of the timer by passing a suitable TIMER.cancel primitive (in an ECB) to the timer task input queue, again using an intertask primitive supported by the real-time kernel. Then, when the timer task is next scheduled to run, it in turn removes the named timer from the timer table.

Agent management task

Each layer, in addition to maintaining state information (variables) relating to the current operational state of the protocol machine, maintains a set of variables relating to various operational statistics for layer management purposes. Some examples of the statistical information gathered by each layer task are as follows:

- ACSE: The number of negative A.ASSOCIATE.response primitives received; the number of ABORT APDUs received and sent.

- Presentation: The number of unsuccessful CPR (connect presentation response) PPDUs received and sent, with the reason codes; the number of unrecognized PPDUs received.

- Session: The number of RF (refuse) SPDUs received and sent; the number of AB (abort) SPDUs received and sent.

- Transport: The number of protocol errors that have occurred; the number of times a timeout expires on a transmitted TPDU; the number of TPDUs that have a bad checksum.

- Network: The number of NPDUs received and sent; the number of NPDUs discarded because of an unknown NSAP.

- LLC: The number of test LPDUs received and sent; the number of protocol errors.

- MAC: The number of collisions and retransmission attempts (CSMA/CD); the number of token pass failures (token bus).

Normally, most of the information is maintained by simple counters whose current contents may be requested by the **agent management task (AMT)** in response to a request from the network manager AP. However, if a particular event occurs in a layer, indicating a possible fault (for example, a predefined threshold limit for a variable being reached), the layer (task) may inform the AMT directly.

The latter must also have a facility for informing a layer of specific operational parameters (characteristics) to be used, such as:

- window limit (T-L),
- timeout interval (all layers),
- routing table contents (N-L),
- maximum retransmission limit (CSMA/CD),
- target token rotation time (token bus).

As with the timer task, a set of service primitives must be defined (together with an associated ECB type and intertask queue structure) to enable these functions to be carried out in an atomic way. A typical set of primitives for the AMT to interact with the various layers is:

- GET_VALUE.request/confirm (parameter value): This is used by the AMT to obtain a statistic from a specific layer.
- SET_VALUE.request/confirm (parameter ID, parameter value): This is used by the AMT to set an operational parameter for a specific layer.
- ACTION.request/confirm (action ID, action value): This is used by the AMT to, say, add one or more entries to a routing table.
- EVENT.indication (layer ID, event identifier, event value): This is used by a layer entity to inform the AMT of, say, a threshold limit being reached.

13.6 RELATED STANDARDS

The goal of an open system protocol suite is to enable application processes running in computer systems from different manufacturers to cooperate to perform a particular distributed processing function. The presentation services associated with the protocol suite are provided to ensure that the syntax of the messages exchanged have the same meanings in all systems. As may be recalled, however, the presentation services are not concerned with the structure or meaning of the information being exchanged. It simply treats the data as a stream of suitably defined data types – for example, character strings – and then uses a suitable transfer syntax and, if necessary, syntax conversions, to ensure these are compatible with the syntax used in each cooperating system. It is the application processes that interpret the structure and meaning of the transferred messages.

Clearly, for application processes to be able to cooperate to achieve a particular distributed processing task, it is necessary for them to agree on the structure and meaning of the messages associated with the application as well as on the order in which they are exchanged. One approach to the latter is to define a virtual device for the application, such as a virtual file server. All messages exchanged must then be ordered according to the order defined for the virtual device. In addition, however, all parties must have knowledge of the type and structure of the messages being exchanged.

In addition to the protocols that are needed within the message handling system to transfer messages to their intended destination – based on the addresses associated with the message envelope – there is a protocol above the communications stack that relates to the type and structure of the messages being exchanged; that is, relating to the body part. The interpersonal message protocol was identified in the last chapter, but in practice there is a range of standards under development that relate to other types of information. For example, the **electronic data interchange (EDI)** standard is being defined for the exchange of trade-related documents such as purchase orders, invoices and dispatch notes. Similarly, standards are being defined for the design, materials and other documentation relating to products associated with the manufacturing industry as are standards relating to the structure and contents of documents associated with office automation. Although all of these standards are of direct relevance to public (and private) X.400 messaging systems, they are also applicable when documents are being exchanged using, say, file transfer. A complete definition of these standards is outside the scope of the book, but two of them are briefly introduced.

13.6.1 EDI

The goal of the electronic data interchange (EDI) standard is to enable possibly non-compatible computers to exchange trade-related documents in a standard message format. As already indicated, these include purchase orders, shipping documents and quotations. In general, these standards are being pushed by the major corporations that utilize a diverse range of suppliers of equipment and products. Clearly, only when all the relevant documentation is in a standard form can the whole trading cycle be automated. This is, of course, on top of an open system stack for communication purposes.

The message standard associated with EDI is a defined common format with a defined structure. The content, quantity and position of all elements that comprise a document can all be defined using the standard. The terminology associated with the standard is given in Figure 13.23(a). It is shown in relation to the structure of a typical form used in such application environments.

As can be seen, each page relating to a document is known as a **transaction set**. This is then made up of a number of **data segments** each of which corresponds to a line or box on the form. A data segment is then made up of one or more **data elements**. The overall format used is shown in part (b) of the figure. As can be seen, the start and end of each component part is signalled by defined character strings and the individual data segments/elements have separators associated with them. The encoding rules are thus relatively simple and the character set is very limited.

For each application a particular set of transactions will be defined and used by each communicating party. A number of message standards have been defined for use in various industries such as the motor trade, rail and grocery.

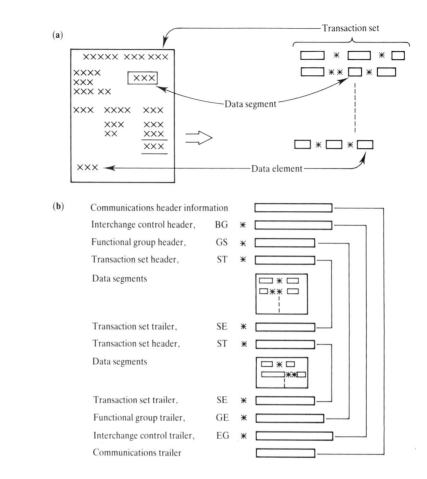

FIGURE 13.23

EDI terminology:
(a) form encoding;
(b) overall document
structure.

13.6.2 ODA

Office documents are considered to be items such as memoranda, letters, forms and reports, which may include not only textual information but also other types of media such as images for company logos or institution crests. The term ODA is an acronym of **open document architecture.**

A document contains information that relates to its content and its structure. The **content** of a document consists of any information that can be presented in a two-dimensional form, such as printed on paper or displayed on a screen. The **structure** is provided to:

- delimit portions within a document, such as areas of a page for images or different types of content elements – its layout structure;
- delimit portions of a document that have a logical meaning, such as chapters and paragraphs – its **logical structure**;
- use different types of coding for the different content types;
- allow documents to be processed.

The rules for representing structured documents are collectively called the **document architecture**.

For the purpose of interchange, a document is represented as a collection of constituent parts, each of which has a set of attributes. Each attribute has a name and a value and expresses a characteristic of a structural element. The types of constituent parts defined include:

- document profile,
- logical structure,
- layout structure,
- content description,
- presentation style,
- layout style.

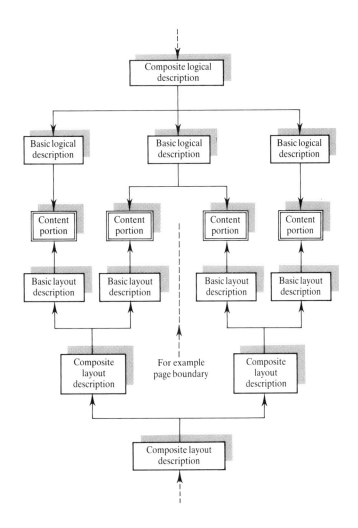

FIGURE 13.24

Example relationship between logical and layout descriptions.

The **document profile** consists of a set of attributes that specify characteristics of the document as a whole. The **content** description consists of the definition of a set of content elements. The **presentation** and **layout styles** are both sets of attributes which relate to the format and appearance of the document content on the presentation media. The separation of styles from the document structures allows the layout and presentation of a document to be modified without affecting its logical structure. This is important in the publishing world, for example. Typically, the author is only concerned with the content and the editor can then modify the layout to fit it with other information. The relationship between the logical and layout descriptions is shown in Figure 13.24.

The layout description includes pages, frames (a rectangular area), blocks, and positioning and dimensioning data for frames and blocks relative to a page. The logical descriptions are independent of the layout (such as page) descriptions. At the lowest level, for example, is a text unit which may be defined as a paragraph or a figure; these may then be grouped into a logical element (object). The logical structure thus defines the correct sequence of elements whereas the layout structure defines how they will be positioned on, say, a page or pages.

Unlike EDI, ODA uses ASN.1 for defining the various structures. It is now supported by all the major vendors of office automation software and equipment and in time will remove the tedious conversion and reformatting operations that are currently necessary with most word processing software.

EXERCISES

13.1   Give an example of a symbolic name that might be used to refer to a networked server.

List the components of the equivalent address associated with the server in:

(a)   the TCP/IP environment,
(b)   the OSI environment.

13.2   Give an example of the symbolic name of a networked server assuming

(a)   a flat naming structure,
(b)   a hierarchical structure.

Identify the implications of using each structure in relation to the management of names and the subsequent partitioning of the resulting directory.

13.3   Give an example of a name hierarchy in relation to the TCP/IP domain system.

Identify selected domain names (labels) in the hierarchy and explain the philosophy behind their assignment in relation to the overall management of the directory.

13.4   Identify the protocols associated with the domain name system.

Produce a sketch of a typical arrangement of these protocols in relation to a client system, a server, and a domain name server. Outline the sequence of messages that are exchanged between these protocols in order to obtain the TCP/IP address of the server.

13.5   With the aid of an outline domain name server hierarchy, give examples, with explanations, of how a name is resolved when the required server is:

(a)   local to the same name server,

(b)   at a higher layer in the hierarchy.

Explain the meaning of the term name cache and how such a mechanism can be used to minimize the use of referrals.

13.6   Explain, with the aid of examples, the meanings of the following terms in relation to the X.500 directory system:

(a)   directory information tree,

(b)   relative distinguished name,

(c)   distinguished name,

(d)   alias name.

13.7   Explain the functions of the directory user agent (DUA) and directory service agent (DSA) in relation to the X.500 directory system.

Explain the messages that are exchanged in order for a DUA to request the PSAP address of a named server. Clearly identify the use of the attribute type and attribute values.

13.8   With the aid of a sketch of an example name server hierarchy, explain the meaning of the terms:

(a)   referral,

(b)   chaining,

(c)   multicasting.

13.9   Identify the communication protocols that are associated with the DUA and DSA application processes.

With the aid of a sketch, trace the sequence of messages that are exchanged between a DUA and DSA through these protocols to determine the address of a named object – a server, for example.

13.10 Explain the meaning of the acronyms MAP and TOP and identify the application domain and protocols associated with each.

13.11 Use a template of the various protocols that make up the TCP/IP suite to trace the sequence of messages that are exchanged in order to carry out a networked request. Use for example purposes the f-open request associated with a networked file server.

13.12 Repeat question 13.11 using an example OSI suite.

13.13 Discriminate between the terms address selector and connection identifier in relation to an OSI suite.

13.14 Describe a typical implementation structure for a TCP/IP and an OSI suite in terms of the processes that are involved and how they interact using the local operating system of the machine in which the various processes are running.

13.15 Explain the role of the user element in relation to an application process that is using an OSI stack for communication purposes. With the aid of an example, clearly describe how it harmonizes the services used by the application process and those provided at the interface with the protocol stack.

CHAPTER SUMMARY

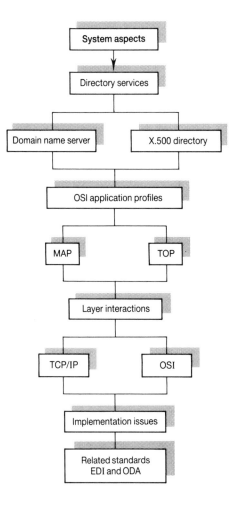

APPENDIX A

Forward error control

A1.1 INTRODUCTION

With an automatic repeat request (ARQ) error control scheme, additional check digits are appended to each transmitted message (frame) to enable the receiver to detect when an error is present in a received message, assuming certain types of error. If an error is detected, additional control procedures are then used to request that another copy of the message be sent. With forward error control (FEC), however, sufficient additional check digits are added to each transmitted message to enable the receiver not only to detect the presence of one or more errors in a received message but also to locate the position of the error(s). Furthermore, since the message is in a binary form, correction is achieved simply by inverting the bit(s) that have been identified as erroneous.

In practice, the number of additional check digits required to achieve error correction is much larger than that needed for just error detection. In most applications involving terrestrial (land-based) links, therefore, ARQ methods similar to those described in Chapter 4 are more efficient than FEC methods, and hence are the most frequently used. Such methods rely, of course, on a return path for acknowledgement purposes. However, in certain applications, it may be that a return path is simply not available or the round-trip delay associated with it is very long compared with the data transmission rate of the link. For example, frequently only a unidirectional link is utilized when transmitting information back from a space probe. Similarly, with many satellite links the propagation delay may be such that several hundred messages may be transmitted by the sending station before a message, and hence an acknowledgement, is received in the reverse direction. In such applications, therefore, FEC methods are often utilized, normally in conjunction with ARQ methods, to reduce the number of retransmissions. The aim of this appendix is to give the reader an introduction to the techniques most widely used with FEC methods.

A1.2 HAMMING SINGLE-BIT CODE

In practice, this FEC method is of limited use for data transmission purposes. Nevertheless, it will be briefly described to give an introduction to the subject and to some of the terms associated with coding theory. Clearly, a comprehensive description of the subject of coding theory is beyond the scope of this book and hence the aim here is simply to give the reader a brief introduction to the subject. For those who have an interest in coding theory and would like to gain a more extensive coverage, the bibliography at the end of the book should be consulted.

The term used in coding theory to describe the combined message unit, comprising the useful data bits and the additional check bits, is **codeword**. The minimum number of bit positions in which two valid codewords differ is known as the **Hamming distance** of the code. As an example, consider a coding scheme that has seven data bits and a single parity bit per codeword. Assuming even parity is being used, consecutive codewords in this scheme will be:

```
0000000   0
0000001   1
0000010   1
0000011   0
```

It can be deduced from this list that such a scheme has a Hamming distance of 2, as each valid codeword differs in at least two bit positions. This means that it will not detect two-bit errors since the resulting (corrupted) bit pattern will be a different but valid codeword. It will, however, detect all single-bit errors since, if a single bit in a codeword is corrupted, an invalid codeword will result.

In general, the error-detecting and error-correcting properties of a coding scheme are both related to its Hamming distance. It can be shown that to detect n errors, a coding scheme with a Hamming distance of $n + 1$ must be used, while to correct for n errors a code with a Hamming distance of $2n + 1$ must be used.

The simplest error-correcting coding scheme is the Hamming single-bit code. Such a code not only detects when a single-bit error is present in a received codeword but also the position of the error. The corrected codeword is then derived by inverting the identified erroneous bit. This type of code is known as a **block code**, since the original message to be transmitted is treated as a single block (frame) during the encoding and subsequent decoding processes. In general, with a block code, each block of k source digits is encoded to produce an n-digit block (n greater than k) of output digits. The encoder is then said to produce an (n, k) code. The ratio k/n is known as the **code rate** or **code efficiency** while the difference $1 - k/n$ is known as the **redundancy**.

To illustrate this, consider a Hamming code to detect and correct for single-bit errors assuming each codeword contains a seven-bit data field – an ASCII character, for example. Such a coding scheme requires four check bits since, with this scheme, the check bits occupy all bit positions that are powers of 2. Such a code is thus known as an $(11, 7)$ block code with a rate of 7/11 and a redundancy of $1 - 7/11$. For example, the bit positions of the value 1001101 are:

```
11  10  9  8  7  6  5  4  3  2  1
 1   0  0  x  1  1  0  x  1  x  x
```

The four bit positions marked with x are used for the check bits, which are derived as follows. The four-bit binary numbers corresponding to those bit positions having a binary 1 are added together using modulo-2 arithmetic and the four check bits are then the four-bit sum:

```
11 = 1 0 1 1
 7 = 0 1 1 1
 6 = 0 1 1 0
 3 = 0 0 1 1
   = 1 0 0 1
```

The transmitted codeword is thus:

```
11  10  9   8   7   6   5   4   3   2   1
 1   0   0  [1]  1   1   0  [0]  1  [0] [1]
```

Similarly, at the receiver, the four-bit binary numbers corresponding to those bit positions having a binary 1, including the check bits, are again added together. If no errors have occurred, the modulo-2 sum should be zero:

```
11 = 1 0 1 1
 8 = 1 0 0 0
 7 = 0 1 1 1
 6 = 0 1 1 0
 3 = 0 0 1 1
 1 = 0 0 0 1
     0 0 0 0
```

Now consider a single-bit error: say bit 11 is corrupted from 1 to 0. The new modulo-2 sum would now be:

```
8 = 1 0 0 0
7 = 0 1 1 1
6 = 0 1 1 0
3 = 0 0 1 1
1 = 0 0 0 1
    1 0 1 1
```

Firstly, the sum is non-zero, which indicates an error, and secondly the modulo-2 sum, equivalent to decimal 11, indicates that bit 11 is the erroneous bit. The latter would therefore be inverted to obtain the corrected codeword and hence data bits.

It can also be shown that if two bit errors occur, the modulo-2 sum will be non-zero, thus indicating an error, but the positions of the errors cannot be determined from the sum. The Hamming single-bit code can thus correct for single-bit errors and detect two-bit errors but other multiple-bit errors cannot be detected.

As was mentioned in Chapter 2, the main types of error occurring in many data communication networks are error bursts rather than, say, isolated single-or double-bit errors. Hence, although the Hamming coding scheme in its basic form would appear to be inappropriate for use with such networks, a simple technique is often used to extend the application of such a scheme.

Consider, for example, a requirement to transmit a block of data, comprising a string of, say, eight ASCII characters, over a simplex channel that has a high probability of an error burst (of, say, seven bits) occurring. The approach in such a case would be for the controlling device first to convert each ASCII character into its 11-bit codeword form to give a block of eight 11-bit codewords. Then, instead of transmitting each codeword separately, the controlling device would transmit the contents of the block of codewords a column at a time. Thus the eight, say, most significant bits would be transmitted first, then the eight next most significant bits and so on, finishing with the eight least significant bits. The controlling device at the receiver then performs the reverse operation, reassembling the transmitted block in memory, prior to performing the detection and, if necessary, correction operation on each codeword.

The effect of this approach is, firstly, that a standard USRT device can be used as the transmission interface circuit and, secondly, and more importantly, that if an error burst of up to seven bits does occur, it will affect only a single bit in each codeword rather than a string of bits in one or two codewords. This means that, assuming just a single error burst in the 88 bits transmitted, the receiver can determine a correct copy of the transmitted block of characters.

Although the approach just outlined provides a way of extending the usefulness of this type of encoding scheme, Hamming codes are used mainly in applications that have isolated single-bit errors; an example is in error-correcting semiconductor memory systems. The preferred method of achieving FEC in data communication systems is based on **convolutional codes** and hence an introduction to this type of encoding process will now be presented.

A1.3 CONVOLUTIONAL CODES

Block codes are *memoryless* codes as each output codeword depends only on the current k-bit message block being encoded. In contrast, with a convolutional code, the continuous stream of source bits is operated upon to produce a continuous stream of output (encoded) bits. Because of the nature of the encoding process, the sequence of source bits is said to be convolved (by applying a specific binary operation on them) to produce the output bit sequence. Also, each bit in the output sequence is dependent not only on the current bit being encoded but also on the previous sequence of source bits, thus implying some form of memory. In practice, as will be seen, this takes the form of a shift register of a finite length, known as the **constraint length**, and the convolution (binary) operation is performed using one or more modulo-2 adders (exclusive-OR gates).

Encoding

An example of a convolutional encoder is shown in Figure A.1(a). With this encoder, the three-bit shift register provides the memory and the two modulo-2

(a)

Encoded (output) sequence ← | Input sequence, I

(b)

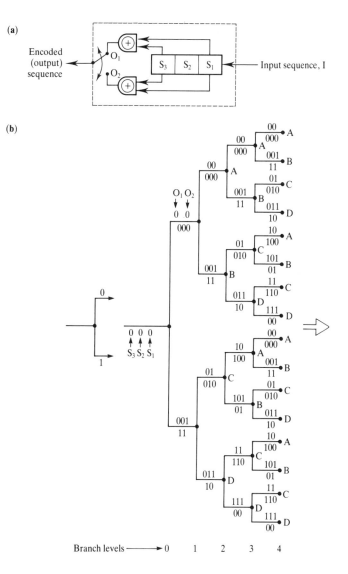

FIGURE A.1

Convolutional codes: (a) example encoder circuit; (b) tree diagram representation.

Branch levels ⟶ 0   1   2   3   4

adders the convolution operation. For each bit in the input sequence, two bits are output, one from each of the two modulo-2 adders. The encoder shown is thus known as a rate $1/2$ (k/n) convolutional encoder with a constraint length of 3.

Because of the memory associated with a convolutional encoder, it is necessary to have a convenient means of determining the specific output bit sequence generated for a given input sequence. There are three techniques that can be used to achieve this, each based on a form of diagrammatic representation: a tree diagram, a state diagram and a trellis diagram. In practice, the last one is the most frequently used method because it is the most useful one for demonstrating the decoding operation. Before this can be drawn, however, it is necessary to determine the outputs for each possible input sequence using either the tree or state diagram.

As an example, Figure A.1(b) shows the **tree diagram** for the encoder shown in Figure A.1(a). The branching points in the tree are known as nodes and the tree shows the two possible branches at each node; the upper of the two branches corresponds to a 0 input bit and the lower branch a 1 bit. The pair of output bits corresponding to the two possible branches at each node are shown on the outside of each branch line.

As can be seen, with a tree diagram the number of branches in the tree doubles for each new input bit. In practice, however, the tree is repetitive after the second branch level since, after this level, there are only four unique branch nodes. These are known as **states** and are shown as A, B, C and D in the figure.

As can be deduced from the figure, from any one of these nodes the same pair of output bits and new node state occurs, irrespective of the position of the node in the tree. For example, from any node C the same pair of branch alternatives occur: 10 output and new state A for a 0 input, or 01 output and new state B for a 1 input.

Once the states for the encoder have been identified using the tree diagram, the **trellis diagram** can then be drawn. As an example, the trellis diagram for the same encoder is as shown in Figure A.2(b). As can be seen, after the second branch level, the repetitive nature of the tree diagram is exploited by representing all the possible encoder outputs in a more reduced form.

As can be deduced from the figure, the trellis diagram shows the outputs that will result from this encoder for all possible input bit sequences. Then, for a specific input sequence, a single path through the trellis – and hence sequence of output bits – will result. As an example, Figure A.2(c) shows the path through the trellis, and hence the output sequence, corresponding to the input sequence 110101 . . .

Initially, the shift register is assumed to be cleared, that is, it is set to all 0s. After the first bit in the input sequence has been shifted (entered) into the shift register, its contents are 001. The outputs from the two modulo-2 adders are then $0 + 1 = 1$ (adder 1) and $0 + 1 = 1$ (adder 2). Thus, the first two output bits are 11 and these are output before the next input bit is entered into the shift register. Since the input bit was a 1, the lower branch path on the trellis diagram is followed and the output is 11, as derived.

After the second input bit has been entered, the shift register contains 011. The two adder outputs are $0 + 1 = 1$ (adder 1) and $1 + 1 = 0$ (adder 2). Thus, the two output bits are 10 and again these are output before the next input bit is processed. Again, since the input bit was a 1, the lower branch on the trellis diagram is followed and the output is 10, as derived. Continuing, the third input bit makes the shift register contents 110 and hence the two output bits are 11; $1 + 0 = 1$ (adder 1) and $1 + 0 = 1$ (adder 2). Also, since the input bit was a 0, the upper branch path on the trellis diagram is followed. This process then continues.

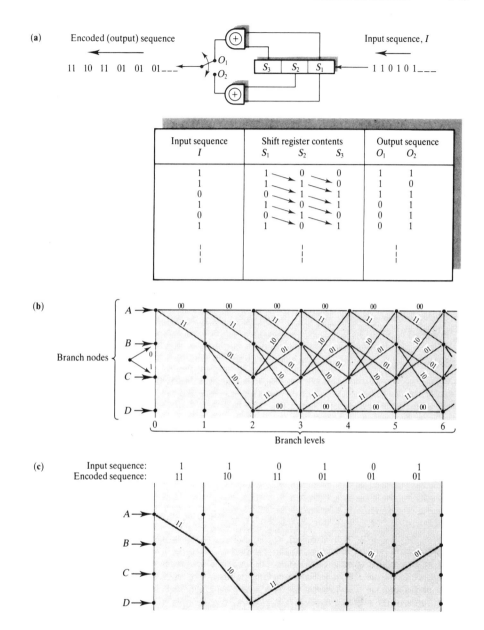

FIGURE A.2

Convolutional encoder: (a) circuit; (b) trellis diagram; (c) example output.

Decoding

The aim of the decoder is to determine the *most likely* output sequence, given a received bit stream (which may have errors) and a knowledge of the encoder used at the source. The decoding procedure is equivalent to comparing the received sequence with all the possible sequences that may be obtained with the respective encoder and then selecting the sequence that is closest to the received sequence.

As was mentioned earlier, the Hamming distance between two codewords is the number of bits that differ between them. Therefore, when selecting the sequence that is closest to the received sequence, the Hamming distance between the received sequence and each of the possible sequences is computed, and the one with the least distance is selected. Clearly, in the limit this would necessitate the complete received sequence being compared with all the possible sequences, and hence paths through the trellis. This is impractical in most cases and hence a compromise must be made.

Essentially, a running count is maintained of the distance between the actual received sequence and each possible sequence but, at each node in the trellis, only a single path is retained. There are always two paths merging at each node and the path selected is the one with the minimum Hamming distance, the other being simply terminated. The retained paths are known as **survivor paths** and the final path selected is then the one with a continuous path through the trellis with a minimum aggregate Hamming distance. This procedure is known as the **Viterbi algorithm**. The decoder, which aims to find the most likely path corresponding to the received sequence, is known as a **maximum-likelihood decoder**. The Viterbi algorithm will now be described by means of an example.

EXAMPLE

Assume that a message sequence of 1001110... is to be sent using the encoder shown in Figure A.1(a). From the trellis diagram for this encoder, it can be deduced that this will yield a transmitted (output) sequence of:

11   01   10   11   10   00   11...

Now assume a burst error occurs so that two bits of this encoded sequence are corrupted during transmission. The received sequence is then:

11   01   00   11   11   00   11...
         ↑   ↑

Use the Veterbi algorithm to determine from this the most likely transmitted sequence.

The various steps associated with the encoding and decoding procedures are shown in Figure A.3. Figure A.3(a) shows the path through the trellis corresponding to the original output from the encoder and Figure A.3(b) shows how the survivor paths are chosen. The number shown by each path merging at a node in Figure A.3(b) is the accumulated Hamming distance between the path followed to get to that node and the actual received sequence.

If the path chosen is that starting at the route node (branch level 0), the received sequence is 11 and the Hamming distances for the two paths are 2 for path 00 and 0 for path 11. These two distance values are then added to the paths emanating from these nodes. Thus, at branch level 1, the received sequence is 01 and the two paths from node A have Hamming distances of 1 for path 00 and 1 for path 11. The accumulated distances are thus $2 + 1 = 3$ for each path. Similarly, the

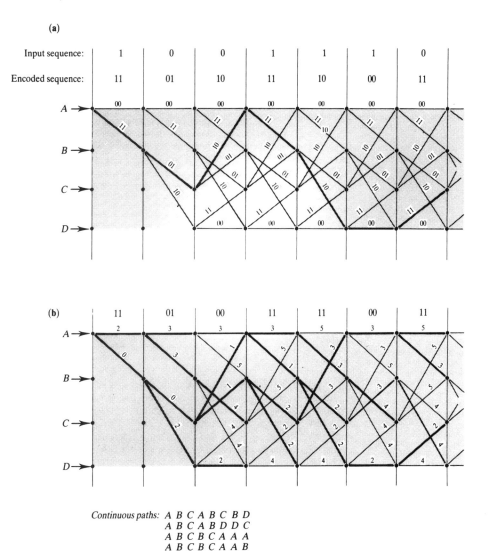

FIGURE A.3

Convolutional decoder:
(a) encoder output;
(b) survivor paths.

Continuous paths: A B C A B C B D
A B C A B D D C
A B C B C A A A
A B C B C A A B

two paths emanating from node *B* have Hamming distances of 0 for path 01 and 2 for path 10, and hence the accumulated distances are 0 + 0 = 0 and 0 + 2 = 2, respectively. A similar procedure is then repeated at branch level 2.

At branch level 3 and onwards, however, the selection process starts. Thus, in the example, the two paths merging at node *A* (at branch level 3) have accumulated distances of 3 and 1, of which the latter is selected to be the survivor path for this node – this is shown as a bold line on the trellis diagram. A similar selection process is then followed at nodes *B*, *C* and *D*. At node *C*, however, it can be seen that the two merging paths both have the same accumulated distance of 4. In such cases, the upper path is selected. Also, after the selection process, all subsequent distances are calculated relative to the accumulated distance associated with the selected path.

It now remains to select the most likely path and hence the output sequence. Although the decoding procedure continues, by inspection of the portion of the trellis shown, it can be seen that:

- only four paths have a continuous path through the trellis, and
- the distance corresponding to the path *ABCABDDC* is the minimum.

Thus, this is the path that is selected, the corresponding output sequence being 11 01 10 11 10 00 11 ..., which corresponds to the original encoded (and hence transmitted) sequence.

Finally, it should be stressed that no FEC methods can identify all errors. In general, therefore, codes like the convolutional code are used primarily to reduce the error probability (bit error rate) of a link to a more acceptable level. A typical reduction with a rate 1/2 convolutional code is between 10^2 and 10^3. Hence, assuming an ARQ error control procedure is also being used, the overall link efficiency is much improved.

APPENDIX B

Transmission control circuits

As was indicated in Section 3.7 of Chapter 3, special integrated circuits are available to perform most of the functions associated with the different types of transmission control scheme. As an example, this appendix describes the circuit used to perform the various control functions associated with character-oriented data transmission. The circuit is known as a **universal synchronous asynchronous receiver transmitter** or **USART**.

The term **universal** is used since the device can be programmed to operate in both character-oriented transmission modes: asynchronous and synchronous. The specific mode and operating characteristics to be used are selected by writing – under program control – a predefined bit pattern into one of the internal control registers of the device. When programmed to operate in the asynchronous mode, the device is normally referred to as a **universal asynchronous receiver transmitter** or **UART** whilst in the synchronous mode it is known as a **universal synchronous receiver transmitter** or **USRT**.

Essentially, a UART accepts a character in parallel form from a controlling device – a microprocessor, for example – and then transmits it out bit serially, together with a start and stop bit(s) and, if selected, a parity bit. Similarly, on input, it receives the serial bit stream, removes the start and stop bits, checks the parity, and then makes the received character available to be read by the controlling device in parallel form. It thus includes all the necessary circuitry to achieve bit (clock) synchronization as well as additional modem control circuitry. A schematic showing the main registers associated with a USART is given in Figure B.1(a); part (b) of the figure shows a typical interfacing arrangement to use the device as a UART.

To use the device, the **mode register** is first loaded with the required bit pattern to define the required operating characteristics; this is known as initialization. With asynchronous transmission, the user may select 5, 6, 7 or 8 bits per character, odd, even or no parity, one or more stop bits and a particular clock rate ratio. The last of these is also referred to as the **baud rate factor**. Then, depending on the required bit rate, a clock source of the appropriate frequency is applied to the transmit and receive clock inputs. The most commonly used bit rates with asynchronous transmission are 110, 300, 1200, 2400, 4800, 9600 and 19200 bps. Hence, if say a $\times 16$ clock rate has been selected, then the transmit and receive clock inputs would be 1760 (110×16), 4800 (300×16) etc, respectively. For the

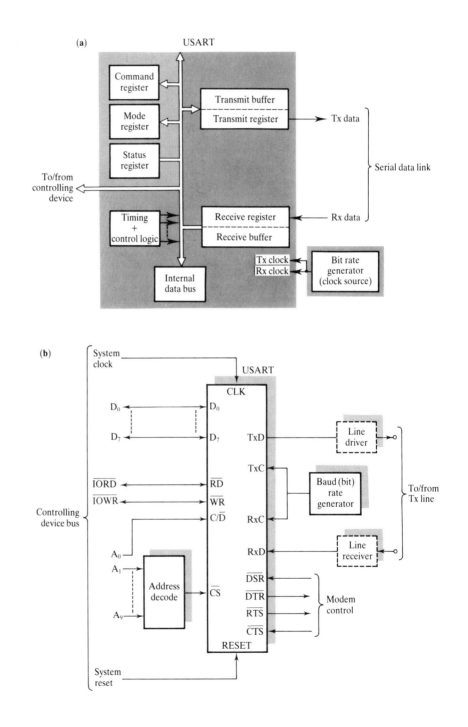

FIGURE B.1

USART schematic:
(a) main device
registers; (b) device
interfacing.

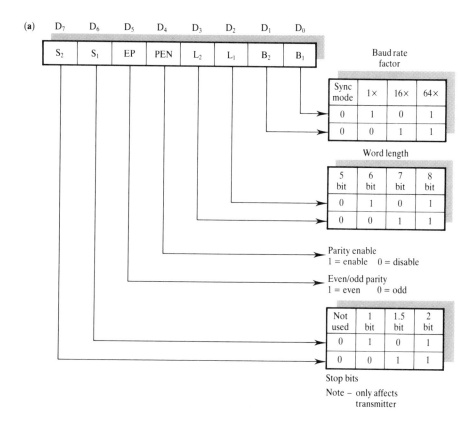

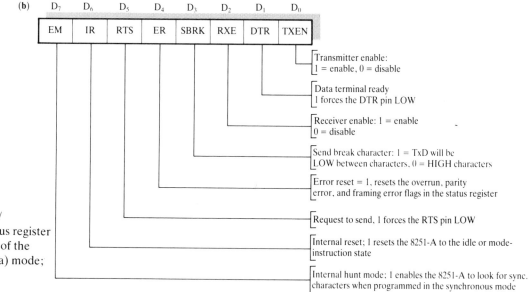

FIGURE B.2

Write to node/
command/status register
bit definitions of the
Intel 8251A: (a) mode;
(b) command.

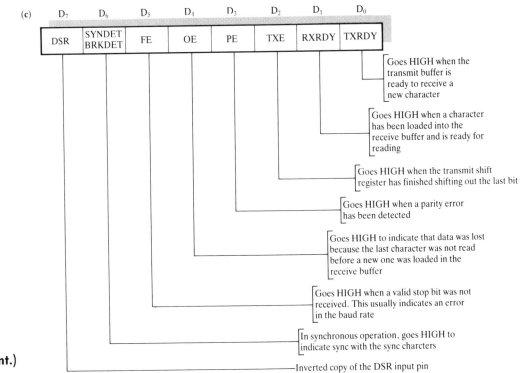

FIGURE B.2 (cont.)

(c) Status.

device shown, it is assumed that the clock circuitry is external to the device, although with some devices it is part of the same integrated circuit.

The meaning of the various bits in the mode register of a typical device – the Intel 8251A – are shown in Figure B.1(a). Hence, assuming a mode byte of 01111010 (7A hexadecimal) was loaded into the mode register at initialization, the device would operate in the asynchronous mode with 7 bits per character, an even parity bit, one stop bit and a clock rate ratio of ×16. A clock source of ×16 the desired bit rate would then be connected to the transmit and receive clock inputs.

The **command byte** is used to control the actual operation of the device. Hence, after selecting the required operational mode (and prior to transmitting data), the command byte must be loaded. The assignments of the various bits in the 8251A command byte are shown in Figure B.2(b). As can be seen, the individual bits perform such functions as enabling the transmitter and receiver sections, and controlling the modem interface. The three bits of general use are the error reset (ER), the receiver enable (RXE) and the transmitter enable (TXEN). Hence, if a command byte of 00010011 (13 Hex) is loaded after the mode byte and prior to the transmission of data, any error conditions would be reset (described later) and the transmitter and receiver sections enabled. The UARTs at both ends of the data link must, of course, be programmed to operate in the same mode and with the same operational characteristics.

The controlling device determines the current state of a UART by reading the contents of a third register (known as the **status register**) and testing specific bits within it. Individually these are referred to as **status** or **flag bits**; the composition of the status register in the 8251A is shown in part (c) of the figure.

To transmit a character, the controlling device first waits until the TxRDY (transmit ready) flag becomes set which indicates the transmit buffer is empty. The character is then loaded into the transmit buffer and is subsequently transferred to the PISO transmit register by the control logic within the device when the last stop bit of the previous character has been transmitted to line. At this point the TxEMPTY flag becomes set and is reset when a new character is loaded into the transmit buffer. The TxEMPTY flag is particularly useful when a line is being operated in the half-duplex mode since in this mode the controlling device must know when the last character in a message – the final stop bit(s), in practice – has been transmitted to line.

On receipt of a character, the individual bits from the line are sampled and shifted bit serially into the SIPO receive register and, on receipt of the final stop bit, the character is transferred by the control logic to the receive buffer. At this point the RxRDY (receive ready) flag becomes set which indicates to the controlling device that a character is ready to be read. The RxRDY flag is then reset by the UART when the received character is read from the receive buffer. In addition, during the reception process, the UART indicates to the controlling device the occurrence (or otherwise) of three possible error conditions:

- PE (parity error) – this is set if the computed parity bit for a character is different from that selected;

- OE (overrun error) – this is set if a received character is transferred to the receive buffer before the previous character was read, thereby losing the latter;

- FE (framing error) – this is set if a valid stop bit was not received and normally indicates the clock rate ratio is incorrect.

To program the USART to operate in the synchronous mode (that is, as a USRT), the two least significant bits of the mode register are both set to binary zero. The next four bits then have the same meaning as for asynchronous transmission: number of bits per character and parity selection – odd, even, or no parity. The ESD (external sync detect) bit is used to indicate whether the character synchronization procedure is to be carried out externally or internally and is normally set to internal. Finally, the SCS bit (sync character select) is used to indicate whether one or two SYN characters are to be transmitted whenever the transmit buffer is empty, for example, prior to transmitting a frame.

Prior to loading the frame contents, as with asynchronous transmission, the command register must first be loaded. The use of the various bits are the same as those used for asynchronous transmission. The additional bit of interest with synchronous transmission is the EH bit (enter hunt mode). Assuming internal sync detect has been selected, then the EH bit is set to start the character synchronization procedure associated with the receive section of the device.

Once the functional definition of the 8251A has been programmed – using the mode register – two or more SYN characters are loaded (to enable the receiver to obtain character synchronization prior to the frame contents being received).

The controlling device determines the current state of the 8251A by reading the contents of the status register and interpreting the individual bits within it. These again are the same as those used with asynchronous transmission. The additional bit of use with synchronous transmission is the SYNDET (sync detect) bit which is used to indicate that the receiver section has achieved character synchronization when it is in the hunt mode. Normally the controlling device will then read each subsequent character as it is received and wait for the start-of-frame character that signals a new frame.

With the 8251A, the controlling device accesses the various registers – control and data – using a combination of the chip select (CS), the read (RD) and write (WR), and the control/data (C/D) lines. The bar above a signal indicates that it is active when low – binary 0 – rather than when it is a binary 1. A summary of the use of the various lines is given in Table B.1.

As can be seen, the C/D line is set to 1 when the controlling device is communicating with a control register and a 0 with a data register, the actual register being determined by the state of the RD and WR lines. For example, to

Table B.1

$\overline{CS}$	$C/\overline{D}$	$\overline{RD}$	$\overline{WR}$	Operation
0	1	1	0	Write to mode/command register
0	0	1	0	Write to transmit buffer
0	1	0	1	Read status register
0	0	0	1	Read receive buffer
1	X	X	X	Device disabled

X = Either 0 or 1

read the status register, the C/D line is set to 1 whilst to read a character from the receive buffer it is set to 0. It should be noted that to write to the mode/command registers two successive write operations must be carried out; the first byte will be loaded into the mode register and the second into the command register.

Finally, although this appendix has described the operation of just a single device type – the USART – all the other transmission control devices operate in a similar way.

APPENDIX C

Summary of standards organizations

American National Standards Institute (ANSI) This is a national standards organization comprised of members from computer manufacturers and users in the United States. It is also the US member body of ISO. Its members are involved in the development of standards at all levels in the ISO Reference Model.

British Standards Institute (BSI) This is a national standards organization concerned with the production of standards for use by all forms of manufacturing and consumer industries. It is the British member of ISO and acts as a source for all their documents.

Electronics Industries Association (EIA) This is a US national standards organization comprised of members from the electronics industry. In the context of data and computer communications, it has produced a range of (physical) interface standards for connecting peripherals to a computer and, more recently, through the contribution of General Motors, has been actively involved in the development of the layer 7 standard for manufacturing message service (MMS). It is a member of ANSI and, through them, ISO.

European Computer Manufacturers Association (ECMA) This is comprised of members from computer manufacturers in Europe including some European divisions of American companies. It produces its own standards and also contributes to CCITT and ISO. Its members are actively involved in the development of standards at all levels of the ISO Reference Model.

European Telecommunications Standards Institute (ETSI) This is a European standards body that produces standards for regulatory purposes by the EC and EFTA countries. It produces standards relating to telecommunication services, public data networks, videotex and digital cellular services which are issued as European Telecommunication Standards (ETSs), also known as NETs.

Institute of Electrical and Electronic Engineers (IEEE) This is a US professional society that also takes part in the development of standards for use by the computer industry. In the context of computer communications, it has been responsible for the production of standards relating to LANs and, in particular, for those concerned with the physical, MAC and LLC (sub) layers.

International Standards Organization (ISO) This is an international standards organization comprised of designated standards bodies of the participating countries. It is concerned with a wide range of standards, each of which is controlled by a separate technical committee. The technical committee that produces standards for the computer industry is TC97 – Information Processing Systems. This committee has been responsible for the production of the basic ISO Reference Model for OSI and also for the production of the various protocol standards for each layer in the reference model.

International Telegraph and Telephone Consultative Committee (CCITT) This is an international standards organization comprised of the Postal, Telegraph and Telephone (PTT) authorities of the member countries. It is concerned primarily with the development and production of standards for interfacing equipment to public telecommunications networks. These include the analogue PSTN. ISDN and PPSDN. It also produces standards for Facsimile, Teletex, Videotex and other value-added services (teleservices).

National Bureau of Standards (NBS) This is a US national standards organization concerned with the production of standards relating to both ISO and CCITT. It issues standards for equipment purchased by the US federal government in the general area of information processing. These are known as federal information processing standards (FIPS).

OSI Network Management Forum (NMF) This is a worldwide organization of telecommunications and computer companies, service providers and service users. The NMF develops standards for network management based on ISO/OSI management protocols.

APPENDIX D

Glossary of terms and abbreviations

Abstract Syntax Notation One (ASN.1) An abstract syntax used to define the structure of the protocol data units associated with a particular protocol entity.

Address resolution protocol (ARP) The protocol in the TCP/IP suite that is used to obtain the network point of attachment address of a host corresponding to its internet-wide IP address.

Advanced Research Projects Agency (ARPA) The former name of the US government agancy that funded the creation of the ARPANET and later the Internet – now DARPA.

American Standards Committee for Information Interchange (ASCII) In normal usage it is used to refer to the character code defined by this committee for the interchange of information between two communicating devices. The ASCII character set is in widespread use for the transfer of information between a computer and a peripheral device such as a visual display unit or a printer.

Amplitude modulation (AM) A modulation technique used to allow data to be transmitted across an analogue network, such as a switched telephone network. The amplitude of a single (carrier) frequency is varied (modulated) between two levels – one for binary 0 and the other for binary 1.

Application layer This corresponds to layer 7 of the ISO Reference Model for open systems interconnection. It comprises a number of application-oriented protocols and forms the user interface to the various distributed information processing services supported.

ARPANET The wide area network funded by ARPA/DARPA that links many universities, research and defense establishments throughout the United States and other countries. In addition to carrying live traffic, it has been used as a development testbed for research into internetworking – now part of the larger Internet.

Association control service element (ACSE) A protocol entity forming part of the application layer. It provides the generalized (common) function of establishing and clearing a logical association (connection) between two application entities.

Asynchronous transfer mode (ATM) The proposed mode of operation of the emerging broadband integrated services digital network. All information to be transmitted – voice, data, image, video – is first fragmented into small, fixed-sized frames known as cells. These are then switched and routed using packet switching principles – also known as cell or post-packet switching.

Asynchronous transmission Strictly, this implies that the receiver clock is not synchronized to the transmitted clock when data is being transmitted between two devices connected by a transmission line. More generally, it is used to indicate that data is being transmitted as individual characters. Each character is preceded by a start signal and terminated by one or more stop signals, which are used by the receiver for synchronization purposes.

Automatic repeat request (ARQ) A technique used for error control over a transmission line. If errors in a transmitted message are detected by the receiving device, it requests the sending device to retransmit the message together with any other messages that may have been affected.

Bandwidth The difference between the highest and lowest sinusoidal frequency signals that can be transmitted across a transmission line or through a network. It is measured in Hertz (Hz) and also defines the maximum information-carrying capacity of the line or network.

Baseband A particular operating mode of a transmission line: each binary digit (bit) in a message is converted into one of two voltage (sometimes current) levels – one for binary 1 and the other for binary 0. The voltages are then applied directly to the line. The line signal thus varies with time between these two voltage levels as the data is transmitted.

Basic mode An ISO international standard protocol defined to control the exchange of data between a master (primary) station and multiple slave (secondary) stations which are connected by means of a multidrop link.

Baud The number of line signal variations per second. It is also used to indicate the rate at which data is transmitted on a line, although this is strictly correct only when each bit is represented by a single signal level on the transmission line. Hence, the bit rate and the line signal rate are both the same.

Binary synchronous control (BSC) The name used by IBM for the ISO Basic Mode protocol.

Bit stuffing (zero bit insertion) A technique used to allow pure binary data to be transmitted on a synchronous transmission line. Each message block (frame) is encapsulated between two flags, which are special bit sequences. Then, if the message data contains a possibly similar sequence, an additional (zero) bit is inserted into the data stream by the sender, and is subsequently removed by the receiving device. The transmission method is then said to be data transparent.

Block sum check This is used for the detection of errors when data is being transmitted. It is comprised of a set of binary digits (bits), which are the modulo-2 sum of the individual characters/octets in a frame (block) or message.

Bridge A device used to link two homogeneous local area subnetworks; that is, two subnetworks utilizing the same physical and medium access control method.

Broadband A particular mode of operation of a coaxial cable. A single coaxial cable can be used to simultaneously transmit a number of separate data streams by assigning each stream a portion of the total available bandwidth. Data are transmitted by modulating a single frequency signal from the selected frequency band and the data is then received by demodulating the received signal.

Broadcast A means of transmitting a message to all devices connected to a network. Normally, a special address, the broadcast address, is reserved to enable all the devices to determine that the message is a broadcast message.

Bus A network topology in widespread use for the interconnection of communities of digital devices distributed over a localized area. The transmission medium is normally a single coaxial cable to which all the devices are attached. Each transmission thus propagates the length of the medium and is therefore received by all other devices connected to the medium.

Check sum *See* Block sum check.

Circuit switching The mode of operation of a telephone network and also some of the newer digital data networks. A communication path is first established through the network between the source (calling) and destination (called) terminals, and this is then used exclusively for the duration of the call or transaction. Both terminals must operate at the same information transfer rate.

Coaxial cable A type of transmission medium consisting of a centre conductor and a concentric outer conductor. It is used when high data transfer rates (greater than 1 Mbps) are required.

Commitment, concurrency and recovery (CCR) A protocol entity forming part of the application layer. It provides the means whereby two or more application processes may perform mutually exclusive operations on shared data. It also provides control to ensure that the operations are performed either completely or not at all. It uses the concepts of an atomic action and a two-phase commit protocol.

Community antenna television (CATV) A facility used in the context of local area data netwoks, since the principles and network components used in CATV networks can also be used to produce a flexible underlying data transmission facility over a local area. CATV networks operate using the broadband mode of working.

Common application service element (CASE) A collection of protocol entities forming part of the application layer that are responsible for providing some common services, such as establishing a logical connection (association) between two application protocol entities.

Common management information protocol (CMIP) The ISO application layer protocol used to retrieve and send management-related information across an OSI network.

Continuous RQ A part of a data link protocol concerned with error control. It endeavours to ensure that, if a frame (message) is corrupted during transmission, another copy of the frame is sent. To improve the efficiency of utilization of the data link, frames are transmitted continuously; hence, retransmission requests relating to corrupted frames may be received after a number of other frames have been transmitted.

Crosstalk An unwanted signal that is picked up in a conductor as a result of some external electrical activity.

CSMA/CD An abbreviation for carrier sense, multiple access with collision detection. It is a method used to control access to a shared transmission medium, such as a coaxial cable bus to which a number of stations are connected. A station wishing to transmit a message first senses (listens to) the medium and transmits the message only if the medium is quiet – no carrier present. Then, as the message is being transmitted, the station monitors the actual signal on the transmission medium. If this is different from the signal being transmitted, a collision is said to have occurred and been detected. The station then ceases transmission and retries again later.

Cyclic redundancy check (CRC) A method used for the detection of errors when data is being transmitted. A CRC is a numeric value computed from the bits in the message to be transmitted. It is appended to the tail of the message prior to transmission and the receiver then detects the presence of errors in the received message by recomputing a new CRC.

Data circuit-terminating equipment (DCE) The name given to the equipment provided by the network authority (provider) for the attachment of user devices to the network. It takes on different forms for different network types.

Data link layer This corresponds to layer 2 of the ISO Reference Model for open systems interconnection. It is concerned with the reliable transfer of data (no residual transmission errors) across the data link being used.

Data terminal equipment (DTE) A generic name for any user device connected to a data network. It thus includes such devices as visual display units, computers and office workstations.

Datagram A type of service offered on a packet-switched data network (*see also* virtual call). A datagram is a self-contained packet of information that is sent through the network with minimum protocol overheads.

Decibel A measure of the strength of a signal relative to another signal. The number of decibels is computed as ten times the log of the ratio of the power in each signal or twenty times the log of the amplitude (voltage or current) of each signal.

Defense Advanced Research Projects Agency (DARPA) *See* ARPA.

Delay distortion Distortion of a signal caused by the frequency components making up the signal having different propagation velocities across a transmission medium.

Directory service (DS) A protocol entity forming part of the application layer in an OSI suite that is concerned with the translation of symbolic names (or titles), as used by application processes, into fully qualified network addresses, as used within the open systems interconnection environment. Also known as X.500.

Distributed-queue, dual-bus (DQDB) An optical fibre-based network that can be used as a high-speed LAN or MAN that is compatible with the evolving broadband ISDN networks. It operates in a broadcast mode by using two buses each of which transmits small fixed-sized frames – known as cells – in opposite directions. Each bus can operate at hundreds of megabits per second.

Domain name system (DNS) The application protocol used in the TCP/IP suite to map the symbolic names used by humans into the equivalent fully-qualified network address.

Error rate The ratio of the average number of bits that will be corrupted to the total number of bits that are transmitted for a data link or system.

Ethernet The name of the local area network invented at the Xerox Corporation Palo Alto Research Center. It operates using the CSMA/CD medium access control method. The early specification was refined by a joint team from Digital Equipment Corporation, Intel Corporation and Xerox Corporation and this in turn has now been superseded by the IEEE 802.3 – ISO 8802.3 – international standard.

Extended Binary Coded Decimal Interchange Code (EBCDIC). The character set used on all IBM computers.

Exterior Gateway Protocol (EGP) A protocol used in relation to large internetworks that comprise multiple smaller internetworks interconnected together. The interconnection devices used are known as exterior gateways and the EGP is the protocol they use to advertise the IP addresses of the networks present in each of the smaller internetworks.

Fast select An optional facility with the X.25 protocol that allows user data to be sent in the call set-up and call clearing packets.

Fibre distributed data interface (FDDI) An optical fibre-based ring network that can be used as a high-speed LAN or MAN. It provides a user bit rate of 100 Mbps and uses a control token medium access control method.

Fibre optic *See* Optical fibre.

File transfer access and management (FTAM) A protocol entity forming part of the application layer. It enables user application processes to manage and access a (distributed) file system.

File transfer protocol (FTP) The application protocol in the TCP/IP suite that provides access to a networked file server.

Flow control A technique used to control the rate of flow of frames or messages between two communicating entities.

Frame The unit of information transferred across a data link. Typically, there are control frames for link management and information frames for the transfer of message data.

Frame check sequence (FCS) A general term given to the additional bits appended to a transmitted frame or message by the source to enable the receiver to detect possible transmission errors.

Frequency-division multiplexing (FDM) A technique used to derive a number of separate data channels from a single transmission medium, such as a coaxial cable. Each data channel is assigned a portion of the total available bandwidth.

Frequency-shift keying (FSK) A modulation technique used to convert binary data into an analogue form comprising two sinusoidal frequencies. It is widely used in modems to allow data to be transmitted across a (analogue) switched telephone network.

Full-duplex A type of information exchange strategy between two communicating devices whereby information (data) can be exchanged in both directions simultaneously. It is also known as two-way simultaneous.

Gateway A device that routes datagrams (packets) between one network and another. Typically, the two networks operate with different protocols, and so the gateway also performs the necessary protocol conversion functions.

Half-duplex A type of information exchange strategy between two communicating devices whereby information (data) can be exchanged in both directions alternately. It is also known as two-way alternate.

High-level data link control (HDLC) An internationally agreed standard protocol defined to control the exchange of data across either a point-to-point data link or a multidrop data link.

Host This is normally a computer belonging to a user that contains (hosts) the communication hardware and software necessary to connect the computer to a data communication network.

Idle RQ A part of a data link protocol concerned with error control. It endeavours to ensure that another copy is sent if a frame (message) is corrupted during transmission. After a frame is sent by the source, it must wait until either an indication of correct (or otherwise) receipt is received from the receiver or for a specified time before sending another frame. It is also known as send (or stop) and wait.

Integrated services digital network (ISDN) The new generation of world-wide telecommunications network that utilizes digital techniques for both transmission and switching. It supports both voice and data communications.

Interior gateway protocol (IGP) The routing protocol used in the gateways of a TCP/IP internetwork to obtain the shortest path routes through the internet.

Intermediate system (IS) The name used by ISO to describe the device that interconnects two networks together – also known as a router or a gateway.

International Alphabet Number 5 (IA5) The standard character code defined by CCITT and recommended by ISO. It is almost identical to the ASCII code.

Internet The abbreviated name given to a collection of interconnected networks. Also, the name of US government funded internetwork based on the TCP/IP protocol suite.

Internet control message protocol (ICMP) A component part of the internet protocol (IP) in the TCP/IP suite that handles error and other control messages that are returned by internet gateways and hosts.

Internet protocol (IP) The TCP/IP protocol that provides connectionless network service between multiple packet-switched networks interconnected by gateways.

Job transfer and manipulation (JTM) A protocol entity forming part of the application layer. It enables user application processes to transfer and manipulate documents relating to jobs (processing tasks).

Local area network (LAN) A data communication network used to interconnect a community of digital devices distributed over a localized area of up to, say, 10km^2. The devices may be office workstations, mini- and microcomputers, intelligent instrumentation equipment, etc.

Logical link control (LLC) A protocol forming part of the data link layer in LANs. It is concerned with the reliable transfer of data across the data link between two communicating systems.

Management information base (MIB) The name of the database used to hold the management information relating to a network or internetwork.

Manchester encoding A scheme used to encode clocking (timing) information into a binary data stream prior to transmission. The resulting encoded signal has a transition (positive or negative) in the middle of each bit cell period with the effect that the clocking information (required to receive the signal) is readily extracted from the received signal.

Manufacturing message service (MMS) A protocol entity forming part of the application layer. It is intended for use specifically in the manufacturing or process control industry. It enables a supervisory computer to control the operation of a distributed community of computer-based devices.

Medium access control (MAC) Many local area networks utilize a single common transmission medium – a bus or ring, for example – to which all the interconnected devices are attached. A procedure must be followed by each device, therefore, to ensure that transmissions occur in an orderly and fair way. In general, this is known as the medium access control procedure. Two examples are CSMA/CD and (control) token.

Message handling service (MHS) A protocol entity forming part of the application layer. It provides a generalized facility for exchanging electronic messages between systems. It is also known as X.400.

Metropolitan area network (MAN) A network that links a set of local area networks that are physically distributed around a town or city.

Microwave A type of communication based on electromagnetic radiation by means of a transmitting aerial and a receiving antenna or dish. It is used for both terrestrial links and satellite links.

Modem The name given to the device that converts a binary (digital) data stream into an analogue (continuously varying) form, prior to transmission of the data across an analogue network (MODulator), and reconverts the received signal back into its binary form (DEModulator). Since each access port to the network normally requires a full-duplex (two way simultaneous) capability, the device must perform both the MODulation and DEModulation functions; hence the single name MODEM is used. As an example, a modem is normally required to transmit data across a telephone network.

Multidrop A network configuration that supports more than two stations on the same transmission medium.

Multiplexer A device used to enable a number of lower bit rate devices, normally situated in the same location, to share a single higher bit rate transmission line. The data-carrying capacity of the latter must be in excess of the combined bit rates of the low bit rate devices.

Multipoint *See* Multidrop.

Network layer This corresponds to layer 3 of the ISO Reference Model for open systems interconnection. It is concerned with the establishment and clearing of logical or physical connections across the network being used.

Network management A generic term used to embrace all the functions and entities involved in the management of a network. This includes configuration management, fault handling and the gathering of statistics relating to usage of the network.

Noise The term given to the extraneous electrical signals that may be generated or picked up in a transmission line. Typically, it may be caused by neighbouring electrical apparatus. If the noise signal is large compared with the data-carrying signal, the latter may be corrupted and result in transmission errors.

NRZ/NRZI Two similar (and related) schemes for encoding a binary data stream. The first has the property that a signal transition occurs whenever a binary 1 is present in the data stream and the second whenever a binary 0 is present. The latter is utilized with certain clocking (timing) schemes.

Open system A vendor-independent set of interconnected computers that all utilize the same standard communications protocol stack based on either the ISO/OSI or the TCP/IP protocols.

Open systems interconnection (OSI) The name of the protocol suite that is based on ISO protocols to create an open system interconnection environment.

Optical fibre A type of transmission medium over which data is transmitted in the form of light waves or pulses. It is characterized by its potentially high bandwidth, and hence data-carrying capacity, and its high immunity to interference from other electrical sources.

Packet assembler/disassembler (PAD) A device used with an X.25 packet switching network to allow character-mode terminals to communicate with a packet-mode device, such as a computer.

Packet switching A mode of operation of a data communication network. Each message to be transmitted through the network is first divided into a number of smaller, self-contained message units known as packets. Each packet contains addressing information. As each packet is received at an intermediate node (exchange) within the network, it is first stored and, depending on the addressing information contained within it, forwarded along an appropriate link to the next node and so on. Packets belonging to the same message are then reassembled at the destination. This mode of operation ensures that long messages do not degrade the response time of the network. Also, the source and destination devices may operate at different data rates.

Parity A mechanism used for the detection of transmission errors when single characters are being transmitted. A single binary digit, known as the parity bit, the value (1 or 0) of which is determined by the total number of binary 1s in the character, is transmitted with the character so that the receiver can thus determine the presence of single-bit errors by comparing the received parity bit with the (recomputed) value it should be.

Phase-shift keying (PSK) A modulation technique used to convert binary data into an analogue form comprising a single sinusoidal frequency signal with a phase that varies according to the data being transmitted.

Physical layer This corresponds to layer 1 of the ISO Reference Model for open systems interconnection. It is concerned with the electrical and mechanical specification of the physical network termination equipment.

Piggyback A technique used to return acknowledgement information across a full-duplex (two-way simultaneous) data link without the use of special (acknowledgement) messages. The acknowledgement information relating to the flow of messages in one direction is embedded (piggybacked) into a normal data-carrying message flowing in the reverse direction.

Postal, Telegraph and Telephone (PTT) The administrative authority that controls all the postal and public telecommunications networks and services in a country.

Presentation layer This corresponds to layer 6 of the ISO Reference Model for open systems interconnection. It is concerned with the negotiation of a suitable transfer (concrete) syntax for use during an application session and, if this is different from the local syntax, for the translation to and from this syntax.

Protocol A set of rules formulated to control the exchange of data between two communicating parties.

Protocol data unit (PDU) The message units exchanged between two protocol entities.

Protocol entity The code that controls the operation of a protocol layer.

Public-switched data network (PSDN) A communication network that has been set up and is controlled by a public telecommunications authority for the exchange of data.

Public-switched telephone network (PSTN) This is the term used to describe the (analogue) telephone network.

Remote operations service element (ROSE) A protocol entity forming part rof the application layer. It provides a general facility for initiating and controlling operations remotely.

Ring A network topology in widespread use for the interconnection of communities of digital devices distributed over a localized area, such as a factory or block of offices. Each device is connected to its nearest neighbour until all the devices are connected in the form of a closed loop or ring. Data is transmitted in one direction only and, as each message circulates around the ring, it is read by each device connected in the ring. After circulating around the ring, the source device removes the message from the ring.

Router A device used to interconnect two or more local area networks together, each of which operates with a different medium access control method – also known as a gateway or intermediate system.

RS-232C/RS-422/RS-423 Standards laid down by the American Electrical Industries Association for interfacing a digital device to a PTT-supplied modem. RS-232C is also used as an interface standard for connecting a peripheral device, such as a visual display unit or a printer, to a computer.

Send and wait *See* Idle RQ.

Service access point (SAP) The subaddress used to uniquely identify a particular link between two protocol layers in a specific system.

Session layer This corresponds to layer 5 of the ISO Reference Model for open systems interconnection. It is concerned with the establishment of a logical connection between two application entities and with controlling the dialogue (message exchange) between them.

Shortest path first (SPF) The algorithm used in gateways/routers/intermediate systems to find the shortest path between itself and all the other gateways in an internetwork.

Signal-to-noise ratio The ratio between the power in a signal and the (unwanted) power associated with the line or system noise. It is normally expressed in decibels.

Simple mail transfer protocol (SMTP) The application protocol in a TCP/IP suite that is used to transfer mail between an interconnected set of (native) electronic mail systems.

Simple network management protocol (SNMP) The application protocol in a TCP/IP suite used to send and retrieve management-related information across a TCP/IP network.

Simplex A type of information exchange strategy between two communicating devices whereby information (data) can only be passed in one direction.

Slotted ring A type of local area (data) network. All the devices are connected in the form of a (physical) ring and an additional device known as a monitor is used to ensure that the ring contains a fixed number of message slots (binary digits) that circulate around the ring in one direction only. A device sends a message by placing it in an empty slot as it passes. This is then read by all other devices on the ring and subsequently removed by the originating device.

Specific application service element (SASE) A collection of protocol entities forming part of the application layer responsible for providing various specific application services, such as file transfer and job transfer.

Star A type of network topology in which there is a central node that performs all switching (and hence routing) functions.

Statistical multiplexer (stat mux) A device used to enable a number of lower bit rate devices, normally situated in the same location, to share a single, higher bit rate transmission line. The devices usually have human operators, and hence data is transmitted on the shared line on a statistical basis rather than, as is the case with a basic multiplexer, on a preallocated basis. It thus endeavours to exploit the fact that each device operates at a much lower mean rate than its maximum rate.

Subnet The name given in the ISO documents to refer to an individual network that forms part of a larger internetwork.

Synchronous transmission A technique used to transmit data between two devices connected by a transmission line. The data is normally transmitted in the form of blocks, each comprising a string of binary digits. With synchronous transmission, the transmitter and receiver clocks are in synchronism; a number of techniques are used to ensure this.

TCP/IP The term used to refer to the complete suite of protocols including IP, TCP and the associated application protocols.

Teletex An international telecommunications service that provides the means for messages, comprising text and selected graphical characters, to be prepared, sent and received.

TELNET The application protocol in the TCP/IP suite that enables a user at a terminal to interact with a program that is running in another computer.

Time-division multiplexing (TDM) A technique used to share the bandwidth (channel capacity) of a shared transmission facility to allow a number of communications to be in progress either concurrently or one at a time.

Token bus A type of local area (data) network. Access to the shared transmission medium, which is implemented in the form of a bus to which all the communicating devices are connected, is controlled by a single control (permission) token. Only the current owner of the token is allowed to transmit a message on the medium. All devices wishing to transmit messages are connected in the form of a logical ring. After a device receives the token and transmits any waiting messages, it passes the token on to the next device on the ring.

Token ring A type of local area (data) network. All the devices are connected in the form of a (physical) ring and messages are transmitted by allowing them to circulate around the ring. A device can only transmit a message on the ring when it is in possession of a control (permission) token. A single token is passed from one device to another around the ring.

TP_4 The term used to refer to the class 4 transport protocol in an OSI suite. This contains error control and flow control functions and is used with connectionless networks/internetworks.

Transmission control protocol (TCP) The protocol in the TCP/IP suite that provides a reliable full-duplex message transfer service to application protocols.

Transmission medium The communication path linking two communicating devices. Some examples are twisted pair wire, coaxial cable, optical fibre cable and a microwave (radio) beam.

Transport layer This corresponds to layer 4 of the ISO Reference Model for open systems interconnection. It is concerned with providing a network-independent, reliable, message interchange service to the application-oriented layers (layers 5 through 7).

Twisted pair A type of transmission medium consisting of two insulated wires twisted together to improve its immunity to interference from other (stray) electrical signals that might otherwise corrupt the signal being transmitted.

User datagram protocol (UDP) A connectionless (best-try) transport layer protocol in the TCP/IP suite.

Videotex A telecommunications service that allows users to deposit and access information to and from a central database facility. Access is through a special terminal comprising a TV set equipped with a special decoder.

Virtual call (circuit) A type of service offered on a packet-switched data network (*see also* datagram). Using this service, prior to sending any packets of information relating to a particular call (message transfer), a virtual circuit is established through the network from source to destination. All information-carrying packets relating to this call then follow the same route and the network ensures that the packets are delivered in the same order as they were entered.

Virtual terminal A protocol entity forming part of the application layer. It enables an application process to have a dialogue with a remote terminal in a standard way, irrespective of the make of the terminal.

V.24/V.35 Standards layed down by the CCITT for interfacing a digital device to a PTT-supplied modem. V.24 is also used as an interface standard for connecting a peripheral device, such as a visual display unit or a printer, to a computer.

Wide area network (WAN) A general term used to describe any form of network – private or public – that covers a wide geographical area.

X.3/X.28/X.29 A set of internationally agreed standard protocols defined to allow a character-oriented device, such as a visual display terminal, to be connected to a packet-switched data network.

X.25 An internationally agreed standard protocol defined for the interface of a data terminal device, such as a computer, to a packet-switched data network.

X.400 *See* Message handling services (MHS).

X.500 *See* Directory services (DS).

Zero bit insertion *See* Bit stuffing.

Bibliography and further reading

The following books cover a similar range of material to that covered in this book:

Stallings W. (1991). *Data and Computer Communications* 3rd edn. Macmillan

Tanenbaum A.S. (1988). *Computer Networks* 2nd edn. Prentice-Hall

The first is more biased towards the electronic engineer and the second towards the computer scientist. Other selected suggestions are as follows:

Chapter 1

Cargill C. (1989). *Information Technology Standardization: Theory, Process and Organizations*. Bedford MA: Digital Press

Cerf V. and Cain E. (1983). *The DOD Architecture Model, Computer Networks*

Clarke D. (1988). The Design Philosophy of the DARPA Internet Protocols. In *Proceedings SIGCOM 88 Symposium*

Day J.D. and Zimmermann H. (1983). The OSI Reference Model. In *Proceedings of the IEEE*, vol. 71, pp. 1334–40

Folts H. (1981). Coming of Age: A Long Awaited Standard for Heterogenous Networks. In *Data Communications*

Green P. (April 1980). An Introduction to Network Architectures and Protocols. In *IEEE Transactions on Communications*

ISO (1984). *Basic Reference Model for Open Systems Interconnection* (ISO 7498)

Vormax M. (June 1980). Controlling the Mushrooming Communications Net. In *Data Communications*

Walker S. (October 1982). Department of Defense Data Network. In *Signal*

Wood D. (1985). Computer Networks: A Survey. In *Computer Communications* Vol. II. Englewood Cliffs NJ: Prentice-Hall

Chapter 2

Bachmann L. (March 1983). Statistical Multiplexers Gain Sophistication and Status. In *Mini Micro Systems*

Bertine H.U. (1980). Physical Level Protocol. In *IEEE Transactions on Communications*, vol. 28(4), pp. 433–44

Bleazard G.B. (1982). *Handbook of Data Communications*. NCC Publications

Chou W. (1983). *Computer Communications* Vol. I. Englewood Cliffs NJ: Prentice-Hall

Cooper E. (1984). *Broadband Network Technology*. Mountain View CA: Sytek Press

Davies D.W. and Barber D.L.A. (1973). *Communication Networks for Computers*. Wiley

EIA (1969). *RS-232C Standard Interface Between Data Terminal Equipment and Data Communication Equipment Employing Serial Binary Data Interchange*

Finnie G. (February 1989). VSATs: A Technical Update. In *Telecommunications*

Freeman R. (1981). *Telecommunication Transmission Handbook*. Wiley

Jennings F. (1986). *Practical Data Communications*. Blackwell

McClelland F.M. (December 1983). Services and Protocols of the Physical Layer. In *Proceedings of the IEEE*, vol. 71, pp. 1372–7

Mehravari N. (November 1984). TDMA in a Random Access Environment: An Overview. In *IEEE Communications Magazine*, vol. 22, pp. 54–9

Mok A.K. and Ward S.A. (November 1979). Distributed Broadcast Channel Access. In *Computer Networks*, vol. 3, pp. 327–35

Nielson D. (1985). Packet Radio: An Area Coverage Digital Radio Network. In *Computer Communications* vol. II. Prentice-Hall

Murano K. *et al* (January 1990). Echo Cancellation and Applications. In *IEEE Comminication Magazine*

Oetting J. (December 1979). A Comparison of Modulation Techniques for Digital Radio. In *IEEE Transactions on Communications*

Roberts L. (1973). Dynamic Allocation of Satellite Capacity through Packet Reservation. In *Proceedings NCC*, pp. 711–16

Schwartz M. (1989). *Telecommunication Networks*. Addison-Wesley

Sklar B. (1988). *Digital Communications: Fundamentals and Applications*. Prentice-Hall

Chapter 3

Bleazard G.B. (1982). *Handbook of Data Communications*. NCC Publications

Fletcher J. (January 1982). An Arithmetic Checksum for Serial Transmissions. In *IEEE Transactions on Communications*

Jennings F. (1986). *Practical Data Communications*. Blackwell

McNamara J.E. (1982). *Technical Aspects of Data Communication*. Digital Press

Peterson W.W. (1981). *Error Correcting Codes*. MIT Press

Ramabadroan T. and Gaitonde S. (August 1988). A Tutorial on CRC Computations. In *IEEE Micro*

Spragus J.D. *et al* (1981). *Telecommunications: Protocols and Design*. Addison-Wesley

Storer J.A. (1988). *Data Compression: Methods and Theory*. Computer Science Press

Vitter J.S. (October 1987). Design and Analysis of Dynamic Huffman Codes. In *Journal of the ACM*

Welch T.A. (June 1984). A Technique for High Performance Data Compression. In *IEEE Computer*

Witten I.H. *et al* (June 1987). Arithmetic Coding for Data Compression. In *Communications of the ACM*, vol. 30, pp. 520–40

Chapter 4

Bleazard G.B. (1982). *Handbook of Data Communications*. NCC Publications

Budkowski S. and Dembinski P. (January 1988). An Introduction to Estelle. In *Computer Networks and ISDN Systems*, vol. 14

Choi T.Y. (January 1985). Formal Techniques for the Specification, Verification and Construction of Communication Protocols. In *IEEE Communications Magazine*, vol. 23, pp. 46–52

Chou W. (1983). *Computer Communications, Vol. I: Principles*. Prentice-Hall

Conrad J. (April 1980). Character-oriented Data Link Control Protocols. In *IEEE Transactions on Communications*

Conrad J. (December 1983). Services and Protocols of the Data Link Layer. In *Proceedings IEEE*

Danthine A.A.S. (April 1970). Protocol Representation with Finite-State Models. In *IEEE Transactions on Communications*. vol. COM28, pp. 632–43

Davies D.W. *et al* (1979). *Computer Networks and their Protocols*. Wiley

Pouzin L. and Zimmermann H. (November 1978). A Tutorial on Protocols. In *Proceedings IEEE*

Schwartz M. (1987). *Telecommunication Networks: Protocols, Modeling and Analysis*. Addison-Wesley

Spragins J.D. *et al* (1991). *Telecommunications: Protocols and Design*. Addison-Wesley

Vissers C.A. *et al* (December 1983). Formal Description Techniques. In *Proceedings IEEE*, vol. 71, pp. 1356–64

Chapter 5

Bleazard G.B. (1982). *Handbook of Data Communications*. NCC Publications

Black U. (June 1982). Data Link Controls: The Great Variety Calls for Wise and Careful Choices. In *Data Communications*

Black U. (1989). *Data Networks: Concepts, Theory and Practice*. Prentice-Hall

Brodd W. (August 1983). HDLC, ADCCP and SDLC: What's the Difference. In *Data Communications*

Brodd W. and Boudrow P. (October 1983). Operational Characteristics: BSC versus SDLC. In *Data Communications*

Carlson D.E. (April 1980). Bit-oriented Data Link Control Procedures. In *IEEE Transactions on Communications*

Field J. (April 1986). Logical Link Control. In *IEEE Infocom 86*

Held G. (May 1983). Strategies and Concepts for Linking Today's Personal Computers. In *Data Communications*

IEEE (1985). *Logical Link Control* (ANSI/IEEE Std. 802.2). IEEE

Jennings F. (1986). *Practical Data Communications*. Blackwell

Schwartz M. (1987). *Telecommunication Networks: Protocols, Modeling and Analysis*. Addison-Wesley

Spragins J.D. *et al* (1991). *Telecommunications: Protocols and Design*. Addison-Wesley

Chapter 6

Bux W. *et al* (November 1983). Architecture and Design of a Reliable Token-Ring Network. In *IEEE Journal on Selected Areas in Communications*

Black U. (1987). *Computer Networks: Protocols, Standards and Interfaces*. Prentice-Hall

Dixon R. *et al* (1983). A Token Ring Network for Local Data Communications. In *IBM Systems Journal*, nos. 1 and 2

Chlamtac I. and Fanta W.R. (April 1980). Message-based priority access to local networks. In *Computer Communications*

Chou W. (1983). *Computer Communications, Vol. I: Principles*. Prentice-Hall

Fine M. and Tobagi F. (December 1984). Demand Assignment Multiple-Access Schemes in Broadcast Bus Local Area Networks. In *IEEE Transactions on Computers*

Finley M. (August 1984). Optical Fibres in Local Area Networks. In *IEEE Communications Magazine*

Hammond J. (1986). *Performance Analysis of Local Computer Networks*. Addison-Wesley

Heyman D.P. (October 1982). An Analysis of the Carrier-Sense Multiple-Access Protocol. In *Bell System Technical Journal*

Heywood P. (July 1981). The Cambridge Ring is Still Making the Rounds. In *Data Communications*

Hopper A. *et al* (1986). *Local Area Network Design*. Addison-Wesley

IEEE (1985). *802.3 CSMA/CD Access Method and Physical Layer Specifications*. IEEE

IEEE (1985). *802.4 Token-passing Bus Access Method*. IEEE

IEEE (1985). *802.5 Token Ring Access Method and Physical Layer Specifications*. IEEE

IEEE (1985). *802.2 Logical Link Control*. IEEE

Schwartz M. (1987). *Telecommunication Networks: Modeling and Analysis*. Addison-Wesley

Spragins J.D. *et al* (1991). *Telecommunications: Protocols and Design*. Addison-Wesley

Stallings W. (1987). *Local Networks – an Introduction*. Macmillan

Stallings W. (1990). *Handbook of Computer Communication Standards Vol. 2: Local Area Network Standards*. Sams

Stallings W. (1990). *Local Networks* 3rd edn.

Stuck B.W. (May 1983). Calculating the Maximum Throughput Rate in Local Area Networks. In *IEEE Computer*, vol. 16, pp. 72–6

Chapter 7

Backes F. (January 1988). Transparent Bridges for Interconnection of IEEE 802 LANs. In *IEEE Network*

Bederman S. (February 1986). Source Routing. In *Data Communications*

Bux W. *et al* (December 1987). Interconnection of Local Area Networks. In *Special issue of IEEE Journal on Selected Areas in Communications*

Dixon R. and Pitt D. (January 1988). Addressing, Bridging and Source Routing. In *IEEE Network*

Hamner M. and Samsen G. (January 1988). Source Routing Bridge Implementation, In *IEE Network*

Hart J. (January 1988). Extending the IEEE 802.1 Bridge Standard to Remote Bridges. In *IEEE Network*

IEEE (1988). *802.1 D, MAC Bridges*. IEEE

IEEE (1988). *802.5 Appendix D, Multiring Networks (Source Routing)*. IEEE

Johnson M. (June 1987). Proof that Timing Requirements of the FDDI Token Ring Protocol are Satisfied. In *IEEE Transactions on Communications*

Joshi S.P. (June 1986). High-performance Networks – a Focus on the FDDI Standard. In *IEEE Micro*, vol. 6, pp. 8–14

Kummerle K. (1987). *Advances in Local Area Networks*. New York: IEEE Press

Limb J.O. (August 1984). Performance of Local Area Networks at High Speed. In *IEEE Communications*, vol. 22, pp. 41–5

Pitt D.A. (January 1988). Bridging – the Double Standard. In *IEEE Network*, vol. 2, pp. 94–5

Ross F.E. (May 1986). FDDI – A Tutorial. In *IEEE Communications*, vol. 24, pp. 10–15

Ross F.E. (September 1989). An Overview of FDDI – the Fiber Distributed Data Interface. In *IEEE Journal on Selected Areas of Communications*

Seifert W.M. (January 1988). Bridges and Routers. In *IEEE Network Magazine*, vol. 2, pp. 57–64

Spragins J.D. *et al* (1991). *Telecommunications: Protocols and Design*. Addison-Wesley

Stallings W. (1990). *Local Networks* 3rd edn. Macmillan

Strole N. (September 1983). A Local Communication Based on Interconnected Token Access Rings: A Tutorial. In *IBM Journal of Research and Development*

Chapter 8

Bleazard G.B. (1982). *Handbook of Data Communications*. NCC Publications

Black U. (1987). *Computer Networks: Protocols, Standards and Interfaces*. Prentice-Hall

Black U. (1989). *Data Networks: Concepts, Theory and Practice*. Prentice-Hall

Burg F. (1983). Design Considerations for Using the X.25 Packet Layer on Data Terminal Equipment. In *Proceedings IEEE Infocom 83*

Bush J. (July 1989). Frame-relay Services Promise WAN Bandwidth on Demand. In *Data Communications*

Deasington R.J. (1988). *X.25 Explained: Protocols for Packet Switched Networks* 2nd edn. Ellis Horwood

Decina M. (May 1986). CCITT Recommendations on the ISDN: A Review. In *IEEE Journal on Selected Areas of Communications*, vol. SAC.4, pp. 320–5

Dhas C.R. and Konangu V.K. (September 1986). X.25: An Interface to Public Packet Networks. In *IEEE Communications*, vol. 24, pp. 118–25

Duc N. and Chew E. (March 1985). ISDN Protocol Architecture. In *IEEE Communications*

Gerla M. and Kleinrock L. (April 1980). Flow Control: a Comparative Survey. In *IEEE Transactions on Communications*

Irland M.I. (March 1978). Buffer Management in a Packet Switch. In *IEEE Transactions on Communications*, vol. COM.26, pp. 328–37

Kostas D. (January 1984). Transition to ISDN – An Overview. In *IEEE Communications*

Lai W. (April 1989). Frame Relaying Service: an Overview. In *Proceedings IEEE INFOCOM 89*

Land J. (1987). *The Integrated Services Digital Network (ISDN)*. NCC Publications

Schwartz M. (1987). *Telecommunications Networks: Modeling and Analysis*. Addison-Wesley

Spragins J.D. *et al* (1991). *Telecommunications: Protocols and Design*. Addison-Wesley

Stallings W. (1989). *ISDN: An Introduction*. Macmillan

Chapter 9

Bell P. and Jabbour K. (January 1986). Review of Point-to-Point Network Routing Algorithms. In *IEEE Communications Magazine*

Boule R. and Moy J. (September 1989). Inside Routers: a Technology Guide for Network Builders. In *Data Communications*

Burg F. and Iorio N. (September 1989). Networking of Networks: Interworking According to OSI. In *IEEE Journal on Selected Areas of Communications*

Comer D.E. (1991). *Internetworking with TCP/IP, Volume 1* 2nd edn. Prentice-Hall

DARPA (1981). *Internet Control Message Protocol* (RFC 792)

DARPA (1983). *Internet Protocol* (RFC 791)

Gopal I. (December 1985). Prevention of Store-and-Forward Deadlock in Computer Networks. In *IEEE Transactions on Communications*

ISO (1988). *Connectionless-mode Network Service (Internetwork Protocol)*. (ISO 8473)

Markley R.W. (1990). *Data Communications and Inter-operability*. Prentice-Hall

McConnell J. (1988). *Internetworking Computer Systems*. Prentice-Hall

McQuillan J. *et al* (May 1980). The New Routing Algorithm for the ARPANET. In *IEEE Transactions on Communications*

Moy J. (1989). *The OSPF Specification, RFC 1131 DDN Network Information Centre*. Menlo Park CA: SRI International

Moy J. and Chiappa N. (August 1989). OSPF: A New Dynamic Routing Standard. In *Network World*

Parulkar G. (January 1990). The Next Generation of Internetworking. In *Computer Communications Review*

Piscitello D. *et al* (May 1986). Internetworking in an OSI Environment. In *Data Communications*

Sheltzer A. *et al* (August 1982). Connecting Different Types of Networks with Gateways. In *Data Communications*

Schoch J.F. (1978). Internetwork Naming, Addressing and Routing. In *Proceedings COMPCON 78*

Spragins J.D. *et al* (1991). *Telecommunications: Protocols and Design*. Addison-Wesley

Weissberger A.J. and Israel J.E. (February 1987). What the New Internetworking Standards Provide. In *Data Communications*

Chapter 10

Black U. (1987). *Computer Networks: Protocols, Standards and Interfaces*. Prentice-Hall

Black U. (1989). *Data Networks: Concepts, Theory and Practice*. Prentice-Hall

Cockburn A. (July 1987). Efficient Implementation of the OSI Transport Protocol Checksum Algorithm Using 8/16-bit Arithmetic. In *Computer Communications Review*

Comer D.E. (1991). *Internetworking with TCP/IP, Volume 1* 2nd edn. Prentice-Hall

DARPA (1983). *Transmission Control Protocol* (RFC 793)

DARPA (1983). *User Datagram Protocol* (RFC 768)

Davidson J. (1988). *An Introduction to TCP/IP*. New York: Springer Verlag

Groenback I. (March 1986). Conversion Between the TCP and ISO Transport Protocols as a Method of Achieving Interoperability Between Data Communication Systems. In *IEEE Journal on Selected Areas in Communications*

ISO (1985). *Connection-Oriented Transport Service and Protocol* (ISO 8072/3)

Karn P. and Partridge C. (1987). Improving Round-trip Time Estimates in Reliable Transport Protocols. In *Proceedings ACM SIGCOMM 87*, pp. 2–7

Limmington P.F. (December 1983). Fundamentals of the Layer Service Definitions and Protocol Specifications. In *Proceedings IEEE*, vol. 71, pp. 1341–5

Markley R.W. (1990). *Data Communications and Inter-operability*. Prentice-Hall

McConnell J. (1988). *Internetworking Computer Systems*. Prentice-Hall

Neumann J. (1983). OSI Transport and Session Layers: Services and Protocol. In *Proceedings INFOCOM 83*

Rose M.T. and Cass D.E. (1987). OSI Transport Services on top of the TCP. In *Computer Networks and ISDN Systems*, vol. 12, pp. 159–73

Spragins J.D. *et al* (1991). *Telecommunications: Protocols and Design*. Addison-Wesley

Sunshine C.A. and Dalal Y.K. (1978). Connection Management in Transport Protocols. In *Computer Networks*, vol. 2, pp. 454–73

Chapter 11

Abbruscato C.R. (September 1984). Data Encryption Equipment. *IEEE Communications*, vol. 22, pp. 15–21

Caneschi F. (July 1986). Hints for the Interpretation of the ISO Session Layer. In *Computer Communication Review*

Diffie W. and Hellman M.E. (November 1976). New Directions in Cryptography. In *IEEE Transactions on Information Theory*, vol. IT-22, pp. 644–54

Diffie W. and Hellman M.E. (June 1977). Exhaustive Cryptoanalysis of the NBS Data Encryption Standard. In *IEEE Computer Magazine*, vol. 10, pp. 74–84

Emmons W.F. and Chandler A.S. (December 1983). OSI Session Layer: Services and Protocols. In *Proceedings IEEE*, vol. 71, pp. 1397–1400

Hellman M.E. (April 1987). Commercial Encryption. In *IEEE Network Magazine*, vol. 1, pp. 6–10

Henshall J. and Shaw A. (1988). *OSI Explained – End to End Computer Communication Standards*. Ellis Horwood

ISO (1986). *Connection-oriented Session Service and Protocol Definitions* (IS 8326/7)

ISO (1987). *Connection-oriented Presentation Service and Protocol Definitions* (IS 8822/3)

ISO (1988). *Commitment Concurrency and Recovery* (IS 8649/50)

ISO (1988). *ASN.1 and its Encoding Rules* (IS 8824/5)

ISO (1988). *Association Control Service Element* (IS 8649/50)

Jueneman J.J. *et al* (1985). Message Authentication. In *IEEE Communications*, vol. 23, pp. 29–40

National Bureau of Standards (1977). *Data Encryption Standard, Federal Information Processing Standard Publication*

Needham R.M. and Schroeder M.D. (December 1978). Using Encryption for Authentication in Large Networks of Computers. In *Communications ACM*, vol. 21, pp. 993–9

Neumann J. (1983). OSI Transport and Session Layers: Services and Protocol. In *Proceedings INFOCOM 83*

Rivest R.L., Shamir A. and Adleman L. (February 1978). On a method for obtaining digital signatures and public key cryptosystems. In *Communications ACM*, vol. 21, pp. 120–6

Tardo J.J. (July 1985). Standardizing Cryptographic Services at OSI Higher Layers. In *IEEE Communications*, vol. 23, pp. 25–9

Chapter 12

Black U. (1987). *Computer Networks: Protocols, Standards and Interfaces*. Prentice-Hall

Black U. (1989). *Data Networks: Concepts, Theory and Practice*. Prentice-Hall

Chilton P. (1990). *X.400: The Messaging and Interconnection Medium for the Future*. NCC Publications

Comer D.E. (1991) *Internetworking with TCP/IP, Volume 1* 2nd edn. Prentice-Hall

Davidson J. (1988). *An Introduction to TCP/IP*. Springer Verlag

Gilmore B. (1987). A User View of Virtual Terminal Standardization. In *Computer Networks and ISDN Systems*, vol. 13, pp. 229–33

Henshall J. and Shaw A. (1988). *OSI Explained: End-to-End Computer Communication Standards*. Ellis Horwood

ISO (1987). *File Transfer Access and Management* (IS 8571/4)

ISO (1987). *Job Transfer and Manipulation* (IS 8831/2)

ISO (1988). *Virtual Terminal* (IS 9040/1)

Klerer S.M. (March 1988). The OSI Management Architecture: an Overview. In *IEEE Network*, vol. 2, pp. 20–9

Lewan D. and Long H. (December 1983). The OSI File Service. In *Proceedings IEEE*

Limmington P.F. (1984). The Virtual Filestore Concept. In *Computer Networks*, vol. 8, pp. 13–16

McLeod-Reisig S.E. and Huber K. (1986). ISO Virtual Terminal Protocol and its Relationship to TELNET. In *Proceedings IEEE Computer Networking Symposium*, pp. 110–19

Svoboda L. (December 1984). File Servers for Network-Based Distributed Systems. In *Computing Surveys*, vol. 16, pp. 353–98

Chapter 13

Baran P. (March 1964). On Distributed Communication Networks. In *IEEE Transactions on Communication Systems*, vol. CS12, pp. 1–9

Black U. (1988). *Data Communications and Distributed Networks*. Prentice-Hall

Comer D.E. (1991). *Internetworking with TCP/IP: Volume 1* 2nd edn. Prentice-Hall

Dolan M. (1984). Minimal Duplex Connection Capability in the Top Three Layers of the OSI Reference Model. In *Proceedings SIGCOM 84*

Henshall J. and Shaw A. (1988). *OSI Explained: End-to-End Computer Communication Standards*. Ellis Horwood

Hutchison G. and Desmond C.L. (October 1987). Electronic Data Exchange. In *IEEE Network Magazine*, vol. 1, pp. 16–20

Langsford A. (1984). The Open System Users Programming Interfaces. In *Computer Networks*, vol. 8, pp. 3–12

Partridge C. (1986). Mail Routing using Domain Names: an Informal Tour. In *Proceedings USENIX Summer Conference*

Sloman M. and Kramer J. (1987). *Distributed Systems and Computer Networks*. Prentice-Hall

Appendix A

Hamming R.W. (April 1950). Error Detecting and Error Correcting Codes. In *Bell System Technical Journal*, vol. 29, pp. 147–60

Peebles P.Z. (1987). *Digital Communication Systems*. Prentice-Hall

Petersen W.W. (1961). *Error Correcting Codes*. MIT Press

Sklar B. (1988). *Digital Communications*. Prentice-Hall

Sweeney P. (1991). *Error Control Coding*. Prentice-Hall

Viterbi A.J. (1971). Convolutional Codes and their Performance in Communication Systems. In *IEEE Transactions on Communication Systems*, vol. 19(5)

IEEE standards can be obtained from: IEEE Press, 345 East 47th Street, New York, NY10017, USA.

ISO and CCITT standards can be obtained from: International Telecommunications Union, Place de Nations, 1211 Geneva, Switzerland.

Index